McGraw-Hill Education
Basic Skills for the
GED® Test

McGraw-Hill Education

Basic Skills for the GED® Test

McGraw-Hill Education Editors

Contributor: Jouve North America

New York Chicago San Francisco Athens London Madrid
Mexico City Milan New Delhi Singapore Sydney Toronto

1 2 3 4 5 6 7 8 9 10   RHR/RHR   1 2 1 0 9 8 7 6 5 (book for set)

1 2 3 4 5 6 7 8 9 10   RHR/RHR   1 2 1 0 9 8 7 6 5 (book alone)

ISBN   978-0-07-183806-1 (book and DVD set)
MHID   0-07-183806-6

ISBN   978-0-07-183849-8 (book for set)
MHID   0-07-183849-X

ISBN   978-0-07-183846-7 (book alone)
MHID   0-07-183846-5

e-ISBN   978-0-07-183847-4 (e-book alone)
e-MHID   0-07-183847-3

Library of Congress Control Number 2014937696

GED® is a registered trademark of the American Council on Education (ACE) and administered exclusively by GED Testing Service LLC under license. This content is not endorsed or approved by ACE or GED Testing Service.

McGraw-Hill Education products are available at special quantity discounts to use as premiums and sales promotions or for use in corporate training programs. To contact a representative, please visit the Contact Us pages at www.mhprofessional.com.

Contents

SCIENCE   485

CHAPTER 1   Life Science   487

CHAPTER 2 Physical Science

To the Student

Welcome to *McGraw-Hill Education Basic Skills for the GED® Test*! This book is designed to develop a firm base of knowledge in all GED® test subject areas: Reasoning through Language Arts, Social Studies, Science, and Mathematical Reasoning. Everything in it has been carefully designed to match the latest GED® test learning objectives. Some special features to note are the Posttests, Chapter Reviews, and the Answer Keys.

Posttests These tests ask questions mainly in multiple-choice and short-answer format, similar to those found on many tests. Some questions are in formats that simulate the technology-enhanced questions used on the actual computerized GED® test. Questions are drawn from the entire range of skills and content in each section.

Chapter Exercises These exercises, also in multiple-choice and short-answer format, review the skills taught in the chapter.

Answer Keys Answer keys for the Posttests are located at the end of each test section. Answer keys for the chapter exercises are located at the end of the book. Answers should be checked as soon as an exercise is completed to ensure mastery of the material.

The instructional sections of this book are organized as follows:

Reasoning Through Language Arts

Grammar and Conventions

Chapters 1 and 2 of this section focus on building knowledge of standard American English grammar and conventions step by step. Lessons cover how to edit writing to correct common problems in English usage, sentence structure, capitalization, and punctuation. Exercises test knowledge of specific grammatical rules and concepts.

Building Sentences and Paragraphs

Chapters 3 and 4 of this section focus on sentences and paragraphs as tools for organizing and conveying ideas effectively. Exercises provide opportunities for writing and editing sentences and paragraphs to promote clarity and coherence.

Vocabulary and Comprehension

Chapters 5 of this section focuses first on building vocabulary skills in order to facilitate reading comprehension. Targeted exercises and questions test vocabulary acquisition. Chapter 6 then focuses the fundamentals of reading comprehension, such as identifying and summarizing main ideas in paragraphs and passages. Exercises provide opportunities to practice these skills using shorter and longer texts.

The Writing Process

Chapter 7 of this section provides an overview of the writing process, including prewriting, drafting, and revising. It includes exercises to provide hands-on writing practice at each stage.

Informational Texts

Chapter 8 of this section focuses on further building reading comprehension skills and applying them to a wide range of informational texts: news articles, textbooks, science and social studies articles, and workplace or other everyday documents (memos, handbooks, brochures, flyers). Some of these texts may include visual elements such as charts and graphs. The emphasis is on the different ways that writers of nonfiction organize their ideas: chronological order, cause and effect, compare and contrast, and problem and solution.

Chapter 9 continues the focus on nonfiction with a discussion of the critical reading and reasoning skills needed to understand and analyze argumentative and persuasive texts such as editorials and speeches. Skills taught include drawing logical conclusions based on textual evidence, evaluating claims and supporting evidence, analyzing two or more sides of an argument, and recognizing persuasive techniques. Exercises provide targeted practice to build these skills.

Understanding Fiction

Chapter 10 of this section provides targeted exercises to develop the ability to comprehend and analyze passages from fiction and nonfiction, including gaining understanding of features unique to storytelling, such as setting, characterization, tone, and theme.

Mathematical Reasoning

Basic Math Skills

The chapters in this section cover a range of mathematics topics including whole numbers, decimals, fractions, signed numbers, ratios, proportions, percents, probability, exponents, polynomials, equations, inequalities, measurement, and geometry. A section on data analysis explains how to read and understand different kinds of tables, charts, and graphs. Exercises build skills in the mathematical operations of addition, subtraction, multiplication, and division.

Word Problems

Because word problems are an important component of the GED® test in Mathematical Reasoning, parts of several chapters pay special attention to the development of problem-solving skills. As computational skills improve with practice, so will the problem–solving skills that are needed to work successfully through the math encountered in daily life.

Science

Key Science Concepts

This section develops the critical reading and thinking skills needed to read and apply scientific information. While some of the skills may have already been mastered, each section is important as the science topics assure a solid grounding in key science concepts. Each chapter addresses a different science topic including: the scientific method, living things, human biology, physics, chemistry, and earth and space science.

Scientific Thinking Skills

Skills covered in this section include how to form a scientific hypothesis, how to use the scientific method, how to tell fact from opinion, how to understand the sequence of events, how to understand cause and effect in a scientific context, and how to read and study scientific information presented the form of diagrams, charts, and graphs. Reading and discussing science topics from newspapers, magazines, radio programs, and television shows will help build these skills not only for school but also for everyday life.

Social Studies

Critical Reading and Thinking Skills

This section develops the critical reading and thinking skills needed to successfully work with social studies material. Each chapter presents text and skill-building exercises based on the four content areas in the GED® social studies test—U.S. civics and government, U.S. history, economics, and geography and world history. Skills covered include how to evaluate historical evidence, how to draw conclusions, and how to read and understand primary source documents and graphic illustrations such as maps, charts, graphs, and photographs. Higher-order thinking skills—understanding, application, analysis, synthesis, and evaluation—are introduced and practiced. In addition, the section covers useful skills such as how to read and understand maps and other geographic tools.

The exercises in this section emphasize the type of questions you will encounter on the GED® social studies test. The question formats are the same as the ones on the real exam and are designed to measure the same skills. Many of the questions are based on historical documents.

Reasoning Through Language Arts (RLA)

The Reasoning Through Language Arts (RLA) Test

The Reasoning Through Language Arts (RLA) section of the GED® test measures your ability to read carefully, write clearly, and understand and use standard English grammar.

Many questions on the RLA test refer to reading passages. About three-quarters of these passages will be informational texts (nonfiction). The rest will be literary texts (fiction). There will not be any poetry selections. Questions about these passages will test your reading comprehension ability. Other questions will test your mastery of basic English usage and vocabulary. Your writing abilities will be assessed through short-answer and extended-response questions.

Basic Skills for Reasoning Through Language Arts

The following section of this book will introduce you to the basic skills that are tested on the RLA test. You will see many examples of the kinds of passages that are included on the test. You will also have the opportunity to test your skills with numerous practice exercises. When you have finished your review, test your mastery of basic RLA skills by taking the RLA Posttest at the back of this book.

This Reasoning Through Language Arts (RLA) review section is organized as follows:

Reasoning Through Language Arts (RLA)

Answers for all of the exercises in these chapters are located in the Exercise Answer Keys section at the back of this book.

## CHAPTER 1

Parts of Speech and Sentence Basics

This chapter introduces the main parts of speech that make up a sentence. You need to master these parts of speech in order to develop your writing skills and to write sentences that express your thoughts clearly and completely.

Parts of Speech

A sentence is made up of parts: the parts of speech. The parts of speech include nouns, pronouns, verbs, and two kinds of modifiers: adjectives and adverbs. When all of its parts work together, a **sentence** expresses a complete thought.

Nouns

A *teacher* is a person. A *classroom* is a place. A *book* is a thing. *Joy* is a feeling. What do these words have in common? They all belong to the same part of speech because they are all **nouns**.

A **concrete noun** names a person, place, or thing that you can identify using your five senses. Examples include *student*, *forest*, or *cup*. However, not all nouns name concrete people, places, or things. Words like *bravery*, *freedom*, and *knowledge* are **abstract nouns**. Abstract nouns name abstractions, or ideas, feelings, or qualities that you cannot identify using your five senses.

For example, you can taste a *cookie*, see a *house*, smell the *ocean*, touch some *velvet*, or hear a *band*. These are all concrete nouns. But you cannot taste, see, smell, hear, or touch *bravery*, *freedom*, or *knowledge*. Therefore, those are all abstract nouns.

Here are some more examples of different nouns:

People	Places	Things	Abstractions
aunt	pond	bicycle	courage
Mrs. Garcia	arena	football	sadness
Nhu	Niagara Falls	cards	beauty
actress	store	parrot	education

Find the three nouns in the sentence below and circle them.

Aunt Betty went to the store to buy a parrot.

Aunt Betty is a person, a *store* is a place, and a *parrot* is a thing. These are all nouns you should have circled.

Now try another example. Circle the two nouns in the sentence below.

My sister is pursuing her education.

Sister and *education* are the two nouns you should have circled. *Sister* is a concrete noun, and *education* is an abstract noun.

Pronouns

Like a noun, a pronoun names a person, place, thing, or abstraction. There are many nouns in the English language, but there are only a few pronouns. The table below lists some of the most common. You will study more about these later.

Singular Pronouns	Plural Pronouns
I, me, mine	we, us, our, ours
you, your, yours	you, your, yours
he, him, his she, her, hers it, its	they, them, their, theirs

When a teacher is absent, a substitute teacher fills in for him or her. In the same way, some pronouns may substitute for nouns in a sentence.

The **woman** ran in a 5K race. **She** got third place in her age group.

Both sentences refer to the same noun, *woman*. In the second sentence, the word *she* substitutes for the noun *woman*.

Many **countries** belong to the European Union. **They** share the same currency.

Both sentences refer to the same noun, *countries*. In the second sentence, the word *they* substitutes for the noun *countries*.

Beauty is in the eye of the beholder. Each of us must define what **it** means.

Both sentences refer to the same noun, *beauty*. In the second sentence, the pronoun *it* substitutes for the noun *beauty* because *beauty* is an abstract noun.

Circle the pronouns in the following sentence.

> The doctor wrote a prescription, and he said it could be filled at a drugstore.

The words *he* and *it* are the pronouns in the sentence. The pronoun *he* fills in for the noun *doctor*. The pronoun *it* fills in for the noun *prescription*.

Now try another example. What are the pronouns in the sentence below? Circle them.

> I paid for the sandwich with the coins in my pocket, but my brother paid with a five-dollar bill.

If you circled *I* once and *my* twice, you correctly picked out the pronouns.

Verbs

Verbs are the parts of speech that describe what something or someone *does* or *is*. The nouns or pronouns in a sentence are generally doing something. An **action verb** describes what a noun or pronoun is doing.

> The class **sang** my favorite song.

> I **wash** the dishes after dinner every night.

Sang is something the class did. *Wash* is what I do to the dishes every night.

Some verbs do not describe action. Instead, they describe being. This kind of verb is called a **linking verb**. Linking verbs do what their name says: They *link*, or connect, a noun or a pronoun to other words that tell you something about it, or what it is.

> Washington, DC, **is** the nation's capital.

> Icy sidewalks **are** slippery.

Is in the first sentence links Washington, DC, to words that tell you what it is—*the nation's capital*. *Are* in the second sentence links *sidewalks* to a word that tells you what the sidewalks are—*slippery*.

Here are some examples of these two kinds of verbs:

Action Verbs	Linking Verbs
jog, swim, fall	am, is, are, was, were
dislike, twirl, grip	appear, become
lose, flee, buy, cry	look, smell, taste

Underline the verbs in the following sentence.

Grace twirls her baton and tosses it in the air.

The verbs in this sentence are *twirls* and *tosses*. They are action verbs.

Now try another example. Again, underline the verb.

That movie was boring.

If you underlined the verb *was*, you correctly identified the verb. It is a linking verb. It connects the noun *movie* to the word *boring*.

Modifiers

Modifiers are words that modify, or change, the meaning of another word in some way. There are two kinds of modifiers: adjectives and adverbs. **Adjectives** describe nouns, and **adverbs** describe verbs.

Adjectives

Adjectives answer a question about a noun: *Which one? What kind? How many?* For example, the words *red* and *sports* in the phrase *red sports car* answer the question *What kind (of car)?*

An adjective tells us more about a noun by describing it more fully. An adjective also makes a noun easier to identify because it provides specific information about it.

Kim is walking two friendly, playful dogs.

Now you know more about the dogs Kim walks. The adjective *two* tells you how many dogs there are, and the adjectives *friendly* and *playful* tell you what kind of dogs they are.

Keep in mind that sometimes an adjective may not come before the word it describes, but after it.

The house Indira bought is bright and spacious.

The adjectives *bright* and *spacious* come after the noun they describe, *house*.

Consider the following three lists of common adjectives:

What Kind?	Which One?	How Many?
round, square	this, that	many, few
weary, energetic	these, those	seven, eight
clean, dirty		

Now read the following paragraph. Find seven adjectives and circle them. Some, but not all, of the adjectives are in the above chart.

Many people brought their dirty cars to our school's car wash on Saturday. I counted at least ten green cars during the seven hours I was working there. I was weary when the day finally ended, but I had a good time.

Did you find all seven adjectives? The first sentence contains the adjectives *many* and *dirty*. The second sentence contains the adjectives *ten*, *green*, and *seven*. The adjectives in the third sentence are *weary* and *good*.

Adverbs

What do adverbs do? They describe verbs, adjectives, and even other adverbs. Adjectives and adverbs have one thing in common—they both answer questions. But the questions that adverbs answer are different from the questions that adjectives answer. Recall that adjectives answer the questions *Which one? What kind? How many?* Adverbs answer the questions *How? When? Where?*

Juan swims.

What has this sentence told you? Not much. You know who is swimming, but nothing else.

Juan swims **slowly**.

The adverb *slowly* adds a detail that describes the verb *swims*. Now you know **how** Juan swims.

Juan swims **daily**.

The adverb *daily* tells you something about the verb *swims*. Now you know **when** Juan swims.

Juan swims **there**.

The adverb *there* tells you something about the verb *swims*. Now you know **where** Juan swims.

The verbs in the following sentences have been underlined, and the adverbs have been circled. Answer the questions that follow each sentence.

The soldier charged (boldly.)

What did the soldier do? _____

How did the soldier do it? _____

She apologized (belatedly.)

What did she do? _____

When did she do it? _____

The answers for the first sentence are *charged* and *boldly*. The answers for the second sentence are *apologized* and *belatedly*.

Parts of Speech

Directions: Read the following advertising flyer. Some words or groups of words are underlined. These underlined words are repeated in the multiple-choice questions that follow. Identify the part of speech for each word or group of words by choosing the correct answer for each multiple-choice question.

The Fremont Nature Museum announces the opening of its new butterfly exhibit. In the exhibit hall, 75 different species of butterflies fly freely under a two-story glass dome filled with the plants and flowers they love. This magical landscape includes trees, walking paths, and an actual stream. Visitors can wander the garden as butterflies fly all around them. In fact, if you stand very still and hold out your finger carefully, a butterfly will land on it.

---

1. Museum

   A. Adverb
   B. Noun
   C. Pronoun
   D. Verb

2. Different

   A. Adjective
   B. Noun
   C. Pronoun
   D. Verb

3. Freely

   A. Adjective
   B. Adverb
   C. Pronoun
   D. Verb

4. Glass

   A. Adjective
   B. Adverb
   C. Pronoun
   D. Verb

5. Love

   A. Adjective
   B. Adverb
   C. Pronoun
   D. Verb

6. Landscape

   A. Adjective
   B. Noun
   C. Pronoun
   D. Verb

7. Them

   A. Adjective
   B. Adverb
   C. Pronoun
   D. Verb

8. You

   A. Adjective
   B. Pronoun
   C. Noun
   D. Verb

9. Carefully

    A. Adverb
    B. Noun
    C. Pronoun
    D. Adjective

10. It

    A. Adjective
    B. Noun
    C. Pronoun
    D. Adverb

Answers are on page 757.

EXERCISE 2

Parts of Speech, continued (Part 1)

Directions: Fifteen words are listed below. What part of speech is each word? Write the word in the correct column identifying the part of speech to which it belongs. One word has been done for you.

lately	messy	Ms. Jay	hears	she
here	cat	sad	eat	they
then	loves	thin	boat	it

Nouns	Pronouns	Verbs	Adjectives	Adverbs
Ms. Jay	_____	_____	_____	_____
_____	_____	_____	_____	_____
_____	_____	_____	_____	_____

Parts of Speech, continued (Part 2)

Directions: Each sentence below contains a blank. Fill in the blank with a noun, pronoun, verb, adjective, or adverb. Then, on the blank following the sentence, tell the part of speech to which your word belongs.

1. Sam rowed a _____ boat across the lake. _____

2. Mrs. Black _____ to the ball game. _____

3. Martin told me about his _____ vacation adventure. _____

4. Aunt Lena strolled _____ across the park. _____

5. Sidney cooked a late-night _____. _____

Answers are on page 757.

Sentence Basics

A **sentence** is a group of words that expresses a complete thought. All sentences always start with a capital letter and end with a specific punctuation mark, such as a period, question mark, or exclamation point.

Four Types of Sentences

There are four different types of sentences. The table below provides definitions and examples of each type of sentence.

Sentence Type	Example
A **statement** gives information and ends with a period.	I play in the school band.
A **command** gives somebody an order to do something. A command usually ends with a period, but may end with an exclamation mark.	Pick me up after today's game. Do your chores now!
With a **question**, you are requesting information about something. A question ends with a question mark.	Have you seen my trumpet?
With an **exclamation**, you are displaying strong feeling. An exclamation ends with an exclamation mark.	That was a great halftime show today!

EXERCISE 3

Four Types of Sentences

Directions: Read the following sentences. On the first blank following each sentence, place the correct punctuation mark, using a period, question mark, or exclamation point. Then identify the sentence type by writing the word *statement*, *command*, *question*, or *exclamation* in the second blank. The first sentence is done for you.

1. This is the old train station _____ . _____ *statement*

2. Did you miss your stop _____ _____

3. Give me the subway map _____ _____

4. Where can I catch the bus _____ _____

5. That van goes to the airport _____ _____

6. Run or we'll miss the taxi _____ _____

Answers are on page 757.

Subjects and Predicates

A complete sentence has two parts: a subject and a predicate.

Subjects

Recall that nouns and pronouns name a person, place, thing, or abstraction. Either nouns or pronouns can serve as the subject of a sentence.

Think of the **subject** of a sentence as the main character in a movie. Just as the main character is the focus of the movie, the subject is the focus of the sentence. The sentence tells about an action that the subject performs, or describes the subject in some way. The subject *does* something or *is* something.

You can find the subject by looking for the **verb** in a sentence. Once you've located the verb, ask yourself the following series of questions.

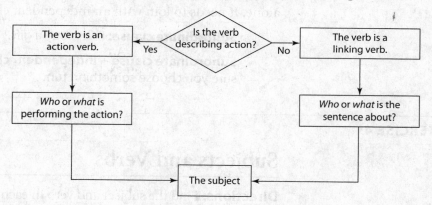

Consider the following sentence.

The brave firefighter saved the dog from the flames.

In this sentence, the verb is the action verb *saved*. Who did the saving? The *firefighter*. The word *firefighter* is a noun, and it is the simple subject of the sentence.

The **simple subject** of a sentence is usually a noun or pronoun.

Remember that not all verbs are action verbs. Recall that there is a second category of verbs, called linking verbs. Linking verbs tell you something about the subject, or what it is. Consider the following sentence.

The dog's owners were happy that their pet was okay.

Here, the linking verb is *were*. It links *happy* to *owners*, the noun that *happy* describes; so *owners* is the subject of the sentence.

Predicates

The subject, as you have seen, is an important part of a sentence. The verb plays an equally important role in the other part of a sentence: the predicate. The **predicate** describes what the subject *does* or *is*.

Consider the following sentence.

Dad cooked the Thanksgiving turkey.

The two parts of this sentence are the subject, *Dad*, and the predicate, *cooked the Thanksgiving turkey*. The verb is part of the predicate. *Dad* is the person who did something, and the predicate tells you what he did (*cooked the Thanksgiving turkey*).

Now consider this next sentence; the verb is a linking verb.

The meal was a great success.

Again, this sentence has two parts: the subject *meal* and the predicate *was a great success*.

Together, the subject and the predicate form an **independent clause** that can stand alone as a sentence.

Independent clause: Fixing cars is my passion.

A **subordinate clause** has a subject and a predicate, but it cannot stand alone. It needs to join with an independent clause to make sense.

Subordinate clause: If you buy a gift.

Subordinate clause + Independent clause: If you buy a gift, make sure you choose something fun.

EXERCISE 4

Subjects and Verbs

Directions: Find the subject and verb in each of the following sentences. Circle the subject, and underline the verb. The first one is done for you.

1. (Four Corners Point) <u>is</u> unique.

2. Four different western states meet here.

3. You reach Four Corners Point after a long drive through the desert.

4. A monument marks the spot.

5. On this spot, you stand in the states of Arizona, New Mexico, Utah, and Colorado at the same time.

Answers are on page 757.

Subject-Verb Agreement

The subject of a sentence may be a noun or a pronoun. The verb is the key ingredient of the predicate. But to work together smoothly, the subject and the verb in a sentence must agree.

Nouns as Subjects

If the subject of a sentence is a singular noun, then the verb must be a singular verb. If the subject of a sentence is a plural noun, then the verb must be a plural verb.

Most of the verbs you use every day are regular verbs. They are called **regular verbs** because they all follow the same pattern when changing from their singular to their plural forms in the present tense. The **present tense** of a verb tells you about an action that is happening *now*. Study the table below, which demonstrates how subject-verb agreement works.

Singular Subject	Regular Verb	Plural Subject	Regular Verb
The camper	sleeps.	The campers	sleep.
The tiger	awakens.	The tigers	awaken.

Camper and *tiger* are both singular nouns, so the correct verb is singular. *Campers* and *tigers* are both plural nouns, so the correct verb is plural.

Now try an example on your own. In the following sentence, underline the verb form that agrees with the subject of the sentence.

The museum (display, displays) dinosaur fossils on the main floor.

What is the subject of the sentence? *Museum.* Is it singular or plural? Singular. So you should have underlined the singular verb *displays*.

Suppose we change the singular subject to the plural version of the noun.

The museums **display** dinosaur fossils on the main floor.

In this case, the correct verb form is the plural verb *display* because regular verbs remove an *-s* to become plural.

There are also a few **irregular verbs**, and these verbs do *not* follow a pattern when changing from their singular to their plural forms. You will learn more about them in a later chapter.

Consider some of the nouns we have been focusing on in this section: *camper, tiger,* and *museum.* These kinds of nouns are called **countable nouns** because they name things that can be counted. It is easy to determine if a countable noun is a singular or plural subject. Are we talking about one camper or two? If we are referring to one camper, then it is a singular subject; otherwise, it is a plural subject.

Are all nouns countable? Think of some abstract nouns, such as *knowledge*, *wisdom*, and *justice*. Could you have more than one *wisdom*? You cannot count these nouns, so they are always singular. In the following sentence, *excitement* is not a countable noun.

Excitement <u>sweeps</u> through the crowd.

Pronouns as Subjects

Recall that pronouns can substitute for nouns in sentences. If nouns can serve as the subject of a sentence, that means that pronouns can be subjects, too. If the subject of a sentence is a pronoun, it still must agree with the sentence's verb. This table shows the subject-verb agreement between various pronouns and the verb *to listen*.

Singular Pronoun	Singular Verb (present tense)	Plural Pronoun	Plural Verb (present tense)
I	listen	we	listen
you	listen	you	listen
he, she, it	listens	they	listen

Note that with regular verbs like *listen*, when you pair the verb with a pronoun, the only time you use the verb form ending in *-s* is with the singular subject pronouns *he, she,* and *it*. Remember that the regular verb form used with the singular pronouns *I* and *you* does not end in *-s*. It looks just like the verb form used with plural pronouns.

In the sentences that follow, underline the verb that agrees with the subject.

They (shop, shops) for groceries at the supermarket every Monday night.

She (take, takes) her recyclables to the recycling center once a month.

I (make, makes) a cake every year for my mother's birthday.

In the first sentence, the plural pronoun *they* agrees with the plural verb *shop*. In the second sentence, the singular pronoun *she* agrees with the singular verb *takes*, which is in the form ending in *-s*. In the third sentence, the singular pronoun *I* agrees with the singular verb *make*.

Pronouns and Subject-Verb Agreement Exceptions

Usually, as you have seen, you can simply add *-s* to the base verb in order to make the verb agree with the singular subjects *he, she,* and *it*. But this rule does not work for every verb. Base verbs that end in *s, x, z, sh,* or *ch* are governed by a different rule. In those cases, you should add *-es* to make the subject and verb agree.

> He **watches** the plane take off.

> She **crosses** the street when the light turns green.

Some pronouns can be hard to figure out. Are they singular or plural? An **indefinite pronoun** does not name a specific person, place, or thing. Here is a list of the singular indefinite pronouns.

Singular Indefinite Pronouns

each (one)	someone, something	anybody
either (one)	somebody	everyone, everything,
neither (one)	no one, nothing,	everybody
one	nobody	
	anyone, anything	

Notice the verbs in the following sentences. They all agree with the indefinite pronouns, which are singular. Indefinite pronouns always take singular verbs.

> Everyone **knows** that exercise is good for you.

> Nobody **is** at the mall after it closes.

EXERCISE 5

Subject-Verb Agreement

Directions: Each sentence below contains two verb choices. Circle the subject in each sentence, and then underline the verb that agrees with the subject. The first one is done for you.

1. Several (tunnels) (claims, <u>claim</u>) the title "world's longest."

2. The length of Norway's Laerdal Tunnel (is, are) fifteen miles.

3. It (is, are) the world's longest car tunnel.

4. You (do, does) not want to get stuck in that tunnel!

5. Japan (has, have) a tunnel, the Seikan Tunnel, that runs 33 miles.

6. It (qualifies, qualify) as the world's longest rail tunnel.

7. The Delaware Aqueduct (put, puts) all the other tunnels to shame.

8. New York City (gets, get) much of its water from this tunnel.

9. Water (flows, flow) 85 miles underground before arriving at your kitchen sink.

10. Nobody (finds, find) this engineering feat more amazing than I do!

Answers are on page 757.

Compound Subjects

You have learned about singular and plural subjects. But sometimes a subject has two parts, sometimes a phrase comes between the subject and verb, and sometimes the word order in a sentence is reversed. How can you make the subject and verb agree in these cases?

A subject that has two parts is called a **compound subject**. Each part is a noun or pronoun, and the parts are connected by a word such as *and*, *or*, or *nor*. These words are a different part of speech called **conjunctions**. They join subjects, verbs, adjectives, phrases, and sometimes even entire sentences. Consider the following sentence, which has a compound subject.

Mom and Dad come to all my Little League games.

Mom and *Dad* are the two parts of the **compound subject**. The conjunction *and* joins these two parts. Because more than one person is mentioned, the compound subject is plural and takes a plural verb.

Compound subjects can also be joined by the words *or* or *nor*. You might expect that the verb in this case also has to be plural because the subject has two parts. But when a compound subject is joined by *or* or *nor*, the verb is plural only if the subject closer to the verb is plural. If the part of the compound subject closer to the verb is singular, the verb is singular. (The words *either* and *neither* are never part of a subject. You can ignore them.)

Underline the two parts of the compound subject in each sentence, and circle the verbs.

The players or the coach boards the bus first.

Neither my aunt nor my cousins know the way to the restaurant.

Players and *coach* are the subjects in the first sentence. Because *coach* is the noun closer to the verb and is singular, the correct verb is the singular *boards*. *Aunt* and *cousins* are the subjects in the second sentence. In this case, the closer noun, *cousins*, is plural, so the plural *know* is the correct verb.

In the following sentence, underline the correct verb.

Either Dad or you (read, reads) the story to us.

Recall that the pronoun *you* requires a verb form that does not end in *-s*. Because *you* is the subject closer to the verb, the correct verb is *read*.

Now see what happens when the order of the subjects is switched. Underline the correct verb in the following sentence.

Either you or Dad (read, reads) the story to us.

Because the singular *Dad* is now the subject closer to the verb, the correct verb form is the one that ends in *-s*. The correct answer is *reads*.

Underline the two parts of the compound subject in this sentence, and circle the verb.

Either Alison or I have to take out the garbage tonight.

Allison and *I* are the subjects of the sentence. *I*, the noun closer to the verb, is singular. Like the pronoun *you*, the pronoun *I* takes a special verb form that is just like the form used with plural pronouns. *Have* is the correct verb form in this case. However, if the subjects were *Allison* and *she*, the correct verb form would be *has*.

The verb in a compound subject joined by *or* or *nor* has to agree with the subject closer to the verb. Ignore the words *either* and *neither* in sentences with such compound subjects.

EXERCISE 6

Compound Subjects

Directions: Each sentence below contains two verb choices. Circle the subjects in each sentence, and then underline the verb that agrees with the compound subject. The first one is done for you.

1. Neither (Jill) nor (I) (enjoys, <u>enjoy</u>) waking up in the morning.

2. The candidates or the debate moderator (has, have) the last word.

3. Fluids and food (is, are) vital for life.

4. Fall and spring (is, are) when we reset the clocks every year.

Answers are on page 758.

Interrupters

In some sentences, an **interrupting phrase** comes between the subject and verb. When the subject is no longer close to the verb, you need to ignore the interrupting phrase, even if that interrupting phrase contains a noun or pronoun. Then, you can identify the subject and determine the correct form of the verb.

Here's an example:

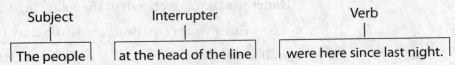

Subject   Interrupter   Verb

| The people | | at the head of the line | | were here since last night. |

The subject *people* is plural. The two singular nouns in the interrupting phrase, *head* and *line*, can be ignored. The plural form of the verb—in this case, *were*—is correct because it agrees with the plural subject, *people*.

Now it's your turn. Try making the subject and verb agree in this sentence. Circle the subject, cross out the interrupter, and underline the correct verb.

The rides at the park (was, were) empty because it was raining.

There are two nouns before the verb, but only one of them, *rides*, is the subject of the sentence, and it is plural. The singular noun *park* is in the interrupting phrase *at the park*, and it is not the subject of the sentence, so it can be ignored. The correct verb, therefore, is *were*.

EXERCISE 7

Interrupters

Directions: Each sentence below contains two verb choices. Circle the subject in each sentence, cross out the interrupter, and then underline the verb that agrees with the subject. The first one is done for you.

1. The steady (rhythm) ~~of the waves~~ (<u>causes</u>, cause) the boat to bob up and down.

2. The baggers at the supermarket in my neighborhood (is, are) very friendly.

3. The people at the back of the crowd (strains, strain) to hear the speaker.

4. The roar of the cannons (makes, make) conversation impossible.

Answers are on page 758.

Inverted Word Order

You may have noticed that the word order is reversed in sentences that ask questions. Because questions are sentences with **inverted word order**, the verb comes before the subject. How do you determine the subject in a sentence with inverted word order? Change the question to a statement, and then identify the subject. Which verb is correct in the sentence below?

(Do, Does) the zoo animals get fed more than once a day?

Put the subject at the beginning of the sentence to change the question to a statement.

The zoo animals **do** get fed more than once a day.

The subject *animals* is plural, so the present-tense verb *do* does not end in -*s*.

Some questions begin with a word that is not the verb, such as *why, how,* or *when*. But even in these kinds of sentences, the verb comes before the subject. Here are some examples:

When (is, are) your relatives due to arrive?

Why (does, do) the car alarm keep going off?

Your relatives **are** due to arrive.

The car alarm **does** keep going off.

When you put the subject first in a sentence, it is easy to see what form the verb should take. In the first sentence, the subject is the plural *relatives*, so the question needs the plural verb *are*. The second sentence contains a singular subject, *car alarm*, so the correct verb is *does*.

Occasionally, a sentence will begin with an introductory phrase that is not the subject. To determine what form the verb should take, find the subject. Who or what is performing the main action in the sentence?

Circle the subject in this sentence. What is the correct verb?

In single file (enter, enters) the students.

Change the word order and place the subject first.

The students **enter** in single file.

EXERCISE 8

Subject-Verb Agreement (Part 1)

Directions: Find the mistake in each of the following sentences. Correct it by crossing out the wrong word and writing the correct word above it. The first one is done for you.

     plan
1. Rob and Michelle ~~plans~~ to go away on vacation this summer.

2. The countries of Europe was their first choice.

3. Does you need a passport to go overseas?

4. How do one get around after arriving in Europe?

5. Either rental cars or the railroad are the best way to see the Continent.

6. In this travel brochure is some amazing images of the Alps.

7. The Internet provide a lot of information about the best places to visit.

8. It sure do take a lot of time and effort to plan a vacation.

Subject-Verb Agreement (Part 2)

Directions: Choose the correct verb to complete each sentence.

1. Vegetables and fruit (is, are) important parts of a nutritious diet.

2. A dog or a cat (provide, provides) companionship for older people who are living alone.

3. (Is, Are) those boots wet or dry?

4. You (has, have) two choices here.

5. Neither a thunderstorm nor blizzards (prevent, prevents) postal carriers from delivering the mail.

6. Neither my twin sister nor I (claim, claims) the aisle seat.

Answers are on page 758.

Sentence Fragments

Recall what you know about sentences. A sentence contains a group of words that expresses a complete thought. If the words are working together like a well-oiled machine, you understand what the writer of the sentence is telling you.

The speedboat skimmed across the water.

This sentence expresses a complete thought, one that is easy to understand. Just as a car will sometimes break down, a sentence can stop working, too. When this happens, a group of words no longer work together as a sentence and become a sentence fragment. A sentence **fragment** is a word or group of words that does not express a complete thought. Consider this group of words:

Blew up the balloon.

Don't you wonder, *Who* blew up the balloon? That is because the subject of the sentence is missing. You can repair this fragment and make it a sentence by adding a subject.

The **clown** blew up the balloon.

The words now express a complete thought. This is a sentence, not a fragment.

Complete Sentences

The dolphin jumped out of the water.

A spray of water washed over the people in the boat.

Do these sentences make sense? Do they express a complete thought? Yes, you can understand what these sentences say because they are complete.

A missing subject is not the only way to produce a sentence fragment. A fragment may also result when a verb or a predicate is missing.

Fragments

Beside the boat.

A pod of whales.

Surfaced.

Considered together, these fragments suggest that someone is describing an incident that happened during a whale-watching trip. *What* happened? *What* surfaced? *Where* did this occur? You can put the fragments together to form a complete sentence with a subject ("A pod of whales") and a predicate ("surfaced beside the boat").

A pod of whales surfaced beside the boat.

EXERCISE 9

Sentence Fragments

Directions: Study the groups of words below. Identify each numbered item as a complete sentence (CS) or sentence fragment (SF). On each long line following a fragment, make the fragment into a complete sentence by adding words. Change capitalization as needed. The first one is done for you.

1. Climbed up to the trapeze. ____SF____

   ___The man climbed up to the trapeze._____

2. The platform at the top of the tower. _____

   _____

3. He gripped the bar. _____

   _____

4. Pushed off from the platform. _____

_____

5. He let go of the bar and somersaulted in the air. _____

_____

Answers are on page 758.

## CHAPTER 2

More About Parts of Speech

In this chapter you will learn more about how to use nouns, pronouns, and verbs correctly. You will learn about the different forms of nouns and pronouns, and about the different tenses of regular and irregular verbs. You will also learn where to place adjectives and adverbs in a sentence so that the meaning is clear.

Nouns

All nouns name a person, place, thing, or abstraction. But different nouns play different roles. You will learn about these different types of nouns in this chapter.

Identifying Common and Proper Nouns

Consider these two sentences.

We are going to the **game** on Sunday.

We are going to the **Super Bowl** on Sunday. *Becurse.*

A **common noun** names a general person, place, or thing: The word *game* is a common noun. A **proper noun** names a specific person, place, or thing: *Super Bowl* is a proper noun.

Common nouns never begin with a capital letter unless they start a sentence. Proper nouns always begin with a capital letter. Notice that when a proper noun is more than one word, all of the words are capitalized.

Incorrect: *Super bowl* or *super Bowl*

Correct: *Super Bowl*

Here are more examples of common nouns and proper nouns.

Common Nouns	Proper Nouns
department	State Department
ship	USS *Enterprise*
month	October
continent	Africa

Some nouns can be common nouns or proper nouns depending on whether they are general or specific. The words *building* and *street*, for example, may be common or proper nouns.

> **Common nouns:** He ducked into a nearby **building** to escape the downpour on the **street.**

> **Proper nouns:** He ducked into the **Empire State Building** to escape the downpour on **34th Street.**

Official titles may also be common or proper nouns. Capitalize a title only when you combine it with the name of a specific person.

> **Common noun:** We invited the **mayor** to our family cookout.

> **Proper noun:** We invited **Mayor Ross** to our family cookout.

In the following paragraph, underline each proper noun that should begin with a capital letter.

> Last summer we took interstate 95 to get to our nation's capital city. We wanted to visit the Washington monument, but we could not find a parking place nearby. We parked on Ohio drive, but then we realized that we were lost. Fortunately, a helpful guide came to our aid. Thanks to ranger Dunn, we found the right way to go.

You should capitalize the words *interstate*, *monument*, *drive*, and *ranger* because they are proper nouns that name specific people, places, and things: *Interstate 95*, *Washington Monument*, *Ohio Drive*, and *Ranger Dunn*.

EXERCISE 1

Identifying Common and Proper Nouns

Directions: On each blank, write the name of a proper noun for each common noun. The first one is done for you.

1. day of the week <u>Saturday</u>

2. ocean _____

3. teacher _____

4. city _____

5. holiday _____

Answers are on page 758.

Forming Singular and Plural Nouns

Consider these two sentences.

"One **man,** one vote" is a guiding principle of the United States.

The Declaration of Independence begins with these words: "All **men** are created equal."

In the first sentence *man* is singular because it is a noun that names one person, place, thing, or abstraction. In the second sentence, the word *men* is plural because it is a noun that names more than one person, place, thing, or abstraction. Here are more examples of singular and plural nouns.

Singular Nouns	Plural Nouns
tiger	tigers
glass	glasses
thought	thoughts
party	parties
woman	women

How do you change a singular noun to a plural noun? There is no one rule that covers all nouns, but the chart below provides some guidelines. Read them and then try making singular into plural nouns yourself by filling in the third column. The first one is done for you.

Forming a Plural Noun	Example	Try It Yourself
For most nouns, add -s.	sun + -s = suns parade + -s = parades	Singular: house Plural: _houses_ Singular: pencil Plural: _____
For nouns that end in s, sh, ch, z, and x, add -es.	fox + -es = foxes kiss + -es = kisses	Singular: branch Plural: _____ Singular: wish Plural: _____
For nouns that end with a consonant and -y, change the y to i and add -es.	baby → babi + -es = babies hobby → hobbi + -es = hobbies	Singular: spy Plural: _____ Singular: county Plural: _____

The correct plurals of the words in the third column are *pencils, branches, wishes, spies,* and *counties.*

Because they are exceptions that are not governed by any rule at all, the plural form of each of the following nouns is unique. You must memorize their singular and plural forms. Again, when in doubt, consult a dictionary to find the correct plural form of any noun.

Forming a Plural Noun	Example	Try It Yourself
Some singular nouns do not change form when they become plural. Check the dictionary to be sure.	Singular: jeans Plural: jeans Singular: offspring Plural: offspring	Singular: sheep Plural: _____ Singular: scissors Plural: _____
Some singular nouns change form in unique ways when they become plural. Check the dictionary to be sure.	Singular: child Plural: children Singular: goose Plural: geese	Singular: tooth Plural: _____ Singular: woman Plural: _____

The correct plurals of the words in the third column are *sheep, scissors, teeth,* and *women.*

EXERCISE 2

Forming Singular Nouns and Plural Nouns

Directions: In each of the following sentences, one of the singular nouns is incorrect because it should be plural. Cross out the incorrect singular noun, and write the correct plural form in the blank. The first one is done for you.

1. Many ~~adventurer~~ want to climb Mt. Everest. ___adventurers___

2. Guide from Tibet take climbers to the top of the mountain. _____

3. Hazardous condition make the climb dangerous. _____

4. It is crucial to take enough supply for the journey. _____

5. Mountaineers must use ax to dig into the ice as they climb. _____

6. Frostbite can damage climbers' hands and foot. _____

Answers are on page 758.

Forming Possessive Nouns

A possessive noun shows ownership:

Singular: the Statue of Liberty's torch

Singular: Boris's book

Plural: the neighbors' yard

Plural: the men's hats

The chart below shows you how to form a variety of possessive nouns. The possessive noun in each example is in **boldface type**. The object the noun possesses is underlined.

Type of Noun	Possessive	Example
All singular nouns	end with an apostrophe followed by an -s	We bought **Mom's** gift at the mall. The **museum's** exhibit closes soon. **Homer's** *Odyssey* recounts the story of **Ulysses's** journey home to Ithaca.
Most plural nouns	end with an apostrophe (')	My **grandparents'** house is on the other side of town. We stored the **musicians'** instruments until the concert.
Plural nouns that do not end in -s	add an apostrophe followed by -s	The **children's** toys are in the car. The **geese's** migration south begins soon.

EXERCISE 3

Forming Possessive Nouns

Directions: On the blank, write the possessive of the first noun in each pair of words. The first one is done for you.

1. car horn _____*car's*_____

2. player bat _____

3. chemists lab coats _____

4. men shoes _____

5. students desks _____

6. diver fins _____

7. wolves cave _____

8. Ross apartment _____

Answers are on page 759.

Pronouns

Recall that pronouns can replace nouns in a sentence. Just as nouns play specific roles within a sentence (subject, object, or possessive), so do pronouns. A pronoun's role in a sentence determines the pronoun's **case**: subjective (subject), objective (object), or possessive (shows ownership).

Using Subject Pronouns and Object Pronouns

A pronoun's **antecedent** is the noun it replaces.

When we moved into our new **house**, **it** was freshly painted.

In this sentence, the pronoun *it* replaces the noun *house*; therefore, *house* is the antecedent of the pronoun *it*. A pronoun must always agree with its antecedent in number, gender, and case. The pronouns that replace a subject noun are called **subject pronouns**. **Object pronouns** replace nouns in the sentence other than the subject. These may include, but are not limited to, the object that receives the subject's action.

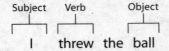

The table below lists the subject and object pronouns.

Subject Pronouns	Object Pronouns
I, we	me, us
you	you
he, she, it	him, her, it
they	them
who	whom

In the following examples, pronouns and their antecedents are in **boldface type**.

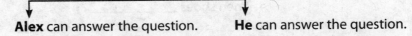

Alex can answer the question.   **He** can answer the question.

He replaces the singular *Alex* in the sentence because it is a singular masculine *subject* pronoun.

The **coins** fell out of my pocket.   **They** fell out of my pocket.

They replaces the plural *coins* in the sentence because it is a plural *subject* pronoun.

Here are some examples of object pronouns.

Elena <u>sent</u> **Hugh** on an errand.   Elena <u>sent</u> **him** on an errand.

Him is a object pronoun that replaces *Hugh.*

Tanya <u>gave</u> a **present** to the **children.** Tanya <u>gave</u> **it** to **them.**

Neither *present* nor *children* is a subject noun, so they *both* take object pronouns. The singular object pronoun *it* replaces *present.* The plural object pronoun *them* replaces *children.*

EXERCISE 4

Using Subject Pronouns and Object Pronouns

Directions: In the blank after each sentence, write the subject pronoun or object pronoun that replaces the underlined noun. The first one is done for you.

1. <u>Aaron</u> met Mrs. Ericson, the driving instructor, at the school parking lot.
   <u>He</u>

2. <u>Mrs. Ericson</u> told Aaron to get behind the wheel. _____

3. <u>Mrs. Ericson and Aaron</u> were ready for the first lesson. _____

4. <u>The car</u> started right away. _____

5. Alex put <u>the book</u> on his nightstand. _____

6. The book had been a gift from <u>his sister</u>. _____

7. She bought <u>Alex</u> the book because his favorite author had written it.
   _____

8. Their parents encouraged <u>Alex and his sister</u> to buy each other gifts.
   _____

Answers are on page 759.

Forming Possessive Pronouns

You have already learned about possessive nouns. **Possessive pronouns** take the place of possessive nouns in sentences. They tell you *who* or *what* has ownership of the noun that follows them. Possessive pronouns must agree with their antecedents in number. This chart lists singular and plural possessive pronouns.

Singular Possessive Pronouns	Plural Possessive Pronouns
my, mine	our, ours
your, yours	your, yours
his	their, theirs
her, hers	
its	

The possessive pronouns in these examples are in **boldface type**.

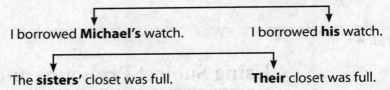

I borrowed **Michael's** watch.   I borrowed **his** watch.

The **sisters'** closet was full.   **Their** closet was full.

Seven of the possessive pronouns in the chart can stand alone in a sentence: *mine, yours, his, hers, ours, yours,* and *theirs.* Consider these examples.

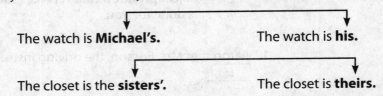

The watch is **Michael's.**   The watch is **his.**

The closet is the **sisters'.**   The closet is **theirs.**

In these sentences, the possessive pronouns *his* and *theirs* stand alone, taking the place of the possessive nouns *Michael's* and *sisters'.*

EXERCISE 5

Forming Possessive Pronouns

Directions: Replace the underlined noun with a possessive pronoun by filling in the blank that follows each sentence. The first one is done for you.

1. The Grimm brothers are famous for <u>the Grimm brothers'</u> fairy tales, which they published during the early 1800s. ___their___

2. Wilhelm Grimm was born in 1786, and <u>Wilhelm's</u> older brother, Jacob, was born a year earlier in 1785. _____

3. Germany, with <u>Germany's</u> rich tradition of myths and folk tales, was a source of inspiration for the brothers' stories. _____

4. People around the world today still enjoy reading <u>Grimm's</u> fairy tales. _____

5. Reading Grimm's fairy tales as a child helped me develop <u>the</u> lifelong fascination with fantasy and folklore. _____

Answers are on page 759.

Pronoun Agreement

Pronouns in a sentence must agree with the antecedents they replace in number (singular or plural), gender (male, female, or neither), *and* case (subjective, objective, or possessive).

> **Temple Grandin** was born with autism. **She** later became a famous scientist and author. *TIME* magazine named **her** one of the world's most influential people due to **her** amazing career.

The pronouns *she* and *her* agree with *Temple Grandin* in number (singular), gender (female), and case (subjective; objective [object of *named*]).

> **Yellowstone Park** is in Wyoming. People visit **it** to enjoy **its** natural beauty. The visitors relax as **they** spend **their** days camping and hiking.

The pronouns *it* and *its* agree with *Yellowstone Park* in number (singular), gender (no gender), and case (the pronoun *it* is the object of *visit*; *its* is possessive).

Like *visitors*, the pronouns *they* and *their* are plural and have no gender. In this sentence, *they* is a subject pronoun and *theirs* is a possessive pronoun.

Fixing Errors in Pronoun Agreement

As you have learned, a pronoun and its antecedent must always agree. Consider these typical agreement errors, one involving a noun antecedent and the other involving a pronoun antecedent.

> **Incorrect:** The **company** stands behind **their** product.

> **Correct:** The **company** stands behind **its** product.

The noun *company* is singular, and therefore it does not agree with the plural possessive pronoun *their*. The correct pronoun is the singular *its*.

Indefinite pronouns can also cause agreement errors. Pronouns such as *no one*, *anything*, *somebody*, and *everybody* do not refer to a specific person, place, or thing. Indefinite pronouns are always singular, but it is easy to mistake them for plurals. In addition, these pronouns have no gender, which can lead to further confusion.

Incorrect: Everyone brought their favorite food to the party.

The indefinite pronoun is *everyone*. Because indefinite pronouns are always singular, *their* is incorrect. You need to change *their* to a singular pronoun. But this raises another issue. The pronoun *everyone* has no gender, so you cannot replace it with either the pronoun *his* or the pronoun *her*. In this instance, you have to replace *their* with the phrase *his or her* containing both pronouns to account for everyone.

Correct: Everyone brought his or her favorite food to the party.

Sometimes, using *his or her* repeatedly this way makes sentences sound too wordy. Changing the indefinite pronoun to a plural pronoun gets around the problem of gender altogether.

Also correct: People brought their favorite food to the party.

EXERCISE 6

Pronoun Agreement

Directions: In the blank in each sentence, write a pronoun that agrees with the underlined noun. The first one is done for you.

1. <u>Les Paul</u> invented the first solid-body electric guitar. With that invention, ___*he*___ changed the course of music history.

2. The TV news report says that there will be <u>shooting stars</u> in the sky tonight. I plan to stay up to watch _____ .

3. The <u>workers</u> who build tall skyscrapers are amazing. _____ must not be afraid of heights!

4. Professional <u>cyclists</u> need to be in excellent shape, and _____ bikes have to be state-of-the-art machines.

5. <u>My dad and I</u> sang "Happy Birthday" to Mom. _____ duet wasn't going to lead to a singing career.

6. The <u>platoon</u> moved forward after _____ commander gave instructions on the battle plan.

7. <u>Anybody</u> wearing a watch should raise _____ hand.

Answers are on page 759.

Verbs

Recall that the verb in a sentence usually describes action: *The dog darts into traffic*. In this sentence, *darts* tells you what the dog does. Sometimes a verb describes a condition or state of being. *Luisa was happy that the dog wasn't hurt*. In this sentence, the linking verb *was* connects *Luisa* and *happy*, telling you how Luisa felt.

Choosing the Correct Verb Tense

You have already learned that verbs tell you *what* is happening. But **verb tenses** tell you *when* something happens: in the present, past, or future. You *did* something yesterday. You *are doing* something right now. You *will do* something tomorrow.

What if you are not sure which verb tense to use? Look for words or phrases in each sentence that tell you when the action takes place, such as *yesterday, at the moment,* or *next year*. This chart defines each verb tense. In each example, the correct form of the verb tense is in **boldface type**. Words or phrases that tell you when the action occurs are underlined.

Verb Tense	Example
Present: Something is happening **now**.	Right now, I **am cooking**.
This tense may also describe something that happens **regularly**.	I **cook** dinner every day at six o'clock.
Past: Something happened **before the present**. It usually ends in -*d* or -*ed*.	Last week, I **cooked** a new recipe.
Future: Something will happen after the present. A future tense verb has the word *will* in front of it.	I **will cook** 10 new *recipes by the end of the year*.

A main verb is called the base verb. Notice that to form the past tense, you generally add -*ed* to the base verb. However, to form the future tense, the verb needs some extra help: combine the base verb (*cook*) with the helping verb *will*.

EXERCISE 7

Choosing the Correct Verb Tense

Directions: Choose the correct verb form based on when the action occurs. The first one is done for you.

1. Eight thousand years ago, people (use, <u>used</u>) livestock, such as cattle or sheep, to pay for things.

2. About 2,500 years ago, the Chinese (start, started) using the first coins: lumps of silver.

3. History (shows, showed) that eventually people began to pay for things with leather money and then paper currency.

4. We (continue, continued) to use money to pay for our purchases today, but the form that money takes is always changing.

5. I believe that someday soon, we (pay, will pay) for everything using electronic money.

Answers are on page 759.

Forming the Present Tense of Regular Verbs

Most verbs in the English language are called **regular verbs** because they follow predictable rules to form the present and past tenses.

Study the table below about how to form a regular present tense verb.

Subject	Present Tense Verb	Example
he, she, it, and all singular nouns	gazes (base verb + -s)	She **gazes** toward the sea.
I, you, we, they, and all plural nouns	gaze (base verb, unchanged)	We **gaze** toward the sea.

Try forming some present tense verbs on your own. In the following sentences, fill in the blank with the word *cheer* or *cheers*.

The fans _____ when the home team scores a run.

My brother _____ for the opposing team.

The verb *cheer* is plural to agree with *fans*. The verb *cheers* is singular to agree with *brother*.

Forming the Past Tense of Regular Verbs

Recall that you generally add -*ed* to a base verb to form the past tense of regular verbs. When a base verb ends in *e*, however, you do not add -*ed*.

Incorrect: I *exerciseed* yesterday. (exercise + -*ed*)

Correct: I *exercised* yesterday. (exercise + -*d*)

When a verb ends with *e*, add only a -*d* to form the past tense of the verb. If you are not sure how to form the correct past tense of a verb, check a dictionary.

This chart shows you how to form the past tense of some regular verbs.

Base Verb	+	Ending	=	Past Tense
talk	+	-ed	=	talked
complete	+	-d	=	completed

Write the past tense of the base verb in each sentence below. The first one is done for you.

Our teacher (join) _joined_ our school's faculty this past September.
She (move) _____ here from another state over the summer.
She (want) _____ to live and teach in the city.
Her parents (live) _____ in the city before she was born.

You should have added -*ed* to the verb *want* to get the verb *wanted*. You should have added -*d* to the verbs *move* and *live* to get *moved* and *lived*.

Forming the Future Tense of Regular Verbs

Recall that the **future tense** describes something that *will* or *might* happen in the future. Consider these two examples of future tense verbs.

Marsha **will get** a summer job this year.

My brother and I **will get** summer jobs this year.

You always pair the helping verb *will* with the base verb to form the future tense. Notice also that you use the word *will* with both singular and plural subjects. The base verb remains the same when the subject changes from singular to plural.

EXERCISE 8

Forming Tenses of Regular Verbs

Directions: There are blanks for the past and future tenses of each verb given below. Write the correct form of the verb in each blank. The first one is done for you.

Base Verb	Past	Future
1. tow	towed	will tow
2. love	_____	_____
3. collect	_____	_____
4. sail	_____	_____
5. place	_____	_____

Answers are on page 759.

Other Tenses and Helping Verbs

Past participles are another kind of past tense verb. The past participle verb describes actions completed at the time of speaking or at or before a past time spoken of. A **past participle verb** has two parts: a helping verb (*has*, *have*, or *had*) and a base verb. The helping verb must agree with the subject in number.

Here are some examples. The subject is underlined and the past participle is in **boldface type**.

Amanda **has boiled** the water to make herself some tea.

We **have arrived** at our destination.

He **had asked** the man for directions because he was lost.

They **had traveled** all the way from California to visit us.

The base verb in each example takes the simple past form: a singular subject is paired with the singular verb *has*. A plural subject is paired with the plural verb *have*. The verb *had* works with both singular and plural subjects.

Forming Tenses with Irregular Verbs

Irregular verbs are words whose base verb changes when you form their past or future tenses. No rule applies to such verbs, so you must remember which ones fall into each category. However, if you are unsure if a verb takes an irregular form, check a dictionary.

Here is a breakdown of different irregular verbs and how they form the simple present, simple past, and past participle.

The simple present, simple past, and past participle take the same form.

Simple Present	Simple Past	Past Participle (with *have, has,* or *had*)
put	put	put
read	read (pronounced *red*)	read (pronounced *red*)
set	set	set

The simple present changes to the same form for the simple past _and_ past participle.

Simple Present	Simple Past	Past Participle (with _have, has,_ or _had_)
catch	caught	caught
hear	heard	heard
lose	lost	lost
say	said	said
stand	stood	stood

The simple present changes to form the simple past or the past participle. All three forms differ.

Simple Present	Simple Past	Past Participle (with _have, has,_ or _had_)
do or does	did	done
drive	drove	driven
go	went	gone
see	saw	seen
speak	spoke	spoken

The simple present changes to form the simple past, but shares the same form as the past participle.

Simple Present	Simple Past	Past Participle (with _have, has,_ or _had_)
become	became	become
come	came	come
run	ran	run

EXERCISE 9

Forming Tenses with Irregular Verbs

Directions: In the blanks below, write the correct form of the indicated verb in either the simple past or past participle form. For those verbs you cannot remember, check the lesson table showing the past tense of irregular verbs. Make sure the verb agrees with the subject in number and tense. The first one is done for you.

Base Verb

1. catch   Dad <u>caught</u> a cold last week. (simple past)

2. set   I _____ the clock this morning. (simple past)

3. drive   Our coach _____ to the gas station. (past participle)

4. go   The manager _____ to the cash register. (simple past)

5. lose   The woman _____ her wallet a month ago. (past participle)

6. stand   The animals _____ their ground. (simple past)

7. see   We _____ our favorite band in concert. (simple past)

8. hear   Nobody _____ the barking dog today. (past participle)

9. run   My neighbor _____ out of sugar. (simple past)

10. read   I loved the new book I _____. (simple past)

11. become   We all _____ members of the track team. (simple past)

Answers are on page 759.

Fixing Errors: Irregular Verbs

A past *tense* verb always stands alone. But the past *participle* of an irregular verb needs to combine with one of three helping verbs, *has, have,* or *had.*

The past participle for some verbs takes the same form as the past tense of the verb. Consider, for example, the present tense verb *meet. Met* is used for both the past tense and the past participle.

     I **met** my friend Jin for dinner today.

     I **had met** Jin at a party last spring.

In contrast, consider the verb *fall*. The past tense of the verb is *fell*, and the past participle is *fallen*.

> I **fell** many times when I practiced skating, but I always got back up.

> I **have fallen** repeatedly while trying to learn my new skating routine.

This difference between the past tense and past participle of a verb causes a common error: You may mistakenly use the past participle form of the verb instead of the past tense. Consider these examples.

> **Incorrect:** I **taken** the shorter route home. (past participle)

> **Correct:** I **took** the shorter route home. (past tense)

> **Incorrect:** She **grown** three inches since last year. (past participle)

> **Correct:** She **grew** three inches since last year. (past tense)

> **Incorrect:** We **eaten** some pineapple. (past participle)

> **Correct:** We **ate** some pineapple. (past tense)

EXERCISE 10

Fixing Errors: Irregular Verbs

Directions: In each of the following sentences, underline the correct form of the verb. The first one is done for you.

1. Becky (gave, given) a donation to her favorite charity.

2. The trainer (rode, ridden) the horse for its workout.

3. Julius Caesar once said, "I (came, come), I saw, I conquered."

4. We had (knew, known) the answer to the riddle.

5. Sketch artists (drew, drawn) pictures of the jurors in the courtroom.

6. When I broke my right arm, I (wrote, written) with my left hand instead.

Answers are on page 759.

Irregular Verbs: Be, Have, and Do

Three irregular verbs in English often cause speakers and writers trouble, *to have*, *to do*, and *to be*.

This table shows the present, past, future, and past participles of the irregular verb *to have*.

Subject	Present	Past	Future	Past Participle (with *has*, *have*, or *had*)
I	have			
he, she, it, and all singular nouns	has	had	will have	had
you, we, they, and all plural nouns	have			

Depending on the subject, you will use *have* or *has* in the present tense. *Had* is always used for the past tense, *will have* for the future tense, and *had* in the past participle; it doesn't matter in any of these instances if the subject is singular or plural.

Here is a table showing the present, past, future, and past participles of the irregular verb *do*.

Subject	Present	Past	Future	Past Participle (with *has*, *have*, or *had*)
I	do			
he, she, it, and all singular nouns	does	did	will do	done
you, we, they, and all plural nouns	do			

- Depending on the subject, you will use *do* or *does* in the present tense.

- You will always use *did* for the past tense whether the subject is singular or plural.

- You will use *will do* for the future tense and *done* for the past participle, making this verb one of those irregular verbs whose past and past participle forms are different.

Read the paragraph below. Cross out the each incorrect verb, and then write the correct replacement above it. Each sentence has at least one error.

You does not want to live in a house or apartment without a smoke

detector. Tenants and homeowners has to be alerted when there is a

fire. The annoying beep of a smoke detector have a way of getting your

attention. The manufacturer of these life-saving devices do its part to

keep you safe by making them in the first place, but smoke detectors

cannot help you if you does not install one.

Here is the correct version of this paragraph:

> You **do** not want to live in a house or apartment without a smoke detector. Tenants and homeowners **have** to be alerted when there is a fire. The annoying beep of a smoke detector **has** a way of getting your attention. The manufacturer of these life-saving devices **does** its part to keep you safe by making them in the first place, but smoke detectors cannot help you if you **do** not install one.

What makes *be* an irregular verb? Study the following chart before you try to answer this question.

Subject	Present	Past	Future	Past Participle (with *has, have,* or *had*)
I	am	was	will be	been
he, she, it, and all singular nouns	is	was	will be	been
you, we, they, and all plural nouns	are	were	will be	been

Among irregular verbs, *be* is unique because it changes so frequently.

- It completely changes its form in the present tense to *am*, *is*, or *are* depending on the subject of the sentence.
- It can take two different forms in the past tense (*was* or *were*), depending on whether the subject is singular or plural.
- The plural form in the present tense is *are*. The future form is *will be*. In the past participle, the verb changes to *been*.

Read the following sentences, and circle the correct form of the verb *be*.

> Early in the movie, the villain declares, "I (be, am) going to conquer the world!"
>
> The hero (was, were) not about to let the villain get away with his evil scheme.
>
> You (is, are) going to be on the edge of your seat if you decide to go see the film.
>
> I had (be, been) wanting to see the movie myself ever since it first came out.

- The verb *am* is correct in the first sentence because it agrees with the singular subject *I*.
- The verb *was* agrees with the singular subject *hero* in the second sentence.
- *Are* is correct in the third sentence because it agrees with the plural *You*.
- In the fourth sentence, the base verb *been* is the past participle form of the verb that is correctly paired with the helping verb *had*.

EXERCISE 11

Irregular Verbs: *Be, Have,* and *Do*

Directions: Each of the following sentences contains a blank. Fill in the blank with the correct form of *be, have,* or *do*. Notice that each sentence specifies the verb tense in parentheses. The first sentence is done for you.

1. (past) Roger Bannister ___was___ the first person to run a mile in under four minutes.

2. (present) _____ I fast enough to run a four-minute mile?

3. (future) I _____ old enough to drive on my next birthday.

4. (past participle) Aliyah _____ in the Coast Guard since last year.

5. (present) Richard _____ a green thumb when it comes to plants.

6. (past) The Nelsons _____ car trouble during their vacation last June.

7. (future) We _____ just enough time to catch our train before it leaves.

8. (present) The presidential oath of office begins, "I _____ solemnly swear . . . ."

9. (past) Erik _____ me a favor by picking me up after work today.

10. (past participle) Padma _____ all the tasks on her to-do list by 11 this morning.

Answers are on page 760.

Forming Continuous Tenses

Some actions happen *now* and then end. They only exist in the moment. But sometimes an action that started in the past continues in the present. You use the **present continuous tense** for verbs that describe these ongoing actions. Use *am, is,* or *are* as the helping verb, and then add *-ing* to the base verb, as shown in this chart:

Subject	Helping Verb	Base Verb + *-ing*
I	am	
he, *she*, *it*, and all singular nouns	is	sweating
you, *we*, *they*, and all plural nouns	are	

Now consider the following example.

The farmer **is plowing** the field behind the barn.

The two words in the verb are the helping verb *is* plus the base verb *plow*. Adding *-ing* to the base verb *plow* signals that the action is ongoing because the farmer continues to plow the field in the present.

Some verbs require that you change their endings to form the present continuous tense as the chart below shows. When in doubt about the correct form of a continuous tense verb, however, check a dictionary.

Verb	Present Continuous Tense	Example
Most verbs	add *-ing* to the base verb.	We are **laughing** at his antics. (*laugh* + *-ing*)
Verbs ending in *-e*	drop the final *e* and add *-ing*.	The street performer is **juggling**. (Drop the final *e* before adding *-ing* to *juggle*.)

Is the continuous tense limited to *present* actions? No. Sometimes actions started in the past and continued in the past but ended before the present moment. To describe such actions, you use the **past continuous tense.**

Present continuous: The street performer **is juggling**.

Past continuous: The street performer **was juggling** when we left the store.

Notice how the helping verb changed from the present *is* to the past *was* as the tense changed.

The chart below shows the forms of the verb *to sweat* in the past continuous tense. Compare this to the chart that shows the forms of *sweat* in the present continuous tense above. What is different? The helping verbs have changed. The helping verbs here are the past tense forms of *be*.

Subject	Helping Verb	Base Verb + *-ing*
I, *he*, *she*, *it*, and all singular nouns	was	sweating
you, *we*, *they*, and all plural nouns	were	

Using the base verb in each sentence below, fill in the blank with the base verb's past continuous form. The first one is done for you.

The blizzard <u>was ending</u> at long last.
(end)

Jerome _____ to the weather report.
(listen)

The two astronauts _____ for liftoff.
(prepare)

- *Jerome* is the singular subject in the second sentence, so you should have written *was listening* in the blank.

- The plural subject *astronauts* in the third sentence requires the verb form *were preparing*.

EXERCISE 12

Forming Continuous Tenses

Directions: To complete each sentence, write a verb in the blank that is in the present or past continuous tense. The first one is done for you.

1. Archaeologists (look) <u>were looking</u> for years for evidence of an ancient civilization.

2. During all that time they (fail) _____ to find enough to prove the civilization existed.

3. Today the location still (provide) _____ important clues about the people who may have lived there.

4. The woman in charge of the new dig (hope) _____ that we will find evidence this time.

5. Now we (get) _____ our funding for this dig from the American Museum of Natural History.

6. I (drop) _____ hints all night that I wanted to leave the party.

7. My fiancé (ignore) _____ me no matter what I said.

8. She (enjoy) _____ herself and did not want to leave.

Answers are on page 760.

Adjectives

Recall what you have learned about the two kinds of modifiers, adjectives and adverbs. An **adjective** tells you something about the noun it modifies by answering a question about that noun: *What kind? Which one? How many?* Adjectives can add help define and add character to the nouns they modify.

> **Without adjectives:** The house sat at the end of the street.

> **With adjectives:** The **mysterious**, **empty** house sat at the **dark** end of the street.

This is not just any house. The adjectives *mysterious*, *alone*, and *dark* tell you specifically what kind of house this is.

Placing Adjectives

Where should you place an adjective, before or after the noun it modifies? This depends on the type of verb that accompanies the noun.

> **Incorrect:** The novel **thrilling** <u>kept</u> me interested from the first page.

> **Correct:** The **thrilling** novel <u>kept</u> me riveted from the first page.

If the verb is not a linking verb, the adjective must come before it: *kept* is not a linking verb, so the adjective *thrilling* must come before it. Now consider this next sentence.

> The novel <u>was</u> **thrilling** and kept me interested from the first page.

In this case you should place the adjective *thrilling* after the noun and the first verb attached to it, the linking verb *was*.

EXERCISE 13

Placing Adjectives (Part 1)

Directions: Each of the following sentences contains an underlined adjective and an action verb. Reposition the adjective in each sentence by rewriting the sentence on the blank using a linking verb. The first one is done for you.

1. The <u>cool</u> summer of 1816 produced something New Englanders had never seen before: snow in June.

   The summer of 1816 was cool and produced something New Englanders had never seen before: snow in June.

2. The <u>strange</u> weather that summer damaged crops throughout the northeastern United States.

   _____

   _____

3. The perplexing cause of the unusual weather remained a mystery for nearly a century.

_____

_____

4. Some insightful scientists concluded that the cause was the eruption of Mount Tambora a year earlier.

_____

_____

Answers are on page 760.

Placing Adjectives (Part 2)

Directions: Each of the following sentences contains a blank and an underlined noun. Fill each blank with an adjective of your own to modify the underlined noun. The first one is done for you.

1. The ___playful___ children frolicked in the ___glittering___ surf.

(what kind)
(what kind)

2. The _____ waves sent the _____ _____ friends scurrying for

(what kind)
(how many)

   the safety of the beach.

3. The _____ boy found a _____ seashell.

(which one)
(what kind)

4. At the end of the day, the _____ families packed up their belongings

(how many)

   and boarded the _____ bus to arrive at the beach stop.

(which one)

Answers are on page 760.

Adverbs

Although adverbs generally modify verbs, they can also tell you something about adjectives or other adverbs as long as they are answering the question *How? When?* or *Where?*

Because many—but not all—adverbs end in *-ly*, you may think that the *-ly* ending is always a sign that a word is an adverb. This is not necessarily true. *Hilly* and *bully*, for example, end in *-ly*, but *hilly* is an adjective that answers the question *What kind? Bully* can be a noun or a verb depending on its use.

The table below shows some common adverbs and the questions they answer.

How?	When?	Where?
slowly	never	alongside
very	always	here
greatly	early	there
badly	yesterday	upstairs

Consider this sentence:

> Marty is <u>tall</u>.

Tall is an adjective that tells you something about Marty. Now let's add an adverb.

> Marty is (very) <u>tall</u>.

The word *very* answers the question, *How tall?* So *very* is an adverb modifying *tall*.

In this next sentence, an adverb modifies another adverb.

> Wanda left the party (rather) <u>early</u>.

Early is an adverb modifying *left* because it tells *when* Wanda left. *Rather* is an adverb telling *how early* Wanda left. *Rather* is an adverb modifying another adverb.

Placing Adverbs

Adverbs are flexible and can modify verbs, adjectives, or other adverbs. Adverbs may appear in various positions within a sentence. In these examples, the adverbs and the questions they answer are in **boldface type**.

How?

Gratefully, she returned the book.

I was **utterly** speechless.

When?

Jay made a plane reservation **yesterday**.

Nadia is **rarely** here.

Where?

I was going to meet Luis **downstairs**.

She ran **alongside** the bus and waved goodbye to her sister.

An adverb usually follows the verb it describes, for example, but adverbs that modify verbs may also show up elsewhere in a sentence. If an adverb modifies an adjective or another adverb, it is likely to precede it.

EXERCISE 14

Placing Adverbs

Directions: This exercise gives you a chance to write sentences of your own that contain adverbs. One of the sentences in each item is done already. You will write the two remaining sentences. Your two sentences should contain adverbs that answer the questions, *How? When?* or *Where?* The first item is finished for you.

1. a. (how)   We speak frequently.

    b. (when)   We speak daily.

    c. (where)   We speak downstairs.

Now use the verb *swim* and adverbs of your own.

2. a. (how)   The twins swim slowly.

    b. (when)   _____

    c. (where)   _____

Use the verb *bloom* and adverbs of your own.

3. a. (how)   _____

    b. (when)   The rosebush blooms annually.

    c. (where)   _____

Answers are on page 760.

Adjective or Adverb?

Because adjectives and adverbs are both modifiers that *describe* something (a noun, verb, adjective, or adverb), it is easy to confuse them with each other. This is especially true because many adjectives and adverbs look so similar. Add the short ending *-ly* to an adjective, and you often produce an adverb. Consider these examples of adverbs and adjectives that look almost identical.

Adjective	Adverb
proud	proudly
weak	weakly

The *-ly* rule is not absolute. Sometimes you have to adjust the spelling of the adjective slightly before adding the *-ly* ending. When an adjective ends in *y*, for example, change the *y* to *i*, and then add *-ly*.

Adjective	Adverb
hazy	hazily
weary	wearily

So how do you know which form to use? Consider the word's role in the sentence. Use the adjective form if the word describes a noun, and the adverb form if it describes a verb, an adjective, or another adverb.

These four sentences show the differences between adjectives and adverbs. In each example, the adjective or adverb is in **bold typeface**, and the word it modifies is <u>underlined</u>.

Part of Speech	Example
Adjective modifying a noun	A solar eclipse is a **rare** <u>event</u>.
Adverb modifying a verb	A solar eclipse is an event that we **rarely** <u>witness</u>.
Adverb modifying an adjective	A solar eclipse is a **truly** <u>amazing</u> event.
Adverb modifying an adverb	A solar eclipse is an event that people **almost** <u>never</u> witness.

EXERCISE 15

Adjective or Adverb?

Directions: Underline the correct adjective or adverb in parentheses for each sentence. Circle the word that it modifies. Then write *adjective* or *adverb* in the blank, The first one is done for you.

1. The (<u>fierce</u>, fiercely) (elephant) charged through the high grass.
   adjective

2. Other animals scattered (wild, wildly) in every direction to escape the rampaging giant. _____

3. In the blink of an eye, the (peaceful, peacefully) landscape had been transformed into a loud and terrifying scene. _____

4. Even the trees seemed to quake (fearful, fearfully). _____

5. Only the cameraman who was filming the scene remained (calm, calmly). _____

6. He knew that the elephant's rage would (quick, quickly) subside. _____

7. The man had (frequent, frequently) filmed in this part of Africa and was familiar with the animal's behavior. _____

Answers are on page 760.

CHAPTER 3

Constructing Sentences

This chapter focuses on developing your writing skills. You will learn how to create sentences with several different kinds of structures. Using those varied structures makes your writing interesting and keeps it flowing smoothly. You will also learn how to fix sentence problems such as wordiness and misplaced modifiers.

Combining Sentences to Make Your Writing Flow Smoothly

Sentence structure is the order of words in a sentence. As you have learned, a simple sentence contains either a simple or compound subject followed by a predicate.

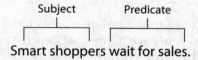

Smart shoppers wait for sales.

However, if you use the same sentence structure over and over, your writing sounds repetitive and choppy.

Smart shoppers want to save money. They wait for holiday sales. They shop online for bargains.

You can fix this problem if you **revise**, or rewrite, sentences by combining them to sound more pleasing to the ear. Be sure that you do not change the sentences' meaning when you revise them. The elements added or changed to revise the sentences are in **bold typeface**.

Because smart shoppers want to save money, **they** wait for holiday sales **and** shop online for bargains.

When the three sentences are combined into one, this writing no longer sounds repetitive and choppy but sounds lively and flows smoothly. Here are several methods you can use to combine sentences.

Combining Sentences with Conjunctions

Words such as *and, but, so, therefore,* and *however* are conjunctions. The word *conjunction* means "an act of joining," and this is exactly what a conjunction does. A **conjunction** is a part of speech that joins two or more words, clauses, or sentences.

Elizabeth Bennett **and** Mr. Darcy are characters in the novel *Pride and Prejudice.*

We had intended to take the day off; **however**, an emergency forced us to change our plans.

Different conjunctions have different purposes. You will learn more about them later in the chapter.

Creating Compound Sentences

Recall that an independent clause contains a subject and predicate and, therefore, can stand alone as a sentence. Here are two examples.

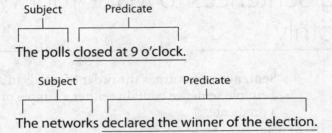

When you join two independent clauses with a conjunction, they form a **compound sentence**. Conjunctions that form compound sentences are called **coordinating conjunctions**. These include *and, but, or, nor, for, so,* and *yet.*

Let's combine the two independent clauses above using a coordinating conjunction. Notice that there are additional revisions you need to make when you combine compound sentences with a conjunction.

The polls closed at 9 o'clock, **and t**he networks declared the winner of the election.

The revisions to the sentence include these steps:

- **Punctuation:** Replace the period at the end of the first sentence with a comma.

- **Transition:** Connect the two sentences with the conjunction *and.*

- **Capitalization:** Change the capital *T* to a small *t* in the second *the* because it is no longer the first word in a sentence.

Now it's your turn. Combine these sentences by inserting the correct punctuation, adding a conjunction, and capitalizing letters correctly.

The loser in the election demanded a recount of the votes.

She refused to admit defeat.

You should have made these changes:

- Replaced the period at the end of the first sentence with a comma.

- Added the conjunction, *and.*

- Replaced the capital *S* in *She* with a small *s* (*she*).

The loser in the election demanded a recount of the votes. ~~She~~ refused to admit defeat. *, and she*

Creating Compound Subjects

When the subjects in two different sentences share the same predicate, you can combine the sentences by creating a **compound subject**. Compound subjects are generally joined by the conjunctions *and*, *or*, or *nor*.

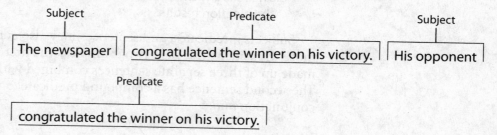

Let's combine these two sentences to form a compound subject:

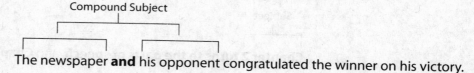

Creating Compound Predicates

When predicates in two different sentences share the same subject, you can join the predicates with a conjunction to make a **compound predicate.**

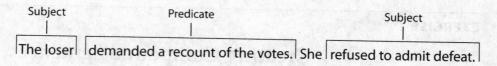

Here's how to combine these sentences using a compound predicate.

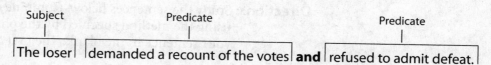

Both predicates share the same subject, *the loser*. Notice that you replace *she*, the subject of the second sentence, with the conjunction *and*. You no longer need the word *she* because the word *loser* now serves as the subject of the compound predicate.

Now you try one. Combine the two sentences below by using a compound predicate. Cross out any word or words that don't belong in the combined sentence, and adjust the punctuation as needed.

The recount changed the vote totals for the two candidates. It reversed the election results.

You should have deleted the period and replaced the subject of the second sentence, *It*, with the word *and*.

The recount changed the vote totals for the two candidates. ~~It~~ ^{and} reversed the election results.

Subjects, predicates, and sentences may also come in groups of three or more. Consider these next two examples. The first is a compound sentence made up of three separate sentences combined with the conjunction *and*. The second sentence has a compound predicate, once again combined by the conjunction *and*.

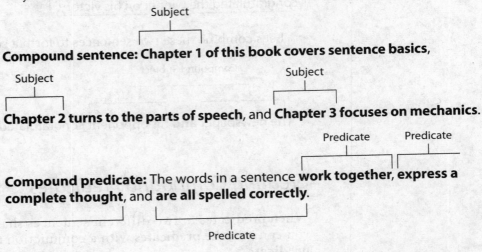

Subject

Compound sentence: Chapter 1 of this book covers sentence basics,

Subject

Subject

Chapter 2 turns to the parts of speech, and **Chapter 3 focuses on mechanics**.

Predicate   Predicate

Compound predicate: The words in a sentence **work together**, **express a complete thought**, and **are all spelled correctly**.

Predicate

EXERCISE 1

Creating Compound Sentences, Compound Subjects, and Compound Predicates

Directions: Study the sentences below. Combine each pair of sentences using the method specified by the phrase in parentheses. Write your sentence in the blank. The first one is done for you.

1. (compound sentence) Today, Earth is divided into different time zones. Each zone represents time on the standard 24-hour clock.

   Today, Earth is divided into different time zones, and each zone represents time on the standard 24-hour clock.

2. (compound subject) Neighboring states can be one time zone apart. Neighboring towns can be one time zone apart.

_____

_____

3. (compound sentence) In the early 19th century, the United States had 300 different time zones. The continental United States has four time zones today.

_____

_____

4. (compound subject) In earlier centuries, towns established the correct time based on the position of the sun. In earlier centuries, villages established the correct time based on the position of the sun.

_____

_____

5. (compound predicate) Today's system of time zones standardizes timekeeping across the United States. Today's system of time zones makes it easier to tell time consistently.

_____

_____

_____

Answers are on page 761.

Combining Sentences with Conjunctive Adverbs

A **conjunctive adverb** modifies an entire sentence. It establishes a relationship between two independent sentences or two clauses in a compound sentence.

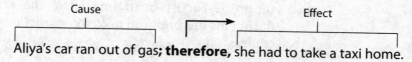

Cause

Effect

Aliya's car ran out of gas**; therefore,** she had to take a taxi home.

In this sentence, the conjunctive adverb *therefore* establishes a cause-and-effect relationship. When Aliya's car ran out of gas, it caused a specific effect: she had to take a taxi home.

The table that follows lists several conjunctive adverbs and their purposes. Notice the relationship each conjunctive adverb establishes between the sentences it connects.

Conjunctive Adverbs	Purpose	Examples
also, furthermore, moreover, namely	Add information.	Angelina Jolie and Russell Brand are both movie stars; **furthermore**, they were born on the same day in the very same year.
conversely, however, nevertheless	Create a contrast.	A person weighing 150 pounds on Earth would weigh 355 pounds on Jupiter; **however**, he or she would weigh only 25 pounds on the moon.
likewise, similarly	Make a comparison.	Paris is the most popular tourist destination. **Likewise**, London draws millions of visitors each year.
finally, next, now, eventually	Establish a time frame.	Learning how to play the banjo was a real struggle; **eventually**, I became good enough at the instrument to entertain my friends.
consequently, hence, therefore	Show cause and effect.	Every spring, we turn the clocks forward one hour; **therefore**, sunset comes one hour later.

The conjunction you choose defines the relationship between the two sentences you combine. Be sure to choose the right conjunction for the job. If you link two sentences with an inaccurate conjunction, the sentence you create will not make sense.

Incorrect: Van Gogh sold only one painting during his life; **therefore,** he became one the greatest artists of all time.

Correct: Van Gogh sold only one painting during his life; **nevertheless,** he became one of the greatest artists of all time.

The first sentence is confusing. *Therefore* is a conjunction that establishes a cause-and-effect relationship between two ideas. But Van Gogh did not become one of the greatest artists of all time *because* he only sold one painting during his lifetime. That makes no sense. Instead, he became one of the greatest artists of all time *despite* the fact that he only sold one painting during his lifetime. You need a conjunction such as *nevertheless* that contrasts the two ideas.

When a conjunctive adverb appears in the middle of a sentence, the first letter is *not* capitalized. Instead, a semicolon comes before the conjunctive adverb and a comma follows it.

Some people prefer dogs as pets**; however,** others prefer cats.

In this sentence, the conjunctive adverb contrasts the first and second parts of the compound sentence: people who prefer dogs as pets versus people who prefer cats. Notice these points:

- A semicolon marks the point where the first part of the compound sentence ends.
- The semicolon is followed immediately by the conjunctive adverb *however*.
- A comma follows the word *however*.

EXERCISE 2

Combining Sentences with Conjunctive Adverbs

Directions: Write a conjunctive adverb in each blank, and add the correct punctuation. Remember to choose an adverb that correctly reflects the meaning of the sentence. The first one is done for you.

1. Rachel and I had an argument; nevertheless, we are still friends.

2. We sent e-mails to Jim for two months _____ he wrote back.

3. Getting through this day has been tough _____ this has been an extremely difficult week.

4. I enjoy playing tennis _____ I like to watch it on television.

5. A hurricane can flatten houses _____ the air inside the eye of the hurricane remains eerily calm.

6. The weather forecast predicted bitterly cold temperatures all week _____ we went to the local pond every afternoon to go ice-skating.

Answers are on page 761.

Combining Sentences with Subordinating Conjunctions

The two independent clauses in a compound sentence are equally important: each clause expresses a complete thought and can stand on its own as a sentence. But a **dependent clause** is a sentence fragment that does not express a complete thought; as a result, it cannot stand on its own as a sentence. A word that introduces a dependent clause is called a **subordinating conjunction**.

Consider the following example:

Because we missed our exit on the drive home.

This clause has a subject (*we*) and a predicate (*missed our exit on the drive home*). But the subordinating conjunction *Because* turns the sentence into a dependent clause that cannot stand on its own, and its meaning is unclear.

What happened "because we missed our exit"? There is no way to answer the question.

You can fix this problem by combining a dependent clause with an independent clause to make a complete sentence. This will make the meaning of your sentence clear. A dependent clause *depends* on, or is subordinate to, the independent clause to give it meaning.

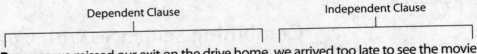

Because we missed our exit on the drive home, we arrived too late to see the movie.

Notice that you must place a comma at the point where the dependent clause ends and the independent clause begins. There is another option for solving the problem. A dependent clause can also *follow* an independent clause. When that happens, you do not need to add a comma, but you do need to change the capital *B* in *Because* to a lowercase *b* since it is no longer the first word in the sentence.

We arrived too late to see the movie **because** we missed our exit on the drive home.

Like conjunctive adverbs, subordinating conjunctions have a special purpose. They form a relationship or connection between the parts of a sentence—in this case, between the dependent clause and the independent clause.

Here are some common subordinating conjunctions and examples of what they do.

Subordinating Conjunctions	Purpose	Examples
after, before, once, since, until, when	Establish a time frame.	**Before** we entered the theater, we bought our tickets.
because, since	Establish cause and effect.	**Since** the police had closed the road ahead due to flooding, we had to take a long detour.
if, unless	Describe a condition.	You get the color green **if** you mix blue and yellow paint together.
although, whereas	Create a contrast.	**Although** he eats lots of food, he never gains weight.
where, wherever	Describe a location.	**Wherever** we went that day, strangers greeted us as if we were long-lost friends.
whether	Describe a choice.	**Whether** you rooted for the winning or losing team, you must agree that it was a great game.

Remember to choose the conjunction that accurately defines the relationship between the sentences. Consider one of the examples given in the table. Notice that the conjunction *because* in the incorrect sentence below makes the sentence confusing.

Incorrect: Because Tim eats lots of food, he never gains weight.

Correct: Although Tim eats lots of food, he never gains weight.

The subordinating conjunction because in the first sentence makes no sense. Tim doesn't gain weight because he eats lots of food. The sentence is meant to show contrast. Tim never gains weight even though he eats a lot of food.

EXERCISE 3

Combining Sentences with Subordinating Conjunctions

Directions: Combine the following pairs of sentences using a subordinating conjunction found in the previous chart. Be sure to choose the appropriate subordinating conjunction based on the information in each sentence. The first one is done for you.

1. Scientists developed the tetanus vaccine in the 1920s. People could die if a small cut became infected.

   Before scientists developed the tetanus vaccine in the 1920s, people could die if a small cut became infected.

2. We cannot wrap up this wedding ceremony. You both say, "I do."

   _____

   _____

3. We saw the coast emerging from the fog. We knew we would reach shore soon.

   _____

   _____

4. You want to excel at anything. You have to work hard.

   _____

   _____

5. I am a defensive driver. I could not avoid the car that ran the stop sign.

   _____

   _____

6. I forgave him. His apology was so heartfelt.

_____

_____

7. I can't decide. I should vote for one of the two-party candidates or for the independent candidate.

_____

_____

Answers are on page 761.

Solving Other Sentence Structure Problems

Other sentence structure problems involve parallelism, wordiness, word order, misplaced or dangling modifiers, split infinitives, comma usage, and run-on sentences. The following sections will describe techniques for solving these sentence problems.

Editing for Parallel Structure

Anytime you see one of the coordinating conjunctions such as *and* or *or*, be on the lookout for parallel structure. **Parallel structure** is a grammatical construction in which specific elements in a sentence are of equal importance. Consider this sentence:

> The five senses include **hearing**, **to see**, **to smell**, **tasting**, and **touching**.

Hearing, *tasting*, and *touching* all end in *-ing*. But *to see* and *to smell* take a different form: they begin with *to* and do not end in *-ing*. In other words, even though the five subjects are equally important in the sentence, they are not parallel because they do not all take the same form.

Fixing this error is simple. Change the subjects so that they all have the same form. Try to make the smallest number of changes possible when you do this. For example:

> The five senses include **hearing**, **seeing**, **smelling**, **tasting**, and **touching**.

By cutting *to* and adding *-ing* to *see* and *smell*, you have made them parallel to *hearing*, *tasting*, and *touching* because now they all share the same *-ing* form.

Here is another example showing failed parallel structure. Can you spot the problem?

The street performer was brash, loud, and was funny.

The problem in this sentence is the second appearance of the verb *was* before the adjective *funny*. What is the simplest way to fix this problem? You do not need to repeat the word *was* more than once.

The street performer was brash, loud, and funny.

EXERCISE 4

Editing for Parallel Structure

Directions: One of the sentences below is correct; the others contain an error in parallel structure. Correct the sentences that contain an error by crossing out the mistake and then writing the correct form of the word or phrase above the error. The first one is done for you. Circle the number of the sentence that contains no error.

city worker
1. Selene is a wife, mother, and ~~works for the city~~.

2. When you come to an intersection, a stop sign is a signal to slow down and to look both ways.

3. Inventor Thomas Edison claimed that genius is 1 percent inspiration and 99 percent to perspire.

4. The singers at the rehearsal came in, waited for their turn on stage, and then performed a musical number together.

5. Running, biking, and to swim are three ways to stay in shape.

Answers are on page 761.

Editing Wordy Sentences

Have you ever heard the expression, "Less is more"? Consider this sentence:

Adding unnecessary words or clauses to a sentence **so that you're increasing the length of the sentence to make it longer** does not improve it.

Do the extra, boldface words in the sentence add anything to the thought that is expressed? No. Wordiness like this distracts readers from what you say because they get tangled in the unnecessary words. Look for opportunities to revise the sentence by saying the same thing with fewer words.

> **Wordy:** I want to take some classes and get some training on account of the fact that people in the medical field make more money and are more financially successful.

> **Revision:** I want to train in the medical field to make more money.

How did we eliminate wordiness from this sentence?

> I want to ~~take some classes and get some training on account of the~~ ~~fact that people~~ in the medical field ^to^ make more money ~~and are more~~ ~~financially successful.~~

Here are some tips for revising wordy sentences:

- Look for words and phrases that have the same meaning. Choose one to use and get rid of the rest. *Some classes* and *some training* have similar meanings, so they are needlessly repetitive. This is also true of *are more financially successful* and *make more money.*

- Look for opportunities to shorten phrases without compromising meaning: shorten *get some . . . training* to *train*, for example.

- Occasionally, you may need to add a word or two to make the sentence grammatically correct. In this case, so much was cut from the sentence that the word *to* had to be added before *make more money.* You should add words under these circumstances only when absolutely necessary.

EXERCISE 5

Editing Wordy Sentences

Directions: Read the sentences below. In the blanks, write a revision of each sentence that expresses the same thought with fewer words. The first one is done for you.

1. The companies that make cars offer a full range of vehicles for you to drive that come in a lot of different sizes and many colors. *Car companies sell vehicles that come in many sizes and colors.*

2. The car we bought was a bargain because we made a good buy and saved some money.

_____

_____

3. There is a house in my neighborhood that has been for sale a long time because it has not had any buyers.

_____

_____

4. The people who had registered to vote in the election waited in line to go into the booths and cast their ballots for the candidates of their choice.

_____

_____

5. All of my favorite shoes are currently on sale at this time.

_____

_____

Answers are on page 761.

Editing for Illogical Word Order

The placement of a modifier affects a sentence's meaning. For example, the placement of the word *only* changes the meaning of each of these three sentences dramatically. The word or words that *only* modifies are underlined.

Only <u>I</u> clean the living room on weekends.

Meaning: No one else but me cleans the living room on weekends.

I **only** <u>clean the living room</u> on weekends.

Meaning: I clean the living room on weekends, not on weekdays.

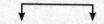

I clean **only** <u>the living room</u> on weekends.

Meaning: I don't clean any other rooms but the living room on weekends.

Placing the modifier in the correct position makes each sentence's meaning clear.

EXERCISE 6

Editing for Illogical Word Order

Directions: Add the modifier *nearly* to each sentence to produce a different meaning. Rewrite the sentence, and write its meaning in the blanks following each sentence.

1. **a.** We lost all our money.

   <u>We lost nearly all our money</u>

   Meaning: We lost almost all the money we had.

   b. We lost all our money.

   _____

   Meaning: _____

2. Add the modifier *quickly* to each sentence to produce a different meaning.

   a. Walking tones your muscles.

   _____

   Meaning: _____

   b. Walking tones your muscles.

   _____

   Meaning: _____

Answers are on page 762.

Editing Misplaced Modifiers

Modifiers such as adjectives and adverbs tell you something about the nouns, verbs, adjectives, or adverbs they describe. But if you place a modifier too far from the word it describes, the sentence may become confusing. Consider this example:

Cooked the day before, the **woman** enjoyed eating the chicken.

In this case, the modifier (*cooked the day before*) is placed too far from the word it should modify (*chicken*), so it modifies the wrong noun (*woman*). As a result, the sentence is confusing: the woman was not *cooked the day before*, the chicken was. You can fix this problem by moving *cooked the day before* next to the word it should modify (*chicken*). Now the sentence makes sense.

The woman enjoyed eating the chicken <u>cooked the day before</u>.

Sometimes a misplaced modifier makes your sentence ambiguous, meaning it has two possible meanings that conflict with each other, making the sentence's meaning unclear.

Lucy told Jorge when the class was over she would drive him home.

Did Lucy tell Jorge she would drive him home after class, or did she tell him after class that she would drive him home? To solve this problem, revise the sentence so the meaning is clear, depending on what you really want to say:

Lucy told Jorge she would drive him home when the class was over.

OR

When the class was over, Lucy told Jorge she would drive him home.

EXERCISE 7

Editing Misplaced Modifiers

Directions: Read the numbered items below. Circle the misplaced modifier that makes the meaning of each sentence unclear. Then correct the mistake by rewriting the sentence on the line that follows so its meaning is clear. The first one is done for you.

1. The lion roarded at the children (in the cage at the zoo).

   The lion in the cage at the zoo roared at the children.

2. The pirate found a chest of gold in the storybook.

   _____

   _____

3. Jacob served cake to his guests on china plates.

   _____

   _____

Answers are on page 762.

Editing Dangling Modifiers

You have learned that certain parts of speech, such as adjectives, can modify, or describe, other parts of speech, such as nouns. But sometimes an entire phrase or clause, not just a single word, modifies another part of speech. Such clauses often come at the beginning of a sentence:

Modifier

Sailing into New York's harbor, many **immigrants** wept with joy.

Who is sailing into New York's harbor? *Immigrants.* This modifier is a dependent clause that describes the subject of the sentence, *immigrants.*

Now consider the following sentence.

Sailing into New York's harbor, the journey was at an end.

Journey is the subject of this sentence, but is journey *sailing into New York's harbor?* No, that does not make sense. So who is sailing? The sentence never names the subject. Because the subject it modifies is missing, the modifier is left hanging, or dangling—thus, the name *dangling modifier.* A **dangling modifier** has no connection to any of the other elements in the sentence. As a result, the sentence's meaning is unclear.

How can you fix this problem? You can add a subject and verb. Now the modifier is no longer dangling because it has a subject to modify.

Sailing into New York's harbor, the **immigrants knew** the journey was at an end.

Editing Split Infinitives

Poorly positioned modifiers also cause another problem, split infinitives. An **infinitive** combines the word *to* with a verb, as in the motto of many police departments: *to protect and serve.* A **split infinitive** occurs when a word or words come between *to* and the verb. Split infinitives have become more acceptable in writing than they used to be, but if you are writing in a formal context, like a business letter or an exam, it always safer to avoid split infinitives.

Incorrect: I intend my words *to **precisely** mean* what I say.

Generally, this is an easy problem to fix. Place the modifier after the infinitive, as long as it does not change the meaning of the sentence.

Correct: I intend my words to *mean **precisely*** what I say.

EXERCISE 8

Editing Dangling Modifiers and Split Infinitives

Directions: In the first blank following each sentence below, identify the error as a dangling modifier (DM) or split infinitive (SI). Circle the error. Then on the second blank, correct the error by rewriting the sentence. The first one is done for you.

1. Hoping to escape, the imprisoned hero had (to noiselessly tiptoe) past the sleeping dragon. **SI** *Hoping to escape, the imprisoned hero had to tiptoe noiselessly past the sleeping dragon.*

2. Peering through the darkness, the door stood only a few feet away.

3. He was going to have to quickly slip out, or all hope was lost.

4. Sneaking toward the door, his sword slipped out of his hand.

Answers are on page 762.

Correcting Comma Usage

A comma is a punctuation mark that appears within a sentence. It has different roles depending on the situation.

For example, commas can help avoid confusion so a sentence's meaning is clear.

Incorrect: Guests who have stayed at our hotel include Dolly Parton's sisters George Clooney and Vice President Joe Biden.

Incorrect: While painting Martha dropped the brush.

The missing commas in these sentences create confusion. George Clooney and Vice President Joe Biden are not Dolly Parton's sisters. Martha is painting, not being painted.

Correct: Guests who have stayed at our hotel include Dolly Parton's sisters, George Clooney, and Vice President Joe Biden.

Correct: While painting, Martha dropped the brush.

The following table demonstrates some of the uses of commas.

Comma Use	Examples
Separate two parts of a compound sentence.	**We came to a fork in the road,** and **we took the path to the left**.
Separate items in a series.	I bought some desserts for the party including **a lemon pie, a chocolate cake, and three flavors of ice cream.**
	The students **walked in, looked around the classroom, and found their seats.**
Separate elements that describe a noun but are not necessary to understand the sentence's meaning.	Darth Vader**, the villain in the original _Star Wars_ movie,** is actually Luke Skywalker's father.
Separate introductory words, phrases, or dependent clauses.	**Although we thought we were finally safe,** our troubles had only just begun.
	On my way out the door, I said goodbye to my cat.
Tell when a quotation begins or ends.	"This was a great day for our city**," said the mayor.**

Watch out for comma splices, one of the most common mistakes when punctuating with commas. Do not combine two independent clauses, or sentences that can stand on their own, with a comma.

Incorrect: He worked at the Italian restaurant, now he works at the coffee shop.

Correct: He worked at the Italian restaurant. **N**ow he works at the coffee shop.

EXERCISE 9

Correcting Comma Usage (Part 1)

Directions: Insert commas in the following sentences to punctuate them correctly.

1. According to rumors the couple's wedding will take place in France.

2. My uncle Carlos an architect for 20 years designed a new school.

3. We planted a garden with corn peas tomatoes and my favorite squash.

4. First Tyrone will visit his aunt in California and then he will travel to Seattle.

5. New York Los Angeles and Chicago are the three largest American cities but Houston is not far behind.

Correcting Comma Usage (Part 2)

Directions: The commas in these sentences are in the wrong place or missing. Cross out the incorrect comma and add commas in the right places. If the sentence needs no comma, write NC after the sentence.

1. Before we went to dinner we went out, to the mall. _____

2. I plan to paint my bedroom blue and green next week. _____

3. The giraffe native to Africa is one of the zoo's most popular exhibits. _____

4. Denise, came to the dance studio but the class, had already started. _____

5. Riding in a hot-air balloon, is the most exciting thing we've ever done. _____

Answers are on page 762.

Revising Run-On Sentences

A **run-on sentence** gets its name from what happens when two sentences run together because end punctuation is missing or incorrect punctuation is used. You can repair a run-on sentence using several different methods. Consider this run-on sentence.

He hit a home run, our team won the game.

Here, you expect to see a period after the words *home run*, but you find a comma instead. Also, where is the capital letter *O* that should begin the second sentence? In a run-on sentence, the capitalization may be incorrect, too.

You have a few options for revising a run-on sentence. Remember that you may have to adjust the sentence's capitalization and punctuation based on your revision. These appear in **boldface type** in this table.

Strategy	Revision
Insert a period.	He hit a home run. **O**ur team won the game.
Insert a semicolon.	He hit a home run**;** our team won the game.
Add a conjunction to form a compound sentence.	He hit a home run, **and** our team won the game.

EXERCISE 10

Revising Run-On Sentences

Directions: Study the groups of words below. On the short line that follows each group of words, write *S* for sentence or *R* for run-on. If you identified the numbered item as a run-on, correct the sentence and write it on the line following the question. The first one is done for you.

1. The forecasters predicted a huge blizzard people rushed to the grocery store to stock up on milk and bread. __R__

   The forecasters predicted a huge blizzard. People rushed to the grocery store to stock up on milk and bread.

2. The snowstorm started at 10:00 in the morning, only a few flakes drifted down from the clouds at first. ___

   _____

   _____

3. The wind grew stronger as the hours passed. It pounded on the windows as if it were going to break them. ___

   _____

   _____

4. By nightfall, the snowdrifts had buried our car, the street had turned into an arctic landscape. ___

   _____

   _____

5. At 9:00, the first snowplows rumbled down our street, they opened up a path for the cars to get through. ___

   _____

   _____

6. In the morning, people emerged from their homes they spent the next two hours shoveling snow to free their cars from the deep drifts. ___

   _____

   _____

Answers are on page 762.

## CHAPTER 4

Building Paragraphs

This chapter focuses on developing your editing skills. You will learn how to construct paragraphs with a topic sentence and sentences that support the main idea. You will also learn how to arrange paragraphs in an order that presents your ideas in a logical sequence that readers can easily follow.

Identifying Parts of a Paragraph

Words are the building blocks of sentences. Sentences, in turn, are the building blocks of paragraphs. A **paragraph** is made up of sentences that join together to express a main idea.

Most well-developed paragraphs include at least three related sentences. Usually, a **topic sentence** states a paragraph's **main idea,** which is the paragraph's central thought. The remaining sentences support, or **develop,** this main idea by providing additional details about it. *All* of these sentences must support the paragraph's main idea.

Identifying a Topic Sentence

Usually, the first sentence in the paragraph is its topic sentence. However, a topic sentence may come somewhere in the middle, or even at the end, of a paragraph. Wherever it appears, the role of a paragraph's **topic sentence** remains the same: it sums up the main idea of the paragraph so the reader can identify what the paragraph is mainly about.

To find a paragraph's topic sentence, check the first sentence. Does it describe, or sum up, the rest of the paragraph fully? If not, look at the last sentence. Does it describe the rest of the paragraph fully? If not, look for the sentence within the paragraph that best sums up what all the other sentences are about.

Here are three examples that show where a topic sentence may appear. The topic sentence in each paragraph is underlined.

1. Designing and building websites is now an essential job skill. Many companies actively seek employees with this ability. A company's website needs to be both attractive and useful. If the website looks good and is easy to use, customers will keep coming back to that business.

2. Many companies actively seek employees who can design and build websites. A company's website needs to be both attractive and useful. If the website looks good and is easy to use, customers will keep coming

back to that business. <u>For this reason, designing and building websites is an essential job skill.</u>

3. Many companies actively seek employees who can design websites. A company's website needs to be both attractive and useful. <u>Designing and building websites is therefore an essential job skill.</u> If the website looks good and is easy to use, customers will keep coming back to that business.

EXERCISE 1

Identifying a Topic Sentence

Directions: Underline the topic sentence in each paragraph.

1. (A) The United States has the most zoos in the world, more than 200. (B) Today there are more than 1,000 zoos located all over the world. (C) Other countries with major zoos include the United Kingdom, Germany, and Japan. (D) The first public zoo did not come into existence until the late 18th century in France.

2. (A) Riding a bus instead of driving a car would reduce the number of drivers on the road. (B) Bicycles are another great alternative, adding valuable health benefits for riders. (C) Subways will actually get you to your destination faster than driving a car. (D) In fact, all three of these forms of public transportation help reduce traffic, pollution, and stress.

Answers are on page 763.

Adding Supporting Sentences

Supporting sentences develop a paragraph's main idea. How do they do this? They provide more details about the main idea in the form of explanations, examples, definitions, descriptions, or other details. Study the following paragraph.

Becoming a veterinarian remains a highly popular career choice. A veterinarian is a licensed doctor who treats animals. Veterinarians not only provide medical and surgical care for animals but also advise owners about animal behavior, feeding, and grooming. Some veterinarians specialize in treating specific types of animals, such as horses, birds, or even reptiles. There are more than 200 million dogs and cats kept as pets in the United States alone, so the demand for veterinarians remains strong.

Topic Sentence

Becoming a veterinarian remains a highly popular career choice.	
Definition	A veterinarian is a licensed doctor who treats animals.
Description	Veterinarians not only provide medical and surgical care for animals but also advise owners about animal behavior, feeding, and grooming.
Examples	Some veterinarians specialize in treating specific types of animals, such as horses, birds, or even reptiles.
Explanation	There are more than 200 million dogs and cats kept as pets in the United States alone, so the demand for veterinarians remains strong.

EXERCISE 2

Adding Supporting Sentences

Directions: Write a short paragraph in which you describe a favorite hobby or area of interest, including sentences that support your main idea. Begin with this topic sentence, and then fill in the blanks that follow using supporting details.

My favorite way to spend my free time is _____.

Definition or Description

_____

Example _____.

Explanation

I enjoy [name of hobby or activity] _____ because

_____

_____.

Answers are on page 763.

Strengthening Paragraphs

Now that you know how a paragraph works, you need to learn how to edit paragraphs to bring out the best in them. Good paragraphs flow smoothly and provide a clear path for your reader to follow from one idea to the next.

When a paragraphs needs revision, it is usually because it has one of the following problems:

- The paragraph has sentences that are off topic or do not support the main idea.
- The paragraph has inconsistent verb tenses.
- The paragraph does not have transitions between sentences or to the next paragraph.
- The paragraph is too long.
- The paragraph has sentences that are not in a logical order.

The strategies in the following sections will help you solve these common problems.

Providing Sufficient Support

If the main idea in a paragraph lacks enough support, a reader may have trouble following what you say or understanding your main idea. You can revise weak supporting sentences by adding supporting details:

> **Weak Support:** (1) Television has taken over our lives. (2) There are so many interesting programs on. (3) There never seems to be enough time to watch them all, but we could watch all day.

How has television "taken over our lives"? This paragraph does not tell you much about how this happens or why. You can revise a paragraph so it truly supports the main idea by adding specific details that tell you how:

> **Strong Support:** (1) Television has taken over our lives. (2) DVRs, streaming, and on-demand channels offer thousands of options from which to choose. (3) I can now watch television virtually anytime, anywhere on my laptop, tablet, or phone, 24 hours a day. (4) It has even become popular to "binge watch" by viewing an entire season or multiple seasons of a television series in one sitting.

The revised sentences add specific examples that now clearly support the main idea, so you can understand exactly *how* television "has taken over our lives."

- Sentence 2 explains how television is now widely available on portable devices.
- Sentence 3 describes television as being available around the clock.
- Sentence 4 defines "binge watching" to show how watching television takes up vast amounts of people's time.

Aim for quality over quantity when you add supporting details—two to three solid supporting details should be enough.

Providing Sufficient Support

Directions: The three numbered sentences below do not provide sufficient support for the main idea sentence. Rewrite the three sentences so they provide stronger support for the main idea.

Cell phones can be distracting. (1) They can distract you on the road. (2) They can distract you in a theater. (3) They can distract you at work.

1. _____

2. _____

3. _____

Answers are on page 763.

Removing Off-Topic Sentences

All the sentences in a paragraph should support its main idea. Sometimes a sentence fails to support a paragraph's main idea because it is a different idea about the topic or it is about another topic altogether. This is distracting and may prevent readers from understanding what the paragraph is actually about. Make sure that the sentences in a paragraph support its main idea so the paragraph's meaning is clear.

For example, identify the main idea in the following paragraph. Which sentence fails to support it?

(1) London, England, is one of the most popular tourist destinations in the world for good reason. (2) It has a long and fascinating cultural history that includes Shakespeare, Sherlock Holmes, and the Beatles, not to mention some of the most powerful kings and queens of all time. (3) You need to budget carefully if you visit, because London is expensive. (4) London's art museums are some of the best in the world.

Sentence 1 is the paragraph's topic sentence. Sentence 3 is about how expensive London is. But while sentence 3 is about traveling to London, it still does not support the paragraph's main idea, which is to describe why London is a popular tourist destination.

Removing Off-Topic Sentences

Directions: Underline the topic sentence in this paragraph. Then, cross out the sentence that fails to support it.

(1) Some people fear public speaking more than poisonous snakes. (2) However, if you are willing, there are many ways to overcome your fears. (3) Many public speakers fear that they will look foolish in front of strangers or coworkers. (4) Perhaps their speech will bore the audience, or their jokes will fall flat. (5) Even worse, they may sound as if they do not know what they are talking about.

Answers are on page 763.

Editing Inconsistent Verb Tenses

Generally, the verbs in a paragraph should all be the same tense, such as present, past, or future, if the events the paragraph describes all take place in the same time frame.

Incorrect: We **stayed** up late last night to watch the total eclipse of the moon. The entire family **watches** the eclipse from our backyard. During this eclipse, Earth's shadow completely **covers** the moon for almost a full hour, and it **was** exciting to watch.

This paragraph is incorrect because it mixes verbs in the past tense (*stayed*, *was*) with those in the present (*watches*, *covers*).

Correct: We **stayed** up late last night to watch the total eclipse of the moon. The entire family **watched** the eclipse from our backyard. During this eclipse, Earth's shadow completely **covered** the moon for almost a full hour, and it **was** exciting to watch.

This paragraph is correct because the events it describes all took place in the past, so all of the verbs are in the past tense.

Writers sometimes make the mistake of shifting tenses from one sentence in a paragraph to the next, even when the sentences all refer to action happening at the same time. Avoid the confusing shift in tenses demonstrated by the following example.

Incorrect: There **will be** a party tonight. The celebration **was** so much fun.

Is this party about to happen, or has it already taken place? The first sentence is in the future tense (*will be*), while the second is in the past (*was*), so it is impossible to tell. Depending on when the party actually takes place, both of the following sentences are correct because their verb tenses are now the same:

Correct: There **was** a party tonight. The celebration **was** so much fun.

Correct: There **will be** a party tonight. The celebration **will be** so much fun.

In the following paragraph, the writer makes the mistake of shifting tenses. "When she was driving" lets you know that the events the paragraph describes take place in the past. Which verbs need to be changed so the verb tenses are consistent in this paragraph? Underline them.

When she was driving in the country yesterday, Mariska pulls off the road when she spots a farm stand. She decided she should stop to check out the produce because she especially likes the look of the corn and tomatoes.

You should have underlined the verbs *pulls*, *spots*, and *likes*. They should be changed to *pulled*, *spotted*, and *liked* to make them verbs in the past tense.

However, not every shift in verb tenses is incorrect. If you describe an action, for example, that shifts from the past to the present or from the present to the future, you need to change the tense of the verbs so they accurately describe when the action occurs.

Past
↓

J. K. Rowling **came** up with the idea for the Harry Potter series during a four-

Present
↓

hour train delay in 1990. Today she **is** one of the world's best-selling authors.

Future
↓

I suspect the Harry Potter books **will delight** generations of children.

EXERCISE 5

Editing Inconsistent Verb Tenses

Directions: The following paragraphs contain some verbs in the incorrect tense. Cross out each incorrect verb, and then write the correct verb above it. The first one is done for you.

Paragraph 1

Even though she is a resident of New York City, Stephanie enjoys

went
going to places that only tourists visit. Last year, she ~~goes~~ to the Empire

saw
State Building for the first time. From the top of the building, she ~~sees~~ all

the way across the city to the river.

Paragraph 2

Next year, she visits the history museum. The museum will feature a traveling exhibit about dinosaurs. Stephanie planned to be first in line to see it.

Paragraph 3

Because she will work during the week, weekends are generally the only time she goes on one of her outings. Sometimes she ventured out alone, and sometimes a friend accompanies her.

Answers are on page 763.

Making Transitions Between Paragraphs

An essay is made up of paragraphs that build upon one another to express a main idea clearly and coherently. These paragraphs form a road map that helps you follow an essay smoothly from one paragraph to the next, and one idea to the next.

You have already learned about transitional words, such as conjunctions and conjunctive adverbs that connect sentences (*and*, *but*, *however*, *nevertheless*, *consequently*, etc.). They can also be used to connect paragraphs. Which transitional word works best to connect one paragraph to the next? This depends on the relationship between the main ideas of the two paragraphs. Recall that each transitional word has a specific purpose. For example, conjunctions such as *however* and *but* establish a contrast between ideas.

Sentence to Sentence

Some people think that art education is not important, **but** learning to play an instrument or paint a picture teaches children valuable skills.

Paragraph to Paragraph

An increasing number of Americans are becoming vegetarians by choosing to cut meat out of their diets. Many do so because they believe it is a healthier lifestyle.

However, some people object to a vegetarian diet because they think that it is bland and provides insufficient protein. It is also difficult to find good vegetarian options in most American restaurants.

The word *however*, which begins the second paragraph, tells you that the essay is about to move in a different direction because the second paragraph will contrast with the first. The first paragraph describes the growing popularity of vegetarianism, but the second paragraph describes objections to vegetarianism.

Similarly, if you describe a series of changes over time, each paragraph should begin with a word that tells you it will discuss the next step in that series: *First, Second, Third,* and so on. These are the topic sentences of three paragraphs that follow one another in an essay about how to plan a trip:

> **First,** you need to narrow down your possible destinations . . .

> **Second,** here are some strategies for finding the lowest priced airfare and hotels . . .

> **Third,** be sure you explore how to find the most interesting sights to visit during your stay . . .

In some cases you may not use connecting words. However, even without connecting words, paragraphs must be written so that they *clearly* signal to the reader that a shift is taking place from one paragraph to the next, as in this case:

> The Thirteenth Amendment to the Constitution radically changed America. The amendment outlawed slavery outright, transforming the lives of millions of African Americans. **It also sparked a long period of social and economic adjustment for Americans in general.**

> **The Civil Rights Act of 1964 was equally revolutionary.** For the first time, a federal law outlawed discrimination based on race, color, religion, sex, or national origin. This eliminated segregation in public places such as schools and voting booths.

The first paragraph focuses on the effects of the Thirteenth Amendment on America. The second paragraph signals that a transition is occurring by connecting the Thirteenth Amendment and the Civil Rights Act with the phrase "was equally revolutionary." The rest of the second paragraph goes on to focus on the effects of the Civil Rights Act of 1964 on America.

EXERCISE 6

Making Transitions Between Paragraphs

Directions: Read the following pairs of sentences. The first sentence in each pair is the final sentence of a first paragraph; the second sentence starts a new paragraph. Choose the answer that best represents how to transition between them.

1. As the first US president, George Washington was also the first to give up the office to another president.
   Nobody knew whether a smooth transfer of power to John Adams was even possible since nothing like this had ever happened before.
   A. Eventually
   B. Consequently
   C. Nevertheless
   D. Likewise

2. In fact, the use of social media is widespread.
    Not everyone believes that all forms of social media are beneficial.
    A. Similarly
    B. Therefore
    C. However
    D. No transitional word needed

3. The California gold rush had changed the state forever.
    Discovery of gold in Alaska a half-century later led to another gold rush.
    A. Conversely
    B. Therefore
    C. Nevertheless
    D. No transitional word needed

Answers are on page 763.

Splitting a Paragraph

If a paragraph you have written is too long, it can tire readers out or confuse them about your main idea. You can often solve this problem by breaking a long paragraph into two or more shorter ones. Read this paragraph:

(1) Regular exercise may save your bones. (2) Bone is a living tissue. (3) It responds to physical activity by becoming heavier, bigger, and stronger. (4) It does this best when we are young. Bone mass usually peaks when we are in our 20s. (5) After that, we often begin to lose bone. (6) Therefore, as we age, we suffer more bone fractures, broken bones, and spinal problems. (7) Studies of animals have shown that exercise during periods of rapid growth can lead to lifelong benefits in bone size and strength. (8) To see if the same holds true for humans, a team of scientists studied more than 100 professional baseball players at different stages of their careers. (9) Baseball players were ideal subjects because their throwing arms get a lot more action than their non-throwing arms. (9) Baseball players also tend to retire from stressful throwing activities once they stop professional play. (10) This allowed the scientists to look at the effects of physical activity long after intense throwing had ended.

Source: Adapted from http://newsinhealth.nih.gov/issue/May2014/Capsule1, a U.S. gov't website (public domain)

This paragraph is too long, and it will likely confuse a reader. A paragraph should focus on only *one* main idea, but this paragraph has two main ideas fighting for space. Can you find them? First, check to see which ideas in the paragraph truly belong together. Which sentences clearly support the same main idea? Then, see if any of the sentences qualify as a topic sentence for them.

In this case, one group of sentences focuses on a description of human bone health. The other focuses on a study on whether exercise improves bone health. Therefore, you should be able to divide this paragraph into two separate paragraphs at sentence 7, the logical transition into the discussion of the scientist's study.

EXERCISE 7

Splitting a Paragraph

Directions: Read the following paragraph, underline the two topic sentences in the paragraph, and then place a slash mark (/) to mark the best place to break the paragraph.

The Hispanic Americans who entered Congress between 1977 and 2012 represent the greatest increase in their ethnic group in congressional history. Of the 91 Hispanic Americans who served in Congress through 2012, 37 were elected or appointed before 1976. This means that nearly 60 percent of the Hispanic Americans in congressional history were elected after 1976. Demographic changes and political reforms likely caused this change. From 1980 to 2010, the US Census shows that the number of Latinos in the United States nearly tripled, to 16 percent of the total population, making Hispanics the second largest ethnic group in the country. Hispanic representation in Congress has also increased because of two major reforms to America's electoral system: the Voting Rights Act of 1965 and a 1962 series of Supreme Court decisions defining voting districts.

Source: Adapted from: http://history.house.gov/Exhibitions-and -Publications/HAIC/Historical-Essays/Strength-Numbers/Introduction /U.S. Gov't publication; public domain

Answers are on page 763.

Arranging a Paragraph in Logical Order

Sentences in a paragraph must all support its main idea. In addition, you should arrange sentences within each paragraph in **logical order**, meaning that they make sense as they build upon one another. There are different strategies for doing this, listed in the chart below.

Transitional words that link one sentence to another can be helpful in placing sentences in a logical order (*before, furthermore, during, then, afterward,* etc.). So can words suggesting steps in a series (*first, second, third,* etc.).

Also look for words and phrases that show the passage of time (*as we age, at the age of, in the past, in the future, now*). The use of the past or future tense, as well as mention of specific time periods (year, dates, etc.) will help you identify the order in which ideas are arranged.

Transitional words that help these sentences follow in a logical order are highlighted **in bold typeface** below. Words or phrases that show the passage of time are underlined.

Strategy	Example
Chronological Order (how they occur in time)	Bone mass usually peaks when we are in our 20s. **After** that, we often begin to lose bone. **Therefore**, as we age, we suffer more bone fractures, broken bones, and spinal problems.
Comparing/ Contrasting Ideas	Studies of animals have shown that exercise during periods of rapid growth can lead to lifelong benefits in bone size and strength. To see if the same holds true for humans, scientists conducted a study.
Cause and Effect	Baseball players were ideal subjects because their throwing arms get a lot more action than their non-throwing arms. Baseball players **also** tend to retire from stressful throwing activities once they stop professional play. **This** allowed the scientists to look at the effects of physical activity long after intense throwing had ended.

The following paragraph is not in logical order. As you read it, circle transitional words and underline words or phrases that show the passage of time.

(4) During construction, builders decided the height of Lincoln's statue should grow from 10 to 19 feet. (5) The memorial was completed in 1922. (3) Finally, an agreement was reached about the design.

(1) Construction on the Lincoln Memorial began in 1914. (2) Before construction could begin, there was much debate over what the memorial should look like.

This is the paragraph now rearranged in logical order.

(1) Construction on the Lincoln Memorial began in 1914. (2) Before construction could begin, there was much debate over what the memorial should look like. (3) Finally, an agreement was reached about the design. (4) During construction, builders decided the height of

Lincoln's statue should grow from 10 to 19 feet. (5) The memorial was completed in 1922.

These sentences now build upon each other in a logical chronological order, from the beginning of the construction of the Lincoln Memorial to its completion,

---

EXERCISE 8

Arranging a Paragraph in Logical Order

Directions: Read the following sentences. Place these sentences in logical order, and write their numbers on the blank that follows.

Passage A

1. Enrollment in computer-related college majors fell as students worried that they would not find jobs.

2. Overall, IT employment actually grew by 8 percent between 2001 and 2007.

3. However, current survey data show that these concerns were largely unfounded.

4. In 2001, employment in Information Technology services began to decline.

_____

Passage B

1. Conflict resolution is the practice of settling disputes peacefully.

2. Rather than continuing to argue, or even fight, they negotiate a fair outcome.

3. Students in a dispute discuss the situation calmly before a committee of fellow students.

4. Now high schools have adopted this method to settle disputes between students.

_____

Answers are on page 763.

EXERCISE 9

Editing Paragraphs

Directions: The following paragraph has multiple problems that require revision. First arrange the sentences in logical order by writing their numbers on the blank below. Cross out any off-topic sentences. Then, mark the spot with a slash (/) where the paragraph should divide into two paragraphs. Underline the topic sentence of each paragraph.

(1) Almost the entire continent is covered by ice and snow, with high winds and extreme cold. (2) There are no towns or cities in Antarctica. (3) Therefore, it is a dangerous climate for humans. (4) Several nature documentaries were made there. (5) Living conditions in Antarctica are extremely harsh. (6) In fact, humans have never set up permanent homes there. (7) Penguins and seals live along the coastline, as do whales and many varieties of fish. (8) Antarctica is, however, the permanent home of a surprising number of animals and plants. (9) In addition, while there are no trees or bushes, many smaller plants have existed there for centuries. (10) Antarctica suffers from global warming, and much of its ice is melting.

Sentences in correct order: _____

Answers are on page 764.

## CHAPTER 5

Building Vocabulary

Language is power. The more words you know, the greater your ability to understand what you read and to communicate your ideas. In addition, the stronger your vocabulary, the more likely you are to succeed at school and in the workplace.

Using a Dictionary

It often feels challenging to encounter a word you don't recognize, but every unknown word is a valuable opportunity to improve your vocabulary. When you come across an unfamiliar word, your first response should be to look it up in a dictionary. The dictionary will tell you the meaning of the word and how to use it correctly. When you know how to use a new word, you can build the vocabulary you need.

Alphabetizing Words

The dictionary lists words in alphabetical order. Words that begin with the letter *a*, such as *apply*, *arrange*, and *awe*, are listed in the *A* section; *b* words, such as *banana*, *bring*, and *bundle*, are listed in the *B* section; and so on. Consider the following words:

> unite   merry   calculate   hot   zoo

How would you list these words in alphabetical order? Start by comparing the first letter in each word.

> **c**alculate   **h**ot   **m**erry   **u**nite   **z**oo

How do you alphabetize words that begin with the same letter, such as *four*, *foul*, *found*, and *fought*? When in doubt, compare the words one letter at a time until you find the letters that do not match.

Consider these words. The first three letters match (*fou*), but the fourth letter in each word is different.

> fo**u**r   fou**l**   foun**d**   foug**h**t

The fourth letter in each word determines how to alphabetize them correctly:

> fou**g**ht   fou**l**   foun**d**   fou**r**

How would you alphabetize these words?

canary   can   cannon   canvas   cane

The word *can* has no fourth letter. So where does this word go in the list? It goes first.

can   canary   cane   cannon   canvas

EXERCISE 1

Alphabetizing Words (Part 1)

Directions: Rearrange each list of words so that the words are in alphabetical order.

1. street   lane   terrace   court   boulevard   avenue

2. Seattle   Boston   Milwaukee   Phoenix   Austin   Omaha

3. iron   aluminum   tin   copper   brass   gold

Alphabetizing Words (Part 2)

Directions: The words that follow are not in alphabetical order. How would a dictionary list them? Rearrange them so that they are in alphabetical order. Use the second, third, or fourth letter, where necessary, to determine the correct order.

1. glow   glove   glory   globe   gloom

2. active   act   actress   actual   action

3. weave   water   wash   welcome   weight

Answers are on page 764.

Using Guide Words

The dictionary has a special feature that can help you look up words faster. Instead of turning page after page trying to find a word, check the top of a page. You will see two boldface words. These **guide words** are the first and last words defined on each page. If the word you seek falls *between* these two guide words, then its definition appears on that page. What if you are looking for the definitions of the words *pioneer* and *pity*? Look at this dictionary page:

pin	pirate
pin *n* a small object, usually metal, used to hold things together	**pine** *v* to yearn for in an intense and persistent way
pin *v* to hold down an opponent in wrestling	**pink** *n* a color that contains some blue and red
pinch *n* a small amount of something, such as a small amount of spice	**pioneer** *n* somebody who is the first to settle in a territory
pinch *v* to squeeze something between thumb and forefinger	**pipe** *n* a tube through which a fluid or gas passes
pine *n* an evergreen tree with needles instead of leaves	**pirate** *n* a person who robs on the high seas

Pioneer falls between the guide words *pin* and *pirate*, so its definition appears on this page in the second column. What about *pity*? The definition of *pity* does not appear on the page because *pit* comes after the *pir* in the guide word *pirate*. The definition of *pity* will appear on a later page.

EXERCISE 2

Using Guide Words

Directions: Each list of words below is preceded by two guide words. Determine where each word on the list would appear. If it would appear on the same page as the guide words, write *same page*. If it would be on a page before the guide words, write *before*. If it would be on a page after the guide words, write *after*. The first one is done for you.

Guide Words: **league—leave**

Word	Where Word Appears
1. leach	*before*
2. left	
3. lead	
4. leer	
5. leak	

Finding Related Words

Sometimes you may not find a word you would expect to find in the dictionary, such as *anonymously*. It's there, but instead of having its own entry, it appears under the entry for the shorter word *anonymous* from which it is formed. Where would you find the word *parental* in the dictionary? Ask yourself, from which word is *parental* formed? You will often find the original word within the longer one. For example, the word *parental* is formed from the word *parent*, so you would find the definition of *parental* under the definition of *parent*.

EXERCISE 3

Finding Related Words

Directions: Each word below in the first column is formed from a shorter word. You would find the longer form of this word in the dictionary entry for the shorter form. Write the shorter form of the word in the blank. The first one is done for you.

To Find	Look Under
1. fundamentally	fundamental
2. discernible	_____
3. softness	_____
4. leadership	_____
5. banishment	_____

Answers are on page 764.

Navigating a Dictionary Definition

Here is a typical dictionary definition for the word *anonymous*. The dictionary contains more than just a word's definition. It also includes:

* the part of speech to which the word belongs;

* how to pronounce it and how it is broken into syllables ("beats");

* its definition and whether it has multiple meanings;

* sample sentences using the word;

* its origin (called *etymology*);

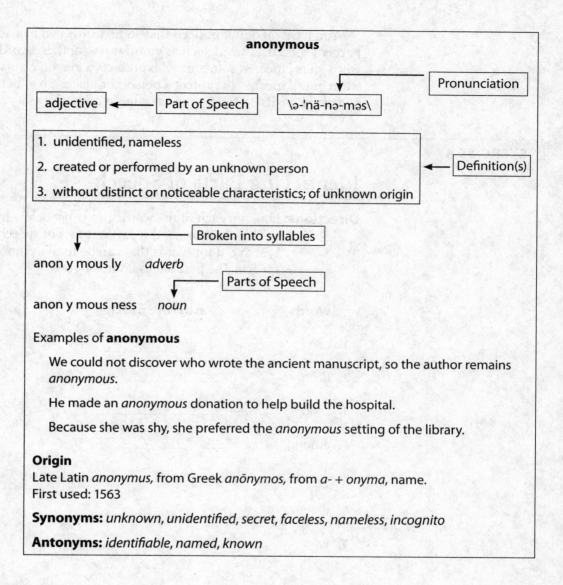

anonymous

Pronunciation

adjective ← Part of Speech \ə-'nä-nə-məs\

1. unidentified, nameless
2. created or performed by an unknown person
3. without distinct or noticeable characteristics; of unknown origin

← Definition(s)

Broken into syllables

anon y mous ly   *adverb*

Parts of Speech

anon y mous ness   *noun*

Examples of **anonymous**

We could not discover who wrote the ancient manuscript, so the author remains *anonymous*.

He made an *anonymous* donation to help build the hospital.

Because she was shy, she preferred the *anonymous* setting of the library.

Origin
Late Latin *anonymus*, from Greek *anōnymos*, from *a-* + *onyma*, name.
First used: 1563

Synonyms: *unknown, unidentified, secret, faceless, nameless, incognito*

Antonyms: *identifiable, named, known*

- words that have identical meanings to it (called *synonyms*); and
- words that have opposite meanings from it (called *antonyms*).

A dictionary definition may seem overwhelming because it includes so much information. Read it slowly, step by step. You will not need to memorize everything in the definition, but reading it will help you understand the word's meaning and remember it.

Identifying Parts of Speech

To save space, dictionaries identify the part of speech for each word with an abbreviation. The abbreviations for the parts of speech generally follow the pronunciation of the word. Common abbreviations include *n.* for noun, *v.* for verb, *adj.* for adjective, and so on.

You have no doubt noticed that some words can be used as different parts of speech. A word such as *guard* is one of these words. As a noun, the word *guard* means "someone who protects a person or place." As a verb, the word *guard* means "to protect a person or place." In a dictionary, a word like *guard* will be listed twice, once as a noun and once as a verb.

EXERCISE 4

Identifying Parts of Speech

Directions: Look up each of the words in the list below in a dictionary. On the blank, indicate the part or parts of speech for each word. Watch out for words that can be used as more than one part of speech. The first one is done for you.

Word	Part(s) of Speech
1. cart	noun, verb
2. drum	
3. solid	
4. among	
5. spark	
6. within	
7. we	

Answers are on page 764.

Determining Multiple Meanings

Many words in the dictionary have multiple meanings. A word may mean one thing as a noun, but as a verb, it may mean something else.

Noun: We found a **row** of empty seats just before the movie started.

Verb: We **row** the canoe on the river every Saturday.

Sometimes, the same word has different meanings within the same part of speech.

Noun: I spread **jam** on my toast this morning at breakfast.

Noun: I got caught in a traffic **jam** on the way to work.

Verb: I **jammed** my clothes into a suitcase and rushed to the airport.

Verb: I **jammed** my finger in the door.

A dictionary will list multiple meanings of the same word. Be sure to look through the full definition to check for these multiple meanings so you know the correct one to use.

EXERCISE 5

Determining Multiple Meanings

Directions: Note that the meaning of the word in boldface type differs in each of the pairs of sentences below. After looking up the word in the dictionary, write the correct definition in each blank. The first one is done for you.

1. **a.** If we **finish** our chores early, we can take the rest of the day off.

   Meaning: _"to bring to an end"_

   b. We applied the **finish** to the furniture and then let it dry.

   Meaning: _"a finishing material, such as varnish"_

2. **a.** The building began to **sway** when the earthquake struck.

   Meaning: _____

   b. The disgraced politician had very little **sway** over his colleagues after the papers reported his wrongdoing.

   Meaning: _____

3. **a.** Last night's **program** on TV got terrific ratings.

   Meaning: _____

   b. I installed a new **program** on my computer.

   Meaning: _____

4. **a.** The workers voted to strike for higher wages.

   Meaning: _____

   b. Because I couldn't sleep, I heard the clock **strike** three in the middle of the night.

   Meaning: _____

5. a. At the end of the performance, the actors take a **bow**.

Meaning: _____

b. The wave crashed over the **bow** of the sailboat.

Meaning: _____

Answers are on page 765.

Building Words from Word Parts

A good way to expand your vocabulary is to understand how words are constructed. For example, many words are constructed by adding a new part to a base word. The **base word** is like a building's foundation; new words are "built" upon it. The new part that is added can be a **prefix** (a part added to the beginning of the base word) or a **suffix** (a part added to the end of the base word). The prefix or suffix alters the meaning of the base word. The base word is like a foundation because it can stand alone; however, the prefixes and suffixes added it to it cannot stand alone. They are dependent on the base word.

Prefix	**Base Word**		
re-	count	→	recount: "to count again"

Base Word	**Suffix**		
peace	ful	→	peaceful: "full of peace or calm"

The following sections will describe how to build new words by adding prefixes and suffixes to base words.

Building Words with Prefixes

A **prefix** is a unit of language placed at the beginning of a word that changes the word's meaning. For example, adding the prefix *un-*, meaning "not," to a word reverses its meaning: *tie* becomes *untie*; *known* becomes *unknown*.

If you know what a word's prefix means, you may be able to figure out the definition of a word. Many prefixes combine with Latin, Greek, or other words to form common English words. For example, the prefix *re-* means "back" or "again." *Review* means "to look again"; *return* means "to turn back" so that you arrive at the point where you started.

Here is a table of some common prefixes and their meanings.

Prefix	Meaning	Example	Definition
auto-	self	autobiography	a biography you write about yourself
en-	bring into the condition of	endanger	to place someone or something in danger
fore-	in advance	foresight	ability to predict
inter-	between	interval	a time or space between events
mid-	middle	midway	halfway point
pre-	before	premature	before the proper time
trans-	across, change	transfer	to change from one place to another

EXERCISE 6

Building Words with Prefixes (Part 1)

Directions: Using the prefixes in the table, make words by adding the prefixes to the base word shown. The first one is done for you.

Prefix	Word or Root	New Word
1. _auto-_	mobile	_automobile_
2. _____	changeable	_____
3. _____	warn	_____
4. _____	section	_____

Building Words with Prefixes (Part 2)

Directions: In the blank, write the letter of the definition that matches the given word.

	Word or Phrase		**Definition**
1.	prevent	_____	**a.** stop something before it happens
2.	forecast	_____	**b.** move from one language to another
3.	translate	_____	**c.** declare in advance

Answers are on page 765.

Prefixes Meaning "Not"

As previously noted, some prefixes create a word that is the opposite, or **antonym**, of the original word. The prefix *un-*, for example, forms *unfriendly*, the antonym of *friendly*.

The following table shows other prefixes that mean "not" or a related idea (such as "against").

Prefix	Meaning	Example	Definition
anti-	against	antibiotic	a medicine that works against infections
de-	remove, take away from	defrost	remove frost; thaw
dis-	not, away from	disembark	to move away from a ship
il-	not	illegible	not readable or legible
im-	not	impossible	not possible
in-	not	inconclusive	not conclusive
ir-	not	irregular	not regular
mis-	wrong, badly	misinterpret	interpret incorrectly
non-	not	nonessential	not essential
un-	not	unwell	not well

EXERCISE 7

Prefixes Meaning "Not" (Part 1)

Directions: Circle the prefix in each of these words, and then write the definition of the word on the blank.

Word	Meaning
1. (un)tested	*not tested*
2. inexcusable	_____
3. imperfect	_____
4. irrational	_____
5. disapprove	_____
6. antihero	_____

Answers are on page 765.

Prefixes Showing Time or Position

Some prefixes indicate time or position (such as a location). Note, for example, that you've already encountered the prefix *in-*, which can mean "not," but it can also signify place, as indicated in the table.

Prefix	Meaning	Example	Definition
ante-	before	antedate	to come before the date (in time)
de-	down, away	depart	to leave, to go away
ex-, extra-	out, outside	exoskeleton	a skeleton that exists outside the body
in-, en-	in, inside	insert	to place inside
		encircle	to draw a circle around (to place something inside a circle)
pre-	before	predawn	the time before dawn
pro-	forward	procession	a line of people moving forward
post-	after	postgame	to come after the game (in time)
sub-	under	submarine	a vessel that goes underwater
super-	above, over	superintendent	a person in charge of something (oversees it)

EXERCISE 8

Prefixes Showing Time or Position (Part 1)

Directions: Match the time phrases in column 1 with their definitions in column 2. Fill in the blank with the letter signifying the definition. You can use a dictionary if you like.

Word or Phrase	**Meaning**
1. prenatal exam _____	**a.** surroundings in which plants or animals live
2. environment _____	**b.** to put off until a later time
3. postpone _____	**c.** before a plane takes off
4. preflight _____	**d.** a health checkup before birth
5. extraterrestrial _____	**e.** to move forward
6. progress _____	**f.** to spoil the shape of
7. deform _____	**g.** from beyond Earth

Prefixes Showing Time or Position (Part 2)

Directions: Match the position phrases in column 1 with their definitions in column 2. Fill in the blank with the letter of the definition. You may consult a dictionary as needed.

Word or Phrase	**Meaning**
1. export goods _____	**a.** to put out on display so it can be seen
2. superimpose an image _____	**b.** front room with no one in it
3. spoken prologue _____	**c.** quick fall
4. exhibit the painting _____	**d.** to place one image over another
5. subway tunnels _____	**e.** materials shipped out of a country

6. empty antechamber _____ **f.** words spoken as an introduction

7. swift descent _____ **g.** network of underground trains

Answers are on page 765.

Prefixes Showing Number

Finally, some prefixes show number. Such prefixes indicate *how many*. Describing something as **universal**, for example, means "applies to all." If you get a paycheck **biweekly**, you get paid every two weeks.

Here is a table of prefixes that show number.

Prefix	Meaning	Example	Definition
bi-	two	bilingual	able to speak two languages
du-	two	duo	a group of two
mono-	one, single	monopoly	a single entity having full control over something
qua-	four	quarter	one-fourth of something
tri-	three	tripod	a three-legged stand (e.g., for a camera)
uni-	one, single	uniform	identical clothing worn by all members of an organization (e.g., a team uniform)

EXERCISE 9

Prefixes Showing Number

Directions: Match the words with number prefixes in column 1 with their definitions in column 2. Fill in the blank with the letter of the definition. You can use a dictionary if you like.

Word		Meaning
1. unify _____		**a.** three-sided figure
2. quadruple _____		**b.** without variety

3. triangle   _____   **c.** bring together as one

4. biannual   _____   **d.** a song for two singers

5. duet   _____   **e.** multiplied four times over

6. monotonous   _____   **f.** twice a year

Answers are on page 765.

Building Words with Suffixes

Suffixes are units of language that come at the end of words. Like prefixes, they affect the meaning of a word, usually by changing the part of speech to which it belongs. For example, the word *love* is a noun or a verb, but if you add the suffix *-ly*, it becomes the adjective *lovely*. Here are a few other examples of nouns changed to adjectives by the addition of a suffix, *-ful*:

bounty   →   bountiful

hate   →   hateful

cheer   →   cheerful

Adding *-er* or *-or* to some verbs changes the verb to a noun that names the kind of person who does the action described by the verb:

act   →   actor

run   →   runner

The suffix *-ish* changes a noun to an adjective, making the word mean "like" or "characteristic of."

child   →   childish

fool   →   foolish

Here is a table showing a few common suffixes.

Suffix	Meaning	Example	Definition
-able, *-ible*	able to	visible	able to be seen
-ful	full of/characterized by	tearful	very sad, full of tears
-hood	state of	brotherhood	the quality or state of being brothers
-ology, *-omy*	study of	zoology	the study of animals
-ship	state of, quality of	kinship	the state of being kin
-tion	act of, state of	recollection	the act of recollecting

EXERCISE 10

Building Words with Suffixes

Directions: Match the words with suffixes in column 1 with their definitions in column 2. Fill in the blank with the letter of the definition. You can use a dictionary as needed.

Word		Meaning
1. admiration	_____	**a.** the quality of being difficult
2. edible	_____	**b.** characterized by loveliness
3. hardship	_____	**c.** the study of the human mind
4. adulthood	_____	**d.** the state of being pleased
5. satisfaction	_____	**e.** the act of approving of
6. beautiful	_____	**f.** capable of being argued about
7. psychology	_____	**g.** able to be eaten
8. debatable	_____	**h.** the state of being grown up

Answers are on page 765.

Other Ways to Build Your Vocabulary

Besides using prefixes and suffixes, you can also build your vocabulary by understanding the Greek and Latin roots that are the sources of many English words. Another way is to become familiar with the **synonyms** (words with similar meanings) and **antonyms** (words with opposite meanings) of common English words. You should also learn to use contractions and **homonyms** (words that sound alike but are spelled differently) correctly.

Identifying Latin and Greek Roots

Base words are often derived from Latin and Greek **roots**. Not all roots form base words, and those roots that don't form base words cannot stand alone.

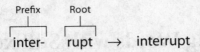

The prefix *inter-* means "between." The root *rupt* comes from a Latin word, *rupere*, which means "to break." When you interrupt, you literally cause a break in the flow of what someone is saying by getting in the middle of what that person is saying when he or she is saying it.

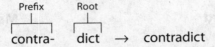

The prefix *contra-* means "against" or "opposed to." The root *dict* comes from a Latin word, *dicere*, which means "to say or tell." When you contradict someone, you oppose, or go against, what that person says.

The following table lists some Latin and Greek roots that are commonly found in English words, including their meanings.

Root	Meaning
ced, ceed, cede	move
cept, ceive	take
cred	believe, trust
hydr	water
scope	see
script, scribe	write
sphere	rounded region

The following words, which have been broken into prefix, base word, and suffix, contain some of the roots shown in the table above.

Word	Prefix	Root or Base Word	Suffix
precede	*pre-*	cede	—
Incredible	*in-*	cred	*-ible*
hydration	—	hydr	*-tion*
microscope	*micro-*	scope	—

EXERCISE 11

Identifying Latin and Greek Roots (Part 1)

Directions: Underline the root or base word in each word using the table that lists common roots. The first one is done for you.

1. sub<u>scribe</u>	5. exceed	9. deceive
2. proceed	6. telescope	10. describe
3. credit	7. inscribe	11. recede
4. dehydrate	8. hemisphere	12. atmosphere

Identifying Latin and Greek Roots (Part 2)

Directions: The following table contains Latin and Greek roots. Use this table to match the words on the left with the definitions on the right. Write the letter of the correct definition in each blank. You can use a dictionary as needed.

Root	Meaning		Root	Meaning
crat, cracy	rule		ject	throw
graph, gram	write		sect	cut

Word or Phrase

1. democracy _____

2. autograph the photo _____

3. movie projector _____

4. bisect an angle _____

5. aristocrat _____

6. celebrity's biography _____

7. inject the vaccine _____

8. section _____

Definition

a. cut an angle in two

b. rule by the people

c. a book written about somebody famous

d. write your name on a picture

e. a part cut from the whole

f. a machine that throws images onto a screen

g. a so-called superior person who rules

h. to shoot medicine into a muscle using a needle

Answers are on page 766.

Using Latin and Greek Roots to Determine Meaning

Latin and Greek roots are clues to the meanings of English words. If you understand what one of these roots means, you can probably figure out what the English word means, too. Consider the words in this table.

Root	Meaning	Example	Definition
tele port	distant carry	teleport	to move (carry) something a long distance
tract	draw, pull	attract	to pull toward

EXERCISE 12

Using Latin and Greek Roots to Determine Meaning

Directions: The following table contains Latin and Greek roots. Use this table to match the words on the left with the definitions on the right. Write the letter of the correct definition in each blank.

Root	Meaning
ex	out of
port	carry

Root	Meaning
tele	distant
tract	draw, pull

Word or Phrase

1. extract _____

2. import _____

3. telegram _____

Definition

a. a message sent over a distance

b. to pull out (e.g., a tooth)

c. to bring goods into a place

Answers are on page 766.

Understanding Synonyms and Antonyms

Some English words mean the same thing or almost the same thing, such as *rage* and *anger*. These words are called **synonyms**. Other words, such as *war* and *peace*, have opposite meanings. These words are called **antonyms**.

Synonyms

English often has several words that have similar meanings or the same meaning. Synonyms provide writers and speakers with options for expressing their thoughts and ideas. Most synonyms are the same part of speech.

Nouns: *story* and *tale*

Verbs: *push* and *shove*

Adjectives: *old* and *ancient*

Adverbs: *bravely* and *courageously*

EXERCISE 13

Synonyms

Directions: The first word in each numbered item in the list below is followed by four other words. Locate and circle the synonym. Use a dictionary as needed. The first one is done for you.

1. sick	healthy	energetic	(ill)	weary
2. pillar	floor	ceiling	wall	column
3. show	hide	demonstrate	discover	comprehend
4. steamy	hot	chilly	lukewarm	cool
5. fish	vegetable	fruit	carrots	seafood
6. teaching	learning	studying	instructing	forgetting

Answers are on page 766.

Antonyms

Did you notice that part of the prefix *anti-* appears in *antonym*? Think of an antonym as the *anti*-synonym. If synonyms are words with the same meaning, it makes sense that antonyms are words with opposite meanings.

Nouns: *heat* and *cold*

Verbs: *push* and *pull*

Adjectives: *tall* and *short*

Adverbs: *boldly* and *shyly*

Sentences that contrast two things often provide enough information for you to figure out the meaning of an antonym.

In the famous Aesop fable, the <u>slow</u> tortoise beats the <u>fleet</u> rabbit in a race. You may not know what the word *fleet* means, although it's clearly not referring to ships in a navy. Still, you should be able to figure out that it means the opposite of *slow*, so it must mean "fast" or "swift."

EXERCISE 14

Antonyms (Part 1)

Directions: The first word in each numbered item in the list below is followed by four other words. Locate the antonym, and circle it. Use the dictionary as needed.

1. loud   deafening   showy   hushed   audible

2. listen   hear   ignore   heed   obey

3. argument   agreement   dispute   quarrel   rebuttal

4. dull   boring   sharp   stupid   tedious

5. certain   sure   some   doubtful   guaranteed

Antonyms (Part 2)

Directions: Each of the following sentences contains a word in **boldface type.** Find the antonym for this word within the sentence and circle it. The first one is done for you.

1. Until midnight the streets were **silent**; then distant shouts were audible from my window.

2. The **prey** managed to escape the hunter that had been tracking it.

3. The store employees **stacked** the merchandise that had toppled off the shelves.

4. The mice retreated **timidly** into the shadows when they heard dogs barking aggressively.

Answers are on page 766.

Using Contractions

Contractions are pairs of words that you combine by removing one or more letters and adding an **apostrophe** (') in their place.

Some contractions combine a helping verb, such as *are* or *has* or perhaps the verb *can,* with the word *not.*

are + not = aren't

has + not = hasn't

There are two exceptions. In these cases, when you form a contraction, you need to drop more than one letter.

cannot = can't

will + not = won't

Here is a list of common contractions made with helping verbs:

Complete Words	Contraction (verb + *not*)
are not	aren't
cannot	can't
did not	didn't
do not	don't
had not	hadn't
has not	hasn't
have not	haven't
is not	isn't
should not	shouldn't
was not	wasn't
will not	won't
were not	weren't
would not	wouldn't

Other contractions are a combination of a pronoun followed by a verb.

you + will = you'll

we + are = we're

In some cases, you will need to drop more than one letter to form a contraction when you combine a pronoun and a verb. Watch out for *will*, *would*, and forms of the verb *to have*.

Form Used in Contraction	Example
'll for *will*	I will = I'll
've for *have*	we have = we've
's for *has*	It has = it's
'd for *would* and *had*	he would = he'd
	they had = they'd

Here is a list of common contractions formed by combining a pronoun and a verb:

Complete Words	Contraction (pronoun + verb)
I would *or* I had	I'd
I will	I'll
I am	I'm
I have	I've
it is *or* it has	it's
she would *or* she had	she'd
we have	we've
who is	who's
you are	you're

EXERCISE 15

Using Contractions

Directions: On each blank below, write the contraction that matches the words for each numbered item. The first one is done for you.

1. had not ___hadn't___

2. I had _____

3. cannot _____

4. they are _____

5. we will _____

Answers are on page 766.

Using Homonyms Correctly

Some English words sound alike but are not spelled the same. These are called **homonyms**. The pronunciations of some homonyms, such as *passed* and *past*, *role* and *role*, or *meat* and *meet* are identical. How can you tell if you are using the correct version of the word? The word's meaning determines the correct spelling.

	Meaning	Example
two	a number between one and three	Rashid expected to receive only one gift, but he got **two** instead!
to	indicates movement toward	The children went **to** the park. The antique doll went **to** the highest bidder.
too	also OR excessively	I invited Latetia to bring a date to the party, **too.** That bright blue coat is **too** expensive.

The table that follows lists some common homonyms. Notice that this list contains a fair number of the pronoun contractions you have already learned. Consult a dictionary if you are not sure if you are using the correct version of the word.

Homonym	Meaning	Example
accept	to agree to receive or recognize	I **accept** the fact that he has a different opinion.
except	not including	I knew everyone at the concert **except** Tom, whom I had never met before.
its	the possessive form of *it*	The team is stunned by **its** loss to its opponent.
it's	it is	**It's** an outcome that hurts our chances to make the playoffs.
knew	the past tense of *know*	Mom **knew** the best way to get to the zoo.
new	not old	Seeing wild animals up close was a **new** experience for us.
their	the possessive form of *they*	Business at **their** restaurant boomed after the celebrity raved about their food in an interview.
there	in that place	After that, everybody wanted to go **there.**
they're	they are	**They're** extremely grateful for what the celebrity said about the restaurant.
your	the possessive form of *you*	**Your** vivid rendering of that tale left us spellbound.
you're	you are	**You're** a master storyteller.

Pronoun homonyms can be challenging. There is a way to test the words in order to determine which one is correct. Which word is correct in the following example?

We always work in a food bank on Thanksgiving.

(Its, It's) a family tradition.

Recall that the contraction *it's* combines a pronoun (*it*) and a verb (*is*). Substitute *it is* into the second sentence above.

> It is a family tradition.

Yes, in this sentence, *it* is the subject and *is* is the verb, so *It's* is correct. Which word, *it's* or *its*, would make this next example correct?

> The food bank can always use volunteers like us on holidays. (Its, It's) staff is thankful for our help.

Again, substitute *It is* into the sentence.

> It is staff is always thankful for our help.

This sentence sounds strange, doesn't it? For one thing, the verb *is* shows up twice. *Its* is correct because, as the possessive pronoun form of *it*, it describes the noun *staff*.

EXERCISE 16

Using Homonyms Correctly

Directions: The sentences below include homonyms that have been used incorrectly. Only one sentence has no errors. Write the incorrect homonym or homonyms in the second column, and the correct homonym that should replace it in the third column. If there are no errors, write "no error" in the second column. The first sentence has been done for you.

1. Weather you love dogs or cats, you can help an animal in need.

2. To many animals have lost there homes, and they need you're help.

3. Support your local animal shelter by adopting a pet.

4. Their are so many wonderful animals that would make great pets and appreciate a knew home.

5. You're donation is also greatly appreciated.

6. Its money that will be put to good use.

Sentence Number	Incorrect	Correct
1	Weather	Whether

Answers are on page 766.

CHAPTER 6
Understanding What You Read

This chapter focuses on helping you to improve your understanding of written communication. You will learn techniques for figuring out the meanings of unfamiliar words. You will also learn how to identify the main ideas in topic sentences, paragraphs, and passages.

Understanding Word Meanings

When you read, it is important to understand the words the writer uses. When you encounter unfamiliar words, you can find the definition in a dictionary, or you can look for clues to the meaning of the word in the surrounding words and sentences. Think also about why the author chooses to use particular words. Words may have shades of meaning, either negative or positive, that can help you understand what the author is trying to say.

Using Context Clues

Context refers to the text surrounding an unfamiliar word or phrase. The context provides extra information that helps you figure out what the word or phrase means. In some cases, the sentence may include a restatement or definition of the word. The definition of the word *botanist* actually follows it in this sentence:

Janice became a **botanist** because she loves to study plants.

In other cases, the definition may not be so obvious. Often, there are examples in the text that reveal the meaning of an unfamiliar word. Look for phrases like *such as*, *for example*, and *including* that tell you an example is about to occur. Notice how the underlined words in the following sentence are clues to the meaning of the word *infraction*.

An **infraction**, *such as* running a red light or driving above the speed limit, often results in a ticket.

Since both underlined examples describe broken traffic rules, you can infer that *infraction* means something you do that violates a law.

In other instances, there may be synonyms or antonyms of the word within the sentence that will help you unlock a word's meaning.

Luis thought the book would be boring, but it was extremely **compelling**.

In this case, the word *but* signals that there is a contrast between the first and second parts of the sentence. Therefore, you can infer that *boring* is the opposite of *compelling*, suggesting that *compelling* means "interesting."

Rachel told us the hotel would be **remote**. It took us hours to get there.

EXERCISE 1

Using Context Clues (Part 1)

Directions: Read the following sentences and then choose the best meaning for each word in **bold** based on the underlined context clues.

1. She was **anxious** about her test results until the doctor **assuaged** her fear by saying he was certain there was nothing seriously wrong with her.

   A. Confirmed
   B. Lectured
   C. Calmed
   D. Insulted

2. The newspaper **maligned** his reputation by spreading false rumors about him. He responded by suing the paper in court for its lies.

   A. Improved
   B. Damaged
   C. Revealed
   D. Concealed

3. John is so **arrogant** that he stops to admire his new haircut in every mirror he passes. He has always been too proud of his good looks.

   A. Vain
   B. Confident
   C. Unhappy
   D. Restless

4. She was **ecstatic** when she got the new job and could not stop smiling. She jumped up and down and squealed with happiness.

   A. Content
   B. Polite
   C. Surprised
   D. Joyful

Answers are on page 767.

Using Context Clues (Part 2)

Directions: Choose the correct definition of the word in **bold**. <u>Underline</u> the context clues in each sentence that help you define the word.

1. Mr. Jones **compensated** his loyal workers with tickets to the theater, or gift cards to the local bookstore.

   A. Fired
   B. Cheated
   C. Promoted
   D. Paid

2. Paula practiced her **culinary** skills by preparing a delicious new pasta recipe.

   A. Mechanical
   B. Musical
   C. Cooking
   D. Language

3. As the sun came up, the view became less **obscure**, and we could see the town ahead.

   A. Interesting
   B. Crowded
   C. Distant
   D. Hidden

Answers are on page 767.

Understanding Connotation and Denotation

The dictionary definition of a word is called its **denotation**. However, a word may evoke different feelings in you, positive or negative, depending on its context. This is called the word's **connotation**. Words with the same denotation can have very different connotations. For example, consider the words in **bold** in these sentences:

When Darlene ran the meeting, she was **bossy** and **controlling**.

When Darlene ran the meeting, she was **assertive** and **confident**.

Although the denotations, their literal meanings, are similar, the connotations of these words are quite different. The words *bossy* and *controlling* describe negative personal characteristics, and therefore they have negative connotations. However, the words *assertive* and *confident* have positive connotations because they describe positive personal characteristics.

Compare the following two sentences. Think about what feeling, or connotation, each expresses.

> Marcus is so **thrifty** that he saved enough for a vacation next month.

> Tony is so **cheap** that he refused to split the dinner check with his friends.

In the first sentence, the word *thrifty* has positive connotations. It refers to a positive trait—saving money to meet a financial goal. In the second sentence, *cheap* has a negative connotation—it means Tony holds on to his money so tightly that he mistreats his friends.

Here is another example:

> The real estate company sold us the oldest **house** on the street.

> We were newly married and loved making a **home** together.

A *house* is a thing, a structure. It has no emotional meaning on its own. *Home*, on the other hand, is a word filled with emotion—it suggests a sense of warmth, safety, and belonging.

EXERCISE 2

Understanding Connotation and Denotation

Directions: Sort the following pairs of words. Based on their connotations, write the words with negative connotations in the **Negative** box. Write the words with positive connotations in the **Positive** box.

1. quiet, isolated

2. job, career

3. proud, egotistical

4. stubborn, persistent

5. young, childish

6. indecisive, thoughtful

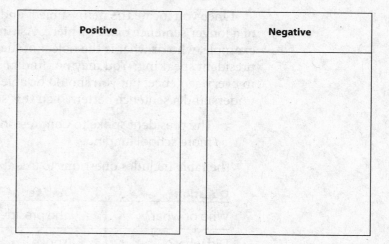

Answers are on page 767.

Understanding Sentences, Paragraphs, and Passages

Following are some useful techniques for understanding the meaning of a sentence, paragraph, or reading passage.

Identifying Key Words

Sometimes a sentence may seem complicated and confusing but breaking it down into smaller, more manageable parts can help you better understand it. One way to do this is by identifying **key words**. First, look for the sentence's main subject and verb, which are key words to its meaning. To identify these key words, ask yourself, "Who (or what) did what?"

For example, read the following sentences:

         What?   *did what?*
Sentence 1: The president spoke.

Key words: president spoke

         What?   *did what?*
Sentence 2: The president spoke to a large crowd about the importance of understanding our national history and passing that knowledge on to future generations.

Key words: president spoke

As you can see, the key words in both sentences are the same. The subject of both sentences is *president*, and the verb is *spoke*. The longer sentence contains extra details that add information about what the president said but the subject and action are identical to the first sentence. You understand the central action: the president spoke.

Once you locate the main subject and verb, you can unpack the rest of a longer sentence piece by piece. Asking these questions can help. For example, who or what is the object of the subject's action? To whom is the president speaking? You may not find answers to all of these questions in every sentence, but you should be able to answer enough of them to understand a sentence better. Read this sentence:

The president spoke to Congress in Washington, DC, about the need for more school funding.

The table includes questions to ask about the sentence:

Question	Answer
Who or what?	the president
Did what?	spoke
To whom or what?	to Congress
Where?	Washington, DC
When?	no information available in sentence
How?	no information available in sentence
Why?	about the need for more school funding

EXERCISE 3

Identifying Key Words

Directions: Read the following sentences. Then answer the questions by filling in the blanks.

1. Amelia Earhart, an American aviation pioneer, mysteriously disappeared in 1937 in the central Pacific Ocean while attempting to fly solo around the world.

   Who or what? _____
   Did what? _____
   Where? _____
   When? _____
   How? _____

2. Beethoven continued to write music even after he went deaf, composing what many consider to be his greatest symphony even though he could not hear.

   Who or what? _____
   Did what? _____
   When? _____

3. The secretary of state expressed her hope to the journalists that the new peace talks would improve relations in the Middle East.

Who or what? _____

Did what? _____

To whom? _____

About what? _____

Answers are on page 767.

Identifying the Main Idea in a Paragraph

The **main idea** is the central, or most important, idea in a paragraph or passage. Writers will often state the main idea of a paragraph **explicitly**, meaning they will tell you what the topic is. As you have learned, this topic sentence may appear anywhere within the paragraph. The main idea in this paragraph is in **bold**:

> No one likes to be proven wrong. But we have become a nation that is too fond of arguing just to prove we are right. Screaming matches on CNN and other news channels, for example, have taken the place of thoughtful debate. **It is time to stop insisting on being right and start listening respectfully to the opinions of others.**

The final sentence in this paragraph is its topic sentence. It tells you clearly what the entire paragraph is about: the writer believes we should stop arguing to prove a point and begin listening to each other with respect.

But sometimes writers will not come out and tell you the main idea. Instead, it is **implicit**, or unstated. In these situations, you must infer the main idea by finding out what the sentences in the paragraph have in common. You can do this by using clues in the paragraph, such as its supporting details, to help you find the main idea.

Here is an example of an introductory paragraph that does *not* state its main idea in a topic sentence. Look closely at the supporting details. Ask yourself: What topic do these sentences have in common?

> Due to health concerns, drinking tea is on the rise because tea contains disease-fighting antioxidants. Not long ago, we were discouraged from drinking coffee because the amount of caffeine was considered harmful. Now that scientists claim that coffee has health benefits, however, Americans are drinking that in larger quantities as well. Soda consumption, on the other hand, is definitely on the decline due to the fear that it contributes to diabetes and stomach cancer.

These sentences all share the same topic: beverages, specifically tea, coffee, and soda. Now, what is the most important point the author makes about this topic? Look at the supporting details:

1. Tea consumption is up because it is healthful.

2. Coffee consumption is up because it is healthful.

3. Soda consumption is down because it is harmful.

Put them all together in one sentence. You may need to add a transition such as *but* or *and* to connect them: People drink more tea and coffee because they are healthful, **but** they drink less soda because it is harmful. This is the paragraph's main idea.

EXERCISE 4

Identifying the Main Idea in a Paragraph (Part 1)

Directions: Read the paragraph. First, circle the main idea. Then, underline three supporting details.

Your skin is the organ that comes into contact with the rest of the world. It holds bodily fluids in, preventing dehydration, and it keeps harmful germs out—without it we would get infections. Your skin is full of nerve endings that help you feel things like heat, cold, and pain. If you couldn't feel these things, you could get badly hurt and not even know it! Since your skin plays such an important role in protecting your body, you should keep it as healthy as you can. This will help keep you from getting sick or having damage to your bones, muscles, and organs.

Identifying the Main Idea in a Paragraph (Part 2)

Directions: Read the paragraph, and then answer the questions that follow.

Middle School 233 in the South Bronx, located in the poorest congressional district in the United States, used to be the most violent middle school in the city. Principal Ramon Gonzalez took over in 2003. Among his numerous reforms, he makes sure his students receive rigorous arts instruction at every grade level. MS 233 students now learn music and math together and take visual arts classes several times a week. Last year the school band won the Northeast Championship. Principal Gonzalez deliberately schedules all the art and music classes for Mondays and Fridays, so that all the kids come to school on those days. Traditionally these days are when the most students skip school, but now these students attend school consistently on both days.

1. What topic do the sentences in this paragraph have in common?

_____

2. What is the main idea the author conveys about this topic?

_____

Answers are on page 767.

Identifying the Main Idea in a Passage

Sometimes breaking a large task into smaller parts can help you accomplish that task. If you can identify the main idea in a paragraph, you can identify it in a longer passage. How? By identifying the main idea of each paragraph first and then figuring out the relationship between those sentences—what they have in common.

> Recently, people have been seeing wild animals in unusual locations—in cities and suburbs. There have been wolves in the streets of suburban Dallas; cougars in San Francisco city parks; and alligators in backyards in Orlando. In late 2013, a woman in Jersey City saw a black bear drinking from her swimming pool.

Main idea: _____

> As their populations increase, many cities need room to grow. In order to expand, they are building new homes and businesses in remote locations where few humans have previously lived. These include forests, woodlands, marshlands, and other wilderness areas.

Main idea: _____

> Animals from deer to bobcats are pushed out of their homes by humans building homes for themselves. Where can these animals go? In the end, they wander away from the smoke and noise of construction in search of food and shelter elsewhere. This leads them deep into human territory, where they face starvation, lack of shelter, and possible destruction.

Main idea: _____

What is the main idea in each paragraph?

Paragraph 1: Recently, people have been seeing wild animals in unusual locations—in cities and suburbs.

Paragraph 2: As their populations increase, many cities need room to grow.

Paragraph 3: Animals from deer to bobcats are pushed of out their homes by humans building homes for themselves.

Now, combine these into a statement of the passage's main idea. You should do this in no more than a couple of sentences. Remember, you may add transitions or other connecting words to help the ideas fit together smoothly as long as they accurately reflect the relationship between the ideas (comparing, contrasting, etc.).

The main idea of the passage is:

> Recently, people have been seeing wild animals in cities and suburbs **because** cities need room to grow **and** animals are pushed out of their homes by humans building homes for themselves.

EXERCISE 5

Identifying the Main Idea in a Passage

Directions: Read the following paragraphs. Write the main idea of each paragraph on the lines that follow. Then write the main idea of the passage.

1   The bee colony offers one of the best examples of what can be accomplished by united effort when harmony prevails. In a beehive, some worker bees gather honey, others are nurses for the queen bee and her babies, others guard the hive and fight intruders, and others care for the hive by mending breaks in the hive's wall. Each bee knows its work and goes about it without interfering with the work of the others.

2   Throughout the long, hot, summer days the worker bees are busy from daylight until dark gathering nectar they use to make food. As long as they are able to gather nectar, they continue to do so, and when they are tired they drop in the field and are forgotten, and others rush to take their place.

3   Ants are closely related to bees and are similar to them in many respects. They live in colonies consisting of workers, drones, and a queen. Like bees, ant workers are divided into various categories according to their duties—warriors, guards, nurses, and other jobs.

4   Ants, however, seem to have real intelligence, and they are far more advanced than the bees in many respects. They do not waste time building a complicated hive, as the bees do, so when food is scarce or for other reasons they need to move, they simply "pack up" and migrate. This, together with the fact that they feed on almost every imaginable kind of plant and animal material, makes them the rulers of the insect world.

Write the main idea for each paragraph here:

Paragraph 1:   _____

Paragraph 2:   _____

Paragraph 3: _____

Paragraph 4: _____

Main idea of the passage: _____

Answers are on page 767.

Summarizing

A **summary** is a short description of the most important elements of a longer text. It "sums up," or briefly states, the main points or highlights of the longer text. To summarize, you need to identify the main idea and the most important details, and then describe them briefly in your own words in no more than two or three sentences. You do not need to include every detail, just the ones that are most important.

Read this paragraph and the chart that follows it. The chart contains questions you should answer in order to make your summary precise.

Service animals are defined as dogs that are individually trained to perform tasks for people with disabilities whenever they are needed. Examples of such tasks include guiding people who are blind, alerting people who are deaf, pulling a wheelchair, alerting and protecting a person who is having a seizure, calming a person with posttraumatic stress disorder (PTSD) during an anxiety attack, or performing other duties. Service animals are working animals, not pets. The task a dog has been trained to provide must be directly related to the person's disability.

Who/What?	service animals
(Do or Did) what?	perform tasks for people with disabilities
When?	whenever they are needed
Why?	some people with disabilities need assistance with specific situations and tasks
How? (list verbs)	*guiding, alerting, pulling, protecting, calming,* or *whatever is needed*

A summary should be brief and to the point. You should include only the *most* important details and the main idea and use no more than one or two sentences. Here is a summary of the paragraph on service animals:

Some people with disabilities need assistance, and service animals perform tasks for them whenever they are needed, such as guiding, alerting, pulling, protecting, and calming them.

EXERCISE 6

Summarizing (Part 1)

Directions: Read the following passage, keeping in mind *Who/What? (Did) What? Where? When? How?* and *Why?* Then answer the questions that follow.

In the life of every human there comes a time, especially in childhood, when he or she wishes to make a collection of some kind. It may be a collection of coins, postage stamps, post-cards, shells, birds' eggs, pressed flowers, or insects kept in a special box. . . . In later life the former child will search in a parent's closet or attic for the old box that contains the remains of his or her youthful efforts, usually covered with dust, but still remembered by the adult in every detail, as if no time had passed. This desire to make a collection . . . tends to make a child observe closely and develop an interest in the surrounding world . . . It will add a store of information that can be gotten in no other way.

1. On the lines, write words from the paragraph that answer each question.

   Who/What? _____
   (Did) what? _____
   When? _____
   Where? _____
   How? _____
   Why? _____

2. Now use your answers to question 1 to write a summary of the paragraph.

   _____
   _____
   _____

3. According to the paragraph, what is the *most* important reason for creating a collection?

   A. It keeps children from getting into trouble and annoying their parents.
   B. It helps children to develop a sense of responsibililty.
   C. It creates positive memories later in life.
   D. It encourages a desire for knowledge of the surrounding world.

Answers are on page 768.

CHAPTER 7

The Writing Process

On the GED® test, you will be asked to write one short essay in the Reasoning Through Language Arts section and another in the Social Studies section. So it's a good idea for you to study the writing process, the technique you can use to create a polished and well-crafted essay.

Parts of an Essay

Most essays explain something or offer an opinion about an issue. The basic parts of an essay are:

- **Introduction:** where you tell your reader what your essay is about
- **Body:** made up of multiple paragraphs, this is where you explain something and include evidence to support what you say
- **Conclusion:** where you summarize what your essay has said

The first paragraph contains the **introduction**; it briefly states the essay topic. This is your main idea, also known as your thesis statement. This helps your readers understand the focus of your essay.

For example, suppose your essay topic is about whether cigarettes should be legal or illegal. The introduction to your essay might be like the following one:

> Everyone knows that cigarettes are dangerous, but you can buy them legally almost anywhere if you are over 18. This is not right. Cigarettes are not just dangerous to smokers but also to nonsmokers. Our government should take the extra step and make cigarettes illegal for the sake of everyone's safety.

In the **body** of the essay, you build from one idea to the next by providing evidence to explain and support the essay's main idea. Types of evidence include examples or definitions, facts, and quotations. Here is the body of the essay on making cigarettes illegal:

> Many studies have proven that smoking cigarettes has dangerous effects. Chemicals in cigarettes cause fatal diseases such as cancer and lung disease, and they increase the risk of diabetes and heart disease. Smoking during pregnancy can cause birth defects. Recently, scientists have shown that smoking even contributes to getting Alzheimer's disease.

> There have been many actions taken to discourage people from smoking, and most of them have worked to some extent. Packs of cigarettes and cigarette ads must carry a warning that "cigarettes

may be hazardous to your health." Cigarettes are taxed more heavily, so they are expensive. Cigarette ads are no longer permitted on television or at sporting events. This has all been helpful, and more people have stopped smoking. But it is not enough.

Many people think it's not the government's business whether people do something harmful to themselves. As long as a person is aware of the risks of cigarettes, he or she has the right to decide whether to smoke. This is fair. However, cigarettes harm more than just the smoker, they harm nonsmokers, too. Nonsmokers may be exposed to secondhand cigarette smoke in any enclosed space or even outdoors by standing downwind from a smoker. Like smokers, they can get sick and even die from breathing this smoke. Some 40 percent of people who get lung cancer have never smoked a cigarette. If people do something that not only hurts themselves but also hurts others, it should be against the law.

The final paragraph, called the **conclusion** or concluding paragraph, wraps up the essay. It should not just repeat what the introduction said. Usually, the conclusion restates the main idea and touches on the main points covered in the body of the essay. Here is a possible conclusion:

Smokers place others in danger, not just themselves. This is why our government needs to take stronger action. Nonsmokers have rights, too. As long as cigarettes are legal, they will continue to have these negative effects. Let's make cigarettes illegal.

The writer has introduced the main idea, offered solid evidence to back it up, and built toward a strong conclusion in favor of making cigarettes illegal. The essay is clear and moves clearly from one sentence to the next and from one paragraph to the next.

The Writing Process

The **writing process** is a three-step method for creating a clear, effective essay or other piece of writing. Here are the steps in the writing process:

- **Prewriting:** planning and gathering information
- **Writing a draft:** putting down thoughts on paper based on prewriting
- **Revising:** reviewing the essay and making changes to build an argument that moves smoothly and includes supporting evidence; checking sentence and paragraph construction

Prewriting

Prewriting is the planning stage of a writing assignment. The goal of prewriting is to help you figure out who your audience is, decide the **purpose** of your writing, and gather supporting ideas.

What do you want your piece to *accomplish*, and how will you support what you will say? Also consider who will be reading your essay—your audience—and what arguments will likely convince them.

For example, suppose your topic is blood donation, and you want to persuade your audience to donate blood. The purpose of your piece, then, is to convince your audience why donating blood is important and that they should do it.

Brainstorming and Idea Maps

Two common types of prewriting are brainstorming and using an idea map.

When you **brainstorm**, you list your ideas as they occur to you without censoring them. You might brainstorm like this about why it is a good idea to donate blood:

> *Saves lives*
>
> *Fast and easy*
>
> *Not very painful*

Consider, too, that if you want to persuade your audience to donate blood, you have to think of some of the reasons that people hesitate to do so. A "pros and cons" list can help you determine the different sides of an issue so that you can better argue for your side.

Donating Blood	
Pros	**Cons**
Donated blood can save lives.	It can hurt.
Giving blood is fast.	You might get an infection from the needle.
Giving blood is easy.	It can be inconvenient to do in the middle of a busy schedule.
Giving blood is safe.	People sometimes pass out or feel weak.
The blood donation center is close to my favorite mall, so I can shop.	There are plenty of people donating blood already.
	It reminds me of a horror movie with vampires.

An alternative to a brainstorm, an **idea map**, sometimes called **webbing or clustering**, is a graphic organizer to help you come up with ideas on a particular topic. Start by writing your topic in the middle of a piece of paper and then jotting down your ideas in the circles around the center circle.

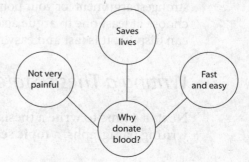

Brainstorming and Idea Maps

Brainstorm ideas for *one* of the following topics. Make sure you brainstorm at least three pros and three cons. Write your ideas in a pros and cons list or in an idea map. Remember to write down whatever comes to mind without censoring yourself. The point is to get some ideas on paper.

Do professional athletes make too much money?

Are celebrities a positive influence on teenagers?

Should bicycle riders have to wear safety helmets?

Answers are on page 768.

Writing a Rough Draft

In this step of the writing process, you come up with a thesis or topic statement, organize your ideas, and write a rough draft. Let's continue, using the topic of the importance of donating blood as an example.

Pick a point of view and stick with it. Let's say you favor blood donation. Now is the time to look at the ideas you have come up with during prewriting and decide which strike you as most persuasive or important.

Think about what you want to say. Read over all your ideas and mark at least two, but no more than three, of the ones you think are most important and convincing. Don't go overboard and pick too many.

Remember your audience. What will be most likely to convince them? Most of the ideas in the pros and cons list are good, but comparing blood donation to a vampire movie and making it an excuse to go shopping do not seem as if they will convince anyone to take your argument seriously.

Helping others is always a strong motive to get people to act. That could be the strongest argument for your point of view. Now consider the cons of the argument: choose at least one to argue against. Not having enough time is something you can dispute. It is fast and easy to donate blood, even if it stings a little.

Writing a Thesis Statement

Next, it's time to write a thesis statement. As discussed in the chapter on writing paragraphs, a **topic sentence** states the main idea of a paragraph so readers know what the paragraph discusses. Just as a paragraph needs a topic sentence, an essay requires a **thesis statement** that presents the main idea of the entire essay in a short number of sentences.

For example, take another look at the pros and cons brainstorm list about donating blood. A good thesis statement for this argument might be: Donating blood is an easy and important way to help others. This thesis statement provides an overview of all the points that the writer is going to make in favor of blood donation—that it is easy, that it is important to do, and that it has benefits for others.

Note that there are two reasons given why blood donation is a good idea. These will help you organize the body of your essay, in which you explain and support your argument.

EXERCISE 2

Writing a Thesis Statement (Part 1)

Here again is the introduction to the essay on making cigarettes illegal. Read it and then underline the sentence that is the thesis statement for the essay.

Everyone knows that cigarettes are dangerous, but you can still buy them legally almost anywhere if you are over 18. This is not right. Cigarettes are not just dangerous to smokers but also to nonsmokers. Our government should take the extra step and make cigarettes illegal for the sake of everyone's safety.

Writing a Thesis Statement (Part 2)

Read the following paragraph.

The faster a vehicle is going when it collides with an object, the more damage is done to the vehicle and the object. Due to inertia, it's harder to stop a fast-moving car than a slow one. Consequently, in a situation requiring sudden braking, a fast-moving car takes more time and a greater distance to slow down to avoid an impact than a slower-moving one. Studies also show that fuel efficiency is higher at 55 mph than at faster speeds. Engines burn more fuel the faster they go.

1. Which of the following would make a good thesis statement for the point of view expressed in the paragraph?

    A. Slower moving cars can stop more quickly than faster moving ones.
    B. A speed limit of 55 mph encourages fuel efficiency.
    C. A speed limit of 55 mph creates safer highways.
    D. A speed limit of 55 mph is safer and better for the environment than faster speed limits.

Answers are on page 768.

Preparing a Rough Draft

Once you've come up with the ideas that you want to include in your writing and you have a thesis statement, it's time to write a rough draft. A **rough draft** is a first pass at organizing your thoughts and ideas into a logical argument that supports your position. Use the rough draft to flesh out your ideas. Don't worry about writing perfect sentences. Don't worry if your ideas are not organized perfectly, either. For the moment, focus on developing the content.

Begin with the thesis statement and then add sentences to support your thesis. If you are worried about where to start, remember that you have identified at least two reasons to back up your point of view. Write a paragraph about one of them. Then write a second paragraph about the other. Follow those paragraphs with a brief concluding paragraph in which you sum up what you have said.

While writing your rough draft, use the following checklist to make sure you have got all the elements necessary for a good essay.

Checklist for a Rough Draft	Yes	No
Do you have a thesis statement?	—	—
Have you included at least two, preferably three, reasons supporting your point of view?	—	—
Have you written a concluding sentence or two?	—	—

Revising

Now it's time to **revise**, a word that comes from a Latin word meaning "to see again" or "to revisit." In other words, it's time to reread your draft, ask yourself the questions in the following checklist, and do some rewriting. Concentrate on whether you have a thesis statement, at least two paragraphs of support for it, and a conclusion. Does your argument make sense?

Checklist for a Revision	Yes	No
Have you focused on your main idea throughout the draft?	—	—
Are there multiple paragraphs—introduction, body, conclusion?	—	—
Have you included reasons that support your position?	—	—
Can you identify any unnecessary details or sentences that can be removed?	—	—
Do you have a concluding paragraph that restates your main idea?	—	—

Creating the Final Draft

Creating the **final draft** is the last step in the writing process. This is the stage in which you **proofread** your work, checking to make sure grammar, punctuation, and spelling are correct. By this stage, the essay needs only minor corrections. If you need to add content or rearrange your examples to strengthen your argument, then you are still revising. That is fine. Most writers revise and rewrite more than once. At this final draft stage, all that is left to do is a last polish.

Final Draft Checklist	Yes	No
Have you checked grammar for subject-verb agreement?	—	—
Are verb tenses consistent?	—	—
Are there sentence fragments?	—	—
Is the punctuation correct?	—	—
Are all words spelled correctly?	—	—

Here is what a final draft of the essay on donating blood might look like:

Donating blood is an easy and important way to help others. It can seem as if you do not have enough time. Maybe you are a little afraid of the needle. But it is a great thing to do.

First, it is easy to donate blood. Saying you are too busy is no excuse. There are three blood donation centers near my neighborhood alone. It takes less than an hour to give blood. There is also a blood mobile that stops frequently at the local malls so you can donate blood on the spot. It is true that it is a little uncomfortable, too, but just for a moment.

Donating blood benefits others. Hospitals are always saying they do not have enough blood. They need it for a reason. Your blood might help someone survive a car accident or a natural disaster. In a hurricane or a tornado, many people can be badly hurt. Hospitals sometimes have to beg people to donate blood to help the wounded. If someone you loved needed blood, wouldn't you want that person to have it?

There are many benefits to giving blood, but the biggest is that you could save someone's life with just a few minutes of your time. It is that easy.

EXERCISE 3

The Writing Process

Directions: Now follow the steps in the writing process to produce a three- or four-paragraph essay. Choose one of the topics in the following list and write what you think about it, taking a position for it or against it. On separate sheets of paper, write a prewriting exercise and a rough draft. Then write your final draft on the lines provided. You can use your brainstorm or idea map from the earlier exercise to get started. Write as if you have to convince someone to agree with your opinion.

Do professional athletes make too much money?

Are celebrities a positive influence on teenagers?

Should bicycle riders have to wear safety helmets?

_____

_____

_____

_____

_____

_____

_____

_____

_____

_____

Answer is on page 768.

Informational Texts

Informational texts convey information based on facts, not opinions. Texts such as news articles and textbooks explain information and ideas. Others, such as office memos, handbooks, brochures, and recipes, provide information and steps to follow in order to reach a specific goal, such as completing a task.

Understanding Informational Texts

The author of an informational text usually writes for a specific purpose. The facts in the text are generally selected and arranged in order to make a particular point, and the author usually has a specific audience in mind. The ideas in the text are also usually organized in a structure and sequence that supports the author's purpose.

Understanding Audience, Purpose, and Evidence

In order to understand any informational text, you need to answer two important questions. First, what is the text meant to accomplish? This is the primary **purpose** of the text. Second, for whom is the text primarily written? This is the text's **audience**. The purpose and audience of a text are usually closely related. For example, doctors and nurses would be the intended audience for a handbook that is designed to explain hospital procedures.

The following chart provides information about types of documents and their audiences and purposes:

Document	Audience	Purpose
Employee handbook	Employees at a specific workplace	To explain the rules and regulations that employees must follow
Newspaper article	People who want to learn about current events	To inform readers about a specific news story
Book about how to prepare for the GED test	People who want to take the GED test	To explain how to prepare for the GED test

What can help you determine the audience and purpose of an informational document? Look for **evidence** in the text. Types of evidence to look for are listed in the following chart.

Type of Evidence	What It Does	Example
Title / headings	Tell you what the passage is about and identifies its parts	*Ten Tips for a Successful Job Search* A. Research the Company B. Dress Appropriately
Definitions	Tell you what something is	"Psychology is the study of the human mind."
Descriptions	Give defining physical and other details, such as size, shape, color, personality, and more. May include visuals such as charts or graphs.	Cats have excellent hearing and a strong sense of smell.
Examples	A specific instance of something	Small dogs, such as poodles and terriers, are delightful. One useful reference book is a dictionary.

Read this text from a brochure about recycling.

Recycling Is Important

Recycling is the process of collecting and processing materials that would otherwise be thrown away as trash and turning them into new products.

Benefits of Recycling

Recycling can benefit your community and the environment because it

- reduces the amount of waste sent to landfills and incinerators,
- conserves natural resources such as timber, water, and minerals,
- prevents pollution by reducing the need to collect new raw materials saves energy,
- reduces greenhouse gas emissions that contribute to global climate change,
- helps sustain the environment for future generations, and
- helps create new well-paying jobs in the recycling and manufacturing industries in the United States.

What Happens
To Stuff We Throw Away?*

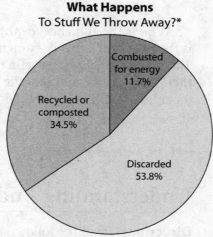

Combusted for energy 11.7%

Recycled or composted 34.5%

Discarded 53.8%

* Based on 2012 MSW Characterization Report

Steps in Recycling Materials

Recycling includes these three major steps:

Step 1: Collecting and processing materials for recycling

Step 2: Manufacturing recycled materials into goods

Step 3: Purchasing products made from recycled materials such as paper towels; aluminum, plastic, and glass soft drink containers; steel cans; and plastic laundry detergent bottles

Here is a chart that lists different kinds of evidence to look for in the brochure to help you determine its audience and purpose. Using this evidence, identify the audience and purpose of the brochure.

What to Look For	Text Evidence
Title	Recycling Is Important
Headings	Benefits of Recycling; Steps in Recycling Materials
Definitions	"Recycling is the process of collecting and processing materials that would otherwise be thrown away as trash and turning them into new products."
Examples	Lists specific benefits of recycling Lists specific steps in the recycling process Lists goods made from recycled materials
Explanations	"Recycling can benefit your community and the environment because it . . ."
Descriptions or visuals (charts, graphs, illustrations)	Chart showing what trash consists of

Who is the audience for this document? People who do not recycle. What is the purpose of this document? To explain the recycling process to them. The brochure defines recycling, tells readers why it is beneficial for them and their community, and lists the steps in the recycling process. The evidence includes definitions, explanations, examples, and even a chart.

EXERCISE 1

Understanding Audience, Purpose, and Evidence

Directions: Read the following passage and then fill in the chart. (The passage may not include every category of evidence in the chart.)

Rare Butterflies in Danger

An endangered species is any animal or plant in danger of disappearing completely from Earth. The Schaus swallowtail is a butterfly that has been on the list of endangered species for 20 years. These butterflies are found only on a single island in Biscayne National Park, Florida. Only 75 Schaus butterflies were recorded there over the past three years combined. The butterflies are dark brown with yellow markings and a broad, rusty patch underneath their hind wing. Their survival is hindered by habitat destruction, insecticide use, droughts, hurricanes, and illegal collection. There is hope that breeding the butterflies in laboratories may help increase their numbers.

What to Look for	Text Evidence
Title	
Headings	
Definitions	
Examples	
Explanations	
Descriptions or Visuals	
Audience:	
Purpose:	

Answers are on page 769.

Understanding How Ideas are Organized

Authors organize what they write for a reason. For example, an instruction manual is organized as a series of steps for readers to follow so they can complete a task, such as connecting a DVD player to a television or putting parts of a table together. A news story is often written in the order in which the events it describes took place so that readers can understand how those events unfolded. Most authors use one or more of these patterns:

- Chronological order/process
- Comparing and contrasting
- Cause and effect
- Problem and solution

Chronological Order/Process

One way to organize a document is in chronological order, the order in which events happened in real time. Authors often do this to show how something changes over time. For example, in a history book, events that happened earlier in history are described early in the book, and as the book progresses, the events move toward modern times.

Chronological order is also used to present a series of steps or instructions so you can make or do something. For example, a recipe is arranged in a series of steps from first to last so you can prepare a specific dish.

Signal words are clues that tell you how an author has organized a piece of writing. The signal words in this chart let you know that an author has arranged a piece of writing in chronological order.

Signal Words/Phrases: Chronological Order	
Transitions	before, first
	then, next
	since, after, later
	finally, last
Dates and time periods	in the early 1980
	1861–1865
	during World War II
Changes over time	As the economy began to improve . . .
	Before . . . after
Verb tenses (past, present, future)	He **went** to California . . .

The following passage is about the first use of email by the US Congress. Underline any words or phrases that show that this paragraph is arranged in chronological order.

(1) Although a precise date is difficult to pinpoint, electronic mail, or email, was first used internally by the House of Representatives in the early 1980s. (2) Next, external email began in the mid-1990s, permitting the public to contact Member offices 24 hours a day. (3) The Internet provided a new level of accessibility to Congress. (4) Finally, in the mid to late 1990s, the launch of congressional websites granted the public instant access to information that once required weeks and even months to obtain.

The words and phrases you should have underlined include: (1) *was first used*; *the early 1980s*; (2) *Next*; *began in the mid-1990s*; (3) *a new level*; (4) *Finally*; *mid to late 1990s*; *once required weeks and even months to obtain*.

The author of the next passage has organized the text as a sequence of steps in a process to follow in order to complete a task, feeding hummingbirds. Again, underline any words that tell you this paragraph is arranged in chronological order.

How to Feed Hummingbirds

(1) You should begin feeding hummingbirds in the spring. (2) First, mix one part sugar to four parts water in a saucepan; then bring this to a boil for no more than two minutes. (3) Next, let the mixture cool. (4) Then, you can freeze any extra mixture to use in the future. (5) Finally, you are ready to fill the feeder with food and watch the hummingbirds arrive.

The words and phrases you should have underlined include: (1) *begin*; *in the spring*; (2) *First*; *then*; *no more than two minutes*; (3) *Next*; (4) *Then*; *in the future*; (5) *Finally*.

EXERCISE 2

Chronological Order

Directions: Underline the clues in each sentence that signal chronological order. Place the sentences in the correct chronological order by writing the letter on the blank. Then, in one sentence, explain the author's purpose in arranging the events chronologically.

1. **A.** Events during the single term of John Adams, our second president, made these divisions even worse.
   B. Although Washington proved to be personally popular and respected, conflict over the proper functions of governmental power dominated his two terms as president.
   C. They continued into the presidency of the third president, Thomas Jefferson (1801–1809).
   D. With a new constitution in place, Americans turned to General George Washington for leadership, this time as the first president of the new republic.

Chronological order: _____

Author's purpose: _____

2. **A.** Separate crushed aluminum cans from tin cans.
   B. Then, sort them into piles according to what they are made of: glass, metal, or paper.
   C. Finally, place the materials in the appropriate bins.
   D. First, gather materials together, including three bins.
   E. Later, clean out all the glass containers, sort the paper into piles, and rinse and crush the aluminum cans.

Chronological order: _____

Author's purpose: _____

Answers are on page 769.

Comparing and Contrasting

Another way authors organize their ideas is to compare and contrast them. To **compare** is to show how two or more things are *similar*. To **contrast** means to show how they are *different*. Using this technique helps authors distinguish between situations or ideas for an audience to prove a point.

Signal words that indicate comparison (and contrast) are listed below:

Signal Words and Phrases	
Compare	**Contrast**
similarly, like, likewise same as, just as in comparison	although, however, but, nevertheless, on the other hand, than, versus, whereas

Read the following paragraph. Underline the signal words that show comparison and contrast.

Like others soldiers in the Union army, African-American soldiers faced all the problems of war. But they also faced additional difficulties created by racial prejudice. Although many served in the infantry and artillery, discriminatory practices resulted in large numbers of African-American soldiers being assigned to perform noncombat, support duties as cooks and laborers.

African-American soldiers were paid $10 per month, from which $3 was deducted for clothing. In comparison, white soldiers were paid $13 per month, from which no clothing allowance was deducted. If captured by the Confederate army, African-American soldiers confronted a much greater threat than did their white counterparts. Nevertheless, in spite of their many hardships, African-American soldiers in the Union army served well and distinguished themselves in many battles.

According to the passage, what are the similarities and differences between African-American soldiers in the Union army and white soldiers in the same army?

African-American and White Soldiers in the Union Army	
Similarities	**Differences**
Soldiers in Union army	African-American soldiers were often assigned to noncombat duties.
Faced problems of war	Pay was lower for African-American soldiers.
Some died in battle	African-American soldiers faced discrimination.
	Capture by enemy was riskier for African-American soldiers.

In this case, the author contrasts the treatment of African Americans who volunteered for the Union army with that of white soldiers in the same army to show that, even after being freed and volunteering to fight, African Americans were still discriminated against and underestimated.

EXERCISE 3

Comparing and Contrasting

Directions: Read the following paragraph and answer the questions that follow.

Money Spent on Eating at Home or Dining Out

Most consumers consider price when deciding whether to eat at home or away from home. They also consider price to determine where they can afford to go out to eat. In 2009, households earning a pretax income of $93,784 and above, which represented the highest 20 percent of all household incomes, spent, on average, more on food away from home than the combined total spent by households in the three income groups below them. Across all income groups, consumers spent more on food at home than food away from home. Consumers in the lowest income group spent the highest amount of annual food expenditures on food at home, about 70 percent. Consumers in the highest income group split their food budget nearly evenly between food at home, 52 percent, and food away from home, 48 percent.

To analyze this passage, answer the following questions.

1. This passage contrasts _____ to _____.

2. According to the paragraph, which group spends the most money dining out?

   _____

   _____

3. According to the paragraph, which group spends the most money eating at home?

   _____

   _____

4. In one sentence, summarize the main idea of this passage.

   _____

   _____

Answers are on page 769.

Cause and Effect

Cause and effect refers to situations in which one condition or event causes another. We refer to cause and effect frequently in our daily lives, and many types of writing deal with cause-and-effect relationships, too. When we say *because*, we are expressing a cause-and-effect relationship. A child cries *because* he skinned his knee, for example. You feel full *because* you ate a big dinner.

Here are some signal words for cause and effect:

Signal Words and Phrases: Cause and Effect	
because, caused	as a result, affected by
determines, due to	therefore
so, so that	thus

When a writer organizes a paragraph or longer piece this way, each sentence builds upon the next to explain how a specific cause or set of causes leads to a specific effect. Here is a paragraph that is organized using a cause-and-effect pattern about how exposure to harmful noise can cause hearing loss. As you read it, underline words that signal a cause-and-effect relationship.

> (1) Exposure to harmful noise can happen at any age. (2) Therefore, people of all ages, including children, teens, young adults, and older people, can develop noise-induced hearing loss (NIHL). (3) Approximately 15 percent of Americans between the ages of 20 and 69—or 26 million Americans—have hearing loss that may have been caused due to exposure to noise at work or in leisure activities. (4) Since 2008, as many as 16 percent of teens (ages 12–19) have reported some hearing loss as a result of loud noise, according to a 2010 report based on a survey from the Centers for Disease Control and Prevention (CDC). (5) NIHL can occur because of a one-time exposure to an intense "impulse" sound, such as an explosion, or continuous exposure to loud sounds over an extended period of time.

Words you should have underlined include: (2) *Therefore*; (3) *may have been caused due to*; (4) *as a result*; (5) *because of*. In this paragraph, loud noise is the cause and NIHL is the effect. The paragraph includes extensive evidence to support this idea, such as statistics.

EXERCISE 4

Cause and Effect (Part 1)

Directions: In the following sentences, circle the words that indicate a cause and underline the words that indicate an effect. The first one is done for you.

1. My pet hamster (ate too much;) therefore, he got fat.

2. Louisa graduated in the top 10 percent of her class because she had a 3.9 GPA.

3. As a result of streaming, fewer people go to theaters to see movies.

4. Due to changes in the climate, migratory patterns of birds are changing.

5. Tyree writes great short stories, so it was no surprise when he won the fiction contest.

Answers are on page 769.

Cause and Effect (Part 2)

Directions: Read the following passages and answer the questions that follow.

Using remote sensing data and computer models, scientists can now investigate how the oceans affect the evolution of weather, hurricanes, and climate. Oceans control Earth's weather as they heat and cool, humidify and dry the air, and control wind speed and direction. The weather determines not just what you'll wear to work in the week ahead, but also whether the wheat crop in Nebraska will get enough rain to mature, whether the snow pack in the Sierras will be thick enough to water southern California, whether the hurricane season in the Atlantic will be mellow or brutal, and whether eastern Pacific fisheries will be decimated by El Niño.

Long-term weather patterns influence water supply, food supply, trade shipments, and property values. They can even foster the growth of civilizations, or kill them off. You can't escape the weather, or even change it—but being able to predict its effects makes its impact manageable. Only by understanding the dynamics of the oceans can we begin to do this.

1. According to the first sentence, what cause-and-effect relationship can scientists now study? _____

2. List two ways that the oceans affect Earth, according to the first paragraph.

A. _____

B. _____

3. Fill in the chart with the possible effects of long-term weather patterns:

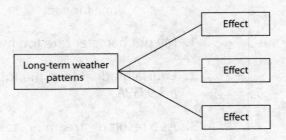

Answers are on page 769.

Problem and Solution

In this organizational pattern, the author poses a problem and then explains a possible solution or solutions, detailing how and why the solution will work. Here is a list of words and phrases that signal a problem and solution pattern: *the problem is, the solution is, the result is, solve this by, if/then.*

In the following paragraph, underline the sentence or sentences that tell you what problem the writer poses and then underline the sentence or sentences that provide the solution.

(1) Marine debris is trash and other solid material that enters ocean and coastal waters. (2) Marine debris threatens wildlife and presents health and safety concerns for humans. (3) Plastics consistently make up a significant percent of all marine debris. (4) There are many sources of marine debris, both on the ocean and on land, including beachgoers, improper disposal of trash on land, stormwater sewers and combined sewer overflow, ships and other vessels, industrial facilities, waste disposal activities, and offshore oil and gas platforms. (5) Proper collection, handling, and recycling or disposal of trash, as well as reduction of consumption and packaging, can help to reduce the marine debris problem. (6) One of the most important ways to address these global challenges is to stop pollutants from entering the marine environment in the first place.

Sentence 2 tells you what the problem is (dangerous marine debris). Sentences 5 and 6 identify a solution to the problem (stopping pollutants from entering marine environments through better trash management).

This next passage is from an emergency preparedness brochure.

Where will your family and friends be when disaster strikes? They could be anywhere—at work, at school, or in the car. How will you find each other? Will you know if your children are safe? What will you do when a disaster strikes to protect yourself and your family?

Develop an Emergency Plan
Know Your Risks

Gather information about hazards. Contact your local emergency management office, American Red Cross chapter, and National Weather Service office. Find out what types of disasters could occur and how best to respond and protect yourself. Learn your community's warning signals and evacuation plans.

Have a Plan

Discuss the information you have gathered and what you need to do to prepare for and respond to different emergencies. Pick two places for family members to meet in case you are separated: a spot outside your home for an emergency, and a location away from your neighborhood in case you cannot return home. Choose an out-of-area emergency contact person as your "family check-in contact" for everyone to call if you get separated. Post emergency telephone numbers by phones and in cell phones.

In this passage, there is a clear set of steps readers can take to ensure that they will not lose touch with family members during a natural disaster. Problem solved.

EXERCISE 5

Problem and Solution

Directions: Read the following passage about helping prevent youth violence. Write the problem the passage discusses on the first set of lines and three solutions the passage proposes to that problem on the lines that follow.

Young people are encouraged to not just wait and watch when violence is about to happen or is occurring around them. When young people see that their friends are getting angry, they can help them calm down and deal with the situation in a nonviolent way. Whenever it is safe to do so, young people can stop an argument from getting violent and let others know that they do not agree with bullying or other forms of violence. Young people should get help from others, like trusted adults, especially when it is not safe to address the problem on their own. It is also important for young people to support others who have been victims of violence so that they do not continue to be victimized or become violent themselves.

Problem:

_____

_____

1. **Solution:**

_____

_____

2. **Solution:**

_____

_____

3. **Solution:**

_____

_____

Answers are on page 770.

Using Different Formats

Sometimes authors choose to use more than words to present their ideas. They may include tables, timelines, or visual elements such as charts and graphs as evidence. These graphic or visual elements are ways to communicate complex information in a format that a reader can grasp quickly. For example, read the following paragraph about an important development in the history of slavery in the United States:

> African Americans had been enslaved in what became the United States since early in the 17th century. Even so, by the time of the adoption of the new Constitution in 1787, slavery was actually a dying institution. As part of the compromises that allowed the Constitution to be written and adopted, the founding fathers agreed to end the importation of slaves into the United States by 1808. By 1800 or so, however, African-American slavery was once again a thriving institution, especially in the southern United States. One of the primary reasons for this was the invention and rapid widespread adoption of the cotton gin. The cotton gin made growing cotton more profitable and thus increased the demand for slaves to work on cotton plantations.

Now read the following timeline of important events in African-American history. Timelines move from earlier to later events to show the passage of time. Look at the earliest and latest dates on a timeline first so you understand its time period.

A Brief African-American History Timeline

1619 First African slaves arrive in Virginia Colony

1787 Slavery is made illegal in Northwest Territory

1808 Congress bans importation of slaves

1820 Missouri Compromise bans slavery north of Missouri's southern border

1861 Confederacy is founded; Civil War begins

1863 President Lincoln issues Emancipation Proclamation freeing many slaves

1868 Fourteenth Amendment is passed, giving citizenship to all persons born in the United States

1870 Fifteenth Amendment is passed, giving adult African-American males the right to vote

Finally, let's look at a bar graph. Bar graphs usually show how something increases or decreases over time. Here is how to read a bar graph:

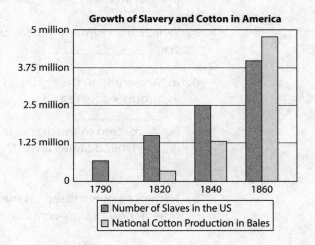

1. A bar graph like this one usually has a title to show you what it is about: *Growth of Slavery and Cotton in America.*

2. Look carefully at the left-hand side of the graph and the bottom of the graph to find out what the graph measures.

   On the left are numbers representing the number of slaves in the United States. On the bottom, you can see four dates moving from 1790 to 1860. The bars show you the number of slaves in the United States in proportion to how much cotton was being produced in 1790, 1820, 1840, and 1860.

3. Find out what the bars represent. Two different colored bars often appear side by side to compare two elements, in this case the number of slaves versus the number of bales of cotton produced.

Each method of communicating information has its advantages and disadvantages:

- The timeline covers a greater span of time and includes a greater number of historical events at once.

- The bar graph shows you a historical trend in a single image.

- The paragraph provides more in-depth information because it explains the situation in greater detail.

EXERCISE 6

Using Different Formats

Directions: Answer the following questions by looking at the paragraph, timeline, or bar graph.

1. When did Congress ban the importation of slaves? _____

2. In what year was the Emancipation Proclamation issued? _____

3. Which amendment gave adult African-American males the right to vote? _____

4. **a.** According to the graph, in what year was the amount of cotton produced lowest? _____ In what year was it highest? _____

   b. According to the graph, in what year was the number of slaves in the United States lowest? _____ In what year was it highest? _____

5. Name one event listed on the timeline that takes place during the same time period as the events discussed in the paragraph. _____

Answers are on page 770.

Workplace Documents

Almost everyone has to write a workplace document at some time to produce a specific result: memos, job application letters, reports, and other documents are common in most workplaces.

When you need to write a workplace document, keep your audience in mind. You will be writing for your coworkers and perhaps your boss or others in your company, not for your friends. So an informal tone, as if you are having a conversation with a friend, is inappropriate. Remember, you are at work, not hanging out at a party in your backyard. If you sound too informal in the workplace, no one will take what you say or write seriously.

Workplace documents should follow these guidelines:

- They should have a clear purpose and stay on message.

- They should include sufficient information.

- They should use formal, rather than informal, language.

- They should use correct grammar and conventions.

Here are two memos written by an employee of a company announcing the relocation of its office. See if you can spot the problems in the first memo:

> **Incorrect:** (1) Hey everyone, how's your day going. (2) OMG, I have got some exciting news 4 u. (3) We are moving to a new office on West Ave. (4) Wait until you guys see the new office, with dope views of downtown. (5) We will go sometime next month, you need to be ready to pack up. (6) And by the way, the office barbeque is coming up to so we need to get redy for that, too.

This memo has several problems. First, the memo fails to provide important instructions about when and how the move will take place, or the address of the new office. Second, the language is too informal for communicating official news with coworkers, starting with the greeting in the first sentence. Texting terminology like "4" as *for* and "u" for *you* is never appropriate in a business setting, nor is slang like "dope." There is a period instead of a question mark in the first sentence, sentence 5 is a run-on, and "redy" is a misspelling of *ready* in the last sentence. Mentioning the barbeque is off-topic.

The following memo, on the other hand, is appropriate, includes all the specifics needed for the move, and stays on topic. It uses a form that is appropriate for business.

Correct:

To: All Office Personnel

From: Jennifer Alvarez

Date: May 11, 20XX

Subject: Upcoming Office Move

I have some exciting news for everyone. We are moving to a new office at 600 West Avenue on Monday, May 21. The office is newly updated and has exciting views of downtown. An IT company will move and install our computers and phones. You need to pack up any files, office supplies, or personal items in boxes by Friday afternoon, May 18. Movers will take them along with our office furniture to the new location. Please let me know if you have any questions.

The second memo

- has a clear purpose and stays on message (announcing and preparing for an office move),

- includes sufficient information (details the schedule for the move and what to pack),

- uses formal, rather than informal, language,

- uses correct grammar and conventions, and

- uses a businesslike memo format, with date, time, etc.

EXERCISE 7

Workplace Documents

Directions: Your company is opening a new branch in Chicago, Illinois. Four people will be chosen to transfer to the new office. People who wish to transfer must apply to the Human Resources Department by Friday, January 15. You must write a paragraph for a memo inviting people to apply for the transfer. Make sure your memo is clear and focused, and that it includes enough information. Make sure to proofread it for any grammatical or spelling errors. Fill in the format below:

To: All Office Personnel

From: Jennifer Alvarez

Date: December 15, 20XX

Subject: Application for Transfer

Answers are on page 770.

Texts Intended to Argue or Persuade

An author's **purpose** is the reason he or she writes a specific work, usually to inform, entertain, or persuade readers. Until now, you have dealt with texts that inform readers using facts, but they do not take positions or express opinions. In this chapter you will learn about argumentative and persuasive texts, in which an author takes a position or expresses an opinion about a topic or issue for a specific audience.

Identifying an Author's Point of View

Point of view is the position an author takes about a topic. Authors often state their point of view directly. Consider this paragraph:

> For the first time in history, we have the tools, technologies, and approaches to end extreme poverty—including widespread hunger and preventable child death—within two decades. But if we're going to tackle this great challenge, we must take stock of what we know, assess what we don't know, and work together to apply new approaches to help us wipe out extreme poverty.

Author's purpose: to bring an end to extreme poverty

Author's point of view: If we work together, we can end extreme poverty within two decades.

Audience: people the author wants to join together to end extreme poverty

However, an author may not state the purpose or point of view directly. Instead, you must use clues from the text, such as words, phrases, and specific details, to infer, or use clues to figure out, the writer's point of view.

Each of these paragraphs starts with the same sentence, but the authors have very different points of view. Look for words, phrases, and specific details that act as clues to each writer's position in the following paragraphs.

Paragraph 1: Austin, Texas, is the fastest growing city in America. The traffic on Austin highways is packed bumper to bumper. Ten years ago, the average commute in Austin was 31 minutes. Today it is 51 minutes, one of the slowest commuting times in the nation. In addition, rents are skyrocketing, as are food and utility costs.

Paragraph 2: Austin, Texas, is the fastest growing city in America. Exciting new businesses from across the country have chosen to relocate there. The unemployment rate is far below the national average. Austin is now home to a new art museum, library, and medical school that will further improve the city's reputation.

Paragraph 1 includes several clues about the author's point of view regarding Austin's role as "the fastest growing city in America." Phrases such as "packed bumper to bumper," "one of the slowest commuting times in the nation," and "rents are skyrocketing" have negative connotations. The statistics the author mentions also show that commute times in Austin have gotten worse. Together, all these details help you infer that the author has a negative point of view about Austin's growth.

In paragraph 2, however, the author includes evidence about Austin that is positive, including Austin's low unemployment rate and a list of new institutions "that will further improve the city's reputation." You can infer, based on these details, that the author's point of view about Austin's growth is favorable.

EXERCISE 1

Identifying an Author's Point of View

Directions: Read the paragraph below. Underline any details that are clues to the author's point of view about the topic of girls' education. Fill in the blanks that follow with a brief statement of the author's purpose and point of view.

Globally, enormous progress has been made in closing the gender gap in primary education over the past 20 years. In most of the world today, a similar percentage of girls and boys attend primary schools. Yet disparities endure—there are 3.6 million more girls out of school compared to boys around the world. Women still comprise the majority (two-thirds) of the illiterate. In Sub-Saharan Africa and South Asia, obtaining an education remains particularly tough for women and girls. The World Bank estimates that half of the out-of-school girls in the world live in Sub-Saharan Africa and one-quarter of them live in South Asia.

Author's purpose: _____

Author's point of view: _____

Answers are on page 770.

Understanding Evidence

Writers often follow this pattern to build an argument:

- **Introduction**: Tell readers what the argument is about and briefly describe his or her point of view.

- **Body:** Use multiple paragraphs, each with a claim and evidence that may build from weakest to strongest evidence or the least dramatic to the most dramatic point.

- **Conclusion:** Restate the main idea.

Within each paragraph, writers often follow this pattern to provide evidence for their point of view:

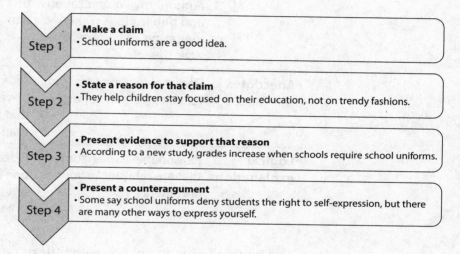

Step 1
- **Make a claim**
- School uniforms are a good idea.

Step 2
- **State a reason for that claim**
- They help children stay focused on their education, not on trendy fashions.

Step 3
- **Present evidence to support that reason**
- According to a new study, grades increase when schools require school uniforms.

Step 4
- **Present a counterargument**
- Some say school uniforms deny students the right to self-expression, but there are many other ways to express yourself.

An author presents a **claim**, or position on a topic, and offers **reasons** to explain it. The author must then include evidence that supports that claim. This evidence helps convince the audience that the author's claims are valid and should be taken seriously. For example, if a writer states that childhood obesity in the United States has become epidemic, the writer must provide supporting evidence to prove that point.

Evidence takes many forms, but you should be able to verify any evidence a writer presents by checking where it comes from to make sure it is trustworthy and accurate.

Here are some examples of valid supporting evidence an author might use to support the claim that childhood obesity has become an epidemic in the United States.

Valid Supporting Evidence		
Facts	Examples and statements that can be proven true	Over the past three decades, childhood obesity rates in America have tripled.
Statistics	Numerical facts and data	In a recent study of 5- to 17-year-olds, almost 60 percent of overweight children had at least one risk factor for cardiovascular disease.
Expert opinions	Quotations or other material from experts or authoritative organizations and publications (*Time* magazine, government agencies, etc.)	The US Surgeon General recently testified before Congress that childhood obesity is at dangerously high levels.
Anecdotes	Personal experiences from reliable, firsthand sources	After he quit swimming regularly, 11-year-old Darius Martin stated that he gained 10 pounds in less than two months.
Logical explanations	Reasonable explanations that are relevant to your argument	Obesity is spreading because only one-third of high school students get the recommended levels of physical activity.

Simply offering an opinion with little or no support is not enough. Arguments must include *sufficient* evidence to support the writer's claims. This evidence needs to be specific and detailed.

Insufficient evidence: There are many reasons children in this country are becoming obese. In fact, this is becoming a national epidemic. It is important to act immediately to stop this situation from becoming worse.

Sufficient evidence: There are many reasons children in this country are becoming obese, including inactivity, growing portion sizes, and choosing junk food over nutritious options. In fact, this is becoming a national epidemic. According to the Centers for Disease Control & Prevention, the rate of childhood obesity has tripled in the last 30 years to 47 percent. It is important to act immediately to stop this situation from becoming worse.

The first example offers no evidence to support its claim that "there are many reasons children in this country are becoming obese" or that it "is becoming a national epidemic." The second example provides specific, verifiable examples and statistics to support the same claims.

EXERCISE 2

Understanding Evidence

Directions: Read this excerpt from a statement by Secretary of State John Kerry celebrating World Oceans Day. Then answer the questions that follow.

1   Life as we know it wouldn't be possible were it not for our oceans. We depend on the ocean for life's essentials: the food we eat and the air that we breathe. It provides jobs for millions of people around the world, and a home for countless unique species.

2   The wonders of the ocean were impressed upon me at an early age in Massachusetts. My father taught me how to fish, and my mother taught me what happens when trash dumped into the ocean ends back up on the shore or kills sea turtles. I learned much more as a senator working for fishing families that saw their way of life threatened when the oceans weren't properly protected.

3   We all have a responsibility to protect our oceans against the threats of overfishing, marine pollution, and ocean acidification. The entire system is interdependent, and we ignore that fact at our peril.

1. Summarize in one sentence the overall claim Secretary Kerry makes in this passage.

     _____

     _____

     _____

2. What is Secretary Kerry's reason for this claim?

     _____

     _____

     _____

3. What type of evidence does Secretary Kerry use to support this claim in paragraph 1?

     _____

     _____

     _____

4. What type of evidence does Secretary Kerry use to support this claim in paragraph 2?

_____

_____

_____

Answers are on page 770.

Identifying Assumptions and Logical Fallacies

Assumptions are ideas that are accepted as true without proof. Sometimes writers attempt to prove a point based on assumptions rather than evidence. Such assumptions provide poor support and weaken an argument because they cannot be verified.

You should watch for these signs that you may dealing with assumptions rather than evidence:

• opinions with insufficient or no support

• examples that are unverifiable

• statements based on stereotypes

• statements that are not relevant to the argument

Which of the following two paragraphs provides stronger support for the writer's point of view?

Paragraph 1

(1) I am against having three new bus routes added to my neighborhood. (2) The buses will bring noise and pollution to our clean, quiet streets. (3) Also, many people prefer to drive their cars because buses are not convenient. (4) A recent study, for example, showed that only 20 percent of people in our town use public transportation. (5) In addition, we cannot afford it—the city budget is already spent for this year.

Paragraph 1	
Evidence	**Appears in which sentence?**
Facts	5
Statistics	4
Expert opinions	none
Anecdotes	none
Reasonable, logical explanations	2, 3

Paragraph 2

(1) I am against having three new bus routes added to my neighborhood. (2) The city council cannot afford to pay for them. (3) In addition, whenever I see buses pass by, they are empty, which clearly proves most people in our town do not use public transit. (4) As we all know, the only people who ride the bus regularly are the unemployed or disabled. (5) People with real jobs drive cars instead.

Paragraph 2	
Evidence	**Appears in which sentence?**
Facts	none
Statistics	none
Expert opinions	none
Reliable anecdote or eyewitness	none
Reasonable, logical explanations	2

The second paragraph is the weaker argument. Sentence 2 does state one legitimate reason why adding the new buses is a bad idea. However, the rest of the paragraph offers little more than a series of assumptions rather than any valid support.

Assumption	**Poor Evidence Because . . .**
Whenever I see buses pass by, they are empty, which clearly proves most people do not use public transit.	The author's random experience seeing empty buses is not enough evidence to prove that this is true for *all* buses. The author incorrectly assumes there is a cause-and-effect relationship.
As we all know, the only people who ride the bus regularly are unemployed or disabled.	The author cannot speak for everyone ("as we all know"). Also, these are not the only people who use public transportation.
People with real jobs drive cars instead.	Not everyone with a "real job" drives a car. Some people own cars and ride the bus.
	You can infer that the author unfairly assumes that people who are unemployed or have disabilities are inferior, thus stereotyping them.

Authors sometimes substitute assumptions and other **logical fallacies** for real support. The word *fallacy* means "a false or mistaken idea." Logical fallacies sound like valid evidence, but they are not the real thing because they are based on unreasonable assumptions. The following table includes a list of common logical fallacies.

Logical Fallacies		
Fallacy	**Definition**	**Example**
Ad hominem	Attacking the person rather than the person's argument	The people who favor new bus routes are pushing their agenda just so they can tell other people what to do.
Ad populum	Appealing to popularity	Most people drive cars, so that is why I do.
Circular logic	Repeating a claim in a slightly different way, rather than supporting it	More people drive cars because fewer people ride the bus.
False dichotomy (either/or)	Claiming there are only two options when there are many	There are two kinds of people, either people drive cars or they take the bus.
Hasty generalization; overgeneralization	Drawing a conclusion based on insufficient evidence; signal words: *all, none, every, always, never*	I never see people riding the bus, which proves that few people use public transportation.
Non sequitur	Drawing conclusions that do not follow from the evidence	If you ride the bus, you must not own a car.
Red herring	Introducing an irrelevant topic to draw attention away from the original issue	The new bus routes are an important issue, but that soccer match yesterday was amazing.
Slippery slope	Declaring that if an action is taken, others will inevitably follow, with an undesired final consequence	If we allow new bus routes on this street, soon we will have to have them on every street.
Stereotyping	Assuming in a negative way that all people who share a characteristic must be the same	People who take the bus are lazy losers who cannot afford a car.
Straw man	Misrepresenting or overstating an opponent's argument so it can be easily attacked	The town council voted to support the new bus routes. Since they obviously do not care about the pollution the buses will cause, they should be voted out of office.

EXERCISE 3

Identifying Logical Fallacies

Directions: Match each of the following sentences to the type of logical fallacy it represents by writing the name of the logical fallacy in the blank.

1. Either you fall into the group that likes books or the group that likes sports.

_____

_____

2. If you vote against building the new playground, you must not care about children and should drop out of this discussion.

_____

_____

3. Women are not as skilled at sports as men; after all, how many women are famous athletes?

_____

_____

4. Most people watch television, so it is silly not to watch.

_____

_____

5. I did not do well in this job interview, so now no one will ever hire me.

_____

_____

6. I agree that discussing the budget is a top priority, but let's talk about the conference we are planning this fall.

_____

_____

7. Cell phone use is on the rise because fewer people use land lines.

_____

_____

Answers are on page 771.

Identifying an Underlying Premise

An **underlying premise** is an unstated idea on which a writer bases an argument. The underlying premise is the underlying belief that makes the writer's argument possible. For example:

> Pretty frequently nowadays, we hear complaints of the selfishness displayed by girls towards their mothers, sons towards their fathers, but in point of fact, they are not one bit more selfish than their parents and grandparents were before them; they were coerced into silence, and, thereby became little sneaks and liars, while the young people of today are aboveboard, and don't pretend to a respect they see no reason to give, if undeserved.

> *from* "Contrast in Generations" by Helen Mathers

In this paragraph, the underlying premise is that it is better for children to express themselves freely and honestly instead of being silent and obedient. The author does not state this directly, but her argument depends on this belief to make its point.

EXERCISE 4

Identifying an Underlying Premise

Directions: Read this paragraph from President Dwight D. Eisenhower's Farewell Address (1961) and answer the question that follows.

> Crises there will continue to be. In meeting them, whether foreign or domestic, great or small, there is a recurring temptation to feel that some spectacular and costly action could become the miraculous solution to all current difficulties. A huge increase in newer elements of our defenses; development of unrealistic programs to cure every ill in agriculture; a dramatic expansion in basic and applied research— these and many other possibilities, each possibly promising in itself, may be suggested as the only way to the road we wish to travel.

1. What is the underlying premise of the paragraph?

    A. A strong military will not solve the nation's problems.
    B. An expensive plan will not solve the nation's problems.
    C. An optimistic attitude will not solve the nation's problems.
    D. A new president will not solve the nation's problems.

Answer is on page 771.

Refuting an Opposing Argument

Writers often refute, or argue against, an opposing point of view. This is also called a **counterargument**. If done properly, this makes their arguments stronger and more convincing.

To refute an opposing point of view, authors must imagine how someone might argue against *their* claims, and consider how to defend them. In addition, they must look for weak spots in an opposing argument, such as unsupported assumptions and logical fallacies.

Read the following argument in which a citizen argues against building a new elementary school:

> Building a new elementary school in our neighborhood this year is impractical. We already tried building a new school in 2010, and we ran out of money. In addition, the old school building is still in good shape, so there is no reason to make this change. We also need money this year for other expenses, like road repairs.

When you refute an opposing argument, the same rules apply as when you make an argument: you must have strong evidence to support your claim that the opposing argument is invalid. Most authors choose one or more of these ways to refute an opposing argument.

Refute an Opposing Argument	Example
Dispute it with specific evidence.	The old school is actually not in good shape: the pipes burst last year, the library has mold, and the classrooms are too small for the growing student population.
Note insufficient evidence.	Our proposal shows the cost of the new school is well within the city's budget. The opposing argument has no current data to back up its claims.
Note outdated or irrelevant evidence.	Referring to the 2010 budget is irrelevant to the current budget.
Respectfully acknowledge a point in the other argument and then offer reasons to dispute it.	It is true that we need road repairs, but our outdated school is a hazard to students and teachers.

EXERCISE 5

Refuting an Opposing Argument

Directions: Read the following paragraph, which argues that advertising is good. Then, come up with two counterarguments that show that advertising is bad.

Many people think advertisements are bad. We all know that advertising may influence us to buy things—but that is what it is supposed to do. Are businesses supposed to stop advertising their products? How will they attract buyers? Eliminating advertisements will hurt the economy.

Counterargument 1:

_____

_____

_____

Counterargument 2:

_____

_____

_____

_____

Answers are on page 771.

Comparing and Contrasting Texts on the Same Topic

Authors have many different opinions, so you may often find essays on the same topic that have different points of view. To understand and evaluate them fairly, carefully compare and contrast the points each author makes. Do not allow your own opinion on the subject to sway you in favor of one essay or the other. Remain neutral and listen to what both authors have to say. Follow this checklist:

1. Identify each author's purpose, point of view, and audience for each passage.

2. Look for valid supporting evidence, including examples and statistics. Compare the type of evidence the authors use. Does one author make a stronger argument than the other based on evidence?

3. Watch out for weak or insufficient evidence, assumptions, and logical fallacies.

4. Check to see if each author shows awareness of counterarguments and attempts to refute them.

EXERCISE 6

Comparing and Contrasting Texts on the Same Topic

Directions: Read the following two essays, which both deal with the use of surveillance cameras. Compare and contrast the authors' points of view. Then answer the questions that follow.

Essay 1: Beware the All-Seeing Eye

1   In a poll conducted after the 2013 Boston Marathon terror attack, 78 percent of respondents approved of surveillance cameras. Our desire for safety is understandable. But we forget that surveillance puts our personal liberties at risk.

2   Cities now have cameras everywhere. They are in and around stores, ATMs, traffic signals, bridges and tunnels, and parks. It is estimated that Chicago alone has between 10,000 and 20,000 publicly and privately owned security cameras. That city claims that the cameras have led to 4,500 arrests between 2006 and 2010.

3   However, such widespread use of cameras invades human privacy and infringes on our rights. History is littered with cases of government surveillance leading to police states where citizens' rights are disregarded.

4   Advocates of increased surveillance say the cameras prevent crime. That claim is debatable. Neil Richards, a professor of law at Washington University, notes in a recent study that although surveillance cameras report crime, they do not *prevent* crime.

5   In fact, Richard notes that any camera connected to the Internet can be hacked. In other words, criminals can use security footage to commit crimes, too. The footage becomes one more tool criminals can use to discover—remotely—what time a potential victim is leaving his home or workplace. So surveillance cameras may actually promote crime.

6   In addition, cameras do not just record criminals' activity, they record *everyone's* activity. It is unclear who controls the surveillance information after it is gathered, or what happens to it. Anyone could own the surveillance footage of you. There are currently no federal laws on the books regulating what happens to that footage.

7   And finally, the hours of video gathered by these cameras are shot without the permission of those being photographed. Great effort goes into protecting the privacy of our medical records and preventing online identity theft. Why, then, is the area of surveillance cameras not equally regulated?

8   Surveillance in the name of safety means trading safety for loss of freedom in the long run. Safeguards are needed—now.

Essay 2: Surveillance Cameras Improve Quality of Life

1. The Boston Marathon bombing in 2013 shook the nation as no disaster had since 9/11. However, the terrorists were located and brought to justice due to the fact that their actions had been caught on video.

2. According to the US Department of Justice, about 75 percent of all crime in the country is property crime. Surveillance cameras on homes or businesses help owners avoid property loss; when people know someone's watching them, they're less likely to do wrong. Indeed, surveillance cameras in stores and businesses are known to decrease theft by customers and employees alike. Business owners can save thousands of dollars in crime-related losses each year by investing in camera installation.

3. Security cameras protect society's most vulnerable members: the very young, the very old, and those who cannot otherwise defend themselves. The kidnapping and subsequent murder of an eight-year-old boy in Brooklyn, New York, in 2011 led to the installation of security cameras in the neighborhood where the crime occurred. In 2014, police used these very cameras to prevent a similar tragedy.

4. A study conducted by the Department of Justice found that increased surveillance in certain areas of Washington, DC, resulted in a decrease of violent crime in those areas. Similar results were observed in Chicago, Illinois, and Baltimore, Maryland. In Chicago, in fact, violent crime in general dropped by about one-fifth.

5. Statistics like these point to real results. Society must use every resource it can to increase public safety, to lower crime rates, and to catch criminals.

1. Fill in the following:
    Essay 1

    Author's purpose: _____

    _____

    Main idea: _____

    _____

    Essay 2

    Author's purpose: _____

    _____

    Main idea: _____

    _____

2. Based on your reading of these passages, list two of the pros and two of the cons of using surveillance cameras. List the evidence the writer includes supporting each pro or con.

Claims (Pro)	Supporting Evidence
1.	1.
2.	2.

Claims (Con)	Supporting Evidence
1.	1.
2.	2.

3. Which of the following statements from the essay against surveillance cameras lacks supporting evidence?

   A. History is littered with cases of government surveillance leading to a police state.
   B. So surveillance cameras may actually promote crime.
   C. Cities now have cameras everywhere.
   D. Cameras do not just record criminals' activity, they record *everyone's* activity.

4. Why are paragraphs four and five in Essay 1 effective as supporting evidence?

   A. They are from an authoritative source.
   B. They present a solid counterargument.
   C. They include verifiable statistics.
   D. They are based on a logical fallacy.

5. Which of these is a flaw in the argument in Essay 2 in favor of surveillance cameras?

   A. The supporting evidence is not specific enough.
   B. The argument is largely based on assumptions.
   C. The writer shows no awareness of counterarguments.
   D. The main idea is based on a hasty generalization.

6. Both arguments open by mentioning the Boston Marathon. How do the arguments differ from each other in their discussion of this event?

   _____

   _____

   _____

Answers are on page 771.

Analyzing Persuasive Texts

The purpose of a persuasive text is to change the audience's minds about an issue and sometimes to inspire them to take action. In a persuasive text, like a speech, writers often use tone and style, along with evidence, to sway the audience by appealing to their emotions. In fact, persuasive writing often builds to an emotional climax for exactly this reason.

The context of a persuasive text is particularly important because it creates a specific relationship between the speaker and the audience. For example, a presidential speech is often an occasion to persuade Americans to see the president and the president's policies in a positive light.

Tone is a writer's attitude toward a subject. A writer's tone may be positive (upbeat, respectful), negative (angry, dismissive), or neutral (objective, impartial).

Style is the distinctive way a writer communicates with an audience, including the writer's choice of words, details, and the use of rhetorical techniques to emphasize specific ideas.

Read this paragraph from President Ronald Reagan's 1981 Inaugural Address and the additional paragraph that follows. Notice how Reagan builds his argument to an emotional climax point by point:

> We have every right to dream heroic dreams. Those who say that we're in a time when there are not heroes, they just don't know where to look. You can see heroes every day going in and out of factory gates. Others, a handful in number, produce enough food to feed all of us and then the world beyond. You meet heroes across a counter, and they're on both sides of that counter. There are entrepreneurs with faith in themselves and faith in an idea who create new jobs, new wealth and opportunity. . . .

> Now, I have used the words "they" and "their" in speaking of these heroes. I could say "you" and "your," because I'm addressing the heroes of whom I speak—you, the citizens of this blessed land. Your dreams, your hopes, your goals are going to be the dreams, the hopes, and the goals of this administration. . . .

Author's purpose: to persuade the audience that Reagan's administration sees them as heroes and has the same goals that they do

Author's point of view: Heroism is not dead because even ordinary Americans (including the audience) are heroes in their daily lives.

Audience: the American public

Tone: upbeat, inspirational

First, President Reagan declares, "Those who say that we're in a time when there are not heroes, they just don't know where to look." Reagan then describes how American workers and entrepreneurs are heroic. Finally, Reagan tells the audience that they are all heroes, too, and his administration will value their hopes and dreams.

The second paragraph highlights Reagan's style through his word choice and direct address of the audience. Reagan asks the audience how his speech would be different if he substituted the words *you* and *your* for *they* and *their* while speaking of these heroes. "I could say 'you' and 'your,' because I'm addressing the heroes of whom I speak—you, the citizens of this blessed land." Through his choice of words, Reagan appeals to the audience's emotions by addressing them personally and telling them they, too, are heroes. This makes it more likely that they will side with his point of view.

Rhetorical techniques are ways writers use language to present their point of view, convey their purpose, and create meaning. In argumentation and persuasion, these techniques are very important because they are the tools authors use to change opinions.

Rhetorical techniques help a writer persuade an audience by making powerful, memorable statements that draw in the audience by emphasizing specific ideas. These are some of the most common rhetorical techniques:

Rhetorical Techniques		
Technique	**Definition**	**Example**
Analogy	Establishes a relationship between two things or ideas based on similarities	"As the plant springs from, and could not be without, the seed, so every act of a man springs from the hidden seeds of thought, and could not have appeared without them."
Enumeration	Dividing a subject into parts or a list of details	"It's imperative that **the best, the brightest and the most creative** should share **their talents, their secrets, their successes—their failures. . . .**"
Juxtaposition of opposites	Placing two or more opposing ideas, places, people, or actions side by side to emphasize one or the other	"We observe today **not a victory of party, but a celebration of freedom— symbolizing an end, as well as a beginning. . . .**"
Parallelism	Using similar grammatical forms or structures to balance related ideas	"The extension of civil rights today means, not **protection of the people against the Government, but protection of the people by the Government.**"
Qualifying statements	Adding information to show conditions under which a claim could be true	**"The arts are not just for those who go on to become professional artists.** Research shows that girls and boys, young men and women who have art classes are more likely to be engaged in their classes. . . ."
Repetition	Repeating the same words, phrases, or sentences	**". . . government of the people, by the people, for the people. . . ."**

EXERCISE 7

Analyzing Persuasive Texts (Part 1)

Directions: Match each sentence to its rhetorical device. Write the letter in
the blank.

1. _____ Men, women, children, young and old, rich and poor, all
deserve fair treatment under the law.

2. _____ We meet at a college noted for knowledge, in a city noted for
progress, in a state noted for strength.

3. _____ The exploration of space will go ahead, whether we join in it
or not.

4. _____ I know not what course others may take; but as for me, give me
liberty or give me death!

5. _____ Yes, we can, to opportunity and prosperity. Yes, we can heal
this nation. Yes, we can repair this world. Yes, we can.

A. Qualifying statement
B. Juxtaposition
C. Repetition
D. Parallelism
E. Enumeration

Analyzing Persuasive Texts (Part 2)

Directions: Read this excerpt from a speech by President Harry Truman
to the NAACP. As you read, think about Truman's choice of
words, including rhetorical devices, and how he builds his
argument about the need to further extend civil rights in the
United States. Then answer the questions that follow.

1   (1) It is my deep conviction that we have reached a turning point in the
long history of our country's efforts to guarantee a freedom and equality to
all our citizens. (2) Recent events in the United States and abroad have made
us realize that it is more important today than ever before to insure that all
Americans enjoy these rights.

2   (3) And when I say all Americans—I mean all Americans.

3   (4) The civil rights laws written in the early years of our republic, and the
traditions, which have been built upon them, are precious to us. (5) Those laws
were drawn up with the memory still fresh in men's minds of the tyranny of
an absentee government. (6) They were written to protect the citizen against
any possible tyrannical act by the new government in this country.

4   (7) But we cannot be content with a civil liberties program, which emphasizes only the need of protection against the possibility of tyranny by the Government.

5   (8) We cannot stop there.

6   (9) We must keep moving forward, with new concepts of civil rights to safeguard our heritage. (10) The extension of civil rights today means, not protection of the people against the Government, but protection of the people by the Government.

7   (11) We must make the Federal Government a friendly, vigilant defender of the rights and equalities of all Americans. (12) And again I mean all Americans.

1. Which sentence best expresses the main idea in this passage?

    A. We must make the Federal Government a friendly, vigilant defender of the rights and equalities of all Americans.
    B. The civil rights laws written in the early years of our republic, and the traditions, which have been built upon them, are precious to us.
    C. It is my deep conviction that we have reached a turning point in the long history of our country's efforts to guarantee a freedom and equality to all our citizens.
    D. But we cannot be content with a civil liberties program, which emphasizes only the need of protection against the possibility of tyranny by the Government.

2. In paragraph 3, Truman says that the first civil rights laws written "in the early years of our republic" served what purpose?

    A. To establish basic civil rights of freedom and equality
    B. To prevent absentee government
    C. To protect citizens from one another
    D. To protect citizens from unjust government actions

3. On the lines below, list two rhetorical devices that Truman includes in this passage. Include the sentence numbers in which these devices appear.

    _____

    _____

4. What happens over the course of paragraphs 3–6?

    A. Truman offers a counterargument to his opponents.
    B. Truman builds his case for further extending civil rights.
    C. Truman asks other nations to join America in a fight for civil rights.
    D. Truman makes a qualifying statement about civil rights.

Answers are on page 771.

## CHAPTER 10

Understanding Fiction

Fiction is literature in the form of stories about imaginary people, places, and events. In order to understand fiction, you need to pay attention to the elements that go into making a story, including plot, characterization, setting, point of view, tone, and theme.

Building Blocks of Fiction

Plot, character, and setting are the most basic building blocks of fiction. Read this excerpt from Mark Twain's *The Prince and the Pauper*. As you read, picture the scene in your mind based on the details the author gives you about the people, places, and events in the passage.

> In the ancient city of London . . . a boy was born to a poor family of the name of Canty, who did not want him. On the same day another English child was born to a rich family of the name of Tudor, who did want him. All England wanted him too. England had so longed for him, and hoped for him, and prayed God for him, that, now that he was really come, the people went nearly mad for joy. Mere acquaintances hugged and kissed each other and cried. Everybody took a holiday, and high and low, rich and poor, feasted and danced and sang, and got very mellow; and they kept this up for days and nights together. By day, London was a sight to see, with gay banners waving from every balcony and housetop, and splendid pageants marching along. By night, it was again a sight to see, with its great bonfires at every corner, and its troops of revellers making merry around them. There was no talk in all England but of the new baby, Edward Tudor, Prince of Wales, who lay . . . in silks and satins, unconscious of all this fuss, and not knowing that great lords and ladies were tending him and watching over him—and not caring, either. But there was no talk about the other baby, Tom Canty, . . . in his poor rags, except among the family of paupers whom he had just come to trouble with his presence.

Plot is the events in a story and the order in which they take place. Plot usually includes conflicts, or challenges characters must face. In this passage, the birth of two babies, one rich and one poor, one wanted, the other unwanted, forms the basis of the plot. What will happen to Tom, born into poverty? What about Edward? Will he have a happy life? The plot will tell.

Characterization is what we learn about characters through the author's description of them. There are two important characters in this passage, Tom Canty and Edward Tudor, and we learn a lot about them in a short period of time, including their family backgrounds, social status, and how others feel about them.

Tom Canty	Edward Tudor
Born to a poor family	Born to a wealthy family
Dressed in rags	Dressed in silk and satin
Unwanted by anyone	Wanted by his family and all of England
No one talks about him but his family	Everyone talks about him

We also learn about the **setting** of the story, England, which is where the story takes place. The story also includes a smaller setting within the larger one: the celebration in the streets of Edward's birth.

Plot

Plot is the sequence of events that build upon each other to form a story. The author may not always spell out the plot for you. You may sometimes need to infer the steps in a plot in order to understand what happens by paying attention to clues in the text.

A plot usually works this way:

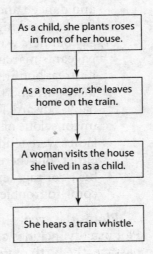

As a child, she plants roses in front of her house.

As a teenager, she leaves home on the train.

A woman visits the house she lived in as a child.

She hears a train whistle.

Steps in a Plot	Examples
Beginning: Main characters and setting are introduced.	A girl lives in a small town with her parents. She wants to go to school to become an artist.
Conflict: There is a problem the characters in a story try to overcome. It may come from circumstances outside the character (war, family conflict) or within the character (self-doubt or other personal struggles).	The girl's parents do not approve of her career choice because it is impractical, and they forbid her from painting or doing other artwork.
Climax: This is the story's most dramatic moment. The problem or conflict reaches the breaking point and is resolved in some way. Often characters undergo a change.	The girl secretly enters a drawing in an art contest without her parents' knowledge. When she wins first place, they realize she is talented and change their minds about her.
Conclusion: This is how the story ends.	The girl reconciles with her parents. She goes to art school.

Plots may take place in chronological order, with the events following each other as they would in real time, such as the birth of Tom and Edward in *The Prince and the Pauper*. Sometimes writers include flashbacks, in which a character remembers something that happened at an earlier point in his or her life. If you put the events of a story in order, remember to place flashbacks where they belong, earlier in the story. For example, suppose a story describes events in this order:

• A woman visits the house she lived in as a child.

• She bends to smell a rose in her old yard.

• Flashback: as a child she planted these roses in front of the house.

• She hears a train whistle.

• Flashback: As a teenager, she leaves home on the train.

What is the chronological order in which these events took place? The first event would be "as a child, she plants roses in front of the house" because it is the earliest event that takes place in real time. The second event would be "as a teenager, she leaves home on the train."

EXERCISE 1

Plot

Directions: Read the story and then answer the questions that follow.

King Midas loved the land he ruled. He loved his subjects, and he loved his only daughter, Marigold. But he spent most of his time in his treasure room, because there he found what he loved most.

This room was filled with gold from floor to ceiling. He spent hours stacking and counting his gold coins. But in the end, he was always dissatisfied. No matter how much gold he had, he always wanted more.

One day, an old man had been traveling a long way. He was so hot and exhausted, he fell asleep in the palace gardens without realizing he was trespassing.

King Midas's servants angrily woke him and took him to King Midas for punishment. To their surprise, King Midas was kind to the old man, invited him to dinner, and let him rest in the palace for the night.

Soon after, Midas was visited by the god Dionysius. The old man was Dionysius's favorite servant, and the god wanted to reward Midas for his kind treatment of him. "Midas, I grant you one wish! Name it, and it is yours."

Midas knew immediately what he wanted. "I want everything I touch to turn to gold!" he exclaimed. And Dionysius granted his wish.

Midas ran around his palace touching chairs, tables, the curtains, the walls, the floor. They all turned to precious gold.

The king's daughter ran in to see her father, as she did every morning. As always, her father was delighted to see her. Without thinking, Midas reached down and embraced Marigold. He stood back and cried out in horror.

It was too late. His touch had turned his beloved daughter into a heavy statue of pure gold.

King Midas broke down and wept. He realized that it was his daughter he had loved more than anything in the world.

1. Which statement BEST states the theme of this story?

   A. Power corrupts everyone.
   B. Destiny is beyond our control.
   C. Greed leads to tragedy.
   D. Love is a dangerous thing.

2. What is the conflict in this story?

   A. The king is greedy.
   B. The king neglects his daughter.
   C. The king is a poor leader.
   D. The king wants to go to war.

3. What happens at the story's climax?

   A. The king is kind to the old man.
   B. The king visits his treasure house.
   C. The king turns his daughter to gold.
   D. The king's wish is granted by Dionysius.

4. What happens at the story's conclusion?

   A. The king realizes he loved his daughter more than gold.
   B. The king realizes he has been tricked by Dionysius.
   C. The king realizes that his people no longer love him.
   D. The king realizes he can never have enough treasure.

Answers are on page 772.

Characterization

Characterization includes all the details that tell you who a character is, including descriptions of a character's physical appearance, thoughts and feelings, words, and actions. Other characters' responses to that character may also reveal important information about him or her.

Read this passage, and see what you can infer about Miss Minchin, the head of a girl's school, when she meets Sara, her latest pupil, and Sara's father, Captain Crewe:

> It was just then that Miss Minchin entered the room. She was very like her house, Sara felt: tall and dull, and respectable and ugly. She had large, cold, fishy eyes, and a large, cold, fishy smile. It spread itself into a very large smile when she saw Sara and Captain Crewe. She had heard a great many desirable things of the young soldier from the lady who had recommended her school to him. Among other things, she had heard that he was a rich father who was willing to spend a great deal of money on his little daughter.

Details	Evidence
Physical appearance	"like her house . . . tall and dull, respectable and ugly"; "large, cold, fishy eyes, and a large, cold, fishy smile"
Thoughts and feelings	You can infer that she is fond of making money.
Words	none
Actions	smiles at Sara and her father because he is wealthy and wants to spend money on his daughter
Other people's reactions	Sara dislikes her.

In a single paragraph, we have learned that Miss Minchin is greedy and sees Sara and her father not as human beings but as a business opportunity. We have also learned that Sara is a smart little girl who can spot an untrustworthy adult quickly.

Characterization also helps us predict what may happen to characters in the story. We can predict that Sara and Miss Minchin will not get along on the basis of their characterizations.

EXERCISE 2

Characterization

Directions: Read the following passage and answer the questions below. Look for clues that describe Randolph Trent's situation and emotions.

Randolph Trent stepped from the Stockton boat on the San Francisco wharf, penniless, friendless, and unknown. Hunger might have been added to his trials, for, having paid his last coin in passage money, he had been a day and a half without food. Yet he knew it only by an occasional lapse into weakness as much mental as physical. Nevertheless, he was first on the gangplank to land, and hurried feverishly ashore, in that vague desire for action and change of scene. . . . Yet after mixing for a few moments with the departing passengers, each selfishly hurrying to . . . rest or business, he insensibly drew apart from them, with the instinct of a vagabond[1] and outcast. Although he was conscious that he was neither, but merely an unsuccessful miner suddenly reduced to the point of soliciting work or alms[2] of any kind, he took advantage of the first crossing to plunge into a side street, with a vague sense of hiding his shame.

---

[1]*vagabond:* a person who wanders from place to place.

[2]*alms:* food or money donated to the poor.

1. Match the characterizations of Randolph Trent to the phrases from the text. Write the letter of the phrases in the blank.

   Hungry _____

   Alone _____

   Poor _____

   Unemployed _____

   a. "unsuccessful miner suddenly reduced to the point of soliciting work"

   b. "penniless"; "paid his last coin in passage money"

   c. "friendless and unknown"; "vagabond and outcast"

   d. "day and a half without food"

2. Why does Randolph Trent cross at the nearest street to get away from the other people on the wharf?

   A. He is going to look for a place to eat.
   B. He is ashamed that he has no money.
   C. He is looking for a place to stay.
   D. He is irritated by the people around him.

3. Based on Randolph Trent's situation in this passage, what do you predict will happen next?

   A. He will return to the ship and sail away from San Francisco.
   B. He will run into an acquaintance, who will take him home and feed him.
   C. He will collapse from hunger and exhaustion.
   D. He will have to beg for work or food.

Answers are on page 772.

Setting and Tone

The **setting** is the time and place where a story happens. For example, the setting of *The Prince and the Pauper* is in London several centuries ago. But a story's setting may take place anywhere, real or imagined. It could be present-day New York City, ancient Egypt, an imaginary planet in the future, a kitchen, a palace, or a zoo. What is important to know is that setting often provides valuable clues about the theme, plot, and characters because it sets the story's mood and tone.

Tone is the writer's attitude toward a subject, which you can infer from the words the writer uses to describe it. This can range from joyful to amused to serious to outraged.

Mood is the feeling the writer wants to inspire in the reader. Consider this description of a house:

> The house sat alone on the edge of a cliff. The gardens that once bloomed around it had become twisted with weeds, and mice ran

through its empty rooms. As the wind howled around the house, it sounded as it was a crying child who would not be comforted. No one had lived there for years, or so we thought.

The author's tone is dark and sinister, and the physical details of this setting build upon each other to create a scary, suspenseful mood for the reader: the house is perched alone on a cliff, the gardens are overgrown, the rooms are overtaken by mice, and the wind howls sadly. The last line suggests that someone or something might still be living there, which makes the house even more disturbing.

EXERCISE 3

Setting and Tone

Directions: Read the two passages below and answer the questions that follow. The first passage describes a countryside in summer. The second passage describes a foggy landscape.

Passage 1

He said the pleasantest manner of spending a hot July day was lying from morning till evening on a bank of heath[1] in the middle of the moors, with the bees humming dreamily about among the bloom, and the larks singing high up overhead, and the blue sky and bright sun shining steadily and cloudlessly. That was his most perfect idea of heaven's happiness.

from *Wuthering Heights* by Emily Brontë

Passage 2

There was a steaming mist in all the hollows, and it had roamed in its forlornness up the hill, like an evil spirit, seeking rest and finding none. A clammy and intensely cold mist, it made its slow way through the air in ripples that visibly followed and overspread one another, as the waves of an unwholesome sea might do.

excerpt from *A Tale of Two Cities* by Charles Dickens

1. **Which word BEST describes the mood of passage 1?**
   A. Lazy
   B. Peaceful
   C. Suspenseful
   D. Hopeful

---

[1]*heath:* an open field of wild, uncultivated land

2. List three words or phrases that establish the mood of passage 1.

_____

_____

_____

3. Which word BEST describes the mood of passage 2?

A. Exciting
B. Complex
C. Eerie
D. Tragic

4. List three words or phrases that establish the mood of passage 2.

_____

_____

_____

Answers are on page 772.

Author's Point of View

Point of view is the perspective an author chooses to tell the story. Most authors choose to tell the story in the **first person**, the **third person limited**, or the **third-person all-knowing**.

Point of View	How You Can Tell	Examples
First person	Told from the point of view of the main character and uses pronoun *I*. Main character speaks directly to reader.	My heart was beating so hard, I thought everyone could hear it as I stepped onstage to dance at last.
Third-person limited	Narrator tells the story from the main character's point of view, using the pronouns *he* or *she*.	Alice thought she knew the way, but then she realized that the houses looked unfamiliar. She was lost, but she knew she would make it home somehow.
Third-person omniscient (all-knowing)	Writer moves from one person's point of view to another's, or writes from outside any character's point of view.	Jackson said nothing, but he felt sad that Isabelle was leaving. Isabelle did not know how to tell Jackson that she loved him. Each was a mystery to the other.

EXERCISE 4

Author's Point of View

Directions: Read each of the following passages and identify the point of view from which it is told by writing *first person*, *third-person limited*, or *third-person omniscient* on the blank.

1. Mrs. Rafferty opened the door. Standing on her freshly painted front porch was a rumpled, ragged looking, very thin young man. He was holding a rope attached to the scrawny neck of a dirty, old dog.

   _____

2. I heard a bark outside, and I opened the door to see where it came from. There was a young man, dirty and starved looking, standing on my porch. He held a rope with a dirty, old dog attached to it. The young man looked terrified. I had never seen such desperation.

   _____

3. The dog hesitated before following her master onto the porch, as if she knew that something dramatic was about to happen. The woman was startled, but she tried to remain calm. The young man was so nervous as he looked at her, he could barely speak.

   _____

Answers are on page 772.

Theme

You learned about unstated main ideas in an earlier chapter. A theme is similar to an unstated main idea. A **theme** is the work's underlying message, what the author wants to express to you about life or some part of human nature. Here are some examples of themes:

- Good always triumphs over evil.

- Nature can be a harsh teacher.

- Together we can do more than we can do alone.

- Love conquers all.

To identify themes, you must do what you do to find unstated main ideas. You must use context clues and draw conclusions based on the language and details of the writing. Plot, characterization, and setting all contribute to the theme.

Read this passage, keeping character, plot, setting, and tone in mind.

Wing Biddlebaum, forever frightened and beset by a ghostly band of doubts, did not think of himself as in any way a part of the life of the town where he had lived for twenty years. Among all the people of Winesburg but one had come close to him. With George Willard . . . he had formed something like a friendship. George Willard was the reporter on the *Winesburg Eagle* and sometimes in the evenings he walked out along the highway to Wing Biddlebaum's house. Now as the old man walked up and down on the veranda, his hands moving nervously about, he was hoping that George Willard would come and spend the evening with him. . . . He went across the field through the tall mustard weeds and climbing a rail fence peered anxiously along the road to the town. For a moment he stood . . . , rubbing his hands together and looking up and down the road, and then, fear overcoming him, ran back to walk again upon the porch on his own house.

from *Winesburg, Ohio* by Sherwood Anderson

First, break the passage into smaller parts. Keep your answers brief and to the point. Look for specific evidence from the text to help support your interpretation.

Plot

What happens in this passage?

Wing goes to see if George is coming down the road to visit him, but he does not see him and goes back to his house.

What conflict does this character face?

Wing does not get along with the other townspeople. Wing is nervous that George might not show up: he rubs his hands together and paces back and forth.

Does Wing change in any way?

No.

Character

Who is this passage mainly about?

Wing Biddlebaum and his only friend, George Willard

How would you describe Wing?

Isolated, lonely, vulnerable, and nervous

Based on what evidence?

Wing's body language, the author's comments about George as his only friend, and the negative reaction of the townspeople to Wing

Setting

Wing's house near the highway, an overgrown field, and the highway that George is supposed to walk down

Tone

What is the author's attitude toward Wing?

Sympathetic—the author shows how vulnerable Wing is, but he does not make fun of him.

What message about human nature does this passage convey? Look at the answers to your questions. What is the common thread? Nearly all of the answers suggest isolation and the need for friendship. The theme of the passage might be that friendship can be a powerful force against loneliness.

EXERCISE 5

Theme

Directions: Read the passage below and then answer the questions that follow. The passage is about a man who is lost in the wilderness and has run out of food.

In the late afternoon he came upon scattered bones where the wolves had made a kill. The debris had been a caribou[1] calf an hour before, squawking and running and very much alive. He contemplated the bones, clean-picked and polished, pink with the cell-life in them which had not yet died. Could it possibly be that he might be that [before] the day was done! Such was life, eh? A vain and fleeting thing. It was only life that pained. There was no hurt in death. To die was to sleep. It meant cessation, rest. Then why was he not content to die?

But he did not moralize long. He was squatting in the moss, a bone in his mouth, sucking at the shreds of life that still dyed it faintly pink. The sweet meaty taste, thin and elusive almost as a memory, maddened him. He closed his jaws on the bones and crunched.

from *The Call of the Wild* by Jack London

1. What word BEST describes the tone of this scene?

    A. Exciting
    B. Sympathetic
    C. Grim
    D. Sarcastic

---

[1]*caribou:* a North American reindeer

2. What is the conflict in this passage?

   A. Man versus man
   B. Man versus nature
   C. Man versus society
   D. Man versus himself

3. Which of these words BEST describes the character of the man in the passage?

   A. Frightened
   B. Thoughtful
   C. Optimistic
   D. Gleeful

4. Based on the first paragraph, what does the man think about life?

   A. We realize too late that life goes quickly.
   B. Life is painful and death brings peace.
   C. People fail to respect life in the wild.
   D. The purpose of life is to survive at all costs.

5. What is a theme of this passage?

   A. Nature defeats humans every time.
   B. There is peace to be found in death.
   C. Humans are superior to animals.
   D. The survival instinct is powerful.

Answers are on page 772.

Mathematical Reasoning

The Mathematical Reasoning Test

The Mathematical Reasoning section of the GED® test measures your ability to use reasoning and mathematics knowledge to make calculations and solve problems. About half of the test focuses on quantitative problem solving, and about half focuses on basic algebraic problem solving. There are some geometry questions as well. There is a short section on which a calculator is not allowed, but for the bulk of the test, a calculator is allowed. The calculator is available on the computer screen.

Some of the test questions simply ask you to make calculations. Others describe real-life situations that you must decide how to solve using mathematics. Many questions are based on graphs or diagrams.

The Mathematical Reasoning Review

The following section of this book will introduce you to the basic skills and topics that are tested on the Mathematical Reasoning test. The chapters cover all of the mathematics topics that appear on the test, and there are practice exercises in every topic area.

This Mathematical Reasoning review section is organized as follows:

Mathematical Reasoning

Answers for all of the exercises in these chapters are located in the Exercise Answer Keys section at the back of this book.

## CHAPTER 1

Whole Numbers

Understanding Whole Numbers

Whole numbers are all the numbers including 0 and all the counting numbers 1, 2, 3, 4, 5, . . . , 999, . . . , and so on. There is no largest whole number.

Place Value

The value of a digit is determined by its place or position in a number. Each digit in a number has its own place value. The number 2,095 is a four-digit number. In this number, each digit has its own place value.

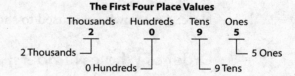

The First Four Place Values

Thousands   Hundreds   Tens   Ones
    2   **0**   **9**   **5**

2 Thousands — | | — 5 Ones
0 Hundreds —   — 9 Tens

Remember: Zero (0) is used as a **placeholder** to show that there are no ones, tens, or hundreds.

Thus, 2,095 = 2,000 + 0 + 90 + 5. You can rewrite the number as: (2 × 1,000) + (0 × 100) + (9 × 10) + (5 × 1). This is the **expanded form** of 2,095. To write the expanded form of a number, write each digit in the number times a one followed by a number of zeroes equal to the number of places to the right of the digit in the number.

Larger Numbers

In larger numbers, commas separate digits into groups of three from the ones place. Notice the pattern of groups in the number given below.

Larger Numbers

Millions			Thousands			Ones		
3	4	5,	8	0	5,	7	1	9
100s	10s	1s	100s	10s	1s	100s	10s	1s

For example, the number 2,367,014,589 is a ten-digit number. The value of each digit is given in the figure below.

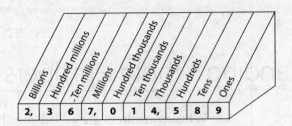

Number LINE

A number line is a line on which numbers are written in order from the least to the greatest. To construct a number line, pick a point on the line and label it as 0. Mark equally spaced units to the right as shown in the figure below and then name each marked point with successive whole numbers.

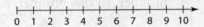

Note: An arrowhead is used to show that the number line continues.

Order of Whole Numbers

Whole numbers can be ordered or compared based on their position on the number line. Use greater than (>) or less than (<) signs to compare two numbers.

- > means "lies to the right of" on the number line.
- < means "lies to the left of" on the number line.

EXAMPLE 1

Using a number line, compare the numbers 2,758 and 2,426.

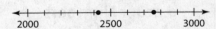

2,756 lies to the right of 2,426 on the number line. Therefore, 2,758 > 2,426.

EXAMPLE 2

Using a number line, order the numbers 1,890, 3,330, and 2,700 from least to greatest.

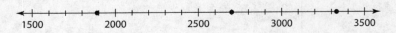

1,890 lies to the left of 2,700 and 2,700 lies to the left of 3,330. Therefore, 1,890 < 2,700 < 3,330.

Place Value (Part A)

Directions: Choose the correct answer.

1. What is the place value of 8 in 2,834?

    A. Ones
    B. Hundreds
    C. Thousands
    D. Ten thousands

2. Which of the following numbers has 9 in the thousands place?

    A. 9,009
    B. 8,991
    C. 10,192
    D. 91,124

3. Which of the following numbers has 0 as a placeholder in the tens place?

    A. 90
    B. 810
    C. 1,023
    D. 1,509

4. Which of the following numbers has 1 in the tens place and 8 in the hundreds place?

    A. 21,018
    B. 12,801
    C. 10,812
    D. 21,108

5. Which of the following numbers has 0 hundreds?

    A. 1,008
    B. 1,800
    C. 10,800
    D. 10,810

Place Value (Part B)

Directions: Fill in each blank with the correct answer.

6. 8,097 has _____ thousands, _____ hundreds, _____ tens, and _____ ones.

7. 17,926 has _____ ten thousands, _____ thousands, _____ hundreds, _____ tens, and _____ ones.

8. The place value of 9 in 1,009 is _____.

9. The place value of 8 in 81,021 is _____.

10. The place value of 0 in 10,965 is _____.

11. The place value of 5 in 350,008 is _____.

12. The place value of 1 in 1,089,726 is _____.

13. The place value of 2 in 1,092 is _____ and the place value of 0 in 1,092 is _____.

14. The place value of 5 in 5,672 is _____ and in 6,753 is _____.

15. The place value of 0 in 6,093 is _____ and in 6,930 is _____.

Place Value (Part C)

Directions: Write the value of each underlined digit.

16. **a.** 8<u>7</u>9 _____ **b.** 10,<u>4</u>52 _____

17. **a.** 1,<u>2</u>11 _____ **b.** <u>1</u>,923 _____

18. **a.** 2,00<u>1</u> _____ **b.** 90<u>1</u> _____

19. <u>3</u>,356,789 _____

20. 1<u>3</u>8,900,001 _____

Answers are on page 773.

Reading and Writing Whole Numbers

To read or write a whole number, think about each group of digits separately: millions group, thousands group, and ones group. There are rules for reading and writing a whole number:

- Read or write the digits in each group as a one-, two-, or three-digit number followed by the group name, except for the ones group.

- When writing a number, place a hyphen in compound words, for example, thirty-two and ninety-six.

- The word *and* is not used when a whole number is written or read in words.

- The commas in the word statements should be placed in the same places as the commas in the number.

EXAMPLES

Ones Group

72   seventy-two

429   four hundred twenty-nine

Thousands Group and Ones Group

6,147   six thousand, one hundred forty-seven

26,400   twenty-six thousand, four hundred

135,356   one hundred thirty-five thousand, three hundred fifty-six

Millions Group, Thousands Group, and Ones Group

1,697,009   one million, six hundred ninety-seven thousand, nine

137,850,000 one hundred thirty-seven million, eight hundred fifty thousand

---

EXERCISE 2

Reading and Writing Whole Numbers (Part A)

Directions: Choose the correct answer.

1. A number has these digits: 5 thousands, 4 hundreds, 7 tens, 2 ones. Which of the following represents the number?

    A. 2,745
    B. 5,247
    C. 5,472
    D. 7,542

2. A number has these digits: 6 millions, 4 hundred thousands, 1 ten thousands, 8 thousands, 6 hundreds, 2 tens, 4 ones. Which of the following represents the number?

    A. 624,418
    B. 418,624
    C. 6,418,426
    D. 6,418,624

3. Which of the following correctly represents the number 12,277 in words?

    A. twelve hundred, two thousand seventy
    B. twelve thousand, two hundred seventy
    C. twelve hundred, two thousand seventy-seven
    D. twelve thousand, two hundred seventy-seven

4. Which of the following correctly represents the number: one hundred thirty thousand, eight hundred fifty-nine?

    A. 13,859

    B. 85,913

    C. 130,859

    D. 859,130

5. The diameter of Earth is seven thousand, nine hundred twenty-six miles. Which of the following correctly represents the number in digits?

    A. 926 miles

    B. 9,267 miles

    C. 7,926 miles

    D. 79,260 miles

Reading and Writing Whole Numbers (Part B)

Directions: Write a number in the blank that has these digits.

6. 6 thousands, 4 hundreds, 2 tens, 3 ones _____

7. 2 ten thousands, 5 thousands, 3 hundreds, 8 tens, 2 ones _____

8. 7 hundred thousands, 5 thousands, 2 hundreds, 9 ones _____

9. 6 millions, 2 hundred thousands, 6 hundreds, 9 tens, 2 ones _____

10. 30 millions, 1 hundred thousands, 3 hundreds, 1 ones _____

Reading and Writing Whole Numbers (Part C)

Directions: Write each number in the blank using digits.

11. four million, seven hundred thousand _____

12. four hundred fifty thousand _____

13. three hundred twenty-six million, fifty thousand, one hundred twenty-five _____

14. twenty-one thousand, eight hundred twelve _____

15. three million, four hundred ninety-one thousand, nine hundred thirty _____

16. three hundred fifty thousand, three hundred eighty-three _____

Reading and Writing Whole Numbers (Part D)

Directions: Write the word name of each number.

17. 200,304 _____

18. 350,359 _____

19. 23,822 _____

20. 8,934 _____

Answers are on page 773.

Operations with Whole Numbers

Whole numbers can be added, subtracted, multiplied, or divided.

Adding Whole Numbers

To **add** is to find the total or sum of two or more numbers.

- The operation of addition is indicated by the **plus** symbol (+).

- Numbers being added are called **addends**. For example, when you write 2 + 3 = 5, 2 and 3 are the addends.

- The answer to an addition problem is called the **sum**. In the previous example, 5 is the sum.

Some Properties of Addition

Understanding the following properties of addition can help you solve problems.

- **The commutative property of addition:** The order of two numbers around an addition symbol does not affect the final sum. In symbols, $a + b = b + a$, for any two numbers a and b.

    EXAMPLES

    $$8 + 7 = 7 + 8 = 15 \qquad\qquad 9 + 3 = 3 + 9 = 12$$

- **The associative property of addition:** The ways in which several whole numbers are grouped do not affect the final sum when they are added. In symbols, $(a + b) + c = a + (b + c)$, for any three numbers a, b, and c.

    EXAMPLES

    $$7 + (6 + 5) = (7 + 6) + 5 = 18 \qquad\qquad (8 + 5) + 2 = 8 + (5 + 2) = 15$$

- **The additive identity property:** The sum of 0 and any whole number is just the whole number. In symbols, $a + 0 = a$, for any number a.

EXAMPLES

$$5 + 0 = 5 \qquad\qquad 7 + 0 = 7$$

Adding Single Digits

Statements such as $2 + 6 = 8$ and $4 + 7 = 11$ are called **basic addition facts**. These addition facts, shown in the following table, are the basis of all additions.

Basic Addition Facts										
+	**0**	**1**	**2**	**3**	**4**	**5**	**6**	**7**	**8**	**9**
0	0	1	2	3	4	5	6	7	8	9
1	1	2	3	4	5	6	7	8	9	10
2	2	3	4	5	6	7	8	9	10	11
3	3	4	5	6	7	8	9	10	11	12
4	4	5	6	7	8	9	10	11	12	13
5	5	6	7	8	9	10	11	12	13	14
6	6	7	8	9	10	11	12	13	14	15
7	7	8	9	10	11	12	13	14	15	16
8	8	9	10	11	12	13	14	15	16	17
9	9	10	11	12	13	14	15	16	17	18

Adding Numbers with Two or More Digits

To add multi-digit numbers, align the numbers vertically so that digits with the same place value are in the same column. Numbers are then added one column at a time. Move from right to left, starting in the ones column. Continue until you have added every column.

EXAMPLE 1

$$
\begin{array}{r} 3471 \\ + 1304 \\ \hline 5 \end{array}
\qquad
\begin{array}{r} 3471 \\ + 1304 \\ \hline 75 \end{array}
\qquad
\begin{array}{r} 3471 \\ + 1304 \\ \hline 775 \end{array}
\qquad
\begin{array}{r} 3471 \\ + 1304 \\ \hline 4775 \end{array}
$$

Add ones   Add tens   Add hundreds   Add thousands

Adding two-digit numbers often involves regrouping (also called carrying). To regroup means to take the tens digit from the sum of one column and place it at the top of the next column to the left.

EXAMPLE 2

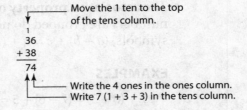

Move the 1 ten to the top of the tens column.

$$
\begin{array}{r} \overset{1}{} \\ 36 \\ + 38 \\ \hline 74 \end{array}
$$

Write the 4 ones in the ones column.
Write 7 (1 + 3 + 3) in the tens column.

STEP 1: Add the ones: 6 + 8 = 14.
Write the ones digit, 4; in the ones place, and carry the tens digit, 1, to the next column.

STEP 2: Add the tens: 1 + 3 + 3 = 7.

ANSWER: 74

When the sum of the digits in the tens columns is greater than 10, write down the ones digit and move the 1 to the top of the hundreds column.

EXAMPLE 3

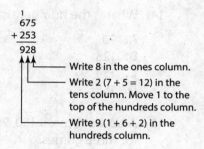

STEP 1: Add the ones: 5 + 3 = 8.

STEP 2: Add the tens: 7 + 5 = 12.
Write the 2; carry the 1.

STEP 3: Add the hundreds: 1 + 6 + 2 = 9.

ANSWER: 928

EXERCISE 3

Adding Whole Numbers (Part A)

Directions: Add (no regrouping is required).

1. 81	**2.** 29	**3.** 32	**4.** 826	**5.** 205	**6.** 2,792
+27	+70	+67	+23	+183	+105

Adding Whole Numbers (Part B)

Directions: Add (regrouping is required).

7. 71	**8.** 191	**9.** 384	**10.** 711	**11.** 9,909	**12.** 8,099
+29	+ 47	+ 277	+ 999	+2,701	+2,890

Adding Whole Numbers (Part C)

Directions: Choose the correct answer.

13. A class contains 21 boys and 16 girls. How many students are in the class?

 A. 9
 B. 27
 C. 37
 D. 82

14. What is the number that is 34 more than 124?

 A. 90
 B. 128
 C. 154
 D. 158

15. A bowler scored 150, 200, and 215 in three games. What is his total score for three games?

 A. 365
 B. 415
 C. 560
 D. 565

Answers are on page 773.

Subtracting Whole Numbers

To **subtract** is to find the difference between two numbers.

- The operation of subtraction is indicated by the **minus** symbol (–).

- The number being subtracted is called the **minuend.**

- The number being subtracted from is called the **subtrahend**. For example, when you write $7 - 4 = 3$, 4 is the minuend and 7 is the subtrahend.

- The **difference** is the answer to the subtraction problem. In the previous example, 3 is the difference.

- Addition and subtraction are often thought of as opposites of each other. For every addition fact, there is a related subtraction fact. If $3 + 6 = 9$, then $9 - 6 = 3$.

EXAMPLE 1

To subtract multi-digit numbers, align the numbers vertically so that digits with the same place value are in the same column. Numbers are then subtracted one column at a time. Move right to left, starting in the ones column. Continue until you have subtracted every column.

$$\begin{array}{r} 7893 \\ -\,6412 \\ \hline 1 \end{array} \qquad \begin{array}{r} 7893 \\ -\,6412 \\ \hline 81 \end{array} \qquad \begin{array}{r} 7893 \\ -\,6412 \\ \hline 481 \end{array} \qquad \begin{array}{r} 7893 \\ -\,6412 \\ \hline 1481 \end{array}$$

Subtract ones   Subtract tens   Subtract hundreds   Subtract thousands

Subtracting two-digit or larger numbers often involves regrouping (also called borrowing). To regroup in subtraction means to take a 1 from one column and move it to the top of the next column to the right.

EXAMPLE 2

When the ones digit of the minuend is larger than the ones digit in the subtrahend, regroup by moving 1 ten from the tens column to the ones column.

STEP 1: Regroup the 6 tens, moving 1 ten to the ones column. Cross out the 6 and write a 5 above it.

$$\begin{array}{r} \overset{\overset{10}{5}}{\cancel{6}2} \\ -\,37 \end{array} \quad \begin{array}{l} \text{Replace 6 with 5.} \\ \text{Move 1 ten.} \end{array}$$

STEP 2: Add 10 to the 2 in the ones column. Think of this as putting 12 ones in the ones column.

$$\begin{array}{r} \overset{5\ 12}{\cancel{6}2} \\ -\,37 \end{array} \quad \begin{array}{l} \text{Add the moved 10 to the} \\ \text{ones column to give a} \\ \text{total of 12 ones.} \end{array}$$

STEP 3: Subtract the ones column: $12 - 7 = 5$.
Subtract the tens column: $5 - 3 = 2$.

$$\begin{array}{r} \overset{5\ 12}{\cancel{6}2} \\ -\,37 \\ \hline 25 \end{array} \quad \begin{array}{l} \text{You can now subtract} \\ \text{each column.} \end{array}$$

ANSWER: 25

Subtracting from Zero

You cannot subtract from 0, so you must regroup. The example that follows shows how to regroup the hundreds column when there is a 0 in the tens column.

EXAMPLE 1

Subtract: $\begin{array}{r} 702 \\ -\,317 \end{array}$

Solution: $\begin{array}{r} \overset{6\ \overset{9}{10}\ 12}{\cancel{7}\cancel{0}\cancel{2}} \\ -\,3\ 1\ 7 \\ \hline 3\ 8\ 5 \end{array}$

STEP 1: You cannot subtract 7 from 2, so you must borrow. You cannot borrow a 1 from the 0 in the tens column, so you must borrow from the 7 as follows:

Cross out the 7 in the hundreds column and write a 6 above it.

Write the borrowed 1 hundred as 10 tens, and place the 10 above the 0 in the tens column.

$$\begin{array}{r} \overset{6}{\cancel{7}}\overset{10}{\cancel{0}}2 \\ -3\ 1\ 7 \\ \hline \end{array}$$

STEP 2: Now borrow from the tens column.
Cross out the 10 and write 9 above it.
Write the borrowed 1 ten above the ones column.
This puts 12 ones in the ones column.

$$\begin{array}{r} \overset{6}{\cancel{7}}\overset{\overset{9}{10}}{\cancel{0}}\overset{12}{\cancel{2}} \\ -3\ 1\ 7 \\ \hline \end{array}$$

STEP 3: Subtract each column.
Ones column: $12 - 7 = 5$
Tens column: $9 - 1 = 8$
Hundreds column: $6 - 3 = 3$

$$\begin{array}{r} \overset{6}{\cancel{7}}\overset{\overset{9}{10}}{\cancel{0}}\overset{12}{\cancel{2}} \\ -3\ 1\ 7 \\ \hline 3\ 8\ 5 \end{array}$$

ANSWER: 385

EXERCISE 4

Subtracting Whole Numbers (Part A)

Directions: Subtract (no regrouping is required).

1. $\begin{array}{r}84\\-23\\\hline\end{array}$	**2.** $\begin{array}{r}75\\-31\\\hline\end{array}$	**3.** $\begin{array}{r}48\\-13\\\hline\end{array}$	**4.** $\begin{array}{r}509\\-401\\\hline\end{array}$	**5.** $\begin{array}{r}781\\-430\\\hline\end{array}$	**6.** $\begin{array}{r}629\\-511\\\hline\end{array}$

Subtracting Whole Numbers (Part B)

Directions: Subtract (regrouping is required).

7. 84 -27	**8.** 75 $-\ 6$	**9.** 48 -19	**10.** 41 -39	**11.** 71 -49
12. 58 $-\ 9$	**13.** 284 $-\ 93$	**14.** 375 $-\ 91$	**15.** 448 $-\ 53$	**16.** 9,591 $-\ 641$
17. 1,372 $-\ 531$	**18.** 3,562 $-\ 940$	**19.** 654 -375	**20.** 736 -559	**21.** 481 -392
22. 509 -318	**23.** 510 -419	**24.** 600 -519	**25.** 8,400 $-7,319$	**26.** 7,000 $-1,999$

Subtracting Whole Numbers (Part C)

Directions: Choose the correct answer.

27. What is the difference between 87 and 33?

    A. 54
    B. 57
    C. 84
    D. 120

28. Jim scored 98 on a math test. Jane's score was 13 less than Jim's. What was Jane's score?

    A. 67
    B. 85
    C. 88
    D. 95

29. The difference between two numbers is 132. If the larger number is 355, what is the smaller number?

    A. 124
    B. 223
    C. 225
    D. 353

30. The sum of two numbers is 650. If one of the numbers is 230, what is the other number?

A. 230
B. 400
C. 420
D. 618

Answers are on page 774.

Multiplying Whole Numbers

Multiplication is the mathematical operation that indicates how many times a number is added to itself. It is shorthand for repeated addition of a number to itself.

- The operation of multiplication is indicated by the **times** symbol ($\times$). For example, when you write 2×5, it means 2 is multiplied by 5. It is also read as "2 times 5." Sometimes multiplication is indicated by a raised dot, as in $2 \cdot 5$.

- In terms of repeated addition, 2×5 means $2 + 2 + 2 + 2 + 2$ or $5 + 5$.

- Numbers being multiplied are called **factors**. In $2 \times 5 = 10$, 2 and 5 are factors.

- The result of a multiplication problem is called the **product**. In the previous example, 10 is the product.

Some Properties of Multiplication

Understanding the following properties of multiplication can help you solve problems.

The commutative property of multiplication: For any two numbers, if you multiply the numbers together in either order, you will get the same result. In symbols, $a \times b = b \times a$, for any two numbers a and b.

EXAMPLES

$$2 \times 7 = 7 \times 2 = 14 \qquad\qquad 3 \times 6 = 6 \times 3 = 18$$

The associative property of multiplication: The ways in which the numbers are grouped in multiplication do not affect the final product. In symbols, $(a \times b) \times c = a \times (b \times c)$, for any three numbers a, b, and c.

EXAMPLE

$$(2 \times 4) \times 9 = 2 \times (4 \times 9) = 72$$

The distributive property of multiplication over addition: When a factor is multiplied by a sum, then multiply the factor by each addend in the sum. Then add the products. In symbols, $a \times (b + c) = (a \times b) + (a \times c)$, for any three numbers a, b, and c.

EXAMPLE

$3 \times (4 + 5) = (3 \times 4) + (3 \times 5) = 12 + 15 = 27$

This property, used extensively in algebra, shows an important relationship between addition and multiplication.

The identity property of multiplication: The product of 1 and any number is just that number. In symbols, $a \times 1 = a$, for any number a.

EXAMPLES

$2 \times 1 = 2$ $1 \times 7 = 7$ $9 \times 1 = 9$

The multiplicative property of zero: The product of 0 and any number is 0. In symbols, $a \times 0 = 0$, for any number a.

EXAMPLES

$14 \times 0 = 0$ $5 \times 0 = 0$ $20 \times 0 = 20$

Multiplying Single Digits

Statements such as $2 \times 6 = 12$ and $3 \times 7 = 21$ are called **basic multiplication facts**. These multiplication facts, shown in the following table, are the basis of all multiplication.

Basic Multiplication Facts Table

×	0	1	2	3	4	5	6	7	8	9
0	0	0	0	0	0	0	0	0	0	0
1	0	1	2	3	4	5	6	7	8	9
2	0	2	4	6	8	10	12	14	16	18
3	0	3	6	9	12	15	18	21	24	27
4	0	4	8	12	16	20	24	28	32	36
5	0	5	10	15	20	25	30	35	40	45
6	0	6	12	18	24	30	36	42	48	54
7	0	7	14	21	28	35	42	49	56	63
8	0	8	16	24	32	40	48	56	64	72
9	0	9	18	27	36	45	54	63	72	81

EXAMPLE 1

To find the product of 7×6:

Find the "7" row.

Find the "6" column.

The square at the intersection of the row and the column gives the product (answer).

ANSWER: 42

EXAMPLE 2

To find the product of 4 × 9:

Find the "4" row.

Find the "9" column.

The square at the intersection of the row and the column gives the product (answer)

ANSWER: 36

Multiplying by One-Digit Numbers

A number with two or more digits is multiplied by one digit at a time. Starting with the ones digit, move from right to left and continue until you have multiplied every digit.

- Write the product of the ones digits in the ones column.
- Write the product of the tens digits in the tens column.
- Write the product of the hundreds digits in the hundreds column.

EXAMPLE 1

$$
\begin{array}{r}
132 \\
\times\ 2 \\
\end{array}
$$

Multiply the ones: 2 × 2 = 4.

Multiply the tens: 2 × 3 = 6.

Multiply the hundreds: 2 × 1 = 2.

ANSWER: 264

EXAMPLE 2

$$
\begin{array}{r}
402 \\
\times\ 4 \\
\end{array}
$$

Multiply the ones: 4 × 2 = 8.

Multiply the tens: 4 × 0 = 0.

Multiply the hundreds: 4 × 4 = 16.

ANSWER: 1,608

Multiplying by Two-Digit Numbers

To multiply by a two-digit number, multiply each digit of the first factor by each digit of the second. To do this, a series of steps are formed. The answer to each step of multiplication is called a partial product. Add these partial products to get the final product.

EXAMPLE 1

Multiply: 32
            × 12

Solution: 32
            × 12
Partial products { 64
                  32   ← Treat this blank space as a 0
                 ———
                  384
                   ↑ Tens column

STEP 1: Multiply 32 by 2, the ones digit: $32 \times 2 = 64$.
Write 64, with 4 in the ones column and 6 in the tens column.

STEP 2: Multiply 32 by 10, the tens digit: $32 \times 10 = 320$.
Write 32, with the 2 in the tens column and the 3 in the hundreds column. The 0 in the ones column is left unwritten.

STEP 3: Add the partial products.

ANSWER: 384

Multiplying and Regrouping

When the product of two digits is 10 or more, then regrouping is required. Write the ones digit of the product of the digits in the appropriate location, and carry the tens digit to the next column to the left (shown in the examples that follow).

EXAMPLE 1

Multiply: 59
            × 5

Solution: $\overset{4}{59}$
            × 5
            ———
            295

STEP 1: Multiply the ones digit: $9 \times 5 = 45$.
Place the ones digit (5) in the ones column.

STEP 2: Move the tens digit (4) to the top of the tens column.

STEP 3: Multiply the tens digit: $5 \times 5 = 25$.
Add the regrouped 4 to 25: $25 + 4 = 29$.
Write 29 in the tens and hundreds columns.

Note: Always multiply digits before adding the carried digit.

EXAMPLE 2

Multiply: 609
            × 3

Solution: $\overset{2}{609}$
            × 3
            ————
            1,827

When multiplying the tens digit, first multiply 3×0. Then add the carried 2 to the product $(2 + 0)$.

EXAMPLE 3

This example shows how a regrouped digit from the product of the tens digit is moved to the hundreds column.

Multiply: 541   Solution: $\overset{2}{5}41$
             × 5   ×   5
                                        ─────
                                        2,705

STEP 1: Multiply the ones digits: $5 \times 1 = 5$.
Write 5 in the ones column.

STEP 2: Multiply the tens digits: $5 \times 4 = 20$.
Write 0 in the tens column.
Carry 2 to the top of the hundreds column.

STEP 3: Multiply the hundreds digits: $5 \times 5 = 25$.
Add 2 to 25: $2 + 25 = 27$.
Write 27, placing the 7 in the hundreds column.

ANSWER: 2,705

Multiplying by 10, 100, and 1,000

The rules to follow when multiplying by 10, 100, or 1,000 are as follow:

Rule 1: To multiply a number by 10, place one 0 to the right of the ones place of the number.

EXAMPLES

     10   89   356
    × 8   × 10   × 10
    ────   ────   ─────
     80   890   3,560

Rule 2: To multiply a number by 100, place two 0s to the right of the ones place of the number.

EXAMPLES

    100   459   4,891
   × 9   × 100   ×   100
   ────   ─────   ───────
    900   45,900   489,100

Rule 3: To multiply a number by 1,000, place three 0s to the right of the ones place of the number.

EXAMPLES

   1,000   159   5,755
  ×   5   × 1,000   × 1,000
  ──────   ───────   ───────
   5,000   159,000   5,755,000

Note: When a whole number is multiplied by a 1 followed by zeroes, the product is just that number followed by as many zeroes as there are following the 1.

EXERCISE 5

Multiplying Whole Numbers

Directions: Multiply.

1. $\begin{array}{r} 8 \\ \times 9 \\ \hline \end{array}$	**2.** $\begin{array}{r} 6 \\ \times 4 \\ \hline \end{array}$	**3.** $\begin{array}{r} 4 \\ \times 9 \\ \hline \end{array}$	**4.** $\begin{array}{r} 8 \\ \times 7 \\ \hline \end{array}$	**5.** $\begin{array}{r} 5 \\ \times 7 \\ \hline \end{array}$	**6.** $\begin{array}{r} 14 \\ \times 2 \\ \hline \end{array}$
7. $\begin{array}{r} 23 \\ \times 3 \\ \hline \end{array}$	**8.** $\begin{array}{r} 41 \\ \times 9 \\ \hline \end{array}$	**9.** $\begin{array}{r} 27 \\ \times 3 \\ \hline \end{array}$	**10.** $\begin{array}{r} 81 \\ \times 9 \\ \hline \end{array}$	**11.** $\begin{array}{r} 82 \\ \times 9 \\ \hline \end{array}$	**12.** $\begin{array}{r} 18 \\ \times 2 \\ \hline \end{array}$
13. $\begin{array}{r} 56 \\ \times 5 \\ \hline \end{array}$	**14.** $\begin{array}{r} 72 \\ \times 9 \\ \hline \end{array}$	**15.** $\begin{array}{r} 89 \\ \times 9 \\ \hline \end{array}$	**16.** $\begin{array}{r} 221 \\ \times 9 \\ \hline \end{array}$	**17.** $\begin{array}{r} 192 \\ \times 91 \\ \hline \end{array}$	**18.** $\begin{array}{r} 203 \\ \times 29 \\ \hline \end{array}$
19. $\begin{array}{r} 503 \\ \times 8 \\ \hline \end{array}$	**20.** $\begin{array}{r} 888 \\ \times 91 \\ \hline \end{array}$	**21.** $\begin{array}{r} 1,000 \\ \times 99 \\ \hline \end{array}$	**22.** $\begin{array}{r} 1,892 \\ \times 100 \\ \hline \end{array}$	**23.** $\begin{array}{r} 824 \\ \times 900 \\ \hline \end{array}$	**24.** $\begin{array}{r} 1,914 \\ \times 213 \\ \hline \end{array}$

Answers are on page 774.

Dividing Whole Numbers

Division asks *how many times* one number is contained in another number. Just as multiplication is repeated addition, division is repeated subtraction.

* The operation of division is indicated by the division symbol ($\div$), by a division bracket ($\overline{)}$), or as a fraction (see Chapter 2).

* The number being divided into is called the **dividend**. For example, in $26 \div 2 = 13$, 26 is the dividend.

* The number being divided by is called the **divisor**. In the previous example, 2 is the divisor.

* The answer to a division problem is called the **quotient**. In the previous example, 13 is the quotient.

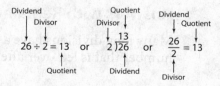

* Multiplication and division are often thought of as opposites of each other. For every multiplication fact, there is a related division fact. If $2 \times 13 = 26$, then $26 \div 2 = 13$.

The process known as *long division* consists of three steps repeated until the end of the process is reached.

- First, a division that is (hopefully) smaller than the entire division problem at hand is performed to generate a single digit in the quotient.
- Then that single digit just generated in the quotient is multiplied by the divisor.
- Finally, this product is subtracted from the dividend and a digit is brought down to form a new dividend.

These steps (division, multiplication, and subtraction) are repeated until the division process is exhausted. Keep an eye out for these steps in the examples that follow.

EXAMPLE 1

$$
\begin{array}{r}
46 \\
3\overline{)138} \\
\underline{12} \\
18 \\
\underline{18} \\
0
\end{array}
$$

STEP 1: Look at the first digit, 1. You cannot divide 3 into 1, and so you look at the first two digits, 13. There are 4 threes in 13, and so you write 4 above the 3 in the dividend as the first digit in the quotient.

STEP 2: Multiply $3 \times 4 = 12$. Place 12 below 13.

STEP 3: Subtract. Because the difference, 1, is smaller than the divisor, 3, you bring down the ones digit of the dividend, 8.

STEP 4: Divide 18 by 3 to get 6. The next digit in the quotient is 6.

STEP 5: Multiply $3 \times 6 = 18$. Place 18 below the 18 obtained by bringing down the 8 at the end of step 3.

STEP 6: Subtract. You have a 0 remainder. So, $138 \div 3 = 46$.

ANSWER: 46

Answers with Remainders

Many long divisions have a remainder as part of the result. A remainder is a number that is left over after division.

EXAMPLE 1

$$3\overline{)17} \quad \begin{array}{r} 5 \\ \hline 17 \\ 15 \\ \hline 2 \end{array}$$

Here, 17 is not evenly divided by 3. It contains 5 three times, but 2 is left over. This leftover is called the remainder in division. You write: $17 \div 3 = 5r2$.

The way to check the result of division when there is a remainder is:

Dividend = Divisor × Quotient + Remainder

For the above example, $17 \div 3 = 5r2$, so $3 \times 5 + 2 = 17$ to check.

More examples of quotients with remainders follow.

EXAMPLE 2

$$\begin{array}{r} 59 \\ 4\overline{)239} \\ 20 \\ \hline 39 \\ 36 \\ \hline 3 \end{array}$$

ANSWER: 59r3

EXAMPLE 3

$$\begin{array}{r} 1197 \\ 2\overline{)2395} \\ 2 \\ \hline 03 \\ 2 \\ \hline 19 \\ 18 \\ \hline 15 \\ 14 \\ \hline 1 \end{array}$$

ANSWER: 1,197r1

Division and Zero

There are two important rules regarding division and zero.

- Zero divided by any whole number (except 0) is 0; for example, $0 \div 6 = 0$.

- Division by 0 is undefined; for example, $6 \div 0$ is undefined.
  From the multiplication facts, you know that 0 times any number can never be 6. So, there is no answer to this problem and thus, you say that $6 \div 0$ is undefined. The same is true of any number other than 6.

EXERCISE 6

Dividing Whole Numbers (Part A)

Directions: Divide.

1. $54 \div 6$ 2. $142 \div 2$ 3. $0 \div 9$ 4. $8 \div 0$ 5. $63 \div 3$

6. $4\overline{)232}$ 7. $7\overline{)346}$ 8. $14\overline{)4,328}$ 9. $2\overline{)1,246}$

10. $5\overline{)43,287}$ 11. $5\overline{)400}$ 12. $10\overline{)9,900}$

Dividing Whole Numbers (Part B)

Directions: Choose the correct answer.

13. There are 63 candy bars in 9 boxes. How many candy bars are there in each box?

    A. 7
    B. 9
    C. 54
    D. 72

14. How many times is 5 contained in 20?

    A. 2
    B. 3
    C. 4
    D. 5

15. In a room there are 48 chairs. Andrew arranged chairs in rows, each row containing 8 chairs. How many rows will it take to set up all 48 chairs?

    A. 6
    B. 8
    C. 10
    D. 12

Answers are on page 774.

Order of Operations

To perform calculations with more than one arithmetic operation, there are some rules for order of operations.

- First perform all the operations inside any grouping symbols such as parentheses.

- Then compute exponents (discussed in a later chapter).

- Next, perform multiplications and divisions as they occur from left to right.

- Finally, perform all additions and subtractions as they occur from left to right.

The common technique to remember this order of operations is "PEMDAS," which stands for "Parentheses, Exponents, Multiplication and Division, Addition, and Subtraction." Notice that multiplications and divisions are performed simultaneously as they appear in the expression when moving from left to right, as are additions and subtractions.

EXAMPLE 1

$120 \div (12 + 3 \times 6) - 3$

STEP 1: $120 \div (12 + 3 \times 6) - 3 = 120 \div (12 + 18) - 3$ (*multiplication inside the parentheses*)

STEP 2: $120 \div (12 + 18) - 3 \quad = 120 \div 30 - 3$ (*addition inside the parentheses*)

STEP 3: $120 \div 30 - 3 \quad\quad\quad = 4 - 3$ (*division*)

STEP 4: $4 - 3 \quad\quad\quad\quad\quad = 1$ (*subtraction*)

ANSWER: 1

Rounding Whole Numbers

Rounding whole numbers is often useful to estimate. To *estimate* means to use or substitute a number that is almost equal to an exact number. To round a number, express it to the nearest hundred, thousand, and so on.

EXAMPLE 1

Round the number 847.

To the nearest ten, 847 rounds to 850.

To the nearest hundred, 847 rounds to 800.

To the nearest thousand, 847 rounds to 1,000.

Steps for rounding whole numbers are:

1. Identify the place of the digit to be rounded.

2. Look at the digit to the right of that place:

• If the digit to the right is 5 or more, that digit and all the digits to the right become 0.

• The digit in the place you are rounding to is increased by 1.

• If the digit to the right is less than 5, that digit and all digits to the right become 0. The digit in the place you are rounding to remains the same.

EXAMPLE 2

Round 5,287 to the nearest hundred.

The hundreds digit is 2. The digit to the right is 8. Since the digit to the right is more than 5, the hundreds digit is increased by 1. The 8 and all the digits to the right of 8 become 0. 5,287 is rounded to 5,300.

EXAMPLE 3

Round 12,493 to the nearest ten.

The tens digit is 9. The digit to the right is 3. Since the digit to the right is less than 5, the tens digit remains the same. The 3 becomes 0. 12,493 is rounded to 12,490.

EXAMPLE 4

Round 13,560 to the nearest thousand.

The thousands digit is 3. The digit to the right is 5. Since the digit to the right is 5, the thousands digit is increased by 1. The 5 and all the digits to the right of 5 become 0. 13,560 is rounded to 14,000.

EXERCISE 7

Rounding Whole Numbers

Directions: Round each number.

1. 59 to the nearest ten _____

2. 1,968 to the nearest thousand _____

3. 831,000 to the nearest ten thousand _____

4. 3,493 to the nearest ten _____

5. 798 to the nearest hundred _____

6. 8,820,000 to the nearest million _____

7. 70 to the nearest hundred _____

8. 841 to the nearest thousand _____

9. 699,779 to the nearest thousand _____

10. 967,982 to the nearest ten thousand _____

Answers are on page 774.

Estimating with Whole Numbers

Sometimes you may want to estimate—to find an approximate answer. For example, when you go to the store, you try to estimate the total price of items by rounding the price of each item. An estimate is a number or amount that is about equal to the exact number.

Estimation can be done for several reasons:

- To give an approximate answer when an exact number is not needed
- To check the accuracy of math when doing an exact calculation
- To help choose among answer choices on a multiple-choice test
- To check a calculator answer

EXAMPLE 1

What is the approximate sum of 983, 478, and 315?

STEP 1: Round each number to the nearest hundred.

$983 \approx 1,000$ $478 \approx 500$ $315 \approx 300$

STEP 2: Add the rounded numbers.

$$
\begin{array}{r}
1,000 \\
500 \\
+\ 300 \\
\hline
1,800
\end{array}
$$

ANSWER: 1,800. The exact sum is 1,776.

EXAMPLE 2

Jane went shopping at a grocery store. She bought items that cost $4.99, $5.88, $1.04, $7.98, and $1.95. What is the approximate total cost of these items?

STEP 1: Round each cost to the nearest whole dollar.

$\$4.99 \approx \$5$ $\$5.88 \approx \$6$ $\$1.04 \approx \$1$ $\$7.98 \approx \$8$ $\$1.95 \approx \$2$

STEP 2: Add the rounded numbers.

$5 + 6 + 1 + 8 + 2 = 22$

ANSWER: $22. The approximate total cost of the items is $22.

EXAMPLE 3

What is the approximate product of 510 and 299?

STEP 1: Round each number to the nearest hundred.

$510 \approx 500 \qquad 299 \approx 300$

STEP 2: Multiply the rounded numbers.

$$\begin{array}{r} 500 \\ \times \quad 300 \\ \hline 150{,}000 \end{array}$$

ANSWER: 150,000. The approximate product is 150,000.

EXERCISE 8

Estimating with Whole Numbers (Part A)

Directions: Estimate an answer by rounding to the indicated place.

Round to the nearest ten.

1.	2.	3.	4.
48	78	89	169
37	21	− 27	× 29
+23	39		
	+ 31		

Round to the nearest hundred.

5.	6.	7.	8.
891	2,679	3,979	5,999
378	197	× 923	− 999
+129	+ 823		

Round to the nearest thousand.

9.	10.	11.	12.
2,138	3,679	8,679	7,999
3,997	4,197	− 3,137	− 3,937
+7,129	+2,823		

Estimating with Whole Numbers (Part B)

Directions: Choose the correct answer.

13. The price of a floor tile is $1.98. What is the approximate total cost of 212 tiles?

    A. $100
    B. $200
    C. $300
    D. $400

14. Jane scored 79, 92, 87, 97, and 61 on her arithmetic tests. What is her approximate total score?

    A. 390
    B. 420
    C. 430
    D. 500

15. Nathan purchased several items from a stationery shop. The items he purchased cost $3.99, $2.12, $6.97, and $4.02. What is the approximate total cost of these items?

    A. $15
    B. $17
    C. $19
    D. $24

16. A whole number rounded to the nearest 10 is 70. What is the smallest possible number?

    A. 62
    B. 65
    C. 74
    D. 75

17. A whole number rounded to the nearest hundred is 5,400. What is the largest possible number?

    A. 5,350
    B. 5,390
    C. 5,449
    D. 5,459

Answers are on page 774.

Whole Numbers Review (Part A)

Directions: Fill in each blank with the correct digit.

1. 3,809 has _____ thousands, _____ hundreds, _____ tens, and _____ ones.

2. 6,798 has _____ thousands, _____ hundreds, _____ tens, and _____ ones.

Whole Numbers Review (Part B)

Directions: Write the value of each underlined digit in the blank.

3. 8<u>9</u>7 _____

4. <u>1</u>25,000 _____

5. 7<u>8</u>,491 _____

6. 3,<u>4</u>67,002 _____

7. <u>8</u>1,980,000 _____

Directions: Write a number that has these digits.

8. 4 thousands, 9 hundreds, 0 tens, 8 ones _____

9. 5 millions, 5 thousands, 5 hundreds, 7 tens, 5 ones _____

Directions: Write each number in standard form.

10. Two hundred fifty thousand, three hundred fifty-one _____

11. Twenty-one thousand, eight hundred thirteen _____

12. Four million, two hundred twenty thousand _____

Directions: Write each number in words.

13. 22,482 _____

14. 200,403 _____

15. 1,532,000 _____

Whole Numbers Review (Part C)

Directions: Add.

16.	24 $+\ 9$	**17.**	35 $+19$	**18.**	274 $+\ 91$	**19.**	565 $+234$

20.	2,894 $+\ 109$	**21.**	7,890 $+\ 6,500$	**22.**	2,900 $+\ 4,590$	**23.**	91,000 $+\ 2,009$

Whole Numbers Review (Part D)

Directions: Subtract.

24.	74 -14	**25.**	94 -73	**26.**	909 $-\ 91$	**27.**	500 -234

28.	2,894 $-\ 789$	**29.**	7,890 $-\ 4,500$	**30.**	9,900 $-\ 4,990$

Whole Numbers Review (Part E)

Directions: Multiply.

31.	9 $\times\ 4$	**32.**	22 $\times\ 4$	**33.**	32 $\times 23$	**34.**	302 $\times\ 25$

35.	455 $\times 200$	**36.**	352 $\times\ 23$	**37.**	300 $\times 500$	**38.**	355 $\times\ 29$

Whole Numbers Review (Part F)

Directions: Divide.

39.	$5\overline{)75}$	**40.**	$9\overline{)72}$	**41.**	$9\overline{)909}$	**42.**	$11\overline{)72}$

43.	$5\overline{)735}$	**44.**	$10\overline{)720}$	**45.**	$11\overline{)444}$	**46.**	$5\overline{)600}$

Whole Numbers Review (Part G)

Directions: Solve the problems by using the proper order of operations.

47. $9 - 5 \div (8 - 3) \times 2 + 6$ _____

48. $(14 - 5) \div (9 - 6)$ _____

49. $5 \times 8 + 6 \div 6 - 12 \times 2$ _____

50. $5 + 6 \times (4 - 3)$ _____

Whole Numbers Review (Part H)

Directions: Round each number to the indicated place.

51. 28, to the nearest ten _____

52. 61 to the nearest ten _____

53. 679 to the nearest ten _____

54. 192 to the nearest hundred _____

55. 324 to the nearest hundred _____

56. 4,235 to the nearest thousand _____

57. 8,812 to the nearest thousand _____

58. 831,000 to the nearest ten thousand _____

59. 18,321,000 to the nearest million _____

60. 9,145,200 to the nearest million _____

61. 11 to the nearest ten _____

62. 190 to the nearest hundred _____

63. 849 to the nearest ten thousand _____

64. 24 to the nearest hundred _____

Whole Numbers Review (Part I)

Directions: Estimate the answer of each problem by rounding to the indicated place.

Round to the nearest ten.

65. 24
　　 +19

66. 65
　　 +11

67. 239
　　 × 92

68. 469
　　 − 233

Round to the nearest hundred.

69. 124
　　 +820

70. 1,395
　　 × 109

71. 184
　　 + 291

72. 565
　　 − 224

Round to the nearest thousand.

73. 5,824
　　 + 1,023

74. 7,824
　　 − 2,059

75. 2,074
　　 +18,291

76. 5,065
　　 − 3,904

Answers are on page 775.

## CHAPTER 2

Fractions

Understanding Fractions

In the previous chapter, you learned about whole numbers and the operations that are performed on them. In this chapter, you will study another type of number—a fraction.

A fraction is written in the form $\frac{x}{y}$, where x and y are whole numbers.

For example, these are fractions: $\frac{3}{4}, \frac{1}{2}$, and $\frac{2}{5}$. The number on the bottom, y, is called the **denominator**. It represents how many equal parts the unit or the whole has been divided into. The number on the top, x, is called the **numerator**. It represents how many parts of the unit or the whole are used or present.

In the fraction $\frac{1}{4}$, the *denominator* is 4 and the *numerator* is 1.

$\dfrac{1}{4}$ ← Numerator
← Denominator

Remember: The whole can represent a single object as well as a group of objects.

EXAMPLE 1

How much of the given figure is shaded?

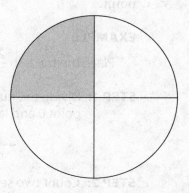

SOLUTION

The whole is divided into four equal parts, so the denominator is 4. One of these parts is shaded, so the numerator is 1.

$\dfrac{1}{4}$ ← Numerator
← Denominator

Read $\dfrac{1}{4}$ as "one-fourth."

EXAMPLE 2

What fraction shows the number of triangles that are shaded?

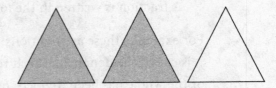

SOLUTION

Two out of three triangles are shaded.

$\dfrac{2}{3}$ ← Shaded triangles
← Total triangles

Fractions on a Number Line

Fractions can be represented on a number line.

- Divide the number line into equal segments, equal to the denominator.
- Mark the first point as 0 and last point as 1.
- Count segments equal to the numerator and place the fraction at that point.

EXAMPLE

Place the fraction $\dfrac{2}{3}$ on the number line.

STEP 1: Divide the number line into three segments and mark the first point 0 and last point 1.

STEP 2: Count two segments and place the fraction at that point.

ANSWER

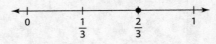

EXERCISE 1

Understanding Fractions (Part A)

Directions: Choose the correct answer.

1. What fraction of the whole shape is shaded?

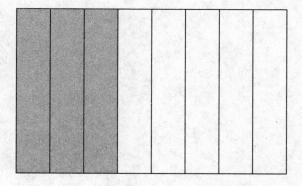

   A. $\frac{8}{3}$

   B. $\frac{3}{8}$

   C. $\frac{1}{3}$

   D. $\frac{1}{8}$

2. How much of the square is shaded?

   A. $\frac{3}{4}$

   B. $\frac{4}{3}$

   C. $\frac{1}{3}$

   D. $\frac{1}{4}$

3. Which figure shows a fraction equal to $\frac{2}{3}$?

A.

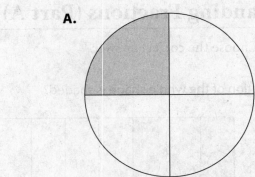

B.

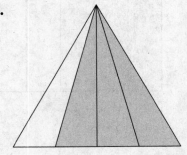

C.

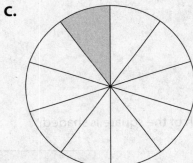

D.

4. What fraction in the given group of circles is shaded?

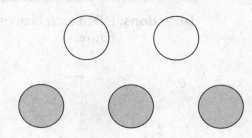

A. $\frac{2}{5}$

B. $\frac{5}{3}$

C. $\frac{3}{5}$

D. $\frac{5}{2}$

5. Which figure shows a fraction equal to $\frac{1}{2}$?

A.

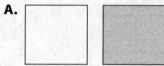

B.

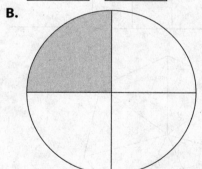

C.

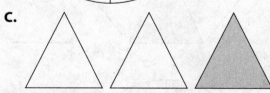

D.

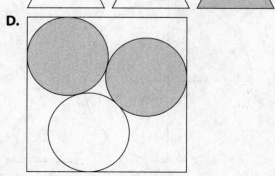

Understanding Fractions (Part B)

Directions: Fill in each blank with a fraction represented by the given figure.

6.

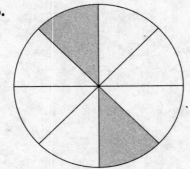

_____

7.

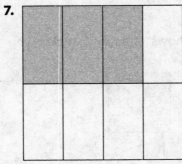

_____

8.

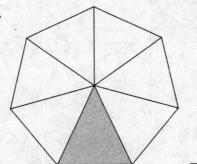

_____

9.

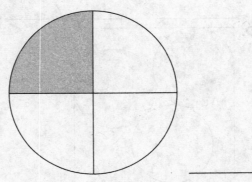

_____

10.

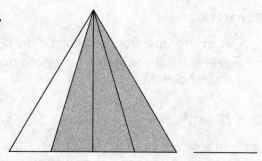

_____

Understanding Fractions (Part C)

Directions: Place the fraction on the number line.

11. $\frac{3}{4}$ ├─────┼─────┼─────┼─────┤

12. $\frac{1}{4}$ ├─────┼─────┼─────┼─────┤

Answers are on page 775.

Proper and Improper Fractions and Mixed Numbers

Fractions can be proper or improper.

Proper Fractions

When the numerator is *less than* the denominator, the fraction is called a **proper fraction**.

> **EXAMPLE**
>
> $\frac{2}{3}$ is a proper fraction because the numerator (2) is less than the denominator (3).

Improper Fractions

When the numerator is *equal to or greater than* the denominator, the fraction is called an **improper fraction**.

> **EXAMPLE 1**
>
> $\frac{5}{4}$ is an improper fraction because the numerator (5) is greater than the denominator (4). In this fraction a whole is divided into four pieces. The numerator refers to five pieces and is one piece more than the whole. Hence, the value of $\frac{5}{4}$ is one piece greater than the whole.

EXAMPLE 2

$\frac{2}{2}$ is an improper fraction because the numerator and denominator are equal. This fraction stands for 2 parts out of 2 total parts and its value is 1 (the whole).

Mixed Numbers

The sum of a whole number and a proper fraction is a **mixed number or mixed fraction**. Although a mixed number is a sum, it is written without a plus sign.

EXAMPLE

$1\frac{1}{4}$ is a mixed number because it is the sum of a whole number (1) and a proper fraction $\left(\frac{1}{4}\right)$. The mixed number $1\frac{1}{4}$ is shorthand for the sum $1+\frac{1}{4}$.

Note: $\frac{5}{4}$ and $1\frac{1}{4}$ are the same. Thus, a fraction in which the numerator is greater than 1 can be written as an improper fraction or a mixed number.

To change an improper fraction to a mixed number:

Divide the numerator by the denominator. The answer will be the whole number part of the mixed number, and the remainder will be the numerator of the fractional part. The denominator of the improper fraction will be the denominator of the mixed number.

EXAMPLE

Change $\frac{31}{7}$ to a mixed number.

Divide 32 by 7:
$$
\begin{array}{r}
4 \leftarrow \text{whole number part of mixed number} \\
7\overline{)31} \\
\underline{28} \\
3 \leftarrow \text{numerator of fractional part}
\end{array}
$$

So $\frac{31}{7}=4\frac{3}{7}$.

Note: If the remainder is 0, the result is a whole number and the fractional part is not written.

To change a mixed number to an improper fraction:

Multiply the denominator by the whole number, and add the numerator. The result is the numerator of the improper fraction. The denominator is the same as the original denominator.

EXAMPLE

Change $2\frac{5}{9}$ to a mixed number.

Multiply the denominator by the whole number: $9 \times 2 = 18$.

Add the numerator: $18 + 5 = 23$.

So $2\frac{5}{9} = \frac{23}{9}$.

Note: To change a whole number to an improper fraction, write the whole number in the numerator and 1 in the denominator. Example: $7 = \frac{7}{1}$.

EXERCISE 2

Proper and Improper Fractions and Mixed Numbers (Part A)

Directions: Fill in the blanks with an improper fraction represented by each figure.

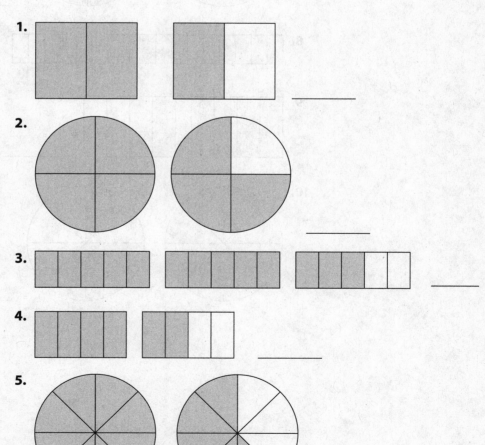

1.

2.

3.

4.

5.

Proper and Improper Fractions and Mixed Numbers (Part B)

Directions: Fill in the blanks with a mixed number represented by each figure.

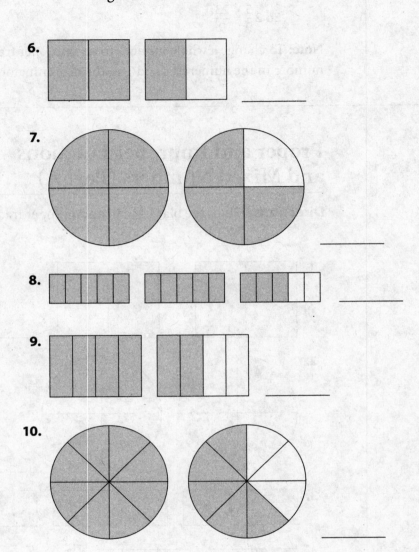

6. _____

7. _____

8. _____

9. _____

10. _____

Proper and Improper Fractions and Mixed Numbers (Part C)

Directions: Change each improper fraction to a mixed number.

11. $\dfrac{14}{5}$

12. $\dfrac{52}{3}$

13. $\dfrac{43}{9}$

14. $\dfrac{87}{13}$

15. $\dfrac{23}{18}$

Proper and Improper Fractions and Mixed Numbers (Part D)

Directions: Change each mixed number to an improper fraction.

16. $3\dfrac{5}{8}$

17. $2\dfrac{7}{11}$

18. $6\dfrac{3}{4}$

19. $12\dfrac{1}{3}$

20. $12\dfrac{3}{5}$

Answers are on page 776.

Equivalent Fractions

A fraction can be written in more than one way to represent a given number. For example, look at the following figures representing the two fractions $\frac{2}{3}$ and $\frac{4}{6}$, respectively.

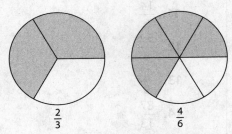

$$\frac{2}{3} \qquad\qquad \frac{4}{6}$$

These two fractions are simply different representations of the same number; thus, they are called **equivalent fractions**.

You can find an equivalent fraction of a given fraction by multiplying the numerator and denominator of the given fraction by the same number.

EXAMPLES

$$\frac{2\times2}{5\times2}=\frac{4}{10} \qquad \frac{3\times3}{4\times3}=\frac{9}{12} \qquad \frac{1\times5}{2\times5}=\frac{5}{10}$$

EXERCISE 3

Equivalent Fractions (Part A)

Directions: Choose the correct answer.

1. Which among the given pairs of fractions are equivalent fractions?

   A. $\frac{2}{3}, \frac{3}{2}$

   B. $\frac{1}{2}, \frac{3}{2}$

   C. $\frac{3}{5}, \frac{6}{10}$

   D. $\frac{2}{3}, \frac{2}{5}$

2. Which fraction is equivalent to $\frac{2}{5}$?

   A. $\frac{5}{2}$

   B. $\frac{2}{10}$

   C. $\frac{10}{5}$

   D. $\frac{6}{15}$

3. Which of the following represents an equivalent fraction of $\frac{4}{8}$?

    A. $\frac{2}{1}$

    B. $\frac{4}{2}$

    C. $\frac{2}{8}$

    D. $\frac{1}{2}$

4. Which of the given pairs of figures represents an equivalent fraction?

    A.

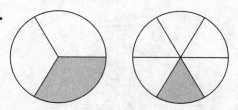

    B.

    C.

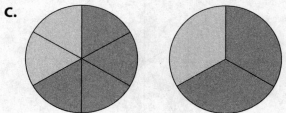

    D.

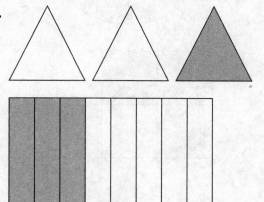

5. Which among the given pairs shows an equivalent figure and fraction?

A.

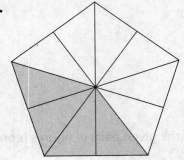

$\dfrac{1}{5}$

B.

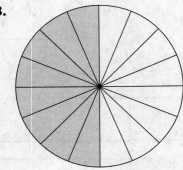

$\dfrac{3}{4}$

C.

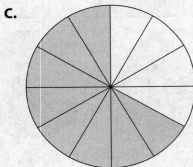

$\dfrac{2}{3}$

D.

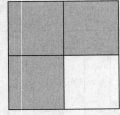

$\dfrac{1}{2}$

Equivalent Fractions (Part B)

Directions: Fill in the blanks.

6. $\dfrac{2 \times 2}{5 \times 2} = \dfrac{}{10}$

7. $\dfrac{3 \times 4}{5 \times 4} = \dfrac{12}{}$

8. $\dfrac{2 \times \underline{\quad}}{3 \times 3} = \dfrac{6}{9}$

9. $\dfrac{1 \times 5}{2 \times 5} = \dfrac{}{10}$

10. $\dfrac{3 \times 2}{4 \times 2} = \dfrac{6}{}$

Equivalent Fractions (Part C)

Directions: Fill in the blanks to make an equivalent fraction.

11. $\dfrac{2}{3} = \dfrac{6}{}$

12. $\dfrac{2}{5} = \dfrac{4}{}$

13. $\dfrac{3}{4} = \dfrac{}{12}$

14. $\dfrac{4}{5} = \dfrac{}{10}$

15. $\dfrac{1}{2} = \dfrac{5}{}$

Answers are on page 776.

Reducing Fractions to Lowest Terms

A fraction is reduced to lowest terms when written as an equivalent fraction using the lowest numbers possible in the numerator and denominator.

EXAMPLES

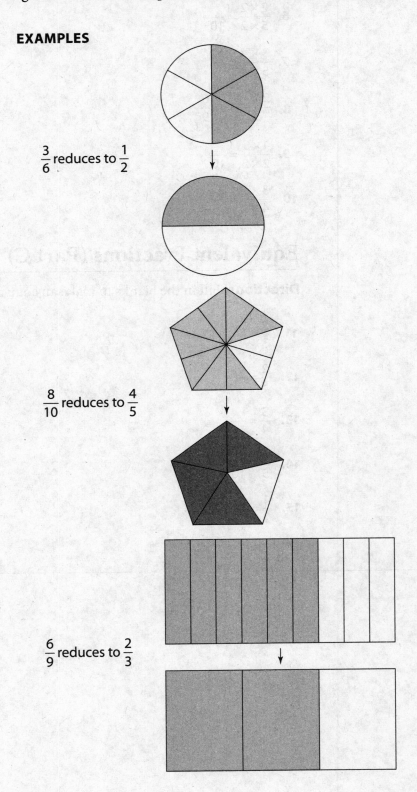

$\frac{3}{6}$ reduces to $\frac{1}{2}$

$\frac{8}{10}$ reduces to $\frac{4}{5}$

$\frac{6}{9}$ reduces to $\frac{2}{3}$

A fraction can be reduced to lowest terms by dividing the numerator and denominator by the greatest number that divides evenly into both.

EXAMPLES

$$\frac{2 \div 2}{4 \div 2} = \frac{1}{2} \qquad \frac{6 \div 3}{9 \div 3} = \frac{2}{3} \qquad \frac{12 \div 4}{20 \div 4} = \frac{3}{5}$$

EXERCISE 4

Reducing Fractions to Lowest Terms (Part A)

Directions: Choose the correct answer.

1. Which of the following is $\frac{6}{15}$ in lowest terms?

   A. $\frac{3}{5}$

   B. $\frac{1}{2}$

   C. $\frac{2}{5}$

   D. $\frac{6}{15}$

2. Which of the following is $\frac{8}{16}$ in lowest terms?

   A. $\frac{4}{8}$

   B. $\frac{2}{4}$

   C. $\frac{8}{16}$

   D. $\frac{1}{2}$

3. Which of the following figures has the same fraction shaded as the given figure?

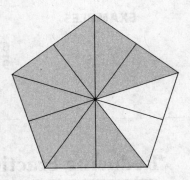

A.

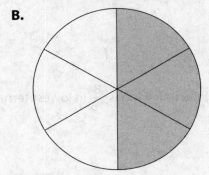

B.

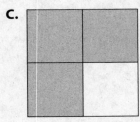

C.

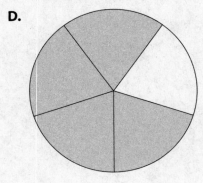

D.

4. Which of the following fractions represents the shaded part of the given figure?

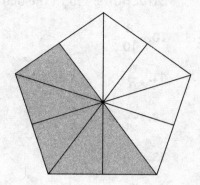

   A. $\dfrac{3}{5}$

   B. $\dfrac{1}{4}$

   C. $\dfrac{2}{3}$

   D. $\dfrac{1}{2}$

Reducing Fractions to Lowest Terms (Part B)

Directions: Fill in the blanks.

5. $\dfrac{4 \div 2}{6 \div 2} = \dfrac{}{3}$

6. $\dfrac{12 \div 3}{15 \div 3} = \dfrac{4}{}$

7. $\dfrac{6 \div 3}{9 \div 3} = \dfrac{2}{}$

8. $\dfrac{10 \div 5}{25 \div 5} = \dfrac{}{5}$

9. $\dfrac{2 \div 2}{4 \div 2} = \dfrac{1}{}$

Reducing Fractions to Lowest Terms (Part C)

Directions: Fill in the blanks to reduce each fraction to its lowest terms.

10. $\dfrac{8}{10} = -$

11. $\dfrac{6}{9} = -$

12. $\dfrac{5}{20} = -$

13. $\dfrac{12}{16} = -$

14. $\dfrac{2}{6} = -$

15. $\dfrac{4}{8} = -$

Answers are on page 776.

Comparing Fractions

Fractions can be **like fractions** and **unlike fractions**.

Like fractions have a common denominator, for example, $\dfrac{5}{4}$ and $\dfrac{3}{4}$. Like fractions are compared by comparing the numerators. The greater fraction is the fraction with the greater numerator. So, $\dfrac{5}{4}$ is greater than $\dfrac{3}{4}$ because 5 is greater than 3. So, use ">" for "greater than" and write as $\dfrac{5}{4} > \dfrac{3}{4}$.

Unlike fractions are those that do *not* have a **common denominator**, for example, $\dfrac{2}{3}$ and $\dfrac{3}{4}$.

To compare unlike fractions, convert them to like fractions by writing each fraction in terms of a common denominator. The lowest possible common denominator is called the **least common denominator (LCD)**. The LCD of two fractions is found by comparing lists of multiples of the denominators.

EXAMPLE

Compare the fractions $\dfrac{2}{3}$ and $\dfrac{3}{4}$.

STEP 1: Write several multiples of the denominators of both fractions, i.e., 3 and 4.

Multiples of 3:	3	6	9	**12**	15	18
Multiples of 4:	4	8	**12**	16	20	24

STEP 2: Find the smallest number that is a multiple of both the denominators. This number is called the LCD.

For $\frac{2}{3}$ and $\frac{3}{4}$, the LCD is 12.

STEP 3: Make each fraction as an equivalent fraction with 12 as the denominator.

$$\frac{2}{3} = \frac{2 \times 4}{3 \times 4} = \frac{8}{12} \quad \text{and} \quad \frac{3}{4} = \frac{3 \times 3}{4 \times 3} = \frac{9}{12}.$$

STEP 4: Compare the like fractions and then the unlike fractions.

$$\frac{9}{12} > \frac{8}{12}, \text{ so } \frac{3}{4} > \frac{2}{3}.$$

Let us see how like and unlike fractions are compared on a number line.

Comparing like fractions:

- Place the fractions on the same number line.
- The fraction at the extreme left is the smallest while the fraction at the extreme right is the greatest fraction.

Comparing unlike fractions:

- Make the fractions like fractions and repeat the process for comparing like fractions.

EXAMPLE

Place the fractions $\frac{2}{3}$, $\frac{3}{4}$, and $\frac{5}{6}$ on the number line, then arrange them in decreasing order.

STEP 1: Find the least common denominator, which is 12.

STEP 2: Make each fraction an equivalent fraction with 12 as the denominator.

$$\frac{2}{3} = \frac{2 \times 4}{3 \times 4} = \frac{8}{12} \qquad \frac{3}{4} = \frac{3 \times 3}{4 \times 3} = \frac{9}{12} \qquad \frac{5}{6} = \frac{5 \times 2}{6 \times 2} = \frac{10}{12}$$

STEP 3: Place the equivalent fraction of each fraction on the same number line.

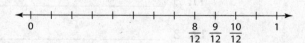

STEP 4: Compare the like fractions and then the unlike fractions.

$$\frac{8}{12} < \frac{9}{12} < \frac{10}{12}, \text{ so } \frac{2}{3} < \frac{3}{4} < \frac{5}{6}. \text{ (The symbol "<" means "is less than.")}$$

ANSWER

$$\frac{5}{6}, \frac{3}{4}, \frac{2}{3}$$

EXERCISE 5

Comparing Fractions (Part A)

Directions: Compare the fractions in each pair using <, >, and =.

1. $\dfrac{7}{6}$ _____ $\dfrac{13}{6}$

2. $\dfrac{4}{5}$ _____ $\dfrac{7}{10}$

3. $\dfrac{2}{3}$ _____ $\dfrac{2}{3}$

4. $\dfrac{12}{13}$ _____ $\dfrac{7}{13}$

5. $\dfrac{4}{8}$ _____ $\dfrac{3}{6}$

6. $\dfrac{2}{5}$ _____ $\dfrac{4}{5}$

7. $\dfrac{2}{3}$ _____ $\dfrac{5}{8}$

8. $\dfrac{1}{4}$ _____ $\dfrac{1}{3}$

9. $\dfrac{6}{8}$ _____ $\dfrac{4}{8}$

10. $\dfrac{9}{15}$ _____ $\dfrac{12}{20}$

Comparing Fractions (Part B)

Directions: Fill in the blanks with the next five multiples of each number.

11. 5 _____ _____ _____ _____ _____

12. 3 _____ _____ _____ _____ _____

13. 8 _____ _____ _____ _____ _____

14. 6 _____ _____ _____ _____ _____

15. 4 _____ _____ _____ _____ _____

Comparing Fractions (Part C)

Directions: Fill in the blanks with the LCD of each pair of fractions.

16. $\frac{7}{10}$ and $\frac{4}{5}$ _____

17. $\frac{5}{8}$ and $\frac{2}{3}$ _____

18. $\frac{5}{6}$ and $\frac{6}{8}$ _____

19. $\frac{3}{6}$ and $\frac{1}{5}$ _____

20. $\frac{1}{3}$ and $\frac{3}{4}$ _____

Answers are on page 776.

Operations with Fractions and Mixed Numbers

Fractions and mixed numbers can be added, subtracted, multiplied, and divided. The following sections will describe techniques for working with fractions and mixed numbers.

Adding and Subtracting Like Fractions

Recall that fractions with the same denominator are called **like fractions**.

EXAMPLES

$$\frac{5}{8} \text{ and } \frac{1}{8}; \frac{1}{3} \text{ and } \frac{2}{3}$$

To add or subtract like fractions:

- **Add** like fractions by adding the numerators and placing the sum over the denominator. Then reduce this fraction to lowest terms.

- **Subtract** like fractions by subtracting the numerators and placing the difference over the denominator. Then reduce this fraction to lowest terms.

EXAMPLE 1

Add: $\dfrac{2}{9} + \dfrac{1}{9}$.

STEP 1: Add the numerators: $2 + 1 = 3$.

$$\dfrac{2}{9} + \dfrac{1}{9} = \dfrac{3}{9}$$

STEP 2: Reduce the fraction $\dfrac{3}{9}$ to lowest terms.

$$\dfrac{3 \div 3}{9 \div 3} = \dfrac{1}{3}$$

ANSWER

$$\dfrac{1}{3}$$

EXAMPLE 2

Subtract: $\dfrac{15}{16} - \dfrac{3}{16}$.

STEP 1: Subtract the numerators: $15 - 3 = 12$.

$$\dfrac{15}{16} - \dfrac{3}{16} = \dfrac{12}{16}$$

STEP 2: Reduce the fraction $\dfrac{12}{16}$ to lowest terms.

$$\dfrac{12 \div 4}{16 \div 4} = \dfrac{3}{4}$$

ANSWER

$$\dfrac{3}{4}$$

EXERCISE 6

Adding and Subtracting Like Fractions (Part A)

Directions: Fill in the blanks.

1. $\dfrac{11}{12} - \dfrac{6}{12} = $ _____

2. $\dfrac{7}{8} - \dfrac{2}{8} = $ _____

3. $\dfrac{7}{5} - \dfrac{3}{5} = $ _____

4. $\dfrac{4}{3} - \dfrac{2}{3} =$ _____

5. $\dfrac{9}{8} - \dfrac{4}{8} =$ _____

6. $\dfrac{1}{5} + \dfrac{2}{5} =$ _____

7. $\dfrac{5}{8} + \dfrac{2}{8} =$ _____

8. $\dfrac{4}{12} + \dfrac{7}{12} =$ _____

9. $\dfrac{1}{4} + \dfrac{2}{4} =$ _____

10. $\dfrac{4}{3} + \dfrac{4}{3} =$ _____

Adding and Subtracting Like Fractions (Part B)

Directions: Add or subtract each pair of fractions. Where possible, write the answer as a mixed number. Reduce all answers to lowest terms.

11. $\dfrac{3}{4} + \dfrac{2}{4} =$ _____

12. $\dfrac{3}{8} + \dfrac{5}{8} =$ _____

13. $\dfrac{4}{5} + \dfrac{2}{5} =$ _____

14. $\dfrac{3}{4} + \dfrac{5}{4} =$ _____

15. $\dfrac{3}{4} + \dfrac{3}{4} =$ _____

16. $\dfrac{3}{4} - \dfrac{2}{4} =$ _____

17. $\dfrac{5}{8} - \dfrac{3}{8} =$ _____

18. $\dfrac{4}{5} - \dfrac{2}{5} =$ _____

19. $\dfrac{5}{4} - \dfrac{3}{4} =$ _____

20. $\dfrac{3}{4} - \dfrac{3}{4} =$ _____

Answers are on page 777.

Adding and Subtracting Unlike Fractions

Recall that fractions that do not have the same denominator are called **unlike fractions**.

EXAMPLES

$\frac{1}{3}$ and $\frac{1}{5}$; $\frac{1}{4}$ and $\frac{2}{3}$

To add or subtract unlike fractions:

- Find the LCD.
- Make each fraction into an equivalent fraction with the LCD as the common denominator.
- Add or subtract numerators and write the sum or difference over the denominator.
- Write the answer as a mixed number and reduce it.

EXAMPLE 1

Add: $\frac{1}{3} + \frac{1}{6}$.

STEP 1: The LCD is 6.

STEP 2: Write $\frac{1}{3}$ as an equivalent fraction with a denominator of 6.

$$\frac{1 \times 2}{3 \times 2} = \frac{2}{6}$$

STEP 3: Add: $\frac{2}{6} + \frac{1}{6} = \frac{3}{6}$.

STEP 4: Reduce the fraction $\frac{3}{6}$ to lowest terms.

$$\frac{3 \div 3}{6 \div 3} = \frac{1}{2}$$

ANSWER

$\frac{1}{2}$

EXAMPLE 2

Subtract: $\frac{4}{5} - \frac{4}{10}$.

STEP 1: The LCD is 10.

STEP 2: Write $\frac{4}{5}$ as an equivalent fraction with a denominator of 10.

$$\frac{4 \times 2}{5 \times 2} = \frac{8}{10}$$

STEP 3: Subtract: $\dfrac{8}{10} - \dfrac{4}{10} = \dfrac{4}{10}$.

STEP 4 Reduce the fraction $\dfrac{4}{10}$ to lowest terms.

$$\frac{4 \div 2}{10 \div 2} = \frac{2}{5}$$

ANSWER

$$\frac{2}{5}$$

EXERCISE 7

Adding and Subtracting Unlike Fractions (Part A)

Directions: Fill in the missing numerators and then find the sum or difference.

1. $\dfrac{1}{2} = \dfrac{}{14}$
    $+\dfrac{1}{7} \; \dfrac{}{14}$

2. $\dfrac{7}{8} = \dfrac{7}{8}$
    $-\dfrac{1}{4} \; \dfrac{}{8}$

3. $\dfrac{1}{2} = \dfrac{}{4}$
    $+\dfrac{1}{4} = \dfrac{1}{4}$

4. $\dfrac{4}{5} = \dfrac{}{15}$
    $-\dfrac{2}{3} \; \dfrac{}{15}$

5. $\dfrac{5}{8} = \dfrac{5}{8}$
    $-\dfrac{1}{4} \; \dfrac{}{8}$

6. $\dfrac{1}{2} = \dfrac{}{6}$
    $+\dfrac{1}{3} \; \dfrac{}{6}$

7. $\dfrac{3}{4} = \dfrac{}{20}$
    $-\dfrac{2}{5} \; \dfrac{}{20}$

8. $\dfrac{1}{3} = \dfrac{}{9}$
    $+\dfrac{1}{9} = \dfrac{1}{9}$

9. $\dfrac{11}{16} = \dfrac{11}{16}$
    $+\dfrac{1}{4} \; \dfrac{}{16}$

10. $\dfrac{1}{3} = \dfrac{}{12}$
    $+\dfrac{1}{4} = \dfrac{}{12}$

Adding and Subtracting Unlike Fractions (Part B)

Directions: Add or subtract and write the answers in lowest terms.

11. $\dfrac{7}{8}$
$-\dfrac{1}{2}$

12. $\dfrac{1}{2}$
$-\dfrac{2}{5}$

13. $\dfrac{3}{4}$
$-\dfrac{1}{3}$

14. $\dfrac{1}{5}$
$+\dfrac{1}{6}$

15. $\dfrac{5}{8}$
$+\dfrac{1}{4}$

16. $\dfrac{1}{2}$
$+\dfrac{1}{3}$

17. $\dfrac{3}{4}$
$-\dfrac{1}{2}$

18. $\dfrac{9}{10}$
$+\dfrac{3}{5}$

19. $\dfrac{1}{2}$
$-\dfrac{1}{4}$

20. $\dfrac{3}{4}$
$+\dfrac{1}{5}$

Answers are on page 777.

Adding and Subtracting Mixed Numbers

To add mixed numbers:

• Whole numbers and fractions are added separately.

• In case the sum of the fractions is an improper fraction (greater than 1), the improper fraction is converted to a mixed number.

• Then add the whole numbers and write the new proper fraction.

EXAMPLE 1

Add: $2\dfrac{2}{3} + 1\dfrac{1}{2}$.

STEP 1: Make each fraction into an equivalent fraction with the LCD.

$$2\dfrac{2}{3} = 2\dfrac{4}{6} \qquad 1\dfrac{1}{2} = 1\dfrac{3}{6}$$

STEP 2: Add the whole numbers and the numerators of the fractions.

$$(2+1)\frac{4+3}{6}=3\frac{7}{6}$$

STEP 3: Convert the improper fraction into a mixed number.

$$3\frac{7}{6}=3+\left(1\frac{1}{6}\right)$$

STEP 4: Add the whole numbers and write the proper fraction.

$$3+1+\frac{1}{6}=4\frac{1}{6}$$

ANSWER

$$4\frac{1}{6}$$

To subtract mixed numbers:

- Whole numbers and fractions are subtracted separately.

- If the second fraction is larger than the first, regroup the first fraction to an improper fraction. This is done by borrowing 1 from the whole number and adding it to the fraction.

- Then subtract the whole numbers and subtract the numerators of the fractions.

EXAMPLE 2

Subtract: $6\frac{1}{4}-3\frac{1}{2}$.

STEP 1: Make each fraction into an equivalent fraction with a common denominator.

$$6\frac{1}{4}=6\frac{1}{4} \qquad 3\frac{1}{2}=3\frac{2}{4}$$

STEP 2: Regroup the fraction $\left(1 \text{ can be written as } \frac{4}{4}\right)$.

$$6\frac{1}{4}=5+1+\frac{1}{4}=5+\frac{4}{4}+\frac{1}{4}=5+\frac{5}{4}=5\frac{5}{4}$$

STEP 3: Subtract the whole numbers and the fractions separately.

$$(5-3)+\left(\frac{5}{4}-\frac{2}{4}\right)=2+\frac{3}{4}=2\frac{3}{4}$$

ANSWER

$$2\frac{3}{4}$$

EXERCISE 8

Adding and Subtracting Mixed Numbers (Part A)

Directions: Add or subtract as indicated.

1. $6\frac{3}{4}$
    $+1\frac{2}{3}$

2. $3\frac{1}{3}$
    $-1\frac{2}{3}$

3. $4\frac{7}{8}$
    $+2\frac{3}{4}$

4. $5\frac{1}{4}$
    $-1\frac{3}{4}$

5. $3\frac{3}{4}$
    $+1\frac{1}{2}$

6. $6\frac{1}{2}$
    $-2\frac{3}{4}$

7. $4\frac{2}{3}$
    $+2\frac{2}{3}$

8. $4\frac{1}{4}$
    $-1\frac{1}{3}$

9. $2\frac{1}{2}$
    $+1\frac{1}{2}$

10. $5\frac{3}{8}$
    $-2\frac{3}{4}$

Adding and Subtracting Mixed Numbers (Part B)

Directions: Choose the correct answer.

11. A person buys two sheets of paper of different types. One is $\frac{3}{8}$ of an inch thick and the other is $\frac{1}{4}$ of an inch thick. How thick are the two sheets together?

    A. $\frac{6}{16}$ of an inch

    B. $\frac{5}{8}$ of an inch

    C. $\frac{20}{32}$ of an inch

    D. $\frac{1}{3}$ of an inch

12. On Monday the recorded snowfall was $\frac{5}{6}$ inch. On Tuesday it was $\frac{3}{4}$ inch. How much more snow fell on Monday than on Tuesday?

A. $\frac{2}{6}$

B. $\frac{5}{8}$

C. $\frac{1}{12}$

D. $\frac{1}{10}$

Answers are on page 777.

Multiplying Fractions

To multiply two fractions:

- Multiply the numerators to find the numerator of the product.
- Multiply the denominators to find the denominator of the product.
- Reduce the fraction to lowest terms, if possible.

Note: Both like and unlike fractions are multiplied in the same way.

EXAMPLE 1

Multiply: $\frac{1}{4} \times \frac{1}{4}$.

STEP 1: Multiply the numerators.

$$\frac{1}{4} \times \frac{1}{4} = \frac{1}{\ }$$

STEP 2: Multiply the denominators.

$$\frac{1}{4} \times \frac{1}{4} = \frac{1}{16}$$

ANSWER

$$\frac{1}{16}$$

EXAMPLE 2

Multiply: $\dfrac{2}{3} \times \dfrac{3}{5}$.

STEP 1: Multiply the numerators.

$$\frac{2}{3} \times \frac{3}{5} = \frac{6}{}$$

STEP 2: Multiply the denominators.

$$\frac{2}{3} \times \frac{3}{5} = \frac{6}{15}$$

STEP 3: Reduce to lowest terms.

$$\frac{6 \div 3}{15 \div 3} = \frac{2}{5}$$

ANSWER

$$\frac{2}{5}$$

EXERCISE 9

Multiplying Fractions (Part A)

Directions: Multiply the fractions and write the answers in lowest terms.

1. $\dfrac{1}{2} \times \dfrac{5}{6} = -$

2. $\dfrac{2}{3} \times \dfrac{4}{5} = -$

3. $\dfrac{1}{4} \times \dfrac{7}{8} = -$

4. $\dfrac{2}{5} \times \dfrac{3}{5} = -$

5. $\dfrac{6}{7} \times \dfrac{1}{5} = -$

6. $\dfrac{3}{4} \times \dfrac{1}{2} = -$

7. $\dfrac{2}{7} \times \dfrac{1}{3} = -$

8. $\dfrac{1}{3} \times \dfrac{1}{5} = -$

9. $\dfrac{1}{2} \times \dfrac{5}{7} = -$

10. $\dfrac{1}{3} \times \dfrac{2}{5} = -$

Multiplying Fractions (Part B)

Directions: Multiply the fractions and write the answers in lowest terms.

11. $\dfrac{1}{2} \times \dfrac{2}{3} = -$

12. $\dfrac{2}{3} \times \dfrac{4}{10} = -$

13. $\dfrac{2}{3} \times \dfrac{3}{4} = -$

14. $\dfrac{3}{4} \times \dfrac{1}{3} = -$

15. $\dfrac{1}{9} \times \dfrac{3}{6} = -$

16. $\dfrac{4}{7} \times \dfrac{1}{2} = -$

17. $\dfrac{2}{5} \times \dfrac{5}{8} = -$

18. $\dfrac{10}{11} \times \dfrac{1}{5} = -$

19. $\dfrac{2}{3} \times \dfrac{3}{5} = -$

20. $\dfrac{1}{6} \times \dfrac{2}{5} = -$

Multiplying Fractions (Part C)

Directions: Choose the correct answer.

21. Katherine eats $\frac{1}{6}$ of a cake that weighs a total of $\frac{7}{9}$ pound. What weight of cake does Katherine eat?

    A. $\frac{7}{54}$ lb

    B. $\frac{1}{14}$ lb

    C. $\frac{1}{54}$ lb

    D. $\frac{1}{8}$ lb

22. Allie has $\frac{6}{8}$ gallons of milk. She uses $\frac{2}{3}$ of the milk. How many gallons of milk has Allie used?

    A. $\frac{12}{24}$

    B. $\frac{6}{12}$

    C. $\frac{2}{4}$

    D. $\frac{1}{2}$

Answers are on page 777.

Multiplying Fractions, Whole Numbers, and Mixed Numbers

When you multiply a combination of fractions, whole numbers, or mixed numbers, first change the whole number or mixed number to an improper fraction. Next, multiply as usual.

EXAMPLE 1

Multiply: $\frac{3}{5} \times 8$.

STEP 1: Rewrite 8 as $\frac{8}{1}$.

STEP 2: Multiply the fractions.

$$\frac{3}{5} \times \frac{8}{1} = \frac{24}{5} = 4\frac{4}{5}$$

ANSWER

$$4\frac{4}{5}$$

EXAMPLE 2

Multiply: $2\frac{2}{3} \times \frac{4}{5}$.

STEP 1: Rewrite $2\frac{2}{3}$ as an improper fraction.

$$2\frac{2}{3} = \frac{8}{3}$$

STEP 2: Multiply the fractions.

$$\frac{8}{3} \times \frac{4}{5} = \frac{32}{15} = 2\frac{2}{15}$$

ANSWER

$$2\frac{2}{15}$$

EXERCISE 10

Multiplying Fractions, Whole Numbers, and Mixed Numbers (Part A)

Directions: Multiply and write the answers as mixed numbers in lowest terms.

1. $\frac{9}{10} \times \frac{2}{1} =$ ___

2. $\frac{3}{4} \times \frac{6}{1} =$ ___

3. $\frac{1}{2} \times \frac{5}{1} =$ ___

4. $\frac{3}{2} \times \frac{5}{2} =$ ___

5. $\frac{4}{3} \times \frac{3}{4} =$ ___

6. $\frac{5}{2} \times \frac{1}{2} =$ ___

Multiplying Fractions, Whole Numbers, and Mixed Numbers (Part B)

Directions: Multiply the fraction and the whole number.

7. $\dfrac{3}{4} \times 5 = -$ **8.** $\dfrac{5}{8} \times 7 = -$ **9.** $\dfrac{1}{3} \times 2 = -$

10. $8 \times \dfrac{3}{4} = -$ **11.** $2 \times \dfrac{3}{8} = -$ **12.** $5 \times \dfrac{2}{3} = -$

Multiplying Fractions, Whole Numbers, and Mixed Numbers (Part C)

Directions: Multiply the fraction and mixed number.

13. $\dfrac{2}{3} \times 2\dfrac{1}{2} = -$ **14.** $\dfrac{3}{4} \times 2\dfrac{1}{3} = -$ **15.** $\dfrac{1}{3} \times 1\dfrac{1}{2} = -$

16. $1\dfrac{3}{4} \times \dfrac{1}{2} = -$ **17.** $2\dfrac{1}{4} \times \dfrac{3}{8} = -$ **18.** $1\dfrac{1}{2} \times \dfrac{3}{4} = -$

Multiplying Fractions, Whole Numbers, and Mixed Numbers (Part D)

Directions: Choose the correct answer.

19. If a hot dog has $\dfrac{1}{4}$ fat, how many ounces of fat are in 48 ounces of hot dog?

     A. 12
     B. 14
     C. 16
     D. 24

20. Danny mixes $\dfrac{6}{7}$ pint of coloring into each gallon of paint he uses. How many pints of coloring will Danny need to complete a job that requires 14 gallons of paint?

     A. 6
     B. 8
     C. 10
     D. 12

Answers are on page 778.

Dividing Fractions

To divide means to find out how many times one number is contained in a second number.

To divide fractions:

First, invert the divisor (the number by which you are dividing).

Second, change the division sign to a multiplication sign.

Last, multiply the two fractions.

Note: Inverting the divisor means interchanging the numerator and the denominator. This is simply switching the top and bottom numbers.

EXAMPLE

Divide: $\dfrac{3}{8} \div \dfrac{6}{10}$

STEP 1: Invert the divisor: $\dfrac{6}{10}$ is inverted as $\dfrac{10}{6}$.

STEP 2: Change the division sign to a multiplication sign and multiply.

$$\frac{3}{8} \div \frac{6}{10} = \frac{3}{8} \times \frac{10}{6} = \frac{30}{48} = \frac{5}{8}$$

ANSWER

$\dfrac{5}{8}$

EXERCISE 11

Dividing Fractions (Part A)

Directions: Invert each fraction.

1. $\dfrac{3}{8} = -$

2. $\dfrac{2}{3} = -$

3. $\dfrac{7}{8} = -$

4. $\dfrac{3}{5} = -$

5. $\dfrac{6}{7} = -$

6. $\dfrac{1}{2} = -$

Dividing Fractions (Part B)

Directions: Divide and write the answer in its lowest form.

7. $\dfrac{1}{2} \div \dfrac{3}{4} = -$

8. $\dfrac{5}{6} \div \dfrac{1}{3} = -$

9. $\dfrac{4}{5} \div \dfrac{3}{4} = -$

10. $\dfrac{1}{6} \div \dfrac{2}{3} = -$

11. $\dfrac{5}{8} \div \dfrac{1}{3} = -$

12. $\dfrac{3}{5} \div \dfrac{1}{10} = -$

Answers are on page 778.

Dividing Fractions, Whole Numbers, and Mixed Numbers

To divide fractions, whole numbers, or mixed numbers:

- Whole number divisor: convert it to a fraction by placing it over 1.
- Mixed number divisor: change it to an improper fraction.
- Invert the divisor.
- Change the division sign to a multiplication sign.
- Multiply the fractions.

Type of Divisor	Example	Write the Divisor as a Fraction	Invert the Divisor and Change the Sign
Proper fraction	$\dfrac{1}{2} \div \dfrac{3}{4}$	$\dfrac{1}{2} \div \dfrac{3}{4}$	$\dfrac{1}{2} \times \dfrac{4}{3}$
Improper fraction	$\dfrac{4}{5} \div \dfrac{3}{2}$	$\dfrac{4}{5} \div \dfrac{3}{2}$	$\dfrac{4}{5} \times \dfrac{2}{3}$
Whole number	$\dfrac{1}{3} \div 4$	$\dfrac{1}{3} \div \dfrac{4}{1}$	$\dfrac{1}{3} \times \dfrac{1}{4}$
Mixed number	$\dfrac{1}{2} \div 1\dfrac{3}{4}$	$\dfrac{1}{2} \div \dfrac{7}{4}$	$\dfrac{1}{2} \times \dfrac{4}{7}$

EXAMPLE

Divide: $\frac{1}{6} \div 1\frac{1}{3}$.

STEP 1: Change the mixed number divisor to an improper fraction: $1\frac{1}{3} = \frac{4}{3}$.

STEP 2: Invert the divisor: $\frac{3}{4}$.

STEP 3: Change the division sign to a multiplication sign and then multiply the fractions.

$$\frac{1}{6} \div 1\frac{1}{3} = \frac{1}{6} \div \frac{4}{3} = \frac{1}{6} \times \frac{3}{4} = \frac{3}{24} = \frac{1}{8}$$

ANSWER

$\frac{1}{8}$

EXERCISE 12

Dividing Fractions, Whole Numbers, and Mixed Numbers (Part A)

Directions: Invert each number.

1. $\frac{8}{3} = -$ 2. $\frac{3}{2} = -$ 3. $\frac{6}{7} = -$

4. $4 = -$ 5. $9 = -$ 6. $5 = -$

7. $1\frac{3}{4} = -$ 8. $2\frac{2}{3} = -$ 9. $3\frac{1}{5} = -$

Dividing Fractions, Whole Numbers, and Mixed Numbers (Part B)

Directions: Divide and write the answer in its lowest form.

10. $\frac{1}{2} \div \frac{5}{4} = -$ 11. $\frac{5}{6} \div \frac{3}{2} = -$ 12. $\frac{4}{5} \div \frac{4}{3} = -$

13. $\frac{1}{6} \div \frac{5}{2} = -$ 14. $\frac{5}{8} \div \frac{5}{6} = -$ 15. $\frac{3}{5} \div 4 = -$

16. $\dfrac{3}{2} \div 3 = -$ **17.** $\dfrac{5}{8} \div 10 = -$ **18.** $\dfrac{4}{5} \div 2 = -$

19. $1\dfrac{1}{2} \div \dfrac{3}{4} = -$ **20.** $\dfrac{1}{2} \div 1\dfrac{1}{2} = -$ **21.** $1\dfrac{1}{4} \div \dfrac{2}{3} = -$

22. $\dfrac{5}{2} \div 2\dfrac{1}{3} = -$

Answers are on page 778.

EXERCISE 13

Fraction Review (Part A)

Directions: Fill in each blank with a fraction represented by the given figure.

1.

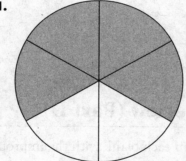

_____

2.

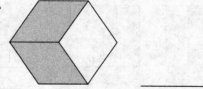

_____

3.

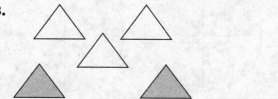

_____

Fraction Review (Part B)

Directions: Fill in the blanks to make an equivalent fraction.

4. $\dfrac{1}{3} = \dfrac{}{6}$

5. $\dfrac{3}{5} = \dfrac{6}{}$

6. $\dfrac{3}{4} = \dfrac{}{12}$

Fraction Review (Part C)

Directions: Fill in the blanks to reduce the fraction to its lowest terms.

7. $\dfrac{6}{10} = -$

8. $\dfrac{3}{9} = -$

9. $\dfrac{2}{8} = -$

10. $\dfrac{5}{15} = -$

Fraction Review (Part D)

Directions: Fill in each blank with the improper fraction represented by each figure.

11.  _____

12. 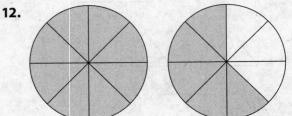

_____

13.   _____

Fraction Review (Part E)

Directions: Compare the fractions in each pair using <, >, and =.

14. $\dfrac{5}{6}$ _____ $\dfrac{7}{6}$

15. $\dfrac{4}{7}$ _____ $\dfrac{7}{8}$

16. $\dfrac{9}{27}$ _____ $\dfrac{4}{12}$

Fraction Review (Part F)

Directions: Solve each problem.

17.
$$\begin{array}{r} \frac{1}{5} \\ +\frac{1}{5} \\ \hline \end{array}$$

18.
$$\begin{array}{r} \frac{3}{4} \\ +\frac{2}{3} \\ \hline \end{array}$$

19.
$$\begin{array}{r} 3\frac{1}{2} \\ +1\frac{1}{4} \\ \hline \end{array}$$

20.
$$\begin{array}{r} \frac{7}{8} \\ -\frac{3}{8} \\ \hline \end{array}$$

21.
$$\begin{array}{r} 1\frac{1}{4} \\ -\frac{3}{4} \\ \hline \end{array}$$

22.
$$\begin{array}{r} 6\frac{1}{3} \\ -2\frac{1}{2} \\ \hline \end{array}$$

23. $\dfrac{2}{5} \times \dfrac{5}{8} = -$

24. $\dfrac{10}{11} \times 2\dfrac{1}{4} = -$

25. $2\dfrac{1}{3} \times \dfrac{3}{5} = -$

26. $\dfrac{1}{2} \div \dfrac{3}{4} = -$

27. $2\dfrac{1}{2} \div \dfrac{3}{8} = -$

28. $\dfrac{3}{4} \div 1\dfrac{1}{2} = -$

Answers are on page 779.

CHAPTER 3

Decimals

Understanding Decimals

In Chapter 2, you studied fractions. This chapter will discuss a special kind of fraction called a **decimal fraction** or **decimal**. Decimal fractions are those fractions in which the denominator is a power of 10. Here are some examples: $\dfrac{3}{10}$, $\dfrac{7}{100}$, $\dfrac{131}{1000}$.

The Place Value System

Look at the number 21.352. The period to the right of the ones place is called a **decimal point**. Each digit to the right of the decimal point represents a fraction whose denominator is a power of 10.

- The first place to the right of the decimal point is the tenths place $\left(0.1 = \dfrac{1}{10}\right)$.

- The second place to the right of the decimal point is the hundredths place $\left(0.01 = \dfrac{1}{100}\right)$.

- The third place to the right of the decimal point is the thousandths place $\left(0.001 = \dfrac{1}{1000}\right)$, and so on.

The figure below illustrates the value of each position as you move right from the decimal point.

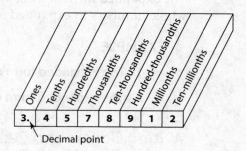

Decimal point

EXAMPLE

Write the place value of each digit in the decimal number 4.5287.

SOLUTION

4	ones
5	tenths
2	hundredths
8	thousandths
7	ten-thousandths

Locating Decimals on a Number Line

The following number line shows that decimal numbers with a single digit to the right of the decimal point correspond to a fraction with a denominator of 10.

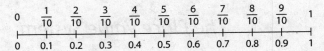

To locate a decimal on a number line, a segment of the number line between consecutive whole numbers is divided into 10 equal parts.

EXAMPLE

To locate 7.6 on a number line, divide the line segment between 7 and 8 into 10 equal parts as shown.

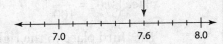

The arrow shows 7.6. The 0.6 represents the 6 parts to the right of 7.

Expanded Form of Decimals

The expanded form of a decimal represents the number as the sum of its whole numbers in expanded form and decimal place values.

EXAMPLE

1. The expanded form of 2.786 is $2 + 0.7 + 0.08 + 0.006$.

2. The expanded form of 12.3253 is $10 + 2 + 0.3 + 0.02 + 0.005 + 0.0003$.

Writing Dollars and Cents as Decimals

A dollar is divided into dimes (tenths of a dollar) and pennies (hundredths of a dollar).

1 dollar = 10 dime = 100 pennies

The decimal point separates whole dollars from parts of a dollar.

$4.26

4 whole dollars ⌐
        └ 6 pennies [6 hundredths of a dollar]
        └ 3 dimes [3 tenths of a dollar]

The values of coins can be written as decimal parts of a dollar.

• One quarter = $0.25 (25 parts out of 100)

• One dime = $0.10 (10 parts out of 100)

• One nickel = $0.05 (5 parts out of 100)

• One penny = $0.01 (1 part out of 100)

25 ¢   10 ¢   5 ¢   1 ¢

EXERCISE 1

The Place Value System (Part A)

Directions: Write the place value of indicated digits in the blanks.

Consider the decimal 3.7892.

1. What is the place value of 8? _____

2. What is the place value of 9? _____

3. What is the place value of 2? _____

Consider the decimal 12.65793.

4. What is the place value of 1? _____

5. What is the place value of 6? _____

6. What is the place value of 7? _____

7. What is the place value of 9? _____

The Place Value System (Part B)

Directions: Write the decimal in expanded form.

8. 2.43 _____

9. 7.809 _____

10. 14.51 _____

11. 12.999 _____

12. 1.001 _____

The Place Value System (Part C)

Directions: Write the amount using a dollar sign.

13.

_____

14.

_____

15.

_____

16.

_____

Answers are on page 779.

Necessary and Unnecessary 0s

The digit 0 has no value and can be used as a **placeholder**.

- When you place 0 between the decimal point and a digit, it changes the value of the decimal fraction.
- When you place 0 at the extreme right of a decimal, 0 does not change the decimal's value but changes the way the decimal is read.

EXAMPLE 1

0.7 and 0.07 differ from each other because in 0.07 the 0 is in the tenths place.

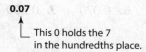

0.07

This 0 holds the 7
in the hundredths place.

So, 0.7 = 7 tenths, and 0.07 = 7 hundredths.

Thus, a **necessary 0** is a 0 that comes anywhere between the decimal point and the last non-zero digit to the right of the decimal point.

You **cannot** remove a necessary 0 without changing a decimal's value.

Examples of necessary 0s: 0.<u>0</u>5   0.2<u>0</u>8   2.<u>0</u>50   0.<u>00</u>9

EXAMPLE 2

The decimals 0.8 and 0.80 have the same value, but they differ in the way they are read. This is similar to the fact that 8 dimes have the same value as 80 pennies.

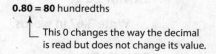

0.80 = 80 hundredths

This 0 changes the way the decimal
is read but does not change its value.

So, 0.8 = 8 tenths, and 0.80 = 80 hundredths.

Thus, an **unnecessary 0** is a 0 that is placed at the far right of the decimal. It *does not* change the value of a decimal.

Examples of unnecessary 0s: 0.8<u>0</u>   0.09<u>0</u>   1.5<u>00</u>   0.76<u>0</u>

Same Values
0.9 = 0.90
0.9 = 0.900
0.25 = 0.250
3.6 = 3.600
8 = 8.00

Different Values
0.9 and 0.09
0.9 and 0.009
0.25 and 0.025
3.6 and 0.036
8 and 0.08

Necessary and Unnecessary 0s (Part A)

Directions: Underline each necessary 0. (Ignore leading 0s.)

1. 0.09   **2.** 0.003   **3.** 0.080   **4.** 6.008   **5.** 4.708

Necessary and Unnecessary 0s (Part B)

Directions: Underline each unnecessary 0.

6. 0.070   **7.** 0.300   **8.** 0.0500   **9.** 6.800   **10.** 4.780

Answers are on page 779.

Reading and Writing Decimals

Here are rules for reading and writing decimals in words:

- Read and write the digit to the left of the decimal point as a whole number.
- Read and write the decimal point as the word "and."
- Read and write the digits to the right of the decimal point as a whole number followed by the place value of the rightmost digit.

EXAMPLE 1

Write 3.67 in words.

SOLUTION

First, write the whole number as "three."

Second, write the decimal point as "and."

Third, write the digits to the right of the decimal point (67) as a whole number, "sixty-seven," and then add the place value of the rightmost digit (7) of the decimal part, which is hundredths, to it.

Thus, 3.67 is read as "three and sixty-seven hundredths."

EXAMPLE 2

Write 0.081 in words.

SOLUTION

The place value of the rightmost digit (1) is thousandths.

Thus, 0.081 is read as "eighty-one thousandths."

EXAMPLE 3

Write 15.371 in words.

SOLUTION

The place value of the rightmost digit (1) is thousandths.

Thus, 15.371 is read as "fifteen and three hundred seventy-one thousandths."

Rules for Writing in Decimal Form

Follow these rules for writing decimals:

* First, identify the place value of the rightmost digit.
* Then write the number so that the rightmost digit is in its proper place.
* Finally write the 0s as placeholders when necessary.

EXAMPLE 1

Write 65 hundredths as a decimal.

SOLUTION

Write 65 so that the 5 is in the hundredths place.

0.65

Leading 0 — Write 5 in the hundredths place.

EXAMPLE 2

Write 43 thousandths as a decimal.

SOLUTION

Write 43 so that the 3 is in the thousandths place.

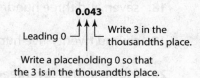

0.043

Leading 0 — Write 3 in the thousandths place.

Write a placeholding 0 so that the 3 is in the thousandths place.

EXERCISE 3

Reading and Writing Decimals (Part A)

Directions: Write each decimal as it is read in words.

1. 0.7 _____

2. 0.4 _____

3. 0.03 _____

4. 0.06 _____

5. 0.34 _____

6. 0.76 _____

7. 0.009 _____

8. 0.056 _____

9. 3.214 _____

10. $0.07 _____

Reading and Writing Decimals (Part B)

Directions: Write each number as a decimal, using digits.

11. six tenths _____

12. eight hundredths _____

13. forty-five hundredths _____

14. two thousandths _____

15. thirty-four thousandths _____

16. four hundred twenty-six thousandths _____

17. two and four tenths _____

18. seven and three hundredths _____

19. six and twenty-five hundredths _____

20. fourteen and seventeen hundredths _____

21. six and three thousandths _____

22. four and thirty-four thousandths _____

23. thirteen and forty-seven thousandths _____

24. nine and six hundred twenty-five thousandths _____

25. sixty-seven and two hundred thirty-four thousandths _____

Answers are on page 779.

Decimal/Fraction Conversions

There are simple methods for converting decimals to fractions and fractions to decimals.

Decimal to Fraction Form

To write a decimal in fraction or mixed number form, first identify the number of decimal places. The number of digits to the right of the decimal point is the same as the number of 0s in the denominator of the fraction. Thus, 0.45 has two 0s in the denominator when written as a fraction. The numerator is the decimal part of the number written as a whole number.

EXAMPLE 1

Write 0.45 as a fraction or a mixed number.

SOLUTION

$$0.\underset{\substack{\text{Two}\\\text{places}}}{\underline{45}} = \dfrac{45}{\underset{\substack{\text{Two}\\\text{zeros}}}{\underline{100}}}$$

Write $\dfrac{45}{100}$ in simplest term.

Thus, $0.45 = \dfrac{45}{100} = \dfrac{9}{20}$.

EXAMPLE 2

Write 3.041 as a fraction or a mixed number.

SOLUTION

Here, the result is a mixed number.

$$3.\underset{\substack{\text{Three}\\\text{places}}}{\underline{041}} = 3\dfrac{41}{\underset{\substack{\text{Three}\\\text{zeros}}}{\underline{1000}}}$$

Remember: The 0 to the right of the decimal point is a placeholder, which is not needed in the fraction form.

Fraction to Decimal Form

If the denominator is a power of 10, then just write the numerator putting the decimal point in the correct place. The number of decimal places will be equal to the number of zeros in the denominator (power of 10).

EXAMPLE

$$\dfrac{7}{\underset{\substack{\text{Three}\\\text{zeros}}}{\underline{1000}}} = 0.\underset{\substack{\text{Three}\\\text{decimal}\\\text{places}}}{\underline{007}}$$

If the denominator is not a power of 10, then the steps to be followed are:

STEP 1: Find a number that you can multiply the denominator of the fraction by to make it a power of 10, such as 10, 100, 1,000, and so on.

STEP 2: Multiply both the numerator and denominator of the fraction by that number.

STEP 3: Then, just write the numerator putting the decimal point in the correct place. The number of decimal places will be equal to the number of zeros in the denominator (power of 10).

EXAMPLE 1

Write $\dfrac{3}{5}$ in decimal form.

SOLUTION

$$\dfrac{3}{5} = \dfrac{3 \times 2}{5 \times 2} = \dfrac{6}{\underbrace{10}_{\text{One zero}}} = 0.\underbrace{6}_{\text{One place}}$$

EXAMPLE 2

Write $7\dfrac{19}{200}$ in decimal form.

SOLUTION

$$7\dfrac{19}{200} = 7\dfrac{19 \times 5}{200 \times 5} = 7\dfrac{95}{\underbrace{1000}_{\text{Three zeros}}} = 7.\underbrace{095}_{\text{Three places}}$$

EXAMPLE 3

Write $\dfrac{3}{25}$ in decimal form.

SOLUTION

$$\dfrac{3}{25} = \dfrac{3 \times 4}{25 \times 4} = \dfrac{12}{\underbrace{100}_{\text{Two zeros}}} = 0.\underbrace{12}_{\text{Two places}}$$

Often it is not possible to multiply the denominator by a whole number to get a power of 10, or it may not be obvious what number to multiply by. These cases will be covered later in the chapter.

EXERCISE 4

Decimal/Fraction Conversions (Part A)

Directions: Write the following in fraction form.

1. 0.029 _____

2. 0.52 _____

3. 0.651 _____

4. 17.001 _____

5. 23.401 _____

Decimal/Fraction Conversions (Part B)

Directions: Write the following in decimal form.

6. $\dfrac{31}{100}$ _____

7. $\dfrac{21}{1000}$ _____

8. $2\dfrac{19}{100}$ _____

9. $7\dfrac{429}{1000}$ _____

10. $9\dfrac{1}{1000}$ _____

11. $\dfrac{3}{4}$ _____

12. $\dfrac{6}{5}$ _____

Answers are on page 780.

Comparing Decimals

It is easy to compare decimals with the same number of digits to the right of the decimal point.

To compare decimals:

• To have the same number of digits to the right of the decimal point of both numbers, add unnecessary 0s wherever required as this does not affect the value of decimal.

• Compare the decimals digit by digit, starting with the tenths digit.

EXAMPLE 1

Is 0.63 or 0.94 larger?

Compare the decimals digit by digit, starting with the tenths digit.

Here, the tenths digits are different.

9 > 6, so 0.94 > 0.63

EXAMPLE 2

Compare 0.45 and 0.453.

Write 0.45 as 0.450. (Add an unnecessary 0 at the end.)

Now, see the thousandths digit in both the decimals.

0 < 3, so 0.450 < 0.453.

Or, 0.45 < 0.453.

Thus, 0.453 (or 453 thousandths) is greater than 0.450 (or 450 thousandths).

EXERCISE 5

Comparing Decimals (Part A)

Directions: Use symbols >, <, or = to compare each pair of decimals.

1. 0.9 _____ 0.5

2. 0.23 _____ 0.12

3. 2.4 _____ 2.06

4. 4.6 _____ 4.60

5. 0.563 _____ 0.53

6. 0.5 _____ 0.213

7. 0.46 _____ 0.5

8. 2.45 _____ 0.89

9. 2.3 _____ 2.333

10. 2.06 _____ 2.095

Answers are on page 780.

Rounding Decimals

When calculating or measuring with decimals, results are often obtained with more digits than are needed. Numbers are then **rounded** to some place value by writing a number as close as possible to the original value but with fewer digits. Rounding is specified to occur to the nearest whole number, nearest tenth, or nearest hundredth, or to some other place value determined by how the number is being used.

The rules for rounding numbers to a decimal place value are:

- Choose the place value to which the decimal is to be rounded.

- If the next digit to the right is equal to or greater than 5, **round up** by increasing the digit in the place you are rounding by 1 and discarding the remaining digits to the right.

- If the next digit to the right is less than 5, **round down** by discarding that digit as well as any remaining digits to the right.

EXAMPLE 1

Round 7.8, 6.28, and 14.567 to whole numbers (nearest one).

Check the digit in the tenths place.

7.8 ≈ 8 (8 in the tenths place is greater than 5, so round up.)

6.28 ≈ 6 (2 in the tenths place is less than 5, so round down.)

14.567 ≈ 15 (The digit in the tenths place is 5, so round up.)

EXAMPLE 2

Round 0.48, 3.73, and 23.457 to the nearest tenth.

Check the digit in the hundredths place.

0.48 ≈ 0.5 (8 in the hundredths place is greater than 5, so round up.)

3.73 ≈ 3.7 (3 in the hundredths place is less than 5, so round down.)

23.457 ≈ 23.5 (The digit in the hundredths place is 5, so round up.)

EXAMPLE 3

Round 0.236, 1.673, and 13.475 to the nearest hundredth.

Check the digit in the thousandths place.

0.236 ≈ 0.24 (6 in the thousandths place is greater than 5, so round up.)

1.673 ≈ 1.67 (3 in the thousandths place is less than 5, so round down.)

13.475 ≈ 13.48 (The digit in the thousandths place is 5, so round up.)

EXERCISE 6

Rounding Decimals (Part A)

Directions: Round each decimal to the nearest whole number.

1. 8.75 cm ≈ _____

2. $22.25 ≈ _____

3. 23.5 mpg ≈ _____

4. $7.85 ≈ _____

5. 21.8 kg ≈ _____

Rounding Decimals (Part B)

Directions: Round each decimal to the nearest tenth.

6. 2.45 cm ≈ _____

7. $13.32 ≈ _____

8. 43.67 km ≈ _____

9. $7.83 ≈ _____

10. 21.845 kg ≈ _____

Rounding Decimals (Part C)

Directions: Round each decimal to the nearest hundredth.

11. 5.673 m ≈ _____

12. $1.675 ≈ _____

13. 8.497 ≈ _____

14. $21.643 ≈ _____

15. 1.665 m ≈ _____

Rounding Decimals (Part D)

Directions: Round each decimal as indicated.

		Nearest Whole Number	Nearest Tenth	Nearest Hundredth
16.	3.437	_____	_____	_____
17.	8.215	_____	_____	_____
18.	4.521	_____	_____	_____

Answers are on page 780.

Estimating with Decimals

Estimating is a good way of checking calculator answers. It also helps on a test to choose the correct answer from a group of answer choices. Estimating is useful when you need a "ballpark figure" and don't need to work out a problem exactly.

To estimate with decimals, round each number before you add, subtract, multiply, or divide.

EXAMPLE 1

Estimate the sum: 7.86 + 2.1.

STEP 1: Round each decimal to the nearest whole number.

$7.89 \approx 8$ $2.1 \approx 2$

STEP 2: Add the whole numbers.

$8 + 2 = 10$

ANSWER

$7.86 + 2.1 \approx 10$

EXAMPLE 2

Estimate the product: 13.8 × 6.4.

STEP 1: Round each decimal to the nearest whole number.

$13.8 \approx 14$ $6.4 \approx 6$

STEP 2: Multiply the whole numbers.

$14 \times 6 = 84$

ANSWER

$13.8 \times 6.4 \approx 84$

EXERCISE 7

Estimating with Decimals (Part A)

Directions: Estimate the answer for each problem.

1.	6.91 + 7.23	**2.**	9.21 − 6.93	**3.**	4.23 × 3.67
4.	5.43 − 2.73	**5.**	9.21 × 3.5	**6.**	1.13 + 4.7

Estimating with Decimals (Part B)

Directions: Choose the best estimate from the given options.

7. What is the approximate cost of 3.9 pounds of flank steak at a price of $2.89 per pound?

    A. $8
    B. $9
    C. $10
    D. $12

8. What is the approximate total cost of four items with prices of $2.31, $5.73, $6.52, and $4.32?

    A. $17
    B. $18
    C. $19
    D. $20

9. If you cut 2.46 meters from a 5.67-meter long ribbon, about how long will the remaining piece be?

    A. 4 m
    B. 3 m
    C. 2 m
    D. 1 m

Answers are on page 780.

Basic Arithmetic Operations with Decimals

The processes for adding, subtracting, multiplying, and dividing decimals are similar to the corresponding operations with whole numbers. The biggest difference is the additional consideration of how to determine the location of the decimal point in the answer.

Adding Decimals

To add decimals:

* First, write the numbers in a column, lining up the decimal points.

* To give the same number of decimal places to all of the numbers, insert unnecessary 0s where needed.

* Add the columns from right to left.

* Place the decimal point in the answer directly below the decimal points of the numbers being added.

EXAMPLE 1

Add: 13.2 + 5.73 + 0.325.

Line up decimal points.

$$\begin{array}{r} 13.2 \\ 5.73 \\ + \ 0.325 \end{array}$$

Write two unnecessary 0s with 13.2 as 13.200.

$$\begin{array}{r} 13.200 \\ 5.73 \\ + \ 0.325 \end{array}$$

Write one unnecessary 0 with 5.73 as 5.730.

$$\begin{array}{r} 13.200 \\ 5.730 \\ + \ 0.325 \end{array}$$

Add each column.

$$\begin{array}{r} 13.200 \\ 5.730 \\ + \ 0.325 \\ \hline 19255 \end{array}$$

Place a decimal point in the answer directly below the decimal points of the numbers being added.

$$\begin{array}{r} 13.200 \\ 5.730 \\ + \ 0.325 \\ \hline 19.255 \end{array}$$

ANSWER

19.255

EXAMPLE 2

Add: 7 + 3.54.

$$\begin{array}{r} 7.00 \\ + \ 3.54 \\ \hline 10.54 \end{array}$$

ANSWER

10.54

Subtracting Decimals

To subtract decimals:

- First, write the numbers in a column and line up the decimal points.
- To give the same number of decimal places to all of the numbers, insert unnecessary 0s where needed.
- Subtract the columns.
- Place the decimal point in the answer directly below the decimal points of the numbers being subtracted.

EXAMPLE 1

Subtract: 8 − 3.62.

Place a decimal point to the right of 8.

$$8 = 8.$$

Line up the decimal points.

$$\begin{array}{r} 8. \\ -\ 3.62 \\ \hline \end{array}$$

Write two unnecessary 0s with 8 as 8.00.

$$\begin{array}{r} 8.00 \\ -\ 3.62 \\ \hline \end{array}$$

Subtract the columns.

$$\begin{array}{r} 8.00 \\ -\ 3.62 \\ \hline 4\ 38 \end{array}$$

Place the decimal point in the answer directly below the decimal points of the numbers being subtracted.

$$\begin{array}{r} 8.00 \\ -\ 3.62 \\ \hline 4.38 \end{array}$$

ANSWER

4.38

EXAMPLE 2

Subtract: 7.42 − 3.2.

$$\begin{array}{r} 7.42 \\ -\ 3.20 \\ \hline 4.22 \end{array}$$

ANSWER

4.22

Multiplying Decimals

To multiply decimals:

- Multiply decimal numbers in the same way as whole numbers. (Temporarily ignore the decimal points.)

- Count the total number of decimal places in each of the numbers being multiplied. This gives you the number of decimal places in the product or answer.

- Place a decimal point so that the number of decimal places in the product is the sum of the number of decimal places in the factors.

EXAMPLE 1

Multiply: 2.86 × 3.

Multiply 286 and 3. There will be 2 + 0 = 2 decimal places in the product.

$$
\begin{array}{r}
2.86 \\
\times\quad 3 \\
\hline
8.58
\end{array}
$$

ANSWER

8.58

EXAMPLE 2

Multiply: 4.16 × 8.3.

Multiply 416 and 83. There will be 2 + 1 = 3 decimal places in the product.

$$
\begin{array}{r}
4.16 \\
\times\quad 8.3 \\
\hline
1248 \\
3328\quad \\
\hline
34.528
\end{array}
$$

ANSWER

34.528

Shortcut: Multiplying by a power of 10

When multiplying a decimal by a power of 10, the digits remain the same, only the position of the decimal point changes. The decimal point should be moved to the right the same number of places as there are zeroes in the power of 10.

EXAMPLE 1

$$
\begin{array}{r}
38.62 \\
\times\quad 10 \\
\hline
386.20, \text{ or } 386.2
\end{array}
$$

EXAMPLE 2

$$
\begin{array}{r}
8.73 \\
\times\quad 100 \\
\hline
873.00, \text{ or } 873
\end{array}
$$

Dividing Decimals

To divide decimals by whole numbers:

* Place the decimal point in the quotient directly above the decimal point in the dividend.

* Divide as you would with whole numbers.

EXAMPLE

Divide 29.82 by 14

$$
\begin{array}{r}
2.13 \\
14\overline{)29.82} \\
\underline{28} \\
18 \\
\underline{14} \\
42 \\
\underline{42} \\
0
\end{array}
$$

ANSWER

2.13

Remember: Place the decimal point in the quotient directly above the one in the dividend.

To divide decimals by decimals:

* Change the divisor into a whole number by moving the decimal point in the divisor to the right. Then move the decimal point in the dividend (the number being divided) an equal number of places to the right. Add unnecessary 0s where needed.

* Divide the numbers as you would with whole numbers.

* Place a decimal point in the quotient (answer) directly above the new decimal point in the dividend.

EXAMPLE

Divide: $1.4\overline{)4.48}$

$$
1.4\overline{)4.48}
$$

$$
\begin{array}{r}
3.2 \\
14.\overline{)44.8} \\
\underline{-42} \\
28 \\
\underline{-28}
\end{array}
$$

STEP 1: Change the divisor (1.4) to a whole number by moving the decimal point one place to the right. Then move the decimal point in the dividend (4.48) one place to the right.

STEP 2: Divide the new dividend 44.8 by the whole number 14.

ANSWER

3.2

Shortcut: Dividing by a Power of 10

When dividing a decimal by a power of 10, the digits remain the same, only the position of the decimal point changes. The decimal point should be moved to the left the same number of places as there are zeroes in the power of 10.

EXAMPLES

1. $34.3 \div 10 = 3.43$ Shift one place to the left.

2. $27.81 \div 100 = 0.2781$ Shift two places to the left.

3. $75.22 \div 1,000 = 0.07522$ Shift three places to the left.

4. $74 \div 10 = 7.4$

5. $5.6 \div 10 = 0.56$

More on Converting Fraction to Decimals

When converting fractions to decimals, it is often difficult or impossible to find a number by which to multiply the denominator so that the new denominator is a power of 10. In this case the fraction can be interpreted as a decimal division, treating the numerator as a decimal and dividing the numerator by the denominator.

EXAMPLE: Convert $\frac{7}{13}$ to a decimal. Round to the nearest hundredth.

To get an answer accurate to the nearest hundredth, the division needs to be carried out to produce the digit in the thousandths place so the rounding can be done correctly. Divide 7.000 by 13.

$$
\begin{array}{r}
0.538 \\
13\overline{)7.000} \\
-65 \\
\hline
50 \\
-39 \\
\hline
110 \\
-104 \\
\hline
6
\end{array}
$$

Because the thousandths digit is 5 or larger, round up to get $\frac{7}{13} \approx 0.54$ to the nearest hundredth.

Basic Arithmetic Operations with Decimals (Part A)

Directions: Add.

1.   0.3
      + 0.5

2.   0.6
      + 0.5

3.   4.2
      + 6.67

4. $0.4
      + $2.73

5. $4.56
      + $3.67

6.   1
      + 4.7

7.   6
      1.2
      + 0.634

8.   5.7
      2.56
      + 0.45

9.   0.23
      7
      + 1.435

10.   0.7
       6.89
       + 4.324

Basic Arithmetic Operations with Decimals (Part B)

Directions: Subtract.

11.   0.9
       − 0.5

12.   6.6
       − 5.5

13.   0.7
       − 0.32

14. $12.4
       − $ 2.73

15. $2.86
       − $1.2

16.   5.784
       − 2.3

17.   4
       − 1.325

18.   7.23
       − 4

19.   1
       − 0.006

20.   0.57
       − 0.3

Basic Arithmetic Operations with Decimals (Part C)

Directions: Multiply.

21.   0.7
       × 0.2

22.   6.6
       × 5

23.   5.4
       × 3

24. $12.4
       × 7

25.   2.45
       × 3.6

26.   5.7
       × 2.3

27.   6.56
       × 0.32

28.   7.23
       × 100

29.   2.48
       × 1000

30.   0.57
       × 10

Basic Arithmetic Operations with Decimals (Part D)

Directions: Divide.

31. $0.04\overline{)24}$ **32.** $2.5\overline{)50}$ **33.** $1.5\overline{)30}$ **34.** $0.12\overline{)0.48}$

35. $2.3\overline{)0.529}$ **36.** $0.02\overline{)1.6}$ **37.** $3\overline{)6.3}$ **38.** $6\overline{)0.612}$

39. $10\overline{)0.842}$ **40.** $100\overline{)49.14}$

Basic Arithmetic Operations with Decimals (Part E)

Directions: Convert to a decimal.

Round to the nearest hundredth.

41. $\dfrac{2}{11} \approx$ _____   **42.** $\dfrac{1}{9} \approx$ _____   **43.** $\dfrac{3}{7} \approx$ _____   **44.** $\dfrac{5}{6} \approx$ _____

Round to the nearest thousandth.

45. $\dfrac{11}{23} \approx$ _____   **46.** $\dfrac{12}{19} \approx$ _____   **47.** $\dfrac{8}{15} \approx$ _____   **48.** $\dfrac{28}{51} \approx$ _____

Answers are on page 780.

EXERCISE 9

Word Problems with Decimals

Directions: Choose the correct answer.

1. Diana's Taffy Shop made 22.2 kilograms of taffy in 2 days. How much taffy, on average, did the shop make per day?

   A. 11.1 kg
   B. 11 kg
   C. 10.3 kg
   D. 10 kg

2. Brenda bought 73 pounds of peanuts and 0.56 pounds of raisins. How many pounds of snacks did she buy in all?

   A. 73.56 lb
   B. 73 lb
   C. 72.34 lb
   D. 72 lb

3. A cafeteria used 91.9 kilograms of beans to make 2 equal batches of chili. What quantity of beans went into each batch?

   A. 44
   B. 45.95
   C. 92.1
   D. 183.8

4. A dump truck is filled with 99.19 pounds of wood chips. It drops off 55.7 pounds at the playground. How many pounds of wood chips are left in the truck?

   A. 16.98
   B. 23.12
   C. 43.49
   D. 154.89

5. Each month, Mimi's family eats 3.5 pounds of granola. How many pounds of granola will Mimi's family eat in 7 months?

   A. 0.5 lb
   B. 4.1 lb
   C. 24.5 lb
   D. 51 lb

6. A scientist collected 3 water samples from local streams. Each sample was the same size, and he collected 1.5 liters of water in all. What was the volume of each water sample?

   A. 5 L
   B. 4.5 L
   C. 1.8 L
   D. 0.5 L

7. Jeanette bought 51.23 ounces of chocolate. Of the total, 0.7 ounces was milk chocolate and the rest was dark chocolate. How much dark chocolate did Jeanette buy?

   A. 50 oz
   B. 50.53 oz
   C. 51.30 oz
   D. 51.93 oz

8. Angie has a set of wooden boards. Each board is 0.8 meters long. If Angie lays 5 boards end to end, how many meters long will the line of boards be?

    A. 1 m

    B. 2 m

    C. 3 m

    D. 4 m

9. Warren bought 8 identical glass paperweights. The paperweights weighed 1.2 pounds in all. What was the weight of each paperweight?

    A. 0.015 lb

    B. 0.15 lb

    C. 1.5 lb

    D. 15 lb

10. A lollipop factory used 42.6 kilograms of sugar to make 2 identical batches of lollipops. How much sugar did the factory put in each batch?

    A. 2.13 kg

    B. 20.13 kg

    C. 21.3 kg

    D. 213 kg

Answers are on page 781.

EXERCISE 10

Decimal Review (Part A)

Directions: Write the place value of the indicated digits in the blanks.

Consider the decimal 9.3712.

1. What is the place value of 1? _____

2. What is the place value of 3? _____

3. What is the place value of 9? _____

Directions: Write each decimal in expanded form.

4. 3.52 _____

5. 9.011 _____

6. 12.201 _____

Decimal Review (Part B)

Directions: Write each decimal number as it is read in words.

7. 0.003 _____

8. 0.7 _____

9. 0.14 _____

10. 0.016 _____

Directions: Write each number as a decimal, using digits.

11. three tenths _____

12. thirty hundredths _____

13. twelve thousandths_____

Decimal Review (Part C)

Directions: Write each decimal in fraction form.

14. 0.19 _____

15. 0.501 _____

16. 0.25 _____

Directions: Write each fraction in decimal form.

17. $\frac{1}{100}$ _____

18. $\frac{11}{1000}$ _____

19. $\frac{303}{100}$ _____

20. $\frac{31}{10}$ _____

Decimal Review (Part D)

Directions: Write >, <, or = to compare each pair of decimals.

21. 2.73 _____ 2.5   **22.** 0.27 _____ 0.7   **23.** 3.2 _____ 2.93

24. 0.5 _____ 0.15   **25.** 0.598 _____ 0.589   **26.** 0.4 _____ 0.40

Decimal Review (Part E)

Directions: Round each decimal as indicated.

	Nearest Whole Number	Nearest Tenth	Nearest Hundredth
27. 14.265	_____	_____	_____
28. 7.124	_____	_____	_____

Decimal Review (Part F)

Directions: Estimate the answer to each problem.

29.	**30.**	**31.**	**32.** $8.4\overline{)121.75}$
16.9	12	4.23	
+ 4.52	− 6.43	× 32	

Decimal Review (Part G)

Directions: Solve each problem by using basic arithmetic operations.

33.	**34.**	**35.**
5	5.07	7.265
4.12	2.5	2.14
+ 0.563	+ 1.645	+ 1.3

36.	**37.**	**38.**
0.94	62.7	8.45
− 0.05	− 12.625	− 5.9

39.	**40.**	**41.**
0.47	16.6	5.04
× 3	× 15	× 7

42. $1.3\overline{)26.52}$　　**43.** $3.4\overline{)74.8}$　　**44.** $0.02\overline{)0.72}$

Answers are on page 781.

## CHAPTER 4

Integers

Understanding Integers

In Chapters 1–3, you learned about whole numbers, fractions, and decimals; the operations that can be performed on them; and various ways in which they may be represented. In particular, you saw that they may be represented by points on a line, called the number line. The convention for a number line is that larger numbers are found farther to the right on the line, so that the number 0 acts as an endpoint. In this chapter you will learn that the number line can be extended to the left of 0 with the invention of negative numbers.

Definitions

The whole numbers are represented on the number line as a series of equally spaced points to the right of a point labeled "0." Values can also be assigned to points to the left of 0. To distinguish these from numbers to the right of zero, numbers to the left of zero are called **negative numbers**.

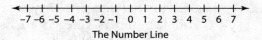
The Number Line

Negative numbers are written with a minus sign preceding the number to indicate that they lie on the left side of 0, thus: −1, −2, −3, and so on. The negative sign is considered part of a negative number. When talking about signed numbers, the numbers to the right of 0 are called **positive numbers**, and can be written +1, +2, +3, . . .; however, it is much more common to write positive numbers without a plus sign. This means that a number that is written without a sign is understood to be positive. All numbers on the number line except zero have a sign, either positive or negative. The only number on the number line that does not have a sign is 0.

Opposites are numbers that are the same distance from 0 but on opposite sides of 0. Opposites are also designated by a minus sign, so the opposite of 3 is written −3. This looks exactly like the number −3, that is, the number that is 3 units to the left of 0. A difference can be seen when writing the opposite of a negative number, for example, the opposite of −6 is written −(−6). This can be simplified to 6, or just 6. The opposite of a positive number is a negative number the same distance from 0, and the opposite of a negative number is a positive number the same distance from 0. The opposite of 0 is 0: −0 = 0.

Note: the symbol − thus has three distinct meanings depending on its use:

1. It can be a subtraction symbol, as in $6 - 4$.

2. It can be a negative sign, indicating a number that lies to the left of 0, as in -4.

3. It can indicate the opposite, as in $-(-4)$.

The meaning of − will nearly always be clear from how it is used. The most common source of confusion is when indicating the opposite of a positive number, as in "the opposite of four," which would be written -4. If a person interpreted -4 as meaning "negative four" the consequences would be unimportant; since $-4 = -4$ (to be read "the opposite of four is negative four"). Likewise, the symbol + has two meanings: (1) addition and (2) positive. Again, the intended meaning should be clear from the particular use of the symbol.

EXAMPLE 1

Find the opposite of each number: 2, 4, −7, +11, −3, −9.

To find the opposites, change the sign of each number: −2, −4, 7, −11, 3, 9.

Integers include the whole numbers, 0, 1, 2, 3, . . ., and their opposites, $-1, -2, -3$, and so on. The numbers 2.5, $\frac{1}{3}$, and $2\frac{1}{2}$ are examples of numbers that are *not* integers. They are neither whole numbers nor the opposites of whole numbers. Integers are used every day for things like counting the days left until rent is due, calculating your checkbook balance, determining the elevation of towns and cities, or counting your age. Including negative integers lets you talk about profit and loss, a negative or overdrawn bank balance like −$10, or places below sea level like Death Valley, California (elevation −282 feet).

EXAMPLE 2

Which of the following numbers are integers? 13, 21, −3.5, −43, 43, 0, $-3\frac{3}{4}$, 7.2

The integers are: 13, 21, −43, 43, 0. The other numbers are either decimals or fractions and are not integers. Note that 0 is also an integer.

EXERCISE 1

Definitions (Part A)

Directions: Circle any number in each sequence that is NOT an integer.

1. 2, 7.25, 4, 30, 3, −5, 6   **2.** 4, 8, $7\frac{1}{2}$, $\frac{4}{3}$, −3.5, 1, −9   **3.** 1, 3, 4, −3, 0

Definitions (Part B)

Directions: Identify which of the following pairs are opposite integers.

4. 7, −7   **5.** 14, −12   **6.** −3, 3   **7.** −11.2, 11.2   **8.** $-\dfrac{1}{2}, \dfrac{1}{2}$

Answers are on page 782.

Integers and the Number Line

Integers can be plotted as points on the number line at places determined by their values.

EXAMPLE 1

Plot the integers 1, 4, −5, and −3 on the number line.

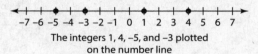

The integers 1, 4, −5, and −3 plotted
on the number line

EXAMPLE 2

Plot the integers 1, 4, −5, and −3 as solid dots on the number line and their opposites as open circles. Connect each pair.

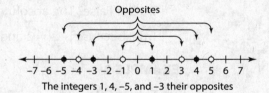

The integers 1, 4, −5, and −3 their opposites

EXERCISE 2

Integers and the Number Line

Directions: Plot each integer listed on a number line with a dot. Plot their opposites with open circles.

1. 1, 4, 7

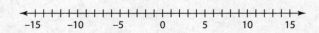

2. −1, −6, 3, 10

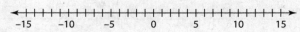

3. $7, 3.25, 5, -8, 1\frac{1}{4}$

Answers are on page 782.

Absolute Value

The rules for adding, subtracting, multiplying, and dividing integers and signed numbers are stated in terms of the absolute value of the numbers. The **absolute value** of a number is its distance from 0. Vertical bars placed on either side of a number indicate the absolute value of the number. Because any distance is measured with a positive number, the absolute value of a number is positive, so $|6| = 6$ and $|-6| = 6$. Also, $|0| = 0$.

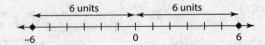

Notice that the distance from each number to 0 is the same so that both −6 and 6 have the same absolute value, that is, 6.

EXAMPLE 1

True or False? The absolute values of 2 and −2 are the same.

True, because $|-2| = 2$ and $|2| = 2$.

EXAMPLE 2

True or False? $|5|, |-5|, -|5|$, and $-|-5|$ are all the same.

False, because $|5| = |-5| = 5$ but $-|5| = -|-5| = -5$. The minus sign outside the absolute value bars means "the opposite of" and is not affected by the absolute value.

EXERCISE 3

Absolute Value

Directions: Simplify the following.

1. $|7|$ **2.** $|-9|$ **3.** $-|4|$ **4.** $-|8|$ **5.** $-|-0|$

Answers are on page 782.

Ordering Integers

Integers are usually listed from the smallest to largest, that is, from left to right on the number line. Given an integer on the number line, anything to its right is larger (or greater) and any integer to its left is smaller (or less). That means 0 is greater than any negative number and that negative 1 (−1) is greater than negative 10 (−10).

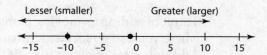

It may help you to think of negative integers as owing money. Which person is better off financially? The person owing one dollar (−$1), or someone owing someone 10 dollars (−$10)? The person owing $1 is better off because he or she is closer to paying off the debt.

Another way is to think of negative integers as heights above (+) or below (−) sea level. The higher the elevation, the "bigger" the integer. Using this idea, −15 is less than −1 because it is deeper under water and farther down in the ocean.

EXERCISE 4

Ordering Integers

Directions: Place the integers in order from the least to greatest.

  1. −11, 12, 3, −3, −5, −4, −2   **2.** −4, −5.2, −1, 1, 5, 0

  3. 6, −3, 1, 5, 7, −4, −1, 3, −6   **4.** $1, -2\frac{1}{2}, 5, 4, 0, 3, 2$

Directions: Place the correct symbol, <, >, or =, between the numbers.

  5. −1 _____ 0   **6.** −2 _____ 6   **7.** 2 _____ −6   **8.** −2 _____ −6

  9. −7 _____ 7   **10.** $|-3|$ _____ −2   **11.** 5 _____ −5   **12.** $|-11|$ _____ $|11|$

Directions: Decide which is largest.

  13. $|7|, |-7|, |-8|$ **14.** $|-7|, |-6|, |-5|$ **15.** $|7|, |-7|, 8$

  16. $|-7|, |7|, 7$ **17.** $|0|, |-1|, |-3|$

Answers are on page 782.

Operations with Integers

The following sections describe how to add, subtract, multiply, and divide integers, including both positive and negative numbers.

Adding Integers

Think of adding as moving along the number line, much like a board game where you can go forward or backward. The first number is a starting point. Addition is taking your turn. If the number being added is positive, move that many spaces to the right (in the positive direction). If the number being added is negative, move that many spaces to the left (in the negative direction).

EXAMPLE 1

What is the sum of 4 and 5? [4 + 5 = ?]

Start at 4 and move 5 places right, ending up at 9. This means 4 + 5 = 9.

EXAMPLE 2

What is the sum of 4 and −5? [4 + (−5) = ?]

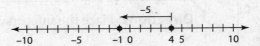

Again, start at 4, but now move 5 places *left*, ending up at −1. This means that 4 + (−5) = −1. This looks more like subtraction than addition.

EXAMPLE 3

What is the sum of −4 and 5? [(−4) + 5 = ?]

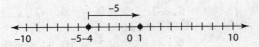

Start at −4 and move 5 spaces right, ending up at 1. So (−4) + 5 = 1. Again, this looks like subtraction.

EXAMPLE 4

What is the sum of −4 and −5? [(−4) + (−5) = ?]

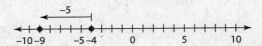

Start at −4 and move 5 spaces left, ending up at −9. So (−4) + (−5) = −9. This looks like addition again.

Collect the results for each of the four previous examples:

$$4+5=9 \qquad 4+(-5)=-1 \qquad (-4)+5=1 \qquad (-4)+(-5)=-9$$

Consider when the two numbers were added or subtracted and the signs of the numbers in each case. When the numbers had the same sign, the sum was found by adding, and when the signs were different, the sum was found by subtracting. All this leads up to the rules for addition.

Rules for Addition of Signed Numbers

If the two numbers have the same sign, add their absolute values and keep the sign, as in $4+5=9$ and $-4+(-5)=-9$. If two numbers have different signs, subtract their absolute values and keep the sign of the number whose absolute value is greater, as in $(-4)+5=1$ and $4+(-5)=-1$.

EXAMPLE 1

Add: $14+(-52)$.

Because $|-52|>|+14|$, the answer will be negative. The signs are different, so subtract the absolute values. $|-52|=52$ and $|14|=14$, and $52-14=38$, so $14+(-52)=-38$.

EXAMPLE 2

Add: $-36+89$.

Because $|+89|>|-36|$, the answer will be positive. The signs are different, so subtract the absolute values. $|89|=89$ and $|-36|=36$, and $89-36=53$, so $-36+89=53$.

EXAMPLE 3

Add: $-24+(-16)$.

The numbers have the same sign, so there is no need to compare their absolute values. The answer will have the same sign as the numbers in the addition problem; it will be negative. Add the absolute values and put a negative sign in front of the sum: $-24+(-16)=-40$.

Adding Several Signed Numbers

When adding several numbers with signs, some of which are positive and some are negative, a handy shortcut can be used. Add all of the positive numbers to get a positive subtotal, add all of the negative numbers to get a negative subtotal, and then add the two subtotals.

EXAMPLE

Add: $4+(-6)+(-2)+9+3+(-7)+5+(-8)$.

Add all the positive numbers: $4+9+3+5=21$.

Add all the negative numbers: $(-6)+(-2)+(-7)+(-8)=-23$.

Add the subtotals by subtracting their absolute values: $23 - 21 = 2$.

Because $|-23| > |+21|$, the final result will be negative:
$4 + (-6) + (-2) + 9 + 3 + (-7) + 5 + (-8) = -2$.

EXERCISE 5

Adding Integers

Directions: Add.

1. $3 + 7$ **2.** $(-4) + 5$ **3.** $-9 + 8$ **4.** $(-9) + (-5)$

5. $(-7) + (-4) + 15$ **6.** $15 + (-2) + 7 + (-4)$ **7.** $7 + 9 + 14 + (-2) + (-9)$

8. $(-3) + (-4) + (-9) + (-12)$ **9.** $(-1) + (-5) + 8 + (-6) + 2$

10. $4 + (-9) + 3 + (-5) + 10$ **11.** $(-8) + 5 + 4 + (-12) + (-3) + 19$

12. $(-7) + 31 + (-2) + (-18) + 6 + (-23) + 5 + 14$

Answers are on page 782.

Subtracting Integers

Subtraction is like addition *except* the subtraction sign is an instruction to *move in the opposite direction* on the number line.

EXAMPLE 1

What is $4 - 2$?

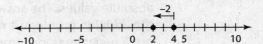

If this were adding, you would start on 4 and move 2 places right. But when subtracting, you *move in the opposite direction*. Start at 4 and move 2 spaces *left*, landing on 2, so $4 - 2 = 2$.

EXAMPLE 2

What is $3 - 7$?

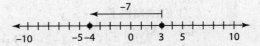

Starting at 3, move 7 spaces left (doing the opposite) and arrive at –4.
$3 - 7 = -4$.

EXAMPLE 3

What is $4 - (-4)$?

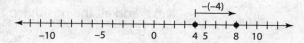

Normally, when adding –4 you would move left. But the subtraction sign tells you to *move in the opposite direction*, to the right. So $4 - (-4) = 8$.

Moving along the number line when adding or subtracting is very much the same process. When using only positive numbers, the direction of movement is a matter of whether the operation is addition or subtraction, but with signed numbers, the direction also has to do with the sign of the number. Also, drawing a number line every time subtraction is used is tedious. Some simplification is called for. Examples like those above lead to the **definition of subtraction**: $a - b = a + (-b)$. This says that subtraction can be changed to addition of the opposite of the subtrahend (the number that follows the subtraction sign), and then the rules for addition are used. Using this definition on the previous examples should lead to the same results.

EXAMPLE 1 (REVISITED)

What is $4 - 2$?

Using the definition of subtraction by changing the sign of the subtrahend and adding, $4 - 2 = 4 + (-2) = 2$, where absolute values were subtracted because the numbers being added had different signs.

EXAMPLE 2 (REVISITED)

What is $3 - 7$?

Changing the sign and adding, $3 - 7 = 3 + (-7) = -4$, where the number with the larger absolute value was negative and so the answer was negative.

EXAMPLE 3 (REVISITED)

What is $4 - (-4)$?

$$4 - (-4) = 4 + (+4) = 4 + 4 = 8$$

Adding and Subtracting Several Signed Numbers

When there are several signed numbers to be combined by adding and subtracting, it is very efficient to change every subtraction to addition and change the sign of each number that followed a subtraction sign, and then use the rules for adding several signed numbers.

EXAMPLE

Evaluate $7 - 9 - (-5) + (-3) - 7 + 5 - (-2) + (-4)$.

Changing the signs and adding gives $7 + (-9) + (+5) + (-3) + (-7) + 5 + (+2) + (-4)$.

Notice how additions are not changed, but every subtraction is changed to addition and the number following the subtraction changes its sign.

Next, add all the positive numbers and add all the negative numbers: $19 + (-23)$.

Finally subtract the absolute values and use the sign of the number that had the largest absolute value to get -4.

EXERCISE 6

Subtracting Integers

Directions: Subtract.

1. $6 - 2$ **2.** $6 - (-2)$ **3.** $2 - 6$ **4.** $2 - (-6)$

5. $-6 - 2$ **6.** $-6 - (-2)$ **7.** $-2 - 6$ **8.** $-2 - (-6)$

9. $7 - 11$ **10.** $-4 - (-7)$ **11.** $-3 - 9$ **12.** $7 - (-9)$

13. $-6 - 5 - (-4) + (-3) - 5 - (-8) + 2$ **14.** $8 - 3 + (-7) - 1 + (-6) - (-5) - 2$

15. $2 - (-6) - 5 + (-2) - (-3) + 9 - (-4)$ **16.** $-5 - 6 + (-7) - 8 + (-3) - 4 - (-6)$

Answers are on page 782.

Multiplying integers

Multiplication is repeated addition, where the second factor counts the number of times the first factor shows up in a repeated addition problem, so that, for example, $5 \times 4 = 5 + 5 + 5 + 5 = 20$.

EXAMPLE 1

What is 7 multiplied by 3?

$$7 \times 3 = 7 + 7 + 7 = 21$$

EXAMPLE 2

What is -7×4?

$$-7 \times 4 = (-7) + (-7) + (-7) + (-7) = -28$$

EXAMPLE 3

What is $4 \times (-7)$?

Here the second factor can't count how many times the first factor shows up in a repeated addition problem because that second factor is a negative number. Because multiplication is commutative, the order of the numbers is unimportant ($2 \times 5 = 5 \times 2$). When you multiply a negative and a positive, you can put the negative integer first. If you have $4 \times (-7)$ you can rewrite it -7×4, which is -28.

In a similar fashion, multiplying a positive and a negative, or a negative and a positive, always leads to a negative answer.

EXAMPLE 4

What is $(-7) \times (-4)$?

If there were just one negative, the answer would be negative. Neither factor can count how many numbers are being added. But the presence of the second negative number flips the answer to *the opposite*, making it positive. $(-7) \times (-4) = 28$.

Another way to understand signs when multiplying is consult an expert, Jack the Mathematical Bunny. When asked to multiply, Jack goes to zero. He looks at the problem and uses the first number to decide which way to face. Very sensibly, if the number is positive, Jack faces right; if it's a negative number, Jack faces left.

Jack then uses the second number to decide whether he should hop forward (positive) or backward (negative).

To multiply 3×4, Jack starts at zero, faces right, and makes 4 jumps forward of 3 spaces each and lands on 12.

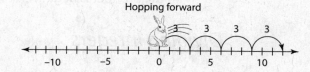

To multiply $3 \times (-4)$, Jack faces right but hops *backward* (to the left) 4 jumps ending up on -12.

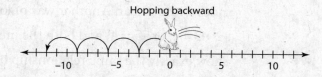

To multiply -3×4, Jack faces left and hops those 4 jumps *forward* also ending up on -12.

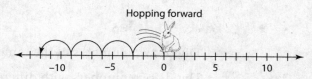

To multiply $-3 \times (-4)$, Jack faces left but jumps *backward* to end up on +12.

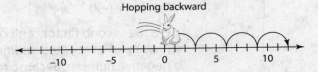

Hopping backward

Great work, Jack!

Multiplication Rules

- Multiplying two numbers with the same sign always gives a positive answer.

- Multiplying two numbers with different signs always gives a negative answer.

Multiplying Several Signed Numbers

When multiplying several numbers together where some are negative and some are positive, determine the sign of the final product by counting how many negative signs there are. Because two negative numbers have a positive product and since positive signs are not usually written, negative signs can be considered to disappear a pair at a time. If there is an odd number of signs, the final product will be negative because there will be one negative sign left behind after all the others disappear a pair at a time. If there is an even number of negative signs, the final product will be positive because there will not be any signs left over after they disappear a pair at a time.

EXAMPLE

$(-1) \times 4 \times (-2) \times (-5) \times 3 \times (-1)$ has an even number of negative signs so the product is positive: $(-1) \times 4 \times (-2) \times (-5) \times 3 \times (-1) = +120$.
$(-1) \times 4 \times (-2) \times (-5) \times 3 \times (-1) \times (-3)$ has an odd number of negative signs so the product is negative: $(-1) \times 4 \times (-2) \times (-5) \times 3 \times (-1) \times (-3) = -360$.

Dividing Integers

The same rules for multiplication apply to division because any division can be turned into multiplication by using the reciprocal of the divisor. That is, because $4 \div 2$ is the same as $\frac{4}{1} \times \frac{1}{2}$, you can use the multiplication rules without fear. Another way of looking at this is that if $3 \times 4 = 12$, then $12 \div 3 = 4$, or $\frac{12}{3} = 4$, and both the multiplication and division statements show exactly the same relationship between the numbers, 3, 4, and 12.

Then, because $-3 \times 4 = -12$, it must also be true that $-12 \div (-3) = 4$; and because $-3 \times (-4) = 12$, it must also be true that $12 \div (-3) = -4$; and lastly because $3 \times (-4) = -12$, it must also be true that $-12 \div 3 = -4$.

Division Rules

- Divide two numbers of the same sign and the answer is positive.

- Divide two numbers with different signs and the answer is negative.

EXERCISE 7

Multiplying and Dividing Integers

Directions: Find the products and quotients, as indicated.

1. $7 \times (-4)$ **2.** $(-4) \times 3$ **3.** $(-2) \times (-5)$ **4.** $-5 \times (-3)$

5. $(-9) \div (-3)$ **6.** $-20 \div 4$ **7.** $32 \div (-8)$ **8.** $(-27) \div 9$

9. $6 \times (-3) \times (-5) \times 3 \times (-1) \times (-2)$ **10.** $(-2) \times 3 \times (-1) \times 5 \times (-3)$

Answers are on page 782.

Integers and Exponents

Raising a number to a power is repeated multiplication. For example, $3^5 = 3 \cdot 3 \cdot 3 \cdot 3 \cdot 3$. As a result, raising integers to powers follows the rules of multiplication. Raising positive integers to powers is no problem—the answer is always positive. In raising negative integers to powers you need to be careful.

Raising a Negative Integer to a Power

Mathematicians agree that if you want to include the sign in raising a negative integer to some power, you must use parentheses. If there are no parentheses, raise the number to the power *without the sign* and the answer stays negative. So, $-3^2 = -9$. If you actually wish to square -3 you need to include the sign in parentheses like this: $(-3)^2 = (-3)(-3) = 9$. If the sign is included in the calculation, and you raise the integer to an even power, the answer will be positive. There will be pairs of integers multiplying each other and any negative signs will disappear. However, if you raise it to an odd power, there will be an unmatched negative integer that will make the answer negative.

Look at $(-5)^4 = (-5) \times (-5) \times (-5) \times (-5) = 25 \times 25 = 625$. Notice how each pair of negative integers gives a positive answer that eliminates all the negative signs.

In contrast, look at $(-5)^3 = (-5) \times (-5) \times (-5) = 25 \times (-5) = -125$. The first pair of numbers multiplies out to a positive number, *but* that unpaired third factor makes the whole answer negative.

Rules of Exponents

If the sign is included and the power is even, the answer is positive. If the sign is included and the power is odd, the answer is negative whenever the original integer is negative.

EXAMPLES

What is the sign of the following?

1. 2^3 : Positive. Even though the power is odd, positive numbers always have positive values when raised to a power.

2. -2^4 : Negative. Even though the power is even, the lack of parentheses tells you to raise the number to the power and then add the negative sign.

3. $(-2)^4$: Positive. Because you have the parentheses, you are actually raising a negative number to an even power. The answer is positive.

EXERCISE 8

Integers and Exponents

Directions: For each integer raised to a power, give the sign of the answer.

1. -4^4 2. $(-7)^2$ 3. 3^3

4. $(-3)^5$ 5. -3^4 6. $-(-3^4)$

Answers are on page 783.

Distance on the Number Line

The distance between points on the number line is always positive. To calculate the distance between two points, use absolute value. Given two points on the number line, a and b, the distance (d) between them is given by:

$$d = |a - b|$$

This works well, but you must pay attention to the signs of the numbers.

EXAMPLE 1

What is the distance between 1 and 7 on the number line?

Let $a = 1$ and $b = 7$. Then $d = |1 - 7| = |1 + (-7)| = |-6| = 6$, as you can see below.

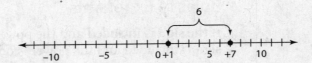

EXAMPLE 2

What is the distance from −4 to 7 on the number line?

Let $a = -4$ and $b = 7$. Now $d = \left|-4-7\right| = \left|-4+(-7)\right| = \left|-11\right| = 11$. Consulting the number line you see that is true.

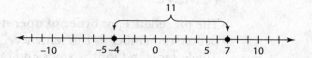

EXAMPLE 3

What is the distance on the number line between −11 and −6?

Letting $a = -11$ and $b = -6$, carefully substitute in the formula to get $d = \left|-11-(-6)\right| = \left|-11+6\right| = \left|-5\right| = 5$. Notice how the double negative affects the answer. This is why you always need to be vigilant with the signs. Again you can see this is correct by looking at the number line.

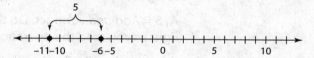

EXERCISE 9

Distance on the Number Line

Directions: Identify which pair of points is farther apart on the number line.

1. 7 and 4 *or* 5 and 7   2. −5 and 5 *or* −3 and 3

3. 4 and −9 *or* 4 and 9 *or* −4 and −9   4. 8 and −9 *or* 7 and −6 *or* −14 and −2

5. −7 and 0 *or* 9 and 0 *or* 0 and −7

Answers are on page 783.

Order of Operations

In working with integers, or actually any numbers, there is a possible serious problem: "Which operations do I do first?" Take the problem $3 \times 2 + 7$. Do you add and then multiply or multiply and then add? The answers are different.

Multiply first	**Add first**
$3 \times 2 + 7 = 6 + 7 = 13$	$3 \times 2 + 7 = 3 \times 9 = 27$

From the start of modern algebra, mathematicians have agreed that multiplication and division hold precedence over (i.e., should be done before) addition and subtraction. Exponentiation, raising numbers to a power or taking the root, holds precedence over multiplication.

PEMDAS

The precedence, or **order of operations** is given by PEMDAS, which many people remember as the sentence, "Please Excuse **My Dear Aunt Sally.**" The letter stand for the steps and operations that should be performed in a complex expression.

Listing these steps vertically,

P = Parentheses: Work within any parentheses first. Follow the order of operations within the parentheses.

E = Exponents: Raise numbers to powers or take roots.

M, D = Multiply *and* Divide: Do these in the same pass in order from left to right as you read the operations.

A, S = Add *and* Subtract: Do these in the same pass in order from left to right as you read the operations.

Looking back at $3 \times 2 + 7$ and applying PEMDAS, the answer is definitely 13.

EXAMPLE 1

Evaluate $(7+2) - 3 \times 2 - 9 \times 2 + 3$.

Following the order of operations,	$(7+2) - 3 \times 2 - 9 \times 2 + 3$
work within the parentheses first to get:	$9 - 3 \times 2 - 9 \times 2 + 3$
Next, multiply from left to right and get:	$9 - 6 - 9 \times 2 + 3$
Followed by:	$9 - 6 - 18 + 3$
Adding and subtracting in order from left to right:	$9 + (-6) + (-18) + 3$
(by changing the signs and adding)	$12 + (-24)$
you get the answer:	-12

EXAMPLE 2

Evaluate $3(1 + 3 \times 2)^2 - (-7 \times 3)$.

Following the order of operations, work within the parentheses to get: $3(1+6)^2 - (-21)$ then:	$3(7)^2 - (-21)$
Then, compute with the exponent to get:	$3(49) - (-21)$
Follow up by multiplying:	$147 - (-21)$
Change the signs and add to get:	$147 + 21 = 168$

Order of Operations

Directions: Evaluate.

1. $6(4+2+7\times3)$ **2.** $6+3-5\times6\div3$

3. $3^2+15\div5\times4+2^3$ **4.** $7(2^3+7)^2+11$

Answers are on page 783.

Rule Review

Here is a recap of the rules governing operations with integers.

Rules of Integer Addition

* If the two integers have the same sign, add and keep the sign.
* If two integers have different signs, subtract and keep the sign of the number whose absolute value is greater.

Rules of Integer Subtraction

* Subtraction follows the rules for addition after using the definition of subtraction: $a-b=a+(-b)$.

Multiplication Rules

* Multiply two numbers with the same sign and the answer is positive.
* Multiply two numbers with different signs and the answer is negative.

Division Rules

* Divide two numbers with the same sign and the answer is positive.
* Divide two numbers with different signs and the answer is negative.

Rules of Exponents

* A negative number raised to an odd power is negative.
* A negative number raised to an even power is positive.

Distance on the Number Line

* The distance (d) between two points a and b is always positive and is: $d=|a-b|$.

## CHAPTER 5

Expressions and Polynomials

In this chapter, you will learn about polynomial expressions. Polynomials are fundamental to using mathematics beyond arithmetic. You will also see other types of expressions in contrast.

Expressions

Expressions can be either numeric or algebraic, as illustrated in the following sections.

Numerical Expressions

A **numerical expression** is two or more numbers combined using the operations of addition (+), subtraction (−), multiplication (× or ·), division (÷ or /), and/or exponents and roots.

These are all numerical expressions: $2+3$, 2×3, $42\div 3$, $24-3$, $\dfrac{2\times 4+3}{4+5}$, $\sqrt{3^2+4^2}$, and 4^2.

$\sqrt{3^2+4^2}$ is an example of a **radical expression** because it includes the radical sign indicating the square root of the expression under the sign.

$\dfrac{2\times 4+3}{4+5}$ is an example of a **rational expression** because it is in the form of a ratio or fraction representing the quotient of two expressions.

Evaluate or simplify a numerical expression by performing the indicated operations. Always follow the order of operations:

- First evaluate any expression inside grouping symbols.

- Grouping symbols include parentheses, the radical symbol, and the numerator and denominator of rational expressions.

- Evaluate exponents, then multiply and divide, and then add and subtract, in order, from left to right.

EXAMPLE

Evaluate the expression: $\dfrac{3+\sqrt{3^2+4^2}}{2}$.

SOLUTION

Inside the radical, evaluate the exponents. $\dfrac{3+\sqrt{9+16}}{2}$

Inside the radical, add. $\dfrac{3+\sqrt{25}}{2}$

Evaluate the square root. $\dfrac{3+5}{2}$

Add. $\dfrac{8}{2}$

Divide. 4

EXERCISE 1

Evaluating Numerical Expressions

Directions: Evaluate each numerical expression.

1. $2+3-4\cdot5\div4$ _____

2. $2\div2\div2$ _____

3. $2+3\times4+5$ _____

4. $\sqrt{5^2+12^2}$ _____

5. $\dfrac{6+5}{6-5}$ _____

6. $2+\dfrac{8-4\times5}{6}$ _____

7. $2+3-\dfrac{4\cdot5}{-4}$ _____

8. $\sqrt{8+4-3\cdot2-2}$ _____

9. $\dfrac{9}{\sqrt{5^2-4^2}}$ _____

10. $1+2-3+4-5+6$ _____

Answers are on page 783.

Algebraic Expressions

An **algebraic expression** is like a numerical expression except it includes one or more variables.

A **variable** is a letter used to represent an unknown or unspecified quantity. Any letter can be used to represent a variable.

As an example, if a worker is paid \$12 per hour, the worker's gross earnings after working x hours is given by the algebraic expression $12x$. The variable x represents the number of hours worked. In this algebraic expression, the number 12 is called the coefficient of x. A **coefficient** is a numeral that a variable is multiplied by. When no coefficient is shown in front of a variable, the coefficient is "1," that is, $x = 1x$. Numerals in algebraic expressions are also called **constants**.

To **evaluate an algebraic expression**, replace each variable with a number and then evaluate the resulting numerical expression.

EXAMPLE 1

Determine a worker's pay for 1 hour, 1 day, 2 days, 1 week, and 1 year by evaluating the algebraic expression $12x$ for $x = 1, 8, 16, 40,$ and 2,000.

SOLUTION

Replace the variable x with its value and evaluate the numerical expression.

$12(1) = 12$

$12(8) = 96$

$12(16) = 192$

$12(40) = 480$

$12(2,000) = 24,000$

If you neglect air resistance, the number of feet that a freely falling object falls is given by the expression $16t^2$. The variable t represents the number of seconds after the object is released. The coefficient of t^2 is 16. The number 2 in the expression is called an exponent. The **exponent** of 2 indicates that the **base** t is used as a factor in the expression two times. Write t^2 instead of writing $t \times t$. The expression $16t^2$ is read as "16 t squared" or "16 t to the second power." Similarly, x^3 is equal to $x \times x \times x$ and is read as "x cubed" or "x to the third power."

Note that for any value of x, $x^1 = x$. Later you will see that as long as $x \neq 0$, $x^0 = 1$.

EXAMPLE 2

Determine how far, in feet, a freely falling object falls after 0, 1, 2, 3, and 4 seconds by evaluating the algebraic expression $16t^2$ for $x = 0, 1, 2, 3,$ and 4 seconds.

SOLUTION

$16 \cdot 0^2 = 16 \cdot 0 = 0 \text{ ft}$

$16 \cdot 1^2 = 16 \cdot 1 = 16 \text{ ft}$

$16 \cdot 2^2 = 16 \cdot 4 = 64 \text{ ft}$

$16 \cdot 3^2 = 16 \cdot 9 = 144 \text{ ft}$

$16 \cdot 4^2 = 16 \cdot 16 = 256 \text{ ft}$

Evaluating Algebraic Expressions

Directions: Evaluate each expression for the indicated value of the variable.

1. $(2x + 3)(x + 4)$ for $x = 4$ _____

2. $\dfrac{2x + 6}{x - 3}$ for $x = 5$ _____

3. $\dfrac{3x + 4x + 5}{10}$ for $x = 5$ _____

4. $\sqrt{x^2 - 6^2}$ for $x = 10$ _____

5. $\dfrac{8 + x}{4 - x}$ for $x = 2$ _____

6. $20 - \dfrac{26 - x}{6}$ for $x = 2$ _____

7. $3.14r^2$ for $r = 7$ _____

8. $\dfrac{4}{3}(3.14)r^3$ for $r = 5$ _____

9. $b^2 - 4ac$ for $a = 1$, $b = 2$, and $c = 9$ _____

10. $x(2x + 1)(x + 12)$ for $x = 22$ _____

Answers are on page 783.

Writing Expressions

Often the first step in solving a real-world math problem is translating the words in the problem into an algebraic expression. Key words can help you write the algebraic expression.

Word Expression	Algebraic Expression
Five *more than* a number or a number plus 5	$x + 5$
10 *times* a number	$10x$
A number *divided by* 3 or one-third of a number	$x \div 3$ or $\dfrac{x}{3}$
Six *less than* a number or a number minus 6	$x - 6$
Twice as many or *two times* as many	$2x$
Half as many as a number	$x \div 2$ or $\dfrac{x}{2}$
An amount *increased by* one-tenth	$x + (0.10)x$

EXAMPLE 1

The volume of a rectangular box is given by the product of its length, width, and height. Write an expression for the volume of a box whose length is 6 feet, width is half of the length, and height is 4 feet less than the length. Evaluate the expression.

SOLUTION

If *l*, *w*, and *h* represent length, width, and height, respectively, the algebraic expression for the product is:

$$V = lwh$$

$l = 6$ ft; $w = 6$ ft $\div$ 2; $h = 6$ ft $- 4$ft; so $\quad V = (6$ ft$)(6$ ft $\div 2)(6$ ft $- 4$ ft$)$

Evaluate inside parentheses. $\quad V = (6$ ft$)(3$ ft$)(2$ ft$)$

Multiply. $\quad V = 36$ ft^3

EXAMPLE 2

In 2014 the federal income tax for a single taxpayer whose taxable income is more than $36,000 but less than $89,350 is $5,081.25 plus one-quarter of the amount by which the taxable income exceeds $36,000. Write an expression for the amount of federal income tax owed by a single person whose taxable income is $50,000. Evaluate the expression.

SOLUTION

You need to translate the expression "$5,081.25 plus one-quarter of the amount by which the taxable income exceeds $36,000" into a numerical expression and then evaluate that expression.

The amount by which income exceeds $36,000:
$\quad \$50,000 - \$36,000$

One-quarter of the amount by which income exceeds $36,000:
$\quad \dfrac{1}{4}(\$50,000 - \$36,000)$

$5,081.25 plus one-quarter of the amount by which income exceeds $36,000:
$\quad \$5,081.25 + \dfrac{1}{4}(\$50,000 - \$36,000)$

Evaluate; first subtract.
$\quad \$5,081.25 + \dfrac{1}{4}(\$14,000)$

Divide by 4.
$\quad \$5,081.25 + \$3,500$

Add.
$\quad \$8,581.25$

Interpreting Expressions in Words

Given an algebraic expression, you also need to be able to translate the expression into words.

EXAMPLE

If *p* is Paul's age and $2p - 10$ represents Paul's dad's age, describe Paul's dad's age in words.

SOLUTION

If p is Paul's age, then $2p$ means "two times Paul's age" or "twice Paul's age." -10 can mean "10 years less than." In words you can say, "Paul's dad is 10 years less than twice Paul's age."

EXERCISE 3

Writing Expressions (Part A)

Directions: Write an expression that represents each situation.

1. You and three friends split the cost of a $10 bucket of fried chicken. Write and evaluate an expression for each friend's share. _____

2. A truck rents for $30 per day plus $0.28 per mile. Write an algebraic expression for the cost of a two-day rental if you drive a total of d miles.
   _____

3. The area of a rectangle is the product of the length and width. If the length is l, write an expression for the area of a rectangle whose width, w, is half its length. _____

4. A salesperson receives a weekly salary of $200 and a commission on sales of 0.03 times her weekly sales total. Write an expression for her total pay if her sales total is s dollars. _____

5. Today Robin's sister is 4 years old. Next year Robin will be twice as old as his sister. Write an expression for Robin's age today. _____

6. This morning the temperature was 45°F. By noon the temperature had increased by $t°$ and by 6 PM the temperature had dropped by half this amount. Write an expression for the temperature at 6 PM.
   _____

Writing Expressions (Part B)

Directions: Translate the algebraic expression into words.

7. $x + 0.06x$ _____

8. $\sqrt{x^2 + y^2}$ _____

9. $\dfrac{V}{h}$ _____

10. $\dfrac{A}{r^2}$ _____

Answers are on page 783.

Monomials and Polynomials

A term is one of the simplest numerical or algebraic expressions. A **term** can be a constant or the product of one or more variables and a constant. These are all terms: 32, $3x$, $-6x^2$, $5x^2$, $5xy$.

A term may begin with a negative sign, but there are no plus or minus signs between coefficients and variables or between variables. Another word for a term is a **monomial**.

A **polynomial** is an algebraic expression consisting of a single term or the sum of two or more terms. These are all polynomials: $x^2 + 2x + 1$, $x^3 + 3x^2 - 3x + 8$, $x^2 + 2xy + y^2$, $x^2 - 1$.

It is standard practice to order the terms of a polynomial in one variable based on the magnitude of the exponent of the variable, from greatest to least. The **degree of a monomial** is the sum of the exponents attached to variables, and the **degree of a polynomial** is the highest degree of all of its monomial terms.

A polynomial with two terms is called a **binomial,** and a polynomial with three terms is called a **trinomial**.

Like terms are terms with all the same variables each raised to the same power.

These are like terms: x^2, $3x^2$, $-5x^2$. None of these are like terms: x^2, $3xy$, $2y^2$, $-5yx^2$.

Operations with Monomials

Monomials can be added, subtracted, multiplied, or divided.

Adding and Subtracting Monomials

Like terms may be combined by adding or subtracting the coefficients. This is an application of the distributive property.

EXAMPLE 1

Find the sum: $x^2 + 2x^2$.

SOLUTION

x^2 and $2x^2$ are like terms because they both have the same variable x with the same exponent of 2.

Because x^2 is the same as $1x^2$ you can write: $\qquad x^2 + 2x^2 = 1x^2 + 2x^2$

Add the coefficients. $\qquad = (1+2)x^2$

Simplify. $\qquad = 3x^2$

EXAMPLE 2

Find the difference: $5x^3 - 2x^3$.

SOLUTION

Check; are these like terms? Yes, the same variable is raised to the same power. $5x^3 - 2x^3 = (5-2)x^3 = 3x^3$

EXAMPLE 3

Find the sum: $3x^2y^3 + 2x^2y^2$.

SOLUTION

Are these like terms? No, the y-exponents are not the same so these terms cannot be combined.

EXERCISE 4

Adding and Subtracting Monomials (Part A)

Directions: Add.

1. $2x + 3x$ _____

2. $3x^2 + 6x^2$ _____

3. $3x + 4x + 5x$ _____

4. $y^2 + x^2$ _____

5. $2xy + 5xy$ _____

6. $20x^3 + 45x^3$ _____

7. $6xy^2 + 4x^2y$ _____

8. $r^3s + 5sr^3$ _____

9. $ax + bx$ _____

10. $x^6 + x^6$ _____

Adding and Subtracting Monomials (Part B)

Directions: Subtract.

11. $3x - x$ _____

12. $6x^2 - 4x^2$ _____

13. $9x - 4x$ _____

14. $y^2 - x^2$ _____

15. $5xy - 3xy$ _____

16. $70x^3 - 45x^3$ _____

17. $6xy^2 - 4x^2y$ _____

18. $7r^3s - 9sr^3$ _____

19. $bx - ax$ _____

20. $x^5 - x^5$ _____

Answers are on page 784.

Multiplying Monomials

Monomials can be multiplied. The product of two monomials is another monomial. When finding the product of two monomials, use the commutative and associative properties to group the numerical coefficients and the variables.

EXAMPLE

Multiply: $(3x^2y^3)(2x^2y^2)$.

SOLUTION

Group the coefficients and the variables. $(3x^2y^3)(2x^2y^2) = (3)(2)x^2x^2y^3y^2$

Because $x^2 = xx$, $y^3 = yyy$, and $y^2 = yy$, $\quad = (3)(2)xxxxyyyyy$

Simplify; write the variables using exponents. $\quad = 6x^4y^5$

When the bases are the same, you add the exponents:
$x^2x^2 = x^{2+2} = x^4$, $\quad y^3y^2 = y^{3+2} = y^5$

Dividing Monomials

Monomials can be divided. Simplify the quotient of two monomials by dividing the coefficients and canceling common factors in the numerator and denominator.

EXAMPLE

Simplify the quotient: $\dfrac{8x^3y^4}{2x^2y^2}$.

SOLUTION

Group the coefficients and the variables.

$$\frac{8x^3y^4}{2x^2y^2} = \frac{8}{2} \cdot \frac{x^3}{x^2} \cdot \frac{y^4}{y^2}$$

Cancel common factors and simplify.

$$= 4 \cdot \frac{xxx}{xx} \cdot \frac{yyyy}{yy}$$

$$= 4xy^2$$

When dividing monomials with the same base you subtract the exponents:

$$\frac{y^4}{y^2} = y^{4-2} = y^2$$

EXERCISE 5

Multiplying and Dividing Monomials (Part A)

Directions: Multiply.

1. $(2x)(3xy)$ _____

2. $(6x^2)(6x^3)$ _____

3. $(3x)(5x)(2x^2)$ _____

4. $(xy^2)(x^2yz)$ _____

5. $(3xy)(5xy^2)$ _____

Multiplying and Dividing Monomials (Part B)

Directions: Divide.

6. $\dfrac{2x}{x}$ _____

7. $\dfrac{8x^3}{2x}$ _____

8. $\dfrac{6x^2y}{3x}$ _____

9. $\dfrac{64x^6}{2x^2}$ _____

10. $\dfrac{x^2y^3z^4}{xy^2z^3}$ _____

Answers are on page 784.

Operations with Polynomials

Like monomials, polynomials can also be added, subtracted, multiplied, or divided.

Adding and Subtracting Polynomials

Polynomials can be added and subtracted. Find the sum of two polynomials by combining like terms.

EXAMPLE 1

Find the sum: $(2x^2+5x+6)+(6x^2+2x+7)$.

SOLUTION

Clear the parentheses.	$=2x^2+5x+6+6x^2+2x+7$
Combine like terms.	$=2x^2+6x^2+5x+2x+6+7$
Simplify.	$=8x^2+7x+13$

To subtract two polynomials, use the distributive property to distribute the minus sign and then combine like terms.

EXAMPLE 2

Find the difference: $(9x^2-5x+6)-(5x^2+2x-5)$.

SOLUTION

Clear the parentheses.	$=9x^2-5x+6-5x^2-2x+5$
Combine like terms.	$=9x^2-5x^2-5x-2x+6+5$
	$=4x^2-7x+11$

EXERCISE 6

Adding and Subtracting Polynomials (Part A)

Directions: Add.

1. $(x^2+2x+9)+(x^2+3x+3)$ _____

2. $(x^2-2x+6)+(x^2+2x-7)$ _____

3. $(2x^2+3x+5)+(3x^2-2x-5)$ _____

4. $(5x^2+5x)+(3x^2+7)$ _____

5. $(x^2+5x+6)+(2x-7)$ _____

6. $(8x^2 - x + 1) + (8 + 2x + x^2)$ _____

7. $(x^2 + 2x - 4) + (3x^2 - 2x + 4)$ _____

8. $(x^2 - 4x + 2) + (3x^2 + 2x - 7)$ _____

9. $(6x^2 - 5x + 6) + (7x^2 + 12x - 9)$ _____

10. $(x^2 + 2xy + y^2) + (6y^2 + 3xy + 7x^2)$ _____

Adding and Subtracting Polynomials (Part B)

Directions: Subtract.

11. $(2x^2 + 3x + 9) - (x^2 + 2x + 6)$ _____

12. $(3x^2 + 2x + 6) - (2x^2 + 3x + 9)$ _____

13. $(x^2 + 3x + 1) - (x^2 - 2x - 1)$ _____

14. $(2x^2 - 2x + 5) - (3x^2 + 3x + 5)$ _____

15. $(x^2 + 9x - 6) - (x^2 + 6x - 9)$ _____

16. $(7x^2 + 2x - 9) - (8x^2 - 3x + 8)$ _____

17. $(x^2 + 2x + 1) - (3x - 2)$ _____

18. $(2x - 9) - (-x^2 - 2x + 3)$ _____

19. $(3x^2 + 2x) - (x^2 - 3)$ _____

20. $(3x^2 + 2xy + 2y^2) - (x^2 + 3xy + 3y^2)$ _____

Answers are on page 784.

Multiplying Polynomials

You can multiply a polynomial by a monomial or by another polynomial.

Multiplying a Monomial times a Polynomial

First use the distributive property and then use the rules for multiplying monomials.

EXAMPLE

Find the product: $2x(3x + 2)$.

SOLUTION

Distribute $2x$.	$2x(3x+2) = 2x(3x) + 2x(2)$
Multiply the monomials.	$= 6x^2 + 4x$

Multiplying a Binomial times a Binomial

You use the distributive property three times to find the product of two binomials.

EXAMPLE

Multiply: $(a+b)(c+d)$.

SOLUTION

Distribute	$(a+b)(c+d) = (a+b)c + (a+b)d$
Distribute c.	$= ac + bc + (a+b)d$
Distribute d.	$= ac + bc + ad + bd$

FOIL, which stands for **First Outer Inner Last**, is an easy way to remember the steps. To use the FOIL method, find the sum of the products of the **f**irst terms, the **o**uter terms, the **i**nner terms, and the **l**ast terms of the two binomials.

$$(a+b)(c+d) = \overset{\text{First}}{ac} + \overset{\text{Outer}}{ad} + \overset{\text{Inner}}{bc} + \overset{\text{Last}}{bd}$$

EXAMPLE 1

Find the product: $(x+2)(2x+3)$.

SOLUTION

Use FOIL.	$(x+2)(2x+3) = x \cdot 2x + 3x + 2 \cdot 2x + 2 \cdot 3$
Simplify.	$= 2x^2 + 3x + 4x + 6$
Combine like terms.	$= 2x^2 + 7x + 6$

Be especially careful when the binomials include minus or negative signs.

EXAMPLE 2

Find the product: $(2x-4)(x-5)$.

SOLUTION

Use FOIL.	$(2x-4)(x-5) = 2x \cdot x + 2x(-5) - 4 \cdot x - 4(-5)$
Simplify.	$= 2x^2 - 10x - 4x + 20$
Combine like terms.	$= 2x^2 - 14x + 20$

Consider the special case of finding the square of a binomial.

EXAMPLE 3

Find the product: $(a+b)^2$.

SOLUTION

Rewrite as a product and use FOIL. $(a+b)^2 = (a+b)(a+b) = a^2 + ab + ba + b^2$

Combine like terms. $\qquad = a^2 + 2ab + b^2$

Another special case is the product of the form $(a+b)(a-b)$.

EXAMPLE 4

Find the product: $(a+b)(a-b)$.

SOLUTION

Use FOIL. $\qquad (a+b)(a-b) = a^2 + ab - ba - b^2$

Combine like terms. $\qquad = a^2 - b^2$

Multiplying Two Polynomials

When finding the product of any two polynomials, you must find the product of every term in the first polynomial times every term in the second polynomial.

EXAMPLE 1

Multiply: $(a + b)(c + d + e)$.

SOLUTION

$(a + b)(c + d + e) = ac + ad + ae + bc + bd + be$

EXAMPLE 2

Multiply: $(x + 6)(x^2 + 3x + 5)$.

SOLUTION

$(x + 6)(x^2 + 3x + 5) = x^3 + 3x^2 + 5x + 6x^2 + 18x + 30$

Combine like terms. $\qquad = x^3 + 9x^2 + 23x + 30$

Here is an example that will prove useful later.

EXAMPLE 3

Multiply: $(a-b)(a^2 + ab + b^2)$.

SOLUTION

$(a-b)(a^2+ab+b^2) = a \cdot a^2 + a \cdot ab + a \cdot b^2 - b \cdot a^2 - b \cdot ab - b \cdot b^2$

Use exponents.　　　　$= a^3 + a^2b + ab^2 - ba^2 - b^2a - b^3$

Collect like terms.　　$= a^3 + a^2b - ba^2 + ab^2 - b^2a - b^3$

Simplify.　　　　　　$= a^3 - b^3$

EXERCISE 7

Multiplying Polynomials (Part A)

Directions: Find the product.

1. $(x^2)(2x^2)$ _____

2. $(-2x)(x^2)$ _____

3. $(3x)(3x^2)$ _____

4. $(5x^2)(3y^2)$ _____

5. $(x^2y)(-2xy^2)$ _____

6. $(-5x)(-2x)$ _____

7. $(2x)(2x)$ _____

8. $(2x^3)(3x^2)$ _____

9. $(6x^2)(7)$ _____

10. $(x^2)(3xy^2)$ _____

Multiplying Polynomials (Part B)

Directions: Find the product.

11. $(9)(x^2+3x+3)$ _____

12. $(-2x)(2x-7)$ _____

13. $(2x^2)(2x-5)$ _____

14. $(5x)(3x^2+7)$ _____

15. $(3x)(x^2-5x+6)$ _____

16. $(-x)(8-2x-x^2)$ _____

17. $(x^2)(3x^2-4)$ _____

18. $(5x^2)(5x^2-2x)$ _____

19. $(-5x)(-7x^2+12x-9)$ _____

20. $(2xy^2)(6xy+x^2)$ _____

Multiplying Polynomials (Part C)

Directions: Find the product.

21. $(2x+9)(3x+3)$ _____

22. $(2x+6)(2x-7)$ _____

23. $(3x+5)(3x^2-2x-5)$ _____

24. $(5x^2-5x)(3x+7)$ _____

25. $(5x-6)(5x+6)$ _____

26. $(x^2-x+1)(8+2x)$ _____

27. $(2x-4)(x^2-2x+4)$ _____

28. $(-4x+2)(2x-7)$ _____

29. $(-5x+6)(6-5x)$ _____

30. $(x^2+y^2)(x^2-y^2)$ _____

Answers are on page 784.

Dividing Polynomials

You can divide a polynomial by a monomial or by another polynomial.

Dividing a Polynomial by a Monomial

You can divide a polynomial by a monomial by rewriting the rational expression as a sum of fractions and then canceling common factors in the numerator and denominator of each fraction.

EXAMPLE 1

Divide: $\dfrac{2x^3 + 4x^2 + 6x}{2x}$.

SOLUTION

Rewrite. $\dfrac{2x^3 + 4x^2 + 6x}{2x} = \dfrac{2x^3}{2x} + \dfrac{4x^2}{2x} + \dfrac{6x}{2x}$

Simplify. $= x^2 + 2x + 3$

EXAMPLE 2

Divide: $\dfrac{12x^2 + 8x}{4x}$.

SOLUTION

Rewrite. $\dfrac{12x^2 + 8x}{4x} = \dfrac{12x^2}{4x} + \dfrac{8x}{4x}$

Simplify. $= 3x + 2$

Dividing a Polynomial by a Polynomial

You can divide a polynomial by another polynomial using long division. This can be demonstrated using the above example problem.

EXAMPLE 1

Divide: $\dfrac{2x^3 + 4x^2 + 6x}{2x}$.

SOLUTION

Rewrite as long division. $2x\,)\overline{2x^3 + 4x^2 + 6x}$

$2x^3$ divided by $2x = \cdot\, x^2$.

Multiply and subtract like terms.
$$2x\,)\overline{2x^3 + 4x^2 + 6x} \quad\quad x^2$$
$$\underline{2x^3}$$
$$0$$

Bring down $4x^2$.
$$2x\,)\overline{2x^3 + 4x^2 + 6x} \quad\quad x^2 + 2x$$
$$\underline{2x^3}$$

$4x^2$ divided by $2x = 2x$.
$$0 + 4x^2$$

Multiply and subtract again.
$$\underline{4x^2}$$
$$0$$

$$\begin{array}{r} x^2 + 2x + 3 \\ 2x\overline{\smash{)}2x^3 + 4x^2 + 6x} \end{array}$$

$$\underline{2x^3}$$
$$0 + 4x^2$$
$$\underline{4x^2}$$

Bring down 6x. $0 + 6x$

6x divided by 2x = 3.

Multiply and subtract. $\dfrac{6x}{0}$

The quotient is $x^2 + 2x + 3$.

Now consider a polynomial divided by a binomial.

EXAMPLE 2

Divide: $\dfrac{4x^2 - 1}{2x - 1}$.

SOLUTION

Rewrite as long division. $2x - 1\overline{\smash{)}4x^2 + 0x - 1}$

Include 0x as a placeholder x-term since
   there was no x-term in the numerator.

Look only at the first terms when you divide. $2x - 1\overline{\smash{)}4x^2 + 0x - 1}^{\,2x}$

$4x^2$ divided by 2x = 2x. Multiply 2x times $\underline{4x^2 - 2x}$
$$0 + 2x - 2x$$

2x – 1 and then subtract by changing signs and adding.

Bring down –1 and divide again. $2x - 1\overline{\smash{)}4x^2 + 0x - 1}^{\,2x+1}$
$$\underline{4x^2 - 2x}$$
$$0 + 2x - 1$$

Subtract; the remainder is 0. $\underline{2x - 1}$
$$0$$

The quotient is $2x + 1$.

Check by multiplying (use FOIL).

$(2x - 1)(2x + 1) = 4x^2 + 2x - 2x + 1 = 4x^2 - 1\ \checkmark$

EXERCISE 8

Dividing Polynomials (Part A)

Directions: Find the quotient.

1. $\dfrac{4x^2}{2x}$ _____

2. $\dfrac{12x^3 + 6x^2}{3x^2}$ _____

3. $\dfrac{3x^3 + 6x^2 + 9x}{-3x}$ _____

4. $\dfrac{5x^2 + x^3}{x^2}$ _____

5. $\dfrac{x^2 y + y^2 x}{xy}$ _____

6. $\dfrac{-15x^2}{-5x}$ _____

7. $\dfrac{64x^4 + 32x^3 + 16x^2}{8x}$ _____

8. $\dfrac{x^3 + 3x^2}{x^2}$ _____

9. $\dfrac{6x^2 - 2}{2}$ _____

10. $\dfrac{x^2 y}{xy}$ _____

Dividing Polynomials (Part B)

Directions: Find the quotient.

11. $\dfrac{x^2 + 5x + 6}{x + 2}$ _____

12. $\dfrac{x^2 + x - 12}{x + 4}$ _____

13. $\dfrac{2x^2 - x - 1}{2x + 1}$ _____

14. $\dfrac{4x^2 - 1}{2x - 1}$ _____

15. $\dfrac{6x^2 + 10x + 4}{3x + 2}$ _____

16. $\dfrac{2x^2 - x - 6}{2x + 3}$ _____

17. $\dfrac{6x^2 - 10x + 4}{2x - 2}$ _____

18. $\dfrac{x^2 + 4x + 4}{x + 2}$ _____

19. $\dfrac{4x^2 + 4x - 8}{2x + 4}$ _____

20. $\dfrac{16x^2 - 4x - 2}{4x + 1}$ _____

Answers are on page 785.

Factoring Polynomials

To **factor a polynomial** means to identify polynomial or monomial factors whose product is the original polynomial. Factoring polynomials is essentially the reverse of multiplying polynomials. Factoring polynomials is often useful when simplifying algebraic expressions and solving math problems.

Factoring the Greatest Common Factor from a Polynomial

Factors common to all of the terms of a polynomial may be factored out. When factoring any polynomial it is always a good practice to first factor out the **greatest common factor (GCF)** from all of the terms of the polynomial.

EXAMPLE 1

Identify the common factors for the terms in the polynomial and write the polynomial as a product of factors: $2x^3 + 4x^2 + 8x$.

SOLUTION

2 is a common factor of each coefficient so

divide each coefficient by 2 and

place a 2 outside the parentheses. $2x^3 + 4x^2 + 8x = 2(x^3 + 2x^2 + 4x)$

x is a common factor of each term so

divide each term by x and place an x

outside the parentheses. $= 2x(x^2 + 2x + 4)$

$2x$ is the GCF; there are no other common factors.

You can do the factoring in one step by identifying and factoring out the GCF for the terms of the original polynomial.

EXAMPLE 2

Identify the GCF for the terms in the polynomial and write the polynomial in factored form: $3x^3 + 6x$.

SOLUTION

$3x^3 = 3xxx$; $6x = 2 \cdot 3x$; $3x$ is the GCF.

Divide each term by $3x$ and place $3x$ outside the parentheses.

$3x^3 + 6x = 3x(x^2 + 2)$

Factoring by Grouping

Some polynomials can be factored by grouping the terms into binomials and factoring the binomials.

EXAMPLE

Factor the polynomial: $x^3 + 6x^2 + 2x + 12$.

SOLUTION

Group the first two terms and the second two terms.

$$x^3 + 6x^2 + 2x + 12 = (x^3 + 6x^2) + (2x + 12)$$

Factor out the GCF from each binomial. $= x^2(x + 6) + 2(x + 6)$

Now factor out $(x + 6)$. $= (x^2 + 2)(x + 6)$

$x^2 + 2$ cannot be factored so you are done.

Factoring a Trinomial of the Form $ax^2 + bx + c$

A simpler case is when $a = 1$. The factored form of a polynomial of the form $x^2 + bx + c$ will look like $(x + \_)(x + \_)$. You need to find two numbers whose product is c and whose sum is b. Depending on the signs of a, b, and c, positive and negative numbers may need to be considered. You can use guess and check to find the factors.

EXAMPLE 1

Factor the polynomial: $x^2 + 7x + 6$.

SOLUTION

Factors of 6 are 2×3, -2×-3, 1×6, and -1×-6.

Check the possible factors. Use FOIL. $(x + 2)(x + 3) = x^2 + 5x + 6$

$(x - 2)(x - 3) = x^2 - 5x + 6$

$(x + 1)(x + 6) = x^2 + 7x + 6$ ✓

$(x - 1)(x - 6) = x^2 - 7x + 6$

EXAMPLE 2

Factor the polynomial: $x^2 - 3x - 10$.

SOLUTION

The factored form will look like $(x + \_)(x - \_)$ because the missing numbers will have opposite signs in order for their product to be negative (-10).

Factors of -10 are 1×-10, -1×10, 2×-5, and -2×5. The sum of the two numbers must equal -3. Since $-5 + 2 = -3$, the factors are $(x + 2)(x - 5)$.

Check. Use FOIL. $(x + 2)(x - 5) = x^2 - 3x - 10$ ✓

If a is not equal to 1 in $ax^2 + bx + c$, then the factored form will look like $(\_x + \_)(\_x - \_)$. Factoring a trinomial in the form $ax^2 + bx + c$ using guess and check is a bit more complicated because you now need to find four numbers: two numbers whose product is a, and two numbers whose product is c. However, it is still possible to solve the factoring problem using guess and check.

EXAMPLE 3

Factor the polynomial: $2x^2 + 7x + 6$.

SOLUTION

Factors of 6 are 2×3, -2×-3, 1×6, and -1×-6. Factors of 2 are 2×1 and -2×-1. Because all of the coefficients are positive, you can limit your guesses to the positive factors.

Check possible factors. $(2x + 2)(x + 3) = 2x^2 + 8x + 6$

$(2x + 1)(x + 6) = 2x^2 + 13x + 6$

$(2x + 3)(x + 2) = 2x^2 + 7x + 6$ ✓

The **"ac" method** is a method for factoring polynomials of the form $ax^2 + bx + c$ when a is not equal to 1. The method provides a systematic way to identify and check the potential coefficients of the binomial factors.

- First make sure the terms of the polynomial are ordered by degree, highest to lowest.

- If a is negative, factor out -1 from all terms in the polynomial.

- Find the factors of the product ac.

- Identify a pair of factors of ac that add up to b.

- Split the middle term of the polynomial into two parts based on this factor pair. There are two possible ways to order the two terms, so if one way does not work, try the other.

- Factor by grouping the first two terms and the last two terms.

EXAMPLE 4

Factor the polynomial: $4x^2 + 8x + 3$.

SOLUTION

Factor ac. $ac = (4)(3) = (2)(2)(3)$

Possible factor pairs: 4 and 3 or 2 and 6; $2 + 6 = 8$

Split the middle term. $4x^2 + 2x + 6x + 3$

Factor the two binomials. $(4x^2 + 2x) + (6x + 3)$

$2x(2x + 1) + 3(2x + 1)$

Factor again. $(2x + 3)(2x + 1)$

If you use the FOIL method to check the answer, you can see that the *ac* method and factoring by grouping is a lot like the FOIL method in reverse.

$$(2x + 3)(2x + 1) = (2x)(2x) + (2x)(1) + (3)(2x) + (3)(1)$$

$$= 4x^2 + 2x + 6x + 3$$

$$= 4x^2 + 8x + 3$$

Factoring a Perfect Square Trinomial

A **perfect square trinomial** is what you get when you square a binomial. $a^2 + 2ab + b^2$ is a perfect square trinomial because

$$(a + b)^2 = (a + b)(a + b) = a^2 + ab + ba + b^2 = a^2 + 2ab + b^2$$

The factored form of $a^2 + 2ab + b^2$ is $(a + b)(a + b)$ or $(a + b)^2$. In a perfect square trinomial, the first and last terms are always perfect squares (a^2 and b^2) and the middle term is always twice the product of the square roots of the first and last terms ($2ab$).

EXAMPLE

Factor the polynomial: $x^2 + 6x + 9$.

SOLUTION

$x^2 + 6x + 9$ is a perfect square trinomial since x^2 and 9 are both perfect squares and $6x = 2 \cdot 3x$. The factored form of $x^2 + 6x + 9$ is $(x + 3)^2$ or $(x + 3)(x + 3)$.

As always, it's a good idea to check your answer by multiplying the factors.

Factoring the Difference of Two Squares

In the lesson on multiplying binomials you saw this example: $(a+b)(a-b) = a^2 + ab - ba - b^2 = a^2 - b^2$. The ab and ba terms added up to 0 leaving only the difference of the two square terms remaining. So, the factored form of the difference of two squares is the product of the sum and difference of the square roots.

$$a^2 - b^2 = (a+b)(a-b)$$

EXAMPLE 1

Factor the polynomial: $x^2 - 16$.

SOLUTION

$x^2 - 16$ is the difference of two perfect squares.

The factored form of $x^2 - 16$ is $(x+4)(x-4)$.

EXAMPLE 2

Factor the polynomial: $3x^2 - 27$.

SOLUTION

$3x^2 - 27$ is not the difference of two perfect squares.

But you can factor 3 from both terms.

$3x^2 - 27 = 3(x^2 - 9)$

Now factor $x^2 - 9$. $= 3(x+3)(x-3)$

Factoring the Difference of Two Cubes

In the lesson on multiplying polynomials you saw this example: $(a-b)(a^2+ab+b^2) = a^3 + a^2b - ba^2 + ab^2 - b^2a - b^3 = a^3 - b^3$. All of the terms *except* a^3 and b^3 added up to 0, leaving only the difference of the two cube terms. The factored form of the difference of two cubes is given by the following: $a^3 - b^3 = (a-b)(a^2+ab+b^2)$.

EXAMPLE 1

Factor the polynomial: $x^3 - 27$.

SOLUTION

$x^3 - 27$ is the difference of two cubes. x^3 corresponds to a^3 in the difference of two cubes factoring formula, and 27 corresponds to b^3 so $b = \sqrt[3]{27} = 3$ and $b^2 = 3^2 = 9$.

Write the formula. $a^3 - b^3 = (a-b)(a^2+ab+b^2)$

Substitute. $x^3 - 27 = (x-3)(x^2+3x+9)$

Because (x^2+3x+9) cannot be factored, you are done.

By replacing b with $-b$ in the difference of two cubes formula, a formula can be derived for factoring the **sum** of two cubes.

- Difference of two cubes formula: $\quad a^3 - b^3 = (a - b)(a^2 + ab + b^2)$

- Replace b with $-b$. $\quad a^3 - (-b)^3 = (a - (-b))(a^2 + a(-b) + (-b)^2)$

- Simplify. $\quad a^3 + b^3 = (a + b)(a^2 - ab + b^2)$

- Multiply to check.
  $(a + b)(a^2 - ab + b^2) = a^3 - a^2b + ab^2 + ba^2 - ab^2 + b^3 = a^3 + b^3 \checkmark$

EXAMPLE 2

Factor the polynomial: $\quad 8x^3 + 125$.

SOLUTION

$8x^3 + 125$ is the sum of two cubes. $8\,x^3$ corresponds to a^3 in the factoring formula so $a = \sqrt[3]{8x^3} = 2x$ and 125 corresponds to b^3 so $b = \sqrt[3]{125} = 5$.

Write the formula. $\quad a^3 + b^3 = (a + b)(a^2 - ab + b^2)$

Substitute. $\quad 8x^3 + 125 = (2x + 5)((2x)^2 - (2x)(5) + 5^2)$

Simplify. $\quad 8x^3 + 125 = (2x + 5)(4x^2 - 10x + 25)$

Since $4x^2 - 10x + 25$ cannot be factored, you are done.

General Strategy for Factoring Polynomials

- First factor out the GCF if possible.

- Look for special cases.

  - Perfect square trinomial $\quad a^2 + 2ab + b^2 = (a + b)^2$

  - Difference of two squares $\quad a^2 - b^2 = (a + b)(a - b)$

  - Difference of two cubes $\quad a^3 - b^3 = (a - b)(a^2 + ab + b^2)$

  - Sum of two cubes $\quad a^3 + b^3 = (a + b)(a^2 - ab + b^2)$

- Use the ac method and factor by grouping.

EXAMPLE

Factor the polynomial: $\quad 30x + 2x^2 - 12x^3$.

SOLUTION

Factor out the GCF. $\quad 30x + 2x^2 - 12x^3 = 2x(15 + x - 6x^2)$

Factor out -1 and reorder terms. $\quad = -2x(6x^2 - x - 15)$

$ac = (6)(-15) = -(2)(3)(3)(5)$; $9 + (-10) = -1$ so rewrite $-x$ as $9x - 10x$.

$= -2x(6x^2 + 9x - 10x - 15)$

Factor the two binomials. $\quad = -2x[3x(2x + 3) - 5(2x + 3)]$

Factor out $(2x + 3)$. $\quad = -2x(3x - 5)(2x + 3)$

Factoring Polynomials (Part A)

Directions: Completely factor each polynomial.

1. $2x^2 - 4x$ _____

2. $4xy - 8y$ _____

3. $27x^3 + 9x^2y$ _____

4. $12 - 8x$ _____

5. $14y - 7xy$ _____

6. $xyz + 2x^2$ _____

7. $2x^3 - 4x^2 + 4x$ _____

8. $2x - 4y + 6z$ _____

9. $3xy + 6xy^2 + 6x^2y$ _____

10. $6x^3 + 3x^2 + 6x$ _____

Factoring Polynomials (Part B)

Directions: Completely factor each polynomial.

11. $x^2 + 3x + 2$ _____

12. $x^2 + 4x + 3$ _____

13. $x^2 + 7x + 12$ _____

14. $x^2 + 2x - 8$ _____

15. $x^2 - 3x + 2$ _____

16. $x^2 - 5x + 6$ _____

17. $x^2 - 6x + 8$ _____

18. $x^2 + x - 20$ _____

19. $x^2 + 3x - 18$ _____

20. $x^2 + x - 6$ _____

Factoring Polynomials (Part C)

Directions: Completely factor each polynomial.

21. $2x^2 + 7x + 6$ _____

22. $6x^2 + 5x + 1$ _____

23. $4x^2 + 12x + 8$ _____

24. $6x^2 + 13x + 6$ _____

25. $4x^2 - 5x - 6$ _____

26. $6x^2 - x - 1$ _____

27. $3x^2 + 5x + 2$ _____

28. $4x^2 - 6x + 2$ _____

29. $12x^2 + 21x + 9$ _____

30. $2x^2 - 3x - 2$ _____

Factoring Polynomials (Part D)

Directions: Completely factor each polynomial.

31. $2x^2 + 10x^2 + 12x$ _____

32. $3x^3 - 12x$ _____

33. $4x^2 + 12x + 9$ _____

34. $2x^2 + 8x + 8$ _____

35. $-15 + 2x + x^2$ _____

36. $12 - 11x + 2x^2$ _____

37. $2x^3 - 2x$ _____

38. $9x^2 - 4$ _____

39. $6x^2 + 7x - 20$ _____

40. $6x^3 - 20x^2 + 6x$ _____

Answers are on page 785.

CHAPTER 6

Equations and Functions

Equations are central to any study of mathematics beyond arithmetic. Equations are used for formulas and to represent conditions that unknown quantities have to satisfy. Real-world problems can be resolved by writing, solving, and interpreting an equation. Once an equation is written, particular steps can, and usually must, be taken to solve it. In this chapter you will learn what those particular steps are and how to apply them to equations and inequalities. You will also learn about functions and how they may be represented.

Equations and Inequalities

An **equation** is a mathematical statement that two quantities are equal. An equation always includes an equal sign (=). Examples of equations:

1. $2 + 2 = 4$
2. $1 + 1 = 2$
3. $2 + x = 7$
4. $y = 2x + 3$

A **solution** to an equation is a value for the variable that makes the equation a true statement. $x = 5$ is a solution to the equation $2 + x = 7$ because $2 + 5 = 7$; $x = 5$ is the only solution to this equation.

Solving an equation means finding all of the solutions to the equation. The equation $y = 2x + 3$ has two variables and an infinite number of solutions. For any value of x you pick, there is a value of y that makes the equation a true statement. It is not possible to list all of the solutions to an equation like $y = 2x + 3$.

An **inequality** is a statement that one quantity is greater than, less than, greater than or equal to, or less than or equal to another quantity. An inequality will include one of the following inequality symbols: < (less than), > (greater than), ≤ (less than or equal to), or ≥ (greater than or equal to).

Suppose a and b represent two expressions.

$a > b$ means that a is **greater than** b.

$a < b$ means that a is **less than** b.

$a \geq b$ means that a is **greater than or equal to** b.

$a \leq b$ means that a is **less than or equal to** b.

Examples of inequalities:

1. $2 + 3 > 4$

2. $1 \leq 1$

3. $x + 5 < 10$

4. $y \geq x + 1$

One solution to $x + 5 < 10$ is $x = 4$. You can tell that $x = 4$ is a solution by substituting 4 for x in the inequality and getting $4 + 5 < 10$, which is a true statement. There are an infinite number of solutions to this inequality. Any number less than 5 is a solution to this inequality. Note that $x = 5$ *is not* a solution. If you substitute 5 for x in the inequality $x + 5 < 10$, you get $5 + 5 < 10$, or $10 < 10$, which is not a true statement.

Linear Equations and Linear Inequalities

A **linear equation** is an equation with one or more variables and both sides of the equation are first degree polynomials. The following are examples of linear equations:

$$x + 3 = 8 \qquad x - 6 = 5 \qquad 2x = 10$$
$$\frac{x}{2} = 8 \qquad 2x + 5 = 15 \qquad 4x - 6 = 10$$
$$2x - 8 = 6x + 10 \qquad 3x + 4y = 10 \qquad 2x + 5y + 7z = 100$$

The following are *not* linear equations because they do not have first degree polynomials on both sides.

$$x^2 + 2x + 6 = 0 \qquad \frac{1}{2x - 1} = 3x + 1 \qquad y = \frac{1}{x}$$

If you replace the equal sign in a linear equation with one of the inequality symbols, you get a **linear inequality**.

Solving Linear Equations and Linear Inequalities

You can use the properties of equality to solve linear equations and inequalities. The idea is to use these properties to isolate the variable and get the equation into the form "$x = \ldots$"; once you have isolated x on one side of the equation or inequality, you have solved the equation or inequality.

The **addition property of equality** states that you can add the same quantity to both sides of an equation without affecting the validity of the equation. Similarly, the **subtraction property of equality** states that you can subtract the same quantity from both sides of an equation without affecting the validity of the equation. These properties also apply to inequalities.

So if $a = b$ is a true statement, then $a + c = b + c$ and $a - c = b - c$ are also true.

And, if $a < b$ is true, then $a + c < b + c$ and $a - c < b - c$ are also true.

Similarly, if $a > b$ is true, then $a + c > b + c$ and $a - c > b - c$ are also true.

The **multiplication property of equality** states that you can multiply both sides of an equation by the same quantity without affecting the validity of the equation. Similarly, you can divide both sides of an equation by the same quantity (just don't divide by zero) without affecting the validity of the equation.

There are also **multiplication and division** properties that apply to inequalities, but with an important difference compared to the multiplication and division properties of equality.

Consider the inequality:

$$4 < 6$$

This is a true statement and if you multiply both sides by a *positive* number the resulting inequality is still a true statement.

$$(5)(4) < (5)(6)$$
$$20 < 30$$

But if you multiply both sides by a *negative* number, the resulting inequality is not true.

$$4 < 5 \ [\text{true}]$$
$$(-5)(4) < (-5)(6)$$
$$-20 < -30 \ [\text{not true!}]$$

Remember that "less than" means "is to the left of" on the number line but -20 is to the right of -30 on the number line. Remember to reverse the direction of the inequality sign and change "<" to ">" to turn the inequality into the true statement.

$$-20 > -30$$

Divide both sides of the original inequality by a negative number to see what happens.

$$4 < 6 \ [\text{true}]$$
$$\frac{4}{-2} < \frac{6}{-2}$$
$$-2 < -3 \ [\text{not true!}]$$

Again, this is not a true statement; -2 *is not* to the left of -3 on the number line. You need to reverse the direction of the inequality sign to make the inequality true.

Whenever you multiply or divide both sides of an inequality by a negative number, you must reverse the direction of the inequality sign in order for the resulting inequality to be a true statement.

Solving Linear Equations and Inequalities by Adding or Subtracting

You can solve addition and subtraction equations by using inverse operations to undo the addition or subtraction.

EXAMPLE 1

Solve for x: $x + 6 = 10$.

SOLUTION

The inverse of adding 6 is to subtract 6.

Subtract 6 from both sides to undo the addition. $x + 6 = 10$

$$x + 6 - 6 = 10 - 6$$

Simplify. $x = 4$

EXAMPLE 2

Solve for x: $x - \dfrac{5}{8} = \dfrac{7}{8}$.

SOLUTION

The inverse of subtracting $\dfrac{5}{8}$ is to add $\dfrac{5}{8}$.

Add $\dfrac{5}{8}$ to both sides to undo the subtraction. $x - \dfrac{5}{8} = \dfrac{1}{8}$

$$x - \dfrac{5}{8} + \dfrac{5}{8} = \dfrac{1}{8} + \dfrac{5}{8}$$

Simplify. $x = \dfrac{6}{8}$ or $\dfrac{3}{4}$

EXAMPLE 3

Solve for x: $9.8 - x = 2.6$.

SOLUTION

The inverse of subtracting x is to add x.

Add x to both sides to undo the subtraction. $9.8 - x = 2.6$

$$9.8 - x + x = 2.6 + x$$

Simplify. $9.9 = 2.6 + x$

Now subtract 2.6 from both sides. $9.8 - 2.6 = 2.6 - 2.6 + x$

Simplify. $7.2 = x$

Note that it's fine that the x ended up on the right side of the equation. You can always rewrite it as $x = 7.2$.

EXAMPLE 4

Solve the inequality for x: $x + 1.2 \geq 2.3$.

SOLUTION

The inverse of adding 1.2 is to subtract 1.2.

Subtract 1.2 from both sides.

$$x + 1.2 \geq 2.3$$
$$x + 1.2 - 1.2 \geq 2.3 - 1.2$$

Simplify.

$$x \geq 1.1$$

The solution is all values of x that are greater than or equal to 1.1.

EXERCISE 1

Solving Linear Equations and Inequalities by Adding or Subtracting (Part A)

Directions: Solve each equation for x.

1. $x - 22 = 76$ _____

2. $x + \dfrac{2}{9} = 3\dfrac{1}{3}$ _____

3. $x - 3.5 = 98.6$ _____

4. $9.8 - x = 5.9$ _____

5. $0.056 + x = 1.01$ _____

6. $x - 0.5 = 5.05$ _____

7. $14 = x - 4$ _____

8. $3\dfrac{3}{4} - x = 1\dfrac{1}{4}$ _____

9. $x + 9\dfrac{3}{16} = 21$ _____

10. $34\dfrac{1}{3} + x = 48\dfrac{1}{12}$ _____

Solving Linear Equations and Inequalities by Adding or Subtracting (Part B)

Directions: Solve each inequality.

11. $x + 6.5 > 4$

12. $x + 5\frac{1}{2} \le 30$

13. $66 - x \ge 25$

14. $x + 10\frac{7}{8} < 27$

15. $100 \ge 207 - x$

16. $x - 198.2 < 13.8$

17. $x + 16.25 > 24.5$

18. $x - \frac{9}{16} \le \frac{3}{32}$

19. $1\frac{5}{8} + x < 3\frac{9}{16}$

20. $x - 2{,}029 < 27$

Answers are on page 785.

Solving Linear Equations and Inequalities by Multiplying or Dividing

You solve a multiplication equation or inequality by isolating the variable using the multiplication property of equality.

EXAMPLE 1

Solve for x: $4x = 36$.

SOLUTION

Isolate the variable by dividing both sides of the equation by 4. $4x = 36$

$$\frac{4x}{4} = \frac{36}{4}$$

Simplify. $x = 9$

EXAMPLE 2

Solve for x: $\dfrac{x}{8} = 6$.

SOLUTION

The inverse of dividing by 8 is multiplying by 8, so multiply both sides of the equation by 8. $\dfrac{x}{8} = 6$

$$8 \cdot \dfrac{x}{8} = 8 \cdot 6$$

Simplify: $x = 48$

EXAMPLE 3

Solve for x: $\dfrac{4}{5}x = 64$.

SOLUTION

Divide by $\dfrac{4}{5}$ to undo the multiplication. To divide by a fraction, multiply by its reciprocal. Multiply both sides by $\dfrac{5}{4}$. $\dfrac{4}{5}x = 64$

$$\dfrac{5}{4} \cdot \dfrac{4}{5}x = \dfrac{5}{4} \cdot 64$$

Cancel common factors. $x = 5 \cdot 16$

Multiply. $x = 80$

EXAMPLE 4

Solve for x: $1.063x \leq 200$.

SOLUTION

Divide by 1.063 to undo multiplication. $1.063x \leq 200$

$$\dfrac{1.063x}{1.063} \leq \dfrac{200}{1.063}$$

$$x \leq 188.15$$

EXAMPLE 5

Solve for x: $\dfrac{x}{-6} > -7$.

SOLUTION

Multiply by −6 to undo the division. Because you are multiplying by a negative number, be sure to reverse the direction of the inequality symbol. $\dfrac{x}{-6} > -7$

$$(-6)\left(\dfrac{x}{-6}\right) < (-6)(-7)$$

Simplify. $x < 42$

EXERCISE 2

Solving Linear Equations and Inequalities by Multiplying or Dividing (Part A)

Directions: Solve each equation for x.

1. $22x = -88$
2. $\dfrac{x}{2.5} = 25$
3. $17x = -306$
4. $\dfrac{1}{2}x = 150$
5. $0.07x = 14$
6. $\dfrac{x}{0.01} = 501$
7. $\dfrac{x}{-11} = 99$
8. $3\dfrac{1}{2}x = 28$
9. $\dfrac{x}{25} = 7.5$
10. $3.3x = -46.2$

Solving Linear Equations and Inequalities by Multiplying or Dividing (Part B)

Directions: Solve each inequality.

11. $13x \geq 169$
12. $-1\dfrac{1}{2}x < -15$
13. $\dfrac{x}{0.05} \geq 2$
14. $\dfrac{x}{-12} \geq 5$
15. $\dfrac{x}{2.5} < 15$
16. $4.5x \leq 180$
17. $3.5x > -140$
18. $\dfrac{2}{3}x \geq 50$
19. $-\dfrac{1}{5}x \leq 8$
20. $2.4x > 96$

Answers are on page 785.

Solving Linear Equations and Inequalities with Combined Operations

Equations often have a variable that is multiplied or divided by a number, and also have a number to be added or subtracted. These equations need to have the operations undone in the proper order to be solved correctly. The order of operations has to be considered in reverse because the idea behind solving an equation is to undo the operations that are being done to the variable. Use inverse operations and the order of operations in reverse when solving equations with both addition or subtraction and multiplication or division.

Consider the expression:

$4 + 2x$

According to the order of operations, the value of x is first multiplied by 2 and then 4 is added to the product.

Now consider the equation:

$4 + 2x = 12$

To solve for x, you need to undo the combined operations of "multiply by 2" and "then add 4." Do this by *first* subtracting 4 and *then* dividing by 2.

Subtract 4 from both sides.

$$4 + 2x = 12$$
$$4 - 4 + 2x = 12 - 4$$
$$2x = 8$$

Divide both sides by 2.

$$x = 4$$

To solve for x, apply the inverse operations in the reverse order.

EXAMPLE 1

Solve for x $\quad 14.5x - 6.9 = 170$.

SOLUTION

Add 6.9 to both sides.

$$14.5x - 6.9 = 170$$
$$14.5x - 6.9 + 6.9 = 170 + 6.9$$
$$14.5x = 176.9$$

Divide both sides by 14.5.

$$\frac{14.5x}{14.5} = \frac{176.9}{14.5}$$
$$x = 12.2$$

EXAMPLE 2

Solve for x: $\quad \dfrac{x - 3}{5} = 12$.

SOLUTION

Solve for x by multiplying both sides by 5 and then adding 3 to both sides.

Multiply both sides by 5.

$$\frac{x-3}{5} = 12$$

$$(5)\left(\frac{x-3}{5}\right) = (5)(12)$$

$$x - 3 = 60$$

Add 3 to both sides.

$$x - 3 + 3 = 60 + 3$$

$$x = 63$$

EXAMPLE 3

Solve for x: $\dfrac{10-x}{4} \geq 9$.

SOLUTION

Multiply both sides by 4.

$$\frac{10-x}{4} \geq 9$$

$$(4)\left(\frac{10-x}{4}\right) \geq (4)(9)$$

$$10 - x \geq 36$$

Subtract 10 from both sides.

$$10 - 10 - x \geq 36 - 10$$

$$-x \geq 26$$

Multiply both sides by –1 and reverse the direction of the inequality.

$$(-1)(-x) \leq (-1)(26)$$

$$x \leq -26$$

EXERCISE 3

Solving Linear Equations and Inequalities with Combined Operations (Part A)

Directions: Solve each equation for x.

1. $9x + 5 = 50$

2. $\dfrac{2}{3}x - \dfrac{1}{3} = 19\dfrac{2}{3}$

3. $200 - 0.45x = 650$

4. $\dfrac{x-15}{5} = 22$

5. $33 - 12x = -111$

6. $\dfrac{x}{5} - 10 = 75$

7. $\dfrac{x}{2.1} + 2.3 = 8.7$

8. $\dfrac{1}{4}x + \dfrac{5}{16} = \dfrac{11}{32}$

9. $\dfrac{x}{8} - 2\dfrac{3}{4} = 4\dfrac{1}{2}$

10. $12 - 2.4x = -48$

Solving Linear Equations and Inequalities with Combined Operations (Part B)

Directions: Solve each inequality.

11. $9x - 49 \geq 5$

12. $36 - 7.5x \leq -114$

13. $\dfrac{x}{10} + 90 \leq 110$

14. $47 - \dfrac{x}{5.5} < 37$

15. $\dfrac{9}{16}x + 4\dfrac{7}{32} \leq 5\dfrac{9}{32}$

16. $72 - 7.5x \leq -153$

17. $2.5x - 130 > -150$

18. $50 - \dfrac{x}{20} < 20$

19. $\dfrac{12 - x}{6} < \dfrac{1}{3}$

20. $32x - 48 \leq 400$

Answers are on page 786.

Solving Linear Equations with Multiple Operations and Parentheses

Equations can have the variable on both sides of the equal sign. Equations can also have grouping symbols. The general strategy is to simplify the equation by removing the grouping symbols using the distributive property and combining terms where possible before using inverse operations.

EXAMPLE 1

Solve for x: $2(3x + 1) + 3(x - 1) = 35$.

SOLUTION

The first step in solving an equation with parentheses is to use the distributive property to remove the parentheses.

Use the distributive property.

$$2(3x+1)+3(x-1)=35$$
$$2\cdot 3x+2\cdot 1+3x-3\cdot 1=35$$
$$6x+2+3x-3=35$$

Collect like terms.

$$6x+3x+2-3=35$$
$$9x-1=35$$

Add 1 to both sides.

$$9x=36$$

Divide by 9.

$$x=4$$

Now consider an example with parentheses and variables on both sides.

EXAMPLE 2

Solve for x: $5(x-2)=32+3(x+4)$.

SOLUTION

Use the distributive property.

$$5(x-2)=32+3(x+4)$$
$$5x-5\cdot 2=32+3x+3\cdot 4$$
$$5x-10=32+3x+12$$

Collect like terms.

$$5x-10=3x+44$$

The next step is to collect all terms with variables on one side of the equation and all other terms on the other side. For this equation, collect the variables on the left side and the constants on the right side.

Add 10 to both sides.

$$5x-10+10=3x+44+10$$
$$5x=3x+54$$

Subtract $3x$ from both sides.

$$5x-3x=3x+54-3x$$
$$2x=54$$

Divide both sides by 2.

$$\frac{2x}{2}=\frac{54}{2}$$
$$x=27$$

You have already solved linear equations involving fractions. The following example shows how you can simplify equations with fractions by first multiplying both sides by a common denominator.

EXAMPLE 3

Solve for x: $\frac{2}{3}(x+6)=\frac{3}{4}(x-6)+1$.

SOLUTION

The common denominator is 12. Multiply both sides by 12.

$$\frac{2}{3}(x+6) = \frac{3}{4}(x-6)+1$$

$$12\left(\frac{2}{3}(x+6)\right) = 12\left(\frac{3}{4}(x-6)+1\right)$$

$$\frac{12\cdot 2}{3}(x+6) = \frac{12\cdot 3}{4}(x-6)+12\cdot 1$$

Cancel common factors and simplify. $4\cdot 2(x+6) = 3\cdot 3(x-6)+12$

$$8(x+6) = 9(x-6)+12$$

Use the distributive property. $8x+48 = 9x-54+12$

Collect like terms on each side of the equation.

$$8x+48 = 9x-42$$

Collect the variable terms on the right side.

$$8x+48-8x = 9x-42-8x$$

$$48 = x-42$$

Add 42 to both sides. $48+42 = x-42+42$

$$90 = x$$

Here is an example of solving an inequality with fractions and parentheses. You will see that by carefully choosing on which side to collect the variable terms, you can avoid having to address division by a negative number and reversing the direction of the inequality symbol.

EXAMPLE 4

Solve the inequality: $\dfrac{x+12}{3} < \dfrac{x+4}{2}$.

SOLUTION

Multiply by the common denominator, 6. $6\cdot\dfrac{x+12}{3} < 6\cdot\dfrac{x+4}{2}$

$$2(x+12) < 3(x+4)$$

Distribute to remove the parentheses. $2x+24 < 3x+12$

Because $3 > 2$, collecting the variable terms on the right side will avoid having a negative coefficient of x and will save a step later.

Subtract $2x$ from each side. $2x+24-2x < 3x+12-2x$

$$24 < x+12$$

Subtract 12 from each side. $24-12 < x+12-12$

$$12 < x$$

Steps for solving a linear equation or inequality can be summarized as follows:

1. Simplify the equation by multiplying both sides by a common denominator to remove fractions.

2. Use the distributive property to remove parentheses.

3. Collect like terms on each side of the equation.

4. Gather the variable terms on one side and the constant terms on the other side.

5. Divide by the coefficient of the variable.

EXERCISE 4

Solving Linear Equations and Inequalities with Multiple Operations and Parentheses (Part A)

Directions: Solve each equation for x.

1. $5(2x+1) - 4(x-2) = 43$

2. $6(4x-1) = 10(3x+2) - 44$

3. $2.5(x-6) + 2x = 0.75$

4. $1.5(x+1.5) = 2.5(x-1.5) + 2.5$

5. $\dfrac{x+4}{2} + \dfrac{x+6}{3} = 14$

6. $\dfrac{2}{3}(2x+1) = \dfrac{1}{3}(3x-4)$

7. $2(2x+1) + 2(x-1) = 36$

8. $1,000 = 100x + 80(50-x)$

9. $(20.5 - x)(20) + (20.5 + x)(10) = 515$

10. $\dfrac{3}{8}x + \dfrac{7}{8}(10-x) = \dfrac{1}{2}(10)$

Solving Linear Equations and Inequalities with Multiple Operations and Parentheses (Part B)

Directions: Solve each inequality.

11. $2(2x+1)+2x \leq 26$

12. $4(3x+1) < 3(2x+2)+34$

13. $1.25(x+6)+2.5x \leq 45$

14. $1.4(10-x) \leq 1.3(x+10)-12.5$

15. $\dfrac{x+5}{6}+\dfrac{x+11}{12} \geq 5$

16. $\dfrac{2}{3}(x-5) \leq \dfrac{1}{3}(x-7)$

17. $4(7-x)-6(5-x) \geq 0$

18. $200x+300(10-x) \geq 2{,}600$

19. $1.1(x+2)+1.2(x+3) \leq 56.4$

20. $\dfrac{1}{3}x+\dfrac{3}{4}(10-x) \geq \dfrac{1}{2}(10)$

Answers are on page 786.

Using Equations to Solve Problems

In order to solve real-world problems, you must be able to translate the "words" or the verbal model into a **mathematical model**. In Chapter 5, you translated word expressions into algebraic expressions. Writing equations from a word problem description is essentially the same skill only now included are the words that correspond to the equal sign and the various inequality symbols. Following are examples and the corresponding mathematical symbols or models.

Words	Math
"is" or "is equal to" or "is the same as"	$=$
"is greater than or equal to" or "is no less than" or "is at least"	$\geq$
"is less than or equal to" or "is no more than" or "is at most"	$\leq$
"is greater than"	$>$
"is less than"	$<$
An amount A is 5 more than x.	$A=x+5$
The length l is twice the width w.	$l=2w$
The length l is at most twice the width w.	$l \leq 2w$
The truck (t) is at least twice as heavy as the car (c).	$t \geq 2c$

Here are some problem-solving tips:

- Read and understand the problem.

- Identify what you know and what you are trying to find, and assign a variable to the unknown quantity.

- Write an equation (or inequality) that fits the situation.

- Solve the equation.

- Check your work. Is the answer reasonable? Does your solution solve the original problem?

EXAMPLE 1

Define a variable; then write and solve an equation.

A group of 20 students and adult chaperones attended the play. Each student ticket cost $5 and each adult ticket cost $8. If the total cost of all of the tickets was $112, how many students and how many adult chaperones attended the play?

SOLUTION

You know that 20 people attended the play.

You know the price of each adult and student ticket.

You know the total cost of all of the tickets.

The question asks "How many students and how many adults attended...?"

Let x = the number of students, so $20 - x$ = the number of adults.

The total cost must equal the total cost of the student tickets plus the total cost of the adult tickets. You can write a verbal model:

$112 = total cost of the student tickets + total cost of the adult tickets

Because the total cost of the student tickets is $5x$ and the total cost of the adult tickets is $8(20 - x)$, you can write the mathematical model:

$$5x + 8(20 - x) = 112$$

Solve for x. First remove parentheses. $\quad 5x + 160 - 8x = 112$

Collect like terms on the left. $\quad -3x + 160 = 112$

Subtract 160 from both sides. $\quad -3x + 160 - 160 = 112 - 160$

$$-3x = -48$$

Divide both sides by 3. $\quad x = 16$

So, 16 students attended the play.

Check the solution.

$$5 \cdot 16 + 8(20 - 16) \overset{?}{=} 112$$

$$80 + 8(4) \overset{?}{=} 112$$

$$112 = 112$$

Are you done yet? No, you still need to determine the number of adults.

$20 - 16 = 4$ adults attended the play.

Is the answer reasonable? Yes.

EXAMPLE 2

Write and solve an inequality.

You have saved $230 toward the purchase of a new laptop computer. If you save $45 each week, how many weeks will it take for you to have at least $400?

SOLUTION

Let x = the number of weeks.

$230 + 45x$ is the total amount saved after x weeks.

The total amount saved needs to be greater than or equal to $400.

Write the inequality.	$230 + 45x \geq 400$
Subtract 230 from both sides.	$230 + 45x - 230 \geq 400 - 230$
	$45x \geq 170$
Divide both sides by 45.	$\dfrac{45x}{45} \geq \dfrac{170}{45}$
It will take at least 4 weeks to save $400.	$x \geq 3.\overline{7}$
Check by substituting 4 for x.	$230 + 45(4) \overset{?}{\geq} 400$
	$410 \geq 400$

Mixture Problems

Consider the following situation: A manufacturing process calls for 100 liters of a 15 percent acid solution. You have on hand a 10 percent solution and a 20 percent solution. How much of each should you combine to get 100 liters of a 15 percent solution? Because 15 percent is halfway between 10 percent and 20 percent, it seems that a 50-50 mixture should work. This is true.

The sum of the acid in the two parts must equal the total acid in the mixture. You can write and simplify an equation to show this.

$$5\% \text{ of } 50 \text{ liters} + 15\% \text{ of } 50 \text{ liters} = 10\% \text{ of } 100 \text{ liters}$$

$$(0.05)(50) + (0.15)(50) = (0.10)(100)$$

$$2.5 + 7.5 = 10$$

$$10 = 10$$

You can also use an equation like this to solve mixture problems when the answer is not 50-50.

EXAMPLE 1

How many liters of a 10 percent acid solution should be combined with a 25 percent solution to get 100 liters of a 13 percent acid solution?

SOLUTION

Let $x =$ the number of liters at 10%, and let $100 - x =$ the number of liters at 25%.

The sum of the acid in the two parts must equal the total acid in the mixture.

Write an equation.	$0.1x + 0.25(100 - x) = 0.13(100)$
Multiply.	$0.1x + 25 - 0.25x = 13$
Collect like terms.	$-0.15x = -12$
Divide.	$x = 80$
Check your answer.	$0.1(80) + 0.25(100 - 80) = 0.13(100)$
	$8 + 5 = 13$

A good way to set up a mixture problem is to organize the information in a table. In the previous example, the equation used to find the answer is based on the bottom row of this table.

	Part	Part	Mixture
Percents	10%	25%	13%
Liters of solution	x	$100 - x$	100
Liters of acid	$0.1x$	$0.25(100 - x)$	$0.13(100)$

You can also solve mixture problems in which the final concentration is unknown.

EXAMPLE 2

Two pounds of mixed nuts containing 30 percent walnuts are combined with 3 pounds of mixed nuts containing 50 percent walnuts. What percent of walnuts is in the final mixture?

SOLUTION

Let x = the percent of walnuts in the final mixture. There will be 5 pounds of nuts in the combined mixture. Organize the information in a table.

	Part	Part	Mixture
Percents	30%	50%	x
Pounds of mixed nuts	2	3	5
Pounds of walnuts	0.3(2)	0.5(3)	x(5)

Write the equation. $0.3(2) + 0.5(3) = x(5)$

Divide by 5 and simplify. $\dfrac{0.3(2) + 0.5(3)}{5} = x$

$$0.42 = x$$

The final 5-pound mix will contain 42 percent walnuts. This is reasonable since the answer is between 30 percent and 50 percent but closer to 50 percent.

It is also possible to have a mixture problem where the percent for one of the parts is zero. See Exercise 5, Part C, item 13.

Rate-Time-Distance Problems

For an object traveling at a constant speed, the speed is given by a ratio: $\text{speed} = \dfrac{\text{distance traveled}}{\text{elapsed time}}$. Speed is the **rate** at which an object travels; it is customary to write $r = \dfrac{d}{t}$, where r is the rate (or the speed), t is the time, and d is the distance.

EXAMPLE 1

If the average speed is 600 miles per hour, how long will it take an airliner to travel from New York to Los Angeles, a distance of about 2,400 miles?

SOLUTION

You know the rate and the distance and need to find the time, t.

Write the equation. $t = \dfrac{d}{r}$

Substitute values for distance and rate. $t = \dfrac{2{,}400 \text{ miles}}{600 \text{ miles per hour}}$

Evaluate. $t = 4 \text{ hours}$

The same principle can be applied in rate problems even when the rate is not a speed.

EXAMPLE 2

The head flipper can make 4 pancakes per minute. How many pancakes can she make in two hours?

SOLUTION

The rate is 4 pancakes per minute. (The "per minute" part tells you that.)

The time is 2 hours, but you must use 120 minutes because the rate is "per minute."

The total number of pancakes corresponds to d in the $rt = d$ equation.

Write the equation. $p = rt$ (p for pancakes)

Substitute values for r and t. $p = $ (4 pancakes per minute)(120 minutes)

Evaluate. $p = 480$ pancakes

The head flipper can make 480 pancakes in two hours.

EXERCISE 5

Using Equations to Solve Problems (Part A)

Directions: Define variables and write an equation or inequality for each situation.

1. The shortest side of the triangle is one less than half the length of the longest side.

2. In three years Jay's son's age will be more than half of Jay's age.

3. The sum of three consecutive integers is 27.

4. The sum of two consecutive even integers is 168.

5. Jake and two friends split the cost of a pizza and a pitcher of iced tea. Each person's share was less than $5.00.

6. The two short sides of a rectangular building lot are one-third the length of the long side.

Using Equations to Solve Problems (Part B)

Directions: Solve each word problem.

7. Regis paid the cashier $20 for five burgers and received $2.50 back in change. What is the price of one burger?

8. Aimee noticed that when the price of gasoline reached $3.99 per gallon, the cost of a fill-up exceeded $60.00. How many gallons did it take to fill the tank?

9. After subtracting deductions amounting to one-third of his gross pay for the week, Arnold calculated that his take-home pay would be $940.00. What is Arnold's gross pay before deductions?

10. The cost to rent a small moving truck is $150 per day plus $1 per mile. How many miles can you travel in a three-day rental period and still keep the total cost of the rental below $800?

11. Your bank charges a monthly fee of $1.00 plus $0.10 for every check you write. Your total fee for January was $3.50. How many checks did you write that month?

12. To calculate your final grade for your math class, your teacher adds your final exam grade, your quiz grade, and your homework grade and then divides the sum by 3. If your homework grade is 83 and your quiz grade is 88, what grade must you get on the final exam in order for your final grade to be at least 90 (for an A in the course)?

Using Equations to Solve Problems (Part C)

Directions: Solve each word problem. If there is no possible solution, write "Not possible."

13. How many liters of pure water must be added to 3 liters of a 20 percent acid solution in order to produce a 5 percent acid solution?

14. How many pounds of peanuts should be added to a 10-pound batch of mixed nuts containing 40 percent peanuts to make the final mixture 50 percent peanuts?

_____

15. If regular gasoline costs $3.50 per gallon and super-premium gasoline costs $3.95, what would be the cost per gallon of a middle grade of gasoline consisting of a blend of 0.3 gallon of the regular gasoline and 0.7 gallon of the super-premium gasoline?

_____

16. How many metric tons of natural uranium (0.711% U-235) must be blended with 100 metric tons of enriched uranium (4.5% U-235) to obtain a mixture with a slightly lower enrichment of 4.05% U-235?

_____

17. How many liters of a 15 percent acid solution must be added to 5 liters of a 10 percent acid solution to make a 20 percent acid solution?

_____

18. What concentration of 2 liters of an acid solution should be added to 3 liters of a 20 percent acid solution in order to obtain 5 liters of a 30 percent acid solution?

_____

Using Equations to Solve Problems (Part D)

Directions: Solve each word problem.

19. How long would it take a passenger train traveling an average of 80 miles per hour to travel 450 miles from Boston to Washington, DC?

_____

20. What is the average speed (in miles per hour) of a race car that can complete one 2.5-mile lap of the Indianapolis Motor Speedway in 50 seconds?

_____

21. A bicycle tourist averages 17 miles per hour. How far can she travel in 6.5 hours?

_____

22. To qualify for the Boston Marathon, a male runner between the ages of 18 and 34 must have completed a marathon (26.2 miles) in less than 3 hours. What is the minimum qualifying average speed?

_____

23. In still water a rower rows at a speed of 5 miles per hour. With a 3-mile-per-hour current, the same rower travels at 8 miles per hour when rowing downstream. The rower rows downstream for one-half hour and then turns around and rows back (against the current) to her starting point.

a. How far did she row altogether?

_____

b. How many hours did the upstream portion of the trip take?

_____

Answers are on page 786.

Functions

A **function** is a relationship between two sets. The set of possible **inputs** is called the **domain** of the function, and the set of possible **outputs** is called the **range** of the function.

For example, consider the relationship between the number of hours worked in a week and gross pay for that week. Gross pay *depends on*, or *is a function of*, the number of hours worked and the hourly pay rate. Suppose the hourly rate is $14.00 per hour and the number of hours worked per week can be any number between 0 and 40 hours. If x represents the number of hours worked and y represents the gross pay, then the equation $y = 14x$ defines the function.

Since the value of y depends on the value of x, the value of x is an **input** of the function and the value of y is the **output** of the function. The set of all possible input values (or all possible x values) is called the **domain** of the function. The set of all possible output values (or y values) is called the **range** of the function.

Not every relationship between two sets is a function. A key property of all functions is that for every value of x in the domain of the function, there is only one value of y in the range of the function.

Representing and Evaluating Functions

The equation $y = 14x$ is one way to represent a function. To emphasize that an equation represents the functional relationship that y is a function of x, it is common to use **function notation** and write $f(x)$ instead of y. The function $y = 14x$ would be written as $f(x) = 14x$. Note that $f(x)$ is read as "f of x," and that $f(x)$ *does not* mean "f times x." Other variables, such as h and g, can also be used to name functions.

To **evaluate a function** means to determine the value of $f(x)$ for a particular value of x. Replace x with its value in the function equation and evaluate the resulting numerical expression. Using the earlier example, if $f(x) = 14x$ then $f(20) = 14(20) = 280$.

EXAMPLE 1

Write the function $y = 30x + 45$ in function notation and evaluate the function for $x = 25$.

SOLUTION

Replace y with $f(x)$.

$$y = 30x + 45$$
$$f(x) = 30x + 45$$

Evaluate $f(25)$.

$$f(25) = 30(25) + 45$$
$$f(25) = 795$$

Functions can also be represented using a table. A table representation of the function $f(x) = 14x$ for $x = 0, 1, 2, 3, 4,$ and 5 would look like this:

x	$f(x) = \mathbf{14}x$
0	0
1	14
2	28
3	42
4	56
5	70

Functions may also be represented using a graph in the xy coordinate plane. Each point on the graph is an **ordered pair** (x, y), where x is the input value and $y = f(x)$. The x-axis represents the domain of the function and the y-axis represents the range of the function. To graph a function given in function notation, create a table of values and then plot the points. The graph of the function $f(x) = 14x$, where $y = f(x)$, is shown below.

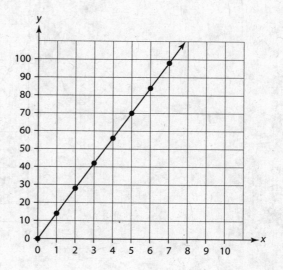

EXAMPLE 2

Write the function $y = 10 - 1.5x$ using function notation.

Evaluate the function for $x = 0, 1, 2, 3, 4, 5,$ and 6.

Display the results in a table of values.

Graph the function.

SOLUTION

Use function notation. $f(x) = 10 - 1.5x$

Create a table of values.

x	$y = f(x) = 10 - 1.5x$
0	10
1	8.5
2	7.0
3	5.5
4	4
5	2.5
6	1.0

Graph the function.

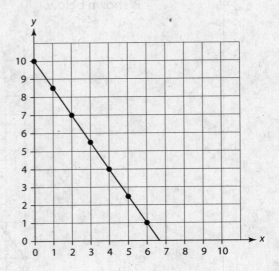

Changing from One Function Representation to Another Function Representation

The previous examples show how you can change from the equation form of a function to a table representation and from a table representation to a graphical representation. Given a graphical representation of a function, it is possible to create a table representation using points from the graph to create the table.

EXAMPLE

Use the information from the graph of the function to complete the table.

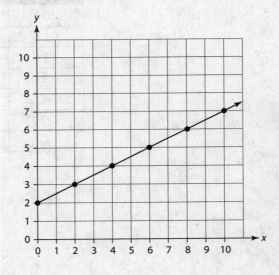

x	y = f(x)
0	
	3
4	
	5
8	
	7

SOLUTION

Start from 0 on the *x*-axis and trace up to the graph and read the corresponding value of *f*(0) on the *y*-axis. *f*(0) = 2. Similarly, find *f*(4) = 4, and *f*(8) = 6. Start from 3 on the *y*-axis and trace horizontally to the graph and read the corresponding value of *x* on the *x*-axis. *f*(2) = 3. Similarly, find *f*(6) = 5, and *f*(10) = 7.

Identifying Functions

A function is defined as a relationship between two sets (called the domain and range of the function) such that for every element in the domain there is exactly one element in the range. Not every relation is a function. You can determine whether a relation is a function by checking to see if there is some value of *x* that is related to two different values of *f*(*x*). If so, then the relation is NOT a function.

EXAMPLE

Is the relation a function?

x	*y*
1	2
2	2
3	4
3	5
4	6
5	9

SOLUTION

The relation **is not** a function. According to the table, *f*(3) = 4 and *f*(3) = 5; this is a violation of the rule that for every value of *x* in the domain there must be only one value of *y* in the range. You cannot have two different values in the range related to the one value in the domain.

It is OK for two different *x* values in the domain to be related to the same *y* value in the range. In the table above we see that *f*(1) = 2 **and** *f*(2) = 2.

There is a test that can be applied to the graph of a relation to determine whether the relation is a function. The test is called the **vertical line test**, and it is used to determine whether there is more than one *y* value for any *x* value. If any vertical line intersects the graph of a relation at more than one point, the graph is said to **fail the vertical line test**, and you can conclude that the graph cannot be the graph of a function. The graphs shown all fail the vertical line test and they are not graphs of functions.

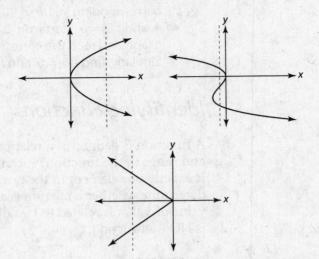

The graphs that follow all satisfy the vertical line test. No matter where a vertical line is drawn, it will intersect the graph in at most one point.

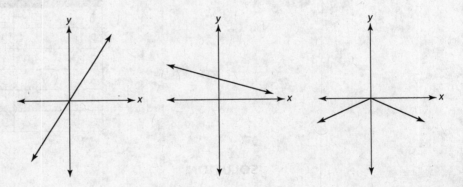

Note that any function whose graph is a line will pass the vertical line test provided the line is not vertical.

Linear and Nonlinear Functions

A **linear function** is a function whose graph is a straight line. By the definition of a function, the graph of the function cannot be a vertical line because a vertical line would not pass the vertical line test. A linear function will have an equation that can be written in the form: $y = f(x) = mx + b$, where m and b are two real numbers. Any function that is not a linear function is called a **nonlinear function**.

Examples of linear functions:

$y = 2.5x + 3.0$

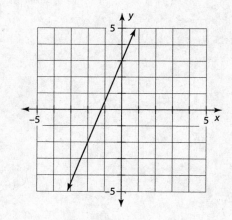

$y = -1.5x$

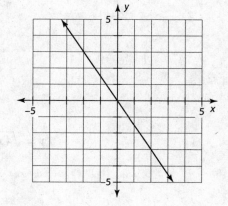

$y = 20 - x$

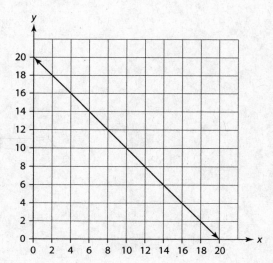

Examples of nonlinear functions:

$y = x^2$

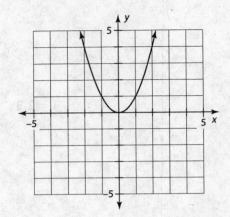

$y = \sqrt{4x + 16}$

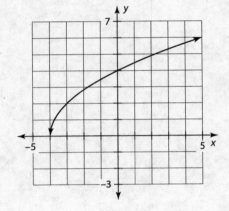

$y = \dfrac{1}{x^2 - 1}$

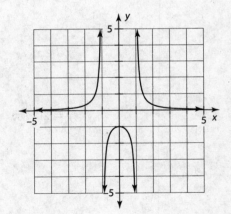

One way to tell if a function represented in table form is a linear function is to graph the table of values and see if the points all lie on a straight line. Another way is to check the differences of the successive x values and y values in the table. If the difference between all successive pairs of x values is constant **and** the difference between all successive pairs of y values is constant, then the function is linear. In the table that follows, the x values are consecutive; they increase by 1 at each step. The *y* values all increase by 4 each step. The function is linear. This can also be seen in the graph.

x	y = f(x)
0	0
1	4
2	8
3	12
4	16
5	20

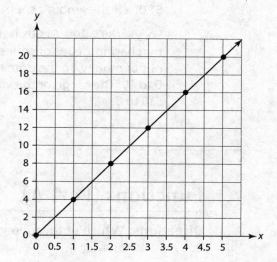

Real-World Functions

EXAMPLE 1

Write a function to calculate the total cost of a restaurant meal including 6 percent sales tax and a 18 percent tip as a function of the cost of the meal before the tax and tip are added. Identify the domain and range of the function.

SOLUTION

Let *x* be the cost of the meal before tax and tip are added.

The sales tax will be 0.06*x*, so the cost of the meal plus tax will be 0.06*x* + *x*, or 1.06*x*.

The tip, calculated on the cost of the meal plus tax, is 0.18(1.06*x*), or 0.1908*x*.

The total cost including tax and tip will be 1.06*x* + 0.1908*x*, or 1.2508*x*.

The function is $y = f(x) = 1.2508x$.

The domain and range of the function is the set of positive real numbers.

EXAMPLE 2

You start the week with $10 for coffee.

A coffee costs $1.00. Write a function equation for the amount of money left after you have purchased x cups of coffee. What is a reasonable domain and range for this function?

SOLUTION

x = the total number of cups of coffee purchased that week.

$1.00x$ is the amount spent on coffee.

So, $y = f(x) = 10 - \$1.00x$ is the amount of coffee money left after purchasing x cups of coffee. You can buy up to 10 cups before you run out of money, so the domain of the function is the set of integers from 0 to 10. The range or the amount of money left can be any integer from $10 to 0.

EXERCISE 6

Functions (Part A)

Directions: Which of the following relations are functions? Justify your answer.

1. $y = 34x - 27$

_____

2. $y = -150x$

_____

3.

x	y
1	1
2	2
3	3
4	2
5	1

_____

4.

x	y
1	2
2	4
1	6
2	8
3	10

5.

x	y
1	3
2	6
3	9
4	12
1	3

Functions (Part B)

Directions: Which of the following graphs are graphs of functions? Justify your answer.

6.

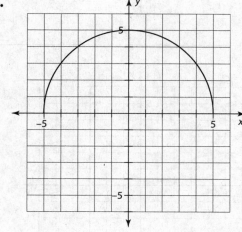

7.

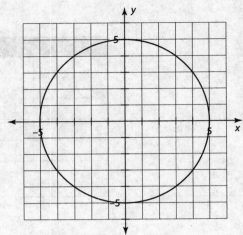

_____

8.

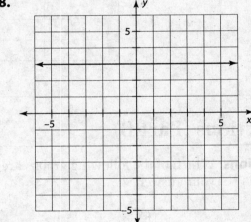

_____

9.

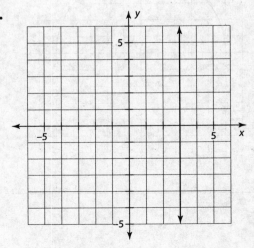

_____

10.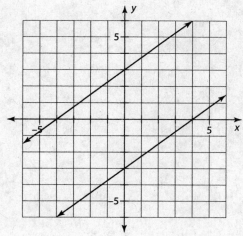

Answers are on page 787.

CHAPTER 7

Ratios, Proportions, and Percent

In Chapter 2, you learned about fractions. A fraction represents the number of parts of a whole. In this chapter, you will learn another meaning of a fraction: a fraction can be a ratio. A **ratio** is a comparison of two numbers or two like quantities. Ratios are a way of talking about relationships between two quantities. You will also learn about proportions, which are comparisons of ratios, and percents, which arise when comparing parts of wholes to 100.

Understanding Ratios

The ratio x to y can be represented as $x{:}y$ or $\dfrac{x}{y}$.

There are three ways in which a ratio can be written.

Using the Word "to"	Writing a Fraction	Using a Colon
3 to 4	$\dfrac{3}{4}$	3:4

Ratios that compare three quantities are written as a:b:c. For example, 4 liters to 3 liters to 5 liters is written as 4:3:5.

Rules for Writing a Ratio

There are three basic rules for writing a ratio.

1. Reduce the ratio to its lowest term.

Reduce a ratio in a same way as the fractions are reduced.

EXAMPLE

$$2{:}8 = \frac{2}{8} = \frac{2 \div 2}{8 \div 2} = \frac{1}{4}$$

2. An improper-fraction ratio should be left as an improper fraction.

EXAMPLE

$$12{:}8 = \frac{12}{8} = \frac{12 \div 4}{8 \div 4} = \frac{3}{2}$$

3. A whole-number ratio should be written as an improper fraction.

EXAMPLE

$$24:6 = \frac{24}{6} = \frac{24 \div 6}{6 \div 6} = \frac{4}{1}$$

Ratios are often used to compare like quantities, that is, quantities with the same units. Take a look at the following examples.

EXAMPLE 1

A rectangle is 6 cm wide and 12 cm long. What is the ratio of its width to its length?

$$\frac{6\,cm}{12\,cm} = \frac{6}{12} = \frac{1}{2}$$

ANSWER: 1:2

Note: When using a ratio to compare like quantities, such as centimeters to centimeters, liters to liters, and oranges to oranges, you should simplify the ratio by canceling the units.

EXAMPLE 2

Two teams, A and B, played 18 football matches against each other. Team A won 12 games. What is the ratio of games Team A won to the games that it lost?

STEP 1: Find out how many games Team A lost.

Games lost = total games played – games won = 18 – 12 = 6

STEP 2: Write the ratio of games won to games lost.

$$12:6 = \frac{12}{6} = \frac{12 \div 6}{6 \div 6} = \frac{2}{1}$$

ANSWER: 2:1

EXERCISE 1

Understanding Ratios (Part A)

Directions: Reduce the ratios to their lowest terms.

1. 2:6 _____

2. 8:4:16 _____

3. 4:16 _____

4. 2:12:6 _____

5. 25:10 _____

Understanding Ratios (Part B)

Directions: Choose the correct answer.

6. A basketball team won 6 matches and lost 8 matches. What is the ratio of games won to games lost?

   A. 4:3
   B. 3:4
   C. 3:7
   D. 4:7

7. In a class, there are 12 boys and 16 girls. What is the ratio of girls to boys in the class?

   A. 4:3
   B. 3:4
   C. 4:7
   D. 7:4

8. In a school, there are 12 science teachers, 15 math teachers, and 9 English teachers. What is the ratio of math teachers to science teachers to English teachers?

   A. 3:5:4
   B. 4:3:5
   C. 5:3:4
   D. 5:4:3

9. A cake recipe requires 3 ounces of cream and 6 ounces of sugar. What is the ratio of cream to the cream/sugar mixture?
   A. 1:2
   B. 2:1
   C. 1:3
   D. 3:1

10. Each month $500 is deducted from Mr. Williams' paycheck for taxes and other withholdings. Mr. Williams takes home $1,500 each month. What is the ratio of the amount of his take-home pay to the amount that is deducted?

    A. 3:1
    B. 1:3
    C. 3:4
    D. 4:3

11. Out of 24 people surveyed, 8 were boys and 16 were girls. What is the ratio of boys to girls?

    A. 2:1
    B. 1:2
    C. 1:3
    D. 2:3

12. In a music class, 16 students are females and 8 males. What is the ratio of male students to the total number of students?

 A. 1:3
 B. 3:1
 C. 1:2
 D. 2:1

Answers are on page 787.

Understanding Unit Rates

A ratio that compares two numbers with different units is called a **rate**. A rate can be used to compare miles and hours, or dollars and pounds, or people and houses, for example. The difference between ratios and rates is that ratios are comparisons between quantities with common units, while rates compare quantities with different units.

A rate where an amount of one quantity is compared to one unit of another quantity is called a **unit rate**. Unit rates are measured in miles per hour (mph), or dollars per pound, or people per house. You can calculate a unit rate by dividing the numbers in the rate. A commonly used term with rates is *per*, which means "for each." Sometimes unit rates are written with a slash, as in miles/hour, or dollars/pound, or people/house. In this case the slash is read "per."

Unit pricing is one of the most common uses of unit rates. A **unit price** is a *price per unit*. The unit used may be pints, pounds, crates, or some other measure. Multiplying unit rates or unit prices by the right quantity can give total amounts.

EXAMPLE 1

A car drives at 150 miles in 3 hours.

What is the speed of the car in mph?

Write a rate comparing miles to hours. After reducing to lowest terms, this is a unit rate called speed.

$$\text{Speed} = \frac{150 \text{ miles}}{3 \text{ hours}} = \frac{50 \text{ miles}}{1 \text{ hour}} \quad \textit{or } \textbf{50 miles per hour (50 mph)}$$

Rate given in problem   Unit rate

How far will the car travel in 5 hours at the given rate?

Distance in 5 hours = 50 mph × 5 hours = 250 miles

EXAMPLE 2

The total price of a cookie purchase is $2.84 for 3 containers.

What is the price per container?

Write the ratio of cost to number of containers and divide.

$$\text{Price per container} = \frac{\$2.84}{3 \text{ containers}} = \$ \, 0.95 \text{ per container}$$

How much would 8 containers cost at the given rate?

Cost of 8 containers = $0.95 \times 8 = \$7.60$

EXERCISE 2

Understanding Unit Rates (Part A)

Directions: Calculate the price of each unit.

1. 6 ounces of nuts for $1.57 _____

2. 5 cold drink bottles for $3.45 _____

3. $0.99 for 8 pencils _____

4. $4.17 for 3 pounds of chicken _____

5. 3 bunches of bananas for $2.34 _____

Understanding Unit Rates (Part B)

Directions: Choose the correct answer.

6. If a man earns $500 for 55 hours, what is his pay rate in dollars per hour?

   A. $0.11 per hour
   B. $9.09 per hour
   C. $10 per hour
   D. $11 per hour

7. If there are 250 calories in 15 ounces of soda, how many calories are there in 50 ounces of this soda?

   A. 3 calories
   B. 75 calories
   C. 800 calories
   D. 833 calories

8. Ramona's heartbeat is 132 beats in 2 minutes. What is Ramona's heart rate in beats per minute?

   A. 60 beats per minute
   B. 66 beats per minute
   C. 70 beats per minute
   D. 72 beats per minute

9. Daniel runs 20 miles in 3 hours. How many miles can he run in 10 hours at the same rate?

    A. 0.66 miles

    B. 1.5 miles

    C. 15 miles

    D. 67 miles

10. Stacey reads 50 pages of a novel having 250 words per page in 125 minutes. What is Stacey's reading rate in words per minute?

    A. 2 words per minute

    B. 25 words per minute

    C. 100 words per minute

    D. 150 words per minute

Answers are on page 787.

Equivalent Ratios

Two ratios with the same value in their simplest forms are called **equivalent ratios**.

For example, 1:5 and 100:500 are equivalent ratios because if you simplify 100:500, you get 1:5.

$$100:500 = 100 \div 100 : 500 \div 100 = 1:5$$

The following methods can be used to find the equivalent ratio for a given ratio:

1. Multiplying the ratio: To find an equivalent ratio of a ratio that is in its simplest form, multiply both numbers of the ratio by the same number.

EXAMPLE

Find the equivalent ratio of 3:7 that compares 6 to a quantity.

Multiply both numbers by 2.

$$3:7 = 3 \times 2 : 7 \times 2 = 6:14$$

ANSWER: 6:14

2. Dividing the ratio: To find an equivalent ratio of a ratio that is *not* in its simplest form, divide both numbers of the ratio by a common divisor.

EXAMPLE

Find the equivalent ratio of 9:15.

Divide both numbers by 3.

$$9:15 = 9 \div 3 : 15 \div 3 = 3:5$$

ANSWER: 3:5

EXERCISE 3

Equivalent Ratios (Part A)

Directions: Choose the correct answer.

1. Which among the given pair of ratios are equivalent ratios?

    A. 2:3, 3:2
    B. 1:2, 3:2
    C. 3:5, 6:10
    D. 2:3, 2:5

2. Which of the following represents the equivalent ratio of 2:5?

    A. 5:2
    B. 2:10
    C. 10:5
    D. 6:15

3. Which of the following represents the equivalent ratio of 4:8?

    A. 2:1
    B. 4:2
    C. 2:8
    D. 1:2

4. Which of the following represents the equivalent ratio of 4:9?

    A. 2:3
    B. 8:27
    C. 16:36
    D. 16:18

5. Which of the following represents the equivalent ratio of 27:30?

    A. 10:9
    B. 9:3
    C. 9:10
    D. 1:10

Equivalent Ratios (Part B)

Directions: Fill in the blanks.

6. $2 \times 2 : 5 \times 2 = \underline{\quad} : 10$

7. $4 \times 3 : 7 \times 3 = 12 : \underline{\quad}$

8. $6 \div 2 : 8 \div 2 = \underline{\quad} : 4$

9. $16 \div 4 : 28 \div 4 = 4 : \underline{}$

10. $2 \times 4 : 5 \times 4 = \underline{} : 20$

Equivalent Ratios (Part C)

Directions: Fill in the blanks to make an equivalent ratio.

11. $2 : 3 = 6 : \underline{}$

12. $2 : 5 = \underline{} : 10$

13. $12 : 24 = \underline{} : 2$

14. $6 : 9 = 2 : \underline{}$

15. $1 : 2 = \underline{} : 10$

Answers are on page 787.

Comparing Ratios

There are three methods to compare ratios. For example, in a fishing competition, Joseph caught 12 catfish and 16 salmon, while Jane caught 18 catfish and 20 salmon.

Who caught a higher ratio of catfish to salmon?

- Joseph → 12 catfish and 16 salmon
- Jane → 18 catfish and 20 salmon

Method 1: Ratios with common denominators

$$\text{Joseph} \rightarrow \frac{12}{16} = \frac{3}{4} = \frac{15}{20}$$

$$\text{Jane} \rightarrow \frac{18}{20}$$

Since $\frac{18}{20} > \frac{15}{20}$, Jane caught a higher ratio of catfish to salmon.

Method 2: Unit ratios

$$\text{Joseph} \rightarrow \frac{12 \div 16}{16 \div 16} = \frac{0.75}{1}$$

$$\text{Jane} \rightarrow \frac{18 \div 20}{20 \div 20} = \frac{0.9}{1}$$

Since $0.9 > 0.75$, Jane caught a higher ratio of catfish to salmon.

Method 3: Ratios with common numerators

$$\text{Joseph} \rightarrow \frac{12}{16} = \frac{3}{4} = \frac{18}{24}$$

$$\text{Jane} \rightarrow \frac{18}{20}$$

Since $\frac{18}{20} > \frac{18}{24}$, Jane caught a higher ratio of catfish to salmon.

EXERCISE 4

Comparing Ratios (Part A)

Directions: Compare each ratio using <, >, or =.

1. 7:6 _____ 13:6

2. 4:5 _____ 7:10

3. 2:3 _____ 8:12

4. 12:13 _____ 7:13

5. 4:8 _____ 3:6

6. 2:5 _____ 4:5

7. 2:3 _____ 5:8

8. 1:4 _____ 1:3

9. 6:8 _____ 4:8

10. 20:30 _____ 2:3

Answers are on page 787.

Understanding Proportions

A **proportion** is made up of two equal ratios or rates, or a pair of equivalent fractions.

EXAMPLES

$$\frac{1}{3} = \frac{3}{9}, \frac{2}{5} = \frac{4}{10}$$

The proportion $\frac{x}{y} = \frac{z}{w}$ is read "x is to y as z is to w" and can be written $x : y :: z : w$. If $\frac{x}{y} = \frac{z}{w}$, then $x \cdot w = z \cdot y$. Likewise, if $x \cdot w = z \cdot y$, then you can say that the ratios $\frac{x}{y}$ and $\frac{z}{w}$ are proportional, or that they are in proportion. This property is called the **proportionality rule**. You can rewrite a proportion such as $\frac{x}{y} = \frac{z}{w}$ as an equation: $x \cdot w = z \cdot y$. This is called **cross-multiplying** because you find the parts to multiply by going across the equal sign:

EXAMPLE 1

Add 1 spoon of protein powder to 2 cups of milk. The ratio of protein powder to milk is 1:2. You will get the same flavor if you add 2 spoons of protein powder to 4 cups of milk.

These two equivalent ratios can be written as the proportion $\frac{1}{2} = \frac{2}{4}$.

In case of proportions, two equal ratios are connected by the word *as*.

$\frac{1}{2} = \frac{2}{4}$ is read "1 is to 2 **as** 2 is to 4."

To check whether these two ratios are in proportion, cross-multiply.

The products are found by multiplying each numerator by its opposite denominator.

Cross-Multiplication	Equal Products
$\frac{1}{2} \diagdown\diagup \frac{2}{4}$	$1 \times 4 = 2 \times 2$
	$4 = 4$

Thus, the two fractions are proportional.

Cross-multiplying is used to check whether two ratios are in proportion. It is also used to find a missing or unknown value in a proportion. You have seen that a proportion consists of four values. If any three of the four values of a proportion are known, then you can find the missing value or unknown value.

Finding the Missing Value in a Proportion

Follow these steps to find the missing value in a proportion.

- Write *n* or any other letter in place of the missing number.
- Cross-multiply to get an equation that will contain *n*.
- To get the value of *n*, divide both sides of the equal sign by the number that multiples *n*.

EXAMPLE 2

Find the value of n: $\dfrac{n}{6} = \dfrac{2}{4}$.

STEP 1: Cross-multiply to get $4n = 12$.

STEP 2: Divide both sides of the equal sign by 4 and simplify to find n.

$$\dfrac{4n}{4} = \dfrac{12}{4}$$
$$n = 3$$

ANSWER: $n = 3$

PROPORTION: $\dfrac{3}{6} = \dfrac{2}{4}$

EXAMPLE 3

Find the value of x: $\dfrac{10}{8} = \dfrac{x}{4}$.

STEP 1: Cross-multiply to get $8x = 40$.

STEP 2: Divide both sides of the equal sign by 8 and simplify to find x.

$$\dfrac{8x}{8} = \dfrac{40}{8}$$

$$x = 5$$

ANSWER: $x = 5$

PROPORTION: $\dfrac{10}{8} = \dfrac{5}{4}$

Proportions can be used to solve word problems involving comparisons.

EXAMPLE 4

A cake recipe calls for 5 cups of milk to 3 cups of cream. To make the cake, how much cream should be added to 15 cups of milk?

STEP 1: Write a proportion where each ratio is of the form $\dfrac{\text{cups of cream}}{\text{cups of milk}}$.

Let n be the unknown cups of cream: $\dfrac{n}{15} = \dfrac{3}{5}$.

STEP 2: Cross-multiply to get $5n = 45$.

STEP 3: To find n, divide both sides of the equal sign by 5 and simplify.

$$\dfrac{5n}{5} = \dfrac{45}{5}$$

$$n = 9$$

ANSWER: $n = 9$ cups of cream

EXERCISE 5

Understanding Proportions (Part A)

Directions: Choose the correct answer.

1. Which pair of fractions is in proportion?

   A. $\dfrac{3}{2}, \dfrac{6}{8}$

   B. $\dfrac{3}{4}, \dfrac{6}{7}$

   C. $\dfrac{3}{4}, \dfrac{6}{8}$

   D. $\dfrac{3}{4}, \dfrac{5}{8}$

2. Which pair of fractions is in proportion?

   A. $\dfrac{8}{12}, \dfrac{2}{4}$

   B. $\dfrac{8}{12}, \dfrac{1}{3}$

   C. $\dfrac{7}{12}, \dfrac{2}{3}$

   D. $\dfrac{8}{12}, \dfrac{2}{3}$

3. Which pair of fractions is NOT in proportion?

   A. $\dfrac{8}{12}, \dfrac{2}{3}$

   B. $\dfrac{4}{8}, \dfrac{2}{4}$

   C. $\dfrac{9}{12}, \dfrac{3}{4}$

   D. $\dfrac{8}{11}, \dfrac{2}{3}$

Understanding Proportions (Part B)

Directions: Find the value of n or x.

4. $\dfrac{x}{8} = \dfrac{1}{4}$ 5. $\dfrac{n}{3} = \dfrac{25}{15}$ 6. $\dfrac{28}{12} = \dfrac{7}{x}$ 7. $\dfrac{3}{n} = \dfrac{18}{12}$

8. $\dfrac{21}{9} = \dfrac{n}{3}$ **9.** $\dfrac{x}{5} = \dfrac{10}{16}$ **10.** $\dfrac{30}{24} = \dfrac{5}{x}$

Understanding Proportions (Part C)

Directions: Choose the correct proportion that can be used to solve each problem.

11. In a management company, 5 out of every 8 managers are women. Which proportion is used to find how many of the 72 managers who work at the company are women?

    A. $\dfrac{n}{8} = \dfrac{72}{5}$

    B. $\dfrac{n}{5} = \dfrac{8}{72}$

    C. $\dfrac{n}{72} = \dfrac{5}{8}$

    D. $\dfrac{n}{72} = \dfrac{8}{5}$

12. Keisha was paid \$108 for 12 hours of work. Which proportion is used to find how much Keisha will earn for working 30 hours?

    A. $\dfrac{12}{30} = \dfrac{n}{108}$

    B. $\dfrac{30}{108} = \dfrac{12}{n}$

    C. $\dfrac{30}{n} = \dfrac{108}{12}$

    D. $\dfrac{30}{n} = \dfrac{12}{108}$

Understanding Proportions (Part D)

Directions: Choose the correct answer.

13. In Highland Middle School, there are 32 teachers, 14 of whom are women. Suppose the same ratio is true for 140 middle-school teachers in the school district. What is the number of male middle-school teachers in this district?

    A. 50

    B. 61

    C. 79

    D. 90

14. Carlos can drive 440 miles in 8 hours. At this speed, what will be the distance traveled in 11 hours?

    A. 300 miles
    B. 320 miles
    C. 600 miles
    D. 605 miles

15. If a machine can produce 16 tin cans in 2 minutes, how long will it take to produce 64 tin cans?

    A. 4 minutes
    B. 8 minutes
    C. 16 minutes
    D. 64 minutes

Answers are on page 787.

Understanding Percent

In Chapters 2 and 3, you learned how to use fractions and decimals to describe parts of a whole. Percent is another way to write part of a whole. **Percents are ratios with 100 in the denominator.** Percent refers to the **number of parts out of 100 parts**.

The symbol for percent is %, which represents multiplication by $\frac{1}{100}$.

- 25 percent means 25 parts out of 100 parts, that is, $\frac{25}{100}$.

- 25 percent is written as 25%.

Relating Decimals, Fractions, and Percents

To convert between decimals, fractions, and percents, follow these steps.

Writing a Percent as a Fraction

To convert a percent to a fraction, replace the percent symbol by $\frac{1}{100}$ and multiply. If necessary, simplify the result.

    EXAMPLES

    Write 9%, 75%, and 125% as fractions.

$$9\% = 9\left(\frac{1}{100}\right) = \frac{9}{100}$$

$$75\% = 75\left(\frac{1}{100}\right) = \frac{75}{100} = \frac{3}{4}$$

If a percent is greater than 100, then the equivalent fraction will be greater than 1 as shown in the following example. Write a percent as a mixed number in such cases.

$$125\% = 125\left(\frac{1}{100}\right) = \frac{125}{100} = \frac{5}{4} = 1\frac{1}{4}$$

Writing a Percent as a Decimal

To convert a percent to an equivalent decimal, remove the percent (%) symbol and divide the number by 100. In other words, move the decimal point two places to the left and remove the percent symbol.

EXAMPLES

Write 7%, 35%, and 128% as decimals.

$7\% = 0.07$

$35\% = 0.35$

$128\% = 1.28$

Writing a Fraction as a Percent

To convert a fraction to a percent, multiply the fraction by $\frac{100}{1}$ and attach a percent sign.

EXAMPLES

Write $\frac{11}{20}$, $\frac{5}{6}$, and $2\frac{14}{25}$ as percents.

$$\frac{11}{20} = \frac{11}{20} \cdot \frac{100}{1}\% = \frac{11}{\underset{1}{20}} \cdot \frac{\overset{5}{100}}{1}\% = \frac{11}{1} \cdot \frac{5}{1}\% = 55\%$$

$$\frac{5}{6} = \frac{5}{6} \cdot \frac{100}{1}\% = \frac{5}{\underset{3}{6}} \cdot \frac{\overset{50}{100}}{1}\% = \frac{5}{3} \cdot \frac{50}{1}\% = \frac{250}{3}\% = 83\frac{1}{3}\%$$

$$2\frac{14}{25} = 2\frac{14}{25} \cdot \frac{100}{1}\% = \frac{64}{25} \cdot \frac{100}{1}\% = \frac{64}{\underset{1}{25}} \cdot \frac{\overset{4}{100}}{1}\% = \frac{64}{1} \cdot \frac{4}{1}\% = 256\%$$

Writing a Decimal as a Percent

To convert a decimal to a percent, multiply the decimal by 100 by moving the decimal point two places to the right and attach a percent sign.

EXAMPLES

Write 0.1357, 5.1, and 3 as percents.

$0.1357 = 13.57\%$

$5.1 = 510\%$

$3 = 300\%$

Solving Percent Problems

To solve percent problems, follow these steps.

Identifying Numbers in a Percent Problem

A percent problem contains three important pieces: the **percent**, the **whole**, and the **part**.

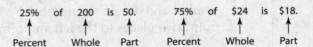

Identifying these pieces is the first step to solving any percent problem. The percent is the easiest to find: it is the quantity followed by the word *percent* or the percent symbol, %. The second easiest to find is the whole: it is the quantity that follows the phrase *percent of.* The part is the quantity that remains; it is usually separated from the percent and the whole by the word *is* or *was* or similar phrasing.

Solving Percent Problems by Using Proportions

In nearly every percent problem, one of the three pieces mentioned above is missing. To identify or compute the missing piece, you can use the **percent proportion**.

$$\textbf{Percent proportion:} \quad \frac{\text{Part}}{\text{Whole}} = \frac{\text{Percent}}{100}$$

EXAMPLE 1

What is 23% of 65?

Here, **part** = not given (n); **whole** = 65; and **percent** = 23.

$$\frac{\text{Part}}{\text{Whole}} = \frac{\text{Percent}}{100}$$

$$\frac{n}{65} = \frac{23}{100}$$

$$100n = 65 \times 23 = 1,495$$

$$\frac{100n}{100} = \frac{1,495}{100}$$

$$n = 14.95$$

ANSWER: 14.95

EXAMPLE 2

If 25% of a quantity is 20, find the quantity.

Here, **part** = 20; **whole** = not given (n); and **percent** = 25.

$$\frac{\text{Part}}{\text{Whole}} = \frac{\text{Percent}}{100}$$

$$\frac{20}{n} = \frac{25}{100}$$

$$20 \times 100 = n \times 25$$

$$25n = 2{,}000$$

$$\frac{25n}{25} = \frac{2{,}000}{25}$$

$$n = 80$$

ANSWER: 80

EXAMPLE 3

20 is what percent of 50?

Here, **part** = 20; **whole** = 50; and **percent** = not given (n).

$$\frac{\text{Part}}{\text{Whole}} = \frac{\text{Percent}}{100}$$

$$\frac{20}{50} = \frac{n}{100}$$

$$20 \times 100 = 50 \times n$$

$$50n = 2{,}000$$

$$\frac{50n}{50} = \frac{2{,}000}{50}$$

$$n = 40$$

ANSWER: 40%

Percent Increase and Percent Decrease

In problems involving a percent increase or decrease, an additional step using addition or subtraction is needed. The whole is always the starting value before the increase or decrease, and the part is the actual increase or decrease.

EXAMPLE 1

A school's enrollment in 2013 was 500 students. If the enrollment increased by 5% from 2013 to 2014, how many students were enrolled in the second year?

Here, **part** = unknown (n = amount of increase); **whole** = 500 (number of students in 2013); and **percent** = 5% (percent increase).

$$\frac{\text{Part}}{\text{Whole}} = \frac{\text{Percent}}{100}$$

$$\frac{n}{500} = \frac{5}{100}$$

$$100n = 2,500$$

$$\frac{100n}{100} = \frac{2,500}{100}$$

$$n = 25$$

Because the amount of increase is 25, the number of students enrolled in the year 2014 must have been:

$$500 \quad + \quad 25 \quad = \quad 525$$
(Students in 2013) (Increase) (Students in 2014)

EXAMPLE 2

At a certain car dealership, sales of cars decreased from 400 units one year to 360 units the next year. What was the decrease as a percent?

First, calculate the amount of decrease = 400 − 360 = 40 units.

Here, **part** = 40; **whole** = 400 (total number of cars); and **percent** = unknown (n = percent decrease).

$$\frac{\text{Part}}{\text{Whole}} = \frac{\text{Percent}}{100}$$

$$\frac{40}{400} = \frac{n}{100}$$

$$4,000 = 400n$$

$$\frac{4,000}{400} = \frac{400n}{400}$$

$$10 = n$$

$$n = 10$$

ANSWER: 10% decrease

EXAMPLE 3

A shopkeeper offers a 40% discount on a product whose cost is $250. How much is the actual discount in dollars, and what is the cost of the product after the discount?

Here, **part** = unknown (n = amount of discount); **whole** = 500 (original cost); and **percent** = 40% (percent decrease).

Let's find the discount and cost after discount.

$$\frac{\text{Part}}{\text{Whole}} = \frac{\text{Percent}}{100}$$

$$\frac{n}{250} = \frac{40}{100}$$

$$100n = 10{,}000$$

$$\frac{100n}{100} = \frac{10{,}000}{100}$$

$$n = 100$$

ANSWER: $100 discount

After the discount the cost of the product is: $250 − $100 = $150.

EXERCISE 6

Understanding Percent (Part A)

Directions: Fill in the blanks. Use percent to describe each situation.

1. Out of 100 students, 23 voted in a student election. _____

2. Out of 100 people surveyed, 49 prefer coffee. _____

3. Out of 20 students, 5 received a grade of A on their class test. _____

4. Of the 25 employees of a company, 9 are females. _____

5. A shopkeeper sold 20 bats of the 100 available. _____

Understanding Percent (Part B)

Directions: Write each percent as a fraction or mixed numbers.

6. 4% _____   7. 19% _____

8. 66% _____   9. 150% _____

10. 130% _____

Understanding Percent (Part C)

Directions: Write each percent as an equivalent decimal.

11. 5% _____   12. 16% _____

13. 27% _____   14. 423% _____

15. 110% _____

Understanding Percent (Part D)

Directions: Fill in the blanks.

16. _____ = 21% of 56   17. 52 = 40% of _____

18. 42 = _____% of 70   19. _____ = 45% of 89

20. 59 = 34% of _____   21. 65 = _____ % of 45

22. 29 = 78% of _____   23. _____ = 64% of 76

Understanding Percent (Part E)

Directions: Choose the correct answer.

24. Austin got a 25% discount on a gadget costing $570. How much is the discount in dollars?

    A. $140.00
    B. $142.50
    C. $200.00
    D. $545.50

25. Which of the following is the largest discount in dollars?

    A. 24% on $50
    B. 32% on $65
    C. 22% on $95
    D. 15% on $72

Understanding Percent (Part F)

Directions: Solve the following word problems.

26. A manager in a company has an annual budget of $39,000. He spent 10% of his budget in July. How much, in dollars, of his annual budget did he spend?

27. Out of 20 students in a physics class, 5 received a grade of A. What percent of students received a grade of A?

28. In a shipment of 800 mobile phones, 4 were found to be defective. What percent of the mobile phones were defective?

29. A chemist has 300-mL solution that is 15% alcohol. How many milliliters of alcohol are in the solution?

30. What interest will you pay on a $3,000 loan for one year if the interest rate is 8%?

31. This year a company hired 18 new employees. Last year, there were 120 employees. What is the percent increase in the number of employees?

32. A storekeeper sells an item for $250. If the store pays $200 for the item, what is the markup rate?

Answers are on page 788.

EXERCISE 7

Ratio, Proportion, and Percent Review (Part A)

Directions: Reduce each ratio to its lowest term.

1. 9:21 _____

2. 10:25:35 _____

3. 18:48 _____

Ratio, Proportion, and Percent Review (Part B)

Directions: Choose the correct answer.

4. In an election a candidate received 300 votes of 1,500 votes cast. What is the ratio of votes received to the votes not received?

A. 1:5
B. 1:4
C. 4:1
D. 5:1

5. Lauren is awake for 16 hours a day and sleeps 8 hours at night. What is the ratio of the hours Lauren sleeps to the hours she is awake?

A. 1:2
B. 2:1
C. 1:3
D. 3:1

6. In a sports club, there are 21 soccer players, 14 badminton players, and 28 tennis players. What is the ratio of badminton players to soccer players to tennis players?

A. 2:4:3
B. 4:3:2
C. 3:2:4
D. 2:3:4

Ratio, Proportion, and Percent Review (Part C)

Directions: Calculate the price of each unit.

7. 3 bottles of milk for $6.23 _____

8. 5 pounds of grapes for $4.30 _____

Ratio, Proportion, and Percent Review (Part D)

Directions: Choose the correct answer.

9. If a man earns $800 for 40 hours, what is his pay rate in dollars per hour?

A. $200 per hour
B. $20 per hour
C. $10.43 per hour
D. $2 per hour

10. If there are 120 calories in 12 ounces of a soft drink, how many calories are there in 30 ounces of this soda?

A. 30 calories
B. 480 calories
C. 300 calories
D. 800 calories

Ratio, Proportion, and Percent Review (Part E)

Directions: Fill in the blanks.

11. $3 \times 4 : 5 \times 4 = \underline{} : 20$

12. $12 \div 3 : 27 \div 3 = 4 : \underline{}$

Ratio, Proportion, and Percent Review (Part F)

Directions: Fill in the blanks to make an equivalent ratio.

13. $4:7 = 12:\underline{\quad}$

14. $16:24 = \underline{\quad}:3$

Ratio, Proportion, and Percent Review (Part G)

Directions: Compare each ratio using <, >, and =.

15. $7:9$ _____ $3:5$

16. $1:2$ _____ $7:14$

17. $6:8$ _____ $9:10$

Ratio, Proportion, and Percent Review (Part H)

Directions: Find the value of n or x.

18. $\dfrac{x}{27} = \dfrac{2}{9}$

19. $\dfrac{3}{7} = \dfrac{n}{28}$

20. $\dfrac{5}{12} = \dfrac{10}{x}$

Ratio, Proportion, and Percent Review (Part I)

Directions: Choose the correct proportion that can be used to solve the problem.

21. Melons are on sale at 15 for $5. How much would 25 melons cost?

A. $\dfrac{5}{15} = \dfrac{25}{n}$

B. $\dfrac{25}{15} = \dfrac{5}{n}$

C. $\dfrac{5}{15} = \dfrac{n}{25}$

D. $\dfrac{n}{15} = \dfrac{5}{25}$

Ratio, Proportion, and Percent Review (Part J)

Directions: Choose the correct answer.

22. A recipe calls for 2 cups of cream for 12 servings of desert. How many cups of cream are needed to make 18 servings?

    A. 2
    B. 3
    C. 4
    D. 5

23. Betty can drive 355 miles in 5 hours. At this speed, how far will she travel in 7 hours?

    A. 469 miles
    B. 476 miles
    C. 483 miles
    D. 497 miles

Ratio, Proportion, and Percent Review (Part K)

Directions: Fill in the blanks.

24. What percent of $300 is $60? _____

25. 112 is 14% of what number? _____

26. 392 is what percent of 2,800? _____

27. Find 110% of 900. _____

28. What percent of 40 is 52? _____

Ratio, Proportion, and Percent Review (Part L)

Directions: Fill in the blanks.

29. _____ = 13% of 76   **30.** 62 = 43% of _____

31. 34 = _____% of 78

Ratio, Proportion, and Percent Review (Part M)

Directions: Solve the following word problems.

32. On a science test, a student had 80% of the problems correct. If he had 20 problems correct, how many questions were on the test?

33. The population of a town increased 15% in 3 years. The population of the town was 6,000 originally. What is the population after the increase?

34. A storekeeper makes a profit of 25% when item A is sold. If item A costs the store $20, what is its selling price?

35. A person pays $300 interest on a $2,500 loan for one year. What is the interest rate for the loan?

Answers are on page 788.

## CHAPTER 8

Data Analysis and Probability

Numbers often come in the form of data. It is difficult to make decisions from individual data values, and ways to represent sets of data have been developed by data users to help them properly make sense of the data as a whole. You will learn about some data representations in this chapter and a little about using probability to predict data.

Data Analysis

A **variable** is a characteristic or measurement that can be recorded and is free to change. **Data** are the values or numbers a variable can have. Often data are the result of measurement, but they don't have to be. Data controlled only by chance are called random data. Data can be people's age, hair color, or blood type; the number of cars in town; or a number connected with anything measured. A single piece of data is called a *data point* or a *datum*.

A **data set** is a collection of data values. A data set might be the age of every student on a school campus or the brand of every fifth car to drive on campus. Here is a data set of the ages of American presidents who were in office on January 1, 1900, or since.

AGE AT INAUGURATION FOR AMERICAN PRESIDENTS SINCE 1900

54 42 51 56 55 51 54 51 60 62 43 55 56 61 52 69 64 46 54 47

Data representation is the process of showing the data to others, usually in a table, graph, or chart.

Data analysis is using mathematics to represent a data set by its characteristics, such as an average.

Data Types

There are two major types of data: continuous and discrete.

Continuous

Continuous data values change smoothly, and you can assume an unlimited number of possible values between two measurements. They often have decimal values. An example of continuous data is the temperature outside your home. Temperature changes continuously from instant to instant and cannot jump from one value to another without passing through the values in between. Suppose you measure the temperature at noon and get 50°. Then, an hour later, at 1 p.m., you measure the temperature and get 60°. Being continuous, the temperature had to pass through every possible value between 50° and 60° during that hour. A measurement such as 55.8° would be real and have meaning.

Discrete

Discrete data naturally come in chunks, and the data values are countable. Count the number of students in a classroom every 15 minutes. One time you count 15. The next time you count 16 students. At no time were there 15.25 or 15.75 students in the room. Students come in discrete units of one at a time and the data reflect that.

EXAMPLE 1

Is the height of alfalfa plants in a test field at a university discrete or continuous?

The plants may be measured periodically, but their height changes slowly and continuously.

EXAMPLE 2

In the data set for Age at Inauguration for American Presidents Since 1900, are the data continuous or discrete?

Although time is continuous, the ages are in whole years and are treated as discrete.

Data Classes

Whether data are continuous or discrete, you often need to bunch the data into *groups* or **classes**. These are then called *grouped* or **classified** data. If you were working with the age of presidents when they took office from the previous data set, you would not try to make sense out of that string of 20 numbers. Instead, you'd collect your results into several groupings or classes. These classes might be five years wide: 40 to 44; 45 to 49; 50 to 54; and so on.

Age at Inauguration	40–44	45–49	50–54	55–59	60–64	65–69
Number	2	2	7	4	4	1

You also might want to look at the party of each president, and you would then have two classes.

Presidential Party Affiliation	
Democrat	Republican
8	12

Whether data values are discrete or continuous, classified or unclassified makes a big difference in how you treat them.

EXERCISE 1

Data Types

Directions: Identify the following data as continuous or discrete.

1. Blood pressure of blood donors _____

2. Number of grapes on a grape vine _____

3. The total amount of gas bought at a filling station during the day _____

4. A person's weight over one day _____

5. The number of dogs and cats at a shelter _____

6. The height of a child as he or she grows up _____

7. The number of bananas in a bunch at a grocery store _____

8. The weight of bananas in a bunch at a grocery store _____

9. The amount of rain from thunderstorms _____

10. Your elevation as you climb a mountain _____

Answers are on page 788.

Data Representation: Tables

Tables are excellent for reporting data in detail. Below is a data table of the information in the data set of presidential ages. The presidents' names are added for convenience. In cases where data must be reported simply and cleanly, as in annual reports of companies or government departments, the use of tables is clear and concise.

Age at Inauguration for American Presidents since 1900		
#	Name	Age at Inauguration
25	McKinley, W.	54
26	Roosevelt, T.	42
27	Taft, W.	51
28	Wilson, W.	56
29	Harding, W.	55
30	Coolidge, C.	51
31	Hoover, H.	54
32	Roosevelt, F.	51
33	Truman, H.	60
34	Eisenhower, D.	62
35	Kennedy, J.	43
36	Johnson, L.	55
37	Nixon, R.	56
38	Ford, J.	61
39	Carter, J.	52
40	Reagan, R.	69
41	Bush, G. H.	64
42	Clinton, W.	46
43	Bush, G. W.	54
44	Obama, B.	47

Tables are also good for reporting classified data such as the following.

Age at Inauguration	40–44	45–49	50–54	55–59	60–64	65–69
Number	2	2	7	4	4	1

EXAMPLE

Given the following data set, expand the table to include party affiliation (listed in order).

R R R D R R D D R D D R D R R D R R D R D

Add a column to the data table. Then, because the data in the set is in order, transfer the data into it in the same order from top to bottom.

#	Name	Age at Inauguration	Party
25	McKinley, W.	54	R
26	Roosevelt, T.	42	R
27	Taft, W.	51	R
28	Wilson, W.	56	D
29	Harding, W.	55	R
30	Coolidge, C.	51	R
31	Hoover, H.	54	R
32	Roosevelt, F.	51	D
33	Truman, H.	60	D
34	Eisenhower, D.	62	R
35	Kennedy, J.	43	D
36	Johnson, L.	55	D
37	Nixon, R.	56	R
38	Ford, J.	61	R
39	Carter, J.	52	D
40	Reagan, R.	69	R
41	Bush, G. H.	64	R
42	Clinton, W.	46	D
43	Bush, G. W.	54	R
44	Obama, B.	47	D

Age at Inauguration for American Presidents since 1900

Data Representation: Tables

Directions: Given the ages at death for these presidents, add them to the data chart. An asterisk (∗) means the president is still alive.

58 60 72 67 57 60 90 63 88 78 46 64 81 93 ∗ 93 ∗ ∗ ∗ ∗

Age at Inauguration and at Death for American Presidents since 1900				
#	Name	Age at Inauguration	Age at Death	Party
25	McKinley, W.	54		R
26	Roosevelt, T.	42		R
27	Taft, W.	51		R
28	Wilson, W.	56		D
29	Harding, W.	55		R
30	Coolidge, C.	51		R
31	Hoover, H.	54		R
32	Roosevelt, F.	51		D
33	Truman, H.	60		D
34	Eisenhower, D.	62		R
35	Kennedy, J.	43		D
36	Johnson, L.	55		D
37	Nixon, R.	56		R
38	Ford, J.	61		R
39	Carter, J.	52		D
40	Reagan, R.	69		R
41	Bush, G. H.	64		R
42	Clinton, W.	46		D
43	Bush, G. W.	54		R
44	Obama, B.	47		D

Answer is on page 789.

Data Representation: Bar Charts and Histograms

Bar charts and histograms are used to show data because they give a much better feel for what the data are doing. You can see how one part of the data relates to another.

At first appearance, there does not seem to be much difference between bar charts and histograms. Both use bars and both have scales. But there is a real difference. The word *histogram* is reserved for charts that have numerical classes. In other words, the data are grouped into classes by numbers or ranges of numbers. Also in histograms, the bars are vertical and touch each other. The following is an example of a histogram.

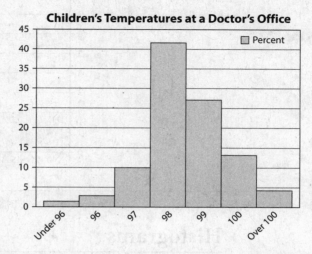

Bar charts have classes that are not numeric. The classes can be things like blood type, the names of states, or anything describing a trait without numbers. In addition, the bars need not be vertical, and they do not touch. The following is a bar chart.

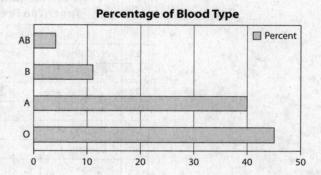

Creating Bar Charts and Histograms

Bar charts and histograms can be used for discrete and/or classified data. Continuous data may be used, but they must be classified before making the chart. For a histogram the classes are located along the horizontal axis, and the height of the bar gives the data value.

EXAMPLE

Create a histogram from the Age at Inauguration for American Presidents Since 1900 data.

Age at Inauguration	40–44	45–49	50–54	55–59	60–64	65–69
Number	2	2	7	4	4	1

The data have been classified in a table so the chart will have six bars, one for each classification. The bars will run across the page with the height of each bar depending upon the number of presidents in each class.

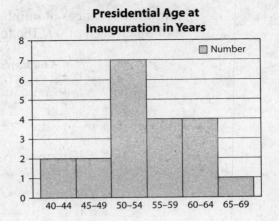

Presidential Age at Inauguration in Years

EXERCISE 3

Histograms

Directions: Using the data provided, construct a histogram of presidential ages at death using four classes: 40–54, 55–69, 70–84, and 85–99 years.

Age at Inauguration and at Death for American Presidents since 1900				
#	Name	Age at Inauguration	Age at Death	Party
25	McKinley, W.	54	58	R
26	Roosevelt, T.	42	60	R
27	Taft, W.	51	72	R
28	Wilson, W.	56	67	D
29	Harding, W.	55	57	R
30	Coolidge, C.	51	60	R
31	Hoover, H.	54	90	R
32	Roosevelt, F.	51	63	D
33	Truman, H.	60	88	D
34	Eisenhower, D.	62	78	R
35	Kennedy, J.	43	46	D
36	Johnson, L.	55	64	D
37	Nixon, R.	56	81	R
38	Ford, J.	61	93	R
39	Carter, J.	52	*	D
40	Reagan, R.	69	93	R
41	Bush, G. H.	64	*	R
42	Clinton, W.	46	*	D
43	Bush, G. W.	54	*	R
44	Obama, B.	47	*	D

Answer is on page 789.

EXERCISE 4

Bar Charts

Directions: Create a bar chart of party affiliation of these presidents.

Presidential Party Affiliation	
Democrat	Republican
8	12

Answer is on page 789.

Reading Histograms and Bar Charts

The other side to using histograms and bar charts is reading them, that is, pulling out data values and using them to answer questions.

EXAMPLE 1

According to the following histogram, how many presidents were between the ages of 60 and 64 when inaugurated?

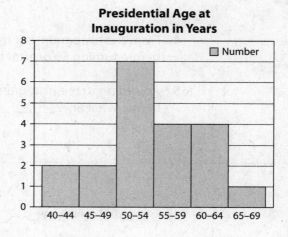

Presidential Age at Inauguration in Years

Go along the horizontal axis and find the bar representing the ages 60–64. It turns out that this bar covers all the years in the question. Running your finger up the bar, you see that the top is at the line labeled 4. So you know that 4 presidents were inaugurated when between 60 and 64 years old.

EXAMPLE 2

According to the histogram, how many presidents were 55 years old or older when inaugurated?

Here you see that just one bar does not cover all the ages in the range. In fact, you need to look at the three rightmost bars to cover the entire range. Follow the bar for 55–59 to its top and find that 4 presidents were between these ages when they took office. Follow the bar for 65–69 to its top and find that 1 president was between these ages when taking office. You need to add this to the 4 from the 60–64 bar to get 9 presidents who were 55 years old or older when they took office.

EXERCISE 5

Reading Histograms and Bar Charts

Directions: Using the histogram "Presidential Age at Inauguration in Years," answer the following questions.

1. What was the most common age range for presidents at inauguration?
    _____

2. What was the least common age range for presidents at inauguration?
    _____

3. How many presidents were younger than 55 years old at inauguration?
    _____

4. From the histogram, is it more likely that a person will become president before turning 50 or after turning 55? _____

5. According to the histogram, just over half of the presidents took office before what age? _____

Answers are on page 789.

Misuse of Bar Charts

A common misuse of bar charts is called the interrupted chart. In this kind of chart only the top of the graph is shown at a large scale. When comparing two or more items, the relationship can easily be exaggerated. Some companies use these types of charts to emphasize increases in sales or profits in order to emphasize the good news. Look at the illustration below of Washing Machines Still Working After 10 Years for companies A, B, and C.

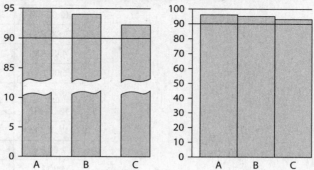

Notice that by breaking the bar chart on the left, a larger scale is used, which makes the difference appear much bigger. The histogram on the right shows a very different picture because the bars go from 0 to 100% without a break. Also, the space between bars in the bar chart makes the differences seem larger. The advertising department of company A would probably favor the interrupted bar chart while those in company C would like the histogram.

Data Representation: Line Graphs

Line graphs are another useful way to display data, particularly how data change over time. Note that line graphs are used only for *continuous* data. Because the graph is a continuous line, it says that every point on that line, even if not measured, represents possible real data. A line graph should have the independent continuous variable (like the time of day) along the horizontal axis. The data values or dependent variable (the readings) will be plotted vertically. The two scales will be set so that the resulting graph is pleasing to the eye; not too flat and wide and not too tall and skinny. The values should be easily read on either scale, and the curve should fill quite a bit of the diagram.

Creating a Line Graph

Let's use the example of the temperature in Phoenix, Arizona, over one day. It is best to start graphing with a data table arranged in some kind of sequence. Here are the data for the temperature for a typical June day in Phoenix. The temperature is recorded every two hours.

Time of Day	Temperature (Fahrenheit)
12:00 AM	91°
2:00 AM	87°
4:00 AM	83°
6:00 AM	82°
8:00 AM	85°
10:00 AM	93°
12:00 PM	100°
2:00 PM	104°
4:00 PM	105°
6:00 PM	104°
8:00 PM	101°
10:00 PM	95°
12:00 AM	92°

Place time along the horizontal axis. Use one division on the graph to represent one hour. Mark and label the times when readings were taken. Establish and label the vertical axis where each division represents one degree of temperature. Plot the temperatures for each recorded time. Here is the result.

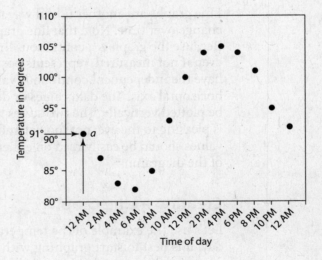

For point *a*, at 12 midnight, the temperature was 91°. Move right until you find 12 AM. Use the vertical scale like a ruler and move vertically up the line passing through 12 AM until you find the proper height, in this case 91°. There, put a point. Do that for each point in the data set (at 2 AM it's at 87°, and so on). Once this is done, connect the points with either straight lines or a smooth curve.

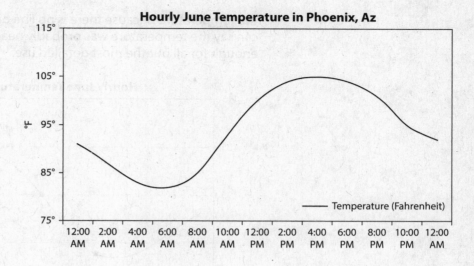

Hourly June Temperature in Phoenix, Az

EXERCISE 6

Data Representation: Line Graphs

Directions: Construct the line graphs.

1. Using the following data, construct a graph of "Height vs. Age for Girls."

Age (years)	2	4	6	8	10	12	14	16	18	20
Height (inches)	34	40	45	50	54	58.5	63	64	64.25	64.5

2. Using the following data, construct a graph of "Height vs. Age for Boys."

Age (years)	2	4	6	8	10	12	14	16	18	20
Height (inches)	34	40	45.5	51	54.5	58.5	65	68.5	69.25	69.5

Answers are on page 789.

Reading Line Graphs

Because line graphs are continuous and the data you need often fall at points in between where readings were taken, a straight edge and pencil are usually very handy to have around.

EXAMPLE 1

What was the temperature in Phoenix at 7 AM according to the graph?

To find the temperature, locate the tick mark on the horizontal axis at 7 AM, halfway between 6 AM and 8 AM. Go straight up until you hit the curve as shown by dashed line *a*. Then go left horizontally, following dashed line *b*, until you hit the vertical axis. Here you need to estimate the temperature because there is no line or tick mark to help. But you can say the temperature was probably near 83° or 84°. This is accurate enough for all but the most detailed use.

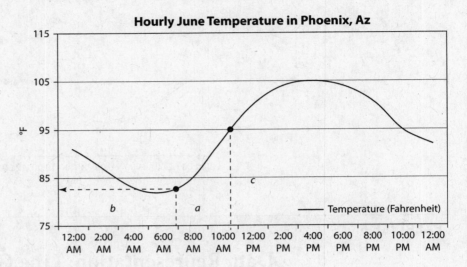

Hourly June Temperature in Phoenix, Az

EXAMPLE 2

At what time did the temperature first reach 95°?

To find this time, locate the point on the line where it first crosses the 95° line. Drop a vertical line (dashed line *c*) down to the horizontal axis. Read the time off the horizontal scale. Here you again need to estimate, but you can say that the temperature first reached 95° sometime around 10:30 to 10:40 AM. That's definitely close enough for you to decide you want your tennis lesson to finish well before 10:30 AM at this time of year. Again, this is close enough for ordinary use.

EXAMPLE 3

Janice went to work at 9 AM and was off work at 5 PM. How much hotter had the day become while she was at work?

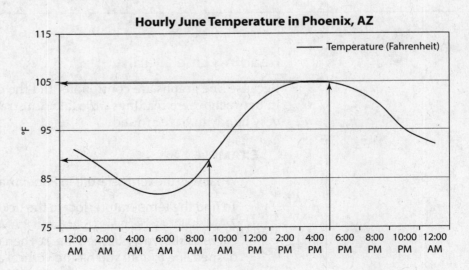

Hourly June Temperature in Phoenix, AZ

Find the 9 AM tick and run vertically up until you hit the curve. Go left until you hit the temperature. You need to estimate, but 89° is pretty close. At 5 PM move vertically up from that tick until you hit the curve. Moving left you see the temperature is very close to 105° if just a bit less. Taking the difference, 105° – 89° = 16°, you see the day has gotten 16° hotter.

EXAMPLE 4

Using the table below, how much had XYZ sold through the end of April?

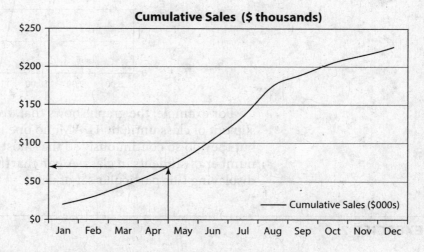

This is a slightly different kind of line graph that plots cumulative amounts (that is, a total, like sales) over time. You read it the same way as any other line graph. First find the tick that represents the end of April. Again, run vertically until you hit the curve. Then run horizontally to the left until you hit the vertical ($) scale. Here, estimate the sales to have been $70,000 by the end of April.

The examples show that a disadvantage to using a line graph to read data values is that it often requires estimation. A line graph is not as accurate as a data table, but it does show things a lot more clearly. On the other hand, an advantage to using line graphs is that trends that are not obvious as raw numeric data are often more noticeable. For instance, you can see how rapidly things change. A rule of thumb is: "The steeper the curve, the faster the change in the data." You can see from the graph that the curve from the middle of August on is less steep. This means that something changed in August to slow the rate of sales. This may be of great interest to management. There may be something going wrong, or if sales depend on the seasons, this may be expected.

Misuse of Line Graphs

The most common misuse of line graphs is with the wrong type of data. Line graphs are often wrongly used to portray discrete data. Remember that line graphs are good only for continuous data. Since line graphs are very easy to follow and look good, this misuse is very common. The following graph shows the number of students in a college professor's classes is constantly changing.

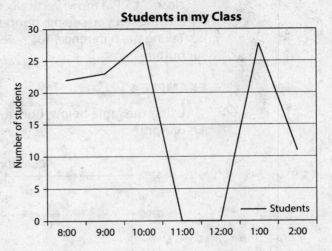

For example, the graph shows that, from 10 AM on, students slowly slip out of class until, by 11 AM, no one is left. Not only do students leave, but they do so continuously so that most of the time there is a fractional number of students in class. A bar chart would have been a better choice for displaying this particular set of data.

EXERCISE 7

Reading Line Graphs

Directions: The following line graph shows the total amount of merchandise sold by XYZ Supply Company over one year. Sales are recorded daily and are assumed to be continuous. Answer the questions.

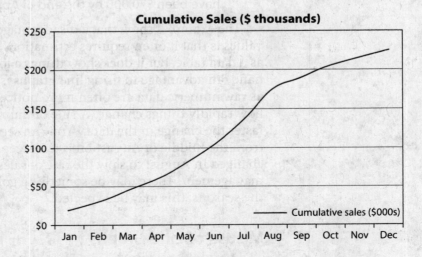

1. What was the total sales number at the end of August? _____

2. What was the total sales number at the end of December? _____

3. What was the increase in sales between the end of August and the end of December? _____

4. In what month or months was the pace of sales the highest as shown by the steepness of the sales curve? _____

5. Use the graph to fill in the table below.

Quarter	Ending Date (end of)	Total Sales
1	March	
2	June	
3	September	

Answers are on page 790.

Data Representation: Pie Charts

Pie charts are so called because they resemble a pie that has been cut into unequal slices. They are good for showing how a whole amount is broken into parts. For example, a pie chart can display the relative percentages of blood types in donors, or show how you spent your paycheck. Displaying how much of a business's expenses go toward salaries, overhead, advertising, and investment is also an appropriate use.

In a pie chart, the size of a slice represents its percentage of the whole. If something is 50% of the total, its slice takes up half the circle. If the amount is 10% of the whole, it gets a slice taking up 10% of the area of the circle. This can be seen in the following Blood Donor Type by Percentage pie chart. Type O donors represent 45% of the donor pool, and their slice on the pie chart occupies 45% of the circle.

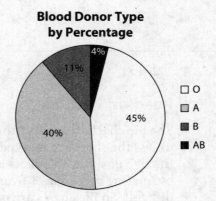

Blood Donor Type by Percentage

- □ O
- ▨ A
- ▨ B
- ■ AB

A pie chart can make some things strikingly obvious. Look at how small the slice is for AB type blood. A graph like this might encourage people with type AB blood to donate more frequently because there are so few of them.

Creating a Pie Chart

How is a pie chart constructed? The size of a slice of a pie chart is proportional to the angle at the center. Let's see how the pie chart of blood types is made.

The pie slice for the type AB donors should take up only 4% of the circle. Remembering that there are 360° in a circle, the 4% slice has an angle of $4\% \times 360° = 0.04(360°) = 14.4°$. Pie charts are not perfectly exact and you can round off the angle to 14°. The entire chart above would have angles as follows:

Type	Percentage	Calculation	Angle
O	45	$0.45 \times 360° = 162°$	162
A	40	$0.40 \times 360° = 144°$	144
B	11	$0.11 \times 360° = 39.6°$	40
AB	4	$0.04 \times 360° = 14.4°$	14
Total	100	360.0	360

Because it is difficult to plot tenths of a degree of an angle, angles to the nearest degree are more than accurate enough.

EXERCISE 8

Creating a Pie Chart

Directions: Given the following data, construct a pie chart for these data.

Recruits to US Military by Region				
Region	Northeast	Midwest	South	West
Percentage of Recruits	13	22	43	22

Answer is on page 790.

Reading Pie Charts

The pie chart is probably the most difficult place to get numbers for the data unless the slices are marked with the actual data. You can easily see whether the size of slices is somewhat the same or quite different, but actually estimating percentages from the chart without measuring angles is very difficult. So pie charts are best used for relative measurement. For example, from the previous chart, you can see at a glance that just two blood types account for the vast majority of blood donors.

EXERCISE 9

Reading Pie Charts

Directions: The Rh factor is another part of your blood type. Two people with the same blood letter type, say two AB types, must have the same Rh factor for a transfusion to be safe. Use the pie chart and the following information to answer the questions.

Blood Types Including Rh Factor

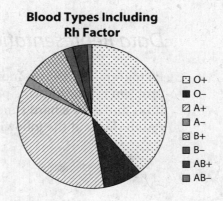

- ☐ O+
- ■ O−
- ▨ A+
- ▩ A−
- ▨ B+
- ◼ B−
- ◼ AB+
- ▩ AB−

1. Which two blood types, ignoring Rh factors (A, B, O, or AB), together account for most of the donors? _____

2. Approximately what percentage of the donors have either of these types? _____

3. In general, which blood types are more common: Rh positive or Rh negative? _____

4. Blood types O+ and O− are called universal donors because as long as the Rh factor matches, anyone can take a type O transfusion. Approximately what percentage of donors have type O blood? _____

5. Which is the "rarest" blood type (i.e., the blood type shared by the fewest donors)? _____

6. Are there more O− or B+ donors? _____

7. From the pie chart, how would you say that the percentage of A− donors compares to the percentage of B− donors? _____

Answers are on page 790.

Misuse of Pie Charts

It is pretty hard to misuse pie charts as a rule. What can be done is to divide items into subcategories and spread them out so the total amount is hidden. Say that you are a company that is spending a lot of money on marketing, in fact way too much. If you lump all that marketing cost into one pie slice, the problem would be obvious. But if you split up these costs by district, or by medium (print, electronic, TV, etc.), you can hide the total amount of expense, at least for a little while.

Data Representation: Pictograms

Pictogram charts are among the most misused of all charts and graphs. The problem is how humans perceive pictures. Humans look at pictures as whole units and have a hard time focusing on specific properties such as area and radius. Look at the following two circles.

The circle on the left represents $100 million and has a radius of one unit. The circle on the right represents twice that amount, $200 million, and is twice as high as shown by the scale on the left. However, looking at the two circles, the one on the right looks much bigger than just twice the other. That's because it is. By doubling its height, the radius is doubled but the area is multiplied by a factor of 4. Of course it looks so much bigger. You see the areas of the circles more than the heights. Next is a chart where the *areas* of the two circles are correctly proportioned, but that makes things look too small.

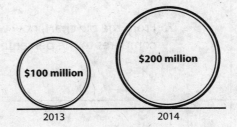

Look at the following pictogram showing home prices. Notice how much bigger the higher priced house in the middle looks because the proportions of the house are kept constant. And the house on the extreme right, although double the height and double the area, looks too skinny.

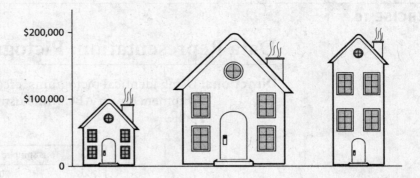

Creating an accurate pictogram is quite difficult. In some cases a pictogram is combined with a bar chart as seen next. Here you get the correct relationship and a graphic for interest, without the problem of size distortion.

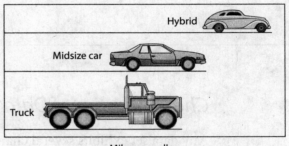

Another way is to use several identical pictograms to tell the story.

EXAMPLE

Create a pictogram showing that ABC Dairy increased its daily milk production from 8,000 gallons per day in 2012 to 12,000 gallons per day in 2013.

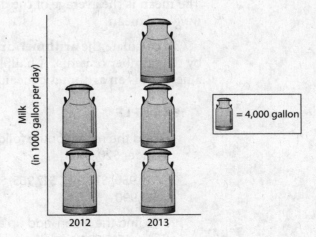

Using milk cans of the same size makes the values plain without distorting the picture.

EXERCISE 10

Data Representation: Pictograms

Directions: Using identical pictograms, create a chart showing the coal shipments from ABC Mine using the data in the following table.

Year	Tons shipped in 100,000s
2009	20
2010	25
2011	40
2012	30
2013	15

Answer is on page 790.

Characteristics of Data Sets

Any data set exhibits several characteristics that describe it. The most basic characteristics are the mean, the median, the mode, and the midrange. These numbers are known as *measures of central tendency* because they give an idea of where the middle of the data set is to be found. An additional measure, the range, is called a measure of variance because it tells you how spread out the values of the data set are.

Mean

The mean is the average of the data set. It can be either an *arithmetic* or a *weighted* mean.

To calculate the **arithmetic mean**, add up all the data values and divide by the number of items. A ballplayer's batting average or the average cost of a new car is an arithmetic mean.

EXAMPLE

Find the mean for the following list prices of 9 compact cars priced under $20,000.

$19,950, $18,990, $17,965, $16,545, $15,995, $14,900, $13,990, $12,995, $11,990

To find the mean, add up all the prices to get $143,320. Dividing by 9 gives $15,924, to the nearest dollar.

A **weighted mean** takes into account the fact that different pieces of data carry more weight, or are more important, than others. An example of a weighted mean is a student's GPA. Weighted means are also used with classified data, with the weights being the numbers of objects that fall into a class.

EXAMPLE

Find the mean monthly water bill for this family.

January/February	$45.00/month
March/April	$46.25/month
May	$42.50/month
June	$100.50/month
July	$127.75/month
August	$133.50/month
September	$95.50/month
October/November/December	$68.75/month

Because some bills represent more than one month, the only thing you *can* calculate is a weighted mean. To account for the fact that some bills represent more than one month, multiply each billed amount by the number of months it covers.

Billed Months	Bill Amount A	Weight No. of Months B	Weighted Amount AB
January/February	$45.00	2	$90.00
March/April	$46.25	2	$92.50
May	$42.50	1	$42.50
June	$100.50	1	$100.50
July	$127.75	1	$127.75
August	$133.50	1	$133.50
September	$95.50	1	$95.50
October/November/December	$68.75	3	$206.25
Sum		12	$888.50

Sum the weighted values and divide by 12, which is the sum of the weights:

$$\frac{888.50}{12} = \$74.0416 = \$74.04.$$

EXERCISE 11

Mean

Directions: Find the means.

1. Find the mean Age at Inauguration for American Presidents since 1900.

2. Find the mean age at death.

3. In finding a weighted mean for classified data, you use the actual midpoints of the classes in the calculation. Because the class 40–44 actually covers ages 40 to 44 years, its midpoint is 42.5 years. Using the following chart, find the weighted mean age for these presidents at inauguration.

Age at Inauguration	42.5	47.5	52.5	57.5	62.5	67.5
Number	2	2	7	4	4	1
Weighted Age = Age Number						

Answers are on page 790.

Median

Just like the median on a highway that splits the road in half down the middle, the median data value splits the data down the middle—half the data points are above the median, half are below. Medians in housing prices are often quoted in magazines. If a neighborhood has a median home price of $75,000, half the homes cost less than $75,000 and half the homes cost more.

To find the median, arrange the data in numerical order. Count from both ends, high and low, toward the center. When you reach the middle, you have the median data point. With an odd number of items in the data set, you end up with one number, an actual data value from the data set. If there is an even number of items in your data set, you end up between two numbers. The median is the average of these two numbers as in the second example below. This may or may not be an actual data value.

EXAMPLE 1

For the following data set of compact car prices, find the median car price.

$19,950, $18,990, $17,965, $16,545, $15,995, $14,900, $13,990, $12,995, $11,990

First, make sure the car prices are in numerical order.

$19,950, $18,990, $17,965, $16,545, **$15,995**, $14,900, $13,990, $12,995, $11,990

Count in four from each end and you end up with $15,995.

EXAMPLE 2

Find the median electric bill of a family that has the following bills.

$32.50, $32.50, $32.50, $34.50, $35.50, $105.50, $110.50, $137.50, $53.50, $33.75, $33.75, $33.75

List the data in ascending order.

$32.50, $32.50, $32.50, $33.75, $33.75, **$33.75**, **$34.50**, $35.50, $53.50, $105.50, $110.50, $137.50

There are 12 values. Counting 6 from each end, you arrive at the space between $33.75 and $34.50. To find the median value in this case, average those two values:

$$\frac{\$33.75 + \$34.50}{2} = \frac{\$68.25}{2} = \$34.13$$

EXERCISE 12

Median

Directions: Find the medians.

1. Using the data provided, find the median Age at Inauguration for American Presidents Since 1900. _____

2. Using the data from Age at Inauguration for American Presidents Since 1900, find the median age at death for those presidents who have died. _____

3. What day of the year (day 1, 2, etc.) is the median day for a regular year of 365 days? _____

4. The median age for a car in the United States is 9.4 years. What percentage of American cars are older than 9.4 years? _____

5. The mean age of an American passenger car is 8.4 years. What, if anything, can you say about the percentage of American passenger cars older than 8.4 years? _____

6. Given the following data set, what is the median value? _____

   7, 5, 8, 11, 4, 23, 17, 21, 25, 19, 14, 20

Answers are on page 790.

Mode

The mode is the data value seen most often in a data set. Not all data sets will have a mode, and some may have two or more.

EXAMPLE 1

What is the mode for the following data set of compact car prices?

$19,950, $18,990, $17,965, $16,545, $15,995, $14,900, $13,990, $12,995, $11,990

There is no one value that occurs more than any other. So there is no mode.

EXAMPLE 2

What is the mode for the following data set of electric bills?

$32.50, $32.50, $32.50, $34.50, $35.50, $105.50, $110.50, $137.50, $53.50, $33.75, $33.75, $33.75

Looking at the data set, two values, $32.50 and $33.75, each show up three times. This set is bi-modal: it has two modes.

EXERCISE 13

Mode

Directions: Find the modes.

1. Using the data from Age at Inauguration for American Presidents Since 1900, what is (are) the modal age(s) for presidents at inauguration?
   _____

2. Using the data from Age at Inauguration for American Presidents Since 1900, what is the mode for the ages at death for the presidents?
   _____

Answers are on page 790.

Range

The **range** of a data set is the difference between the highest and lowest values. You may know the median home price in a neighborhood, but you would have a better picture of the prices of homes in the neighborhood if you also knew the range.

EXAMPLE 1

What is the range of the compact car prices in the example in the previous section?

To find the range, subtract the minimum value from the maximum.

$19,950 - $11,990 = $7,960

EXAMPLE 2

What is the range of the family's electric bills in the example in the previous section?

Again, take the difference between the maximum and minimum values.

$137.50 - $32.50 = $105

EXERCISE 14

Range

Directions: Find the ranges.

1. Using the data from Age at Inauguration for American Presidents Since 1900, what is the range of presidential ages at inauguration?

   _____

2. From that same data, what is the range of ages at death for these presidents? _____

3. California, the most populous state in the United States, has 38,332,000 residents. Wyoming is the least populous with 582,000 residents. What is the range in population between the most and least populous states?

   _____

Answers are on page 790.

Midrange

The **midrange** is the number halfway between the maximum and minimum data values. It is the average of the maximum and minimum data values.

EXAMPLE 1

What is the midrange value for the list of compact car prices?

Add the maximum and minimum values and divide by 2.

$$\frac{\$19,950 + \$11,990}{2} = \frac{\$31,940}{2} = \$15,970$$

EXAMPLE 2

What is the midrange for the list of the family's electric bills?

$$\frac{\$137.50 + \$32.50}{2} = \frac{\$170.00}{2} = \$85$$

Midrange

Directions: Find the midranges.

1. Using the data from Age at Inauguration for American Presidents Since 1900, what is the midrange for the ages of presidents at inauguration?

   _____

2. Using the same data, what is the midrange for presidents' ages at death?

   _____

3. The population of California, the most populous state in the United States, is 38,332,000. Wyoming is the least populous with 582,000 residents. What is the midrange of population between the most populous and least populous states? _____

Answers are on page 791.

Probability

Probability is the likelihood that a given event will occur. Mathematically it is *the number of desired outcomes divided by the number of possible outcomes*. Probabilities are expressed as decimals, percentages, or fractions.

For example, a coin has two sides: heads and tails. The probability of flipping the coin and getting tails is 1 (the number of desired outcomes—tails) divided by 2 (the number of possible outcomes—heads or tails). The probability is $\frac{1}{2}$, 50%, or 0.50. This assumes the coin is "fair."

Probabilities range from 0 for an impossible outcome (like flipping a two-headed coin and getting tails) to 1 for a guaranteed outcome (like the sun setting in the west). The sum of the probabilities of all outcomes for a situation must add up to 1 (or 100%).

Probabilities are found by counting outcomes either directly or through the use of formulas. For the simplest problems, it is easy to count outcomes. Flipping a coin or tossing a single die are examples.

Counting Outcomes

In very simple situations, you can calculate probabilities by listing all the outcomes and selecting those you want.

EXAMPLE 1

Given a fair six-sided die, what is the probability of throwing a 6?

There is one desired outcome, throwing a 6, out of all possibilities (1, 2, 3, 4, 5, and 6). The probability is $\frac{1}{6}$.

EXAMPLE 2

What is the probability of throwing a number *greater than* 4 with that same die?

There are two possibilities that satisfy the criteria, throwing a 5 or a 6. Therefore, the probability is $\frac{2}{6} = \frac{1}{3} = 33.33\%$.

EXAMPLE 3

What is the probability of throwing *at least a* 4 with that same die?

Now there are 3 desired outcomes, throwing a 4, 5, or 6. The probability is now $\frac{3}{6} = \frac{1}{2} = 50\%$.

Notice from these examples that it is *very* important to read and understand the question being asked! This is true not just for probability or even not just for math. A little extra time spent in re-reading questions until you are sure you understand what is being asked will pay off in higher test scores.

EXAMPLE 4

What is the probability of throwing a 7 *or* an 11 using two dice?

This is a little more difficult because each die can have its own value regardless of what the other shows. There are $6 \times 6 = 36$ different ways for the two dice to stop rolling after being tossed. You can represent all 36 possible dice throws with a chart that shows the sums for any throw. For an example, if die 1 shows 2 spots and die 2 shows 4, go on row 2 to column 4 and find the sum is 6.

		Die 2					
		1	2	3	4	5	6
	1	2	3	4	5	6	7
	2	3	4	5	6	7	8
	3	4	5	6	7	8	9
Die 1	4	5	6	7	8	9	10
	5	6	7	8	9	10	*11*
	6	7	8	9	10	*11*	12

From the chart you see there are 6 ways to throw a 7 and 2 ways to throw an 11 (highlighted and in italics in the chart). That gives 8 desired outcomes out of 36 possible outcomes.

$$\frac{8}{36} = \frac{2}{9} = 0.222 = 22.2\%$$

EXAMPLE 5

What is the probability of throwing anything other than a 7 or an 11 using two dice?

Because probabilities must add up to 100% or 1.00, the probability of throwing something other than a 7 or an 11 is $1 - \dfrac{2}{9} = \dfrac{7}{9} = 0.7777 = 77.8\%$.

EXERCISE 16

Counting Outcomes

Directions: Count outcomes to answer the questions.

1. Given a bowl with 6 red and 3 blue balls, what are the chances of picking a blue ball in a blindfolded test? _____

2. A gamer's die has ten sides numbered 1 to 10. What is the probability of the gamer rolling a number less than 4? _____

3. Using the same gamer's die, what is the probability of throwing an even number? _____

4. Using the same gamer's die, what is the probability of throwing a 6, 7, or 8? _____

5. There are 14,000,000 tickets sold in the week for the Texas Lottery. If each ticket is different and you have bought 2 of them, what is the probability of your holding the winning ticket? _____

6. Given a bowl with 6 red balls, 8 green balls, and 4 white balls, what is the probability of picking a white ball in a blindfolded test? _____

7. Given the same bowl as in #6, what is the probability of picking either a green ball or a red ball? _____

8. You have a drawer of screws with a mixture of 55 screws that are $3\frac{3}{4}$ inches long and 85 screws 4 inches long. If you pick a screw without looking, what is the probability of picking a $3\frac{3}{4}$-inch long screw? _____

9. In a deck of 52 playing cards, what are the chances of picking an ace at random? _____

10. In a deck of 52 playing cards, what are the chances of picking a club? _____

11. In a deck of 52 playing cards, what are the chances of picking something other than a club? _____

12. In your closet you have 3 pairs of athletic shoes, 1 pair of boots, 3 pairs of casual shoes, and 2 pairs of dress shoes. You are going to the boss's barbecue this afternoon. What is the probability that by picking a pair at random, you will get either your dress or casual shoes to wear to the barbecue? _____

13. You just had a small flood and all the labels on the cans in your pantry have washed off. To make things worse, all the cans have been mixed up by the waters. Before the flood you know you had 14 cans of baked beans, 10 cans of spinach, and 3 cans of succotash. What is the probability that any one can you pick will contain succotash? _____

14. Given a pair of fair dice, what is the probability of throwing a total of 9? _____

15. With that same pair of dice, what is the probability of throwing a 7 or higher? _____

Answers are on page 791.

Combining Probabilities—Addition Rules

When combining probabilities, follow these addition rules.

Mutually Exclusive Events

If two or more events cannot happen at the same time, such as throwing a heads and tails on the same coin flip, winning and losing a tennis match, or being in two places at the same time, they are called *mutually exclusive*.

If two or more events *are mutually exclusive*, the probability of any one of them occurring is found by adding the probabilities of the individual events. In mathematical terms, for mutually exclusive events, P(X) is the probability of event X occurring; so P(A or B) = P(A) + P(B).

EXAMPLE 1

What is the probability of drawing an ace of clubs or a 2 of hearts from a deck of 52 cards?

These possibilities are mutually exclusive because the card cannot be an ace of clubs and a 2 of hearts at the same time, so follow the equation above. Add the probabilities: $\frac{1}{52} + \frac{1}{52} = \frac{2}{52} = \frac{1}{26} = 3.8\%$

EXAMPLE 2

What is the probability of throwing a 5 or a 6 on a regular six-sided die?

Because you can't throw a 6 and a 5 at the same time, they are mutually exclusive. Add the probabilities: $\frac{1}{6} + \frac{1}{6} = \frac{2}{6} = \frac{1}{3} = 33.33\%$.

Nonmutually Exclusive Events

If two events are *not* mutually exclusive, they may occur at the same time. Using the formula for exclusive events would include the probability of this possibility twice. To account for this, the probability of both events occurring must be subtracted. Let's consider picking cards from a deck of 52.

EXAMPLE 1

What is the probability of picking a black card or an ace from a deck of 52 cards?

For the ace the probability is $\frac{4}{52}$. For picking a black card it is $\frac{26}{52}$.

But there are two cards that are both black **and** an ace and these have to be taken into account by subtracting. The probability becomes

$\frac{4}{52} + \frac{26}{52} - \frac{2}{52} = \frac{28}{52} = \frac{7}{13}$, which takes into account the existence of two

aces that belong to the black suits, spades and clubs.

In mathematical language, for events that are not mutually exclusive, where P(A) is the probability of A happening, P(A or B) = P(A) + (B) − P(A and B).

EXAMPLE 2

The probability of having an accident while driving is 0.19. The probability of driving at night is 0.40. The probability of driving at night and having an accident while driving is 0.22. What is the probability of either driving at night or having an accident while driving?

Note the difference in meaning between "driving at night *and* having an accident while driving" and "driving at night *or* having an accident while driving." The first phrase refers to having an accident while driving at night, while the second refers to driving at night without regard to having an accident or having an accident while driving during the day or the night. Add the probabilities of the separate events and subtract the probability of the simultaneous event:

$$0.19 + 0.40 - 0.22 = 0.37$$

EXERCISE 17

Combining Probabilities: Addition Rules

Directions: Find the probabilities.

1. Two events, A and B, are not mutually exclusive. The probability of event A is 0.5 and the probability of event B is 0.4. The probability of A and B occurring together is P(A and B) = 0.2. What is the probability of either event A or B occurring? _____

2. Given a bowl with 10 red balls numbered 1 to 10 and 10 white balls numbered 1 to 10, what is the probability of drawing a red ball or a ball marked 7? _____

3. What is the probability of picking an ace, king, queen, jack, or a spade from a deck of 52 playing cards? _____

4. A litter of eight Lab puppies is divided as in the following chart. What is the probability of picking a black or a female puppy at random? _____

	Black	Yellow	Total
Male	1	2	3
Female	4	1	5
Total	5	3	

5. For the same litter, what is the probability of picking a yellow or a female puppy? _____

Answers are on page 791.

Combining Probabilities—Multiplication Rules

Probabilities can be combined for a series of events by multiplying individual probabilities. Outcomes of events may depend on previous outcomes, or they may have nothing to do with previous outcomes.

Independent Events

Independent events are those events that do not depend upon each other in any way. The results of any event do not affect the results of any other event. Examples of independent events are throwing two dice or consecutive flips of a fair coin. When events are independent, the probability of all of them occurring together is the product of their individual probabilities.

EXAMPLE

What is the probability of throwing a heads followed by a tails with a fair coin?

There is a $\frac{1}{2}$ probability of the first throw being a head. There is also a $\frac{1}{2}$ probability that the second is a tails. If you multiply these two probabilities together, you get $\frac{1}{2} \times \frac{1}{2} = \frac{1}{4} = 25\%$.

Looking at this in a different way, let's list all the possible combinations for the two throws.

1. Heads followed by heads

2. Heads followed by tails

3. Tails followed by heads

4. Tails followed by tails

There are four possible results, and only one is the desired outcome—heads followed by tails. According to the definition of probability, this is a probability of $\frac{1}{4}$, or 25%.

If you are picking objects from a group and putting back the picked items, this is called *selection with replacement*. In such a case, the probabilities remain the same. Consider a bowl with 4 red and 6 white balls. What is the probability of picking 3 white balls on three tries if balls are replaced after each pick? The probability of picking a white ball on the first pick is $\frac{4}{10} = \frac{2}{5}$.

After a pick, the ball is replaced. Every time you choose there will be 4 red balls and 6 white ballsin the bowl. The probability of picking a white ball will be $\frac{2}{5}$ for each pick, and the outcome of the second and third events do not depend on earlier events in any way. The events are independent, so the probabilities are multiplied. The probability of picking 3 white balls is $\frac{2}{5} \times \frac{2}{5} \times \frac{2}{5} = \frac{8}{125} = 6.4\%$.

Dependent Events

Dependent events occur whenever the results of one event change the probability of following events. If items are being chosen from a group without returning the item to the group for subsequent picks, this is known as *selection without replacement*.

Consider the same ball problem just described, picking from a bowl with 4 white and 6 red balls, if you do not put the balls back after each pick. What is the probability of picking 3 white balls on three tries if the balls are not replaced? Let's slow down and take a close look at the problem. The probability of picking a white ball on the first pick is $\frac{4}{10} = \frac{2}{5}$.

But on the second pick there are only 9 balls left, 3 of which are white. The probability of picking a white ball on the next pick is $\frac{3}{9} = \frac{1}{3}$.

On the last try there are 2 white balls to choose from out of a total of 8, so the probability is $\frac{2}{8} = \frac{1}{4}$. Multiplying these together, you get

$$\frac{4}{10} \times \frac{3}{9} \times \frac{2}{8} = \frac{2}{5} \times \frac{1}{3} \times \frac{1}{4} = \frac{2}{60} = \frac{1}{30} = 3.3\%.$$

EXAMPLE 1

Susan has 2 red dresses, 4 blue dresses, and 6 yellow dresses. What is the probability of picking a red dress followed by a yellow one?

It makes no sense for Susan to replace dresses in this case, so this is a selection without replacement. The probability of picking the red dress is $\frac{2}{12} = \frac{1}{6}$. The probability of picking the yellow one is now $\frac{6}{11}$ because there are only 11 dresses left. The combined probability is $\frac{1}{6} \times \frac{6}{11} = \frac{6}{66} = \frac{1}{11}$.

EXAMPLE 2

For the problem in Example 1, what is the probability of picking a yellow dress first and then a red one?

The probability of picking the yellow dress first is $\frac{6}{12} = \frac{1}{2}$, and then the probability for picking the red one is now $\frac{2}{11}$. The combined probability is $\frac{1}{2} \times \frac{2}{11} = \frac{1}{11}$.

EXERCISE 18

Combining Probabilities: Multiplication Rules

Directions: Identify each of the following events as dependent or independent.

1. Throwing a 6 and then a 2 with one die _____

2. Selecting three committee members from a group of people _____

3. Owning a television and that television being an LED TV _____

4. Picking 4 black cards from a deck of 52 _____

5. Picking three red jelly beans from a bag of jelly beans _____

6. A first child being a boy and a second child being a girl _____

7. Throwing a heads after six tails _____

8. Owning a dog and owning a cat _____

Answers are on page 791.

Probability Review

Directions: Find the probabilities.

1. What is the probability of throwing three heads followed by three tails with a fair coin? _____

2. What is the probability of throwing H T H T H T with six flips of a fair coin? _____

3. What is the probability of having a family with three children in the order boy, girl, boy, if the probability of having a boy is 0.512 and that of having a girl is 0.488? _____

4. What is the probability of selecting 2 aces in two picks from a deck of 52 cards if cards are replaced and shuffled between picks? _____

5. What is the probability of selecting 2 aces in two picks from a deck of 52 cards if cards are *not* replaced? _____

6. What is the probability of picking a club followed by a spade followed by a heart from a deck of 52 cards if no cards are replaced? _____

7. Given a six-sided die, what is the probability of throwing two 5s in a row? _____

8. A bowl has 3 white and 6 green balls in it. What is the probability of selecting 4 white balls in a row if the selection is done with replacement? _____

9. A bowl has 3 white and 6 green balls in it. What is the probability of selecting 4 white balls in a row if the selection is done without replacement? _____

10. What is the probability of your ticket being picked 3rd in a drawing with 20 tickets? (*Hint:* What represents a "win" for you on the first two picks?) _____

Answers are on page 791.

CHAPTER 9

Exponents and Roots

Multiplication is the repeated addition of the same number. For instance, 3×5 is shorthand for $3+3+3+3+3$. As a result of this simple concept, multiplication inherits several properties of addition and has several of its own. In this chapter you will learn about a similar shorthand for repeated multiplication of the same number, called **exponentiation**.

Exponents

Exponents are a shorthand form for writing repeated multiplication. An exponent is commonly a positive integer.

Positive Integer Exponents

Consider a number x multiplied repeatedly by itself, such as $x \cdot x \cdot x \cdot x \cdot x \cdot x \cdot x$. A shorthand way to write the seven x's is x^7, which is read as "x to the seventh power" or simply "x to the seventh." For another example, instead of writing $3 \cdot 3 \cdot 3 \cdot 3 \cdot 3$, you can write 3^5. The small number written as a superscript is the **exponent**, or **power**, and the quantity that is repeatedly multiplied is the **base**. The exponent tells you how many bases are multiplied, not how many multiplications to do. An expression of this type is written in **exponential notation**. In these examples, the exponent is a positive integer. If there is only one factor, the exponent is understood to be one: $x = x^1$. When the exponent is 2, as in x^2, it is often read as "squared," and when it is 3, as in x^3, it is often read as "cubed," both of these references come from geometry formulas.

Note: For any real number x and any natural number n, $\underbrace{x \cdot x \cdot x \cdot \ldots \cdot x}_{n \text{ factors}} = x^n$.

When the base is more than a single number or variable, grouping symbols should be used, as in $5a \cdot 5a \cdot 5a = (5a)^3$.

EXERCISE 1

Positive Integer Exponents

Directions: Write each expression using exponential notation.

1. $c \cdot c \cdot c \cdot c \cdot c \cdot c$ _____

2. $2y \cdot 2y \cdot 2y$ _____

3. $3xy \cdot 3xy \cdot 3xy \cdot 3xy \cdot 3xy \cdot 3xy$ _____

4. $a^2y \cdot a^2y \cdot a^2y \cdot a^2y$ _____

5. $5a^2bc \cdot 5a^2bc \cdot 5a^2bc \cdot 5a^2bc \cdot 5a^2bc$ _____

Answers are on page 792.

Properties of Exponents

The properties of exponents include the Product Rule, the Quotient Rule, the Power Rule, the Factor Rule, and the Fraction Rule.

The Product Rule

When several quantities are being multiplied, the order in which the factors are turned into products doesn't matter. An expression such as $(x \cdot x \cdot x) \cdot (x \cdot x \cdot x \cdot x \cdot x)$ may as well be written $x \cdot x \cdot x \cdot x \cdot x \cdot x \cdot x \cdot x$; the expressions are equal. In terms of exponents, this would be written $x^3 \cdot x^5 = x^8$. How does 8 come from 3 and 5? By addition, and this is an example of the Product Rule, a property of exponents.

The Product Rule: For any real number x and positive integers m and n, $x^m \cdot x^n = x^{m+n}$.

In words, this means to multiply quantities with the same base, add exponents.

EXAMPLE 1

$$x^6 \cdot x^9 = x^{6+9} = x^{15} \qquad 13^6 \cdot 13^8 = 13^{6+8} = 13^{14} \qquad (7x)^3(7x)^2 = (7x)^{3+2} = (7x)^5$$

This rule can be extended to any number of factors whose bases are all equal.

EXAMPLE 2

$$a^2 \cdot a^5 \cdot a^4 = a^{2+5+4} = a^{11} \qquad 5 \cdot 5^2 \cdot 5^7 \cdot 5^4 \cdot 5 \cdot 5^3 = 5^{1+2+7+4+1+3} = 5^{18}$$

If there are coefficients (numbers in front of the variable) when dealing with variables raised to powers, multiply the coefficients and add the exponents.

EXAMPLE 3

$$(3c^3)\cdot(5c^7)=(3\cdot5)c^{3+7}=15c^{10} \qquad (9x^2)(7x^4)=(9\cdot7)x^{2+4}=63x^6$$

When there is more than a single variable, add the exponents for each variable separately.

EXAMPLE 4

$$(2x^3y)\cdot(6xy^7)=(2\cdot6)(x^3\cdot x)(y\cdot y^7)=12(x^{3+1})(y^{1+7})=12x^4y^8$$

EXERCISE 2

Properties of Exponents: The Product Rule

Directions: Simplify using the Product Rule.

1. $x^7\cdot x^5$ _____

2. $a^3\cdot a^6\cdot a$ _____

3. $(2xy)^6(2xy)^2$ _____

4. $5p^3q\cdot3p^2q^6$ _____

5. $a^2b^5c\cdot ab^2c$ _____

6. $4x^5y^2z^3\cdot3x^2z^4\cdot2xy^3$ _____

Answers are on page 792.

The Quotient Rule

Just as there is a Product Rule, there is a Quotient Rule. It is used to tell how many factors are left over after canceling one factor at a time in an expression like $\dfrac{x^5}{x^3}$. If the numerator and denominator of $\dfrac{x^5}{x^3}$ were written as several xs being multiplied, and then xs were canceled a pair at a time, the process might look like this:

$$\frac{x^5}{x^3}=\frac{x\cdot x\cdot x\cdot x\cdot x}{x\cdot x\cdot x}=\frac{x\cdot x\cdot\not x\cdot\not x\cdot\not x}{\not x\cdot\not x\cdot\not x}=\frac{x\cdot x}{1}=\frac{x^2}{1}=x^2$$

How does 2 come from 3 and 5? By subtraction, and subtraction is the operation used to tell how many are left over after things are taken away, or as in this case, canceled. This leads to the Quotient Rule.

The Quotient Rule: For any nonzero real number x and positive integers m and n, $\dfrac{x^m}{x^n} = x^{m-n}$.

In words, this means to divide quantities with the same base, subtract exponents.

EXAMPLE 1

$$\frac{a^7}{a^4} = a^{7-4} = a^3 \qquad \frac{6^{13}}{6^5} = 6^{13-5} = 6^8 \qquad \frac{(3b)^7}{(3b)^5} = (3b)^{7-5} = (3b)^2$$

If there are coefficients when dealing with variables raised to powers, divide the coefficients and subtract the exponents.

EXAMPLE 2

$$\frac{64c^9}{4c^2} = \frac{64}{4}c^{9-2} = 16c^7 \qquad \frac{15x^{10}}{25x^6} = \frac{15}{25}x^{10-6} = \frac{3}{5}x^4$$

When there is more than a single variable, subtract the exponents for each variable separately.

EXAMPLE 3

$$\frac{72x^3y^5}{9x^2y^3} = \frac{72}{9}x^{3-2}y^{5-3} = 8x^1y^2 = 8xy^2 \qquad \frac{x^7y^3z^5}{x^3yz^4} = x^{7-3}y^{3-1}z^{5-4} = x^4y^2z^1 = x^4y^2z$$

The Product Rule and the Quotient Rule can both be used to simplify a single expression.

EXAMPLE 4

$$\frac{x^7 \cdot x^3}{x^2 \cdot x^4} = \frac{x^{7+3}}{x^{2+4}} = \frac{x^{10}}{x^6} = x^{10-6} = x^4 \qquad \frac{8x^5 \cdot 9x}{12x^3} = \frac{72x^5}{12x^3} = 6x^2$$

EXERCISE 3

Properties of Exponents: The Quotient Rule

Directions: Simplify using the Quotient Rule.

1. $\dfrac{p^8}{p^2}$ _____

2. $\dfrac{(2d)^{15}}{(2d)^{10}}$ _____

3. $\dfrac{32x^6}{8x^4}$ _____

4. $\dfrac{30x^5y^3}{20x^2y}$ _____

5. $\dfrac{12r^5 \cdot 4r^7}{2r^3 \cdot 3r^6}$ _____

6. $\dfrac{a^5b^9 \cdot a^7b^6}{a^3b^4 \cdot a^6b^8}$ _____

Answers are on page 792.

The Power Rule

How can an expression like $(x^3)^5$ be simplified? First, the definition of exponent can be applied to the exponent on the outside to write $x^3 \cdot x^3 \cdot x^3 \cdot x^3 \cdot x^3$. Then applying the Product Rule gives $x^{3+3+3+3+3}$. Following the reminder at the beginning of the chapter, the repeated addition can be written as multiplication: $x^{3 \cdot 5}$, so the simplified form is x^{15}. The connection between addition and multiplication is the justification for the Power Rule.

The Power Rule: For any real number x and natural numbers m and n, $(x^m)^n = x^{mn}$.

In words, to simplify a quantity raised to a power and raised to a power again, multiply the powers.

> **EXAMPLE 1**
>
> $$\left(2^2\right)^4 = 2^{2\cdot4} = 2^8 \qquad \left(x^7\right)^9 = x^{7\cdot9} = x^{63} \qquad \left[\left(3t\right)^8\right]^2 = \left(3t\right)^{8\cdot2} = \left(3t\right)^{16}$$

The Power Rule can be used together with the Product Rule and the Quotient Rule to simplify an expression.

> **EXAMPLE 2**
>
> $$\left(x^4\right)^7\left(x^5\right)^2 = x^{4\cdot7} \cdot x^{2\cdot5} = x^{28} \cdot x^{10} = x^{38} \qquad \frac{\left(5^6\right)^5}{\left(5^4\right)^3} = \frac{5^{6\cdot5}}{5^{4\cdot3}} = \frac{5^{30}}{5^{12}} = 5^{18}$$

EXERCISE 4

Properties of Exponents: The Power Rule

Directions: Simplify using the Power Rule.

1. $\left(x^4\right)^2$ _____

2. $\left(5^6\right)^3$ _____

3. $\left[\left(4q\right)^3\right]^5$ _____

4. $\left(b^6\right)^2\left(b^3\right)^5$ _____

5. $\dfrac{\left(k^4\right)^3}{\left(k^2\right)^5}$ _____

6. $\dfrac{\left(x^7\right)^3\left(x^2\right)^6}{\left(x^5\right)^2\left(x^3\right)^5}$ _____

Answers are on page 792.

The Factor Rule

Often, expressions with two or more factors raised to a power need to be simplified. An expression like $(ab)^3$ can be expanded to $(ab)(ab)(ab)$. Then, again using the fact that several multiplications can be carried out in any order desired, this can be written $(a \cdot a \cdot a)(b \cdot b \cdot b)$, which is the same as a^3b^3. This is the basis for the Factor Rule.

The Factor Rule: For any real numbers x and y, $(xy)^m = x^m y^m$.

In words, a product raised to a power can be written with each factor raised to the same power.

EXAMPLE 1

$$(bc)^7 = b^7 c^7 \qquad (2b)^4 = 2^4 b^4 = 16b^4 \qquad (-4y)^3 = (-4)^3 y^3 = -64y^3$$

Like the Product Rule, the Factor Rule can be extended to any number of factors.

EXAMPLE 2

$$(5xy)^3 = 5^3 x^3 y^3 = 125x^3 y^3 \qquad (-2abc)^4 = (-2)^4 a^4 b^4 c^4 = 16a^4 b^4 c^4$$

The Factor Rule can be used together with the previous rules.

EXAMPLE 3

$$(3x^2)^5 = 3^5 (x^2)^5 = 3^5 x^{10} \qquad \frac{(5x^3)^7}{(5x^4)^4} = \frac{5^7 (x^3)^7}{5^4 (x^4)^4} = \frac{5^7 x^{21}}{5^4 x^{16}} = 5^3 x^5 = 125x^5$$

$$(a^2 b^4)^3 = (a^2)^3 (b^4)^3 = a^6 b^{12} \qquad (p^3 q^5)^2 (p^2 q^3)^3 = p^6 q^{10} \cdot p^6 q^9 = p^{12} q^{19}$$

EXERCISE 5

Properties of Exponents: The Factor Rule

Directions: Simplify using the Factor Rule.

1. $(xy)^3$ _____

2. $(2ab)^6$ _____

3. $(3x^4)^2$ _____

4. $(s^4 t^3)^2 (s^3 t^2)^4$ _____

5. $\dfrac{(x^4 y^6)^5}{(x^2 y^4)^6}$ _____

6. $\dfrac{(p^4 q^2)^2 (p^3 q^4)^5}{(p^2 q^5)^3}$ _____

Answers are on page 792.

The Fraction Rule

A fraction may be raised to a power. So $\left(\dfrac{a}{7}\right)^5$ can be expanded as $\dfrac{a}{7} \cdot \dfrac{a}{7} \cdot \dfrac{a}{7} \cdot \dfrac{a}{7} \cdot \dfrac{a}{7}$. To multiply fractions, multiply the numerators together and multiply the denominators together to get $\dfrac{a \cdot a \cdot a \cdot a \cdot a}{7 \cdot 7 \cdot 7 \cdot 7 \cdot 7}$, which is the same as $\dfrac{a^5}{7^5}$. The shortcut is to apply the exponent to the numerator and the denominator. This is the Fraction Rule.

> **The Fraction Rule:** For any real numbers x and y, $y \neq 0$, $\left(\dfrac{x}{y}\right)^n = \dfrac{x^n}{y^n}$.

In words, raise a fraction to a power by raising both the numerator and the denominator to the power.

Caution: When writing a fraction raised to a power, you have to use grouping symbols around the fraction. The expression $\dfrac{a^5}{7}$ means $\dfrac{a \cdot a \cdot a \cdot a \cdot a}{7}$, not $\dfrac{a}{7} \cdot \dfrac{a}{7} \cdot \dfrac{a}{7} \cdot \dfrac{a}{7} \cdot \dfrac{a}{7}$.

EXAMPLE 1

$$\left(\frac{4}{5}\right)^3 = \frac{4^3}{5^3} = \frac{64}{125} \qquad \left(\frac{3}{x}\right)^4 = \frac{3^4}{x^4} = \frac{81}{x^4} \qquad \left(\frac{c}{d}\right)^9 = \frac{c^9}{d^9}$$

The Fraction Rule can be used with the other rules.

EXAMPLE 2

$$\left(\frac{1^7}{2^4}\right)^2 = \frac{\left(1^7\right)^2}{\left(2^4\right)^2} = \frac{1^{14}}{2^8} = \frac{1}{256} \qquad \left(\frac{a^4}{b^3}\right)^3 = \frac{\left(a^4\right)^3}{\left(b^3\right)^3} = \frac{a^{12}}{b^9}$$

$$\left(\frac{ab}{xy}\right)^5 = \frac{(ab)^5}{(xy)^5} = \frac{a^5 b^5}{x^5 y^5} \qquad \left(\frac{3x^5}{2y^3}\right)^2 = \frac{\left(3x^5\right)^2}{\left(2y^3\right)^2} = \frac{3^2 \left(x^5\right)^2}{2^2 \left(y^3\right)^2} = \frac{9x^{10}}{4y^6}$$

EXERCISE 6

Properties of Exponents: The Fraction Rule

Directions: Simplify using the Fraction Rule.

1. $\left(\dfrac{2}{3}\right)^4$ _____   2. $\left(\dfrac{x}{y}\right)^7$ _____   3. $\left(\dfrac{7x}{9y}\right)^2$ _____

4. $\left(\dfrac{x^3}{y^6}\right)^4$ _____   5. $\left(\dfrac{3a^4}{5b^2}\right)^3$ _____   6. $\left(\dfrac{2x}{y^2 z}\right)^5$ _____

Answers are on page 792.

Properties of Exponents

Directions: Write the exponential expressions in simplified form.

1. $(-3x)^2(-3x)^3(-3x)^5$ _____

2. $-2 \cdot a^3 \cdot a^4 \cdot a^7$ _____

3. $(x^2yz)(xy^2z^3)(x^3yz)(xyz)$ _____

4. $\dfrac{x^4z^5}{xz^3}$ _____

5. $\dfrac{a^9b^5c^4}{a^2b^4c^3}$ _____

6. $\dfrac{2^{18}}{2^8}$ _____

7. $\left(\dfrac{a}{5}\right)^3$ _____

8. $(-x^2)^5$ _____

9. $\left(\dfrac{2}{3}\right)^3$ _____

10. $(x^2)(2x^5)(3x^3)(3x^2)$ _____

11. $\dfrac{6x^3y^2 \cdot x^5y}{xy \cdot 5x^2y}$ _____

12. $\dfrac{6x^3y^3z^2 \cdot xy}{xy \cdot 2xyz}$ _____

Answers are on page 792.

Zero and Negative Integer Exponents

In previous sections of this chapter, you learned about properties of exponents that were positive integers. In this section, you will look at properties of zero and negative integers.

Zero Exponent

You know that any fraction with an identical numerator and denominator is equal to 1. This includes fractions with exponents raised to powers, such as $\dfrac{x^6}{x^6}$. The Quotient Rule can be used on this fraction: $\dfrac{x^6}{x^6} = x^{6-6} = x^0$.

The definition of *exponent* does not apply to an exponent of 0 because the exponent is supposed to count factors. But since $\dfrac{x^6}{x^6} = 1$, it makes sense to say $x^0 = 1$. This is the motivation for the definition of a **zero exponent**.

Zero exponent: For any nonzero real number x, $x^0 = 1$.

EXAMPLES

$$8^0 = 1 \qquad \left(a^2bc\right)^0 = 1 \qquad \left(x^4\right)^0 = 1 \qquad (-100)^0 = 1$$

Negative Integer Exponents

An expression such as $\dfrac{x^3}{x^5}$ can be simplified by canceling: $\dfrac{x^3}{x^5} = \dfrac{x \cdot x \cdot x}{x \cdot x \cdot x \cdot x \cdot x} =$

$\dfrac{\overset{1}{\cancel{x \cdot x \cdot x}}}{\cancel{x \cdot x \cdot x} \cdot x \cdot x} = \dfrac{1}{x \cdot x} = \dfrac{1}{x^2}$. If you were to try using the Quotient Rule, you

would come up with a negative exponent: $\dfrac{x^3}{x^5} = x^{3-5} = x^{-2}$. Comparing these

results, $\dfrac{1}{x^2} = x^{-2}$, leads to the definition of a **negative exponent**.

Negative exponent: For any nonzero real number x and natural number n, $x^{-n} = \dfrac{1}{x^n}$ and $\dfrac{1}{x^{-n}} = x^n$.

EXAMPLE 1

$$5^{-3} = \frac{1}{5^3} = \frac{1}{125} \qquad\qquad (2x)^{-3} = \frac{1}{(2x)^3} = \frac{1}{2^3 x^3} = \frac{1}{8x^3}$$

$$(-3)^{-3} = \frac{1}{(-3)^3} = \frac{1}{-27} = -\frac{1}{27}$$

The second part of the definition of negative exponent can be used to simplify expressions where there is a negative exponent in a denominator.

EXAMPLE 2

$$\frac{1}{x^{-5}} = x^5 \qquad \frac{1}{3^{-4}} = 3^4 = 81 \qquad \frac{1}{\left(x^2 y\right)^{-4}} = \left(x^2 y\right)^4 = \left(x^2\right)^4 y^4 = x^8 y^4$$

Both parts of the definition may be used to move any factor with a negative exponent to the other side of the fraction bar, changing the sign of the exponent.

EXAMPLE 3

$$\frac{2^{-5}}{3^{-2}} = \frac{3^2}{2^5} = \frac{9}{32} \qquad \frac{a^5 x^{-4}}{b^{-7} y^2} = \frac{a^5 b^7}{x^4 y^2} \qquad \frac{7^{-1} x^4 y^{-2}}{4^{-2} x^{-3} y} = \frac{4^2 x^3 x^4}{7^1 y^2 y} = \frac{16 x^7}{7 y^3}$$

EXERCISE 8

Zero and Negative Integer Exponents (Part A)

Directions: Write the exponential expressions in simplified form. Write answers with only positive exponents.

1. 2^{-9} _____

2. $\dfrac{1}{4^{-3}}$ _____

3. $\left(\dfrac{1}{4^{-3}}\right)^{0}$ _____

4. $\left(a^2 b^9\right)^0$ _____

5. $\left(5^{-3}\right)^0$ _____

6. $\left(\dfrac{1}{3^{-3}}\right)^4$ _____

7. $\left(2^{-5}\right)^4$ _____

8. $\left(5^{-4}\right)^2$ _____

Zero and Negative Integer Exponents (Part B)

Directions: Simplify each expression. Write answers with only positive exponents.

9. $\left(2m^2 n^{-3}\right)\left(3m^{-4} n^{-2}\right)$ _____

10. $\dfrac{24x^3 y^{-4}}{36x^{-3} y^{-2}}$ _____

11. $\dfrac{m^{-5} n^{-7}}{m^0 n^{-4}}$ _____

12. $\left(\dfrac{a^2}{b^{-2}}\right)^{-3}$ _____

Answers are on page 793.

Scientific Notation

An important use of exponents is scientific notation. Scientific notation is used to write very large numbers (such as the diameter of the Milky Way) and very small numbers (such as the radius of an atom). Any positive number written in the form $x \times 10^n$ is written in **scientific notation**, where n is an integer and x can take the values $1 \le x < 10$.

EXAMPLES

Write each number in scientific notation.

90,000	9×10^4
40	4×10^1
0.0027	2.7×10^{-3}
.000005	5×10^{-6}

Here, the exponents show the **number of places you move the decimal point** so that the multiplier x is a number between 1 and 10. The decimal point of a number in scientific notation should be placed to the right of the leftmost nonzero digit. Note that small numbers correspond to negative exponents and large numbers correspond to positive exponents. To convert the number in scientific notation to standard notation, reverse the process.

EXAMPLES

Write each expression in standard notation.

4.7×10^{-5}	0.000047
2.1×10^3	2,100
7×10^5	700,000
2×10^{-3}	0.002

EXERCISE 9

Scientific Notation (Part A)

Directions: Write each number in scientific notation.

1. 0.0003 _____
2. 110,000 _____
3. 5,200,000 _____
4. 230 _____
5. 2,120,000 _____

Scientific Notation (Part B)

Directions: Write each number in standard notation.

6. 7.9×10^{-3} _____

7. 9×10^{-5} _____

8. 2.1×10^2 _____

9. 6.1×10^4 _____

10. 7×10^{-1} _____

Scientific Notation (Part C)

Directions: Choose the correct answer.

11. Which of the following is the correct scientific notation for 80?

    A. 8×10^1
    B. 8×10^{-1}
    C. 0.8×10^{-1}
    D. 0.8×10^2

12. The average distance from the Earth to the sun is 93,000,000 mi. Which of the following correctly represents this distance in scientific notation?

    A. 9.3×10^6 mi
    B. 9.3×10^7 mi
    C. 9.3×10^{-7} mi
    D. 9.3×10^{-6} mi

13. The radius of an atom is 0.0000000021 m. Which of the following correctly represents the radius in scientific notation?

    A. 2.1×10^9 m
    B. 2.1×10^{-9} m
    C. 21×10^{-10} m
    D. 21×10^{10} m

14. Which of the following correctly represents the standard notation for 3.1×10^4?

    A. 0.0031
    B. 0.00031
    C. 31,000
    D. 310,000

15. The size of a grain of sand is 2×10^{-5} m. Which of the following correctly represents the size of a grain in standard notation?

    A. 200,000 m
    B. 20,000 m
    C. 0.000002 m
    D. 0.00002 m

Answers are on page 793.

Roots

In previous sections of this chapter, the properties of exponents are discussed. In this section, you will look into the *reverse* of raising a number to a power.

If $x^2 = 36 = 6^2$, then x is called a **square root** of 36. As indicated by the last part of this equation, one possible value for x is 6, but because $(-6)^2 = 36$, x could also be –6. Positive square roots are indicated by the symbol $\sqrt{}$, called a **radical sign**. Thus, $\sqrt{36} = \sqrt{6^2} = 6$, and 6 is also called the **principal square root** of 36. The principal square root of a number is designated by use of the word *the*, and when both possible signs must be allowed for, the word *a* is used.

In general, if $x^2 = m$, and m is positive, then x is a square root of m, and $\sqrt{m}$ is the principal square root of x. It is the nonnegative number whose square is m.

The following table shows the squares of the numbers from 1 to 15. The numbers 1, 4, 9, 16, and so on are called the **perfect squares** because their square roots are whole numbers.

Table of Perfect Squares				
$1^2 = 1$	$4^2 = 16$	$7^2 = 49$	$10^2 = 100$	$13^2 = 169$
$2^2 = 4$	$5^2 = 25$	$8^2 = 64$	$11^2 = 121$	$14^2 = 196$
$3^2 = 9$	$6^2 = 36$	$9^2 = 81$	$12^2 = 144$	$15^2 = 225$

Finding the square root of a negative number is something that can't be done. For instance, there are only two possible values for the square root of –36. It isn't 6 because that is the square root of +36. And it isn't –6 either because $(-6)^2 = +36$. In fact, the square root of any negative number is not a real number.

EXAMPLES

Find the principal square roots of 225 and 400.

SOLUTIONS

$$\sqrt{225} = \sqrt{15^2} = 15$$

$$\sqrt{400} = \sqrt{20^2} = 20$$

You can also estimate a square root by using the table of perfect squares.

EXAMPLES

$\sqrt{50} \approx 7$, because $50 \approx 49$ and $\sqrt{49} = 7$

$\sqrt{20} \approx 4.5$, because $16 < 20 < 25$

Parts of Radical Expression

Just as x is a square root of m if $x^2 = m$, x is called an nth root of m if $x^n = m$. The principal nth root of x is written $\sqrt[n]{x}$. Here, n is called the **index**, x is the **radicand**, and $\sqrt{}$ is the radical sign. Thus, the principal cube root of x is written $\sqrt[3]{x}$. With square roots, the index is understood to be 2.

EXAMPLES

$$\sqrt[3]{27} = \sqrt[3]{3^3} = 3, \text{ because } 3^3 = 27$$

$$\sqrt[3]{-125} = \sqrt[3]{(-5)^3} = -5, \text{ because } (-5)^3 = -125$$

In the similar manner, fourth root of x is represented as $\sqrt[4]{x}$.

EXAMPLES

$$\sqrt[4]{625} = \sqrt[4]{5^4} = 5, \text{ because } 5^4 = 625$$

$$\sqrt[4]{81} = \sqrt[4]{3^4} = 3, \text{ because } 3^4 = 81$$

Remember:

- $\sqrt{x}$ is the positive square root of x. It is the nonnegative number.

EXAMPLE

$$\sqrt{25} = 5$$

- You must square $\sqrt{x}$ to get x.

EXAMPLE

$$(\sqrt{25})^2 = 25$$

- $-\sqrt{x}$ is a negative square root of x.

EXAMPLE

$$-\sqrt{25} = -5$$

- The square root of a negative number is *not* a real number.

EXAMPLE

$$\sqrt{-36} \text{ is not a real number.}$$

- $\sqrt{0} = \sqrt{0 \times 0} = 0$

- $\sqrt[3]{x}$ is the cube root of x.

   EXAMPLE

   $\sqrt[3]{27} = 3$

- $\sqrt[4]{x}$ is the fourth root of x.

   EXAMPLE

   $\sqrt[4]{625} = 5$

EXERCISE 10

Roots (Part A)

Directions: Find the square root.

1. $\sqrt{900}$ _____   **2.** $\sqrt{196}$ _____

3. $\sqrt{729}$ _____   **4.** $\sqrt{441}$ _____

5. $\sqrt{121}$ _____   **6.** $-\sqrt{225}$ _____

Roots (Part B)

Directions: Estimate each square root.

7. $\sqrt{37}$ _____   **8.** $\sqrt{11}$ _____

9. $\sqrt{72}$ _____   **10.** $\sqrt{110}$ _____

11. $\sqrt{42}$ _____   **12.** $\sqrt{82}$ _____

Roots (Part C)

Directions: Find the cube root.

13. $\sqrt[3]{125}$ _____   **14.** $\sqrt[3]{-8}$ _____

15. $\sqrt[3]{-64}$ _____

Roots (Part D)

Directions: Choose the correct answer.

16. Which of the following is NOT a real number?

    A. $\sqrt[3]{-8}$

    B. $\sqrt{-3}$

    C. $\sqrt{4}$

    D. $-\sqrt{9}$

17. Which of the following is a real number?

    A. $\sqrt[3]{-27}$

    B. $\sqrt{-9}$

    C. $\sqrt{-120}$

    D. $\sqrt[4]{-81}$

18. Which of the following is NOT a perfect square?

    A. 9

    B. 16

    C. 120

    D. 625

19. Which of the following is a perfect square?

    A. 8

    B. 63

    C. 125

    D. 729

20. Between which two whole numbers is $\sqrt{30}$?

    A. Between 1 and 2

    B. Between 2 and 3

    C. Between 4 and 5

    D. Between 5 and 6

Answers are on page 793.

EXERCISE 11

Exponents and Roots Review (Part A)

Directions: Write each expression using exponential notation.

1. $m \cdot m \cdot m \cdot m \cdot m$ _____

2. $3yz \cdot 3yz \cdot 3yz$ _____

Exponents and Roots Review (Part B)

Directions: Write each expression in simplest form. Use the properties of exponents.

3. $(-2x)^2(-2x)^5(-2x)^5$ _____

4. $-8 \cdot m \cdot m^4 \cdot m^7 \cdot m^2$ _____

5. $(x^2yz)^5(x^2yz)^3(x^2yz)^2(x^2yz)^0$ _____

6. $\dfrac{m^9 n^5}{m^2 n^3}$ _____

7. $\dfrac{3^{15}}{3^6}$ _____

8. $\left(\dfrac{a}{3}\right)^3$ _____

9. $(-a^3)^5$ _____

10. $\left(\dfrac{3}{5}\right)^3$ _____

11. $(x^0)(2x^5)(5x^3)(x^2)$ _____

12. $\left(\dfrac{3a^3 b}{ab}\right)\left(\dfrac{ab}{2a^2 b}\right)$ _____

Exponents and Roots Review (Part C)

Directions: Simplify each expression. Write answers with only positive exponents.

13. 3^{-3} _____

14. $\dfrac{1}{5^{-3}}$ _____

15. $\left(\dfrac{1}{5^{-2}}\right)^0$ _____

16. $\left(6^{-2}\right)^0$ _____

17. $\left(\dfrac{1}{2^{-3}}\right)^5$ _____

18. $\left(3^{-5}\right)^5$ _____

Exponents and Roots Review (Part D)

Directions: Simplify each expression. Write answers with only positive exponents.

19. $(5a^2b^{-3})(3a^2b^3)$ _____

20. $\dfrac{16x^3y^{-6}}{32x^{-7}y^{-2}}$ _____

Exponents and Roots Review (Part E)

Directions: Write each number in scientific notation.

21. 0.00007 _____

22. 10,000 _____

23. 22,000,000 _____

Exponents and Roots Review (Part F)

Directions: Write each number in standard notation.

24. 8.1×10^3 _____

25. 5×10^{-3} _____

Exponents and Roots Review (Part G)

Directions: Find the square root.

26. $\sqrt{1,600}$ _____

27. $\sqrt{256}$ _____

28. $\sqrt{529}$ _____

Exponents and Roots Review (Part H)

Directions: Find the cube root.

29. $\sqrt[3]{-1,000}$ _____

30. $\sqrt[3]{343}$ _____

Answers are on page 793.

CHAPTER 10

Measurement and Geometry

The word *geometry* is derived from the Greek *ge* ("earth") + *metria* ("measure"). Ancient Greeks developed rules and formulas to measure many common objects. In this chapter you will learn some of these formulas and also the means of measuring the parts of the objects needed to use the formulas.

Measurement

No one knows when humans started measuring things, but archeologists digging at Lothal, in Pakistan's Indus River Valley, found one of the oldest rulers. The ruler, made of ivory, dates back to 2400 BC. It is divided into units about $1\frac{1}{3}$ inches long. Each unit was split into 10 equal parts to an accuracy of 0.005 inch! Bricks in the area seem to have been made using this as a measure.

Measurement Systems

Several different measurement systems are in use. The major ones are the US measurement system, which developed from the English system, and the metric system.

English System

Because the English system grew over time, the units were confusing and varied from area to area. The first English units were based on parts of people's bodies or familiar objects. That was convenient because it is hard to mislay a finger or foot. But everyone is built differently, so no two people measured things the same. To solve that problem people used measurements based on the king's body parts. This worked until that king died and then all the measurements changed when a new king was crowned. Eventually, a standard set of measurements was introduced.

Metric System

The metric system was created in France in 1799. Napoleon's conquests before 1815 helped spread the system throughout Europe. Whenever the French took over an area, the metric system became the official system. But the simplicity of the system kept people using it even after the French were defeated. Originally, given a meter stick, you could derive all the other units of measure.

The meter was defined as one ten-millionth of the distance between the North Pole and Equator on a line running through Paris, France. But soon a physical, "standard meter" was made in France that everyone could copy from. Today, units of the metric system are defined so that anyone with the right lab equipment can create their own standard measures. For example, the meter is defined as a certain number of wavelengths of a particular color of light.

The metric system has a few drawbacks. For example, there is no dry volume measure. Where US recipes ask for 1 cup of flour, recipes in metric countries ask for a specific weight of flour. You need a scale or a special measuring cup to bake using metric measurements.

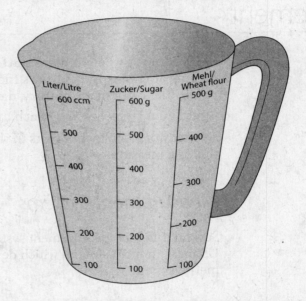

The metric system is also called the SI system, which stands for its French name Système International.

The Metric System in Detail

The metric prefixes are based on Greek and Latin words, and unit names are based on multiples of 10, which makes the metric system easy to use. The metric system uses the same titles, or prefixes, for each grouping or division regardless of what is being measured. For example, one-thousand (1,000) of one makes a kilo, one-hundredth $\left(\dfrac{1}{100}\right)$ of one is a centi, and one-thousandth $\left(\dfrac{1}{1,000}\right)$ of one is a milli. The prefix is added to the unit being measured. The meter is a unit of length so you could have a kilometer, centimeter, or millimeter.

The chart shows all the official prefixes for the metric system. Those in everyday use are shaded darkly while less common prefixes are lightly shaded. The unshaded prefixes have a scientific and technical use.

Prefix	Symbol	Size	Mathematical	Scientific
tera	T	1,000,000,000,000	trillion	10^{12}
giga	G	1,000,000,000	billion	10^{9}
mega	M	1,000,000	million	10^{6}
kilo	k	1,000	thousand	10^{3}
hecto	h	100	hundred	10^{2}
deca	da	10	ten	10^{1}
		1	*unit name*	10^{0}
deci	d	$\frac{1}{10}$	tenth	10^{-1}
centi	c	$\frac{1}{100}$	hundredth	10^{-2}
milli	m	$\frac{1}{1,000}$	thousandth	10^{-3}
micro	μ	$\frac{1}{1,000,000}$	millionth	10^{-6}
nano	n	$\frac{1}{1,000,000,000}$	billionth	10^{-9}
pico	p	$\frac{1}{1,000,000,000,000}$	trillionth	10^{-12}

LEFT divide

RIGHT multiply

Metric units are converted by moving the decimal point in the number left or right. This is the same as multiplying or dividing by factors of 10. The arrows on the chart tell in which direction to slide the decimal. Move the decimal point one place every time you change a box. Also included are the arithmetic operations involved.

The following diagram is useful in converting the most common unit prefixes.

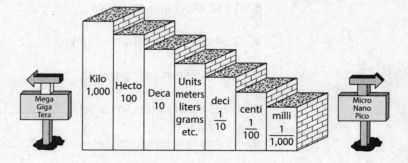

To use this diagram:

• start with the given prefix and then step up or down to the desired unit prefix.

• for each step, move the decimal one place in the same direction. If you go up two steps left, move the decimal two places left.

EXAMPLE 1

Convert 1.275 meters to millimeters.

Starting at meters (units) and going to millimeters, jump three steps to the right and move the decimal point three places right. This is also the same as multiplying by 1,000 (10^3).

1.275 m = 1,275 mm

EXAMPLE 2

Jeanne needs 50 lengths of ribbon, each 35 centimeters long. How many meters of ribbon should she buy?

First calculate the total length of the ribbon. 50×35 cm = 1,750 cm

To go from centimeters to meters on the diagram, move two steps left. Move the decimal two places left.   1,750 cm = 17.50 m

---

EXERCISE 1

The Metric System in Detail

Directions: Convert the measurements into the specified units.

1. 185 millimeters to centimeters _____

2. 1,355 centimeters to meters _____

3. 8,245 grams to kilograms _____

4. 0.450 liters to milliliters _____

5. 1.250 kilograms to grams _____

6. 2.54 centimeters to millimeters _____

7. 350 milliliters to liters _____

8. 0.245 centimeters to meters _____

9. 850 millimeters to meters _____

10. 72 centimeters to meters _____

Answers are on page 794.

The US Measurement System in Detail

The American system follows the English system that traveled across the Atlantic Ocean over hundreds of years. No one person designed this system. Instead it sprung up in many different industries and places, and at many different times. Because of that, there are many conversion factors and unit conversions. Who can be expected to remember that 1,760 yards equals one mile or that there are 64 tablespoons in one quart?

Although the US system may someday be replaced by the metric system, the foot, mile, rods (16.5 feet), and chains (66 feet) will survive for a long time because our country's land was divided and surveyed using those measures.

The following chart shows the most common measurement units in the United States and how they relate to one another.

U.S. Units

Distance

Foot	12 inches
Yard	3 feet
Furlong	660 feet
Mile	5,280 feet; 1,760 yards; 8 furlongs

Weight

Pound	16 ounces
Ton (short)	2,000 lbs
Ton (long)	2,200 lbs (approx. 1,000 kg)

Liquid Volume

Teaspoon, tsp.	$\frac{1}{6}$ liquid ounce
Tablespoon, Tbsp.	3 tsp.
2 Tablespoons	1 liquid ounce
Cup	8 liquid ounces; 16 Tbsp.; 48 tsp.
Pint	2 cups
Quart	2 pints; 4 cups; 32 liquid ounces
Gallon	4 quarts; 8 pints; 16 cups; 128 liquid ounces

Measuring Length

You can measure length with a metric ruler or with a ruler that uses the US measurement system.

Using a Metric Ruler

The unit of distance in the metric system is the *meter,* which is about 10 percent longer than a yard.

- Each meter is divided into 100 equal parts or *centimeters*.

- Each centimeter is divided into 10 equal parts or *millimeters* (because there are $10 \times 100 = 1,000$ millimeters to a meter).

Metric rulers are divided into millimeters. The distance between two of the closest lines is 1 millimeter regardless of the numbers on the ruler.

There are two common ways metric rulers and tape measures are numbered. Longer rulers or tape measures, often labeled "cm," are numbered like the first one that follows. Short rulers are labeled in millimeters (each number represents 10 millimeters) like the second ruler. Notice that both rulers have millimeters as the smallest division.

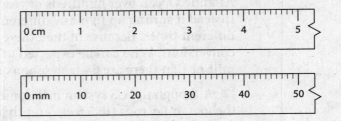

EXAMPLE

What is the length of the following line in metric units?

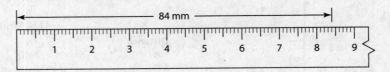

The line measures 8 centimeters plus an extra 4 millimeters. In other words, it measures 8.4 centimeters or 84 millimeters because 1 centimeter = 10 millimeters. Because these measurements are equal, use whichever form of the measurement makes sense at the time.

EXERCISE 2

Using a Metric Ruler

Directions: Using a metric ruler, measure the length of each of the following lines, giving the measurements in both centimeters and millimeters.

1 |————————————————|

2 |————————————————————|

3 |——————————————————————————————————|

4 |———|

1. _____

2. _____

3. _____

4. _____

Answers are on page 794.

Using a US System Ruler

Although many rulers and tape measures have both metric and US measurement scales, everyday measurements in the United States are still done in feet and inches.

Unlike meters, centimeters, and millimeters, which are related by multiples of 10, the US foot is broken into 12 inches. Partial inches are usually indicated by fractions. Inches are divided by factors of 2 into: halves, quarters, eighths, sixteenths, or smaller lengths.

To determine how the inch is divided on a ruler, look at the marks between the inches. Some rulers are marked with the smallest divisions. Most rulers are divided into sixteenths $\left(\dfrac{1}{16}\right)$, but some metal rulers are divided into thirty-seconds with $\dfrac{1}{32}$ of an inch between the closest lines.

Look at the following ruler. the marks between inches are different length lines. Each shorter line indicates a smaller division.

- Start in the middle of the inch where there is the line indicating the half $\left(\dfrac{1}{2}\right)$ inch.
- Halfway on either side are the slightly shorter one-quarter $\left(\dfrac{1}{4}\right)$ lines.
- Halfway between quarter lines are the eighths $\left(\dfrac{1}{8}\right)$.
- Between the eighths are the sixteenths $\left(\dfrac{1}{16}\right)$.

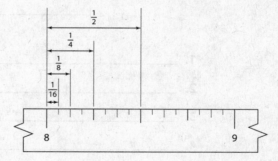

EXAMPLE

What is the length of the following line?

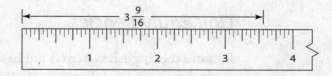

The line is one division longer than $3\dfrac{1}{2}$ inches.

Add $\dfrac{1}{16}$ to the $3\dfrac{1}{2}$ and get $3\dfrac{9}{16}$ inches.

Here are some charts to help with converting divisions of the inch to each other.

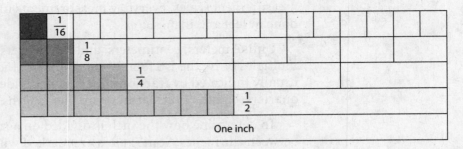

One inch

Using a US System Ruler

Directions: Measure the following lines to the nearest $\frac{1}{16}$ of an inch.

1 ├─────────┤

2 ├───────────┤

3 ├─────────────┤

4 ├──────────────────┤

1. _____

2. _____

3. _____

4. _____

Answers are on page 794.

Unit Equivalencies

Because the English system is not based upon factors of 10, unit equivalencies in the US system are needed. Conversion factors between the US and metric systems are required to transfer measurements from one system to another.

The following charts are not complete but should cover the most common units of measure.

U.S.–Metric and Metric–U.S. Equivalents

Distance	**Liquid Volume**
1 meter = 3.281 feet	1 liter = 0.264 gallons
= 1.09 yards	= 1.057 quarts
1 kilometer = 0.6214 miles	
1 inch = 2.54 centimeters; 25.4 millimeters	1 cup ≈ 237 milliliters
1 foot = 0.305 meters	1 pint ≈ 473 milliliters
1 yard = 0.9144 meters	1 quart ≈ 946 milliliters
1 mile = 1.61 kilometers	1 gallon = 3.785 liters

Weight

1 kilogram = 2.205 pounds
1 ounce = 28.35 grams
1 pound = 0.454 kilogram

Unit Conversions Using Dimensional Analysis

An easy way to do conversions, especially between US and metric measurements is called **dimensional analysis**. Dimensional analysis does away with the need to remember whether to multiply or divide units because you *always multiply*!

EXAMPLE 1

A European fairy tale talks about "7 league boots," which let the wearer take steps that are 7 leagues long. How far is 7 leagues in miles?

In dimensional analysis, always start out with the given units on the left.

Then multiply it by a conversion factor or factors (see next examples), to get the result you want, on the right.

$$7 \text{ leagues} \times \text{conversion factor} = \underline{\quad\quad} \text{ miles}$$

1 league is 3.452 miles. That means you will multiply in the previous equation by either of two forms of the conversion: $\dfrac{1 \text{ league}}{3.452 \text{ miles}}$ or $\dfrac{3.452 \text{ miles}}{1 \text{ league}}$.

Using the first form of the conversion factor $\dfrac{1 \text{ league}}{3.452 \text{ miles}}$ in the equation, you get:

$$\frac{7 \text{ leagues}}{1} \times \frac{1 \text{ league}}{3.452 \text{ miles}} = \underline{\quad\quad} \text{ miles}$$

But multiplying across the top gives 7 square leagues divided by 3.452 miles, which does not make sense for an answer.

The second form of the factor $\dfrac{3.452 \text{ miles}}{1 \text{ league}}$ is better because it gives you:

$$\dfrac{7 \text{ leagues}}{1} \times \dfrac{3.542 \text{ miles}}{1 \text{ league}} = \underline{\hspace{1cm}} \text{ miles}$$

The units of leagues in the denominator and the numerator of the equation cancel out. That leaves the unit "miles" on top and where you want it. Then canceling out leagues and multiplying, you get:

$$\dfrac{7 \, \cancel{\text{leagues}}}{1} \times \dfrac{3.452 \text{ miles}}{1 \, \cancel{\text{league}}} = 7 \times 3.452 \text{ miles} = 24.164 \text{ miles}$$

EXAMPLE 2

How far in miles is the 1,500 meters race in the Olympics?

This is a two-step conversion.

First convert meters to feet.

$$\dfrac{1,500 \text{ meters}}{1} \times \underline{\hspace{1cm}} (\text{meters to feet}) = \quad \text{feet}$$

Then convert feet to miles. Writing out the problem, you need:

$$\dfrac{\text{feet}}{1} \times \underline{\hspace{1cm}} (\text{feet to miles}) = \quad \text{miles}$$

Or you can combine the two parts of the problem to get:

$$1,500 \text{ meters} \times \underline{\hspace{0.5cm}} \times \underline{\hspace{0.5cm}} = \underline{\hspace{1cm}} \text{ miles}$$

In converting meters to feet, the fact that 1 meter = 3.281 feet gives a choice of

$$\dfrac{1 \text{ meter}}{3.281 \text{ feet}} \text{ or } \dfrac{3.281 \text{ feet}}{1 \text{ meter}} \text{ as a conversion factor in the equation.}$$

Looking at the units, the second fraction will cancel meters, so plug that one in.

$$\dfrac{1,500 \, \cancel{\text{meters}}}{1} \times \dfrac{3.281 \text{ feet}}{1 \, \cancel{\text{meter}}} \times \underline{\hspace{0.5cm}} = \underline{\hspace{1cm}} \text{ miles}$$

For the second conversion, because 5,280 feet = 1 mile, you have either

$$\dfrac{1 \text{ mile}}{5,280 \text{ feet}} \text{ or } \dfrac{5,280 \text{ feet}}{1 \text{ mile}} \text{ to choose from.}$$

Looking at units again, you see that the first one eliminates feet and leaves miles, right on top where you want it.

$$\dfrac{1,500 \, \cancel{\text{meters}}}{1} \times \dfrac{3.281 \, \cancel{\text{feet}}}{1 \, \cancel{\text{meter}}} \times \dfrac{1 \text{ mile}}{5,280 \, \cancel{\text{feet}}} = \underline{\hspace{1cm}} \text{ miles}$$

$$\frac{1,500 \times 3.281 \times 1}{5,280} \text{ miles} = 0.932 \text{ miles}$$

Dimensional analysis can be used for purely metric units, too.

EXAMPLE 3

What is 123 centimeters per second in kilometers per hour?

Here you need conversion factors for distance (centimeters to meters and meters to kilometers) and for time (seconds to hours).

Combine three conversions: centimeters to meters, meters to kilometers, and seconds to hours. These conversion steps are not labeled in the equation because the order in which you do them is not a problem—*any order works*!

$$\frac{123 \text{ cm}}{\text{second}} \times \underline{} \times \underline{} \times \underline{} = \underline{} \frac{\text{kilometers}}{\text{hour}}$$

Distance conversion factors are:

Centimeters to meters: $\dfrac{100 \text{ cm}}{\text{meter}}$ or $\dfrac{\text{meter}}{100 \text{ cm}}$

Meters to kilometers: $\dfrac{1000 \text{ meters}}{1 \text{ kilometer}}$ or $\dfrac{1 \text{ kilometer}}{1000 \text{ meters}}$

In the first group (centimeters to meters), the second fraction cancels out centimeters.

$$\frac{123 \cancel{\text{ cm}}}{\text{second}} \times \frac{1 \text{ meter}}{100 \cancel{\text{ cm}}} \times \underline{} \times \underline{} = \underline{} \frac{\text{kilometers}}{\text{hour}}$$

In the second set (meters to kilometers), the second fraction cancels out meters leaving kilometers on top.

$$\frac{123 \cancel{\text{ cm}}}{\text{second}} \times \frac{1 \cancel{\text{ meter}}}{100 \cancel{\text{ cm}}} \times \frac{1 \text{ kilometer}}{1000 \cancel{\text{ meters}}} \times \underline{} = \underline{} \frac{\text{kilometers}}{\text{hour}}$$

To convert between hours and seconds, look it up and find you have either

$$\frac{3600 \text{ seconds}}{1 \text{ hour}} \text{ or } \frac{1 \text{ hour}}{3600 \text{ seconds}}$$

The first fraction above takes care of the time by eliminating seconds and introducing hours in the denominator.

$$\frac{123 \cancel{\text{ cm}}}{\cancel{\text{second}}} \times \frac{1 \cancel{\text{ meter}}}{100 \cancel{\text{ cm}}} \times \frac{1 \text{ kilometer}}{1000 \cancel{\text{ meters}}} \times \frac{3600 \cancel{\text{ seconds}}}{1 \text{ hour}}$$

$$= \underline{} \frac{\text{kilometers}}{\text{hour}}$$

The units work out and so does the arithmetic.

$$\frac{123 \times 1 \times 3600}{100 \times 1000 \times 1} = \frac{442,800}{100,000} = 4.428 \frac{\text{kilometer}}{\text{hour}}$$

Notice that the seconds to hours conversion (3,600 seconds equals 1 hour) could be found with two conversions (60 seconds = 1 minute and 60 minutes = 1 hour) in its place.

Sometimes it helps to split the problem into pieces, say distance and time, or length and volume. Practice will make this easier. The key to using dimensional analysis is to cancel out units by doing conversions.

EXERCISE 4

Unit Conversions Using Dimensional Analysis

Directions: Convert these measurements to the specified unit. (Refer to the tables found in "The US Measurement System in Detail" and "Unit Equivalencies.")

1. 24 ounces to pounds _____

2. $1\frac{1}{2}$ gallons to cups _____

3. 220 yards to meters _____

4. 210 kilometers to miles _____

5. 100 kilometers per hour to meters per second _____

6. 88 feet per second to kilometers per hour _____

7. A common piece of building lumber is called a "2 by 4" and measures 2 inches thick and 4 inches wide. What would a 2 by 4 be called in metric measure to the nearest millimeter? _____

8. Two by four lumber is usually sold in lengths of either 6 or 8 feet. How long are these pieces of lumber to the nearest centimeter? _____

9. 176 centimeters to inches _____

10. 6 feet 2 inches to centimeters _____

Answers are on page 794.

Geometry

Geometry is the study of forms in two or three dimensions. The beginning of geometry is hard to date, but by 1800 BC the Egyptians were calculating the area of triangles and the volumes of hemispheres. By 1650 BC they were estimating the constant π, which relates a circle's radius to its perimeter.

By 800 BC, Indian mathematicians had become highly skilled in geometry. But they must have been working on it well before the oldest existing records because the earliest records show they were highly advanced.

The ancient Greeks established many of the ideas used in geometry today. Then from about AD 1000 until the 1500s, Islamic thinkers made significant contributions to the field. By the 1600s the center of geometric studies shifted to Western Europe where it has remained.

Angles

The size of an angle, or its *arc*, is measured in degrees. A circle contains 360 degrees of arc. Each degree is divided into 60 minutes of arc, and each minute is further divided into 60 seconds. The point where two lines meet to form the point of the angle is called the angle's *apex*.

There are four major groups of angles: straight, obtuse, right, and acute.

- A *straight angle* looks like a straight line and measures 180 degrees.

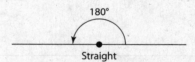

- An *obtuse angle* measures more than 90 degrees but less than 180 degrees.

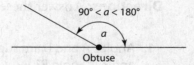

- A *right angle* measures exactly 90 degrees.

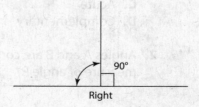

- An *acute angle* measures less than 90 degrees but more than 0 degrees.

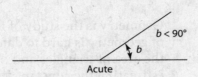

Acute

Angles are also named based upon their relationship to other angles.

- Two angles whose measures add up to 180 degrees are *supplementary* angles. Two angles creating a straight line are definitely supplementary.

Supplementary Angles

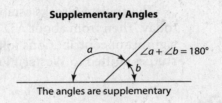

The angles are supplementary

- Two angles adding up to 90 degrees are *complementary* angles. Two angles that create a right angle are definitely complementary.

Complementary Angles

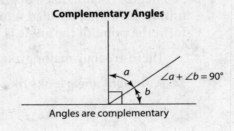

Angles are complementary

EXERCISE 5

Angles

Directions: Answer these questions about angles.

1. Angles A and B are supplementary. If angle A measures 78°, what kind of angle is angle B?

   A. Straight
   B. Obtuse
   C. Acute
   D. Complementary

2. Angles A and B are complementary. If angle A measures 30°, what is the measure of angle B?

3. If two angles are complementary, what can you say about their sizes?
   A. They are equal angles.
   B. One must be an acute angle.
   C. Both must be acute angles.
   D. Not enough information is given.

4. Draw the situation in which angles A and B are supplementary and angle B is complementary to angle C. *(Hint: you will need three lines and one angle will be below the line.)*

Answers are on page 794.

Intersecting Lines, Parallel Lines, and Angles

Although lines can go in any direction, there are two separate special cases for two lines: where the two lines never meet and where two lines cross at exactly 90 degrees to each other, forming four right angles.

- When lines never meet they are called *parallel*. The sides of a road are parallel.

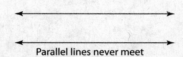

Parallel lines never meet

- When lines cross at exactly 90 degrees they are *perpendicular* to each other. Walls and floors should be perpendicular to each other.

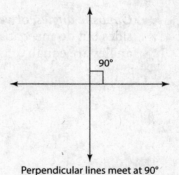

Perpendicular lines meet at 90°

• A piece of regular graph paper has both parallel and perpendicular lines.

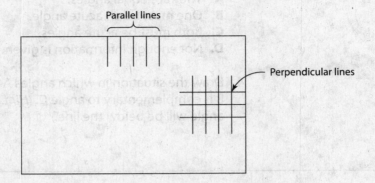

Parallel lines

Perpendicular lines

Relationships for Intersecting Lines

When two lines intersect, they create different kinds of angles with each other.

• *Adjacent angles* share a common side and share the same point, or *apex*. When two lines meet, adjacent angles are supplementary; together they form a straight line.

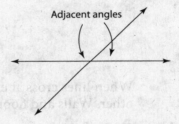

Adjacent angles

• *Opposite angles*, or *vertical angles* as they are also known, do not share sides but do meet at and share a common apex point. As shown, opposite angles are equal.

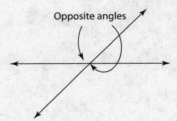

Opposite angles

EXAMPLE 1

For the following diagram, calculate the measure of all unlabeled angles.

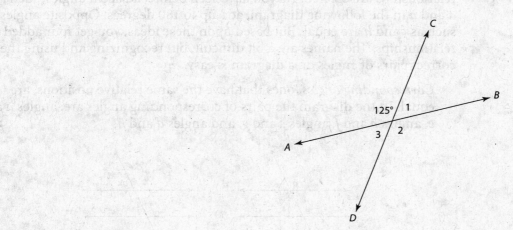

Note that angle 2 is opposite the given angle, so it has the same measure: 125°.

Angle 1 shares a side with the given angle, so it is supplementary and the measures of angle 1 and the given angle add up to 180°.
So, $\angle 1 + 125° = 18°$.

Subtracting: $\angle 1 = 55°$.

Angle 3 is opposite angle 1, so it too has a measure of 55°.

In summary:

$\angle 1 = 55°$

$\angle 2 = 125°$

$\angle 3 = 55°$

EXAMPLE 2

The following figure is of a right angle. What is the measure of the remaining angle?

The measure of a right angle is exactly 90°. If one angle measures 32°, subtract that from 90° and find the measure of the remaining angle.

$90° - 32° = 58°$

Angle Relationships in Parallel Lines

When two parallel lines are cut by a third line, a number of angle relationships are created. As you have seen before, adjacent angles, such as *a* and *d* in the following diagram, add up to 180 degrees. Opposite angles such as *f* and *h* are equal. But based upon these ideas, you get four added relationships. The names are a bit difficult, but recognizing and using the correct pairs of angles on a diagram is easy.

- *Corresponding angles*, ones that have the same relative positions, are equal. In the diagram the pairs of corresponding angles are: angles *a* and *e*, angles *b* and *f*, angles *c* and *g*, and angles *d* and *h*.

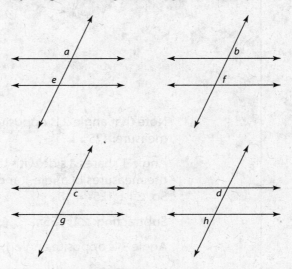

- *Alternative interior angles* are inside the parallel lines on opposite sides of the nonparallel line. Each pair is equal. In the diagram these pairs are: angles *d* and *f* and angles *c* and *e*.

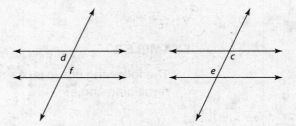

- *Alternative exterior angles* are on the outsides of the parallel lines and are pairs of equal angles. The pairs of alternative exterior angles in the following diagram are angles *b* and *h* and angles *a* and *g*.

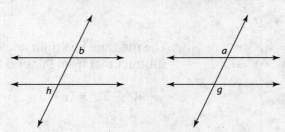

• Perhaps the least obvious pairs are the *consecutive interior angles*. These angles are supplementary, that is, their measures add up to 180 degrees. These pairs are angles *d* and *e* and angles *c* and *f*. By the way, this also implies that angle pairs *b* and *g* along with *a* and *h* are also supplementary.

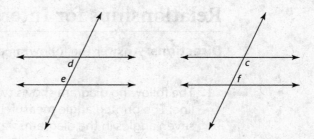

EXAMPLE

Given two parallel lines cut by a third straight line: (a) list all pairs of equal angles along with the reason you know they are equal, and (b) list all pairs of supplementary angles and the reason you know they are supplementary.

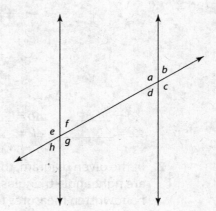

Angles *a* and *c*, *b* and *d*, *e* and *g*, and *h* and *f* are equal pairs because they are opposite angles. Angles *a* and *e*, *b* and *f*, *c* and *g*, and *d* and *h* are pairs of equal angles because they are corresponding angles. Angles *a* and *g* along with angles *d* and *f* are pairs of equal angles because they are alternate interior angles, while the pairs of alternative exterior angles, *b* and *h* plus *c* and *e*, are also part of the answer.

There are eight pairs of supplementary angles, four at each place two lines meet:

a and *b*	*e* and *f*
b and *c*	*f* and *g*
c and *d*	*g* and *h*
a and *d*	*e* and *h*

In addition, angles *a* and *d*, *d* and *g*, *g* and *f*, and *f* and *a* are supplementary pairs because they are consecutive interior angles.

EXERCISE 6

Relationships for Intersecting Lines

Directions: Answer the following questions.

1. The following diagram shows two parallel lines intersected by a straight line. The printed angle measure is given. Supply the measures of the other seven angles in the diagram.

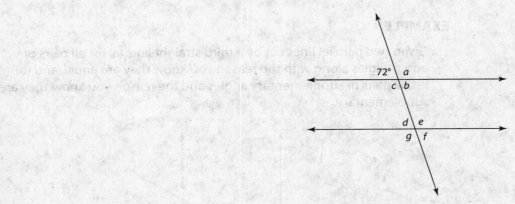

∠*a* = _____ ∠*b* = _____ ∠*c* = _____ ∠*d* = _____
∠*e* = _____ ∠*f* = _____ ∠*g* = _____

2. In the given diagram, the horizontal lines are parallel and the triangles are right angle triangles. Given the first angle, a student turned in the handwritten measures for all the other angles. Find and correct any mistakes by writing the correct measure on the diagram.

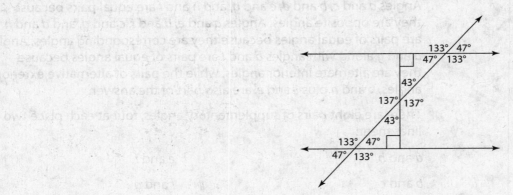

Triangles

A triangle is a three-sided figure in which the three angles always add up to 180 degrees. While all triangles have internal angles adding up to 180 degrees, certain special types of triangles have special angle relationships. Triangles come in four major classes: equilateral, isosceles, right, and scalene.

Equilateral Triangles

Equilateral triangles have all three sides of equal length, and each inside angle is exactly 60 degrees.

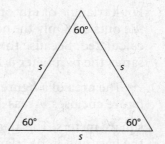

Isosceles Triangles

Isosceles triangles have two sides of equal length. The angles adjacent to these two sides are equal, while the third or apex angle completes the 180-degree total for the triangle.

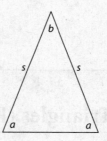

Right Triangles

Right triangles have one 90-degree angle and two other angles that are complementary.

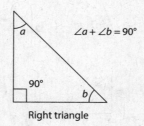

Right triangle

Scalene Triangles

These triangles include all those that do not fit one of the previous three definitions.

Height of Triangles

An important measure of a triangle is its height. The height of a triangle is the distance from the base to the point of the triangle (its apex), measured on a line perpendicular to the base. Height can be measured internally on many triangles but must be measured externally on some triangles.

Perimeter and Area of Triangles

For a triangle or any other figure, the **perimeter** is the distance around the outside. Only the equilateral triangle has a perimeter that can be easily calculated. Because the length of each side of an equilateral triangle is the same, the perimeter is $P = 3s$.

The **area** of a figure such as a triangle is the amount of real estate the figure encloses. Areas are measured in square units such as square feet or square meters. The area of *any* triangle is $A = \frac{1}{2}bh$, where b is the length of the base and h the triangle's height.

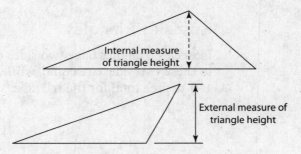

Internal measure of triangle height

External measure of triangle height

EXERCISE 7

Triangles (Part A)

Directions: Given the following triangles, identify each one using a term from the list.

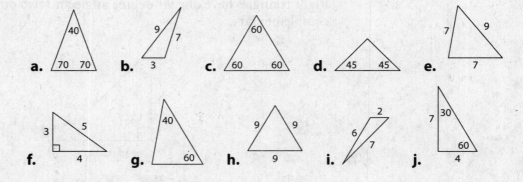

1. Isosceles triangles _____

2. Scalene triangles _____

3. Right triangles _____

4. Equilateral triangles _____

Triangles (Part B)

Directions: Calculate the perimeters and areas of the following figures. Some of these figures are combinations of simpler figures and may require you to split figures into pieces.

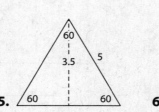

5.

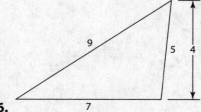

6.

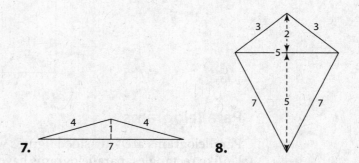

7.

8.

5. Perimeter: _____ Area: _____

6. Perimeter: _____ Area: _____

7. Perimeter: _____ Area: _____

8. Perimeter: _____ Area: _____

Answers are on page 794.

Quadrilaterals

A quadrilateral is a four-sided figure in which the inside or internal angles add up to 360 degrees. Special kinds of quadrilaterals include squares, rectangles, and parallelograms.

Squares and Rectangles

These are regular quadrilaterals in which each of the four internal angles is equal to 90 degrees. Together, the four angles add up to 360 degrees. In a square, all four sides are equal in length. In a rectangle, opposite sides are equal in length.

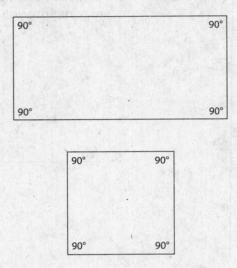

Parallelograms

Parallelograms are four-sided figures with opposite sides of equal length. Unlike rectangles, parallelograms have four angles that are not 90 degrees, and two sides are sloped as shown in the following diagram. The flat sides are called the bases, and the distance between bases is called the height. In parallelograms, opposite angles are equal, and successive angles, those "next to" each other, are supplementary angles.

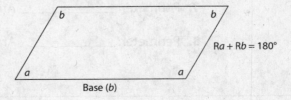

$Ra + Rb = 180°$

Base (*b*)

Perimeter and Area of Squares, Rectangles, and Parallelograms

- **Squares:** The four sides of a square are all equal and the perimeter is $P = 4s$, where s is the length of a side. The area of a square is $A = s^2$. In fact, this is why numbers to the second power are said to be "squared."

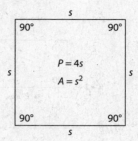

- **Rectangles:** Because rectangles have sides of two different lengths, called length (l) and width (w), the perimeter is $P = 2l + 2w$. The area of a rectangle is $A = l \times w$. It will help to think of a square as a special rectangle with equal sides.

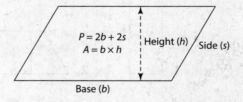

- **Parallelograms:** A parallelogram is not a rectangle, but its perimeter is still the sum of the sides or $P = 2b + 2s$, where b is the length of a base and s the length of a side. For the area of the parallelogram, you need the height, that is, the distance between the two bases. It may be measured either inside or outside the parallelogram as on the diagram. The area is then $A = b \times h$.

Quadrilaterals (Part A)

Directions: Supply the missing lengths and angle measures in the diagrams below.

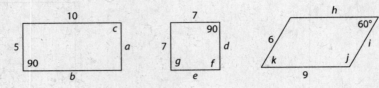

a. _____

b. _____

c. _____

d. _____

e. _____

f. _____

g. _____

h. _____

i. _____

j. _____

k. _____

Quadrilaterals (Part B)

Directions: In each of the following diagrams, calculate the perimeter and area.

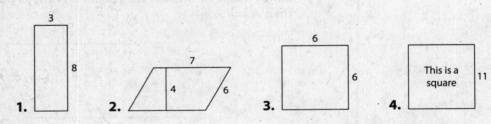

1. Perimeter: _____   Area: _____

2. Perimeter: _____   Area: _____

3. Perimeter: _____   Area: _____

4. Perimeter: _____   Area: _____

Answers are on page 795.

Circles

The basic measurement for circles is the radius, *r*, which is the distance from the center to any point on the outside of the circle. The *diameter* is the distance across the circle. It is twice the length of the radius.

Perimeter and Area of Circles

The perimeter of a circle, its circumference, is $P = 2\pi r$ where *r* is the radius and π (*pi*) is a constant. Use 3.14 for π.

The area of a circle is $A = \pi r^2$.

EXERCISE 9

Circles (Part A)

Directions: Calculate the areas area of the shaded portion of each figure.

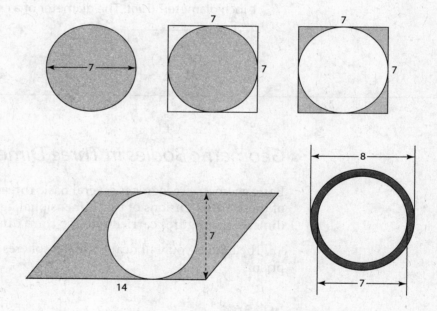

1. _____

2. _____

3. _____

4. _____

5. _____

Circles (Part B)

Directions: Calculate each measurement.

6. Calculate the perimeter and area of a circle with a 1-inch radius.
   _____

7. What is the difference between the area of this circle and a circle with 1-inch diameter? (*Hint*: The diameter of a circle is twice the radius.)
   _____

Answers are on page 795.

Geometric Bodies in Three Dimensions

Basic geometry recognizes several basic three-dimensional objects. All of these are extensions of two dimensional figures; that is, they are two-dimensional figures carried into the third dimension.

The bodies you will deal with are: spheres (balls), cubes, pyramids, and prisms.

Spheres

Spheres are basically three-dimensional circles. As such, the primary measurement of the sphere is the radius, *r*.

The surface area of a sphere, what you need to cover if you want to paint it, is $A = 4\pi r^2$. The volume of a sphere, how much it will hold, is $V = \frac{4}{3}\pi r^3$.

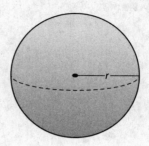

Cylinders

Cylinders are the familiar shape of a soda can or can of soup.

Their surface area is $A = 2\pi r^2 + 2\pi rh$ including the two ends. If the cylinder has no ends or open ends, the surface area is $A = 2\pi rh$. The volume is $V = \pi r^2 h$.

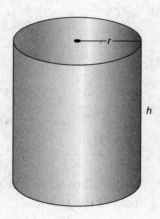

Cubes

Cubes are three-dimensional squares. So all edges of a cube (l) are equal and all faces have the same area.

The area of the face of a cube is l^2 which means the surface area of a cube is $A = 6l^2$.

The volume of a cube is $V = l^3$. This is why numbers to the third power are called "cubed."

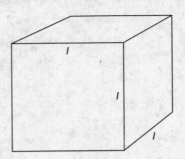

Prisms

Prisms are the three-dimensional extension of the circle, rectangle (or square, which is just a well-behaved rectangle), triangle, or other figure.

In each case, the plane figure forms the ends of the body with the third dimension being called the height.

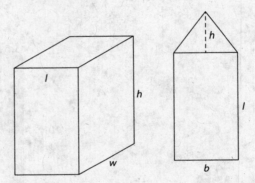

For all of these, the surface area is twice the area of the base, plus the areas of the sides.

The volume is easier. It is the area of an end times the height.

EXAMPLE

What is the volume of the following triangular prism?

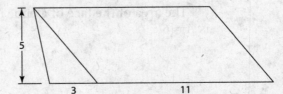

First calculate the area of the triangle at the end.

$$A = \frac{1}{2}bh = \frac{1}{2}(3)(5) = \frac{1}{2}(15) = 7\frac{1}{2}$$

Next, multiply by the height of the prism (which is on its side, but the height is still $h = 11$).

$$V = \left(7\frac{1}{2}\right)(11) = 82\frac{1}{2} \text{ cubic units}$$

Note that you really don't need to know the units for problems like this, or for area problems either. Areas are square units; volumes are cubic units.

EXERCISE 10

Geometric Bodies in Three Dimensions

Directions: For each body below, give the surface area and volume.

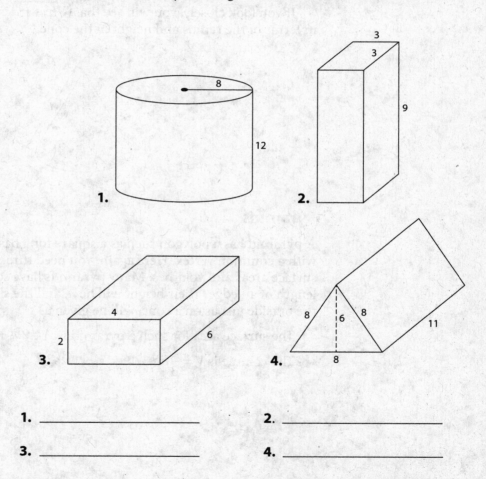

1. _____   2. _____

3. _____   4. _____

Answers are on page 795.

Cones

Cones are a bit different because they start out as circles at the base but disappear in a point at the top. There are three measures needed to describe a cone: the radius of its base (r), the vertical height (h), and the slant height (l), which is measured on the cone's surface.

- The surface area of a cone, including its base, is $A = \pi r\left(r + \sqrt{h^2 + r^2}\right)$, if you are given the radius (r) and the height of the cone (h), or $A = \pi r^2 + \pi r l$, if you have the radius (r) and the slant height (l).

- The surface area *without the base* (the area of just the sides) is $A = \pi r\left(\sqrt{h^2 + r^2}\right)$ or $A = \pi r l$.

- The volume of a cone is $V = \pi r^2 \dfrac{h}{3}$ or $\dfrac{1}{3}\pi r^2 h$.

If you look closely, you will see that $\left(\sqrt{h^2 + r^2}\right)$ is actually the slant height in terms of the radius and height of the cone.

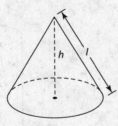

Pyramids

A pyramid has a polygon such as a square for a base and triangular sides with a common vertex. Here again, you need three measurements to find the surface areas and volumes. Many pyramids have square bases of side b, the length of an edge. Their height will be h, and the slant height, measured on the outside just as on a cone, will be given as s.

- The surface area for such a pyramid is $A = 2bs + b^2$.
- The volume is $V = \dfrac{1}{3}b^2 h$.

• If the base is not a square, then this formula becomes

$V = \frac{1}{3}$(area of the base)h, or $V = \frac{1}{3}lwh$, where l and w are the dimensions of the base.

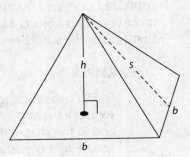

EXERCISE 11

Cones and Pyramids

Directions: Provide the surface areas and volumes for the cone and pyramid.

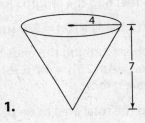

1.

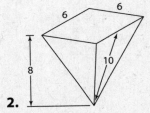

2.

1. Cone: _____

2. Pyramid: _____

Answers are on page 795.

Complex Constructions

Many everyday items require you to calculate their surface areas and volumes. Any time you need to estimate the amount of paint needed to paint something, you need a surface area. And if you are going to hold gasses in a container or even air-condition a building, you need a volume. Fortunately, most common objects can be broken down into separate, simpler parts and that makes the whole process easier.

EXAMPLE

Sam is constructing and painting a propane tank. The tank is a cylinder 14 feet long and 2.5 feet in radius. At each end of the tank is a rounded end in the shape of half a sphere with a radius of 2.5 feet. How many square feet of surface will Sam need to paint, and what is the volume of the tank in cubic feet?

Break down the tank into its component shapes. The middle portion is a cylinder 14 feet long and 2.5 feet in radius. The two ends together make one sphere 2.5 feet in radius. You can calculate the surface area for each part and add those numbers together. Then you can calculate the volume for each part and add those numbers together.

Calculating the surface area:

- For the cylinder, the area *without the ends* is $A = 2\pi rl$, where the radius r is 2.5 feet and the length l is 14 feet.

  $A = 2\pi(2.5)(14) = 70\pi = 220$ square feet, rounded up to the nearest foot.

- The sphere forming the ends has a surface area of
  $A = 4\pi r^2 = 4\pi(2.5)^2 = 4\pi(6.25) = 25\pi = 79$ square feet, rounded up to the nearest foot

- Adding the total area to be painted is $220 + 79 = 299$ square feet.

  Calculating the volume:

- The volume of the cylinder is $V = \pi r^2 h$, which is
  $V = \pi(2.5)^2(14) = \pi(6.25)(14) = 87.5\pi = 275$ cubic feet, rounded up.

- For the sphere the volume is $V = \dfrac{4}{3}\pi r^3$, or

  $V = \dfrac{4}{3}\pi(2.5)^3 = \dfrac{4}{3}\pi(15.625) = \dfrac{62.5}{3}\pi = 20.8\pi = 65$ cubic feet, rounded up.

- Adding, you get $275 + 65 = 340$ cubic feet.

EXERCISE 12

Complex Constructions

Directions: Solve these problems.

1. An Olympic swimming pool measuring 50 meters by 25 meters is surrounded by a cement walkway exactly 2 meters wide.

   a. What is the area of the walkway in square meters?

   _____

   b. If the walkway is 400 millimeters thick, what volume, measured in cubic meters, of concrete does it contain? _____

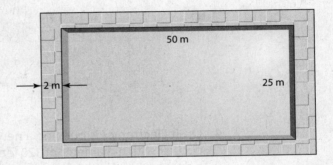

2. The Farmer family is constructing a new silo out of concrete. The silo will be 20 feet in diameter and 55 feet high, and it will have walls 1 foot thick. The top will be metal and is NOT part of the problem.

   a. How many cubic feet of concrete will be needed to build the silo?

   _____

   b. What area of concrete will need to be painted with sealer on the *inside* of the silo? (The outside will be left raw concrete.)

   _____

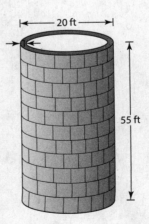

3. Awning Attractions is creating a square four-sided tent with a pyramidal top for Jiffy Auto Jalopy Jobbers. The tent is to measure 25 meters by 25 meters and has 2-meter tall straight sides. The pyramid top will have a slant height of 40 meters. Ignoring seams and such, how many square meters of cloth will be needed? _____

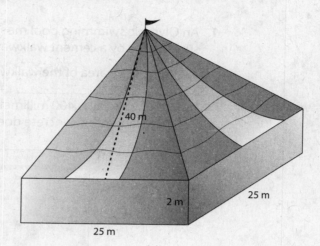

4. Orbit Electronics is building a new multifloor showroom that will be circular with a diameter of 120 feet. It will have 14-foot walls and have a dome on top in the form of a hemisphere (half sphere). To design the air-conditioning system, the engineer needs to calculate the volume of the space. What is the volume in cubic feet of the building, ignoring wall thickness? _____

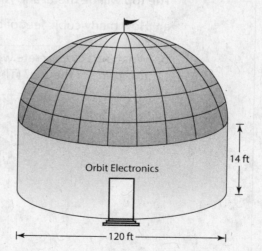

5. One description of a Plains tribe tepee lists the diameter at the base as 18 feet and the slant height as $19\frac{1}{2}$ feet.

A. Using these dimensions, what area of material is needed to construct a tepee of this size? _____

B. If the average buffalo hide measures 27 square feet, how many buffalo hides went into the average Plains tepee? Round up your answer to the nearest whole buffalo hide. _____

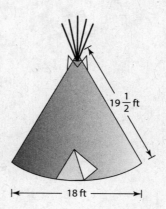

$19\frac{1}{2}$ ft

18 ft

Answers are on page 795.

Science

The Science Test

The Science section of the GED® test measures your knowledge of key science topics and how well you understand basic scientific practices.

Questions on the Science test may ask about the information in a short passage, a graph, a table, or some other graphic presentation of scientific data. Sometimes two or three questions will refer to the same passage, graph, or table. These questions measure your ability to interpret scientific data.

The Science Review

The following section of this book will introduce you to the basic skills and topics that are tested on the Science test. Each main topic is followed by an exercise to measure how well you have mastered that subject. When you are finished with your review, test your mastery of basic science skills by taking the Science Posttest at the back of this book.

This Science review section is organized as follows:

Science

Chapter 1	Life Science
Chapter 2	Physical Science
Chapter 3	Earth and Space Science

Answers for all of the exercises in these chapters are located in the Exercise Answer Keys section at the back of this book.

Life Science

This chapter focuses on many of the life sciences topics tested on the GED® test, including the history of life on Earth, life functions, the human body and its organ systems, evolution, and ecology. It begins by reviewing some basic science skills: how to understand scientific language and how to use the scientific method.

Understanding Scientific Language

Science textbooks attempt to explain and describe all the things that exist in our world. If you find it difficult to understand scientific terms and ideas, it is important to pick apart the sentences and find out the meaning of the words used. Once you understand the terms, you can reword the sentence in your head in a way that makes sense to you.

Use the following steps to help you read and understand difficult passages.

Understanding Difficult Passages

1. When you find a sentence that does not make sense, read the sentence again more slowly.

2. Look for words you do not know. Try to determine their meanings using word parts and context clues. If necessary, look up words in a dictionary.

3. Look at the next few sentences in the passage to find clues about the sentence you are reading.

4. Reread the sentence one more time. This time, try to replace the hard words with simpler words to help you understand the sentence.

5. Reread the entire passage again at regular speed and see if it makes more sense.

Restating Ideas

Sometimes breaking a sentence into parts and rewriting it can help you understand its meaning. Read the following example and consider how restating it may help the sentence make sense to you:

> In considering the experimental results, it would not be wise to take too optimistic a view of the eventual effectiveness of the new drug in the treatment of cardiovascular diseases.

Begin by defining any words you do not recognize such as *optimistic*, *eventual*, and *cardiac*. *Optimistic* means "hopeful and confident about the future." *Eventual* means "occurring at the end of an event." The prefix *cardio-* deals with things related to the heart. Rewrite the sentence in simpler terms using the new definitions:

> When you look at the results of the experiments, you shouldn't be too hopeful that in the future the new drug will help people with heart disease.

EXERCISE 1:

Restating Ideas

Directions: Rewrite the following sentences using simpler words or word parts. Follow the steps listed under "Understanding Difficult Passages" for help.

1. Observing the evaporative properties of water requires the utilization of an apparatus such as a Bunsen burner.

   _____

   _____

2. The advent of nuclear fission permitted electricity providers to utilize a cleaner method of production than the combustion of fossil fuels.

   _____

   _____

3. It has been argued in the media that cellular telecommunications have an adverse effect on human physiology.

   _____

   _____

Answers are on page 796.

Using the Scientific Method

Scientists solve problems the same way that nonscientists do. The first step scientists use is to identify the problem. Then they collect facts the scientists think are important for solving the problem. Next, scientists make a guess about what they think is causing the problem. After making a guess, scientists test their guess, usually by conducting an experiment. Finally, they use the results of the tests to conclude whether or not their guess was correct. Although we solve problems the same way as scientists, their process has a name, the scientific method. The **scientific method** is a process to observe, understand, and explain the world we live in. Read the following story to understand the scientific method:

> Henry is driving down a long, deserted highway late at night. He has been driving for a few hundred miles on his way to his parents' house. The radio volume is loud while Henry sings along to pass the time. Suddenly, Henry feels the car shudder, and he immediately swerves the car thinking he hit something in the road. As he steers the car back into the lane, he wonders if one of the car's tires went flat. Henry slows the car and parks on the shoulder of the road, turning on the hazard lights. Henry gets out of the car and shines a flashlight on each of the tires, inspecting each one to see if the tires seem to have enough air. None of the tires looks flat, so Henry gets back in the car.

> Because no tire was flat, Henry guesses that because he has been driving for a few hundred miles, the car shuddered because it is running out of gas. Henry starts the engine and notices that the fuel gauge is on empty. He realizes that he had better find a gas station before the car stops for good.

There are six steps to the scientific method. Based on this story, you can see how Henry followed these steps to solve the problem.

Solving the Problem	The Scientific Method
1. Henry feels the car shudder and wonders if one of the tires went flat.	1. Identify the problem.
2. Henry pulls the car over and gets out to inspect each tire for damage.	2. Find facts and information.
3. Henry guesses that the car must be running low on gas.	3. Form a hypothesis.
4. Henry turns on the car to see the fuel gauge.	4. Test the hypothesis.
5. Henry observes that the fuel gauge is on empty.	5. Collect the data.
6. Henry concludes that he was correct: the car is running low on gas.	6. Draw conclusions.

Step 1: Identify the Problem

Scientists have many scientific questions that they can answer. They decide which question or problem they want to study. Outside of the scientific world, people tend to solve problems whenever one arises.

How do you come up with questions? Look or observe around you. An **observation** is something you hear, feel, smell, taste, or see to gather information. All you need is curiosity about the world around you.

Step 2: Find Facts and Information

After you identify your question, you need to gather and organize information. Several ways exist to research information such as reading books, looking in newspapers, and searching the Internet. It is important to use trusted websites such as those belonging to universities, governmental agencies, and scientific organizations. To measure your information-finding skills, read the following question and then answer the three numbered questions that follow.

Question: How much rain falls each year in the Amazon forest?

1. What kind of answer is best for this question: a word, a number, or a place?

   _____

2. What unit of measure is appropriate for this answer: inches, gallons, or pounds?

   _____

3. Where would you research to find this answer?

   _____

For question 1, you probably thought that the answer would be a number. For question 2, it is common to measure rainfall in inches, although the amount of rain that falls in the rainforest may be many gallons! However, if you listen to weather reports, you already know that rainfall measurements are in inches. For question 3, you might search the Internet for international weather reports, graphs about rainfall in the Amazon, or perhaps a news article about tropical forests. This type of information changes over time, so although you may have an idea, you would want to get the most up-to-date information.

Let's try another item:

Question: What would happen if all the honeybees died?

1. Would you expect this answer to be in numbers or words?

_____

2. Where might you find the answer to this question?

_____

For question 1, you would most likely expect an answer in words. If you know something about honeybees, you probably know that bees help to pollinate plants that animals and humans use for nutrition. A world without honeybees might experience starvation. For question 2, you could read about this potential problem in science magazines or books about the environment.

Fact vs. Opinion

Sometimes you are told that something is true, but after careful examination, you find out that it is not a fact. A **fact** can be supported with evidence from observations or measurements that can be gathered in the natural world.

It can be difficult to determine if a statement is a fact or an opinion. If a person starts a sentence with the phrase "I think" or "I believe," then it is possible that he or she is stating an opinion. An **opinion** is something that someone believes although it may not be true. Opinions are based on beliefs, culture, values, or the way someone wishes to live. Values cannot be proven right or wrong.

Here are a few examples of opinions:

• The sounds of a thunderstorm are quite relaxing.

• Hockey is the most exciting professional sport.

• It is best to vacation on the beach during spring break.

You may have feelings about each of these statements, but you cannot prove that any of them are right or wrong. These are all opinions and not facts.

EXERCISE 2

Fact vs. Opinion

Directions: Write the letter *F* before each statement that is a fact. If the statement is an opinion, write the letter *O* before the statement. Write three sentences of your own at the end and indicate if they are facts or opinions.

_____ **1.** New York has the largest population of any city in the United States.

_____ **2.** Mining for coal is better than drilling for oil.

_____ **3.** Phoenix is the capital of Arizona.

_____ **4.** The Pittsburgh Steelers are the greatest team in the history of sports.

_____ **5.** The moon is 240,000 miles from Earth.

_____ **6.** The length of your foot is about the same as the length of your forearm.

_____ **7.** Studying while listening to jazz music is a better way to learn.

_____ **8.** _____

_____ **9.** _____

_____ **10.** _____

Answers are on page 796.

Step 3: Form a Hypothesis

Once all the facts available about a specific problem are collected, scientists use these facts to make an educated guess about the answer or solution. A **hypothesis** is a guess or possible explanation based on the available facts. Hypotheses must be scientific. To be considered scientific, a hypothesis must be testable in the natural world.

Scientific hypotheses are best when based on more than one or two facts. For example, to diagnose a health problem, doctors collect many facts about you such as your blood pressure, temperature, and medical history. The doctor develops a hypothesis based on many factors. A good hypothesis must work with all of the facts available. It is best not to ignore a fact because it does not match your guess about a problem. Instead, change your hypothesis to include all the facts you observed.

Each of us makes careful guesses, or hypotheses, about things that happen in our daily lives. Consider a situation where you see a person walking out of a grocery store looking very angry. What might you **hypothesize**, or guess, about why he is angry? Read this chart:

Fact: A person walks out of a grocery store looking very angry.

Hypothesis 1: The person forgot to bring his wallet into the store.

Hypothesis 2: The store did not have the main ingredient for the person's special meal.

Hypothesis 3: The person just lost his job at the grocery store.

A hypothesis is a best guess based on the facts available. Make a hypothesis for the following situation:

You wake up and notice your digital alarm clock isn't working and your bedside lamp won't turn on. Why do you think this is occurring?

_____

_____

Is it correct to guess that the bedside lamp's lightbulb burned out? How would this explain that the alarm clock is not working? Your first hypothesis might be that there may be something wrong with the electricity in your bedroom.

EXERCISE 3

Forming Everyday Hypotheses

Directions: Write a hypothesis for each real-life situation.

1. When using your gas grill in the backyard, you notice that the food is not cooking.

    Your hypothesis: _____

    _____

2. You wake up from sleeping overnight and immediately put on your running shoes and start to jog around the neighborhood. You begin to feel lightheaded and weak.

    Your hypothesis: _____

    _____

3. Your parents invite you to come to their house for dinner. When you arrive, you notice that all the lights inside the house are off, but you can make out the shapes of people hiding behind furniture and balloons floating around the house.

Your hypothesis: _____

_____

Answers are on page 796.

EXERCISE 4

Forming Scientific Hypotheses

Directions: Write a hypothesis for each real-life situation.

1. Tests prove that a creek is polluted with arsenic, oil, and soap. Upstream past a city, the creek shows signs of arsenic and oil, but no soap. Further upstream, past a manufacturing plant, the water is clean and not polluted. Remember that water in a creek flows downstream.

Your hypothesis: _____

_____

2. Amelie uses a handheld magnet to experiment what it can pick up. The results are shown in the table.

Things Picked Up	Things Not Picked Up
Steel paper clip	Saltine cracker
Iron nail	Copper wire
Steel wire	Crystal rock

Your hypothesis: _____

_____

Answers are on page 796.

Step 4: Test the Hypothesis

Once a hypothesis is formed, a scientist will test it to see if his or her guess is correct. Testing helps scientists to disprove or to support their hypotheses. They conduct **experiments**, which are processes used to test a hypothesis. Experiments usually involve observations and **measurements** with tools like scales, thermometers, or rulers.

Before designing an experiment, scientists make a **prediction** of what will happen in their experiment based on their hypotheses. People make predictions every day when they make decisions. For example, you might hypothesize that premium gas is more efficient than other types of gas. Then you might predict that cars that use premium gas run more efficiently than cars that do not use premium gas. This prediction can then be tested using experiments.

A scientist needs to make many decisions in designing an experiment. These decisions include: what things to test, what steps to follow, and how to collect information or data from the experiment.

Parts of an Experiment

What you choose to study is your study **subject**. For your experiment, your subjects will be separated into two groups: the control group and the experimental group. The **experimental group** is the group that is being exposed to one factor or **variable** being tested. The **control group** is treated exactly the same way as the experimental group *except* it is not exposed to the variable. For example, to test gas efficiency your study subject might be a particular brand of car. You decide to test five cars of that brand with premium gas (the experimental group) and another five cars of that brand with regular gas (the control group). Let's examine an example so you can understand the process.

A paint manufacturer in western Pennsylvania has an outdoor laboratory for testing paints. Scientists who work for the manufacturer develop new paints. They hypothesize that a certain new paint brand will hold colors in outdoor environments longer than the paint brand the manufacturer currently sells.

For the test, the scientists use 20 identical wooden boards mounted on poles. On 10 of these boards, the scientists paint three coats of the existing paint brand. These are the control group. On the other 10 boards, the scientists paint three coats of the new paint brand. The new paint brand is the variable.

The boards stay on the poles for two months. The scientists observe the paint on each of the boards and notice that the boards painted with the existing brand faded more than the boards with the new brand of paint.

These results of the experiment support the scientists' hypothesis correctly—the new paint brand will hold its color better.

Let's summarize the parts of this experiment:

- Subjects—wooden boards
- Variable—the new brand of paint
- Control group—boards painted with the existing brand
- Experimental group—boards painted with the new brand of paint

Well-Designed Experiments

Results of a poorly designed experiment are not valid or reliable. **Valid** means that the results are true. **Reliable** means that each time the experiment is repeated or reproduced, the same results occur. An experiment without valid and reliable results is not useful. In our example, the paint scientists may conduct the same experiment a hundred times using another set of boards each time to make sure that nothing in the first test was missed. Reproducing the same results over and over is the key to testing the validity of the hypothesis.

The requirements for a well-designed experiment are summarized as follows:

- Subjects need to be the same, and the more subjects, the more reliable the results.
- Subjects in the experimental group should be treated the same as the subjects in the control group for all conditions except for the one variable being tested.
- A control group is necessary.
- The results should be able to be reproduced when repeated.

Now, read the following experiment and try to determine what went wrong.

> A baker wanted to see if a sugar substitute would make her cookie mix taste better while being healthier. She mixed up batter for a dozen cookies using the sugar substitute and batter for a dozen cookies using sugar. While both the sugar cookies and sugar-substitute cookies were still baking, she took out one of the sugar-substitute cookies for a taste. She compared this cookie to a sugar cookie she baked yesterday. She decided that the cookie with sugar substitute tasted better and she would change her recipe for the future.

What is wrong with the baker's results? _____

_____

_____

The problem with this experiment is that too many things were changed. The baker mixed up the same amount of batter using sugar versus a sugar substitute, but she removed one of the sugar-substitute cookies from the oven ahead of the sugar cookies. Then she compared that sugar-substitute cookie to some cookies she had baked the day before. As a result, she cannot be certain that her sugar-substitute cookies are better than the sugar cookies that she was baking at the same time. This experiment is not valid or reliable.

EXERCISE 5

Errors in Experiments

Directions: Identify the problem with each experiment listed below. Choose from the following list of errors and write your answer on the line provided.

- Not enough subjects were included in the test.
- The subjects are not similar.
- The conditions of the experiment were not kept the same.
- The experiment results were not reproduced.

1. A gardener wanted to find out if distilled water would be better for flowers. She used distilled water on her roses but used water from the hose for her petunias. The roses suffered, but the petunias grew tall and strong. The gardener decided that distilled water is not good at all for flowers.

   _____

2. A machine that affixed postage stamps to envelopes was having problems. About 25 percent of the envelopes going through the machine came out missing a stamp. A mailroom worker adjusted the timing wheel in the machine and ran a few envelopes through the machine, noticing that the stamps were affixed properly. The worker was satisfied, turned the machine back on, and left to work on another task.

   _____

Answers are on page 796.

Step 5: Collect the Data

For any experiment, you will collect data. Data may be qualitative (observational) or quantitative (measureable). For example, noticing that using premium gas made a car run more smoothly is qualitative data. Recording the actual gas mileage for a car using premium gas is a quantitative measurement.

When you make observations or collect numerical data, it is best to record your data in a lab notebook or computer file. Organizing your data is important. Thus, tables and spreadsheets are useful for recording data. This will make it easier for you to determine the meaning of your data and to **analyze** your data to identify trends. During data analysis, look for patterns in the data. For example, you might check whether cars with premium gas are more gas efficient than cars with regular gas. Computers with statistical programs are commonly used to analyze data.

Step 6: Draw Conclusions

So far, you have learned how to identify the question, find the facts and information, form the hypothesis, test the hypothesis, and collect and analyze data. You have also learned that it is important to repeat an experiment many times to make sure the results are reliable and valid. The final step is to form a conclusion about the data. In other words, based on the results of your experiment, you accept or reject your hypothesis. If you reject your hypothesis, then you create a different hypothesis based on your data and retest.

When there is enough data accumulated to support a hypothesis, scientists move to the next step called a theory, such as Newton's theory of gravity or Darwin's theory of natural selection. A **scientific theory** summarizes a hypothesis or group of hypotheses that have been supported with repeated testing. Theories may be revised over time if new data are discovered that contradict, or go against, the original findings.

Let's look at examples of scientific theories that were later contradicted.

Example 1	**Scientific theory:** Pre-1900 astronomers believed that the universe was static, that it was not expanding or contracting. All of the solar systems held their place in the universe.
	Contradiction: In the 1920s astronomer Edwin Hubble observed that distant objects in the universe were moving away more quickly than closer objects. Following Hubble's discovery, later astronomers found that the expansion is occurring far more rapidly than Hubble originally theorized.
Example 2	**Scientific theory:** In ancient Greece, Aristotle claimed that the speed at which an object falls is related to the object's mass.
	Contradiction: In the late 1500s the Italian scientist Galileo proved through experimentation that Aristotle's theory was incorrect. The speed of a falling object is not related to its mass.

Making Decisions Using the Scientific Method

All of us use the scientific method in our daily lives. We have a question or problem to solve and so we take the time to collect the facts to help make our decision. Then we choose possible solutions or hypotheses.

Sometimes we ask friends or family to help us figure out the solution. We might attempt to solve the problem by trying different things to see what would happen. Sometimes we just think through the situation and come to a conclusion. Even when we make our decision, there is always the possibility that it is not correct. Then we go through the scientific method again.

You can even adapt the scientific method when taking a test. Read a question, collect facts by reading the question again, and study any available illustrations. Then examine every possible answer, considering each one to determine the answer that makes the most sense.

EXERCISE 6

Making Decisions Using the Scientific Method

Directions: Read each passage and then answer the questions about each step of the scientific method.

Smallpox was a deadly disease that doctors believe is no longer a danger. An English doctor named Edward Jenner worked to end this disease in the early 1800s. During that time, smallpox killed thousands of people each year.

When Jenner was a young doctor, a sudden spread of smallpox occurred. He was unable to save many of his patients from dying from this disease. Jenner observed something odd, however. Women who worked milking cows on dairy farms did not catch smallpox. This fact made Jenner curious.

1. For the first step in Jenner's scientific process, what question do you think he asked?

_____

_____

Jenner spoke with a lot of dairy workers. He found out that although the women did not get sick with smallpox, they would catch a disease called cowpox from the cows. This was not a serious disease. The milkmaids would get spots on their hands only, while smallpox victims developed spots all over their bodies. Nobody ever died of cowpox, and nobody who ever caught cowpox seemed to catch smallpox.

2. What facts did Jenner collect from talking to the dairy workers?

_____

_____

3. What hypothesis would you make if you were the doctor studying this disease?

_____

_____

Jenner hypothesized that a person who caught cowpox would not catch smallpox for the rest of his or her life.

4. Can you explain how Jenner decided to test this hypothesis?

_____

_____

_____

_____

Jenner tested his hypothesis by infecting healthy people with cowpox. He injected the disease into them using a needle. He observed his patients to see if they caught smallpox, but none of them got sick. He tested this on several people and got the same result.

This idea to inject people with a mild disease to keep them from getting a serious disease was the beginning of modern vaccinations. However, many people were not happy with Jenner's testing of healthy people. But over time, people realized that Jenner's work was helping to save more and more people. His vaccination process made him famous.

5. What can you conclude about cowpox based on the results of Jenner's experiment?

_____

_____

Answers are on page 797.

Foundations of Life

Biology is the study of life. It is difficult to define the word _life_, but the scientific community agrees that living things share certain qualities. For example, all living things have genetic material, respond to the environment, and reproduce more of the same kind.

All living things are also organized internally and externally as shown here:

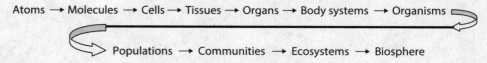

Organization of Living Things

Atoms → Molecules → Cells → Tissues → Organs → Body systems → Organisms

Populations → Communities → Ecosystems → Biosphere

In this flowchart, each arrow stands for the words *make up*. For example, cells make up tissue, and tissues are organized into parts of the body called organs. Different organs work together to perform the functions of an organ system. Several body systems make up an organism like a human. Organisms that live and breed together in one area make up a population. Populations interact and form a community, which interacts with the nonliving world in an ecosystem on Earth. That is the hierarchy of life.

Cells

All living things are made up of cells. **Cells** are the smallest unit of life. A cell is microscopic, something too small to see without a microscope. Cells are organized structures that help living things complete tasks like breaking down food for nutrients, reproducing, growing, and moving around in the environment. Scientists made observations to develop a theory about cells. There are three main ideas of **cell theory**:

1. All living things are made of cells.

2. Cells are the basic building units of life.

3. All cells come from preexisting cells.

There are several different types of cells, and each may have a different job in living things. Cells within animals may be different from cells in a plant. However, all cells have some similarity in their structure. They have four basic parts:

- A **cell membrane** that controls the materials that enter and leave the cell

- A watery **cytoplasm**, in which cell parts are suspended

- Many small grains called **ribosomes**, where proteins are made

- One or more **chromosomes**, the strands of the genetic material

Basic Cell Structure

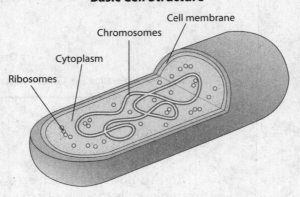

Simple Cells: Bacteria

There are two main types of cells—prokaryotic cells and eukaryotic cells. **Prokaryotic cells** are the simplest cells with few internal parts, as shown in the diagram. These microscopic organisms are called **bacteria**. In the diagram, notice the bacterium's **flagellum**, a tail-like structure to help it move, and **pili**, tiny hair-like structures that allow the bacterium to attach to other cells.

Bacterium

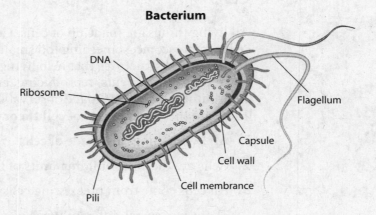

Bacteria can either cause disease or be helpful to other living things. Some bacteria cause strep throat, tuberculosis, and staph infections that are the common cause of skin infections. Antibiotics can cure most harmful bacterial infections. Beneficial bacteria help the cycle of life by breaking down organic matter. Dead plants and animals decompose as bacteria recycle nutrients from them for other living things to use. Our intestines use bacteria to help our body produce certain vitamins.

Complex Cells: Animal Cells and Plant Cells

The cells that make up protists, fungi, plants, and animals are **eukaryotic cells**. These are complex cells with many internal parts. Organisms composed of eukaryotic cells may be **unicellular** (having one cell) or **multicellular** (having many cells).

The control center of every complex cell is the **nucleus**, a dark spot near the middle of the cell, as shown in the cells in the diagram that follows. A nuclear membrane separates the nucleus from the cytoplasm. Inside the nucleus are chromosomes that are the cell's blueprints or **DNA**. Cells that make up different animals and plants may have a different number of chromosomes. For instance, fruit flies have 8 chromosomes, humans have 46, and some plants can have more than 1,000.

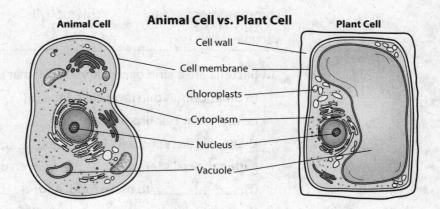

Notice in the diagram that animal and plant cells have **vacuoles** that store water and nutrients for the cell. The difference between animal and plant cells is that the vacuole in a plant cell often takes up a lot of available space in the cell. Another difference between an animal cell and a plant cell is the outer protection. An animal cell has a thin **cell membrane** that holds the cell together. A plant cell has both a cell membrane and an extra outer **cell wall**. The plant cell wall is made of **cellulose**, a strong supportive material that helps the cell keep its shape.

Most plant cells have **chloroplasts**, structures in which plants make their food. Chloroplasts contain a green pigment known as **chlorophyll**. The presence of this pigment helps green plants make food using energy from sunlight. Organisms that make their own food are called **autotrophs**. Animal cells do not have chloroplasts and cannot make food. Organisms that cannot make their own food and must eat food to survive are called **heterotrophs**.

EXERCISE 7

Cells

Directions: Write the word from the list that best completes each sentence.

cell membrane	pili	nucleus
chromosomes	chlorophyll	cell wall
vacuole		

1. Bacteria are a kind of prokaryotic cell that uses **(a)** _____ to attach to other cells. A thin layer called the **(b)** _____ protects animal cells. A plant cell also has a **(c)** _____ that helps the cell keep its shape. A eukaryotic cell's **(d)** _____ are made up of DNA, protected within the cell's **(e)** _____. Green plants use pigments called **(f)** _____ to make food. A **(g)** _____ is empty space within the cell that stores water and nutrients for the cell.

Directions: Choose the best answer to the question.

2. Which statement is NOT a main idea about cell theory?

    A. Cells are the building unit of living things.
    B. All cells contain a nucleus and DNA.
    C. All cells come from other cells.
    D. All living things are made up of cells.

Answers are on page 797.

Viruses

Viruses are extremely tiny microbes made of genetic material inside a protein coat, as shown in the illustration. Unlike bacteria, a **virus** is not a cell and thus is not alive. Most scientists classify viruses as "nonliving" because they lack the ability to reproduce and perform other self-sustaining life processes on their own. A virus is a parasite that must infect living cells to reproduce. It is unable to reproduce without the help of a host cell. A virus infects a cell and begins to create copies by using the host cell's nutrients and energy.

A Virus that Infects Bacteria

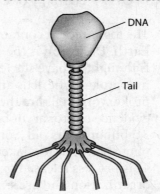

DNA

Tail

Viruses are responsible for the common cold, influenza (the flu), and chickenpox. These diseases are caused by different kinds of viruses. Scientists have worked to find and cure cancer-causing viruses and the virus that causes AIDS. Unlike bacteria, viruses are not killed by antibiotics. For the most part, humans infected with a virus must let their bodies fight the virus until the cells are healthy again.

With microbes like bacteria and viruses, you might expect that humans would be sick all of the time. But the human body can build up immunity to disease by learning how to kill the microbes it has had to fight in the past. In addition, **immunizations** and **vaccinations** enable the body to practice building defenses against dead or weakened germs injected through a needle. It is important for people to be immunized throughout their childhood to help their bodies learn to fight diseases as they grow.

History of Life

Earth is about 4.6 billion years old. Young Earth was a very different place from the planet we see today. It started out as a hot brew of molten rock and gases, churning and cooling to form a crust covered with mountains, plains, and valleys. As Earth cooled, some gases formed clouds that rained on the planet, filling the valleys with water that eventually formed the oceans. Between three and four billion years ago, it is believed that life started in the oceans.

Scientists use fossils to research the history of life on Earth. **Fossils** are the remains or impressions of organisms that have died. Layers upon layers of soil and sand covered their bodies over millions of years. With each additional layer pressing down, hardened rock formed around the remains, preserving the structure of prehistoric life. The collection of fossils in layers of rock is called the **fossil record**. Using the fossil record and age-dating methods, scientists can infer the order and timing of events in the history of life on Earth. Scientists continue to find new evidence of ancient life as more fossils are discovered.

From Prokaryotes to Eukaryotes

The fossil record contains direct evidence of the evolution of life on Earth. **Evolution** is the change over time of living things on Earth. Life is thought to have started as simple one-celled organisms. These were the first prokaryotic cells and similar to modern-day bacteria. Recall that prokaryotic cells are the simplest cells with few internal parts. The oldest evidence of prokaryotic life comes from rocks that are dated at about 3.5 billion years old. Some early bacteria, called blue-green algae, used photosynthesis to make their own food using sunlight and inorganic matter. This process released oxygen into the atmosphere. Prokaryotes have less organization and are smaller than the eukaryotic cells that make up all other organisms. One explanation for these differences is that prokaryotic cells evolved before eukaryotic cells. In fact, it took about another two billion years until our planet became populated by single-celled eukaryotes called protists. These single-celled organisms evolved into the complex, multi-celled organisms we now know as fungi, plants, and animals.

Animals: From Invertebrates to Vertebrates

Starting about 600 million years ago, the oceans became filled with multi-celled organisms known as animals. The first animals were soft-bodied, and because they lacked a backbone, they are classified as **invertebrates**. Today, invertebrates are still the predominant animal form. They include worms, insects, and crustaceans such as crabs and lobsters. About 550 million years ago, the first **vertebrates** with backbones evolved. They were the ancestors of all backboned animals that exist on Earth today. The earliest vertebrates were jawless fish. Fish later evolved jaws and diversified during the era called the **Age of Fishes**. Having jaws enabled the fish to bite and chew their food. Soon some fish developed into large predators.

About 360 million years ago, a special group of fish, called lungfish, evolved into the first group of land vertebrates by crawling on four legs out of the water. These ancestors of **amphibians** had leg-like fins to walk on the ocean bottom. They also had primitive lungs allowing them to swim to the surface for extra oxygen. Their amphibian descendants, such as the modern-day frog, are still tied to the water. They have smooth, thin skin that is good for taking in oxygen for breathing. Unfortunately, this skin allows moisture to escape. This is one reason why amphibians have to stay close to moist locations and live part of their life in the water.

If you have ever seen a frog develop, you know that it started its life in the water as an egg and then as a tadpole. Amphibians keep close to the water because this is where they reproduce and lay eggs. Hatchlings swim in the water like fish, breathing through gills underwater. As they grow, fins and gills change into legs and lungs. This allows the animals to crawl onto dry land.

After another 50 million years had passed, **reptiles**, which are a different kind of cold-blooded vertebrates, evolved and began to inhabit the Earth. The term **Age of Reptiles** describes this time period when many large reptiles, including **dinosaurs**, roamed the planet. Reptiles are adapted to live in a drier environment than amphibians. Another difference between amphibians

Amphibian

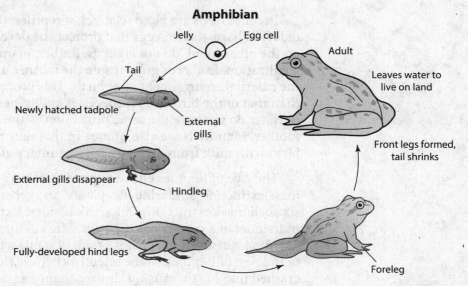

and reptiles is that reptiles lay their eggs on land rather than in the water. So the young immediately breathe through lungs, not gills. Reptile eggs have hardened shells to protect the developing animal **embryo**. The eggshell protects the embryo and accompanying nourishment from drying out. Reptiles are also better suited for dry land than amphibians because their bodies are covered with scales. Scales are a type of waterproof outer skin that helps the reptile hold moisture in its body. Today, the descendants of prehistoric reptiles, such as snakes, turtles, and alligators, still walk the Earth and bask in the sun.

By the end of the Age of Reptiles, two new groups of organisms had evolved: **mammals** (evolved from reptiles before dinosaurs) and **birds** (evolved from smaller dinosaurs). Unlike amphibians and reptiles, which absorb heat from their environment, mammals and birds keep a steady body temperature by producing heat internally. To insulate their bodies, mammals are covered with hair and birds are covered with feathers. These unique characteristics help these animals survive weather changes, such as seasonal temperature shifts. To understand how mammals and birds have evolved, examine the diagram.

Animals

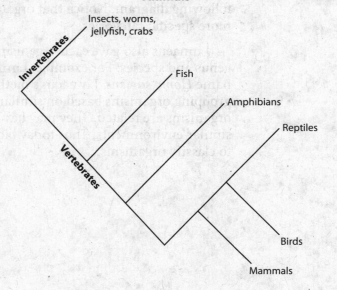

Because birds are close relatives of reptiles, they share the characteristic of laying hard-shelled eggs that protect the developing embryo. Mammals, on the other hand, do not lay eggs. Rather, mammals have internal fertilization. Embryos grow inside the mother until they are ready to handle the external environment after birth. This process protects the young better than that of the bird and reptile. Eggs laid in nests, underground, or even in water do not have the same protection as the embryo carried inside the mother. Mammals are also unique in that they nourish their young after birth with milk from the mother's mammary glands.

The Age of Reptiles ended approximately 65 million years ago during a mass extinction of marine life, plants, and other animals. There have been six such mass extinctions in Earth's history. **Extinction** means that every individual of a species has died out. Mass extinctions involve many species. The dinosaurs were the major group of reptiles to become extinct at the end of the Age of Reptiles. Some scientists believe that a comet or a large asteroid crashed into Earth, causing climate change and loss of food that wiped out many species. Although many species became extinct at this time, certain life-forms, such as small mammals, survived and flourished afterward. The **Age of Mammals** started the next phase in the history of Earth. Many of the familiar animals on Earth today are mammals, such as cats, bats, dogs, cattle, and even humans.

Classification of Life

The total number of different kinds of living things on Earth is unknown. Recent estimates put the possible number at more than eight million species. How do we classify all these species? Scientists needed to describe and name each type of organism in order to share information about living things.

In the 18th century, Swedish botanist Carolus Linnaeus contributed an important classification system to biology. **Classification** is the science of categorizing things such as organisms into groups based on their similarities. Linnaeus organized living things into groups. We still use the hierarchical classification system developed by Linnaeus as shown in the following diagram. Notice that organisms are grouped into progressively more specific categories.

Linnaeus also gave each organism a unique scientific name denoting its genus and species. For example, Linnaeus assigned humans the scientific name *Homo sapiens*. Linnaeus's method of classification has limits because grouping organisms based on similarities does not always mean that organisms are related. They may have common features because they live in similar environments. Thus today biologists use evolutionary relationships to classify organisms.

Classification System

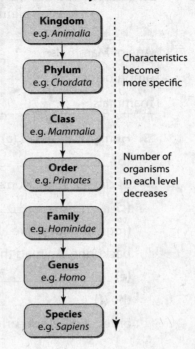

EXERCISE 8

History of Life

Directions: Choose the best answer to each question.

1. Which statement correctly identifies an advantage that reptiles gain from having scales?
   A. Scales provide protection from predators.
   B. Scales prevent the skin from losing water.
   C. Scales improve the speed of a moving reptile.
   D. Scales keep embryos from drying out.

2. Rabbits and horses are familiar examples of animals in the class Mammalia. Therefore, rabbits and horses are all classified into the same_____.
   A. kingdom, phylum, and class
   B. phylum, class, and family
   C. class, genus, and family
   D. kingdom, species, and order

Directions: Choose the word or phrase from the following list that best fits in each blank in the passage.

Age of Mammals	reptiles	vertebrates
amphibians	fossil record	order
mammals	invertebrates	Age of Fishes

3. Humans, a class of **(a)** _____, are grouped in the
   (b) _____ of primates, based on Linnaeus's system
   of classification. Humans are not grouped among the
   (c) _____, which include snakes and lizards. Humans,
   frogs, and toads are all **(d)** _____, animals that have a
   backbone. Animals that begin life in the water and move to land are
   (e) _____. Dinosaurs existed during a time period before
   the **(f)** _____. It is possible for scientists to infer the time
   order of different early life-forms from the **(g)** _____.

Answers are on page 797.

Life Functions and Energy Intake

All living things need energy and organic matter for their life functions. Organisms need **nutrients**, substances needed for growth and other activities. They get their nutrients in one of two ways. Organisms are either producers or consumers. **Producers**, such as plants, take in energy from their surroundings as well as inorganic matter to make their own organic matter or food. **Consumers**, such as animals, have to catch and eat food to get energy and organic matter needed for life functions. Consumers feed on the producers or on other consumers.

Producers and consumers are also grouped into the related terms *autotrophs* and *heterotrophs*, respectively. The term **autotroph** comes from the Greek, meaning "self-feeder." These living things do not need to eat food because they make their own food. For example, plants absorb the sun's energy to make sugars. The producers and autotrophs include green plants, algae-like seaweed, and some bacteria.

Heterotrophs, or consumers, eat other living things for organic nutrients. The term **heterotroph** is a combination of Greek words, meaning "other-feeder." Heterotrophs cannot make organic matter from inorganic materials. So heterotrophs rely on autotrophs or other heterotrophs for nutrients. Common heterotrophs are some bacteria, some protists, all fungi, and all animals.

Photosynthesis

Like other autotrophs, plants make their own food. Plants can do this through the activity of **photosynthesis**, using the sun's energy to produce sugars. This process is shown in the following chemical equation:

$$6\ CO_2 + 6\ H_2O + \text{light energy} \rightarrow C_6H_{12}O_6 + 6\ O_2$$

carbon dioxide + water + light energy → sugar + oxygen

This process requires a chemical reaction, and only cells that contain chlorophyll can complete the process. **Chlorophyll** is a green pigment found in plants. In plants, chlorophyll is located in the **chloroplasts**, organelles that conduct photosynthesis. Chlorophyll traps the sun's light energy. This energy is used to convert carbon dioxide gas from the air and water from the soil into the chemical energy of sugars. Plants store sugars and use this energy for carrying out life functions. In addition to synthesized sugars, notice in the diagram that oxygen gas is given off to the air.

Photosynthesis

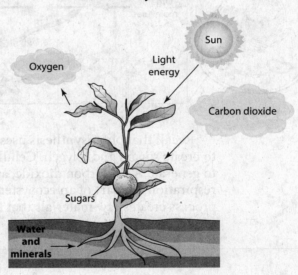

Almost all of the oxygen gas in the atmosphere is the result of photosynthesis by autotrophs like plants. Heterotrophs, including humans, breathe in oxygen and exhale carbon dioxide for plants to use. This is an important partnership between autotrophs and heterotrophs.

Cellular Respiration

Organisms cannot perform cell processes without energy. Cells use a special type of energy that is a made during cellular respiration. **Cellular respiration** is an aerobic (oxygen-requiring) process that burns sugars to make **ATP**, which is the main energy for cells, as shown here:

$$C_6H_{12}O_6 + 6\ O_2 \rightarrow 6\ CO_2 + 6\ H_2O + \text{ATP energy}$$

sugar + oxygen → carbon dioxide + water + energy

Cellular respiration is a process that resembles the way in which an automobile burns gasoline. In simplistic form, a car engine burns gas, and the energy released pushes the pistons that turn the crankshaft that turns the axle to make the wheels spin. Cellular respiration uses the oxygen we breathe to make energy for our cells, and the output we produce is carbon dioxide. All organisms, including plants, carry out some form of respiration.

Cellular respiration occurs in the **mitochondria**, the "powerhouse" of eukaryotic cells, as shown in the following figure. Respiration powers the cell's metabolism to complete functions such as building molecules to promote cellular health.

Cellular Respiration in Cells

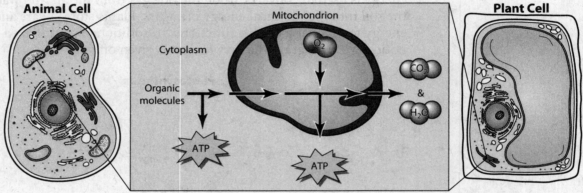

Recall that photosynthesis uses light energy, water, and carbon dioxide to create sugars and oxygen. Cellular respiration uses oxygen and sugar to generate ATP, carbon dioxide, and water. Photosynthesis and cellular respiration are part of an ecosystem's energy flow and cycle of carbon. Each process creates raw materials that the other process needs.

EXERCISE 9

Life Functions and Energy Intake

Directions: Choose the best answer to each question.

1. Which is an output from the process of photosynthesis?
   A. Chloroplasts
   B. Carbon dioxide
   C. Oxygen
   D. Water

2. Which BEST describes an autotroph?
   A. Organisms that feed on inorganic and organic matter to survive
   B. Bacteria that use the process of photosynthesis to make food
   C. Producers that take in inorganic matter and energy to make food
   D. Consumers that catch and eat organic matter for food

Directions: Choose the word or phrase from the following list that best fits in each blank in the passage.

chloroplast	ATP	mitochondria
chlorophyll	plants	animals
anaerobic bacteria	prokaryotic	eukaryotic

3. Cellular respiration is a process that occurs in cells of organisms such as (a) _____ and (b) _____. The process burns sugars to create (c) _____ and it occurs in the (d) _____ of (e) _____ cells.

Answers are on page 797.

Genetics and Heredity

Each of us has similar features to our parents, just as a lion cub shares traits with the lions that birthed it. **Heredity** is the study of how and why characteristics are passed from one generation to another. For all organisms, the continuation of life from one generation to the next depends on cell division.

Cell Division

Cell division is the process by which cells reproduce themselves and make more of the same kinds. Cells must divide when they reach a certain size. At a certain point, the cell is no longer able to take in nutrients and get rid of wastes fast enough to maintain itself. Cell division allows multicellular organism to grow bigger and replace old or injured cells. We take for granted that many of our cells, such as those of our skin and nails, are being replaced each day. Your blood cells are constantly duplicating to replace blood cells that are worn out.

Cell division allows for simple organisms to reproduce themselves. **Reproduction** is a process by which a cell or an organism produces offspring. Many organisms begin as a single cell. As it divides, one cell becomes two cells. Then 2 cells divide to form 4 cells, followed by the formation of 8 cells, 16 cells, 32 cells, and so on. More complex organisms have more complex processes of reproduction, but the end result is the same—more offspring or organisms of the same kind.

Unlike cutting an orange in half, a cell cannot slice itself down the middle to reproduce. Cell division is a complex and well-orchestrated process. Recall that cells require energy to complete cellular tasks. One of those tasks is powering the cell cycle. The **cell cycle** is the life cycle of cells in which they grow, reproduce, and die. The eukaryotic cell cycle in animals and plants involves several stages, including growth and preparation for division. As you can see in the illustration on page 514, eukaryotic cells spend the longest period of time in the interphase portion of a cell's life cycle. **Interphase** is the period during which the growth and development of a cell occurs. There are three stages of interphase—cell growth and development, the copying of its chromosomes, and preparation for cell division. During the first stage of interphase, the cell is rapidly growing and making enzymes and proteins.

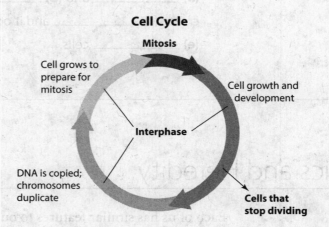

Cell Cycle

Mitosis

Cell grows to prepare for mitosis

Cell growth and development

Interphase

DNA is copied; chromosomes duplicate

Cells that stop dividing

During the second stage of interphase, the cell makes a copy of its chromosomes that reside within the nucleus. The cell cannot divide until the DNA making up its chromosomes is duplicated. If a cell did not replicate its DNA, the next generation of cells would have only half of the total genetic information. This is similar to making a copy of a photo of you and a friend, but only giving your friend half of the picture.

Once the cell has made a copy of its DNA, the cell moves into the third and last stage of interphase. The cell grows larger until it is ready to begin cell division. There are two ways in which the cell can divide. One way, called **mitosis**, leads to two identical new cells. The other way, called **meiosis**, leads to the formation of four new cells, each of which has half of the genetic material. Mitosis will be discussed first. Meiosis will be discussed in relation to the process of sexual reproduction.

There are four main steps or stages in mitosis, as shown in the diagram. First, during a long stage called **prophase**, the duplicated chromosomes coil up into visible rods and the nuclear membrane breaks down. Next, during the **metaphase** stage, the chromosomes line up in a single file within the nucleus in the center of the cell. During the **anaphase** stage, the chromosomes separate to opposite sides of the cell. In the last stage of mitosis, called **telophase**, the chromosomes arrive at opposite ends of the cell and the cell then splits into two cells.

Once mitosis is complete, the two new cells move into the interphase period and start the cell cycle all over again. Some cells, such as nerve and heart muscle cells, spend their entire time in interphase after they mature.

Mitosis

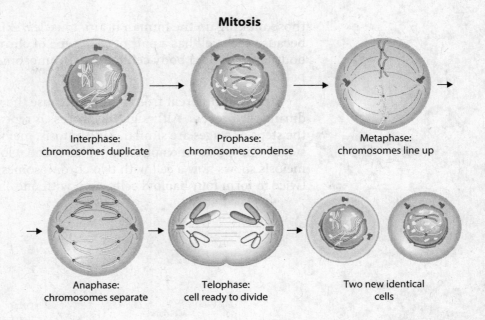

Interphase:
chromosomes duplicate

Prophase:
chromosomes condense

Metaphase:
chromosomes line up

Anaphase:
chromosomes separate

Telophase:
cell ready to divide

Two new identical
cells

But other cells, including single-celled organisms, must move through the entire cell cycle to reproduce. Depending on the type of cell, the cell cycle can take minutes or hours to complete.

Reproduction

All organisms have the ability to reproduce and make more of their own kind. There are two main types of reproduction—asexual and sexual. **Asexual reproduction** requires only one parent and leads to offspring that are almost identical to the parent. Plants, such as potatoes and strawberries, can asexually reproduce by regrowing from a part of the plant. A few animals can asexually reproduce as well. **Budding** is another kind of asexual reproduction that allows certain animals, such as sponges and coral, to reproduce a whole new organism as an outgrowth of the parent's body.

Sexual reproduction involves two parents and leads to genetically different offspring. Sexual reproduction involves two events. First, sex cells called **gametes** are made by meiosis. Second, a male gamete and a female gamete, such as the egg and sperm, join during **fertilization**. **Eggs** are formed in the female reproductive organs, and **sperm** are formed in the male reproductive organs. When fertilization occurs, the resulting cell is called a **zygote**. The zygote cell will have a combination of chromosomes from both the male and female parents.

Meiosis is the type of cell division that leads to sex cells, each with half the number of chromosomes as the original cells. Sex cells are called **haploid** cells because each cell has only one of each type of chromosome instead of the usual pair. For example, humans have only 23 chromosomes in each sex cell instead of the usual 46. Organisms require haploid cells to complete the process of sexual reproduction so that they end up with the correct number of chromosomes after fertilization. The body cells, such as those making up the human brain, muscles, skin, and bones, are **diploid** because each cell has a pair of each type of chromosome. In the human body, each diploid body cell has 46 chromosomes, or 23 chromosome pairs.

Meiosis is different from mitosis because the nucleus divides twice during the process. Although the process is repeated twice, the names of the steps or stages are similar. Like mitosis, meiosis includes the same four stages—prophase, metaphase, anaphase, and telophase. The diagram of meiosis shows how a cell with two chromosomes duplicates and divides twice to form four haploid cells, each with one chromosome.

Meiosis

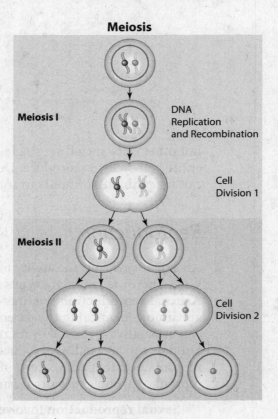

The first stage of this process is called meiosis I. During this stage, unlike in mitosis, chromosomes with the same length, shape, and genes align with each other in **homologous chromosome pairs** and then separate to different cells. During the aligning, **crossing-over** or an exchange of chromosome sections occurs between the paired-up homologous chromosomes. This is a type of **genetic recombination**. After meiosis I, the two new cells have one of each chromosome but the chromosomes are still in duplicate form.

During meiosis II, each chromosome replicates into two copies of itself. The copies are called **sister chromatids.** The sister chromatids that make up each homologous chromosome then separate from each other. The process of meiosis II is similar to mitosis, but it leads to four genetically different new cells. Each of the four new cells has one single, unduplicated chromosome. These genetically diverse sex cells will combine with the sex cells from another parent to create a diploid cell that has genetic properties from both parents. In the diploid cell, the original chromosome number of two is restored.

EXERCISE 10

Reproduction

Directions: Choose the best answer to the question.

1. Which is true about asexual reproduction and sexual reproduction?
   A. Cells do not split during sexual reproduction as they do in asexual reproduction.
   B. Fertilization is a necessary step in both sexual and asexual reproduction.
   C. Haploid cells are created during sexual reproduction so that each sex cell has half of a chromosome pair.
   D. Meiosis is the cell division process that occurs during asexual reproduction.

Answer is on page 798.

Genes and DNA

Chromosomes within the nucleus of a cell consist of genetic material called DNA. **Deoxyribonucleic acid**, or **DNA**, contains the genetic information that dictates how an organism looks, functions, and grows. Recall that during interphase of cell reproduction, the chromosomes and their DNA are duplicated. Every single cell in your body, with the exception of your gametes, contains the same DNA so that every cell knows everything about you.

In 1953, scientists James Watson and Francis Crick created a model of the DNA molecule that looks like a spiraling ladder. DNA is made up of two strands of repeating units called **nucleic acids**. The nucleic acids are composed of chains of subunits called nucleotides, each of which contains a sugar, a phosphate group, and one kind of nitrogen base. The key ingredient to how DNA replicates itself is the four types of **nitrogen bases**—adenine, guanine, cytosine, and thymine—that connect the two strands together. Within a DNA molecule, the bases of the nucleotides form pairs, called **base pairs**. The makeup of the pairs is based on the following base-pair rules: adenine always pairs with thymine and guanine always pairs with cytosine.

During DNA replication, the two DNA strands separate and each strand can replicate the other strand. DNA contains the guidelines for the continuity of all life.

DNA

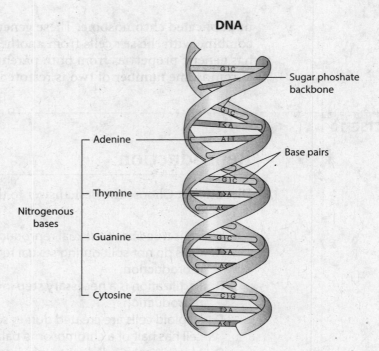

- Sugar phoshate backbone

Base pairs

Nitrogenous bases

Adenine

Thymine

Guanine

Cytosine

A cell's DNA molecules contain the instructions for producing all the parts of the living thing to which the cell belongs and for controlling when these parts are made. These instructions are encoded in the sequence of the four different kinds of nucleotide bases found in DNA molecules. Within each strand of DNA, the order of the four different bases in the series of nucleotides that make up the strand can vary in countless ways. This order of nucleotides is called the **DNA base sequence**.

Genes are specific regions along a DNA strand that code for a characteristic in an organism, such as height or eye color. Each chromosome can be made up of many genes. Each gene is an instruction guide for a cell to make a protein. **Proteins** are made up of amino acids. An **amino acid** is a small compound with an amino group, a carboxyl group, and one or more atoms called the "R" group, as shown in the figure.

General Amino Acid Structure

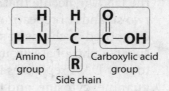

Amino group

Carboxylic acid group

Side chain

The gene determines the sequence or order of amino acids to build a protein. Changes to the DNA, called **mutations**, can change the order, kind, or number of amino acids in a protein. This may have no significant effect on an individual. Some mutations may be helpful if the new protein is beneficial. Other mutations are harmful if they lead to conditions and diseases.

Scientists have been able to identify certain genes within chromosomes that cause genetic disorders. For example, within chromosome #1, scientists mapped the genes that cause prostate cancer, glaucoma, and Alzheimer's disease. For individuals, knowing about this genetic information early in life can bring important health benefits. Medical professionals can use this information to develop treatments before symptoms even occur. But knowing about a person's genetic defects may also give rise to difficult ethical issues.

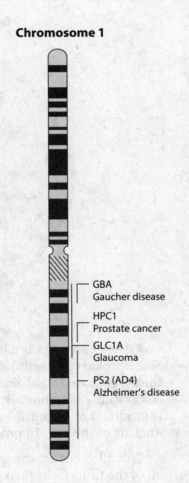

Chromosome 1

GBA
Gaucher disease

HPC1
Prostate cancer

GLC1A
Glaucoma

PS2 (AD4)
Alzheimer's disease

Aside from locating genes that are connected with disease, gene mapping can determine hair color, eye color, and other traits. Identifying genes helps us understand why zebras have stripes, why some animals have two different colored eyes, and why children look like a combination of their parents.

Gene Expression

Recall that a gene is a segment of DNA that contains the code for a protein. Genes direct the synthesis or making of proteins. Protein synthesis happens in two steps—transcription and translation. In **transcription**, the base sequence in a segment of DNA acts as the template for making another biological molecule called **mRNA** ("messenger" RNA). In other words, the information in the DNA is copied, or transcribed, into the mRNA. In **translation**, the base sequence in the mRNA molecule acts as the template for assembling a chain of amino acids. The amino acids are combined to form a protein. So, the information in mRNA is translated into the end product, a protein. Translation occurs at ribosomes in the cytoplasm of both prokaryotic and eukaryotic cells. An overview of transcription and translation in eukaryotes is shown here.

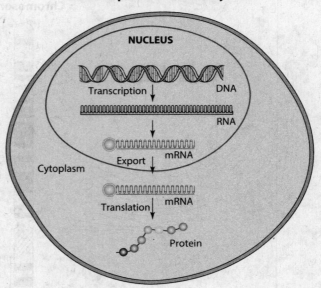

Gene Expression in Eukaryotes

Gene expression is a little different in prokaryotes and eukaryotes. Since prokaryotic cells do not have a nucleus, transcription happens in the cytoplasm. In eukaryotes, transcription happens in a cell's nucleus. In eukaryotic cells, the early mRNA is called pre-mRNA. This pre-mRNA is modified or changed before it becomes the final mRNA that leaves the nucleus of the cell. In prokaryotic cells, polypeptides are not modified.

Not all genes are expressed in every cell, nor are many genes expressed all of the time. Cells turn genes "on and off" in response to signals they receive from the environment. These signals come from outside of cells and from inside of cells. Gene expression is a complex process and is well-controlled at every step of the way.

Gene Expression

Directions: Choose the best answer to the question, which is based on the following:

The flow of genetic information is summarized as follows:

DNA → mRNA → protein

1. What does the arrow between mRNA and protein represent?
   A. Translation
   B. Transcription
   C. Meiosis
   D. Mitosis

Answer is on page 798.

Inheritance of Traits

Have you ever wondered why you and your siblings look similar? You and your siblings look similar but not identical as a result of the meiosis that produced the different gametes leading to each of you. The types of genes, or **alleles**, you inherit from gametes influence all your traits—your weight, hair color, and even the shape of your earlobes. A **genotype** is the alleles that an organism has for each gene. A **phenotype** is the expression of the genotype or the observable traits in an organism. Heredity is the passing of these traits from the parents to offspring. Figuring out how genes control the nature of an organism's traits began with the work of a 19th-century scientist named Gregor Mendel.

Mendel studied plants, specifically pea plants. He used scientific methods to experiment how traits pass from one generation of pea plants to another. Mendel cross-bred thousands of plants with different traits. He found that the relationships among alleles (or what he called "factors") influence their expression in the plant. For example, when he crossed a parent plant with green peas with a parent plant with yellow peas, all of the offspring in the first generation had green peas. When he crossed the plants from the first generation, he found that in the second generation, 75 percent of the offspring had green peas and 25 percent had yellow peas. Thus, he determined that in regard to the color of the peas, green is dominant and yellow is recessive. In other words, only one **dominant** allele from a parent is needed to express the condition of having green peas. But two alleles—one from each parent—are needed to express the **recessive** condition of having yellow peas.

Scientists use a diagram called a **Punnett square** to predict the results of a genetic cross and the probability of a trait occurring in offspring. The Punnett square lists the possible alleles from the parents on the outside of the square. The boxes within the square show all the possible combinations of the alleles in the offspring. By counting the combinations, you can predict the probability of each genotype occurring in the offspring. The genotypes will determine the ratios between different phenotypes in the offspring.

The Punnett square in the following illustration shows how the genes from two parents might influence a child's height. Height is determined by two alleles. The allele can be dominant (T) or recessive (t). If the dominant allele is present, the trait will be expressed. For height, that means that the individual will be tall. If only recessive alleles are present, the individual will not be tall; that is, he or she will be short. An individual with two of the same alleles (TT or tt) for a trait is said to be **homozygous**. An individual with two different alleles for the trait (Tt) is said to be **heterozygous**.

In this case, the father and the mother each have one dominant tall gene (T) and one recessive short gene (t). The Punnett square shows the likelihood of each possible combination of alleles from the two parents. Each child of these parents has a 75 percent chance of being tall (TT or Tt) and a 25 percent chance of being short (tt).

Punnett Square

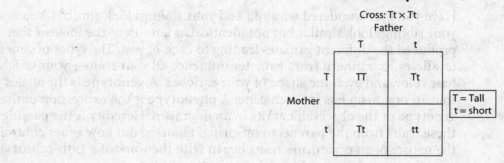

Mendel discovered the basic laws of inheritance for simple traits. Since Mendel's studies, scientists have discovered traits that do not follow Mendel's patterns of heredity. For example, sometimes different genes interact or are inherited together. Some traits are controlled by more than two alleles, such as blood types in humans. Finally, some human traits are controlled by more than one gene, as in height and skin color.

EXERCISE 12

Genetics and Heredity

Directions: Match each word with its definition by writing the correct letter in the blank provided.

_____ **1.** The division process during which chromosomes pair up in the nucleus during metaphase

a. telophase

_____ **2.** The phase during which the chromosomes arrive at opposite ends of the cell

b. mitosis

_____ **3.** The longest period in the cell cycle

c. anaphase

_____ **4.** The phase during which the chromosomes separate to opposite sides of the cell

d. metaphase

_____ **5.** The division process that leads to two identical new cells

e. meiosis I

_____ **6.** The phase during which the chromosomes align in the center of the nucleus

f. interphase

Directions: Fill in the blanks in the diagram below with the correct allele combinations. Then circle the letter of the best answer to the question.

Punnett square for eye color: B = blue   b = green

	B	b
b	1._____	2._____
b	3._____	4._____

7. Which describes the correct probability of eye color based on the dominant and recessive genes?
   A. 100 percent chance that the child will have green eyes
   B. 75 percent chance that the child will have green eyes
   C. 50 percent chance that the child will have green eyes
   D. 25 percent chance that the child will have green eyes

Directions: Fill in the blanks in the diagram below with the correct DNA sequence.

8. What is the complementary DNA sequence of the DNA strand shown below?

T A T – G G C – T A T – C T G – G G G – G A C

_____ – _____ – _____ – _____ – _____ – _____

Answers are on page 798.

The Human Body and Health

So far, you have learned that cells are the smallest units of life. Everything that a cell can do is performed by an organism as well. Both cells and organisms reproduce to replicate themselves from one generation to the next. Organisms developed from single cells to complex, multicelled organisms.

There are anywhere from 5 billion to 200 million trillion cells in the body, and each cell has a unique task to complete. In multicellular organisms, cells of a similar kind are grouped together to form **tissues**, such as groups of cells that form nerve tissue and muscle tissue. Tissues are organized into body parts called **organs**. For example, the heart is an organ that is made up of layers of loose connective tissue, nerve tissue, and muscle tissue that work to pump blood throughout your body. Different organs work as a team to form an **organ system** or body system. For example, the circulatory system is made up of the heart and blood vessels. Several organ systems make up an organism. The human body is composed of several systems.

Skeletal System

Humans and many other animals have an **endoskeleton**; the structures that support the body are located inside the body. Other animals have **exoskeletons**, which are structures on the outside of the body. The **skeletal system**, shown in the diagram, is composed of bones and connecting tissues that form the framework of our bodies and function in support, protection, and movement. Without the skeletal system, our bodies would be slumped to the ground. Our internal organs like our lungs would be unable to inflate, and therefore we would be unable to breathe or move.

An adult's skeletal system has 206 separate bones. Some bones, such as the leg bones, hip bones, and spine, allow us to stand upright. Other bones,

The Human Skeleton

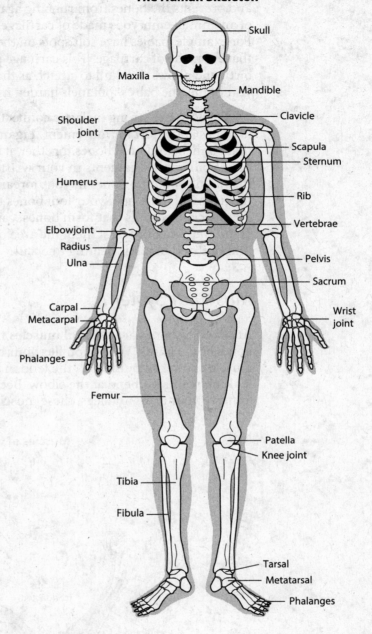

Skull

Maxilla

Mandible

Shoulder joint

Clavicle

Scapula

Sternum

Humerus

Rib

Vertebrae

Elbowjoint

Radius

Ulna

Pelvis

Sacrum

Carpal

Metacarpal

Wrist joint

Phalanges

Femur

Patella

Knee joint

Tibia

Fibula

Tarsal

Metatarsal

Phalanges

such as the skull and the rib cage, protect vital organs. Even the ear is made of tiny bones that help to capture sound. The outer layer of bones is hard, but the inside of some bones is bone marrow. **Bone marrow** is a soft substance within which red and white blood cells are made.

Our skeletal system not only contains all the bones in the body, but also the tissues such as cartilage, tendons, and ligaments that connect them. The skeleton diagram does not show a bone where the nose or outer ear should be. The reason is that your nose and outer ears are made of cartilage. **Cartilage** is a tough but flexible tissue that holds its shape when undisturbed. It is often found where bones come together at joints. Cartilage cushions the joints between bones, such as the elbow and knee joints, and prevents the bones from rubbing against each other. Most of the skeleton of an animal embryo is made of cartilage, which is replaced by bone over time. For example, babies have soft spots on the top of their skull called fontanels that are made of cartilage. This cartilage protects the newborn's brain during birth and allows the skull to stretch as the brain develops. Within the first year of life, the baby's fontanels harden into the bones of the skull.

Tendons are strong inelastic connective tissues that attach muscles to bones and allow for movement. **Ligaments** are strong inelastic bands that connect and hold bones together at the joints. For example, when you bend your wrist, ligaments in your wrist keep the carpal bones attached to the radius and ulna bones in your forearm. When you sprain your ankle, the ligaments that hold your foot bones to your leg bones stretch or tear. The specialized cells that form bones, cartilage, and ligaments divide to mend the break or tear. Often, the area of the break or injury needs to be immobilized to allow healing to occur.

Muscular System

Attached to bones are **skeletal muscles** that expand and contract to bend the bones at the joints. When you flex your biceps as shown in the diagram, the muscle contracts, pulling on the tendon attached to the lower arm bones, making your arm bend at the elbow. Because you can control these muscles to move your arms and legs, these muscles are called **voluntary** muscles.

Muscles of the Arm

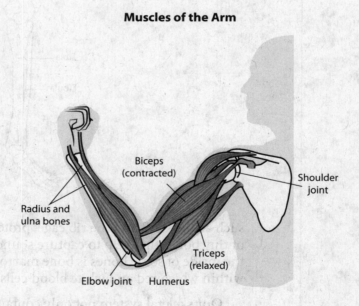

Other muscles are **involuntary** and work without conscious control. A certain part of your brain automatically controls these muscles' movements because they are critical to body function. There are two groups of involuntary muscle: smooth and cardiac. **Smooth muscles** in the digestive system expand and contract to move food through the stomach and intestines. **Cardiac muscles** contract and expand your heart.

EXERCISE 13

Skeletal and Muscular Systems

Directions: Match each word with its definition by writing the correct letter in the blank provided.

_____	**1.** Strong connective tissue that holds a muscle to a bone	**a.**	cartilage
_____	**2.** Bands that connect bones together at a joint	**b.**	involuntary
_____	**3.** Responsible for controlling organs such as the stomach	**c.**	tendon
_____	**4.** Tissue inside bones where new blood cells are formed	**d.**	tissue
_____	**5.** Flexible tissue that protects a newborn's brain until the tissue hardens into bones	**e.**	ligament
_____	**6.** A collection of specialized cells that carry out a function	**f.**	smooth muscle
_____	**7.** A muscle that contracts without conscious control	**g.**	bone marrow

Answers are on page 798.

Respiratory and Circulatory Systems

When your muscles expand or contract, whether voluntarily or involuntarily, they need oxygen to operate. The body carries oxygen to the muscles and to other body systems through blood cells. The **respiratory system** is composed of organs in your body to help you breathe. It takes in oxygen and works with the circulatory system to move oxygen into the blood and remove wastes such as carbon dioxide out of the body. The **circulatory system** moves blood, oxygen, and nutrients throughout the body. These systems are vital to life because without oxygen, the brain ceases to function.

Respiration

Your respiratory system contains organs that help you to breathe. Examine the respiratory system in the following diagram. The main respiratory organs, the lungs, are made of a soft, spongy material that contains no muscle at all. The lungs rely on external muscles and bones to allow for respiration. Have you ever thought about your breathing and then found you had difficulty breathing? This happens because breathing is both involuntary and voluntary. The diaphragm is a muscle that works as an involuntary muscle and a voluntary muscle when you hold your breath or control your breathing.

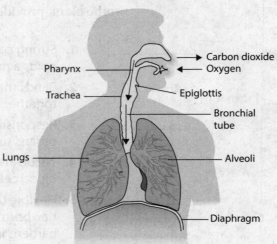

Respiratory System

How do you breathe air in? Suction in the chest occurs when the **diaphragm,** a dome-shaped muscle, pulls down while the chest muscles expand outward. This action pulls air through the mouth or nose and into the **pharynx,** an opening that has two different paths. One path leads to the stomach while the other leads to the lungs. At the end of the pharynx is the **epiglottis,** a small, elastic strip of cartilage that covers the tube leading to the lungs. When you breathe in, the epiglottis opens to allow air to flow in and out. The epiglottis closes when you eat so that food does not enter the breathing pathway. This is why you can choke if you talk while you eat.

Beyond the pharynx, the air flows down the trachea and through the bronchus tubes, inflating the lungs. Inside the lungs, the air flows through small tubes to the **alveoli,** little air sacs. Blood vessels called **capillaries** surround the alveoli. These tiny blood vessels are where gas exchange takes place; oxygen is delivered to body cells and carbon dioxide is removed from body cells.

Because carbon dioxide is a waste product from the body cells, it is removed from the body when you exhale. To do this, the muscles surrounding the lungs reverse the process of breathing in. The diaphragm and chest muscles contract inward, pushing on the lungs and forcing air out, up the bronchus tubes and the trachea, past the epiglottis, through the pharynx, and then out through the mouth or nose. Recall that plants take in carbon dioxide and output oxygen during photosynthesis. Although plants do not breathe, the exchange of oxygen and carbon dioxide is a process that animals and plants share.

Circulation

The body systems need more than just oxygen to operate. The circulatory system, also called the cardiovascular system, carries nutrients and antibodies through the bloodstream to fuel and protect the body. The circulatory system has three organs that work together: the heart, the lungs, and the blood vessels. There are two circulation loops. The first loop, which is called the **pulmonary circulation**, is the flow of blood through the heart to the lungs and back to the heart. This process sends blood to the lungs to expel carbon dioxide and to take in oxygen from the lungs for the next route. In the second loop, the oxygen-rich blood is sent out to the body in a process called **systemic circulation**.

An average adult has five to six quarts of blood. Blood is a tissue that is composed of plasma, **red blood cells** that carry oxygen, **white blood cells** that fight infections, and **platelets** that seal off cuts in blood vessels by the process of **clotting**.

Follow the following diagram to understand the flow of blood through the heart into the body. If you were able to look at a person's heart, this is what you would see.

The Path of Circulation

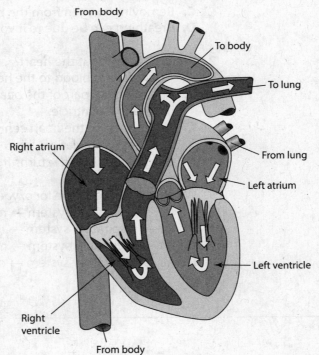

From body

To body

To lung

From lung

Right atrium

Left atrium

Left ventricle

Right ventricle

From body

Notice that the deoxygenated blood (often shown as blue in color) returns through the right atrium and passes into the right ventricle. Then the blood is sent to the lungs to expel carbon dioxide and take in oxygen. The oxygenated blood (red in color) returns to the heart by the left atrium and then is pumped throughout the body by the left ventricle. Because the heart is a muscle, it expands to pull blood into both the right and left atria, and it contracts to pump blood out of the two ventricles. In a person at rest, the heart expands and contracts between 60 and 80 beats per minute.

Blood travels through blood vessels that stretch all over the body. The blood vessels that generally carry blood away from the heart are called **arteries**, and the blood vessels that often carry blood back to the heart are called **veins**. Arteries are made of connective tissue and smooth muscle tissue and have thick, elastic walls. Veins are designed to take blood in only one direction—straight to the heart. The skeletal muscles contract to help push blood through the veins.

EXERCISE 14

Respiratory and Circulatory Systems

Directions: Choose the best answer to each question.

1. Which is NOT true about the respiratory system?
   A. The diaphragm expands to create suction so that air is pulled into the lungs.
   B. The epiglottis allows air to pass into the trachea but not food.
   C. Removing oxygen from the body is a function of respiration.
   D. Breathing can be due to involuntary or voluntary muscle movement.

2. Which is true about the heart?
   A. Arteries carry blood to the heart.
   B. An atrium is a part of the heart that blood first enters before being passed to a ventricle.
   C. The process of the heart sending blood throughout the body is called pulmonary circulation.
   D. Oxygenated blood returns from the lungs into the right atrium.

3. Which is the correct path for oxygen to reach a muscle cell in the human body?
   A. Air → circulatory system → respiratory system → muscular system
   B. Air → respiratory system → muscular system
   C. Air → circulatory system → muscular system → respiratory system
   D. Air → respiratory system → circulatory system → muscular system

Answers are on page 798.

Digestive System

In addition to oxygen, you need food to provide nutrients for your body cells to operate. The **digestive system** is a group of organs working together to convert food into energy to feed the entire body. It includes all of the functions that break down food into simple chemicals for the body to use. Many of the digestive system's organs conduct mechanical digestion and/or chemical digestion. **Mechanical digestion** involves physically breaking food into smaller pieces and pushing it through the digestive system. **Chemical digestion** occurs when the food is chemically broken down using various enzymes to release nutrients. An **enzyme** is often a protein that speeds up a chemical reaction.

Examine the diagram of the digestive system. Digestion involves four things: ingestion, digestion, absorption, and elimination. The process of digestion begins with ingestion in the mouth where the teeth tear apart food. Inside the mouth, the salivary glands coat the teeth and tongue with saliva, helping to soften the food and begin to chemically break it down. Digestion begins in the mouth. **Saliva** is 98 percent water and includes electrolytes, mucus, antibacterial compounds, and various enzymes. The enzymes in saliva break down starches into sugars. Coating the food with saliva helps us to swallow the food particles, sending the particles down the esophagus.

Digestive System

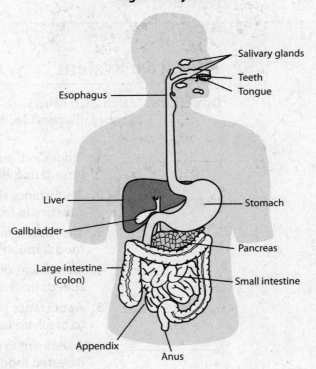

The food particles pass through the long esophagus by a series of smooth muscle contractions called **peristalsis**. These contractions happen throughout the digestive tract, moving food and waste along. Food particles then enter the **stomach**, a smooth muscle organ that churns and mixes the food with enzymes and acids to further break it down. Your stomach contains hydrochloric acid, which dissolves the food particles so that enzymes can digest the protein from the food. This partially broken down mass of food that is now a semi-fluid is called **chyme**. Chyme moves from the stomach into the small intestine where most absorption of nutrients occurs.

Important digestive organs like the liver, gallbladder, and pancreas do not have food pass through them, but rather secrete enzymes needed to further break down food. Fats and proteins are digested by these enzymes as the chyme travels through the **small intestine**, a tube about 15 to 20 feet long. The liver produces **bile** that breaks up large fat particles in the small intestine. Nutrients are mainly absorbed in the small intestine. Absorption occurs at capillaries in places called **villi**, finger-like ridges with high surface area inside the small intestine. Nutrients are carried by blood to the rest of the body. The remaining material that moves from the small intestine into the large intestine is waste and water. The large intestine, or **colon**, is wider than the small intestine but about one-third the length. The large intestine absorbs water and vitamins back into the body. Also, undigested materials begin to turn into solids. This waste is pushed through the end of the large intestine and eliminated from the body through the anus in the form of feces.

The digestive process takes about six to eight hours from the time food enters the mouth and goes through the small intestine. The amount of time that the remaining materials take to pass through the large intestine varies from 30 to 50 hours, depending on health and gender.

EXERCISE 15

Digestive System

Directions: Match each word with its definition by writing the correct letter in the blank provided.

_____	**1.** Ridges in the small intestine that absorb nutrients	**a.** colon
_____	**2.** A substance that coats and contains substances for breaking down food	**b.** bile
_____	**3.** The muscle motion that pushes food through the digestive tract	**c.** chyme
_____	**4.** A chemical, often a protein, that speeds up chemical reactions	**d.** peristalsis
_____	**5.** A substance produced by the liver to break up fats	**e.** villi
_____	**6.** A semi-liquid mass of partially digested food that passes through the small intestine	**f.** enzyme
_____	**7.** The organ where water and vitamins are absorbed	**g.** saliva

Directions: Choose the best answer for each question.

8. Which is the correct order of the four main stages of food processing?
   A. Ingestion → digestion → absorption → elimination
   B. Digestion → ingestion → absorption → elimination
   C. Absorption → elimination → ingestion → digestion
   D. Elimination → ingestion → digestion → absorption

9. Where does the digestion of proteins occur?
   A. Mouth
   B. Stomach and small intestine
   C. Liver
   D. Large intestine

Answers are on page 798.

Nervous System

The body systems we have discussed are set in motion through their connection to the brain. The muscles expand and contract, the heart pumps blood, the lungs inhale and exhale air, and the digestive system breaks down food because the brain sends signals to these systems. The brain is part of the **nervous system**, the communication center of the body. Just like wires and connections in a computer, the nervous system transmits signals throughout the body to control movement and organ functions and to operate the senses. The nervous system consists of the brain, spinal cord, sensory organs, and nerves that connect these organs with the entire body.

Nervous System

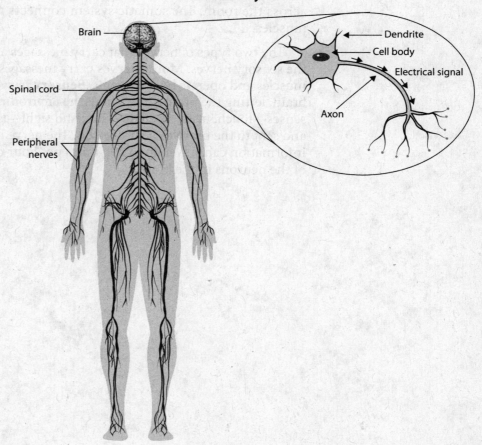

The brain has billions of neurons. **Neurons** are one of the main types of cells making up the nervous system. They have three main parts—a cell body, dendrites, and axons. The **cell body**, which is the main portion of the cell, is covered with branches called **dendrites** for receiving signals, and long **axons** that carry and transmit signals to another neuron. These signals or messages are called **nerve impulses**. When you move a part of your body, nerve impulses are sent from one neuron to another neuron signaling the muscle groups to move in unison. As an impulse is transmitted from one neuron to another, the message crosses a space between the axon and the receptors of the next neuron called a **synapse**. The synapse is an extremely small gap that chemicals called **neurotransmitters** pass across to stimulate the next neuron.

The brain sends signals through the **spinal cord**, which is the main connection for almost all of the nerves in the body. The spinal cord is protected within the vertebrae in the backbone much like a copper wire within an insulating sheath. The brain and the spinal cord make up the **central nervous system**. Messages are passed to and from the brain and the spinal cord through the **peripheral nervous system** that connects to each organ and muscle, reaching the furthest extremities. There are two divisions of peripheral nerves in the system, the autonomic system and the somatic system. The **autonomic system** controls involuntary actions, such as the heartbeat, digestion, and breathing. The **somatic system** controls voluntary movements, such as when you lift something or walk across the room. The somatic system connects your brain to your skeletal muscles.

The two types of nerves that carry messages are the motor nerves and the sensory nerves. **Motor nerves** carry messages from the brain to control muscles and operate body systems. **Sensory nerves** carry messages to the brain, letting the brain know about the environment. Information from the senses—touch, taste, smell, hearing, and sight—is collected from the body and sent to the brain to be processed. The nerve impulses carrying this information can travel up to 200 miles per hour depending on the structure of the neurons in the brain.

EXERCISE 16

Nervous System

Directions: Choose the best answer to each question.

1. When you touch something very hot with your fingers, which BEST describes what happens?
   A. Motor nerves connected to the autonomic system carry impulses to the brain telling it that the fingers are touching something hot. The brain signals the sensory nerves to pull the hand away to safety.
   B. Motor nerves connected to the somatic system carry impulses to the brain telling it that the fingers are touching something hot. The brain signals the sensory nerves to pull the hand away to safety.
   C. Sensory nerves connected to the somatic system carry impulses to the brain telling it that the fingers are touching something hot. The brain signals the motor nerves to pull the hand away to safety.
   D. Sensory nerves connected to the autonomic system carry impulses to the brain telling it that the fingers are touching something hot. The brain signals the motor nerves to pull the hand away to safety.

2. Which is NOT true about neurons in the brain?
   A. Neurons are important nerve cells that send and receive messages.
   B. A synapse is a message sent from one neuron to another.
   C. Dendrites of the cell body receive messages for neurons.
   D. Axons carry and transmit messages to other neurons.

Directions: Use the following diagram to answer question 3.

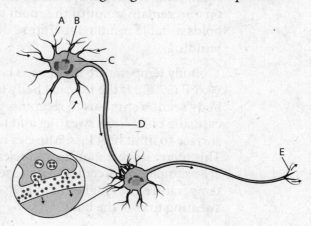

3. In the diagram, which letter identifies the axon?
   A. A
   B. B
   C. C
   D. D

Answers are on page 799.

Homeostasis

All organisms maintain homeostasis within their cells and body systems. **Homeostasis** means that the cell or body system keeps a stable internal environment as the external environment changes. Cells and body systems monitor their internal environments and adjust the internal conditions if a change occurs. These adjustments may be made through a negative feedback system or a positive feedback system.

Cells tend to use a negative feedback system to maintain homeostasis. A **negative feedback** system is a process in which an initial change will bring about an additional change in the opposite direction. Negative feedback systems control the amount of water in the body, blood pressure, and levels of carbon dioxide, calcium, and sugar in the blood, as well as the body temperature. All negative feedback systems have a set of common parts as shown in this diagram.

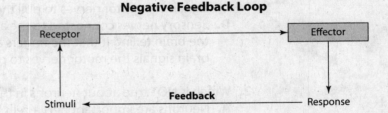

Negative Feedback Loop

How does negative feedback regulate body temperature? The process is similar to that by which a thermostat controls the heating and cooling of a house or apartment. If the room thermostat is set at 23°C and the room temperature drops below the set temperature, the heater will turn on and remain on until the room temperature becomes 23°C. The room holds a stable room temperature despite temperature changes outside the building.

Body temperature in humans is normally at a **set point** that is close to 98.6°F (37°C). If the internal body temperature falls below this level, the body sends a stimulus to receptors in the body that cause a change. In this case, the body stops sweating and blood flow is directed away from the body surface to limit heat loss. Muscles may begin to contract, causing shivering. This increases metabolism and releases heat. The muscles and sweat glands are examples of **effectors** that cause a response in the body. If the body temperature goes higher than the set point, the opposite occurs such as sweating to cool the body.

A **positive feedback** system is a process in which an initial change will bring about an additional change in the same direction. Such feedback is rare in living things. An example of a positive feedback system is control of labor contractions during childbirth. The fetus secretes a hormone that stimulates contractions of the uterus. The contractions cause the mother's body to release more hormones. More hormones cause stronger uterine contractions. This stimulates the release of more hormones, and so on. The contractions and hormone release increase until the system is reset after the birth of the child.

EXERCISE 17

Homeostasis

Directions: Choose the word or phrase from the following list that best fits in each blank in the passage.

homeostasis	positive	negative
set point	effectors	stable

1. Your normal internal body temperature is known as its
   (a) _____, which is 98.6°F. When your body maintains its
   temperature on a hot summer day by sweating, your body is maintaining
   its **(b)** _____ by using a **(c)** _____ feedback system.
   Sweat glands are examples of **(d)** _____ because they cause a
   response in the body.

Answers are on page 799.

Health

The foods you eat, the lifestyle choices you make, and your activity level can affect your overall health. If you choose to eat unhealthy fatty foods, your eating habits can increase your risk of certain diseases, such as cancer and cardiovascular disease. Having chronic stress may negatively affect your ability to fight off infections. In addition to eating unhealthy foods and having stress, using tobacco products will increase your chance of developing various cancers. Inactivity can also have an impact on your health by weakening muscles and bone growth. Although there is a genetic component to disease, the choices you make can promote or reduce your health and well-being.

Nutrition

The human body absorbs nutrients from the foods it digests. The six types of nutrients necessary for the human body are proteins, carbohydrates, fats, vitamins, minerals, and water. They are necessary to keep body cells healthy to fight off infection and viruses, such as the common cold and the flu. Without nutrients, your body becomes susceptible to health problems, such as high blood pressure, fatigue, depression, and even memory loss.

Proteins are made from amino acids. The body uses proteins to replace and repair body cells as well as to help the body grow. Proteins perform many functions within living organisms, including enzymatic reactions, replicating DNA, fighting infections, responding to stimuli, and transporting molecules from one location to another. Body cells need only 20 amino acids to produce the proteins used. Most of the amino acids can be made in the body cells, but some of them must come from the foods you eat. These amino acids are called essential amino acids. You can get these amino acids by eating eggs, milk, cheese, and meat. You can also obtain these essential amino acids from eating certain vegetables, fruits, and grains.

Carbohydrates or sugars provide energy for the body. They come in many forms in the human diet, such as simple sugars, disaccharides, and complex polysaccharides (e.g., starches and fibers). Simple sugars and disaccharides can be found in foods such as fruits, honey, and milk. Starch is found in potatoes and grains. Eating whole-grain breads, cereals, peas, and other fruits and vegetables is the way to get fiber. Fiber is not digested but is used to help the digestive system work well.

Lipids, sometimes called fats, have been connected to diseases and obesity, but the body needs a certain amount to stay healthy. Lipids provide energy and help to absorb vitamins into the body. Fat tissue protects internal organs, and every cell membrane is made of a special type of lipid. Foods such as processed and baked goods, poultry, and nuts contain lipids.

Vitamins are **organic** (always having carbon and hydrogen) substances necessary to strengthen bones, clot blood, and help enzymes carry out chemical reactions in the body. Two types of vitamins help the body: water-soluble vitamins that must be eaten daily and fat-soluble vitamins that can be stored in fat cells to be used later. Vitamins are found in most of the foods you eat.

Minerals are inorganic nutrients that conduct most of the chemical reactions in the body. Although the body uses about 14 minerals, calcium and phosphorus have the greatest impact on body functions. Minerals make strong bones and help muscles and nerves operate properly.

Finally, water is one of the most important nutrients the body needs. About 70 percent of all body weight is made up of water. Water can be taken in through milk, fruit juices, and of course, drinking water.

Nutritionists are professionals who create programs to help people choose a healthy diet. Over time, nutritionists change the amounts of different foods that should be eaten based on their studies and scientific experiments. It is difficult to develop a nutrition guide for all people because infants, children, teenagers, and adults have different needs. The **food pyramid** has been a guide that has helped people determine how many servings to eat each day of grains, fruits, vegetables, meats, dairy products, and fats. The US Departments of Agriculture and Health and Human Services have developed a new guideline intended to simplify a healthy diet for everyone.

Food Guide

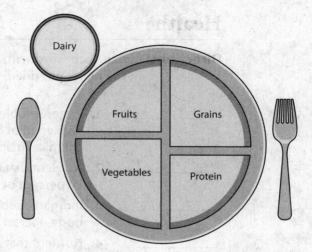

The new guideline suggests that each meal should consist of half fruits and vegetables. Fruits and vegetables should also be eaten as snacks. Half of the grains eaten should be of a whole-grain variety as found in certain breads. The protein choices should be a mixture of seafood, beans, lean meats, and poultry. A small portion of dairy is important too.

Body Maintenance

Keeping your body healthy goes beyond maintaining a good diet. There are many things you can do to give yourself the best chance for a long, healthy life. As you recall, the human body is very complex with multiple body systems working in unison when conditions are ideal. The environment around you can add stress to your body systems, sometimes making it difficult for your body to operate well.

Researchers study how sleep, exercise, diet, drugs, and alcohol affect the human body. Although one person may be physically similar to another, each person may react differently to these lifestyle choices. It is well known that children need more sleep than adults, roughly 10 hours as compared to 8 hours for adults. During restful sleep, the body repairs itself and prepares you for the next day. Have you ever noticed how difficult it is to function when you have not had enough sleep? Perhaps you came down with a cold when deprived of sleep when you normally are healthy.

Exercise is another important life choice because of its benefits to the body. Exercising strengthens muscles and bones as well as increases your energy level, improves sleep, lowers blood pressure, and reduces stress. Eating a nutritious diet is important when adding exercise to your routine. Avoiding tobacco products reduces your risk of getting cancers, respiratory infections, heart disease, and strokes. When you stop smoking, your body will repair the damage to your lungs and other vital organs. Reducing or eliminating alcoholic consumption can also help repair damage to brain cells and liver and kidney functions.

EXERCISE 18

Health

Directions: Match each word with its definition by writing the correct letter in the blank provided.

_____ 1. Water-soluble and fat-soluble nutrient that helps to carry out chemical reactions in the body

a. mineral

_____ 2. Nutrient that makes up about 70 percent of body weight

b. amino acid

_____ 3. Inorganic substance that helps the body operate efficiently

c. lipid

_____ 4. Nutrient that helps to repair and replace body cells and to replicate DNA

d. water

_____ 5. Energy-releasing nutrient found in fruit and honey

e. protein

_____ 6. The main building block of proteins

f. vitamin

_____ 7. An important part of the cell membrane; provides energy

g. carbohydrate

Answers are on page 799.

Evolution

Evidence shows that living organisms have a common ancestry and also that organisms have changed over time. **Evolution** is a theory of change over time in the genetic composition of interbreeding groups of organisms called **populations**. Some of these evolutionary changes are of a small scale, such as a new beneficial trait that spreads through a population. Other changes are of a larger scale and lead to new species and even higher levels of classification. The source of evolutionary change is DNA mutations. Such genetic changes may be passed on from parents to their offspring. As DNA mutations are transmitted from one generation to the next, the frequency of genes can change, and thus the population evolves.

Evidence of Evolution

Paleontologists are scientists who collect and study fossils. **Fossils** are the remains or impressions of organisms that lived a long time ago. Fossils provide direct evidence of evolution. They can consist of the imprints of organisms that became trapped under layers of materials—sand, mud, small rocks—until the layers formed sedimentary rock. Fossils collected from sedimentary rock have been dated and form what scientists call the **fossil record**.

The geological timescale, a calendar of evolutionary events in the past, organizes life's history and records changes in the fossil record, meaning all the fossils ever found. This is the history of living things on Earth. Paleontologists and geologists discover new fossils each year, continuously adding entries to the fossil record. The fossil record helps scientists determine how Earth looked hundreds of millions of years ago and how it has changed over time. For example, similar fossils found in continents separated by oceans provide clues that at one time there was a single landmass.

Geologic Time Scale

Era	Period Millions of years ago (mya)	
Cenozoic	Quanternary (1.8 mya-present)	
	Tertiary (65-1.8 mya)	
Mesozoic	Cretaceous (146-65 mya)	
	Jurassic (200-146 mya)	
	Triassic (251-200 mya)	
Paleozoic	Permian (299-251 mya)	
	Carboniferous (359-299 mya)	
	Devonian (416-359 mya)	
	Silurian (444-416 mya)	
	Ordovician (488-444 mya)	
	Cambrian (542-488 mya)	
Precambrian (4570-542 mya)		

There are two ways of estimating the age of fossils—relative dating and absolute dating. For **relative dating**, the deeper the rock layer, the older the rock and the older the fossils are within the rocks. Younger fossils are found in the more recent upper layers of rock formations. Depending on the depth that fossils are found in the rock layers, scientists can estimate the relative period during which these organisms lived. This method of fossil dating is best used with undisturbed rock layers. If a geologist can determine the age of the layers below and above a fossil, a relative date range can be made.

A more specific approximation for the age of rocks is done through **absolute dating**. This method uses radioactive elements within the rocks and determines each element's age based on its decay. Radioactive elements decay over time. Scientists then can measure how much decay has occurred to estimate the age of the rock. The oldest fossils are unicellular prokaryotes that are about 3.5 billion years old.

Not all organisms become fossils, however. This creates gaps in the fossil record that make it difficult to rely solely on fossils to determine Earth's living history. Scientists study other types of data for evidence of evolution. For example, similar structures or molecules in organisms can indicate evolutionary relationships among organisms. **Homology** is the term for similar characteristics of related organisms. The strongest evidence of shared ancestry is homology in genetic molecules, such as DNA and RNA. The greater the difference in DNA sequences of any two organisms, the longer these organisms have been moving down separate evolutionary paths. The greater the matching of sequences in organisms, the more closely related the organisms are.

Another type of homology is similarity in anatomy or body parts, as shown here in the limbs of mammals.

Homologous Limb Structures

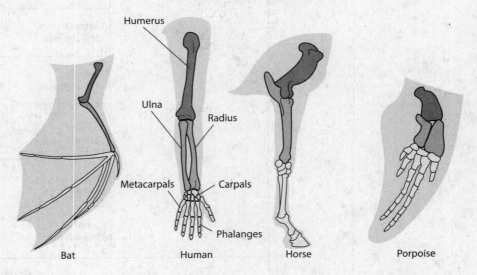

Bat   Human   Horse   Porpoise

Notice from this diagram that each of these mammals has the same arrangement of internal bone structures in its forelimb. Although each forelimb is shaped differently and may function differently, this illustrates that all of these mammals are related.

Natural Selection and Adaptation

You now know what evolution is, but how does it happen? Several mechanisms can cause evolution. One of the most famous and important mechanisms of evolutionary change is natural selection. **Natural selection** is a process whereby organisms with favorable traits in a specific environment breed and survive more successfully than organisms without these traits. As a result, organisms with these favorable traits become more prevalent in the population over time. Natural selection is responsible for the diversity not only within species, but among species.

Charles Darwin developed the theory of evolution by natural selection in the 1800s. One of many influences on Darwin was an essay written by economist Thomas Malthus. Malthus noted in 1798 that plants and animals produce many more offspring than can survive. Malthus's concern as an economist was the possible doubling of the human population every 25 years and rapidly using up Earth's resources. Darwin spent many years thinking about what he read while collecting fossils and making observations of nature. In his 1859 book *The Origin of Species*, Darwin provided ample evidence that organisms have a common ancestry and have evolved or descended with modifications over time due to natural selection.

Natural selection and evolution are not the same things. Natural selection is one way, or mechanism, for evolution to occur in a population. There are four main requirements for evolution to occur by natural selection:

1. A population of organisms must vary in characteristics.

2. Variation is inherited and thus can be passed from parents to offspring.

3. Populations produce more offspring than can survive, and offspring compete for resources.

4. There is **differential reproductive success** among organisms—those with favorable genetic variations survive and reproduce better than those without these variations.

Nature seems to select for the fittest organisms and to select against the less fit. However, fitness is not necessarily about strength and vigor. Evolutionary fitness is the ability to pass on your genes. The end result of evolution by natural selection is a population with **adaptations** or favorable characteristics that allow organism to better survive and reproduce in a specific environment.

Let's consider a real-life example of evolution by natural selection in insects. Insects play good and bad roles in agriculture. They help pollinate important food crops, but some insects eat the crops. This pressure led farmers to spray pesticides in their fields to control the populations of harmful insects. However, some insects had a genetic mutation that enabled them to resist the harmful effects of pesticides. When they passed on this mutation to their offspring, their offspring were better able to survive, compete, and reproduce in the pesticide-filled environment. As a result, over time, more and more insects in the population had this pesticide-resistant mutation. The mutation spread quickly in the population because insects have short lifespans, and the generations succeed each other rapidly. The ability of insects to resist the effects of pesticides is considered an adaptation and evolves due to natural selection favoring those insects with resistance.

Species that can adapt in this way to a changing environment have a better chance of surviving and reproducing. However, species that cannot adapt to a changed environment may die off or become **extinct**.

Another type of adaptation is **mimicry**. Many animals survive by mimicking other species as a way to avoid predators. For example, certain flies mimic the appearance and sound of bumblebees. Predators avoid the bumblebees, so they avoid the mimic flies too.

Adaptations are part of the amazing diversity we see in species.

EXERCISE 19

Evolution

Directions: Choose the best answer to each question.

1. Which is true about the fossil record?
   A. The fossil record is a complete history of organisms on Earth.
   B. The fossil record contains important evidence of evolution.
   C. Each rock layer has fossils of organisms that existed during different eras.
   D. The fossil record shows that the first fossils were multicellular.

2. Fossils of an extinct mammal that was larger than an elephant are only found in South America and Africa. Radioactive dating data show that the mammal existed more than 250 million years ago. Which is the best hypothesis to support this information?
   A. South America and Africa were separated by water 250 million years ago.
   B. A land bridge thousands of miles across joined South America and Africa.
   C. South America and Africa were once one landmass and then separated.
   D. The ancient mammal swam across the ocean from South America to Africa.

3. Plants need sunlight to produce food by photosynthesis. Which trait is MOST likely to be an adaptation for a plant living in a forest of dense vegetation?
   A. Small leaves
   B. Climbing stems
   C. Poisonous leaves
   D. Protective thorns

4. Which is NOT necessary for a population to evolve by natural selection?
   A. Environmental variation in a population
   B. Offspring that compete with each other for resources
   C. Differential reproductive success
   D. Genetic traits in a population

Answers are on page 799.

Understanding Sequence and Cause and Effect

A part of studying science is discovering how and why things work. Scientists determine this by examining data and hypothesizing a reason for the results. They make observations and form opinions based on the information gathered. The results must make sense and should explain how things work logically. Part of establishing how and why things work is by studying the order in which things happen and the factor(s) associated with making something happen.

Sequencing Events

You have likely read a question that asked you to sequence the steps of a process. **Sequencing** is arranging events in the order in which they occur. When an automobile mechanic diagnoses a problem in an engine, he or she needs to understand the source of the problem. To fix the engine, the mechanic must understand the order in which the belts turn, the pistons pump, and combustion within the engine occurs. Understanding the big picture allows the mechanic to notice other vehicle functions that may indirectly affect the performance of the engine.

Read the following sentences and locate the words that help to describe the order in which things happen.

Before mixing the cookie dough, mix the eggs, butter, and vanilla in a separate bowl.

While watching fireworks at a park, you will see the colorful lights first and then you will hear the sound of the explosion.

The next thing that happens is that the crash dummy slams into the airbag after the car crashes into the wall.

Although the actions in these sentences were written out of order, you can figure out the sequence in which things happened. There are key words that describe the order of events. The words may be numerical like *first*, *second*, and *third* or words that list an order such as *before*, *after*, and *next*. It may help to add numbers to each sequential part of the reading passage.

EXERCISE 20

Sequencing Events

Directions: Read the passage. Then determine the sequence of events and answer the questions that follow.

Have you ever noticed that when you bake something in an oven, a metal pan sitting on top of the oven gets hot? First, the oven's heating element increases the temperature of the metal surrounding the oven. Then, the energy created from heating the metal causes the particles in the metal to vibrate faster and bump into one another. Finally, the metal pan sitting on the stove heats up after the metal particles surrounding the oven transfer heat into the metal particles of the pan. **Conduction** is the process of heat transfer from one object to another through the interaction and collision of adjacent particles.

1. What happens inside the oven before the particles of the surrounding metal begin to vibrate?

   _____

2. Once the particles begin to vibrate quickly, what happens to them?

   _____

3. How does the pan on the top of the oven get hot?

   _____

4. Which conducts heat, the vibration of particles or the collision of particles?

   _____

Answers are on page 799.

Cause and Effect

We just discussed the sequencing of events. Let's now consider why things happen. Understanding why things happen in a specific way requires studying **cause and effect**. When questions arise, we think about why things happen. Why does the foundation in a new house crack? Why does lightning tend to strike metal objects?

An action, or **cause**, has an **effect**, which is the outcome of an occurrence. Another way to understand cause and effect is that *cause* answers the question *why* and *effect* answers the question *what happened*. There are key words that you might read in a passage that clue you in on a cause and effect. These words and phrases include *because, since, as a result*, and *therefore*. Read the following passage and label each sentence as a cause or an effect:

> According to news reports, there has been an increase in house burglaries in our neighborhood. Many homeowners purchased alarm systems. Police also advertised neighborhood watch programs.

The second and the third statements above are effects of the first statement. An increase in burglaries (cause) motivated homeowners to purchase alarm systems (effect) and the police to activate neighborhood watch programs (effect). Sometimes a single cause can have multiple effects, and vice versa, multiple causes can result in a single effect.

It is important to understand that sometimes one event does not cause another event to happen, but rather is associated with another factor that caused the event. It may be a coincidence that one event occurred at the same time as another unrelated event. Incorrectly labeling an unrelated event as a cause is called reaching a false conclusion. You need to determine if the two events are related to one another. For example, if you watered a plant once a week but it wilted and died in a month, is the true cause a lack of watering or something else? What if the plant was a cactus? Perhaps the temperature was too cold for the cactus to survive. Read the following passage and see if you can tell if the writer reached a false conclusion.

> I walked into my bedroom last night and flipped the switch to turn on the bedside lamp, but the light did not work. Normally, flipping the switch opens the circuit to send electricity to the lamp. So, I thought to myself that there must be something wrong with the wiring in the house.

Consider that there might be something else besides faulty wiring in the house that caused the lamp not to turn on. Maybe the light bulb burned out, or perhaps the bedside lamp is no longer plugged into the wall socket. Perhaps the power to the house has been knocked out by a thunderstorm. You do not have enough information. The conclusion made in the passage is a false conclusion because it was made without enough investigation to eliminate other possible causes. Read the following passages and determine which ones end with false conclusions.

1. I could not start my car's engine this morning. Last night was the coldest night on record with temperatures in the teens. The car's battery could be dead or the fuel line could be frozen.

2. I never take vitamins over the weekend. On Monday, I caught a cold. If I took my vitamins on Saturday and Sunday, I would not have gotten sick.

3. I was using a helium tank to fill party balloons. One of the balloons exploded. The package of balloons I purchased must be defective.

4. Sara wore shoes with rubber soles instead of wooden soles to her ballroom dance class. She couldn't glide well on the dance floor. If Sara wore her wooden-soled shoes, she might have been able to move her feet more easily.

If you selected passages numbered 2 and 3 as the false conclusions, you are correct. Catching a cold on Monday did not have anything to do with not taking vitamins over the weekend. Maybe that person's immune system was weakened by lack of sleep or a poor diet. Furthermore, just because one balloon exploded does not necessarily mean that the entire package of balloons is faulty. Perhaps that person overinflated the balloon.

Sometimes a passage will not present obvious information about a cause and an effect. The writer may **imply** or indirectly hint that something caused a certain effect. Consider this statement:

> After I calculated the amount I spend each month on gasoline, I realized that I made a bad choice when I purchased the wrong vehicle.

There are several things that are implied by this statement. Although the statement does not mention how much gasoline the vehicle uses, it implies that the quantity is more than the speaker wishes to pay for. The statement does not mention the type of vehicle, but it was not a good choice based on the amount of gasoline the vehicle requires for a month's driving.

When cause and effect are implied, the reader must determine what the writer means to say by making **inferences** or conclusions reached on the basis of evidence and reasoning. The reader must be a detective and decipher the meaning of the passage. What do you think the writer is implying in this passage?

> A study published in the newspaper states that electricity generated from burning coal is the cleanest method of all the options. But, interestingly, the study was conducted by the National Council for Coal Energy.

You can infer that the writer believes the study is biased because the coal producers were involved.

As you look for cause-and-effect relationships in your reading, recall the difference between fact and opinion. A **fact** is a statement or information that can be proven. An **opinion** is a statement or information that cannot be proven. Opinions are someone's beliefs or personal judgments. Understanding cause-and-effect relationships and avoiding false conclusions will help you better understand the topics you read and study.

EXERCISE 21

Cause and Effect

Directions: Read the cause and write two possible effects.

1. **Cause:** There was a severe decrease in rainfall during winter and spring months.

    Effect: _____

    Effect: _____

Directions: Read the following effect and write two possible causes.

2. **Effect:** Motorcyclists began wearing helmets every time they rode.

    Cause: _____

    Cause: _____

Directions: Determine if the following statements are fact or opinion. Write *F* for fact or *O* for opinion.

3. _____ LeBron James is the greatest basketball player of all time.

4. _____ Riding in a car without wearing your seatbelt is illegal.

5. _____ *Hamlet* was written by William Shakespeare.

Answers are on page 799.

Ecology

All living things interact with each other and with the nonliving things in their environment. **Ecology** is the scientific study of interactions among living things and between the living and nonliving world. Ecologists categorize the living and nonliving environmental factors that affect organisms into two groups: biotic and abiotic. The living parts of an environment are **biotic factors**, such as different species. For example, species interact with other species of plants and animals. The nonliving parts of an environment are called **abiotic factors**, such as water, sunlight, and temperature. Species are affected by how they obtain and use these nonliving resources.

Ecology can be studied at different levels of organization, such as the population level, the community level, or the ecosystem level, as shown in the following illustration. Populations of different species form a **community** in which the species interact with one another. Communities of species interact with nonliving things in an **ecosystem**. All of this interactivity occurs within Earth's biosphere. The **biosphere** is all areas of Earth's water, crust, and atmosphere where living things exist.

Levels of Organization

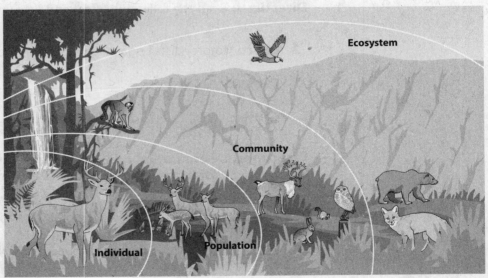

Populations

A group of organisms of a specific species, such as deer, that lives and reproduces together in a specific area is a **population**. Populations exist in a delicate balance. Too many individuals of a species can use up necessary resources quickly. However, there must be enough individuals in the population to ensure sufficient numbers for future generations. For example, individuals making up a population of deer compete with each other and with other species for food, water, and shelter. If there are too many deer, there will not be enough resources to sustain them all. But the population must be large enough to ensure that enough offspring survive to pass on their genes to future generations.

Members of a population interact. They signal or communicate with each other to warn of dangers like predators, to identify each other, and to attract mates. Communication is an example of animal behavior that occurs among individuals of a population. **Animal behavior** is how species relate to their environment as well as to other species. There is also individual behavior. For instance, bird songs change depending on the situation. One bird call or song will warn about predators in the area. Another song will notify the population about a food source that was found, and another song could attract a mate.

Members of a population also will work and interact together as a group; this is called **group behavior**. Members of the group cooperate to carry out a task such as group foraging for food or flocking and herding to protect the entire group. Some monkeys will care for the young of the entire population even if something happens to the parents. Ants work in a similar manner by building and protecting colonies including those born from a different queen. Group behavior may have evolved because group membership can increase the chances of survival for genetically related individuals.

Population Growth

The number of individuals in a population is constantly changing. This occurs because individuals are added and subtracted through birth, death, and migration. When birds move into a new area and join an existing population, the birds have **immigrated** into the population. Immigration and birth increase the size of the population. As birds mature and fly away from their original population, they **emigrate** from the population. Emigration and death reduce a population. Populations tend to fluctuate around a point of equilibrium. There are times when populations will increase rapidly to a point at which the environment can no longer support all of the individuals. Likewise, if environmental resources are suddenly scarce, perhaps because of a drought, the population may shrink dramatically.

There are two types of population growth—exponential growth and logistic growth.

Population Growth

Exponential versus logistic population growth

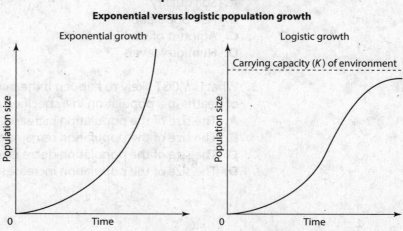

Each of the graphs on the preceding page shows a population growing over time. In **exponential growth**, there is no external limitation to the size of a population and the growth curve shows a characteristic *J*-shape in the graph. Such growth can take place only if the environment in which the population lives has sufficient resources to support large additional numbers of individuals. Because bacteria reproduce quickly and have a short generation time, they may initially exhibit exponential growth. However, no population can grow forever.

Logistic growth occurs in most populations when environmental factors limit the number of individuals that can be sustained in a population. Factors like competition and predation limit population growth. At some point, equilibrium, or the carrying capacity of the population's environment, is reached. **Carrying capacity (K)** is the maximum number of individuals in a population that a given environment can support. At this point, birth rates begin decreasing, while death rates begin increasing. Different interacting populations may fluctuate in sync around the carrying capacity. For example, predatory animals may decline in numbers when the number of prey animals diminishes but then begin increasing once again as soon as the prey animals rebound and increase again in number.

EXERCISE 22

Populations

Directions: Choose the best answer to each question.

1. A population grows to a specific size and then begins to level off around a set point. Which term BEST describes this limitation?
   A. Immigration
   B. Carrying capacity
   C. Exponential growth
   D. Emigration

2. Which term does NOT describe a nonliving resource that affects a community of species?
   A. Soil quality
   B. Fish population
   C. Amount of sunlight
   D. Humidity levels

3. What is MOST likely to happen if the number of births exceeds the number of deaths in a population in a specific time period?
   A. The size of the population increases.
   B. The size of the population remains constant.
   C. The size of the population decreases.
   D. The size of the population increases and then decreases.

Directions: Use the information in the graph to answer question 4.

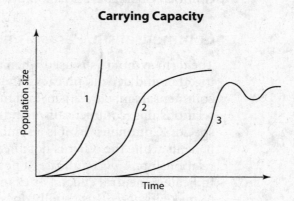

Carrying Capacity

4. Which line(s) of the graph show(s) the existence of a carrying capacity?
   A. 1
   B. 2
   C. 1 and 3
   D. 2 and 3

Answers are on page 800.

Community Interactions

A group of different species living and interacting in the same area is known as a **community**. The water you drink comes from reservoirs that are also used as resources by animals, fish, and plants. All these different living things interact as a community. You might live in an apartment or a house, and aside from interacting with your neighbors, you interact with insects and animals that live nearby or within your residence.

Each species in a community has a specific role known as an ecological niche. **Ecological niche** refers to the manner in which a species interacts with other living and nonliving things in the community. The basic characteristics of a niche include where a species lives, the conditions under which it thrives, the type of food it consumes, and its competition with other species. An ecological niche also includes the activity of a species, such as the time of day it is active, and the temperature ranges the species can tolerate. No two species can occupy the exact same ecological niche or they would compete until one perishes. A community can host similar species if the available resources are used in different ways. The number of species living together in a specific area is a measure of **species diversity**.

As you will recall, populations of living things compete for resources like food and shelter to survive. Competition is an example of an interaction between members of the same species or different species. Whether or not these interactions are positive or negative depends on the situation and the relationship. Five main types of species interactions are commensalism, parasitism, mutualism, competition, and predation.

Commensalism, Parasitism, and Mutualism

The term **symbiosis** is used when two species live and associate closely together and depend on each other. There are three symbiotic relationships: commensalism, parasitism, and mutualism. Two of these symbiotic relationships (commensalism and parasitism) are not beneficial to both species. **Commensalism** is a symbiotic relationship in which one species benefits while the other is not affected. You might think of this as a *plus/zero* relationship. A *plus* indicates a positive effect on a species' fitness and a *zero* indicates a neutral effect. For example, a bird will use the protection of a tree to make its nest. This usually doesn't affect the tree while giving the bird a safe place to lay its eggs.

Parasitism is a symbiotic relationship in which one species benefits while the other is harmed. This is a *plus/minus* relationship. In this case, a *minus* indicates a negative effect on a species' fitness. A **parasite** lives on or inside a living host, feeding off it but not killing it. Ticks, tapeworms, and hookworms are examples of parasites that live in the bodies of other living things.

Mutualism is the third kind of symbiotic relationship in which both species benefit from the interaction. It is a *plus/plus* relationship. Have you heard the expression "a dog is man's best friend"? This describes a symbiotic relationship because the dog receives food and shelter while the owner obtains affection and perhaps protection from the dog. In the wild, we see other examples of mutualism. The remora, or suckerfish, is a small fish that lives around larger sea animals like sharks, turtles, and whales. The remora attaches itself to a larger animal, and while the animal swims along, the remora will feed on parasites that infect the larger animal. Other mutualism relationships are seen in plants interacting with birds and bees. Plants develop flowers to attract birds and bees. The birds and bees get nectar to eat while the flower gets an assist in reproduction when the birds and bees involuntarily take away pollen to be dropped off at another plant's flowers.

Competition

Each community has a limited amount of resources such as food and habitat. When two or more species need the same resources, this leads to **competition** among organisms. Competition occurs within a species as well. Competition is a potentially mutually harmful interaction or a *minus/ minus* relationship. For example, lions and tigers roaming the same prairie may compete for water and food. This interaction can become violent if, for example, individuals fight over a prey animal that one of them has killed. Competition can also be indirectly harmful to both species if the populations rapidly use up the available resources. Different species often evolve in a way that enables them to coexist by using resources in different ways. This may make competition hard to recognize between closely related species.

Predation

Similar to parasitism, predation is a *plus/minus* relationship. One species, the **predator**, will kill and eat another species, the **prey**. This interaction differs from the symbiotic relationship of parasitism because the two species do not live together. The predators diminish the number of prey population. A smaller number of prey animals eventually limit the number of predators that can exist in a community. Sometimes, predators and prey co-evolve together due to their constant, close interaction. As the prey species evolves better adaptations for avoiding or escaping predators, the predator evolves better adaptations for detecting and catching its prey. This process increases the fitness of the predator and prey species over time. Predator and prey co-evolution can lead to an evolutionary "arms race." The two sides continue developing defense and counterdefense strategies without either side ever winning.

EXERCISE 23

Community Interactions

Directions: Choose the best answer to each question.

1. A flowering vine climbs on the trunk of a tree to better reach the sunlight, but it does not affect the tree. This is which type of interaction?
   A. Commensalism
   B. Mutualism
   C. Predation
   D. Competition

2. A herd of elephants and a herd of rhinoceros fight for the use a small pond in a mostly dry African savanna. This is which type of interaction?
   A. Commensalism
   B. Competition
   C. Mutualism
   D. Predation

3. A cowbird feeds on insects that pester a bison. Which type of interaction is this?
   A. Predation
   B. Mutualism
   C. Commensalism
   D. Competition

Answers are on page 800.

Ecosystems

An **ecosystem** is a community of species and their nonliving environment. Ecosystems can encompass an area as big as an ocean or a forest and as small as a pond or a garden. Ecologists study the delicate balance between the living things that make up communities and the nonliving resources they use.

Cycles of Matter

Matter moves through ecosystems and is continuously recycled. The **law of conservation of matter** states that matter can be transformed or changed but cannot be created or destroyed. The elements that make up your body were here before you were born, and these same elements will be here after you die. Some of the most important substances in living organisms, such as water, carbon, and nitrogen, are continuously recycled. These materials cycle through an ecosystem in **nutrient cycles**.

You are probably aware of the **water cycle**, the process in which water moves on, in, and above Earth's surface. A water molecule is made up of two hydrogen atoms and one oxygen atom, and its chemical formula is H_2O. Most species, including humans, cannot live without regular water replenishment. Most of our body, approximately 70 percent by weight, is made up of water. Water is found underground, in the atmosphere, and on Earth's surface.

This diagram shows how water cycles through an ecosystem.

The Water Cycle

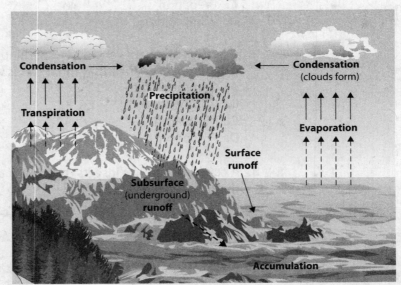

Water molecules accumulate in bodies of water such as lakes, seas, and oceans. Heat from the sun causes the liquid water molecules to transition into a gas. The transition of a liquid into a gas is **evaporation**. Water in the atmosphere is called water vapor. Water vapor rises and cools into droplets around dust particles, forming clouds. Cloud droplets, which are small drops of condensed water, attract other droplets and fall from the sky as **precipitation**, bringing water back to Earth's surface. Some of the groundwater and runoff from land flow back into bodies of water, while some of the water is absorbed by soil. Green plants take in water through their roots, and the plants release water molecules back into the air by a process called **transpiration**.

Carbon cycles through Earth's ecosystems, atmosphere, and oceans in a process called the **carbon cycle**. Carbon is one of the major building blocks of living organisms. For the most part, carbon is confined to Earth's crust and ocean sediments. Carbon moves through the environment and is used by some organisms while being released by others. Recall that photosynthesis is a process in which plants take carbon dioxide (CO_2) from the atmosphere and use the carbon to build carbohydrates. Carbon is then released back into the atmosphere as CO_2 during cellular respiration. When organisms die, their bodies decay, releasing carbon back into the environment through soil and sediment. The oceans are host to marine organisms that have carbon dioxide within their shells in the form of calcium carbonate. When these organisms die, their shells compress into ocean sediment and form limestone. Earthquakes and wave movements break down limestone, releasing carbon dioxide back into the atmosphere.

Nitrogen makes up almost 80 percent of the air we breathe. If you ever fertilized your lawn, you know that nitrogen is an important nutrient for grasses and plants. Organisms use nitrogen to make proteins and nucleic acids that are used to help body cells function. Although air holds a great deal of nitrogen, most organisms cannot take in nitrogen in a gaseous form. The process of nitrogen conversion for use by plants and animals is called the **nitrogen cycle**. **Decomposer** organisms such as bacteria and fungi convert nitrogen into a form plants can obtain from the soil. You will learn more about decomposers in the next section. Animals eat plants and thus take in nitrogen-containing molecules. Some of the nitrogen trapped in the soil is released back into the atmosphere by other types of decomposing bacteria.

Energy Flow

Energy also cycles through an ecosystem. The transferable energy in many instances requires sunlight as a starting point. Ecologists develop models that reflect how energy transfers from one organism to another.

The flow of energy in an ecosystem can be modeled as a simple **food chain** as shown:

Producer → primary consumer → secondary consumer
(herbivore)   (carnivore)

This model describes the feeding relationships between organisms within an ecosystem, or "who eats whom."

A typical food chain includes the following:

- **Producers** are organisms that make their own food, usually by photosynthesis. They are also called **autotrophs** and include plants, algae, and some bacteria.

- **Consumers** are organisms that cannot make their own food and must eat producers or other consumers to get energy and carbon. They are also called **heterotrophs.** Animals are heterotrophs.

- Primary consumers are heterotrophs that feed directly upon autotrophs. Primary consumers include **herbivores**, such as birds, rabbits, and beetles, that eat plants and seeds.

- Secondary consumers are animals that feed on the primary consumers. Secondary consumers tend to be **carnivores** because they eat animals and insects. For example, frogs eat beetles and snakes eat rabbits,

- Tertiary consumers feed on secondary consumers. They include eagles, lions, and humans. Humans and some animals are **omnivores** because they eat both plants and animals.

Another type of diagram that shows energy flow through an ecosystem is an energy pyramid. An **energy pyramid** is a diagram in which each feeding level (or **trophic level**) is represented by a block. The energy pyramid shows that there are more organisms on the bottom of the pyramid than at the top. There are many more producers than primary, secondary, or tertiary consumers.

Human beings ultimately depend for their nourishment and energy on the largest level of the pyramid, the producers, which convert the sun's energy into carbohydrates. When humans or other consumers eat plants, they take in the **biomass**, or organic matter, that is present in the plants. The carbohydrates in the biomass provide energy to the consumers. As you move up the energy pyramid from primary consumers to secondary consumers to tertiary consumers, the amount of biomass present decreases from one level to the next.

Energy Diagram

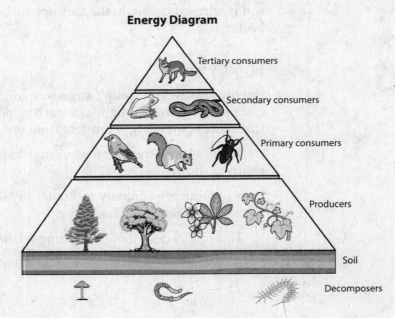

As organisms are eaten, waste is left behind, including animal carcasses, plant parts, and digestive wastes. **Decomposers,** such as bacteria and fungi, break down dead and decaying organic matter. They connect to all levels of the energy pyramid and fill the soil with nutrients for the plants. Decomposers are as essential to ecosystems as are producers. Without decomposers, nutrients would never return to the soil.

Not all of the energy created by the producers is passed all the way up through the energy pyramid. At each level, some of the energy is used for life functions and metabolism, and much is lost as heat generated by metabolism. Only about 10 percent of energy moves from one level of the energy pyramid to the next. This inefficiency in energy transfer limits ecosystems to four or five trophic levels.

Human Impact

The nutrient cycles have been and continue to be affected by the growing human populations. Humans first changed ecosystems through agriculture and domestication of animals. The environment was forever altered when mass manufacturing processes were developed in the mid-1800s. Horse-drawn carriages were replaced by automobiles. Steam-powered trains evolved into diesel-powered engines. Today the burning of nonrenewable resources drives much of our lives. This human impact has put a strain on the water, carbon, and nitrogen cycles.

As cities grow, the rainfall part of the water cycle is disturbed because much of the water is not returned to rivers and oceans. The concrete and asphalt in cities does not allow water to seep into the ground. Water also gets polluted from industrial processes. Humans also impact natural cycles through deforestation. **Deforestation** is the mass removal of forests for use in as building houses and other structures. As you recall, trees store carbon and produce oxygen. Without forests, many species lose their natural habitats.

Humans also impact Earth's natural cycles through the use of fossil fuels. **Fossil fuels** are made from carbon deposits left by decaying plants and animals. These fuels include coal, crude oil, and gasoline. Industries and consumers burn these fuels, releasing more carbon into the atmosphere than can be taken in by green plants. The overabundance of carbon in the atmosphere, in gaseous forms such as CO_2, is the cause of the **greenhouse effect**. Greenhouse gases hold solar heat in the atmosphere, functioning in much the same way as the glass panels in a greenhouse. This effect is likely to cause climate change and unusual weather patterns, some of which can already be observed.

The nitrogen cycle is also disrupted by human activity. Decomposers that provide organisms with nitrogen in usable form are removed when their habitat is covered by concrete and asphalt. Nitrogen builds up in soils and in water sources when crops are overfertilized, causing rapid growth of algae and other water plants. Large algae "blooms" block sunlight from reaching sea life, destroying marine habitats. The burning of fossil fuels releases nitrogen into the atmosphere that can cause acid rain. Too much nitrogen in the atmosphere can deplete the ozone layer that protects Earth from the sun's ultraviolet radiation.

The disturbance of nutrient cycles by humans has already caused some permanent damage. Some species have not survived the changes in ecosystems and have become **extinct**; every individual of the species has died out. Deforestation, growth of urban areas, and expansion of agriculture and mining have eliminated the habitats of many species and led to their extinction. At times, humans have also inadvertently introduced species from other geographic areas, such as fire ants and Africanized bees, into ecosystems that are not adapted to these novel residents. In their new habitat, these exotic species have few or no natural limiting factors, such as competitors and predators. As a result, they are able to displace or exterminate the native species in an ecosystem.

However, it is possible to remedy the negative impact on ecosystems caused by human populations. Reintroducing and conserving biodiversity is an important step in this process. **Biodiversity**, the presence of a variety of species, is valuable as a way of keeping ecosystems in balance. By replanting forests, protecting natural habitats, and promoting breeding programs, ecosystems can be rebuilt. Reducing the use of fossil fuels will cut down on carbon and nitrogen pollution and help restore Earth's atmosphere. Developing water conservation programs, including the reduction of artificial landscaping, can restore the water cycle, allowing green plants to flourish. Every person can make a difference in reducing negative factors in the environment.

EXERCISE 24

Ecosystems

Directions: Choose the best answer to each question.

1. In an energy pyramid, only a small amount of energy is transferred from one trophic level to the one above it. If frogs eat insects and are themselves later eaten by snakes, what share of the energy stored in the insects reaches the snakes?
   A. 0 percent
   B. Approximately 1 percent
   C. Approximately 10 percent
   D. Approximately 50 percent

2. Human activities can produce an overabundance of nitrogen in rivers, lakes, and other bodies of water. Why does this sometimes cause rapid growth of aquatic algae?
   A. Nitrogen depletes oxygen from the water.
   B. By absorbing more nitrogen, algae can produce more proteins.
   C. High levels of nitrogen in the water generate CO_2 for plants.
   D. Algae take in nitrogen through the air.

3. There is much concern about the buildup of carbon dioxide and other greenhouse gases in Earth's atmosphere. Which is NOT a source of carbon dioxide emissions?
   A. Burning of gasoline in automobile engines
   B. Cellular respiration in the bodies of animals
   C. Deforestation to make way for agriculture
   D. Burning of coal to generate electricity

Answers are on page 800.

## CHAPTER 2

Physical Science

Graphical information is one of the main ways that scientists share information with other scientists and with the public at large. This chapter will help you develop your skills in reading and interpreting scientific graphical information.

Understanding Graphical Information

Visual representations of complex information, such as diagrams, tables, and graphs, help you understand a topic better. Images also bring interest to information. If you are reading a large amount of text about the human body systems without having images to refer to, it would make for a very difficult read. By understanding how to use these images, you will become a better learner.

Diagrams

The previous chapter discussed topics such as the human body systems and photosynthesis in plants. These topics are best described with **diagrams**, or images that display a visual representation of a subject or an idea.

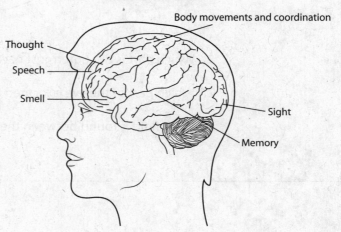

Areas of the Brain

Notice that the diagram has a **title** that provides a simple description of the purpose of the image. A diagram like this one may be useful by itself if, for example, you wish to identify locations in the brain where certain functions occur. But the purpose of other diagrams will be to clarify or simplify information found in the accompanying text.

This diagram you just looked at has labels that identify specific parts of the brain. Other diagrams may have labels that point to parts of a machine or labels that name the steps in a process. Being able to connect a diagram with the story being told helps you answer questions about the subject matter.

EXERCISE 1

Diagrams

Directions: Study the diagram and then answer the questions that follow.

The Human Eye

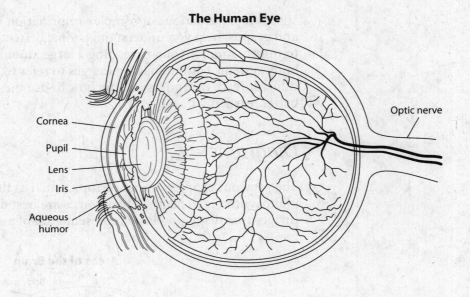

1. Which part is the outermost covering of the eye? _____

2. Which part of the eye is located behind the pupil? _____

3. What fluid is found between the lens and cornea? _____

Answers are on page 800.

Tables

Another type of graphical illustration that helps to communicate information is a chart or **table**. A table has columns and rows.

Columns and rows separate information so that the reader can notice similarities and differences. For example, the table below shows the relationship between blood types and blood donation.

Blood Types and Blood Donation

Blood Type	Can Take Blood From	Can Give Blood To
O	O	O, A, B, AB
A	O, A	A, AB
B	O, B	B, AB
AB	O, A, B, AB	AB

This table has three columns and four rows. The first column lists the blood type. The second and third columns represent the blood types of blood donors and blood recipients, respectively. The rows show four different blood types: O, A, B, and AB. For example, people with blood type O can receive blood only from a donor with blood type O. A person with type O blood cells has A and B antibodies that would reject the cells of a donor with A, B, or AB blood cells. However, a person with blood type O can donate blood to a person with any blood type.

EXERCISE 2

Tables

Directions: Use the blood-type table to answer the questions.

1. People with which blood type are likely to have the greatest number of donors available? _____

2. People with which blood types are the most similar in their pattern of receiving and donating blood? _____

Answers are on page 800.

Line Graphs

A **graph** is a useful way to show a trend over time or a change based on a series of measurements. With a graph, you can easily determine trends, make comparisons, and draw conclusions from a set of data. For example, consider a scientist testing a new growth hormone that can increase the weight of holiday turkeys. The scientist tested different amounts of the hormone using nine turkeys (subjects) and charted the following data.

Subject #	Amount of Hormone Used	Increase in Weight
1	2 oz	4 lb
2	4 oz	10 lb
3	6 oz	16 lb
4	8 oz	20 lb
5	10 oz	23 lb
6	12 oz	26 lb
7	14 oz	28 lb
8	16 oz	20 lb
9	18 oz	13 lb

Notice that there appears to be a relationship between the amount of the hormone used and the amount of weight gained by the turkeys. However, the last two rows representing subjects #8 and #9 show a smaller weight gain than the other data would lead you to expect. Let's examine this same data using a line graph. A **line graph** is a graphical representation that shows trends in data in a way that is easier to grasp by a reader.

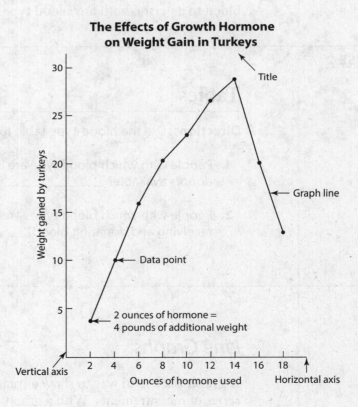

The Effects of Growth Hormone on Weight Gain in Turkeys

The graph is a visual way of showing that up to the amount of 14 ounces, there is a positive linear relationship between the amount of hormone used and weight gain in turkeys. That is, as the amount of hormone increases, the weight gain also increases. But for higher amounts of 16 and 18 ounces, that relationship turns negative; the weight gain decreases. The graph makes this shift immediately and visibly clear in a way that the table did not. However, tables and graphs are both useful ways of presenting information.

Graphs are created using two **axes**, a vertical line and a horizontal line that are used to plot data. The horizontal line is the x-axis or horizontal axis. The x-axis is where you plot the **independent variable**, which is the data that you can control and manipulate. The line that runs up and down is the y-axis or vertical axis. The y-axis is where you plot the **dependent variable**, which is the data that is determined by and dependent on the independent variable on the x-axis. The dependent variable is often what you seek to measure when plotting the independent variable on the x-axis. In the graph shown, the independent variable plotted on the x-axis is the amount of growth hormone given to the turkeys. The dependent variable, plotted on the y-axis, is the amount of weight gain that resulted for each amount of growth hormone.

Creating and analyzing a graph requires an understanding of the data being displayed. In the data table on hormones and weight gain, the amount of hormone used increases by 2 ounces in each row. This seems like a natural scale to use on the x-axis in the graph. The **scale** is the numerical interval used on the x-axis or y-axis to help organize the data. The scale on each axis should be uniform so that the points on the graph are spaced evenly.

When you create a graph from a data table, start by determining which values are independent variables and which values are dependent variables. In the example, the independent variables are the numbers in the second column, the amounts of hormone used. The dependent variables are the numbers in the third column, the resulting increases in weight. The numbers in each row are coordinates that help you plot a data point on the graph. For each row, count the number of spaces to the right along the x-axis that correspond to the independent variable. Then count up (parallel to the y-axis) the number of spaces that correspond to the dependent variable. The point where you stop is your data point. For example, for the first row in the table, you would count two spaces to the right on the x-axis and four spaces up parallel to the y-axis. Your first data point would have the coordinates (2, 4). When giving coordinates, the x-axis coordinate is always shown first. After all the data points are plotted, you draw a connecting line to help illustrate any **trend** or pattern that may be present. The trend shown in the graph is that more hormones produce more weight gain until a limit, or threshold, is reached at 14 ounces.

Line Graphs

Directions: Study the line graph and then answer the questions that follow.

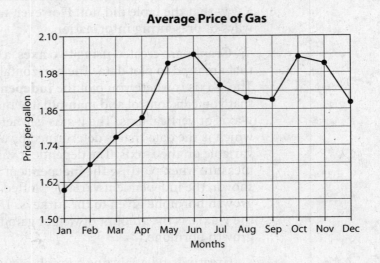

Average Price of Gas

1. What do the values on the *x-axis* represent? _____

2. During which month did the price of gas reach its peak? _____

3. Why do you think the price of gas was highest during this month?

   _____

Answers are on page 801.

Bar Graphs

A bar graph is a kind of graph that is best suited to compare **discrete** (separate) items, such as the populations of different cities or the heights of different mountains. The purpose of a bar graph is generally to show how different items compare, not to illustrate a trend as in a line graph.

You create a bar graph in the same way as a line graph, with a title and labels for both axes. There is an *x*-axis and a *y*-axis. The bars representing each item to be compared are arranged along the x-axis. The height of the bar is determined by the scale on the *y-axis*.

EXERCISE 4

Bar Graphs

Directions: Study the bar graph and then answer the questions that follow.

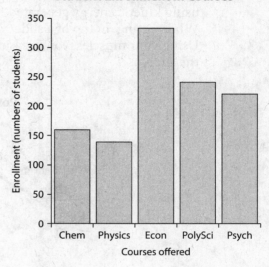

Student Enrollment in Courses

1. Which course offered has the smallest enrollment? _____

2. Estimate how many more students enrolled in Econ versus Poly Sci.

   _____

3. Why is a line graph NOT ideal to show this data? _____

Answers are on page 801.

Energy

Energy is the ability to do work. Energy can be derived from physical or chemical sources. For example, you use physical energy when you lift a book up off of a table. An example of chemical energy is the electricity produced from chemicals in a battery. The combustion in an automobile engine is another example of chemical energy. The two main categories of energy are potential and kinetic energy.

Potential and Kinetic Energy

To understand how energy is used in everyday life, you need a basic understanding of potential and kinetic energy. **Potential energy** is the stored energy that can be used to perform work. Nutrients that animals consume contain stored chemical energy. The opposite of stored energy is energy of motion. **Kinetic energy** is the energy of motion. Muscles move using kinetic energy generated from the stored potential energy of nutrients. When sitting on top of a slide, you have potential energy to slide downward. Using your muscles, you use kinetic energy to glide down to the bottom of the slide.

Potential and Kinetic Energy

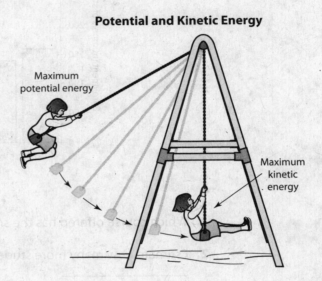

Maximum potential energy

Maximum kinetic energy

In the diagram, the child on a swing displays both potential and kinetic energy in action. Potential energy is at its highest level when the child has reached the top of the swinging motion. Kinetic energy increases as the child begins to swing back toward the center of the swing set. Kinetic energy is at its highest level at the bottom of this curve, while potential energy is at its lowest value there.

This conversion of energy from potential to kinetic or kinetic to potential is known as energy transformation. **Energy transformation** is the process of changing from one form of energy to another. The food that you eat contains chemical energy. This chemical energy in foods is then transformed into kinetic energy, which gives you the power to move.

Forms of Energy

There are many forms of energy that can be either potential or kinetic, such as chemical energy, gravitational energy, mechanical energy, radiant energy, thermal energy, sound energy, and electrical energy. Two types of potential energy are chemical energy and gravitational energy.

- **Chemical energy** is potential energy stored in the bonds of molecules. This energy is found in food, batteries, and combustible natural fuels such as coal and gas.

- **Gravitational energy** is the energy an object has because of its position in relation to Earth. Gravitational energy is dependent on mass and height. A book located on the top shelf of a bookcase has more gravitational energy than a book located on the bottom shelf. In other words, the higher an object is away from the center of Earth, the greater the gravitational energy.

Chemical and gravitational energy are summarized in the table.

Energy Type	Description	Examples
Chemical energy	potential energy stored in the bonds of molecules	gasoline, coal, food
Gravitational energy	Potential energy due to the downward pull of gravity	Books on a shelf

Kinetic energy is energy of motion. Any object that is in motion uses a form of kinetic energy. There are many types of kinetic energy.

- The **mechanical energy** of an object is the sum of its energy in motion and stored energy. An example of mechanical energy in use is a wind turbine. The kinetic energy of the wind is combined with the potential energy of the turbine to produce mechanical energy.

- **Radiant energy** is the energy of electromagnetic waves that travel through a medium such as air, water, or solid matter. Some examples of radiant energy include radio waves, X-rays, gamma rays, and light.

- **Thermal energy** is the vibration of atoms and molecules within a material. As the material's temperature increases, the intensity of molecular vibration causes collisions that release thermal energy. When thermal energy is transferred to or from an object, it is called heat. When combustion engines ignite fuel, chemical potential energy is converted to thermal energy.

- **Sound energy** is energy produced by vibrating sound waves moving through a medium. An example of sound energy is the plucking of a guitar string sending vibrating waves into the air around it. Sound energy requires a force to cause the object to vibrate.

- **Electrical energy** is the energy produced by the movement of electrons. Storm clouds release electrical energy in the form of lightning, which is similar to the static electricity created when you shuffle your feet across a heavy carpet while wearing socks.

The many forms of kinetic energy are summarized in the table below.

Kinetic Energy Type	Description	Examples
Mechanical	The sum of potential energy and kinetic energy in motion	Wind power generator, a moving car
Radiant	The energy of electromagnetic waves	Sunshine, X-rays
Thermal	The vibration of atoms and molecules within materials	Boiling water in a pot
Sound	The energy produced by vibrating sound waves moving through a medium	Clapping your hands, a car horn
Electrical	The energy produced by the movement of electrons	Lightning

Conservation of Energy

The energy that exists in the universe cannot be created or destroyed, although its form may change. Potential energy converts to kinetic energy and back again through cycles. This constant amount of energy is described by the law of conservation of energy. The **law of conservation of energy** states that the total amount of energy in the universe is constant.

Recall that gravitational potential energy (GPE) is the energy possessed by an object due to its mass or its position. For example, a boulder that begins to roll down from the top of a hill contains its maximum potential energy at the top of the hill. The higher that hilltop, the more potential energy there is within the boulder. This can be shown by using the equation for GPE.

$$GPE = m \times h \times g$$

where m = mass (kg), h = height (m), g = gravitational constant

The gravitational constant is 9.8 meters per second squared (m/s²). Energy is measured in joules (J). The GPE is affected by the object's vertical position on Earth—the higher the object, the greater the GPE.

Thus, a boulder that weighs 5,000 kg that is resting on a hill 100 m in height will have a GPE of approximately 4,900,000, or 4.9×10^6 J.

$$GPE = 5{,}000 \text{ kg} \times 100 \text{ m} \times 9.8 \text{ m/s}^2 = 4.9 \times 10^6 \text{ J}$$

As the boulder rolls down the hill, its kinetic energy increases and its potential energy decreases.

Recall that kinetic energy is the energy created by moving objects. The kinetic energy of an object depends upon the object's mass and velocity. The following equation is used for calculating kinetic energy:

$$KE = 0.5 \times m \times v^2$$

where m = mass (kg), v = velocity (m/s)

If the 5,000 kg boulder is rolling at a velocity of 5 m/s, its kinetic energy at that moment is 62,500 J.

$$KE = 0.5 \times 5{,}000 \text{ kg} \times (5 \text{ m/s})^2 = 62{,}500 \text{ J}$$

The conservation of energy states that the total amount of energy is constant. Therefore, the total energy of an object is the sum of its potential energy and kinetic energy. Recall that mechanical energy is the sum of an object's potential and kinetic energy. In this case, the total mechanical energy of the boulder is equal to the sum of its GPE plus its kinetic energy.

At the boulder's highest point on the hill, the total amount of energy is solely present as potential energy. As the boulder rolls down the hill, some of the potential energy is converted to kinetic energy. The height of the boulder from Earth is decreasing, which decreases the GPE. At the same time, the velocity of the boulder as it rolls increases, which increases its kinetic energy. When the boulder lands at the bottom of the hill, there is no more GPE and the kinetic energy is at its maximum. The total mechanical energy of the boulder is conserved as the boulder rolls down the hill.

We calculated the maximum GPE of the boulder at the top of the hill to be 4.9×10^6 J. Since the total amount of energy is constant and is equal to the sum of potential and kinetic energy, the maximum kinetic energy of the boulder as it crashes at the bottom of the hill must be equal to 4.9×10^6 J. You know the mass of the boulder is unchanged at 5,000 kg. Knowing this, you can determine the velocity of the boulder at the bottom of the hill. The kinetic energy equation can be used to determine the velocity of the boulder at the bottom of the hill by incorporating our known maximum kinetic energy of 4.9×10^6 J.

$$KE = 0.5 \times 5{,}000 \text{ kg (mass)} \times (5 \text{ m/s})^2 \text{ (velocity)}$$

$$0.5 \times 5{,}000 \text{ kg} \times v^2 = 4{,}900{,}000 \text{ J}$$

$$v^2 = 4{,}900{,}000 \text{ J} / (0.5 \times 5{,}000 \text{ kg})$$

$$v^2 = 1{,}960$$

$$v = \sqrt{1{,}960}$$

$$v = 44.27 \text{ m/s}$$

The boulder must reach the velocity of about 44.27 m/s as it crashes at the bottom of the hill, ensuring that the total energy is conserved.

EXERCISE 5

Energy

Directions: Choose the best answer to each question.

1. Which statement is true about energy?

   A. Kinetic energy is a form of stored energy.
   B. The potential energy of an object increases as the object moves.
   C. Thermal energy is released by charged particles.
   D. Potential energy is found in the nutrients we eat.

2. A crane lifts a 100-kg weight 10 m off the ground. The weight is released and falls to the ground. At the instant the weight is released, what is its GPE?

   A. 0 J
   B. 98 J
   C. 980 J
   D. 9,800 J

3. A baseball is thrown by the pitcher at a velocity of 50 m/s. The resulting kinetic energy from this action is equal to 187.5 J. What is the approximate weight of the baseball in kilograms?

   A. 0.015 kg
   B. 0.150 kg
   C. 1.500 kg
   D. 6.7 kg

Answers are on page 801.

Thermodynamics

Thermodynamics is the study of relationships between heat and other energy forms. The law of conservation of energy is the **first law of thermodynamics**. Another aspect of thermodynamics is the principle of which energy can be used. The **second law of thermodynamics** discusses the idea of **entropy**, which is the measure of disorder in a closed system containing energy. The less order in a system, the greater its entropy is.

In thermodynamics, entropy is given in terms of the heat transferred to or from a substance at a known temperature. Consider an ice cube taken from the freezer and placed on a kitchen counter. The counter and the surrounding air are warmer than the freezer. Over time, the ice cube melts because the heat of the countertop transfers thermal energy to the ice cube. One of the principles of the second law of thermodynamics is that thermal energy is transferred from an object of higher temperature to an object of lower temperature. This transfer of heat energy continues until both objects are the same temperature or there is uniformity in the system. Thermal energy can never be transferred from an object with a lower temperature to an object with a higher temperature.

EXERCISE 6

Thermodynamics

Directions: Choose the best answer to the question.

1. What is the name of the law that states that energy cannot be created or destroyed?

   A. Conservation of matter
   B. Newton's third law
   C. First law of thermodynamics
   D. Second law of thermodynamics

Answer is on page 801.

Forces and Interactions

When you move a chair from one spot to another, you are using energy to move that chair. Recall that energy is the ability to do work. To move an object, such as a chair, a force is required. A **force** is the pushing or pulling on an object. Once the chair is placed where you want it, no forces are at work. Another example of force is a satellite orbiting Earth. The satellite has a force pulling it toward the planet. When you push a lawnmower across the yard, you exert a force to complete this task.

When a moving object slows down, it is due to friction. **Friction** is a force that resists and opposes motion and has the result of slowing or stopping an object from moving. Galileo Galilei, the famous Italian astronomer, mathematician, and physicist, imagined a world where no friction forces existed. This allowed him to study only the simple forces needed to do work.

Simple Machines

When people say that they have to go to work, what does it mean? In everyday language, going to work is going to a location, such as an office, where one earns a paycheck. In scientific terms, **work** is the activity of a force being applied to move an object. The equation *Work (W) = Force (F) × distance (d)* measures the amount of work done to move an object. For instance, to lift a 100-pound barbell 5 feet off the ground, how much work is required?

Use the work equation to determine the answer:

$W = F \times d$

where $F = 100$ pounds and $d = 5$ feet

$W = (100 \text{ pounds}) \times (5 \text{ feet}) = 500 \text{ foot-pounds} = 500 \text{ ft-lbs}$

You have to do 500 ft-lbs of work to move the barbell.

Sometimes the force required to move objects goes beyond human strength, requiring assistance from some type of machine. The lever is one of the most common simple machines that many of us have used. A **lever** is a rod used to move an object. A crowbar and a seesaw are levers. The lever allows you to lift or move a heavier object than you would be able to by using just your muscles. The purpose of simple machines is to reduce the force you need to use to do work. Examples of the six types of simple machines are shown below.

Simple Machines

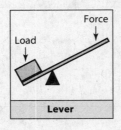

Lever

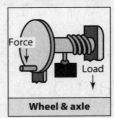

Wheel & axle

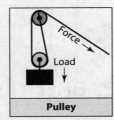

Pulley

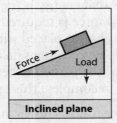

Inclined plane

Wedge

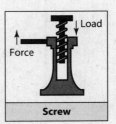

Screw

Each of these machines makes it easier to move heavy objects. What are some of the items around your house or at your job that look like these machines? What looks similar to a wedge or a pulley? The **wedge** is an inclined plane that moves. Examples of a wedge are an axe used to cut trees and logs or a doorstop. The **pulley** is a wheel with a cable attached to it. A crane has a pulley. Another example of a pulley is the weight machines at an exercise facility. A **screw** is an inclined plane wrapped around a rod. Examples are light bulb bases, construction screws, and jar lids. The **wheel and axle** is a simple machine consisting of a wheel mounted on an axle. A car's steering wheel, a doorknob, and a bicycle tire are examples of a wheel and axle.

The wedge and the screw are based on an inclined plane. An inclined plane is a ramp or a slope. For example, say that you own a motorcycle that will not start. You need to put it onto a truck to take to a mechanic. If the motorcycle weighs 500 pounds and the truck bed is 4 feet high, how much force would you need to apply to lift the motorcycle onto the truck bed? And how much easier would the job be if you pushed the motorcycle up a ramp?

Inclined Plane

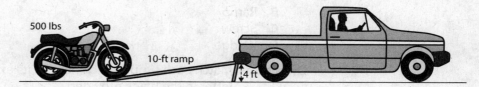

First, determine the amount of work involved in in simply lifting the motorcycle 4 feet to the truck bed. The amount of work (W) is calculated using the work equation:

$$W = F \times d$$

The force F that you would need to apply is equal to the weight of the motorcycle: 500 pounds. The distance d is 4 feet.

$$W = (500 \text{ pounds}) (4 \text{ feet}) = 2000 \text{ ft-lbs}$$

So lifting the motorcycle to the truck bed will be 2000 ft-lbs of work. Lifting it straight up will require 500 pounds of force. But what if you pushed the motorcycle up a 10-foot ramp instead? The same amount of work would be involved, but it would be spread over a longer distance (10 feet *vs.* 4 feet), so you would not need to apply as much force. Plug the numbers into the work equation:

$$W = F \times d$$

$$2000 \text{ ft-lbs} = (x \text{ pounds}) \times 10 \text{ feet}$$

$$2000 \text{ ft-lbs} \div 10 \text{ ft} = 200 \text{ pounds}$$

So now, instead of applying 500 pounds of force, with the ramp you would need to apply only 200 pounds of force to accomplish the same amount of work.

EXERCISE 7

Simple Machines

Directions: Choose the best answer to each question.

1. You are moving into a third-story apartment and have a grand piano weighing 800 lbs that needs to be moved. The third floor is 30 ft off the ground. How much work must be done to move the piano?

   A. 26.7 ft-lbs
   B. 267 ft-lbs
   C. 2,400 ft-lbs
   D. 24,000 ft-lbs

2. A knife is an example of which simple machine?

   A. Pulley
   B. Ramp
   C. Screw
   D. Wedge

Directions: Match each simple machine with its example by writing the correct letter in the blank provided.

3. _____ screw   **a.** doorknob

4. _____ pulley   **b.** doorstop

5. _____ lever   **c.** slope

6. _____ inclined plane   **d.** seesaw

7. _____ wedge   **e.** crane

8. _____ wheel and axle   **f.** light bulb

Answers are on page 801.

Newton's Laws of Motion

When you use a lawnmower, you exert a force on the lawnmower. Recall that a force is the pushing or pulling on an object. The amount of force necessary to push or pull an object depends on its mass. If an object cannot be moved by one force, an additional force may be added that results in the object being moved. For example, you try to move a desk but cannot due to its size. With the help of a friend, the desk gets moved. A net force was applied to move the desk. A **net force** is the sum of two or more forces being applied to set an object in motion.

When you push a lawnmower across tall grass, the friction of the grass requires you to push harder. The lawnmower moves because the force of pushing the lawnmower is greater than the force of friction. This reflects an unbalanced force. You are exerting a force on the lawnmower that is greater than the friction that pushes back. An **unbalanced force** results in a net force that is not equal to zero. If you push the lawnmower against a tree, the lawnmower will not move. The forces that both you and the tree are exerting on the lawnmower are equal. This reflects a **balanced force** where the net forces are equal to zero. An object will not move if the net force is zero.

In the 17th century the English physicist Sir Isaac Newton developed a theory about the movement of objects and their interaction with forces. Newton studied the works of previous scientists to explain how objects act with regard to motion. These discoveries have been verified over time and have become our way of understanding motion. These discoveries are now known as Newton's laws of motion.

The classic example of Newton's first law is a skateboarder. If a person is standing on the skateboard and not moving, that person will continue to be motionless until a force is exerted. Once the force is exerted upon the skateboarder, the skateboarder will stay in motion until friction slows the skateboarder down. Newton understood that it took a force to set an object in motion in the same manner that it takes a force to stop or slow an object that is moving. Newton's first law demonstrates the motion of objects when an unbalanced force is exerted upon that object. **Newton's first law of motion** states that an object at rest tends to stay at rest unless an unbalanced force is applied, and an object in motion tends to stay in motion unless acted on by an unbalanced force.

Newton's First Law of Motion

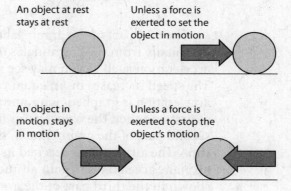

An object at rest stays at rest

Unless a force is exerted to set the object in motion

An object in motion stays in motion

Unless a force is exerted to stop the object's motion

A force can be applied to change a moving object's speed or direction. The change in motion of an object is known as **acceleration**. We use the term *acceleration* in our daily lives when discussing increasing the speed of a vehicle. Acceleration happens when an object slows down, speeds up, or changes direction. When you push a lawnmower across the yard, you are applying a force that accelerates the lawnmower. If a ball is rolling down a hill and you catch it, you are applying a force that changes the ball's acceleration. The relationship between force, acceleration, and an object's mass is addressed by Newton's second law. **Newton's second law of motion** states if an object is acted upon by a force, it will accelerate in the direction of that force. In mathematical terms, Newton's second law is stated as:

$$F = m \times a$$

where F = force, m = mass, and a = acceleration

Force is measured in Newtons, or N, each of which is equivalent to kg•m/s². The equation can be used to determine any of the terms as long as you know two of the three terms. You can calculate the force exerted on an object of a known mass affected by a known acceleration. Or the equation can be used to calculate the mass of an object for a known force and acceleration. Finally, acceleration can be calculated for a known mass and force applied.

To support Newton's second law of motion, the acceleration of an object can be graphed as a function of time, as shown in the graph below.

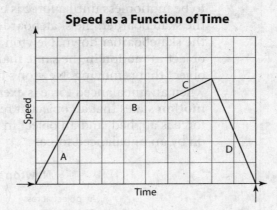

Speed as a Function of Time

The first part of the graph, labeled *A*, shows a straight line rising diagonally from the coordinates 0,0 on the *x-y* axis. This line shows a steady acceleration such as you may see when an airplane takes off from a runway. The speed increases by an equal value over a period of time. Sometimes this acceleration is graphed as an upward curve if the speed increases slowly at first and then the object gains more speed in a short period of time. The second part of the graph, line *B*, shows an unchanging speed over a period of time. The airplane has reached its cruising speed at a certain altitude. If the airplane accelerates to gain altitude, its speed over time may be graphed as shown in the third part of the graph above. A gradual acceleration is a slight increase of speed, as shown in line *C*. Finally, as the airplane descends to its final destination, there is a steady deceleration (line *D*) until the airplane touches down and halts its movement.

EXERCISE 8

Newton's Laws of Motion

Directions: Choose the best answer to each question.

1. A baseball is hit high into the air. As the ball travels downward, the outfielder positions himself under the ball, ready to catch it. How much force will the outfielder need to exert on the ball if the ball weighs 0.150 kg and has an acceleration of 10 m/s^2 as it falls?

   A. 0.15 N
   B. 1.5 N
   C. 15.0 N
   D. 150 N

2. Which term is defined by a push or a pull?

   A. Acceleration
   B. Force
   C. Friction
   D. Mass

Answers are on page 801.

Momentum

A motorcycle and a bicycle are traveling at the same speed. Suddenly, a deer runs across the road, causing both riders to stop their vehicles. The bicyclist stops a lot quicker than the motorcycle because the motorcycle has more mass. A larger mass creates a bigger momentum. Sports reporters use the term *momentum* to describe the unstoppable nature of a winning team. **Momentum**, known as mass in motion, is a measure of how hard it is to stop an object. In physics, momentum is the product of an object's mass and its velocity. **Velocity** is the speed and the direction an object is traveling. The equation for momentum is:

$$p = m \times v$$

where p = momentum, m = mass, and v = velocity

The unit measurement of p is kg•m/s.

Two vehicles of equal mass traveling at different speeds will have different momentum. The vehicle moving faster will have a greater momentum and a more difficult time stopping its motion. Vehicles of different mass but similar speeds also have different momentum; the larger vehicle will take a longer distance to stop. For example, suppose that two vehicles are traveling in the same direction. Vehicle A, traveling at 16 m/s, has a mass of 4,000 kg. Vehicle B, traveling at 17 m/s, has a mass of 7,000 kg. Which vehicle has the greater momentum? Use the momentum equation, $p = m \times v$, to determine which vehicle has the greater momentum.

Vehicle A

$p = 4,000 \text{ kg} \times 16 \text{ m/s} = 64,000 \text{ kg} \bullet \text{m/s}$

Vehicle B

$p = 7,000 \text{ kg} \times 17 \text{ m/s} = 119,000 \text{ kg} \bullet \text{m/s}$

Vehicle B has greater momentum than Vehicle A.

Momentum is an important factor when looking at collisions. One object strikes another and the result of the collision depends on the direction of the velocity. In any collision, one object transfers momentum to another object. There are two types of collisions—inelastic and elastic. An **inelastic collision** occurs when the two objects stick together after the collision. **Elastic collisions** occur when two objects strike each other but do not stick together. The following image shows the different ways elastic collisions occur.

Elastic Collisions

In each of these diagrams, each ball has the same mass. In addition, the velocity of the balls is occurring along a similar plane. In row "a," the dark-colored ball is traveling slowly toward the white ball that sits idle. An object at rest does not have any momentum since its velocity is zero. As when a cue ball strikes a billiard ball, after the collision the momentum of the first ball is transferred entirely to the second ball. The first ball stops and the second ball rolls away.

In row "b," the two balls are rolling toward each other at a similar velocity. Upon striking one another, each ball transfers its momentum is to the other. Given that the balls' masses are the same, the transfer of momentum means that each ball will take the directional velocity from the other. The dark-colored ball that was moving from left to right now shifts direction backward, while the opposite happens to the white ball.

In row "c," both balls are moving in the same direction, but the dark-colored ball is bearing down on the white ball. Upon collision, momentum is transferred from one ball to the other essentially resulting in a switch of velocity between the two. When a speeding car hits a slower car from behind, the car in front suddenly speeds up while the trailing car slows down.

In all of these cases, the total momentum of the system cannot change. Total momentum equals the momentum of object 1 plus the momentum of object 2, or $p_{total} = (m_1 \times v_1) + (m_2 \times v_2)$. Total momentum is measured prior to the collision and after the collision.

The **law of conservation of momentum** states that the total momentum of two objects before the collision is equal to the total momentum of the two objects after the collision. When momentum transfers from one object to another, the total amount of momentum these objects had before the collision must equal the amount of momentum afterward, or $p_{ta} = p_{tb}$.

EXERCISE 9

Momentum

Directions: Choose the best answer to each question.

1. After a collision, two objects of equal mass of 10 kg have different momentums. Object A has a momentum totaling 50 kg·m/s. Object B has a momentum of 100 kg·m/s. Prior to the collision, object A had a velocity of 8 m/s. What was object B's velocity prior to the collision?

   A. 7 m/s
   B. 8 m/s
   C. 10 m/s
   D. 18 m/s

2. A car and a bicycle are traveling at the same velocity. Which statement is true?

   A. The car and bicycle have the same momentum.
   B. The car and bicycle have the same mass.
   C. The car has more momentum than the bicycle.
   D. The bicycle has more momentum than the car.

Answers are on page 801.

Forces and Energy

There is a relationship between energy and forces. For example, rubbing a balloon on a wool sweater will cause the balloon to become electrically charged. This action increases the electrostatic potential energy on the surface of the balloon. Then if you hold the balloon above your head, your hair will become attracted to the balloon, effectively standing on end. This attractive force is called **electrostatic force**. The electrostatic force exerted by the balloon caused your hair to become attracted to the balloon. Charged objects exert electrostatic forces on other objects regardless if those objects are charged.

Objects have charges in one of two ways. An object with more protons than electrons is **positively charged**. Conversely, an object with more electrons than protons is **negatively charged**. The rule of "opposites attract" is the simplest way to describe the relationship between charged objects as shown in the diagram.

Attraction of Charged Objects

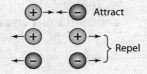

When two charged objects are coming into close proximity with each other, a pushing or pulling force will occur. Consider the following scenario of electrostatic potential energy. Two similarly charged objects will require work to bring them together. This work increases the potential energy of both objects. The opposite occurs when you attempt to separate oppositely charged objects. Work is required to increase the distance between these objects, and the potential energy of the objects increases.

The electrostatic force between two charged objects follows Newton's third law, or the action-reaction law. **Newton's third law** states that for every action, there is an equal and opposite reaction. In the diagram above, the positively charged object exerts a force upon the negatively charged object. Because opposites attract, both objects exert an equal force on one another, bringing them together. The similarly charged objects in the diagram reflect equally exerted forces by both objects to repel one another.

EXERCISE 10

Forces and Energy

Directions: Fill in the blanks.

1. Newton's third law states that two negatively charged objects will exert a force that is _____ and _____ on each other.

Answer is on page 802.

Noncontact Forces

When you jump off a diving board, you fall into the pool. A person jumping out of an airplane falls to Earth. Both the diver and the skydiver are affected by gravity. **Gravity** is the force that Earth exerts on objects to pull them toward the ground. This is an example of a **noncontact force**, or a force that is applied from one object to another without touching. Celestial objects, such as Earth, have a noncontact gravitational pull that pulls objects toward them.

Another one of Newton's theories is the **law of universal gravitation**, which states that the amount of the force of gravity between two objects depends on their masses and the distance between them. As the mass increases for either or both of the objects, the gravitational value increases. The gravitational pull will decrease as the two objects are separated by a greater distance. Newton's law of universal gravitation is represented by this mathematical equation:

$$F_g = G \times (m_1 \times m_2) / r^2$$

where F_g = the gravitational force, G = Newton's gravitational constant, m_1 and m_2 = the mass of the two objects, and r = the distance between the two centers of the objects

Gravitational forces exist no matter the mass of the objects in question. Each of us has gravitational forces pulling on us from larger objects and our mass pulling on smaller objects. These gravitational forces are extremely small and therefore practically impossible to detect. The heavier an object is on the surface of Earth, the greater the gravitational force.

Noncontact forces come in other forms aside from gravity. **Magnetic forces** are exerted from magnets onto certain metals. Electrostatic force is an exchange of positive and negative charges when two surfaces come in contact with each other. An electric field surrounds an electrically charged object and exerts this noncontact force on another electrically charged object. Depending on the positive or negative electric field of the second object, the electrostatic force exerted either attracts or repels the two. Recall that opposite charges attract while similar charges repel.

Prior to the discovery by the French physicist Charles Augustin de Coulomb in 1785, the attractive force between objects was thought to be qualitative in which a positive and negative charge is present. **Coulomb's law** describes the strength of the electrostatic force quantitatively between two distant objects. As the distance between two objects increases, the electrostatic force decreases, an inverse relationship.

Noncontact Forces

Directions: Choose the best answer to the question.

1. A spaceship heading for Mars is launched from the surface of Earth. Initially, the force of gravity on the spaceship is equal to its mass times 9.8 m/s^2. The spaceship leaves Earth's atmosphere and travels through space past the distance of the moon. Which sentence describes the gravitational force exerted on the spaceship by Earth?

   A. The gravitational force exerted on the spaceship does not change.
   B. The gravitational force exerted on the spaceship decreases.
   C. The gravitational force exerted on the spaceship increases.
   D. Not enough information is provided to make a determination.

Answer is on page 802.

Electricity and Magnetism

Our world today would be very different if American inventor Thomas Edison had not worked on electricity. Most of the items we take for granted, such as cars, televisions, and computers, would not be in existence.

In 1882 Edison built the first electric power plant. When you turn on the television, you are starting the flow of electricity to the television set. **Electricity** is the movement of electrons from one place to another. Electricity flows in a complete circle called a circuit. This flow of electricity is called an **electric current**. If the circuit is broken, the electric current will find a different path from its normal path. Sometimes this can become dangerous and possibly start a fire. Electricity and magnetism are strongly related. Electricity can be used to produce a magnet. Magnets can be used to make electricity.

An object that can attract iron, a metal, is considered **magnetic**. Many of the devices we use daily such as hairdryers and computer hard drives contain powered magnets, which have a magnetic field. A **magnetic field** is the area surrounding the magnet. Magnetic fields also surround electric currents. When you hold a compass near a wire that is carrying a current, the compass needle will move as it is affected by the magnetic field around the electric circuit. As the current increases in the wire, the magnetic field becomes stronger. **Electromagnets** are powered magnets built by wrapping a current-carrying wire, such as copper or aluminum, around a core made of iron or a similar material.

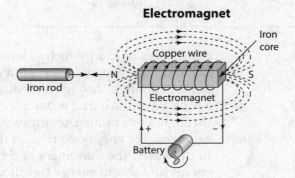

Electromagnet

In this diagram, the battery or power source connects a positive charge on one end of the coil and a negative charge on the other end of the coil. The electrical force of the coil converts the iron core into an electromagnet, exerting a noncontact force on the iron rod. The core produces a north and south pole, similar to the magnetic forces that are exerted from Earth. An electromagnet can be manipulated to create a greater magnetic force. The more loops the coil makes around the core, the greater is the strength of the magnetic field. In addition, increasing the electric current through the coil also increases the magnetic field's strength.

EXERCISE 12

Electricity and Magnetism

Directions: Match the words on the left with their description on the right. Write the correct letter on the line.

1. _____ electric current   **a.** object attracted to metal

2. _____ electricity   **b.** flow of electricity

3. _____ electromagnet   **c.** magnet built by wrapping a coil around a metal core

4. _____ magnetic   **d.** movement of electrons

Answers are on page 802.

Waves

Some types of energy such as light and sound move through space or substances as a wave. A **wave** is a disturbance that transfers energy from one point to another through a medium. A **medium** is a material through which a wave passes. Air and water are examples of mediums that waves move through. For example, tossing a stone into a pool of still water creates ripples or waves. The energy exerted on the surface of the water creates waves in the water. The movement of the waves in water is similar to how light energy and sound energy travel. Sound energy travels through a medium by vibrating the molecules in the material.

It is important to understand that when an energy wave passes through a medium, the matter in the medium may vibrate, but it is not set in motion the way a baseball moves when struck by a bat. After the wave passes through, the matter in the medium returns to its original position. In this way, waves are different from the other kinds of energy discussed previously.

Properties of Waves

Waves can be described by how they transfer energy. They can be classified based on whether or not they transfer energy through a vacuum. The two types of waves are mechanical and electromagnetic. **Mechanical waves** are waves that use matter to transfer energy. A wave caused from a stone splashing in a pool of water is an example of a mechanical wave. Mechanical waves can travel through solids, liquids, and gases. However, the main difference between mechanical waves and electromagnetic waves is that electromagnetic waves do not need a medium to be able to travel. **Electromagnetic waves** are waves that can travel through a vacuum. Light energy is an example of a wave that can travel through a vacuum as light from the sun. Surrounding stars send light energy to Earth through the void of space. Unlike electromagnetic waves, mechanical waves cannot travel through a vacuum.

Another way to describe waves is the relationship of the direction of the wave as compared to the direction of the disturbance that creates the wave. Three types of waves are transverse, longitudinal, and surface waves as shown in the illustration.

Types of Waves

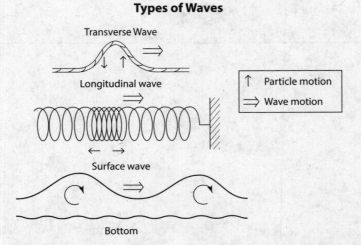

A **transverse wave** occurs when the disturbance is perpendicular to the direction of the wave. For example, if you tied a rope to a doorknob and then shook it up and down, a transverse wave would run the length of the rope from your hand to the doorknob. The motion of your hand is vertical while the resulting wave travels horizontally. In the following diagram, the original position of the rope before the wave occurred is called the **equilibrium position**. The highest points and lowest points of a transverse wave are **crests** and **troughs,** respectively. The distance from the equilibrium position to the crest is the wave's **amplitude**. The distance between two crests or two troughs is the **wavelength**.

Parts of a Transverse Wave

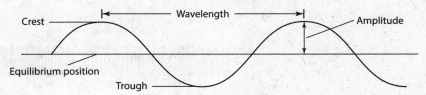

Several measurements can help describe the speed and intensity of a wave. Counting the number of wave crests that pass a certain point each second provides the wave's **frequency**, which is measured in hertz (Hz). One hertz is equal to one cycle per second. The **velocity** of a wave is the distance a wave travels every second, measured in meters per second. The time it takes a wave to complete a full cycle from crest to crest is a wave's **period**. A wave's frequency is unchanged as a wave passes from one medium to another.

An inverse relationship exists between a wave's frequency and period. With this equation, you can calculate either the frequency or the period, depending on the known value. The equation is:

$$f = 1/T$$

where f = the frequency and T = the period

For example, if a bird pecks at a tree three times a second, what is the frequency? The frequency is 3 Hz. Each peck must be for one-third of the time. The period of the bird pecking is 0.33 s. The difference between frequency and period is that frequency measures rate and period measures time.

In visible light waves, frequency provides the colors that we see. A stoplight sends a wave of red light through the air in the direction of your car, and you see the color red as the wave passes through the windshield. However, as the light wave passes into the glass, its speed decreases. The speed of a wave is equal to the product of the frequency and the wavelength. For example, what is the speed of a wave with a frequency of 70 Hz and a wavelength of 8 m?

$$v = f \times \lambda$$

where v = wave speed, f = frequency, and λ = wavelength

f = 70 Hz or 70/s λ = 8 m

v = 70/s $\times$ 8 m = 560 m/s

The wave speed is 560 m/s.

We know that a light wave's frequency does not change as it passes from air to glass, but its speed does. If the wave speed is reduced, then the wavelength and speed must be directly proportional.

A **longitudinal wave** causes the molecules in a medium to move parallel to the direction of the wave. Instead of a rope tied to a doorknob, imagine a long spring attached to the doorknob. The wave disturbance causes the coils of the spring to compress and then stretch farther apart before returning the spring to its original position. This type of wave describes how sound passes through a medium. An earthquake is another type of longitudinal wave.

Longitudinal Wave

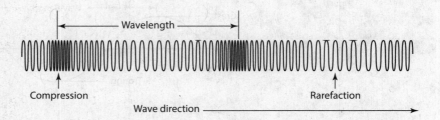

Whereas transverse waves have crests and troughs, longitudinal waves have compressions and rarefactions. At rest, the spring's coils are spaced evenly. The illustration shows that the wave produces **compression** or closeness in the spring, followed by **rarefactions**, or the expansion of the spring. As with transverse waves, the wavelength is measured between two points of compression.

A **surface wave** is a wave in which the medium moves in a circular motion. It differs from the transverse and longitudinal waves because the medium does not travel perpendicularly or parallel to the direction of the wave. For example, waves in the ocean cause circular rifts in the water primarily at the surface. This motion does not affect water deep below the wave. Although watching a wave in the ocean gives the appearance of a transverse wave, its properties as a surface wave are different.

Surface Wave

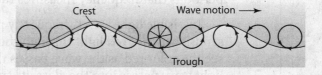

EXERCISE 13

Properties of Waves

Directions: Fill in the correct terms to complete the following sentences.

1. One end of a 3-m long rope is tied to a fixed point on a wall. When you shake the other end of the rope up and down, you create a _____ wave.

2. Using a 3-m rope that is attached to the wall, each time you shake the rope up and down, the wave created takes three seconds to reach the wall. What is the velocity of the wave you created? _____ m/s

3. An earthquake or other seismic activity is a type of wave, similar to the wave properties of a coil that moves through the Earth as a series of _____ and _____.

4. The height of a wave, measured from the equilibrium position to the _____ of the wave, is known as the wave's _____.

Answers are on page 802.

Digital Information and Waves

Music recording technology has evolved over time from analog to digital. Analog audio recordings, such as defunct VCR tapes and music records, are created from recording continuous changes in sound. The sound waves captured by a microphone are converted to an electronic voltage representing the changes in frequency and amplitude. These electronic voltages burn an image of the sound into a tape or vinyl record. The playback of these recordings comes close to reproducing the original sound waves. But there is a disadvantage to analog recordings. The analog recording over time will degrade.

However, digital recording has replaced analog because of its efficiency and accuracy of the stored information. Unlike the continuous recording of the analog process, digital recording samples amplitude and frequency at certain time intervals. These samples are captured in **binary form**, which is a series of ones and zeroes that describes the information that is captured.

The benefit of storing information digitally is that the information cannot be easily damaged or corrupted. In an analog system, the continuous recording can be corrupted because the data is stored on a magnetic device such as a tape. These magnetic tapes stretch and wear over time, which can result in a continuous wave of data that does not sound like the original recording. With digital data stored as ones and zeroes, the pulses of information can still be recognized even if some of the binary information is lost.

Another benefit of digital information is the speed of duplication. To duplicate information stored on an analog medium, the entire recording must be played back and recorded simultaneously. With digital information duplication, the recording does not need to be played back. It only requires that the reader and writer recognize the discrete low and high signal pulses. This function of copying digital information eliminates a great deal of corruption from one copy to another. Conversely, copying analog information can cause a great deal of corruption as each additional copy is made.

With digital information being stored as values of ones and zeroes, enhancing this information only requires tweaking the strings of binary data. In addition, digital systems are a great deal faster than analog systems at retrieving and configuring data. Finally, advanced technology benefits digital information because instead of using moving parts to decipher data, closed circuitry is used to eliminate wear and tear on the reading and writing devices.

The low cost of digital systems allows for a greater amount of data to be stored. But one disadvantage of digital systems compared to analog systems is that companies and consumers that use digital systems must spend more money on protecting data. Because digital information is stored electronically instead of on an analog tape, theft of data can occur. A hacker at a remote location can break into a digital system to access data that previously may have been stored on a magnetic tape that was inaccessible to outsiders. Lastly, digital data can be lost at the click of a mouse. Analog data stored on magnetic tapes must be physically destroyed to be lost.

The sheer amount of data stored for each bit of information has increased as technology improves. Transferring this data from one location to another requires a large amount of **bandwidth**, which is the amount of data that can be transferred each second.

EXERCISE 14

Digital Information and Waves

Directions: Choose the best answer to the question.

1. Which is NOT a benefit of storing information digitally versus using analog systems?

   A. State-of-the-art closed circuitry
   B. Better protection of information
   C. Information not as easily corrupted
   D. Speed of reproducing information

Answer is on page 802.

Electromagnetic Radiation

What do cell phones, microwave ovens, and X-ray machines have in common? They all use waves in the **electromagnetic spectrum**. The electromagnetic spectrum ranks the electromagnet waves from lowest energy/longest wavelength to highest energy/shortest wavelength. The energy put out by this electromagnetic wave or radiation spreads out as it travels, or radiates. The waves interpreted by your car stereo, the light generated from your desk lamp, and the heat generated by your microwave oven occur because of electromagnetic radiation. The following diagram shows the spectrum of electromagnetic radiation. Radio waves have the longest wavelength in the spectrum. Their waves can be longer than a football field. On the other end of the spectrum are gamma rays. They have the shortest wavelength with the most energy. Visible light, in the middle of the spectrum, can travel through a vacuum and through mediums such as water, air, and glass.

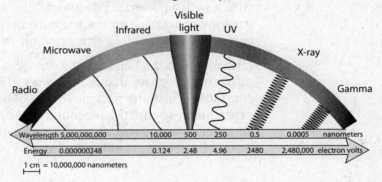

Electromagnetic Spectrum

Electromagnetic radiation behaves just like any other type of wave energy. Waves can be reflected, refracted, and diffracted. Electromagnetic radiation can be reflected just like light hitting a mirror. **Reflection** occurs when a wave strikes an object and bounces back to its source. An echo is an example of a sound reflection.

Many times when listening to a car radio, the radio signal gets weak. This is known as interference. **Interference** takes place when a solid object blocks the waves of electromagnetic radiation from being received. In addition, electromagnetic radiation can be refracted as in the case of light passing through a prism as shown in the following diagram. **Refraction** is the bending of a wave as it moves from one medium to another medium. White light going through a prism will separate into many different colors, as shown.

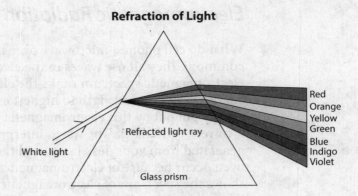

Refraction of Light

Refracted light ray

White light

Glass prism

Red
Orange
Yellow
Green
Blue
Indigo
Violet

The German-born physicist Albert Einstein proposed that light is emitted as tiny particles called **photons**. Over the past century, scientists conducted experiments that support Einstein's particle theory. The photoelectric effect is a phenomenon discovered that supports Einstein's work. The **photoelectric effect** is observed when light shines on a metal object and electrons are emitted from the metal. If a surface of metal is struck with a powerful photon of light, an electron can be separated from its atom, generating an electric current. Photoelectric cells found in solar energy collectors utilize this principle through Einstein's theory.

Diffraction is the bending of a wave. Scientific experiments have used diffraction to prove that light can act like a wave. This might seem to contradict Einstein's particle theory of light. However, depending on the experiment, scientists have found that light can behave as either a wave or a particle stream. This discovery suggests that electromagnetic radiation cannot be defined as either a wave or a particle stream.

EXERCISE 15

Electromagnetic Radiation

Directions: Fill in the correct terms to complete the sentence.

1. The photoelectric effect supported Einstein's theory that light is a
_____ wave. The opposing wave theory of light was proven
through the use of _____.

Directions: Choose the best answer to the question.

2. Sunlight entering the water of a swimming pool changes direction as the rays pass from air to water, distorting the appearance of objects underwater. What wave behavior is this?

   A. Diffraction
   B. Reflection
   C. Refraction
   D. Interference

Answers are on page 802.

Effects of Electromagnetic Radiation

Radio waves, microwaves, light, and gamma rays are types of electromagnetic radiation. The intensity of electromagnetic radiation differs in each of these types of waves. For example, radio waves contain the least amount of electromagnetic radiation because they have long wavelengths and low frequencies. Gamma rays are the most dangerous type of electromagnetic radiation because of their short wavelengths and high frequencies.

When microwaves and light waves are absorbed into matter such as water or other solids, thermal energy or heat is created. Shorter-wavelength electromagnetic radiation, such as gamma rays, x-rays, and ultraviolet rays, can cause damage to living cells. This occurs with overexposure to natural light without proper UV protection like sunscreen and sunglasses. Fortunately, Earth's ozone layer protects us from most of the sun's UV rays sent to our planet. Without the ozone layer, most living things on Earth might be destroyed by the power of electromagnetic radiation.

EXERCISE 16

Effects of Electromagnetic Radiation

Directions: Choose the best answer to the question.

1. According to their position on the electromagnetic spectrum, which types of waves can cause damage to living cells?

   A. x-rays and microwaves
   B. microwaves and gamma rays
   C. infrared rays and gamma rays
   D. x-rays and gamma rays

Answer is on page 802.

Matter and Chemical Interactions

If you look around your family room, what would you see? The room will contain objects, such as a table, a lamp, and possibly a bookcase. What do these objects have in common? They are all matter. **Matter** is a substance that occupies space and has mass. Matter is found in four different states—solid, liquid, gas, and plasma. Recall that water exists in three states of matter as ice (solid), water (liquid), and vapor (gas). **Plasma** is a gaseous state containing a significant number of electrically charged particles. But it is rare on Earth. Celestial stars including our sun are composed of plasma.

Atoms and Their Properties

Everything around you is made of matter. But what makes up matter? Matter is composed of tiny particles called atoms. An **atom** is the smallest unit of matter and is the basic unit of elements. In the center of the atom is the **nucleus**, which contains positively charged **protons** and noncharged **neutrons**. Surrounding the nucleus are **electrons**, which are negatively charged particles. Electrons orbit the nucleus in a series of levels called shells. There are always two electrons in the first shell, and no more than eight electrons in each of the following shells until the electron count is satisfied. The outermost shell is where atoms combine with each other.

Over the past century, many new elements have been discovered. There are 92 natural elements. The remaining 30 elements were created by scientists. An **element** is a substance that cannot be broken down into simpler substances. An element is defined by its atomic number. The **atomic number** is the number of protons in the nucleus of an atom. You might be familiar with common elements such as hydrogen, oxygen, and iron. For example, each atom of the element oxygen has the same number of protons, which is eight. The aluminum atom has the atomic number 13, which means that it has 13 protons in its nucleus. Aluminum also has 13 electrons that surround the nucleus. In order for an element to have a neutral charge, the number of protons has to be equal to the number of electrons.

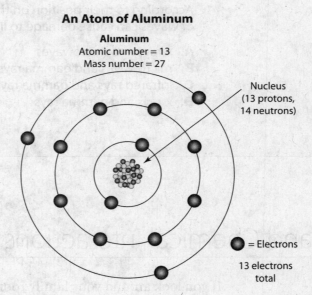

An Atom of Aluminum

Aluminum
Atomic number = 13
Mass number = 27

Nucleus
(13 protons,
14 neutrons)

= Electrons

13 electrons
total

Scientists identify atoms by the atomic number. The elements hydrogen and sodium have the atomic numbers 1 and 11, respectively, because their nuclei have 1 proton and 11 protons, respectively.

Isotopes

Although all atoms of a specific element have the same number of protons, each individual atom can have a different number of neutrons. This means that atoms of the same element can have different masses. Atoms that have the same atomic number but different masses are called **isotopes**. The atom's **mass number** is the sum of its protons and neutrons. Each kind of isotope has a different mass number. For example, hydrogen has three kinds of isotopes, labeled H-1, H-2, and H-3.

	H-1	H-2	H-3
Number of Protons	1	1	1
Number of Neutrons	0	1	2
Number of Electrons	1	1	1
Mass Number	1	2	3

The most common hydrogen atom has one proton and no neutrons, so its mass number is 1. This hydrogen isotope is labeled H-1. When an isotope of hydrogen has one proton and one neutron, it is labeled H-2. Very rare hydrogen isotopes, labeled H-3, have one proton and two neutrons.

The Periodic Table

Charting and organizing the elements was the work of several scientists. One notable scientist, Dmitri Mendeleev, developed a periodic table similar to today's version. Elements are ordered in rows, or **periods**, from left to right by an increasing number of protons in their nucleus. The columns of the table, or **groups**, organize elements with similar chemical properties due to a common number of electrons in the outermost shell. This organization of the periodic table is based on the periodic law. The **periodic law** states that as the atomic number increases, physical and chemical properties of the elements are found to repeat. Here is the current periodic table of the elements:

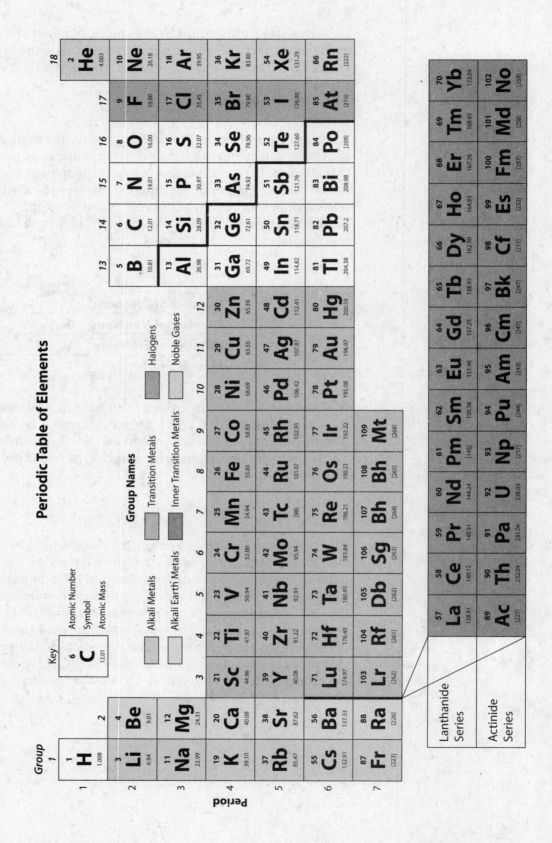

Periodic Table of Elements

Each element in the table is separated in its own box and is labeled by the symbol representing that element. The number above the element's symbol is the atomic number. The number below the element's symbol is the **atomic mass**, or the average weight of all the isotopes for that element.

Similar properties repeat as the atomic number increases for elements in a group. For example, the first five Group 1 elements are hydrogen (H), lithium (Li), sodium (Na), potassium (K), and rubidium (Rb). Their atomic numbers are 1, 3, 11, 19, and 37, respectively. This group contains chemically active elements because each element has one electron in its outermost shell. This allows the atoms of these elements to bond easily with atoms of other elements. Sodium reacts explosively with water, and rubidium catches fire once exposed to air.

Physical and Chemical Properties

How would you describe the physical characteristics of a car? Would you mention the color, type, and weight of the car? Color, weight, and type are descriptions of the car's physical properties. A **physical property** is a characteristic of a substance that can be observed without changing the substance into another substance. Examples of physical properties are color, density, boiling point, melting point, and states of matter. Recall that matter can be a solid, liquid, or gas. In addition to having physical properties, elements also have chemical properties. **Chemical properties** of an element determine whether an element has the ability to form new substances. The ability to burn is an example of a chemical property. Another example is the ability to rust.

Solutions

When you mix sugar in your iced tea or coffee, you are creating a solution. A **solution** is formed when one substance dissolves in another substance. When you mix sugar in your drink, sugar is known as a solute. A **solute** is the substance being dissolved. Your liquid drink is known as the **solvent,** or the substance that the solute dissolves in. Other examples of solutions are antifreeze, salt water, and lemonade.

Have you noticed that dissolving sugar in iced tea is difficult, but the same amount of sugar will dissolve easily in hot tea? The reason is that temperature affects the way in which solutes will dissolve in water or other solvents. Generally, most substances will dissolve in greater quantity in hot water than in cold water. The term for how a substance dissolves is **solubility**.

EXERCISE 17

Atoms and Their Properties

Directions: Match the description with the correct term. Write the letter of the term on the line.

1. _____ a negatively charged particle   **a.** nucleus

2. _____ a positively charged particle   **b.** neutron

3. _____ a noncharged particle   **c.** isotope

4. _____ the number of protons in a nucleus   **d.** electron

5. _____ the center of an atom   **e.** atomic number

6. _____ elements with differing mass but the same atomic number   **f.** proton

Directions: Choose the best answer to the question.

7. Which statement about Group 1 of the periodic table is FALSE?

     A. Every element in the group has the same number of protons.
     B. Every element has the same number of electrons in its outer shell.
     C. The elements in the group have similar properties.
     D. The elements in the group can bond with another element easily.

Answers are on page 802.

Conservation of Mass

Similar to the laws of conservation of energy and matter, the **law of conservation of mass** states that when chemical reactions occur, the mass of a closed system must stay the same. In other words, the mass before the chemical reaction must equal the mass after the chemical reaction. A closed system is one that particles cannot escape or enter.

Water molecules are produced when hydrogen gas reacts with oxygen gas. The chemical equation that describes the reaction is:

2 hydrogen atoms + 1 oxygen atom → 1 water molecule

Making a large quantity of water requires an accurate measurement of a large quantity of hydrogen and oxygen atoms. To simplify counting of atoms and molecules, scientists use a unit of measurement called the mole. A **mole** is the mass of a pure substance that contains 6.02×10^{23} atoms or molecules. The number 602 is followed by 21 zeroes.

The mass of a mole of atoms or molecules is measured in grams. The atomic mass of a particular atom is equal to one mole of that atom in grams. For example, the atomic mass of hydrogen is 1.008. A mole of hydrogen atoms has a mass equal to 1.008 grams of hydrogen. Oxygen has an atomic mass of 15.999; therefore, a mole of oxygen has a mass equal to 15.999 grams of oxygen atoms. With this information, you can alter the chemical reaction equation for water to look like this:

2 hydrogen atoms + 1 oxygen atom → 1 water molecule

becomes

2 moles of hydrogen atoms + 1 mole of oxygen atoms → 1 mole of water molecules

which equals

2.016 (1.008 × 2) g hydrogen + 15.999 g oxygen → 18.015 g water

The sum of the masses of the reacting particles equals the resulting mass of the water produced. This supports the law of conservation of mass.

EXERCISE 18

Conservation of Mass

Directions: Use the periodic table of the elements and the following chemical equation to answer the question.

Na + Cl → NaCl

1. Sodium (Na) and chlorine (Cl) combine to form sodium chloride, or table salt. If one mole of sodium atoms and one mole of chlorine atoms are used, how many grams of sodium chloride would be created?

_____

Answer is on page 803.

Chemical Bonding

Sodium chloride is formed by a chemical reaction. A **chemical reaction** is a chemical change that creates a new substance with different properties. For example, when a sodium atom (Na) bonds with a chlorine atom (Cl), a new substance, sodium chloride (NaCl), is formed. Sodium chloride is a **compound**, which is a pure substance that cannot be separated into other compounds by physical methods. Sodium chloride has properties that are different from those of the individual sodium and chlorine atoms. Sodium chloride is a white crystal solid, whereas sodium is a silvery metal and chlorine is a yellow-green gas.

When two or more different atoms combine to form a compound, the compound consists of particles known as molecules. **Molecules** are made up of two or more atoms that are bonded together. A **chemical bond** is a force that holds together two or more atoms. Atoms form chemical bonds either by sharing electrons or by transferring electrons. The two main types of chemical bonding are ionic and covalent.

Ionic Bonding

Sodium and chlorine atoms are electrically neutral because they have the same number of electrons as they have protons. When the sodium and chlorine atoms bond together, the sodium atom donates or transfers an electron from its outer shell to the chlorine atom. With the donation of the electron, the sodium atom now has more protons than electrons, making it a positively charged ion. An **ion** is an electrically charged atom, either positive or negative. The transfer of the additional electron by sodium now means that chlorine has more electrons than protons. The chlorine atom is now a negatively charged ion. The positively charged sodium ion and the negatively charged chlorine atom are attracted to each other, thus forming an ionic bond. An **ionic bond** is an attraction between oppositely charged ions, as shown here.

Ionic Bond

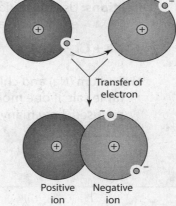

Atoms

Transfer of electron

Positive ion   Negative ion

Elements found in the same group in the periodic table will bond in a similar manner. For example, potassium and sodium are in Group 1. Bromine and chlorine are in Group 17. In the same manner that sodium atoms and chlorine atoms form an ionic bond, potassium atoms and bromine atoms can also form an ionic bond, resulting in potassium bromide. The strength of various ionic bonds may differ based on the atoms involved.

Covalent Bonding

Some chemical reactions involve two atoms that share electrons instead of transferring electrons. When two hydrogen atoms form a hydrogen molecule, the two atoms form a covalent bond. A **covalent bond** occurs when two atoms share one or more pairs of electrons. A covalent bond is stronger than an ionic bond. The following diagram shows two atoms sharing electrons in a covalent bond.

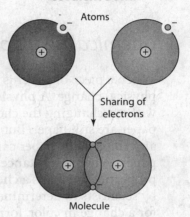

Covalent Bond

Atoms

Sharing of electrons

Molecule

When looking at the periodic table, you will notice that sulfur and oxygen are in the same Group 16. Sulfur will react with hydrogen in a manner similar to oxygen. Two hydrogen atoms share electrons with one sulfur atom, resulting in hydrogen sulfide gas.

Although covalent bonds are strong, they can be broken with thermal or electrical energy. For example, the two covalent bonds of water are broken when an electrical current is applied to water. The result of electrifying water is oxygen atoms forming bonds with other oxygen atoms and hydrogen atoms bonding with other hydrogen atoms. These atoms released from the water molecule bond form oxygen gas and hydrogen gas.

EXERCISE 19

Chemical Bonding

Directions: Choose the best answer to each question.

1. Potassium bromide has an ionic bond created by reactions between atoms of potassium and bromine. Which statement is true about potassium bromide?

    A. Bromine transfers one electron to potassium.
    B. The potassium bromide ionic bond is impossible to break.
    C. The potassium atom is positively charged.
    D. The bromine atom is positively charged.

2. Which statement about covalent bonds is FALSE?

    A. Covalent bonds are stronger than ionic bonds.
    B. Thermal energy can break a covalent bond.
    C. Energy is absorbed when a covalent bond is formed.
    D. Hydrogen and sulfur can form a covalent bond.

Answers are on page 803.

Chemical Reactions

When a piece of paper is torn into many pieces, the paper goes through a physical change. A **physical change** occurs when a substance changes form without changing the chemical nature of the substance. The torn pieces of paper are still paper. But if the paper is burned, the paper turns into ashes and smoke. The paper cannot be reformed because the paper is no longer paper. When a substance changes into another substance with different properties, it means a **chemical change** has occurred. Several signs are used by scientists to determine if a chemical change took place. Scientists look for a change in color, formation of a solid, and formation of gas bubbles. As you may recall, a chemical change is also known as a chemical reaction. Chemical reactions occur in many forms.

Types of Chemical Reactions

Many types of chemical reactions are used to create new substances. They can be classified in several ways. For example, chemical reactions can be classified as combustion, synthesis, and decomposition.

- A **combustion reaction** is any reaction that uses oxygen as a starting substance. For example, burning logs in a fireplace uses oxygen from the air to produce heat, light, ash, and smoke.

- A **synthesis reaction** is a reaction in which two substances react to form one new substance. Substances can be two different elements, two different compounds, or one element and one compound. A synthesis reaction might also be called a combination reaction. An example of a synthesis reaction is the reaction of sodium and chlorine. Recall that the reaction of sodium and chlorine forms the compound sodium chloride.

- A **decomposition reaction** occurs when a compound breaks down into simpler compounds or elements. If enough electricity is applied to water, it will decompose into its components of hydrogen gas and oxygen gas.

Chemical Reactions and Energy

When chemical reactions occur, energy may be used to aid in the reaction. For example, when you cook an egg on the stove, heat energy from the burner is used to cook the egg. The energy is absorbed into the egg.

A reaction absorbing energy from its surrounding is called an **endothermic reaction**. Other examples of endothermic reactions are melting ice cubes and baking bread. The opposite of absorbing energy is releasing energy. Many chemical reactions release energy as heat. This releasing of heat is an **exothermic reaction**. Examples of exothermic reactions are a burning candle and making ice cubes.

The Balanced Chemical Equation

When substances react to form new substances, the law of conservation of mass is observed. Recall that the law of conservation of mass states that the mass of the starting substances has to equal the mass of the final substances. Scientists use chemical equations to determine how much material is needed for a chemical reaction. A **chemical equation** is a representation of a chemical reaction. It would be very difficult and time consuming for scientists to write out the names of the substances each time. Instead of writing *sodium plus chlorine reacts to form sodium chloride*, it is much easier to write *Na + Cl → NaCl*. To help write chemical equations, scientists use the terms *reactant* and *product*. A **reactant** is any starting substance in a chemical reaction. In the sodium chloride reaction, sodium and chlorine are reactants. Sodium chloride is the **product,** or substance formed by the reaction. To ensure that the chemical reaction is in agreement with the law of conservation of mass, the chemical equation has to be balanced. A **balanced chemical equation** has the same number of atoms of each element on both sides of the equation. The following chemical equation is *not* balanced:

$$H_2 + O_2 \rightarrow H_2O$$

2 H atoms + 2 O atoms → 2 H atoms + 1 O atom

Reactants → product

The hydrogen molecule has two hydrogen atoms. The numeral 2 by the H indicates that there are two hydrogen atoms. The oxygen molecule also has two oxygen atoms. The total number of atoms on the reactants side is four. On the product side, there are only three atoms. The equation is not balanced because the number of atoms is not the same on both sides of the equation.

Here is the same equation, now balanced.

$$2 H_2 + O_2 \rightarrow 2 H2O$$

4 H atoms + 2 O atoms → 4 H atoms + 2 O atoms

The numeral 2 that is in front of H_2 and H_2O tells you that there are two molecules of H_2 and two molecules of H_2O. If you have two molecules of H_2, you have four atoms of hydrogen. On the reactants side, four atoms of hydrogen plus two O atoms are equal to the four hydrogen atoms and the two oxygen atoms on the product side. The law of conservation of mass is observed.

Chemical Reactions

Directions: Choose the best answer to each question.

1. What is another name for a chemical reaction?

    A. Chemical property
    B. Physical property
    C. Chemical change
    D. Physical change

2. What type of chemical reaction is represented by a burning candle?

    A. Combination
    B. Combustion
    C. Decomposition
    D. Synthesis

Directions: Use this chemical equation to answer the question.

$$4\,Na + O_2 \rightarrow 2\,Na_2O$$

3. How many atoms are there are on the reactants side of the equation?

    A. 2
    B. 4
    C. 6
    D. 12

Answers are on page 803.

Reaction Rates

Atoms or molecules are moving particles that can collide, resulting in chemical reactions. These collisions cause atoms or molecules to bond together or split apart. **Collision theory** states that in order for a reaction to occur, the reactants must collide in a specific orientation and with enough energy. Not all collisions between particles result in a reaction. For a chemical reaction to occur, two conditions must be met. First, there must be sufficient energy to break existing bonds and form new ones. Second, the particles reacting with each other must be aligned properly to allow the bonding to occur. A greater number of collisions can increase the chances of a successful reaction. The reaction rate usually increases as the number of collisions between particles increases. **Reaction rate** is the measure of how fast a reaction occurs.

Scientists use a number of methods to increase a reaction rate. One method is to increase the temperature of the reaction. By increasing the temperature, the particles have increased speed and energy. Higher speed and energy result in more collisions, which increase the odds of a reaction occurring. Another method to increase the reaction rate is to increase the number of reacting particles. The closer the particles are to each other, the more the potential for chemical reactions. For example, hydrogen peroxide is a combination of two molecules of hydrogen and two molecules of oxygen. Hydrogen peroxide can be decomposed into water molecules and oxygen gas. Chemists can produce oxygen gas at a faster rate by increasing the concentration of the hydrogen peroxide solution. **Concentration** is the amount of solute in a solvent. Finally, scientists may use a catalyst to speed up chemical reactions. A **catalyst** lowers the energy needed for particles to react. This increases the potential for collisions between reacting molecules. For example, automobiles use a catalytic converter to burn up and reduce the amount of toxic by-products of combustion engines.

EXERCISE 21

Reaction Rates

Directions: Choose the best answer to the question.

1. Which is NOT a method to increase reaction rates?
   A. Increasing the energy of the reaction
   B. Increasing the energy of the particles
   C. Increasing the speed of the particles
   D. Increasing the number of the particles

Answer is on page 803.

Chemical Equilibrium

There are times when chemical reactions produce multiple results. The products of a chemical reaction might react with each other and thereby change back into the original reactants. For instance, the reaction between methane gas (CH_4) and water vapor (H_2O) produces carbon monoxide gas (CO) and hydrogen gas (H_2).

$$CH_4 + H_2O \leftrightarrow CO + 3\,H_2$$

(left to right)   reactants → products

(right to left)   products ← reactants

CO and H_2 are formed as the reaction moves forward from left to right. In the other direction, the reverse reaction of CO and H_2 produces CH_4 and H_2O. This equation illustrates a chemical equilibrium. **Chemical equilibrium** happens when the rate of the forward reaction and the rate of the reverse reaction are equal. French chemist Henri Le Châtelier developed a rule regarding chemical equilibrium. **Le Châtelier's principle** states that any disturbance by a change in conditions will cause the equilibrium to shift to minimize those changes.

Le Châtelier's principle explains several changes that occur during a disturbance. Increasing the concentration of a reactant to a system in equilibrium causes the system to use up the added reactants by creating more products. The reverse will also happen if the concentration of reactants decreases. The reaction will move to the left to create more reactants, returning the system to equilibrium. An increase in temperature of an endothermic system has the same effect as increasing the concentration of reactants. The reaction will shift to the right, creating more products. Increasing the temperature of an exothermic reaction will shift the reaction to the left to create more reactants.

EXERCISE 22

Chemical Equilibrium

Directions: Choose the best answer to the question.

1. What does Le Châtelier's principle state?

   A. Product output is increased in the absence of thermal energy in an energy-absorbing system.
   B. Product output is increased with an endothermic reaction in the system.
   C. Product output is increased without the addition of reactants.
   D. Product output is increased in a system at equilibrium.

Answer is on page 803.

Nuclear Processes

Recall that atoms of the same elements with the same number of protons in their nucleus but with different number of neutrons are isotopes. In cases where the isotope is unstable, the atom becomes radioactive.

When an atom is unstable, it will emit particles in order to become stable. This process of emitting particles to become stable is called **radioactive decay**. The nucleus will emit different particles depending on the type of radioactive decay.

Radiation

Radioactive decay can be classified as alpha (α) decay, which emits alpha particles; beta (β) decay, which emits beta particles; and gamma (γ) decay, which emits gamma rays. Alpha particles do not penetrate very far and can be stopped by a piece of paper. This form of radiation is the least harmful to humans. **Alpha particles** contain two protons and two neutrons. Beta **particles** are high-speed, high-energy electrons. They penetrate farther than alpha particles but can be stopped by several sheets of paper. Beta particles are also smaller than alpha particles. **Gamma rays** are waves of energy without mass or charge. Lead and water can stop them. Gamma rays are the most damaging type of radiation.

Decay of Uranium-238

The following diagram illustrates a radioactive decay event that starts an unstable uranium nucleus emitting an alpha particle. The resulting particle is a thorium nucleus with fewer protons and neutrons than its parent uranium-238. Thorium is also an unstable element. So the decay process continues with the thorium nucleus emitting beta particles. This decay continues until a stable nucleus results.

Alpha Decay of Uranium-238

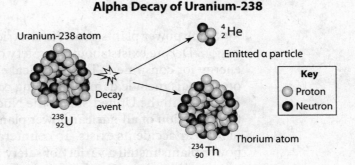

Nuclear Fission

Another nuclear process is **fission**, which is the splitting of an atomic nucleus. Fission can occur in two ways—naturally by unstable nuclei or by a forced reaction, such as a neutron shooting into a nucleus causing it to split. Regardless of how fission occurs, the splitting of the nucleus produces gamma radiation, thermal energy, and visible light.

When a neutron collides with the nucleus of a uranium atom, the neutron causes the nucleus to become unstable. Fission occurs as the uranium nucleus splits apart into two elements—krypton and barium nuclei. Upon splitting, energy is released and neutrons are ejected. These neutrons crash into other uranium nuclei causing additional krypton and barium nuclei to form, along with additional neutrons. This chain reaction progresses quickly and releases a great deal of energy:

Fission Process

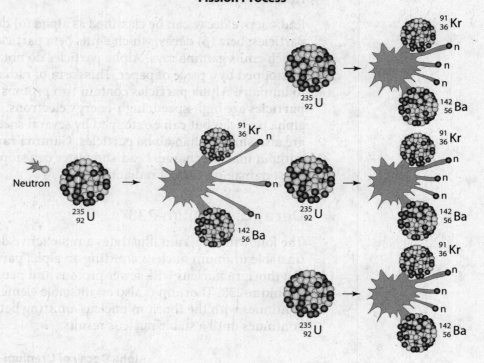

Some power plants generate electricity through the process of nuclear fission. Debate exists about the safety of using nuclear processes to create energy for consumers. The biological effects of radiation from fission on animals include damaging living cells, cancer, and genetic defects in offspring. In the United States, the Nuclear Regulatory Commission governs the operation of all nuclear power plants. Even with oversight, the possibility of nuclear accidents exists. To counteract the potential of accidents, nuclear power plants install a variety of safety measures.

Nuclear Fusion

The most violent of the nuclear processes is fusion. **Nuclear fusion** is the fusing of small atomic nuclei that forms a nucleus with a larger atomic mass. Similar to fission, energy is released, but fusion results in a much larger amount of energy. However, no containment systems exist to protect life-forms from this type of radioactive reaction. A constant fusion process powering the sun is an example of nuclear fusion.

In the following diagram, two hydrogen nuclei fuse together to form a helium nucleus. This helium is unstable as it has three neutrons but only two protons. In an effort to gain equilibrium, the helium nucleus ejects one neutron with a large quantity of energy. Similar to other nuclear processes, a chain reaction occurs until all of the hydrogen is used up.

Fusion Process

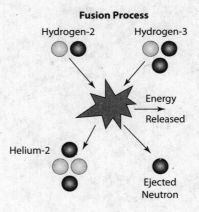

EXERCISE 23

Nuclear Processes

Directions: Choose the best answer to each question.

1. Radioactive decay can occur

   A. when a stable isotope exists.
   B. when an atom has an equal number of protons and electrons.
   C. when an isotope releases a particle, but only once.
   D. when a nucleus has more protons than neutrons.

2. Which statement about nuclear fission is FALSE?

   A. Gamma radiation can be released.
   B. Coolants are needed to remove excess heat in fission power plants.
   C. Fission cannot occur unless a neutron is shot into a nucleus.
   D. Krypton and barium are products of uranium fission.

3. Which statement about nuclear fusion is correct?

   A. Nuclear fusion releases radiation through alpha decay.
   B. Nuclear fusion releases more energy than nuclear fission.
   C. Nuclear fusion releases radiation through gamma decay.
   D. Nuclear fusion releases radiation through beta decay.

Answers are on page 803.

## CHAPTER 3

Earth and Space Science

For many people, their introduction to Earth and space science was gazing at the stars. For others, it was collecting rocks, and maybe a fossil or two. This chapter will explore the systems of Earth and space. It will also examine how the human population has affected Earth's climate and weather.

Space Systems

Studying the universe is a practice that dates back thousands of years. Today, astronomers are scientists who research the universe, the galaxy, the solar system, and Earth with hopes of increasing our understanding of the beginning of the universe and how all things are related.

The Big Bang Theory

In 1929 the American astronomer Edwin Hubble discovered through his research that the universe is expanding. He noticed that some stars appear to be redder in color than other stars. He realized that this was due to a light wave phenomenon called **redshift**. When an object that emits light is moving away, its light appears to shift toward the red end of the spectrum. Thus to Hubbell and other astronomers observing stars from Earth, some stars and galaxies appear redder than others. Those stars and galaxies are moving away from Earth, and moving away from each other as well.

Following this discovery, astronomers developed a new theory to explain the origin of the universe. According to this so-called "**big bang**" **theory,** nearly 14 billion years ago all the matter in the universe was contained in an extremely small but extremely dense, super-heated ball no larger than a tiny point. The universe was born when this tiny point exploded in an event informally called the "big bang." This explosion had such force that the universe expanded rapidly more than a hundred thousand years until the expansion slowed. Over time, the expanding material cooled to allow atoms to form. Hubbell's observations of redshift indicate that the universe is continuing to expand away from the center of that initial enormous explosion.

The big bang theory is now widely accepted because of the amount of evidence available. In addition to redshift, the theory is also supported by another discovery made in the 1960s. Astronomers detected faint microwave radiation striking Earth from all directions. This radiation is believed to be cosmic microwave background radiation, or remnants of energy left over from the big bang.

The early universe was composed of interstellar gases, roughly 75 percent hydrogen and 25 percent helium. Gravitational forces pulled these particles together to form clouds called nebulae. In many of those nebulae, those forces compressed the gas particles, and particle collisions created tremendous amounts of thermal energy. The particle collisions continued until the temperature within the nebulae reached approximately 11 million degrees Celsius. At that temperature, a nuclear fusion reaction began, forming a star. New stars continued to develop in this manner throughout the universe. Gravitational forces attracted billions of these stars together into galaxies. A galaxy is a large group of stars, gas, and dust held together by gravitation.

EXERCISE 1

Big Bang Theory

Directions: Choose the best answer to the question.

1. Which statement supports the big bang theory?

    A. A dense ball of matter and energy exploded to form the universe.
    B. Hydrogen and helium atoms were compressed until stars were formed.
    C. A light-emitting object moving away appears redder in color than other objects.
    D. At a temperature of 11 million degrees Celsius, a nuclear fusion reaction may begin.

Answer is on page 803.

Stars and Elements

During the early growth of the universe, gravitational forces pulled hydrogen and helium atoms together to form stars through a reaction called nuclear fusion. As you may recall, **nuclear fusion** is the fusing of small atomic nuclei, which collide at high speeds to form a new atomic nucleus with a larger atomic mass. Our sun, just like most stars, is composed of large amounts of hydrogen along with smaller amounts of helium and oxygen. Nuclear fusion produces heavier elements including helium, oxygen, and iron. The process releases visible light and other electromagnetic energies.

The Spectrum of Starlight

Stars emit a **light spectrum**, a range of different colors of light. Astronomers cannot observe the surface of stars, so they study the light spectrum, which varies in color and brightness.

The spectrum of starlight is similar to a rainbow, although some of the basic colors are missing. The elements that make up a star can be determined by analyzing its light spectra. When exposed to a large amount of energy, the atoms of each element emit and absorb combinations of colors of light in a unique manner. Thus each element produces its own distinct light spectrum. Knowing this, scientists can detect the presence of an element by analyzing its light spectrum. Through this research, astronomers have determined that most stars contain the elements hydrogen, helium, oxygen, calcium, iron, and magnesium.

The light spectrum for hydrogen is illustrated in the following diagram. Notice the four vertical lines in the spectrum. These lines are the wavelengths emitted by hydrogen. Three of the four lines are closer to the violet end of the spectrum. If the star being observed is approaching Earth, the spectral lines are more toward the violet end of the spectrum. Conversely, as the star moves away from Earth, these wavelengths may shift to the red side of the spectrum. A star's speed may be determined by analyzing the amount of shift of its spectral lines.

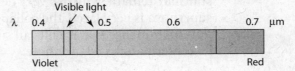

Balmer Series Light Spectrum of Hydrogen

Astronomers can also use a star's brightness, or **magnitude**, to determine a star's position in the universe. Astronomers consider two types of magnitude—apparent magnitude and absolute magnitude. **Apparent magnitude** is how bright an object, such as a star, appears from Earth. **Absolute magnitude** is how a star's brightness appears from the standard distance of 32.6 light-years. A **light-year** is a measurement of distance that light can travel during one Earth year, roughly 9.5 trillion kilometers. Scientists use absolute magnitude to compare the brightness of several stars that are far apart from each other. Two stars that have similar absolute magnitudes may not share similar apparent magnitudes. It may be that one of the stars is farther away. A star farther from Earth most likely will have a smaller apparent magnitude.

Death of a Star

Throughout a star's life, nuclear fusion is responsible for the output of the star's energy. The average lifespan of a star ranges from several hundred thousand years to many billions of years. A star dies because its supply of hydrogen is exhausted by the nuclear fusion reaction. Without hydrogen, the process of nuclear fusion ends. This reduces the temperature of the star. The star's gravity pulls and compresses the remaining particles toward the center. But without hydrogen, very little energy is produced. As the star's particles compress in the center, the outer layers of the star swell to a large size. The effect of the star's death on its outer layers depends on the size of the star.

Our sun is considered a small- or medium-sized star. When it dies in the distant future, the outer layers will swell, creating a red giant. A **red giant** is a star that is in the last stages of its life. When our sun turns into a red giant, its surface will cool significantly without nuclear fusion. The sun will expand to become 100 times larger than it is today, and it will be thousands of times more luminous. Its light energy output will be enough to boil all the water off the Earth's surface. Eventually, the outer layers of a red giant are cast off into space, and the star becomes what is called a nova. The center of the nova is hot and dense, and astronomers describe this as a **white dwarf**.

Larger stars than our sun die in a more violent manner. The outer layers swell to a vast size; the star becomes a **red supergiant**. By comparison, a red supergiant is about a thousand times larger than the sun. The supergiant's gravity is so intense that when the outer layers are pulled in, the star explodes into a supernova. This process creates new atomic nuclei from existing protons and neutrons in a process called **nucleosynthesis**. This process occurs in the center of the mass, producing elements like plutonium and uranium, which are much heavier than iron. A supernova expels gas and dust into space, forming a nebula. Following the explosion, a **neutron star** may remain, which is very dense with a very small mass. However, if the supernova is very large, the collapsing star within it may have a gravitational pull so immense that it pulls all surrounding particles, including light, into its center to form a **black hole**.

EXERCISE 2

Stars and Elements

Directions: Read the passage and then answer the question.

Two stars, labeled A1000 and B1000, are monitored and measured for light magnitude. Astronomers determine that the stars have a similar apparent magnitude. Star A1000 is known to be a red giant. B1000 is known to be an active star about the size of our sun. It is known that A1000 is farther away from Earth than B1000.

1. What can be said about the absolute magnitudes of the two stars?

   A. The absolute magnitudes of A1000 and B1000 are equal.
   B. The absolute magnitude of A1000 is greater than the absolute magnitude of B1000.
   C. The absolute magnitude of A1000 is less than the absolute magnitude of B1000.
   D. There is not enough information to answer this question.

Answer is on page 803.

The Sun

Earth receives most of its energy from the sun. Light and heat from the sun are necessary for all living things on Earth. The sun contains more than 90 percent of all the mass that exists in our solar system. It is a rather average-sized star when compared to the hundred billions of stars in the Milky Way galaxy.

Our sun has been alive for four to five billion years. Based on astronomical predictions, it may be alive for another four billion years. Astronomers cannot study the inside of the sun, but they can draw conclusions about its age by observing its energy output. The sun emits energy through nuclear fusion just like every other star. During this process, four hydrogen nuclei collide to form the nucleus of one helium atom, producing a remarkable amount of energy. This radiant energy emitted by the sun is **solar radiation**. The radiation is expelled into space in all directions as electromagnetic waves. Only a fraction of the sun's total solar radiation strikes the Earth, but enough reaches our planet to warm it and provide energy.

The magnitude and type of energy produced by the sun varies slightly over time. Sunspots and solar flares are events that hinder or magnify the sun's energy production. **Sunspots** are visible dark areas on the surface of the sun with temperatures about 1,500°C less than the sun's average temperature. The number of sunspots on the surface of the sun differs from year to year over what astronomers deem an 11-year cycle. Astronomers have determined that even though sunspots create cooler areas on the surface of the sun, they lead to an increase in the sun's radiation output.

The other events that affect the sun's energy output are solar flares. A **solar flare** is a blast of energy that, from Earth, appears as an area of additional brightness. Solar flares release a great deal of energy. On Earth, they can affect satellite transmissions and can cause auroras, which are streams of colored lights around Earth's North or South Pole. The auroras are the result of solar winds caused by solar flares colliding with charged particles in the upper atmosphere.

EXERCISE 3

The Sun

Directions: Choose the best answer to the question.

1. A period of 500 years starting in 1300 has been called the "The Little Ice Age." The agricultural growing season was shortened, and a lack of sunspots was observed during this period. Which statement may support a correlation between these observations?

   A. Sunspots do not affect Earth's temperature.
   B. An increase in sunspots causes lower temperatures on Earth.
   C. A decrease in sunspots causes higher temperatures on Earth.
   D. A decrease in sunspots causes lower temperatures on Earth.

Answer is on page 803.

The Sun–Earth System

Ancient philosophers developed a model of the universe that placed Earth at the center of everything. According to this model, all of the planets, as well as the sun, orbited Earth. Later, the Egyptian astronomer Claudius Ptolemy refined this model to help predict the location of the planets in the sky during certain parts of the year. These models reflect a **geocentric**, or Earth-centered, idea. This was the accepted model for over a millennium.

In the 1500s, the Polish astronomer Nicolaus Copernicus went against common beliefs by proposing that Earth and the other planets orbited the sun. Later during that century, the Italian astronomer Galileo Galilei invented a telescope that produced evidence to support Copernicus's hypotheses. It was then understood that Earth was part of a solar system, with the sun at its center. This idea is called the **heliocentric** model.

Shortly after Galileo's work, the German astronomer Johannes Kepler expanded on the sun-centered model and developed three laws of planetary motion. The first law, the **law of ellipsis**, states that planets orbit the sun in an elliptical or oval-shaped path, with the sun situated in a single focus or fixed point of the orbit. Second, the **law of equal areas** states that as a planet orbits the sun, it travels the same distance in space in the same amount of time throughout its elliptical orbit. This is true even though there are periods where the planet is closer to the sun. Essentially, the planet's speed increases as it nears the sun and decreases as the planet travels away from the sun. As shown in the diagram, Earth will travel an equal distance in space in the same amount of time despite its position relative to the sun.

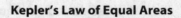

Kepler's Law of Equal Areas

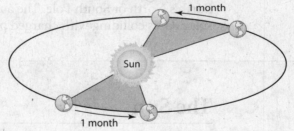

The third law, the **law of harmonies**, is a mathematical relationship between the planet's **orbital period** and its **radius of orbit**. The orbital period is the amount of time it takes the planet to complete one orbit around the sun. The radius of orbit is the average distance between the sun and the planet. The law states that the square of a planet's orbital period is equal to the cube of its radius of orbit:

$$P^2 = a^3$$

where P = a planet's orbital period a = its radius of orbit

With this information, scientists can calculate the distance from the sun for any planet given its orbital period. In addition, scientists can apply

Newton's law of universal gravitation to further describe the orbit of one object around a second object. Recall the equation:

$$F_g = G \cdot (m_1 \cdot m_2)/r^2$$

where F_g = the gravitational force, G = Newton's gravitational constant, m_1 and m_2 = the mass of the two objects, and r = the distance between the two centers of the objects

According to this model, the closer two objects are to each other, the greater the force of gravity the objects exert on one another. Consider what would happen if an enormous asteroid struck Earth's moon. If the moon were pushed farther away from Earth, this would lessen the effect of the gravitational pull that Earth exerts on the moon. If another celestial body exerted a greater force of gravity on the displaced moon, it is possible that the moon would break free of Earth's gravitational pull.

EXERCISE 4

The Sun–Earth System

Directions: Choose the best answer to each question.

1. Which statement about Kepler's law of harmonies is correct?

    A. There is a direct relationship between the orbital period and the radius of orbit.

    B. There is an indirect relationship between the orbital period and the radius of orbit.

    C. The smaller a planet's orbital period, the greater is its radius of orbit.

    D. The smaller a planet's radius of orbit, the greater is its orbital period.

2. Many early scientists and philosophers believed that the sun was at the center of the universe. Who developed the model that the sun, not Earth, was the center of the universe?

    A. Ancient philosophers

    B. Galileo Galilei

    C. Johannes Kepler

    D. Nicolaus Copernicus

Answers are on page 804.

The Planets

Our solar system is comprised of eight planets that orbit the sun. These eight planets are divided equally into two groups, terrestrial and Jovian. **Terrestrial planets** are made up of rock and metallic substances, and they are small and dense compared to the larger Jovian planets. The terrestrial planets are Mercury, Venus, Earth, and Mars, which have the closest orbits to the sun. Terrestrial planets rarely have orbiting satellites.

Our Solar System

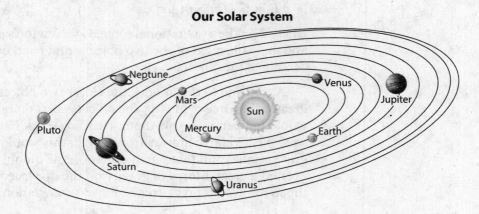

Jovian planets are composed of gases like hydrogen, helium, methane, and ammonia. The Jovian planets are Jupiter, Saturn, Uranus, and Neptune. Due to their immense size, Jovian planets tend to have multiple satellites orbiting them. These planets collect space material that surrounds them in a series of rings, in which the planetary moons orbit.

An object previously classified as one of the nine planets orbiting the sun, called Pluto, was downgraded to a dwarf planet based on its relative size to other objects in the solar system.

The History of Planet Earth

Scientists have collected evidence that shows that Earth formed about 4.6 billion years ago when the rest of the solar system developed. During that time, the solar system was a whirling cloud of hot debris called the solar nebula. For the most part, the solar nebula was a mixture of helium, hydrogen, and other elements. The hydrogen and helium atoms collided to form the sun at the center of the nebula. The other components, mostly metallic and rocky materials, cooled and collided to form asteroids that began to orbit the new sun. These asteroids were the early beginning of the four terrestrial planets. They continued to build in size as more and more material crashed into their surfaces, much like a snowball gaining in size as it rolls down a snowy slope. Light gases, such as helium and hydrogen, continued to circle the sun and eventually combined farther away from the terrestrial planets to form the gaseous, giant Jovian planets.

Earth's Formation

The solar nebula materials that formed Earth continued to crash into its surface. These collisions generated a great deal of heat that caused the materials surrounding Earth's core to be a molten mass. Heavier and denser elements like nickel and iron sank through this liquid toward the center of the planet. Lighter rocks floated to the top of the molten soup, slowly forming Earth's crust. The constant churning of heavy and light materials over time formed the layers of Earth. Those layers are the crust, mantle, outer core, and inner core.

The dramatic geological changes throughout the formation of Earth changed and destroyed many of the oldest rock formations that would help scientists pinpoint the planet's age. However, early in the 20th century, geologists developed a technique called radiometrics to estimate the age of Earth. **Radiometrics** is a way of measuring gamma radiation from decaying elements in Earth's materials. This radiation was measured and compared to measurements taken from meteorites that had struck Earth billions of years ago. This data allowed geologists to determine that Earth's continental rocks are as much as four billion years old. These rock formations are older than the rocks making up the ocean floor, which are estimated to be only 200 million years old. How can the difference be explained? Ocean rocks are constantly being churned and moved by volcanic displacements, whereas continental rocks are able to age undisturbed. Following the lunar landings by NASA astronauts, radiometric analysis of moon rocks verified geologist's estimates of the age of Earth.

Plate Tectonics

Studies of Earth's history led to the theory of **plate tectonics**, which describes how Earth's crust moves and interacts with itself. The theory also explains how mountains and ocean trenches are formed through the physical activities of earthquakes and volcanic eruptions.

Plate tectonics provides support for a theory proposed in the early 1900s by the German scientist Alfred Wegener. Wegener theorized that the continents are in constant motion in a process that he called **continental drift**. He suggested that the seven continents we know today, North America, South America, Europe, Asia, Africa, Australia, and Antarctica, were once connected in a giant continent called Pangaea. The supercontinent later split into several landmasses that drifted apart. The original Pangaean continent is shown in the diagram.

Pangea

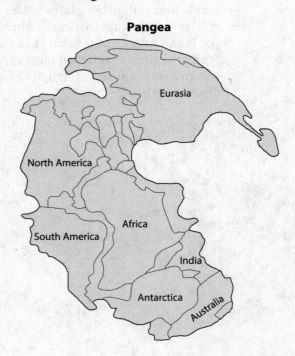

In the diagram of Pangaea, you can make out the familiar shapes of several of the continents. Although the theory of continental drift explained why the borders of these continents seemed to fit together so well, scientists were unable to determine why the continents split apart. The theory of plate tectonics, developed in the 1960s, provides an explanation for this phenomenon.

Earth's crust is made up of eight large tectonic plates and nine smaller plates. These plates float on the liquid mantle, which is the layer of Earth beneath the crust. The continents and ocean floor rest on top of the plates. The plates shift along the mantle at a very slow pace, anywhere from a half inch to four inches per year. The illustration shows the locations of the tectonic plates.

Tectonic Plates

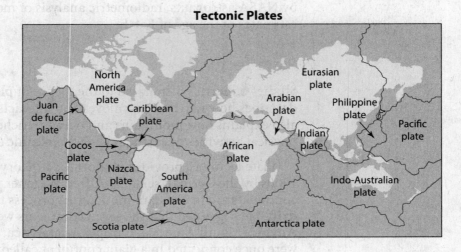

The convection process in Earth's mantle moves the tectonic plates. **Convection** is the slow rising of hot materials that push some plates aside and pull other plates under the molten mantle. Convection causes plates to press against each other. The pressure can cause earthquakes, or it can break open fissures in the plates to form volcanoes. Sometimes the pressure of colliding plates is enough to thrust up rocks to form mountains. These constructive forces continue to develop land features on Earth's crust.

EXERCISE 5

The History of Planet Earth

Directions: Choose the best answer to each question.

1. Which describes the order in which objects in our solar system formed?

   A. Terrestrial planets, sun, Jovian planets, solar nebula
   B. Jovian planets, sun, terrestrial planets, solar nebula
   C. Solar nebula, sun, terrestrial planets, Jovian planets
   D. Solar nebula, Jovian planets, sun, terrestrial planets

2. Which BEST describes an example of continental drift?

   A. North America and Europe are moving away from each other.
   B. Volcanoes form new landmasses in the Pacific Ocean.
   C. Large meteors slammed into Earth, forming giant craters.
   D. Hot materials rise up, pushing the crust of Earth in different directions.

Answers are on page 804.

Earth's Systems

The planet Earth is constantly changing as its systems of air, land, water, and life interact with each other. There are four systems that make up Earth—atmosphere, lithosphere, hydrosphere, and biosphere. The **atmosphere** is the air that surrounds Earth. It provides for life and protects the planet from harmful radiation from space. The **lithosphere** is the planet's land areas such as mountains, valleys, and plains. The **hydrosphere** contains the rivers, lakes, seas, and oceans that hold Earth's water resources. The fourth system is the **biosphere**, or all the areas on the planet that support life. Earth's systems work together just like the systems in the human body.

The Hydrosphere

When you look at Earth from space, you notice that the planet is blue. It is no wonder that astronauts call Earth the *blue marble*. About 71 percent of the surface of Earth is covered with water. The oceans hold more than 95 percent of all of Earth's water. The chemical compound for water is simple, containing two atoms of hydrogen and one atom of oxygen. Its chemical and physical properties are able to support Earth's environment. Water has the ability to absorb, store, and release large amounts of thermal energy. It also absorbs and reflects sunlight, expands upon freezing, and has the ability to dissolve materials and transport them.

Earth's Oceans

Earth's oceans vary in depth as shown in the diagram. The oceans sit atop the **continental crust** and the **oceanic crust**. The shallowest area of the ocean is the **continental shelf**, which is a shallow extension of the landmasses. A wedge of sediment provides for the **continental slope**, which forms the transition from the continental shelf to the ocean floor. At the base of the continental slope, thick amounts of sediment make up the **continental rise**. The ocean floor is called the **ocean basin**, an underwater area that is equal in size to the land above sea level. The ocean basin makes up about 30 percent of all of Earth's surface area. It is not a smooth surface, however. Deep-ocean trenches, ridges, and seamounts make the bottom of the ocean look a lot like the valleys, cliffs, and mountains that we see above water.

Geographic Regions of the Oceans

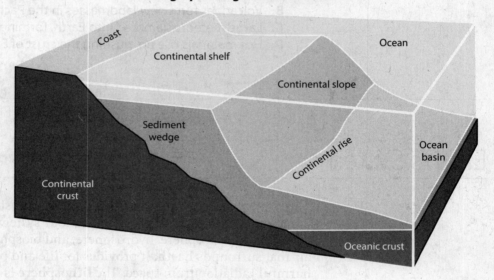

Tides

The ocean is not a still body of water. Tides keep the oceans moving. They are the rising and falling of water across the ocean's surface due to the gravitational pull of the sun and the moon as well as the rotation of Earth. Recall Newton's law of universal gravitation, where gravity is inversely proportional to distance. The gravitational force is greater on the side of Earth closest to the moon. Because of this, the water on the side closest to the moon moves toward the moon, causing high tides. On the opposite side of Earth, the water is also being pulled toward the moon but with not as much force, also creating high tides. Ocean water also flows in **currents**, which are caused by the rising and falling of tides. The tides also create currents in bays and coastal estuaries, areas where lake and stream freshwater meets ocean salt water.

Marine Life

A quarter of Earth's marine life lives in coral reefs, a living ecosystem. **Corals**, or polyps, are very small, invertebrate animals. A multitude of coral polyps bunch together to form a coral reef, which provides food and shelter for diverse populations of living organisms. Phytoplankton are algae and bacteria that live in coral reefs and have the distinction of providing more than half of the oxygen we breathe through photosynthesis.

Recall the description of the water cycle in the review of ecosystems. Water is constantly moving and carrying materials and nutrients. Heat from the sun evaporates water, transferring it from the hydrosphere to the atmosphere, where it rains on the lithosphere and feeds the living things in the biosphere. Water makes its way back to the hydrosphere where the process starts over again.

EXERCISE 6

The Hydrosphere

Directions: Choose the best answer to the question.

1. Phytoplanktons are responsible for providing about half of the oxygen humans breathe. Because these organisms use photosynthesis, how do phytoplanktons receive the necessary carbon dioxide to complete the process?

    A. Carbon dioxide is not available to marine life, so phytoplanktons do not use carbon dioxide.
    B. Carbon dioxide is available to marine life only through the decomposition of plants and animals.
    C. Carbon dioxide is available to marine life because it dissolves in the surface water of oceans.
    D. Carbon dioxide is available to marine life because it is trapped in estuaries.

Answer is on page 804.

Earth's Atmosphere and the Weather

The water cycle has an effect on Earth's atmosphere in the form of weather. Meteorologists understand this and apply their knowledge of the water cycle. They study the interaction between the atmosphere and hydrosphere. Wind, humidity, and temperature also affect Earth's weather.

Air Masses

Weather is the result of interactions between humidity, temperature, and the air masses that flow through the atmosphere. **Air masses** are bodies of air that retain climate characteristics derived from the land or water over which they were formed. For example, air masses flowing out of Canada are usually cold and dry. Air masses flowing north from the Gulf of Mexico are usually warm and humid. It is important for meteorologists to track different air masses since the characteristics of each can affect the atmosphere in different ways. For the most part, air masses passing through the United States travel in an easterly direction.

Warm air generally rises. Conversely, cold air sinks. When two different air masses meet, a boundary, or a **front,** is formed. A **warm front** forms when warm, humid air rises up over denser, cold air. A **cold front** forms when cold, dry air slides under warm air like a wedge. Because cold fronts move faster than warm fronts, this wedge-like action quickly pushes the warm air upward, resulting in heavy rainstorms. Sometimes warm fronts and cold fronts collide with each other, creating violent weather patterns. For example, the central part of the United States experiences the convergence of warm, moist air from the Gulf of Mexico and cold, dry air from Canada. These two fronts collide to form thunderstorms and tornadoes.

Severe Weather

Tornadoes are funnel-shaped columns of circulating wind that occur primarily on land. A **mesocyclone**, the precursor to a tornado, develops from the spinning air within an updraft of a thunderstorm. The updraft may take on a counterclockwise spin. While spinning, it can generate wind speeds of almost 300 miles per hour. The direction of the spin is due to the easterly rotation of Earth. For the most part, tornadoes in the Northern Hemisphere spin counterclockwise while tornadoes in the Southern Hemisphere spin clockwise. Tornadoes occur only under certain conditions during storms. Most tornadoes occur in the central plains of the United States, which include Oklahoma, Kansas, Missouri, and parts of Texas, Iowa, and Illinois. This area is known as "tornado alley." There are about 1,000 tornadoes each year in the United States. This total represents the bulk of tornadoes that occur worldwide, roughly 10 times as many as in Canada, the country with the second most tornadoes.

Hurricanes are another kind of seasonal weather pattern. A tropical depression forms when a group of thunderstorms converges over a warm region of ocean. The hot and moist air of the thunderstorms collects the evaporating water from the warm ocean to build powerful atmospheric elements. Tropical depressions are upgraded to tropical storms when the wind speed reaches 40 miles per hour. As the storm gains power, wind speeds can reach 75 miles per hour, which is the definition of a category one hurricane. Hurricanes tend to form during the summer months when water temperatures are at their highest. Because hurricanes need warm water to generate power, the Caribbean waters to the southeast of the United States create about a dozen storm systems each year that have the potential for hurricane status.

Ecosystem Changes

As violent wind storms, tornadoes and hurricanes have the potential to inflict heavy damage on anything in their path. Tornadoes destroy homes, buildings, farmland, and plant life, including trees. Hurricanes cause tidal waves that can flood river basins and marshes, displacing wildlife and destroying property. Hurricanes and tornadoes can cause economic damage on the local level in both the short term and long term. In addition, they can wipe out natural ecosystems that have taken decades to develop. The loss of plant life can have an adverse effect on the carbon cycle. As coastal areas grow in population, governments attempt to thwart the effects of hurricanes by building storm shelters and levees and dikes to hold back the rising tides.

Climatologists and meteorologists believe that destructive weather events such as tornadoes and hurricanes are increasing, and that the increase is related to climate changes that are now under way. Global temperatures have been rising because large quantities of so-called "greenhouse gases" have become trapped in Earth's atmosphere. These gases block heat from the sun from escaping back into space. In addition, the rising temperatures have caused ice at Earth's poles and elsewhere to melt. That ice normally plays an important role in reflecting heat from the sun back into space. When the ice melts, more heat remains in the atmosphere. The result is warmer oceans that feed hurricanes and odd weather patterns that foster tornadoes.

EXERCISE 7

Earth's Atmosphere and the Weather

Directions: Choose the best answer to the question.

1. Which statement describes a short-term effect of tornadoes and hurricanes?

    A. Human populations move away from coastal regions for inland areas.
    B. Wildlife is displaced by the destruction of wetlands and forests.
    C. New construction standards are enacted to make buildings better able to withstand the effects of storms.
    D. "Greenhouse gases" are trapped in Earth's atmosphere.

Answer is on page 804.

The Lithosphere

The lithosphere contains Earth's landmasses. Three types of rocks make up the lithosphere—igneous, metamorphic, and sedimentary. When underground molten rock, called magma, cools and hardens, or when lava cools on Earth's surface, **igneous rocks** are formed. **Metamorphic rocks** are rocks that change from one form to another within Earth's crust due to high pressure and temperature. **Sedimentary rocks** are formed from pieces of other rocks that have been pressed together.

Earth's Layers

Geologists compare the layers of Earth to the layers of an apple. Earth's crust is similar to an apple's peel. An apple has an inner layer as well as a core, just like Earth. The following illustration shows Earth's layers—the crust, mantle, outer core, and inner core—as well as the thickness of each layer.

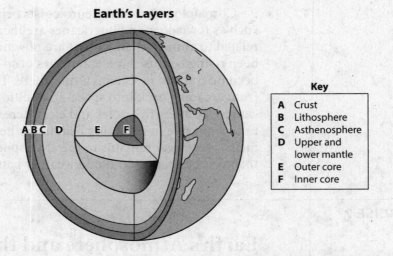

Earth's Layers

Key

A	Crust
B	Lithosphere
C	Asthenosphere
D	Upper and lower mantle
E	Outer core
F	Inner core

The **crust** is the outermost layer of the planet. Relative to the inner parts of the planet, the crust is a cool, rocky layer with two distinct areas: continental and oceanic. The crust is composed of igneous, metamorphic, and sedimentary rocks. Because the rocks in the continental crust tend to go untouched by the heat and pressure that transform Earth's other layers, these rocks are dated at more than four billion years old. The oceanic crust undergoes more frequent changes than the continental crust, and as a result, most oceanic rock is less than two million years old.

Below the crust is the **mantle**, which contains more than 80 percent of all of Earth's volume. The mantle has several layers: the lithosphere, asthenosphere, and the upper and lower mantle. Each layer has its own unique characteristics. The mantle is partially solid, composed mostly of igneous rock. The area of the mantle bordering the crust is soft rock. The upper mantle contains soft, flowing rocks that are at a temperature close to their melting point. This is the flowing rock that erupts during volcanic activity. Further down is the lower mantle that borders the outer core. It is composed of both hard and soft igneous rock.

Deeper still, roughly 1,800 miles under Earth's crust, is the **outer core**. This is a layer of liquid iron and nickel. Iron is a solid metal in Earth's crust, but the outer core temperatures between 4,000°C and 5,000°C keep this a molten layer. The iron within the outer core produces Earth's magnetic field.

At the center of Earth is the inner core. The **inner core** is a solid sphere of mostly iron, about the size of Earth's moon. Although temperatures are between 5,000°C and 7,000°C, the immense pressure exerted on the inner core by the rest of the planet keeps this a solid mass. The inner core has a temperature range similar to the surface of the sun. This extremely hot ball of minerals is buried more than 3,000 miles under Earth's crust.

The Rock Cycle

The **rock cycle** is a continuous process in which rocks are created, destroyed, and re-created. Geologists have studied the rock cycle by examining igneous rock as it progresses from Earth's inner layers to the crust. Deep within Earth, magma is formed when rocks melt under extreme temperatures. The magma escapes to Earth's crust and solidifies as it cools, forming igneous rock. As this igneous rock is exposed to wind, water, collisions with other rocks, or manipulation by living things, it breaks down. The broken pieces of rock, called sediments, may compact with other sediments to form sedimentary rocks. Water, glaciers, wind, and gravity may further affect these rocks. If the motion of Earth's tectonic plates pushes the sedimentary rock deep underground, intense heat and gravitational pressure will transform it into metamorphic rock. Even greater pressures and temperatures may be exerted on the metamorphic rock, melting it into magma. From there, the rock cycle starts again. The diagram shows the rock cycle and how the various rock types go through the cycle.

The Rock Cycle

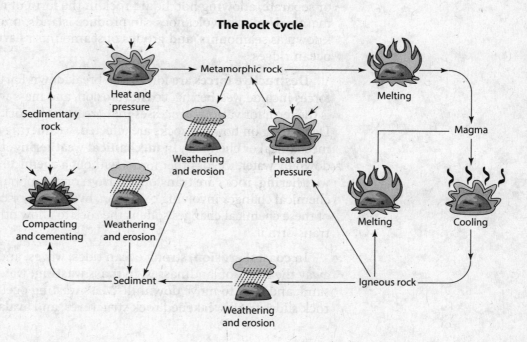

Tectonic Plate Motion

The landmasses of the lithosphere are divided into **tectonic plates**. Thermal convection in the mantle keeps the tectonic plates moving, although at a very slow pace. **Thermal convection** is the movement of heated molecules from one surface to another, much like the warmth you feel when holding your hands near a fire. Earth's crust and mantle contain radioactive elements that decay, generating the heat that causes thermal convection. As tectonic plates move, seismic waves are emitted that scientists can measure. This analysis provides the measurement of intensity of seismic activity such as earthquakes.

Thermal convection over millions of years caused the tectonic plates in the supercontinent called Pangaea to separate into the continents we know today. Scientists determined that about 170 million years ago, violent tectonic plate activity started the formation of the Rocky Mountains in the western United States. It took roughly 130 million years for this tectonic plate movement to complete the construction of this tremendous mountain range.

Constructive and Destructive Forces

Mountains, canyons, and plateaus are **landforms** created by **constructive forces** that help build up Earth's surface. Three categories of constructive forces are orogeny, tectonic uplift, and some types of volcanic activity. **Orogeny** forces construct mountains when tectonic plates collide with each other. **Tectonic uplift** results when tectonic collisions raise an entire geographical area. The rising land may trap large bodies of water, forming inland lakes and seas. Finally, **volcanism**, or volcanic activity, occurs at tectonic plate boundaries. Volcanism results when tectonic plates **diverge**, or separate, allowing hot, liquid rock in the form of magma to escape the mantle. Undersea volcanoes can produce islands, underwater mountains known as seamounts, and groups of seamounts as arranged in lines called ocean ridges.

Destructive forces are forces that break down Earth's surface. These forces include weathering, coastal erosion, and mass wasting. **Weathering** is the term for various processes that break down rocks on Earth's surface. Depending on how the rocks are affected, weathering can be either mechanical or chemical. In **mechanical weathering**, rocks are broken down by water, ice, or other forces without a chemical change. In **chemical weathering,** rocks are transformed from one compound to another through chemical changes involving oxidation, hydrolysis, or carbonation. Each of these chemical changes softens the rock to allow other forces to further transform it.

In **coastal erosion,** strong ocean tides, waves, and water drainage wear away the edges of landmasses. In **mass wasting**, water drainage causes soil, sand, and rock to move downhill. Mass wasting occurs through landslides, rock slides from weakened rock structures, and avalanches.

Natural Hazards

Living things on Earth's surface are subject to various kinds of natural hazards. Tectonic plate motion causes earthquakes and volcanic eruptions. Hurricanes and tornadoes occur from adverse weather systems.

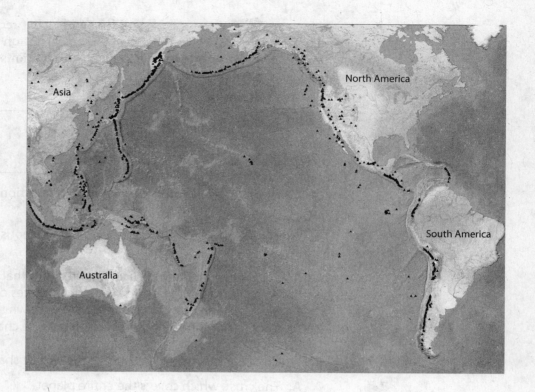

When tectonic plates press against each other or slide one over another, earthquakes occur. Fault lines are fractures in Earth's crust caused by tectonic plate movement. In the western United States, there is a 1,300-km fault line called the San Andreas Fault. Scientists observe that the landmasses adjacent to this fault move on average one inch per year. However, the movement is not constant. Pressure builds up at the fault line until the two landmasses slip past each other violently, causing some of the world's worst earthquakes. The land areas that rim the Pacific Ocean contain so many fault lines that the region is called the "Ring of Fire." The diagram illustrates the fault lines and fissures in Earth's crust where volcanoes occur.

Underwater volcanoes tend to be constructive forces because they form islands and other underwater surface features. Conversely, land-based volcanoes can have destructive effects on geographic areas, the atmosphere, and living things. In 1980, the volcano called Mount St. Helens in the state of Washington erupted, spewing a cubic kilometer of ash and upsetting ecosystems in more than 10 states. When lava poured down the mountain, glaciers on the mountainside melted, creating mudslides that spread out over an area of 65 square kilometers. The destructive force of this volcano killed or displaced thousands of animals.

In recent years, tsunamis (huge ocean waves) caused by undersea earthquakes devastated coastal populations in Japan and Thailand in the eastern Pacific. Many people living in or near these hazard zones take preventive measures to alleviate the impact of natural disasters.

Many earthquake zones have building codes that require buildings to be more flexible to allow movement. Transportation authorities work on developing evacuation plans that enable populations to seek refuge when danger threatens.

The Lithosphere

Directions: Choose the best answer to each question.

1. Which destructive process may transform igneous rock into sedimentary rock?

   A. Volcanic eruptions producing molten lava that melts igneous rock
   B. Tectonic uplift that results when rocky plates collide with each other
   C. Mass wasting that causes rocks to slide down a mountainside
   D. Underground heat and pressure that cause changes in igneous rocks.

2. Which of Earth's layers accounts for the largest share of the planet's mass?

   A. The crust, which covers the entire planet
   B. The mantle, which is comprised of mostly soft rock
   C. The outer core, which is 1,400 miles thick
   D. The inner core, which has a size equal to the moon

Answers are on page 804.

Interactions of Earth's Systems

Living things have been able to develop on Earth because the planet's interacting systems have created a favorable environment for life. The atmosphere regulates the amount of solar radiation that reaches Earth's surface. The carbon cycle provides the carbon that is the basis for all life. The water cycle provides nutrients to living things all across the planet's surface. Plants use the process of photosynthesis to convert sunlight, water, and carbon dioxide into energy while also providing oxygen to other life forms. Water and solar energy in the atmosphere produce the weathering of rocks in the rock cycle. The four systems of Earth—atmosphere, lithosphere, hydrosphere, and biosphere—continue to interact, sustaining life on the planet.

Carbon Cycle

Each of the Earth's systems interacts with the others. You can see this interaction by examining the carbon cycle. You might recall that carbon is an essential building block of life. It bonds with other elements to form compounds such as carbon dioxide. Carbon dioxide is exhaled into the atmosphere by animals living in the lithosphere as well as some living in the hydrosphere. Carbon dioxide also dissolves into the surface water of the hydrosphere.

Plants and algae living in Earth's systems use the process of photosynthesis to convert sunlight, water, and carbon dioxide into energy. The carbon dioxide is converted into carbohydrates. The animals that feed on plants and algae break down the nutrients in the plants and exhale carbon dioxide back into the atmosphere. When plants and animals die, the carbon dioxide in their bodies is released into the atmosphere, lithosphere, and hydrosphere.

Climate Change

Earth has undergone climate changes throughout its history. Millions of years ago, Earth experienced severe atmospheric changes due to asteroid impacts and planet-wide volcanic activity. Earth also follows a 40,000-year cycle in which it changes its axis of rotation in conjunction with its orbit. Earth rotates on an imaginary axis that runs through the North and South Poles. The axis of rotation changes over a two-degree difference during the 40,000-year cycle, in what is called Earth's "wobble." This change in the axis of rotation can cause seasonal fluctuations that have produced several ice ages during the past hundred thousand years.

Other natural phenomena can cause climate change. Volcanic eruptions emit huge amounts of carbon dioxide into the atmosphere. The carbon dioxide can trap heat and cause a rise in temperatures. Volcanoes also emit clouds of ash, which can reflect solar heat back into space and cause large-scale cooling. Other natural causes of climate change include changes in ocean currents and fluctuations in heat output by the sun.

Greenhouse Gases

In recent times, human activities have begun to have an impact on Earth's climate. In particular, the burning of fossil fuels such as coal, petroleum, and natural gas has released huge quantities of so-called **greenhouse gases**, mainly carbon dioxide, into the atmosphere. In the atmosphere, these gases tend to trap heat that would otherwise radiate out into space, and the result has been a slight increase in average temperatures worldwide. This rise in temperatures is called the **greenhouse effect**.

The greenhouse effect does not just alter the balance in Earth's atmosphere. It also affects the hydrosphere. As temperatures rise, wetlands dry up. When that happens, humidity levels decrease, and vegetation and wildlife populations decline. Higher temperatures also melt and shrink glaciers and polar ice caps, and as a result, less solar radiation is reflected back into space. In addition, the melting of these large expanses of ice raises the level of seas and oceans, which causes coastal flooding, coastal erosion, and other kinds of destruction in Earth's lithosphere. The higher temperatures also introduce more energy into atmospheric systems, resulting in stronger and more frequent storms. Efforts are now under way in countries worldwide to reduce greenhouse gas emissions and to slow the pace of climate change.

EXERCISE 9

Interactions of Earth's Systems

Directions: Choose the best answer to the question.

1. Which of the following does NOT contribute to climate change?

   A. Earthquakes caused by shifts in tectonic plates
   B. Ash emitted into the atmosphere during volcanic eruptions
   C. Carbon dioxide released through the burning of fossil fuels
   D. Changes in Earth's axis of rotation

Answer is on page 804.

Earth, Human Activities, and Natural Resource Sustainability

Ancient cultures began the process of manipulating Earth's natural resources to create farms, towns, and cities. As people discovered new uses for forests, waterways, and lands, the impact on Earth grew exponentially. Our modern culture started with the industrial revolution that began in the late 18th century. Since then, agricultural and industrial development has led to a huge increase in population worldwide.

Modern agriculture and industry require the use of vast amounts of natural resources. Minerals are mined and used to create countless kinds of industrial and consumer products. Forests are cut down and used for lumber and paper. Land is cleared and used for farms, cities, highways, and industrial development Modern agriculture uses huge amounts of water and chemical fertilizers. All of these activities require huge amounts of energy and produce large amounts of waste.

Much of the energy for industrial development has come from the burning of fossil fuels. **Fossil fuels** are naturally occurring hydrocarbons found in coal, petroleum, and natural gas. They are produced from the anaerobic decomposition of organisms over hundreds of millions of years. Petroleum provides power for modes of transportation such as automobiles, ships, and airplanes. Coal and natural gas are used to produce heat and electricity.

Fossil fuels are a nonrenewable resource; that is, there is only a finite supply available on Earth. Once petroleum, coal, and natural gas deposits are used up, they cannot be replaced. And according to the laws of supply and demand, as fossil fuels become scarce, the cost to extract, manufacture, distribute, and consume them is sure to increase.

The environmental impact of the expanding human footprint is visible in the destruction and depletion of natural resources, in the waste output that endangers wildlife, and in atmospheric changes due to the burning of fossil fuels. Scientists agree that Earth's climate is changing. Dramatic weather patterns, extreme seasonal temperatures, and the melting of glaciers and polar ice caps are evidence of the changing conditions on Earth. Evidence indicates that human activities such as deforestation, mining, manufacturing, and population growth have played a significant role in causing climate change. The evidence also indicates that action is necessary to rebalance Earth's ecosystems that permit humans and animals to survive.

Climate and Weather

What is the difference between *weather* and *climate*? **Weather** describes short-term conditions in the atmosphere, such as precipitation in the form of rain or snow, temperatures, humidity, and periodic storms. Weather conditions usually do not last for a significant period of time because of environmental changes and other variables. **Climate** is the term used for longer-term weather trends in a particular area. Meteorologists can predict climate conditions with high accuracy because a large amount of historical information is available. For example, they can predict the potential strength of hurricanes in a particular season based on warming trends in the oceans because they have decades of data. **Climate change** refers to alterations in long-term climate patterns that continue for decades and centuries. The same historical information that meteorologists use to predict weather patterns can be used to predict the long-term effects of climate change.

Climate change has begun impacting weather in certain parts of the United States. For example, some areas that normally receive significant rainfall have experienced severe droughts. In other parts of the country, late summer and early fall weather patterns are occurring later and later in the year. In October 2012, Hurricane Sandy devastated the northeast coast of the United States. Unseasonably warm ocean temperatures adjacent to New Jersey and New York were a major factor fueling the strength of this hurricane and making it so destructive.

EXERCISE 10

Climate and Weather

Directions: Choose the best answer to the question.

1. Which is NOT true in regard to weather?

   A. Weather lasts for only a short time period.
   B. Weather stays the same over years and decades.
   C. Weather is affected by changing atmospheric conditions.
   D. Weather is influenced by changes in heat and humidity.

Answer is on page 804.

Natural Resources and Human Activity

The climate changes observed today may be caused by increased levels of carbon dioxide in the atmosphere, which keep solar radiation from escaping. Much of this increase in carbon dioxide is the result of human activity: carbon dioxide is produced from the burning of fossil fuels. Huge amounts of these fuels are consumed worldwide in order to keep modern economies running, and the consequence has been a steady upward trend in the amount of carbon dioxide in the atmosphere. The following chart displays this upward trend and the corresponding increase in global temperatures.

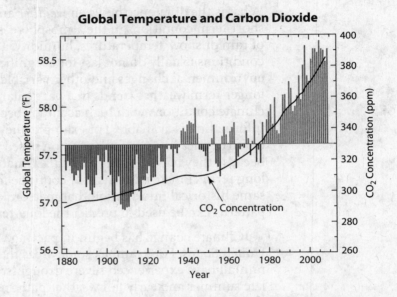

Global Temperature and Carbon Dioxide

Another human activity with harmful environmental consequences is deforestation. **Deforestation** is the cutting down of trees for lumber and the clearing of tree-covered areas for farming, housing, and industry. Trees perform the important function of taking in carbon dioxide from the atmosphere and producing oxygen through the process of photosynthesis. When large areas of forests are removed, the remaining trees cannot filter sufficient amounts of carbon dioxide out of the atmosphere. Deforestation not only contributes to increased atmospheric carbon dioxide levels, but it also displaces and destroys **biodiversity**, the remarkable variety of living things that inhabit forests.

Carbon dioxide from the atmosphere is also absorbed in the oceans. Evidence now shows higher-than-normal carbon dioxide levels in seawater. When the concentration of carbon dioxide in seawater rises, the pH of the seawater decreases. This decrease results in an acidic ocean ecology that threatens marine life. Shellfish and coral reefs cannot form hard calcium shells under acidic conditions. Coral reefs are host to about 25 percent of Earth's marine life. Without coral reefs, a domino effect ensues, threatening food chains and the future growth of animal populations.

The increase in atmospheric carbon dioxide, if left unchecked, is likely to have major consequences. Global warming and climate change can cause odd and extreme weather patterns, including an increase in devastating hurricanes. Droughts and other climate shifts can harm agriculture and reduce food production. Melting glaciers and polar ice caps can raise sea levels, causing flooding and coastal erosion and displacing human and animal populations. In short, there may be severe and harmful effects on national economies, societies, and even politics. For these reasons, it is becoming increasingly important for human societies worldwide to take major steps to control the factors that are leading to global warming and climate change.

EXERCISE 11

Natural Resources and Human Activity

Directions: Choose the best answer to the question.

1. Which statement describes a result of increased carbon dioxide levels in the atmosphere?

   A. An increase in hydrocarbons in the lithosphere
   B. An increase in the melting of ice caps in the arctic zones
   C. An increase in the amount of forested areas
   D. An increase in the number of coral reefs

Answer is on page 804.

Reducing Human Impact on the Earth

The damage that climate change is causing is not irreversible. People can change the way they interact with Earth's systems and restore the necessary balance that allows living things to exist on Earth. Two positive actions we can take are recycling and conserving resources.

Recycling is the reuse of consumer waste materials. Items such as paper, aluminum, steel, and copper are all recyclable materials. Recycling plants currently help communities by processing these wastes, reducing the amount of garbage that is deposited in landfills.

Conserving resources means decreasing the use of nonrenewable natural resources such as fossil fuels. For example, automobile manufacturers now make hybrid vehicles that conserve petroleum by switching to electric power produced by batteries.

In agriculture, there are "best practices" that farmers can use to minimize damage to the land and keep it productive. One is **contour plowing**, which is the plowing of fields across rather than along hillside slopes. This method reduces the amount of water run-off and soil erosion. Another is **strip cropping**, which is the practice of planting crops with differing nutrient requirements next to each other. This practice prevents depletion of nutrients in the soil.

But even some attempts to reduce the human impact on the environment can have adverse effects. For example, many homes and industries have switched from petroleum to natural gas because natural gas is relatively "clean burning"; that is, it releases only half as much carbon into the air as petroleum. However, one major technique for mining natural gas is actually harmful to the environment. This technique is called **hydraulic fracturing**, or "**fracking**." It is used to release natural gas from oil shale or sedimentary rock located deep within Earth's crust. In fracking, water mixed with sand and chemicals is injected under high pressure into the oil shale. The pressure causes cracks in the shale, allowing the natural gas to be extracted. Opponents of fracking claim that the chemical wastewater is not only bad for the environment but also pollutes and depletes people's water supplies. The following diagram shows how fracking can release chemicals into the water table.

Hydraulic Fracturing

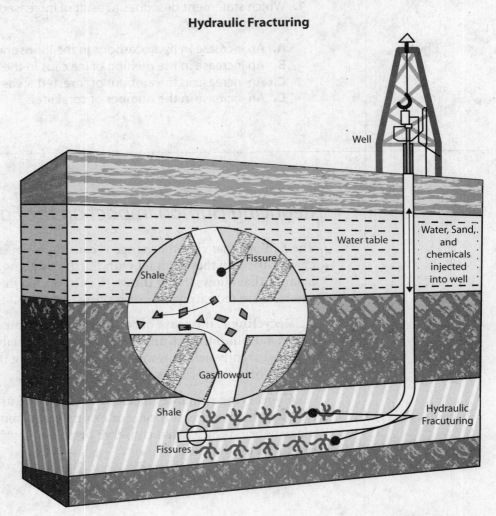

Developing conservation methods and better ways of using Earth's natural resources can be a complex task. For each new idea, the costs, safety, reliability, and impact to the environment must be considered. The potential societal benefits need to be weighed against the environmental impacts over the short term and long term.

Today when planners consider major new projects, such as factories, housing developments, or highways, they need to consider issues such as minimizing the environmental impact, managing natural resources efficiently, reducing waste and pollution, and sustaining biodiversity in the surrounding area. Only by considering these factors can they ensure that they are building human communities that are sustainable in the long term.

Of course, incorporating these factors into development plans has a cost. For example, **waste management**, or the collecting, transport, and proper disposal of waste materials, costs money to implement and operate. Proper waste management can require building water treatment facilities, recycling centers, and safe landfills for nonrecyclable garbage. When these kinds of major costs are involved, government officials may need to make sure that regulations are followed and community interests are met.

Today entire industries are focused on developing new technologies to reduce the human impact on the environment. "Green spaces" are created in city centers. New buildings limit the amount of electricity used. Offices and homes install "green roofs" with vegetation that absorbs heat and carbon dioxide and emits oxygen. With the help of these and numerous similar initiatives, human beings hope to build and maintain a healthy relationship with the environment.

EXERCISE 12

Reducing Human Impact on the Earth

Directions: Choose the best answer to the question.

1. Hydraulic fracking is now used in many areas of the United States to extract natural gas and petroleum products. Which statement BEST describes the benefits and costs of hydraulic fracking to the United States?

   A. Fracking may extract more natural gas, but it will cause conflicts between the United States and other countries that mine fossil fuels.

   B. Fracking reduces the cost of extracting natural gas, but it does not produce sufficient volumes to meet demand.

   C. Fracking enables people to use more cleaner-burning natural gas, but it may adversely affect the delicate balance of the ecosystem.

   D. Fracking may help reduce imports of foreign oil, but it does not generate an economic benefit.

Answer is on page 804.

Social Studies

The Social Studies Test

The Social Studies section of the GED® test measures your knowledge of key social studies topics and how well you are able to analyze and interpret documents and other social studies information. Half of the questions focus on US government and civics. The rest cover US history, world history, economics, and geography.

Questions on the Social Studies test may ask about the information in a short passage, a map, a graph, a table, or some other graphic presentation of social studies data. Sometimes two or three questions will refer to the same passage, graph, or table.

The Social Studies Review

The following section of this book will introduce you to the basic skills and topics that are tested on the Social Studies test. Each main topic is followed by a short exercise to measure how well you have mastered that subject. When you are finished with your review, test your mastery of basic social studies skills by taking the Social Studies Posttest at the back of this book.

This Social Studies review section is organized as follows:

Social Studies

Answers for all of the exercises in these chapters are located in the Exercise Answer Keys section at the back of this book.

CHAPTER 1

US Civics and Government

This chapter examines the principles that have contributed to the development of American constitutional democracy, as well as the structure and design of the US government.

Early Forms of Government

Throughout history, different cultures have tried various forms of government. At the dawn of civilization, with the emergence of agriculture, early peoples found that they had to organize themselves beyond the tribal structures that had dominated hunter-gatherer societies. A growing population in need of a steady supply of food and adequate defense led to the development of government. Governments could organize and regulate human activity while providing order among various groups and individuals.

The earliest form of government to emerge was the *monarchy*, centered on the rule of kings and queens. These monarchs normally gained power by inheritance and usually ruled for life. They organized armies to protect the population, made laws to regulate daily life, and managed the maintenance and stability of the food supply. Their power was often absolute, meaning that their authority could never be challenged.

Out of monarchy, new forms of social order emerged based on economic power and education. In time, monarchs were supported by an *aristocracy*, a ruling upper class whose wealth was based on land ownership and whose power passed from one generation to the next. Farmers, artisans, craftspeople, and slaves made up the lower class. In this structure, the demand for luxury goods by the upper class, such as jewelry and pottery, spurred economic development in the lower class.

As time went on, the form of monarchy became more complex. In ancient Mesopotamia (modern Iraq), for example, a form of monarchy called *theocracy* emerged, in which government was presumed to be based on divine authority. Kings were believed to get their power from the gods, and in some instances it was believed that they represented the gods. In ancient Egypt this took on a very literal form, in which monarchs, called *pharaohs*, were considered gods themselves. Authority over all of society rested with the pharaohs. However, the rule of the kingdom soon proved to be too much for any one person, and a *bureaucracy*—an administrative organization that relies on appointed officials and regular procedures—was developed. In ancient China, where kings ruled as well, most power actually lay in the hands of a landowning aristocracy.

With the development of writing, expanding wealth, and a growing educated class, more and more people began to demand a voice in government. Struggles emerged over the right to rule. In ancient Greece, tyrants emerged around the year 700 BC. Unlike the modern, often negative meaning of the word *tyrant*, Greek tyrants were members of the newly empowered lower class who sought to seize power from the kings and aristocracy. Support for the tyrants came from peasants who were in debt to the former rulers. With the help of paid armies, the tyrants were able to lead ancient Greece for close to 200 years.

The rule of the tyrants is significant because it ended the rule of monarchs and aristocrats and allowed more people to participate in government. In some Greek cities, this led to the development of *oligarchy* (government by a small group of people usually distinguished by wealth or family ties) and *democracy* (government by all eligible members of a population, often through elected representatives). The Greek experiments in government would become a model for later civilizations, most notably Rome, which would eventually establish a *republic* (a state in which power is exercised by elected representatives rather than a monarch) that lasted for several hundred years.

EXERCISE 1

Early Forms of Government

Directions: Choose the best answer to each question. Question 1 is based on the following passage.

As time went on, the form of monarchy became more complex. In ancient Mesopotamia (modern Iraq), for example, a form of monarchy called *theocracy* emerged, in which government was presumed to be based on divine authority. Kings were believed to get their power from the gods, and in some instances it was believed that they represented the gods.

1. What is the BEST definition of *theocracy*?

  A. Rule by a small group
  B. Rule by all eligible members of a population
  C. Rule by divine right
  D. Rule based on land ownership

2. Why did the pharaohs require the assistance of a bureaucracy?

  A. To help manage the affairs of the kingdom
  B. To perform religious rites
  C. To satisfy the demand for jewelry and pottery
  D. To lead armies into battle

3. What led to the development of democracy?

   A. The development of more complicated agricultural techniques
   B. The demand of the lower class to have a say in government
   C. The emergence of the aristocracy
   D. The demand for luxury goods

Answers are on page 805.

Athenian Democracy

The best example of Greek democracy comes from the city of Athens, where around the year 600 BC the city was thrown into turmoil due to an economic crisis. Many members of the lower class found themselves in debt, often forced into slavery when they were unable to pay. As a result, much of the population rebelled against the aristocracy that ruled the city. Hoping to avoid a tyranny, the aristocrats appointed a reformer named Solon to rule and end the crisis. Solon canceled all land debts, freed peasants who had been sold into slavery, and even took land from the rich and gave it to the poor. Despite Solon's best efforts, however, a tyrant named Peisistratus seized Athens in 560 BC.

Peisistratus immediately began his own campaign of reforms. He increased trade to please merchants and gave even more land to the poor. Despite these efforts, the people of Athens rebelled again in 510 BC, ending the tyranny, and they appointed a reformer named Cleisthenes as their ruler.

Cleisthenes created a ruling council of 500 that oversaw the main functions of government and gave ultimate authority to an assembly made up of male citizens. For the first time in history, a ruling majority had the power to negotiate treaties, make laws, and declare war. Democracy was born.

Athenian democracy went through many reforms and revisions after Cleisthenes, eventually becoming a direct democracy led by a statesman named Pericles. Under this system, all male citizens had a voice in the decisions of government through debate and direct vote. Any male citizen could speak on any issue, and poor citizens as well as those of the upper class were eligible for any public office. Judges and generals were elected, and to guard against the ambitions of any one man, a majority of citizens could at any time banish anyone considered harmful to the state in a practice known as *ostracism.*

Under democratic rule, Athens became the preeminent power in Greece, building for itself a vast and wealthy empire known as the Delian League. Using these vast riches, Pericles launched several impressive building projects, including the construction of the Parthenon, regarded as one of the greatest temples of the ancient world. Athens also became the center of art and education, its citizens pioneering the fields of mathematics, astronomy, biology, and philosophy.

Despite these accomplishments, though, it is important to note that the vast majority of Athenians did not take part in Athenian democracy. Noncitizen males, women, and slaves were excluded from the government. Despite the fact that there were as many as 40,000 male citizens in Athens at any given time, on average the number of participants in debate and voting seldom reached 6,000.

Ultimately, direct democracy led to the collapse of the Athenian empire, as the majority of people called for war against the city's chief rival, Sparta. Despite Pericles' best efforts, the majority ruled in favor of hostilities, beginning a long series of conflicts known the Peloponnesian War. The war between Athens and Sparta lasted decades, during which the city of Athens endured several losses, including a plague that wiped out more than a third of the city's population and resulted in the death of Pericles himself. Still the war dragged on until finally in 405 BC, the majority of the once powerful Athenian fleet was destroyed. Within a year, Athens surrendered and the Athenian empire was destroyed.

EXERCISE 2

Athenian Democracy

Directions: Read the passage and then answer the questions that follow.

Pericles, a statesman of ancient Athens, made this speech at a public funeral after the first battle of the Peloponnesian War in 431 BC.

Sculpture of the ancient Greek
statesman Pericles

Excerpt from Pericles's Funeral Oration, 431 BC

Our form of government does not enter into rivalry [competition] with the institutions of others. Our government does not copy our neighbors', but is an example to them. It is true that we are called a democracy, for the administration is in the hands of the many and not of the few. But while there exists equal justice to all and alike in their private disputes, the claim of excellence is also recognized; and when a citizen is in any way distinguished, he is preferred to the public service, not as a matter of privilege, but as the reward of merit. Neither is poverty an obstacle, but a man may benefit his country whatever the obscurity of his condition. There is no exclusiveness in our public life, and in our private business we are not suspicious of one another, nor angry with our neighbor if he does what he likes; we do not put on sour looks at him which, though harmless, are not pleasant. While we are thus unconstrained in our private business, a spirit of reverence pervades [spreads through] our public acts; we are prevented from doing wrong by respect for the authorities and for the laws. . . .

1. Which phrase from the excerpt BEST expresses a central idea of democracy?

   A. "Our government does not copy our neighbors'"
   B. "administration is in the hands of the many"
   C. "we are not suspicious of one another"
   D. "a spirit of reverence pervades our public acts"

2. Which phrase BEST completes the chart?

How Pericles Defines Democracy
Respect for authorities
Respect for the laws
Equal opportunity for all

   A. Equal justice for all
   B. Competition with other governments
   C. Discrimination against the poor
   D. Better treatment for the wealthy

3. According to Pericles, one responsibility of a citizen in a democracy is to do which of the following?

   A. Elect only the wealthy to public office.
   B. Avoid sharing opinions with others.
   C. Operate a private business.
   D. Take part in the civic affairs of the nation.

Answers are on page 805.

The Roman Republic

At the same time that Athens was moving toward democratic rule, people known as the Romans began their own experiment in government. The people who would eventually become the Romans first settled in modern-day Italy around 1500 BC, and they established the city of Rome soon after. Little is known about these people except that they spoke Latin and soon fell under the influence of several other groups, most notably the Etruscans and the Greeks, who had established colonies on the southern tip of the Italian peninsula. After a short period of conquest and unification, the Romans overthrew their kings, and in 509 BC they established a republic. A republic is a form of government in which the leader is not a king, is usually elected, and certain citizens have a right to vote.

Rome was divided into two classes—the patricians and the plebeians (plih BEE unhz). The patricians were the wealthy, landowning elite, who under the Roman Republic became Rome's ruling class. The plebeians were the poor landowners, farmers, merchants, artisans, and craftspeople who made up the majority. All male citizens, regardless of class, paid taxes, served in the military, and had the right to vote, although only patricians could hold political office.

A Senate, a ruling body of patricians who served for life, was the focal point of Roman politics. At first the Senate served only in an advisory capacity, but by the third century BC it had come to dominate rule in the Republic. Below the Senate were several people's assemblies, most importantly the centuriate assembly, which elected officials and passed laws. The plebeians also had their own assembly, called the council of the plebs, to serve as a check on the power of the patrician class.

The chief political officers in Rome were the consuls and praetors. Two consuls, elected annually, ran the government and commanded Roman armies, taking turns as to prevent any one man from gaining too much power. The praetors oversaw all civil laws—laws governing Roman citizens—and eventually as Rome's power grew, they also judged cases involving noncitizens.

Central to the Roman Republic was a deep mistrust of total rule by any one man, and so a series of checks and balances were established. Each assembly and each office had the power of veto over another, and they were able to effectively block any decision deemed unpopular or dangerous. The most powerful veto was given to the tribune of the plebs, a powerful office designed to protect the plebeians from the Senate. Although checks and balances were seen as crucial to maintaining order, the power of veto often stood in the way of legislative progress. Class struggle and mistrust dominated the Roman Republic throughout its existence.

Possibly the most enduring legacy of the Roman Republic was its system of law. The Romans were the first to establish concepts of natural law, or universal law, ensuring that all Roman citizens, and by extension all people, had some basic rights. Many of these Roman standards of justice endure today, including the presumption of innocence and the right to a fair trial.

Ultimately, the Roman Republic collapsed because of the ambitions of a few people. Rome was driven by conquest, and triumphant generals were considered celebrities in their own right. Some were able to use their fame to gain greater political power. One such general, Julius Caesar, was able to exploit his popularity to make himself dictator in 47 BC. Although the position of dictator was meant to be used only in emergencies, Caesar declared his appointment for life. Knowing that to maintain power he had to keep the plebeians happy, Caesar gave land and money to the poor while weakening the power of the Senate. Resentful of his growing power and determined to restore the Republic, a group of senators assassinated Caesar in 44 BC. More than a decade of civil war followed. Eventually, Julius Caesar's grandnephew, Octavian, became the first emperor of Rome. The Republic would never return again.

EXERCISE 3

The Roman Republic

Directions: Read the passage and then answer the questions that follow.

Polybius (puh LIH bee uhs) was an ancient Greek historian best known for writing about the Roman Republic in his work *The Histories*. In Book 6 of *The Histories*, Polybius describes the structure of the Roman government as a balance of interests between the consuls, the Roman Senate, and the plebeians' assemblies and officials, known as tribunes. He outlined how each part of the government had ways to check, or limit, the powers of the other two parts. For example, the Senate had the power to pass laws, but the people's assembly had the power to approve or reject laws. The consuls had the power to direct the government and the army, but consuls were limited to a one-year term and each consul had the power to veto the actions of the other. While the consuls could command the army, only the people's assembly and tribunes had the power to decide to go to war, and only the Senate had the power to fund the military. Polybius's work would later influence the framers of the US Constitution. Several of the delegates at the Constitutional Convention, including James Madison, were familiar with Polybius and had studied *The Histories*. The system of checks and balances that the framers built into the Constitution were based in part on Polybius's analysis of the structure of the Roman government.

1. Based on the passage, which statement BEST supports the conclusion that the structure of Roman government influenced the framers of the US Constitution?

   A. James Madison studied *The Histories*.
   B. The framers outlined a system of checks and balances in the Constitution.
   C. Polybius described checks and balances in Rome's government.
   D. Roman senators had the power to pass laws.

2. What evidence does the passage provide to support the claim that Polybius's work had an impact on the framers of the Constitution?

A. Polybius invented the Roman Republic's system of checks and balances.
B. The framers rejected the idea of a system of checks and balances.
C. Polybius outlined the structure of the Roman government.
D. Several framers had studied *The Histories*.

3. In the US system of checks and balances, Congress checks the power of the executive branch by controlling taxes and spending. Based on the passage, what feature of Roman government is MOST similar to this check?

A. The Senate had the power to pass laws.
B. Consuls were limited to one-year terms.
C. The Senate had the power to fund the military.
D. The consuls commanded the military.

Answers are on page 805.

The Rise of Modern Government

After the collapse of the Roman Empire, absolute monarchies once again dominated governments in much of the world. It was not until 1215, when King John of England signed the Magna Carta, or Great Charter, that government again began to include the voice of the people.

After a series of dictatorial kings, the English aristocracy began to demand more power in the government. Central to their demands were basic civil liberties, or personal rights and freedoms that cannot be taken away. Members of the English ruling class argued that they were entitled to certain rights. The Magna Carta gave written recognition of basic civil liberties and was the first step in establishing a limited monarchy. In the decades that followed, English nobles took a further step in establishing Parliament, a representative body that would eventually consist of two houses, a House of Lords made up of members of the church and nobility, and a House of Commons made up of knights and townspeople. Parliament quickly became the center of government in England, acting as a crucial check on the king's power.

Another political revolution began in England during the 1600s. In 1628, Parliament passed a Petition of Right in response to the rule of Charles I, who tried to restore absolute monarchy. The petition put even greater limits on the king and expanded the notions of basic civil rights. At first Charles seemed to accept the petition, but he soon began to ignore its provisions. In 1642 England descended into civil war. Under the leadership of Oliver Cromwell, parliamentary forces won the struggle. In 1649 Charles I was executed, and the monarchy was abolished. England was declared a republic known as the Commonwealth—a nation founded on law and united by agreement for and by the people.

The Commonwealth did not last long. Finding Parliament to be a roadblock to his power, Oliver Cromwell eventually declared himself dictator, and in 1689, after his death, the monarchy was completely restored. However, the power of the king would be even weaker than before. In accepting a new ruler, Parliament strengthened the rights of citizens and its own checks on the monarchy with the English Bill of Rights. This document gave several key powers to Parliament, including the right to raise armies, and it confirmed for people the right to bear arms and have a jury trial. Parliament did not have complete control of government, but it had abolished the idea of the divine right of kings by dethroning one king and establishing another, and it had asserted its right to be a permanent part of government. Over the next century, the powers and influence of Parliament only expanded, and England became a true constitutional monarchy.

The turmoil of the 1600s was reflected in English legal and political thought. In 1651 Thomas Hobbes, appalled by the events surrounding the rise of Oliver Cromwell, wrote a political work called *Leviathan*. In this work, Hobbes argued that people were naturally cruel, only concerned with self-preservation above all else, and thus had to be ruled by an absolute ruler with unlimited power who could suppress rebellion and maintain order. John Locke, on the other hand, believed that people naturally craved peace and freedom. In his 1689 work, *Two Treatises on Government*, Locke argued that human beings were born with certain natural rights, including the rights of life, liberty, and property. According to Locke's philosophy, government existed to protect these natural rights. If a government failed in its obligation, the people had the right to alter or abolish that government.

Locke was not a supporter of democracy, believing instead that only an aristocracy had the right to rule. His ideas, however, greatly influenced future generations of political thinkers and revolutionaries. Many of Locke's ideas, and sometimes his exact words, can be found in both the Declaration of Independence and the US Constitution.

The Rise of Modern Government

Directions: Choose the best answer to each question.

1. Why did English monarchs object to the idea of granting civil rights?

   A. It would create disorder in society.
   B. It would lead to civil war.
   C. It would require the writing of new laws.
   D. It would limit the king's power.

Question 2 is based on the following passage.

Excerpt from the English Bill of Rights, 1689

. . . suspending the laws or the execution of laws by regal authority without consent of Parliament is illegal. . . .

2. Which form of government does the passage support?

   A. Rule by divine right
   B. Limited monarchy
   C. Absolute rule
   D. Dictatorship

Question 3 is based on the following passage.

Excerpt from the Declaration of Independence, 1776

We hold these truths to be self-evident, that all men are created equal, that they are endowed by their Creator with certain unalienable Rights, that among these are Life, Liberty and the pursuit of Happiness.

3. Based on the passage and what you have read in "The Rise of Modern Government," what inference can be made about some of the ideas in the Declaration of Independence?

   A. They were shaped by the philosophy of John Locke.
   B. They were based on the work of Thomas Hobbes.
   C. They reflected a belief in the divine right of kings.
   D. They established a constitutional monarchy.

Answers are on page 805.

The US Government

Ideas about civil rights and civil liberties were very much at the forefront when the American colonies declared their independence from Britain in 1776. The Revolutionary War that followed demonstrated John Locke's belief that a government that failed in its obligation to its people should be changed or abolished. The struggle for independence was long and bloody, but in the end the colonists won and created a new representative democracy, based on the foundations of Greek and Roman government and strengthened by the English ideas of natural rights.

Colonial leaders recognized that they could not foresee every problem that the new nation might face in the future, and so they created a government that would be flexible enough to change peacefully. In this regard, the US Constitution served as a framework for government open to ongoing interpretation and change, as opposed to a strict and unchanging set of laws and regulations. This basic idea made the government of the United States unlike that of any other nation on Earth.

Under the Constitution, power was divided between a chief executive and a legislature. As in Athens, citizens had the right to voice their opinion and debate the issues, but a series of checks and balances would prevent one branch of government from overpowering the others. As in the Roman Republic, citizens would have the right to vote for their representatives. As in England, the government guaranteed basic civil rights, but these rights were extended to all citizens, not just members of a landowning aristocracy.

The US government was founded on the ideals of shared power—between branches of government, between state government and the federal government, and between citizens and their elected representatives. Citizens' rights were protected, but citizens also had certain duties, including the duty to obey the law, pay taxes, and gain an education. In this way, it became a responsibility for citizens to be informed on issues and to vote.

Over time, through protest and negotiation, the idea of who could be considered a citizen and who could benefit from the right of citizenship has changed. When the Constitution was written, full citizenship was granted only to landowning free men over the age of 21. Over time, citizenship and voting rights were extended to nonlandowning white men. Passed by Congress and ratified by the states after the Civil War, the Fourteenth Amendment granted citizenship to former slaves, and the Fifteenth Amendment guaranteed voting rights and equal protection of the law to all male citizens regardless of race. In 1920 the Nineteenth Amendment granted voting rights to women. Later, in 1971, the Twenty-Sixth Amendment lowered the voting age for all citizens to 18.

In addition to voting rights, American history has seen several movements meant to extend full civil rights to all citizens. This includes the struggle for equality by African Americans in the 1960s, women in the 1970s, and gays and lesbians today. As time goes on, the roles and rights of citizens, the definition of natural rights, and the form of government will continue to change.

The US Government

Directions: Read the passages. Then complete the writing assignment that follows.

Excerpt from the Fifteenth Amendment, Ratified in 1870

The right of citizens of the United States to vote shall not be denied or abridged by the United States or by any State on account of race, color, or previous condition of servitude.

Excerpt from the Nineteenth Amendment, Ratified in 1920

The right of citizens of the United States to vote shall not be denied or abridged by the United States or by any State on account of sex.

Excerpt from the Twenty-Sixth Amendment, Ratified in 1971

The right of citizens of the United States, who are eighteen years of age or older, to vote shall not be denied or abridged by the United States or by any State on account of age.

Write a paragraph that traces the expansion of civil rights in the United States. When you write your response, be sure to follow these steps:

1. Create a sound, logical response based on the passages and your reading of "The US Government."

2. Cite evidence from the passages to support your main idea.

3. Organize and present information in a sensible sequence.

4. Show clear connections between main points and details.

5. Follow standard English conventions in regard to grammar, spelling, punctuation, and sentence structure.

Write your response in the box. This task may take 25 minutes to complete.

Answers are on page 805.

## CHAPTER 2

US History

This chapter examines some of the most important ideas and key historical documents that have shaped American constitutional government.

Ideas from Greece and England

Modern American democracy has its foundations in ancient Greece, where in the city of Athens, democracy, or rule by the people, was first developed some 2,500 years ago. Under this system, the majority elected leaders, and those deemed eligible voted on the policies of their government. Laws could be proposed by anyone, and trials were held in public. The idea of direct rule through popular election was then later adopted in ancient Rome, which set up a representative democracy in which eligible citizens were allowed to elect officials to act on their behalf. A senate devised laws, and magistrates passed sentences at trial.

Although these early attempts at democracy ultimately failed, they became the model for future experiments in majority rule. One such place where democratic ideas took root was medieval England.

After the victory of William of Normandy at the Battle of Hastings in 1066, the French-speaking Normans gradually merged with the native Angles and Saxons of England. William established himself as a powerful monarch, and he greatly expanded the system of taxation and royal courts begun by the Anglo-Saxon kings. The power of the king expanded further under the reign of William's heirs, who could, without justification, banish, execute, or imprison their subjects.

Resentful of the growing king's power, the English nobility rebelled under the reign of King John. At Runnymede in 1215, a group of English nobles forced John to accept and sign a document of rights called the **Magna Carta**, or Great Charter. Its principles, or ideas, had a great influence on the development of constitutional government. One of the most important principles established by the Magna Carta was due process of law. The Magna Carta said that "no freeman shall be seized or imprisoned . . . except by the lawful judgment of his equals or by the law of the land." The Magna Carta made it clear that everyone, including the monarch, must follow the law.

The Magna Carta also defined English nobles' individual rights that the monarch could not take away. For example, the monarch could not levy taxes

657

without consent from the nobles. The document also guaranteed individuals accused of crimes to a trial by a jury of their peers. The Magna Carta was originally intended to guarantee the rights of English nobles. In time, these rights would be extended to most English people.

Later in the 1200s, **Parliament** was established to give voice to the people in dealings with the state. In 1628, a conflict between Parliament and King Charles I led to another important document called the **Petition of Right**. The Petition of Right further limited the monarch's power by requiring the king to get approval from Parliament before setting new taxes. It also outlined rules under which individuals could be punished or when martial law could be declared.

EXERCISE 1

Ideas from Greece and England

Directions: Read the passage and then answer the questions that follow.

Excerpt from the Magna Carta

No freeman shall be taken, imprisoned, disseised, outlawed, banished, or in any way destroyed, nor will We proceed against or prosecute him, except by the lawful judgment of his peers or by the law of the land.

To no one will We sell, to no one will We deny or delay, right or justice.

1. Based on the excerpt, which of the following is the BEST example of "lawful judgment"?

   A. A king who banishes a subject for stealing
   B. A jury finding a man guilty of murder
   C. A teacher taking a phone away from a student for disrupting the class
   D. A judge inventing a punishment to fit a crime

2. Based on the excerpt, which of the following would NOT be a denial of justice?

   A. A defendant buying his way out of criminal charges
   B. A government denying an accused person a trial
   C. A judge postponing a trial for months without reason
   D. A jury failing to reach a verdict

Answers are on page 805.

The Mayflower Compact

After European explorers reached America in the 1400s, the powers of Europe began to colonize the territories that they claimed across North America. The English, competing against the French and Dutch, began to send ships to what is now New England, and they eventually dominated the eastern seaboard of what would become the United States. Although many of the ships sent from England went in search of trade and wealth, some were filled with groups of people seeking freedom from political and religious persecution at home. Among these groups was a sect of Puritans we know today as the **Pilgrims**.

The Pilgrims were separatists from the Church of England who believed that the church needed reform and restoration from corruption. Facing increased persecution for their beliefs, a group of Pilgrims left England in 1620 aboard a ship called the *Mayflower*. After crossing the Atlantic Ocean, the Pilgrims eventually settled near what is now Plymouth, Massachusetts. Upon arrival, with limited contact with royal or colonial authorities, the Pilgrims drew up the **Mayflower Compact**, a plan for self-government. Essentially, the Pilgrims, while avowing their loyalty to the king of England, also empowered themselves to create laws and regulations through majority rule. The Mayflower Compact drew heavily on English democratic tradition that was born out of the Magna Carta, and it represented the first attempt at majority self-rule in the New World.

EXERCISE 2

The Mayflower Compact

Directions: Read the passage and then answer the questions that follow.

Excerpt from the Mayflower Compact

In the name of God, Amen. We whose names are underwritten, the loyal subjects of our dread sovereign Lord, King James, by the grace of God, of Great Britain, France, and Ireland King, Defender of the Faith, etc.

Having undertaken, for the glory of God, and advancement of the Christian faith and honor of our King and Country, a voyage to plant the first colony in the northern parts of Virginia, do by these presents, solemnly and mutually, in the presence of God, and one another, covenant and combine ourselves together into a civil body politic; for our better ordering, and preservation and furtherance of the ends aforesaid; and by virtue hereof to enact, constitute, and frame, such just and equal laws, ordinances, acts, constitutions, and offices, from time to time, as shall be thought most meet and convenient for the general good of the colony; unto which we promise all due submission and obedience....

1. What is the BEST definition of the phrase "combine ourselves together into a civil body politic"?

   A. Start a new religion
   B. Declare independence
   C. Form a government
   D. Rebel against the king

2. Based on the excerpt, what does the phrase "enact, constitute, and frame" refer to?

   A. Making laws
   B. Choosing a new king
   C. Building houses
   D. Rejecting government

3. The Mayflower Compact can BEST be described as

   A. a royal order to establish a colony.
   B. a written framework for self-government.
   C. a plan for planting new crops.
   D. an agreement to name a new king.

Answers are on page 805.

The Declaration of Independence

Throughout the 1600s and 1700s, the British colonies continued to grow. As territories and trade expanded, tensions began to rise between the American colonists and the British government. Central to the issue was the lack of colonial representation in Parliament along with increased taxation on colonial exports and the imposition of increasingly strict laws by the king. Drawing on the precedent of majority rule, many colonists believed that they had a right to have a say in how the colonies were governed. By 1775 these tensions had escalated into armed conflict. Colonial militia and British troops fought at Lexington and Concord in Massachusetts, marking the first time colonists had taken up arms against British rule. The fighting at Lexington and Concord was the start of the **Revolutionary War**.

Colonial leaders met in Philadelphia in 1776 to discuss the problems, and after prolonged debate and vote, they agreed that the only viable course of action was to separate from the British Empire. Thomas Jefferson, the representative from the wealthy Virginia colony as well as a renowned scholar and political philosopher, was tasked with the job of writing the document that officially called for independence from the Crown.

Influenced heavily by Enlightenment thinkers such as John Locke, Jean-Jacques Rousseau, and Baron de Montesquieu, Jefferson believed that all men had certain unalienable, natural rights, and among these were the right to life, liberty, and property. Jefferson also believed that there existed a social contract between a government and its people based on upholding these rights. When a government failed in its duty and denied its citizens justice and liberty, it was the right of the people to abolish the government and establish a new one in its place.

On July 4, 1776, the Second Continental Congress adopted the **Declaration of Independence**. The main purpose of the Declaration of Independence as a whole was to announce that the colonies had separated from Britain. The nation it established was the newly formed United States of America.

EXERCISE 3

The Declaration of Independence

Directions: Read the passage and then answer the questions that follow.

Excerpt from the Declaration of Independence

IN CONGRESS, July 4, 1776.

The unanimous Declaration of the thirteen united States of America,

When in the Course of human events, it becomes necessary for one people to dissolve the political bands which have connected them with another, and to assume among the powers of the earth, the separate and equal station to which the Laws of Nature and of Nature's God entitle them, a decent respect to the opinions of mankind requires that they should declare the causes which impel them to the separation.

We hold these truths to be self-evident, that all men are created equal, that they are endowed by their Creator with certain unalienable Rights, that among these are Life, Liberty and the pursuit of Happiness.—That to secure these rights, Governments are instituted among Men, deriving their just powers from the consent of the governed,—That whenever any Form of Government becomes destructive of these ends, it is the Right of the People to alter or to abolish it, and to institute new Government, laying its foundation on such principles and organizing its powers in such form, as to them shall seem most likely to effect their Safety and Happiness. . . .

1. The introduction of the Declaration is the paragraph that begins with "When in the Course of human events." The introduction identifies that the purpose of the Declaration is to

   A. describe the system of government the new nation will have.
   B. announce the reasons causing the colonies to separate from the British Empire.
   C. argue that the colonies should be allowed to name their own king.
   D. present terms for a peace treaty between the colonies and Britain.

2. The paragraph that follows the introduction of the Declaration is known as the preamble. According to the preamble, where does a government get its power?

   A. From God
   B. From an absolute ruler
   C. From the consent of the people it represents
   D. From a wealthy upper class

3. The preamble of the Declaration states that the purpose of government is to

   A. expand national territory.
   B. add to a nation's wealth.
   C. make and carry out laws.
   D. protect the rights of the people.

Answers are on page 806.

The Constitution of the United States

Once the colonies declared independence from Britain, the Second Continental Congress faced a larger problem. They had to devise a new national government. The United States' first attempt at self-rule came in the form of the **Articles of Confederation**, adopted by Congress in 1777 and ratified by the states in 1781. After fighting for independence against British rule, the colonies did not want a powerful government that might become tyrannical. As a result, the Articles loosely unified the colonies as states under Congress, which had only a few limited powers. Congress could negotiate with other countries, raise armies, and declare war, but it had no authority to regulate trade or impose taxes. In addition, there were no separate branches of government, and each state had one vote in Congress, regardless of population.

After several political and economic problems threatened to undo the young republic following the end of the Revolutionary War, the political leaders of the United States met again to discuss the weaknesses of the Articles of Confederation. It was agreed that although balance and oversight must be maintained, a strong national government was essential to the nation's success.

In 1787, 55 delegates representing the 13 states met in Independence Hall in Philadelphia to discuss the formation of a new government. First, they agreed that the government should be divided into executive, legislative, and judicial branches to ensure that no one part of government could grow too powerful. Second, the delegates greatly increased the powers and responsibilities of Congress. Third, they divided the Congress into two houses, a House of Representatives in which states would be represented on the basis of population, and a Senate in which each state would receive two votes regardless of size. Finally, the delegates created a representative system known as federalism, in which power would be divided between the national government and the state governments.

In September, the **Constitution** was voted on by the Congress and submitted to the states for ratification. Once all state concerns were satisfied, including the addition of a Bill of Rights, the Constitution was formally ratified by all 13 states on May 29, 1790. The US government as we know it was born.

The Constitution of the United States

Directions: Read the passage and then answer the questions that follow.

Preamble of the Constitution of the United States

We the People of the United States, in Order to form a more perfect Union, establish Justice, insure domestic Tranquility, provide for the common defence, promote the general Welfare, and secure the Blessings of Liberty to ourselves and our Posterity, do ordain and establish this Constitution for the United States of America.

1. In your own words, explain some of the reasons given in the Preamble for why the Constitution was written.

_____

_____

_____

_____

_____

_____

_____

_____

_____

_____

2. Why is the phrase "We the People" significant?

_____

_____

_____

_____

_____

_____

_____

_____

_____

Answers are on page 806.

The Supreme Court of the United States

Under the Constitution, the national government was divided into the legislative, executive, and judicial branches. The legislative branch, made up of the House of Representatives and the Senate, is responsible for passing laws. The executive branch is headed by the President of the United Sates and is responsible for carrying out laws. The judicial branch includes all courts up to and including the Supreme Court, the final authority in the federal court system. Most of the Supreme Court's cases come from appeals of lower court decisions. Since the writing of the Constitution, the power of the Supreme Court has gradually expanded, most notably in 1803 when Chief Justice John Marshall struck down an act of Congress in the case of *Marbury v. Madison*, thus establishing the principle of judicial review. Since then, the Supreme Court has greatly shaped American democracy through numerous landmark decisions.

Plessy v. Ferguson

In 1892, an African American named Homer Plessy took a seat in a whites-only section of an East Louisiana Railway train in violation of an 1890 segregation law. After refusing to move from his seat, Plessy was arrested and later convicted at trial. Plessy appealed his case first to the Louisiana Supreme Court and then to the US Supreme Court. In 1896 the Supreme Court upheld the Louisiana law and the doctrine of so-called "separate but equal" public facilities for people of different races. The ruling in *Plessy v. Ferguson* established the legal basis for segregation in the South.

EXERCISE 5

Plessy v. Ferguson

Directions: Read the passage and then answer the questions that follow.

Excerpt from the Supreme Court Ruling on *Plessy v. Ferguson*

We consider the underlying fallacy of the plaintiff's argument to consist in the assumption that the enforced separation of the two races stamps the colored race with a badge of inferiority. If this be so, it is not by reason of anything found in the act, but solely because the colored race chooses to put that construction upon it. . . . The argument also assumes that social prejudice may be overcome by legislation, and that equal rights cannot be secured . . . except by an enforced commingling of the two races. We cannot accept this proposition. . . . Legislation is powerless to eradicate racial instincts or to abolish distinctions based upon physical differences, and the attempt to do so can only result in accentuating the difficulties of the present situation. If the civil and political rights of both races be equal, one cannot be inferior to the other civilly or politically. If one race be inferior to the other socially, the Constitution of the United States cannot put them upon the same plane. . . .

1. In this case, the plaintiff argued that the law that enforced segregation created "a badge of inferiority"? Did the Court agree? In the Court's view, where did that idea come from?

   _____

   _____

   _____

2. Would this Supreme Court have supported a civil rights bill? Explain.

   _____

   _____

   _____

   _____

Answers are on page 806.

Brown v. Board of Education

In 1952 the questions of segregation and basic natural rights again came before the Supreme Court. In the case that would become known as **Brown v. Board of Education of Topeka, Kansas**, the National Association for the Advancement of Colored People (NAACP) challenged the "separate but equal" principal first established in *Plessy v. Ferguson* as it pertained to public schools.

In 1954 the Supreme Court ruled unanimously in favor of the NAACP and the plaintiffs in the case, thus overturning *Plessy v. Ferguson* and effectively making segregation in public schools illegal in the United States. *Brown v. Board of Education* also marked the first in a series of landmark decisions passed down by Chief Justice Earl Warren.

EXERCISE 6

Brown v. Board of Education

Directions: Read the passage and then answer the questions that follow.

Excerpt from the Supreme Court Ruling in
Brown v. Board of Education

Segregation of white and colored children in public schools has a detrimental effect upon the colored children. The impact is greater when it has the sanction of the law, for the policy of separating the races is usually interpreted as denoting the inferiority of the negro group. A sense of inferiority affects the motivation of a child to learn. Segregation with the sanction of law, therefore, has a tendency to [retard] the educational and mental development of negro children and to deprive them of some of the benefits they would receive in a racial[ly] integrated school system. . . .

We conclude that, in the field of public education, the doctrine of "separate but equal" has no place. Separate educational facilities are inherently unequal. Therefore, we hold that the plaintiffs and others similarly situated for whom the actions have been brought are, by reason of the segregation complained of, deprived of the equal protection of the laws guaranteed by the Fourteenth Amendment. . . .

1. According to the ruling, what effect does segregation have on children?

   A. It creates a sense of inferiority in the discriminated group.
   B. It limits diversity in public schools.
   C. It puts unnecessary strains on the educational system.
   D. It encourages bad behavior from students in the classroom.

2. What might be a benefit of an integrated school system?

_____

_____

3. Rewrite the ruling in *Brown v. Board of Education* in your own words.

_____

_____

_____

_____

Answers are on page 806.

The Warren Court

In 1953 President Dwight D. Eisenhower appointed the governor of California, Earl Warren, to be the Chief Justice of the Supreme Court. With a reputation as a fair but tough law–and-order politician, Warren became an activist on the bench, greatly expanding the power of the Supreme Court.

Under Warren the Supreme Court handed down several landmark rulings. In 1954 the Court ruled on *Brown v. Board of Education*, which effectively ended segregation in public schools. The *Brown* decision was not just a powerful moral statement, it also demonstrated the power of the Court to affirm individual rights.

Between 1962 and 1964, the Warren Court considered what would collectively become known as the "one man, one vote" cases of **Baker v. Carr** and **Reynolds v. Sims**. In *Baker v. Carr*, the Warren Court held that federal courts have the power to determine the constitutionality of a state's voting districts. In *Reynolds v. Sims*, the Warren Court ruled that state legislative districts must be equal in population. In these cases the Warren Court ruled in favor of cities and suburbs, which were underrepresented in state legislatures in favor of rural areas. In his opinion, Chief Justice Warren wrote that the power of a person's vote should not depend on where that person lives. As a result, states immediately reapportioned their legislators, in essence transforming the political landscape of the country.

The area in which the Warren Court was most active was in criminal law. In 1961 the Court ruled in the case of **Mapp v. Ohio** that evidence seized illegally could not be used as evidence at trial. In 1963, in **Gideon v. Wainwright**, the Court ruled that criminal defendants were entitled to publicly funded counsel. In 1966, in the famous **Miranda v. Arizona** case, the Court ruled that police had to explain legal rights clearly to people in custody. Collectively these cases and others remade the United States' legal framework and made Earl Warren a major figure in the shaping of the way citizens interacted with their government.

EXERCISE 7

The Warren Court

Directions: Match each case to the correct Warren Court ruling.

1. _____ *Mapp v. Ohio*

    a. Segregation was deemed illegal in public schools.

2. _____ *Brown v. Board of Education*

    b. Evidence seized illegally could not be used as evidence at trial.

3. _____ *Gideon v. Wainwright*

    c. State legislative districts must be equal in population.

4. _____ *Reynolds v. Sims*

    d. Criminal defendants were entitled to publically funded counsel.

5. Would you describe the Warren Court as activist? Explain.

_____

_____

_____

Answers are on page 806.

Roe v. Wade

In addition to major shifts in civil and criminal rights, the 1960s and 1970s saw profound changes in the right to privacy as well. As women began to take a more active role in society and demand equal treatment in the workplace, the issues of contraception and later reproduction came before the Supreme Court.

In 1965 the Supreme Court heard the case *Griswold v. Connecticut*, in which the justices struck down a Connecticut state law banning contraceptive drugs. Although the Bill of Rights does not expressly mention a right to privacy, the justices ruled that the right to privacy exists in spirit throughout the Constitution, including the self-incrimination clause of the Fifth Amendment.

The notion that constitutionality protected privacy was put to its greatest test eight years later in 1973 when the Supreme Court decided the landmark case *Roe v. Wade*. Prior to 1973 abortion was regulated by the states and was largely illegal across the country. A shift began in the 1960s when several states began to relax their rules about abortion, especially in cases of rape or incest. With *Roe v. Wade* the court ruled that states could not regulate abortion during the first three months of pregnancy, as this period was deemed protected under the right to privacy. It was only during the second three months that abortion could be regulated, and in the final three months that it could be banned. The decision gave rise to a right-to-life movement whose members consider abortion morally wrong. The impassioned debate between pro-choice and pro-life factions eventually led to alterations to abortion rules, but the struggle to define the limits of privacy continues until this day.

EXERCISE 8

Roe v. Wade

Directions: Read the passage and then complete the writing assignments that follow.

Excerpt from Justice Byron White's Dissenting Opinion in *Roe v. Wade*

I find nothing in the language or history of the Constitution to support the Court's judgment. The Court simply fashions and announces a new constitutional right for pregnant women and, with scarcely any reason or authority for its action, invests that right with sufficient substance to override most existing state abortion statutes. The upshot is that the people and the legislatures of the 50 States are constitutionally disentitled to weigh the relative importance of the continued existence and development of the fetus, on the one hand, against a spectrum of possible impacts on the woman, on the other hand. As an exercise of raw judicial power, the Court perhaps has authority to do what it does today; but, in my view, its judgment is an improvident and extravagant exercise of the power of judicial review that the Constitution extends to this Court. . . .

1. Describe in your own words Justice Byron White's main objection to the Court's decision in *Roe v. Wade*.

   _____

   _____

   _____

   _____

2. Write a response to *Roe v. Wade* either in support or in opposition to the case.

   _____

   _____

   _____

   _____

Answers are on page 806.

## CHAPTER 3

Economics

This chapter examines some fundamental concepts in economics and some of the key economic developments that have shaped American history and politics.

Foundations of Economics

As long as people have organized themselves into groups, some type of economic activity has existed. People have always produced, consumed, and traded goods not only in order to survive but also to create wealth. People living in ancient times relied heavily on **bartering**, or trading goods for other goods or services. As societies became larger and more complex, **currency**, or money, was invented. Currency could be used to buy goods and services without having to trade goods or services in return. The earliest currencies were grains or other trade goods that were small and easily carried.

The earliest currency-based economies were centered around **markets**. Farmers, artisans, and craftspeople would bring their goods to the market in towns or cities, where people would gather to make purchases. The money earned by the producers of goods could then be used to produce even more goods, thus growing the economy, the market, and the cities that housed them. Cities grew because goods and services could more easily be concentrated in one place. In the cities of ancient Mesopotamia (modern Iraq), for example, temples became the first money-lending institutions, allowing people to borrow money at interest, or money paid for the use of money lent.

By the late Bronze Age (1500–1200 BC), trade had become multinational, taking place among many countries. Goods produced by one society were now traded for goods produced by other societies. This trade led to the development of trade routes, or pathways used for the transportation of goods. By 650 BC merchants had developed coins, made from precious metals such as gold and silver, which could be exchanged across borders.

The ancient world was also witness to the first developments in economic awareness and thought. Beginning with the ancient Greeks and philosophers such as Plato and Aristotle, people began to examine the ways in which trade and business were conducted and how those interactions could be improved. The first economist is considered to be a Greek poet named Hesiod, who, in an 800-line poem titled *Works and Days*, wrote that labor, or work performed by people, was the source of all good.

After the fall of Rome, the world's economy grew slowly. New trade routes were established. The most famous among them was the **Silk Road**, which extended more than 4,000 miles and connected Europe and China. Silk and spices traveled west, while horses, fruits, and jewels flowed east. The trade along the Silk Road helped transform Europe from relatively poor to rich, with cities such as those in Italy emerging as rich trade centers. It was in these trade cities that the first modern accounting systems were developed to help people keep track of goods being transported and the wealth they were earning.

EXERCISE 1

Foundations of Economics

Directions: Choose the best answer to each question.

1. What were the first money-lending institutions?

   A. Banks
   B. Temples
   C. Markets
   D. Palaces

2. Which describes multinational trade?

   A. Trade within a country
   B. Trade controlled by one company
   C. Trade among many countries
   D. Trade conducted in a city market

3. What was the Silk Road?

   A. An overland trade route from Europe to Asia
   B. A sea trade route from Europe to Asia
   C. An overland trade route from Europe to America
   D. A sea trade route from Europe to America

Question 4 is based on the following passage.

Excerpt from *The Politics* by Aristotle, around 340 BC

Property should be in a certain sense common, but, as a general rule, private; for, when everyone has a distinct interest, men will not complain of one another, and they will make more progress, because every one will be attending to his own business.

4. Based on the passage, what is Aristotle's idea about the importance of private property in regulating human behavior?

A. Private property will make society less productive.
B. Private property will encourage society to progress.
C. Private property will make people more greedy.
D. Private property will make people happy.

Answers are on page 807.

The First Global Economic System

Throughout much of the Middle Ages, Europeans did not travel far beyond their small corner of the world. Trade with Asia along the Silk Road had encouraged some Europeans, such as Marco Polo in the late 13th century, to travel east, but with the conquests of the Ottoman Turks in the 14th century, Europeans found themselves restricted from travel by land to Asia. The closing of land routes to China also meant that the silk and spices that had fueled economic growth for almost a thousand years all but stopped flowing west. Thus, European merchants, adventurers, and state officials began looking for new ways to grow wealth. This desire for new trade opportunities, along with a religious zeal to expand Christianity and recent advances in sailing technology, all made it possible for Europe to enter an age of exploration.

Beginning in the early 1400s, Portuguese explorers sponsored by Prince Henry the Navigator and equipped with a new ship, the caravel, began to probe the western coast of Africa. Encouraged by an abundant spice trade, Portuguese ships charted new routes along the southern tip of Africa to India and captured several trading cities to serve as waypoints for the passage east. Eager to share in the wealth of its neighbor, Spain agreed to sponsor expeditions of its own. Christopher Columbus, who sailed from Europe in the fall of 1492 to reach the Americas, led the first of these trips. Columbus believed that he had found a westerly route to Asia. It took later explorers to realize that he had instead discovered a new world in the Western Hemisphere.

The 1500s saw the mass expansion of European power. Spanish conquerors, known as **conquistadors**, flooded the Americas in search of "gold, God, and glory." Relying on superior technology such as gunpowder, these Spanish profiteers were able to conquer several civilizations, including the Aztecs and Incas, enslaving the populations and looting their cities for precious goods. The flood of gold and other precious metals from the Americas quickly made Spain the dominant power in Europe and motivated other nations to send expeditions of their own. Although the Dutch failed at their attempts at colonization, the British and French had established control over most of the eastern seaboard of North America by the 1600s.

Dominating the rush to colonize the Americas and to establish centers of trade was the theory of **mercantilism**, which held that the prosperity of a nation depended on a large supply of gold and silver. Mercantilists believed in creating balanced trade, which favored exports over imports. It was the role of government to create this favorable balance by building bridges and roads and by stimulating the growth of businesses through subsidies, or payments made to support industries. Governments also placed **tariffs**, or taxes, on foreign imports to make foreign goods more expensive and thus less attractive to consumers. Colonies were crucial to this new economy as they provided raw materials and import goods.

All of the economic activity between European governments and their colonies created the world's first truly global trade network. Goods, plants, and animals flowed across the Atlantic Ocean in what became known as the **Columbian Exchange**. Colonies in the Americas established plantations, or large agricultural estates, to grow cash crops such as sugar, cotton, vanilla, and tobacco for export, while bringing in imports such as wheat, citrus, and horses. The exchange not only created wealth and new markets for goods on both sides of the Atlantic but also transformed the ecology of both the Americas and Europe.

The Columbian Exchange also proved to be deadly. Diseases from Europe devastated Native American populations. Europeans enslaved people from Africa and brought them to work on colonial plantations, where they provided the labor to produce crops. Millions of people died or were forcibly relocated as a result of the Columbian Exchange and what became known as the **triangular trade**, a flow of goods and slaves connecting Europe, Africa, and the American continents. In this system, European goods were traded for African slaves, who were then sold in the American colonies in exchange for cash crops that were then shipped back to Europe. The results of this system were devastating to some of the people. Native Americans were all but wiped out, while parts of Africa were depopulated and suffered culturally, politically, and economically. Slavery as an institution endured well into the 1800s, and in some parts of the world it continues even until this day.

EXERCISE 2

The First Global Economic System

Directions: Choose the best answer to each question.

1. What was the primary motivation of European explorers?
   A. Converting people to Christianity
   B. Establishing new colonies
   C. Mapping the world
   D. Finding new trade routes to Asia

2. Which is the BEST definition of *mercantilism*?

   A. "The belief that a nation's wealth is directly linked to its supply of gold and silver"
   B. "The belief that an economy functions best when it is free of government controls"
   C. "The belief that trade should be free of tariffs and taxes"
   D. "The belief that societies only advance through the building of new markets"

3. What was a major positive effect of the Columbian Exchange?

   A. It halted the spread of disease.
   B. It brought an end to slavery.
   C. It provided labor for plantations.
   D. It created new markets for goods.

Question 4 is based on the following map.

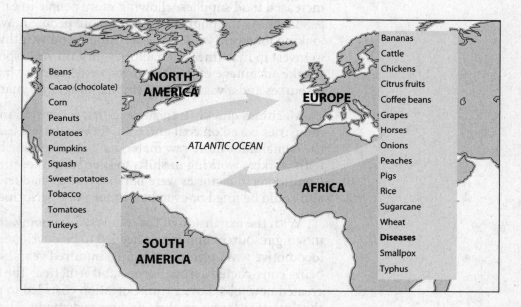

4. What evidence does the map give to show a negative effect of the Columbian Exchange?

   A. People on both sides of the Atlantic learned to use new crops.
   B. More nutritious food was available worldwide.
   C. New diseases were introduced to the Americas.
   D. People in Europe discovered they could eat corn.

Answers are on page 807.

The Rise of Modern Economics

The greatest changes to the ways in which people thought about labor and the creation of wealth came in the Enlightenment of the 1700s and from the Scottish philosopher Adam Smith, considered to be the father of modern economics. Smith believed that if individuals were free to pursue their own economic self-interest, then all of society would benefit. The government should leave the economy alone. This doctrine became known as **laissez-faire**, a French term roughly translated as "to let people do what they want." In his book *The Wealth of Nations*, Smith argued that the state had only three basic roles. Those roles were to protect society from invasion, defend citizens from injustice, and maintain public works—such as roads and canals—that individuals could not afford but that were necessary for trade.

While Smith was developing his ideas about modern economics, a major event was transforming the way economies functioned. Beginning in the 1780s in Great Britain, the **Industrial Revolution** was beginning to take place. It began with major advances in agriculture that dramatically increased food supplies, allowing more people to eat at a lower cost with less labor. As the population grew, more people moved to towns and cities looking for work, while the government and wealthy individuals began to invest in machines and factories. Britain was especially well positioned to take advantage of these changes as the country had abundant natural resources and a vast colonial empire hungry for manufactured goods.

Machines quickly transformed first the cotton industry and then industries based on coal and iron. Raw materials fed factories, thus growing the demand for more raw materials. Labor became highly systematized, with workers working in shifts to keep machines producing at a steady rate. Conditions in factories were harsh. Workers had few rights or protections and could be fined or even beaten for poor performance or bad behavior.

With the expansion of the industrial economy, more efficient means of moving resources and goods needed to be developed. In 1804 the first steam locomotive was invented. Within a hundred years, vast railway systems were being constructed across Europe and America. The building of the railroads created new jobs. Lower transportation costs led to more affordable goods, thus creating larger markets and more demand. The new industrial economy became self-feeding, ensuring steady growth and greater wealth than had ever been known before.

Society was forever transformed as a result of the Industrial Revolution. Cities grew as never before. In 1800, for example, London's population was about one million. By 1850 that number had more than doubled. A better-fed population meant the decline of famine and disease and an increase in life span, which only added to the population boom. Soon reform movements sprang into existence calling for greater political participation and better sanitation.

Perhaps the most important result of the Industrial Revolution was the development of a new middle class. Throughout history, society was chiefly divided between a small, wealthy upper class and a large, poor lower class.

Doctors, lawyers, bankers, and teachers, and also the people who built and ran the factories, made up the new industrial **middle class**. The middle class did not have enough wealth to be considered rich but had just enough wealth to afford bigger homes and some luxury goods. As this new class grew, so did new industries, most notably businesses that provided entertainment, such as theaters and restaurants.

However, as some people prospered under the Industrial Revolution, many others struggled with poverty and harsh working conditions. This gave rise to a political movement favoring the establishment of **socialism**, a system in which society, usually the government, owns the means of production, such as factories. Developed chiefly by a German philosopher named Karl Marx, socialism maintained that the industrial economic system was essentially unfair, with only a few getting rich at the expense of the majority. Socialists believed that only government-controlled industry could promote true and fair economic equality. The conflict between capitalism and socialism would become the defining struggle for the next one hundred years.

EXERCISE 3

The Rise of Modern Economics

Directions: Choose the best answer to each question.

1. What conclusion BEST supports the idea that Adam Smith is the father of modern economics?

   A. Most people work to earn their living.
   B. Today most developed nations practice some form of *laissez-faire* capitalism.
   C. Developing nations such as India and China have growing economies.
   D. Western governments routinely regulate their economies.

2. What conclusion can BEST be made about the Industrial Revolution?

   A. It changed the way governments interact with their citizens.
   B. It heavily influenced art and music.
   C. It was not very long or meaningful.
   D. It transformed the economies of most Western countries.

3. What conclusion BEST supports the claims of socialism?

   A. The Industrial Revolution gave people new economic opportunities.
   B. As a result of the Industrial Revolution, cities grew larger.
   C. The Industrial Revolution made some people very rich and many more very poor.
   D. The Industrial Revolution led to the spread of reform movements.

Answers are on page 807.

Developments in American Economics

The American Revolution was fought in part as a protest against unfair taxation of the American colonies by Great Britain. Once the colonies gained independence and established the United States of America, the country was formed as a common market with no internal tariffs or taxes restricting trade between the states. Although this system encouraged the free and open exchange of goods and services, it did nothing to regulate and fund the new, struggling federal government.

Alexander Hamilton, the first US secretary of the treasury, proposed the creation of a government-sponsored bank and tariffs on foreign imports to encourage economic growth. Furthermore, he consolidated the debt amassed by the colonies during the Revolutionary War, building national credit and encouraging investment in the federal government through the sale of bonds. There was much resistance to Hamilton's ideas of a strong central bank to regulate the economy, most notably from Thomas Jefferson, who favored a smaller, weaker federal government. However, conflict between France and England, and later the War of 1812, forced many opponents of the national bank to support the institution as a stabilizing force in times of crisis. Thus, the American economy became a compromise, in which states were encouraged to trade goods freely and without restriction, while the federal government, through the national bank, would regulate the economy overall.

When the Industrial Revolution spread to the United States from England, the American government invested millions in infrastructure improvements. These included building the **intercontinental railroad**, a railway linking the eastern and western halves of the United States, and the building of canal systems throughout the East Coast and Great Lakes region. The US economy was further improved in 1793 when Eli Whitney invented the cotton gin, a machine that could quickly and easily separate cotton from its seeds. Suddenly the cost of cotton production dropped, and Southern plantations, worked by slaves, began exporting enormous amounts of cotton to mills in Europe. The boom in cotton production led to a land rush into the West while greatly increasing the demand for slave labor. Disputes over the spread of the slave labor system to the Western territories led directly to the Civil War in the 1860s.

After the Civil War and the collapse of the Southern plantation system, the North ramped up manufacturing. Immigrants flocked to the North in search of jobs. Cities grew rapidly. New factories sprang up to meet growing demand for goods by European nations and a fast-growing American middle class. When the Civil War ended in 1865, the United States began a period of rapid economic growth. By 1890 the United States surpassed Great Britain to become the world's largest manufacturer. New discoveries and inventions exploded on to the American scene, including electricity, the light bulb, the telephone, the phonograph, and the typewriter. The automobile began to replace the horse-drawn carriage, slowly at first, until in 1913 Henry Ford installed the first **assembly line** to manufacture cars. Mass production, or the production of goods in large quantities, usually by machinery, made the automobile affordable for most Americans. As a result, the US government invested heavily in roads and oil exploration.

This was the Gilded Age, a period of time lasting into the early 1900s, when the economy of the United States created more wealth than all the nations that came before. Wealthy individuals, known as **tycoons**, built vast fortunes. Among them were John D. Rockefeller, who built a vast oil empire; J. P. Morgan, who did the same in banking; and Jay Gould, who dominated the railroad industry. Individuals such as these created **monopolies**, industrial or commercial organizations with complete control over the production or sale of a specific commodity. Monopolies stifled competition, thus eliminating choice and increasing prices. Angry over monopolies and poor working conditions, workers began to organize **unions**, organizations of workers formed to protect and expand their rights and interests. At the same time, progressive politicians and reformers began to call for the break-up of monopolies to encourage greater competition. The result was not only greater economic equality but also increased political participation.

EXERCISE 4

Developments in American Economics

Directions: Study the graph and then answer the questions that follow.

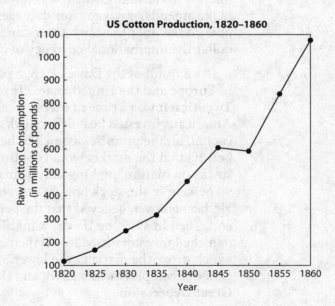

US Cotton Production, 1820–1860

1. Based on the graph, what was the trend in cotton production following the invention of the cotton gin in the late 1700s?

   A. Cotton production increased.
   B. Cotton production decreased.
   C. Cotton production remained relatively unchanged.
   D. Cotton production stopped altogether.

2. Based on the graph and what you learned from the reading, what conclusion can be made about slavery from 1820 to 1860?

A. Demand for slaves decreased.
B. Demand for slaves increased.
C. Demand for slaves stayed the same.
D Demand for slaves stopped altogether.

Answers are on page 807.

The Globalized Economy

Between 1914 and 1918 much of the world was engaged in World War I. Although the United States participated in the fighting, no actual combat took place in America. The war devastated countries such as France and Germany, and it led to the rise of a socialist government in Russia, which was renamed the Soviet Union. But the United States remained strong and was in a good position to lend money to other countries for postwar rebuilding. The Dawes Plan, for instance, named after American banker Charles G. Dawes, was a plan in which the United States lent money at interest to Germany, which was forced to pay reparations (money paid to make amends or pay for war damages) to France and England. This loan opened the door to heavy American investment in Europe and made the dollar the international currency of choice.

As a result of the Dawes Plan, a period of economic prosperity followed in Europe and the United States. This period was known as the **Roaring Twenties**. It was a time of excess when the US stock market boomed. Americans invested heavily in **stocks**, or shares in companies issued to raise capital, on the promise of quick riches. Buyers engaged in **speculation**, or betting that the market would continue to climb. Many investors bought stocks on margin, making only a small cash down payment, with as much as 90 percent of the stock bought on credit. Some people, including President Herbert Hoover, believed that the period of postwar prosperity would never end. Then in 1929 the US stock market crashed. As stock prices plummeted, panicked investors tried to sell their stocks before prices dropped too far, which drove the market even lower. After the crash, banks and companies closed, unemployment soared, and the world found itself in the grip of the **Great Depression**.

There were many factors for the Great Depression beyond stock speculation and overinvestment. Overproduction of goods was an important factor. Supply outpaced demand, meaning that there were more goods than people to buy them. Another major factor was the uneven distribution of income. While the wealthiest Americans saw their incomes increase, the majority of workers dealt with wages that remained low.

The Great Depression devastated the globally connected economy. Trade and investment slowed as unemployment spread across Europe and America. In response, countries such as the United States, Great Britain, and France invested heavily in social relief programs. American president Franklin Roosevelt, for example, led the passage of a series of sweeping reforms called the **New Deal**, which included public works programs such as the Works Progress Administration and welfare programs such as Social Security. The idea was to put able Americans back to work while providing protections for Americans who could not work. At the same time, the response to the Great Depression in countries such as Italy, Germany, and Japan was a political shift toward dictatorship. Germany, for instance, saw the rise of the Nazi Party in the 1930s. Adolf Hitler, a former German soldier, promised to restore the country to economic prosperity through a campaign appealing to German militarism and nationalism. Hitler blamed Jews, Communists, and other minorities for Germany's defeat in the war and subsequent economic collapse.

World War I led to the Great Depression, which in turn led to World War II, as the dictatorships in Europe and Japan began an aggressive campaign of conquest and expansion. The war, which lasted from 1939 to 1945, devastated most of Europe and much of Asia, but just as in the previous conflict, it left the United States relatively undamaged. As a result of this, as well as the nation's unmatched industrial output, the United States became the leading global economic power. The US dollar became the monetary standard for the world. American investment and American-made goods dominated international trade. Although the Soviet Union (formerly Russia) tried to challenge American dominance, the global economy continued to grow ever more connected, fueled by US capital.

By the 1990s the Soviet Union had collapsed and the world had firmly entered an age of globalization, defined as the movement toward a more integrated and interdependent world economy. Under the direction of the World Bank and International Monetary Fund (IMF), two organizations set up after World War II to help prevent economic crisis, multinational corporations rose to dominate economic activity. Multinational corporations are companies that operate in more than two countries.

While economic prosperity has increased and global conflict continues to decline, globalization is not without problems. Poverty and income inequality remain major concerns, especially as most wealth is concentrated in Europe and North America. Critics of globalization have accused multinational corporations of putting profits ahead of worker safety and wages. In addition, companies have been accused of ignoring environmental concerns. Despite these issues, one point remains clear: the world's economy is more connected than ever before.

EXERCISE 5

The Globalized Economy

Directions: Write a short response to each question.

1. What are some of the benefits of a globalized economy?

   _____

   _____

   _____

   _____

2. What are some of the negative consequences of a globalized economy?

   _____

   _____

   _____

   _____

Answers are on page 807.

CHAPTER 4

Geography and World History

Geography is the study of Earth's physical features and of human activity as it affects these features. The word *geography* comes from the Greek language and means "to describe Earth's surface." The study of geography has two major branches. Physical geography focuses on the processes and patterns of physical features, such as air, water, or landforms. The other major branch of geography is human geography. Human geographers study interactions between people and environments in order to explain the nature of these interactions, why they happen, and how they affect the population. This chapter will discuss how human geographers explore relationships between the environment and the development of societies.

Environment and Society

For the majority of our existence, human beings have been at the mercy of the environment. Before the development of agriculture, humans survived as hunter-gatherers, living in small nomadic tribes and traveling with the food supply. As technology was still in its infancy, natural barriers such as mountains and oceans prevented people from moving far beyond their immediate environments. This changed approximately 10,000 years ago with what is called the **Neolithic Revolution** that took place during the Neolithic, or "new stone," Age. During this change, hunter-gatherers developed systematic agriculture. Historians regard this revolution as the single most important development in human history.

As people started growing their food, they stopped moving and settled near their crops. Farming provided a more stable food supply, thus allowing for a larger population. The first agricultural communities developed in what is today the Middle East with the cities of Çatalhöyük in modern-day Turkey and Jericho, which still exists today as an Israeli-controlled town. This region is called the Fertile Crescent because its abundant water sources make it especially well-suited for growing crops. There is also pasture land for grazing animals such as sheep and cattle.

The first civilizations developed in river valleys where people could carry on large-scale farming. As populations grew, so did cities and the need for more crops. These river valley civilizations, such as those developed by the Sumerians, Egyptians, and Indus peoples, developed techniques for irrigation and canal building, diverting the flow of rivers to feed their crops. As the power and influence of these early civilizations grew, they also built vast road networks and cleared entire forests for building materials and additional land for use in agriculture.

Rulers found themselves having to organize and feed growing numbers of farmers and workers. Over time, the idea of states and nations emerged. With more complex social structures came economic and technological innovation. Agricultural techniques were refined so that more crops could be produced from less land. Surplus crops could be sold to generate wealth.

With increased prosperity came war and conflict, and soon societies found themselves in need of more natural resources. As societies fought over territory and resources, they also changed the environment to better suit their needs. Rivers were dammed, tunnels were dug, and forests were cleared. Some civilizations, such as the Romans, built vast aqueducts to transport water to cities, allowing populations to settle away from rivers. Later, natural springs were tapped, and plumbing brought water directly into people's homes. In every step technology led the way, as people shaped the environment to grow and prosper.

These changes were not without negative consequences, which occurred over a long period of time. Overfarming led to crop failure, diverting rivers turned once lush environments into deserts, and deforestation resulted in erosion and soil loss. Many animal species were reduced in number or driven completely into extinction. As human populations grew and industry developed, pollution became a serious concern. In modern times, reformers began to call for conservation and environmental protection, but the damage to the environment continued, and it continues today.

Today geographers study the relationship between people and the environment to understand how geography has influenced historical development, and also the impact human societies have had on the planet. Some examples include the building of dams and canals, polluting the air and water, building highways and railroads, and even planting grass or gardens. Even the smallest changes to the environment can affect animals and the ecosystem. Positive change might include planting trees and building wild habitats, while negative change might include building landfills.

One of the most important ways in which people impact the environment is through population growth. Before the 20th century, world population was well below one billion. Advances in farming, medicine, and refrigeration led to a population boom that tripled the population by 1960, and then it doubled again just 50 years later. Even today this population boom continues, leading many researchers and scientists to grow increasingly concerned about the human impact on Earth. Another area of concern is that the greatest population increase is happening in some of the poorest countries. As these countries often lack the tools to limit pollution, negative change is likely to increase as time goes on. Understanding the impact of the environment on people and people on the environment can help societies create better policies and avoid ecological disasters.

EXERCISE 1

Environment and Society

Directions: Study the map and then answer the questions that follow.

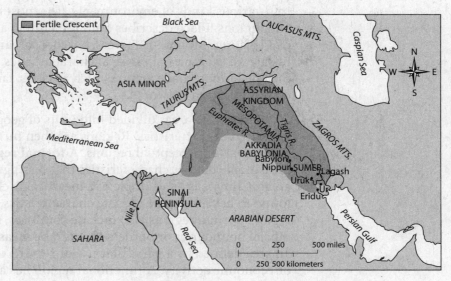

Early Civilizations of the Fertile Crescent

1. The Fertile Crescent extends from the eastern coast of the Mediterranean Sea to the

   A. Red Sea.
   B. Black Sea.
   C. Caspian Sea.
   D. Persian Gulf.

2. Based on the map, what natural features were important to the development of civilizations in the Fertile Crescent?

   A. Mountains
   B. Deserts
   C. Rivers
   D. Forests

3. According to the map, Mesopotamia was an area of land between the Tigris and the _____ Rivers.

4. What natural features MOST LIKELY limited the expansion of early Fertile Crescent civilizations?

   A. Rivers and valleys
   B. Mountains and deserts
   C. Roads and canals
   D. Irrigation dikes and dams

Answers are on page 807.

Geographic Concepts and Tools

One of the most important innovations in how people related to their environment was in how they classified the world. As humans began to settle beyond their immediate surroundings, they began to divide the world into various kinds of environments. The most basic of these are places and regions. **Place** describes both the human and physical characteristics of a location. Mountains, rivers, beaches, oceans, and animal and plant life are all examples of physical characteristics. Human characteristics include human-made features such as cities, farms, and transportation and communication networks.

Regions are areas divided into units of geographic study, usually linked by shared characteristics. Regions are then further broken down into formal, functional, or perceptual regions. A **formal region** is an area defined by measurable data or characteristics that distinguish it from surrounding areas. Climate is an example of a measurable characteristic. When an area is found to have the same climate characteristics, geographers call it a climate region. Formal regions also include countries, states, and cities. They have official boundaries or borders that can be measured. A **functional region** is an area defined by a particular use or service, usually related to a business or economic activity. A functional region has a center that connects it to that use or service. One example of a functional region is a metropolitan transportation system. In the case of the New York metropolitan area, New York City represents the center of the region. **Perceptual regions** are areas defined by people's opinions, attitudes, or perceptions. These regions are not based on measureable data and therefore are more likely than other regions to change over time. Examples of perceptual regions are the Midwest, the North, or the Middle East.

Another important way humans study the world is in terms of its **cultural geography**, or the ways in which concepts such as language, religion, economics, and government vary or remain the same from one place to another. By looking at how different people in different regions relate to each other and to the world, geographers better understand how the environment shapes human behavior.

People who study geography use various tools to help them. These include maps, or drawings of all or part of the Earth's surface, and globes, a model of Earth. Because a globe is round like Earth, it represents land areas and bodies of water in their accurate sizes and shapes. A map, however, is flat and therefore cannot represent land and water accurately. The larger the area shown on a flat map, the greater the distortion because of the curve of Earth's actual surface. However, a map can show small areas of Earth with much more accuracy than can ever be represented on a globe.

Other tools used in geography include the lines drawn on maps and globes. The line running horizontally around the middle of a globe, for example, is the **equator**. The equator is an imaginary line halfway between the North and South Poles and divides Earth into the Northern and Southern Hemispheres. The **prime meridian** is an imaginary vertical line running from the North Pole to the South Pole, dividing the globe into the Eastern and Western Hemispheres. The prime meridian runs north and south through Greenwich, England, a location near London.

In addition to the equator and prime meridian, there are other imaginary lines that geographers use to locate specific areas on maps and globes. Horizontal lines running parallel to the equator are **parallels of latitude**. They show distances measured in degrees north or south of the equator. Vertical lines running parallel to the prime meridian are **lines of longitude**. These lines measure distances in degrees east or west of the prime meridian.

Latitude and longitude form a grid that allows geographers to give an absolute location for every place on Earth. The equator is 0 degrees latitude. The prime meridian is 0 degrees longitude. New York City is located at about 40°N and 74°W. This means that New York City is 40 degrees north of the equator and 74 degrees west of the prime meridian.

EXERCISE 2

Geographic Concepts and Tools

Directions: Study the chart and then answer the questions that follow.

Types of Geographic Regions	Characteristics	Examples
Formal	Defined by measurable data or characteristics that distinguish it from surrounding areas Defined by official boundaries or borders that can be measured	Country State City Rocky Mountains
Functional	Defined by a particular process, use, or service Usually related to a business or economic activity Has a center around which processes are organized	Metropolitan transportation system Telecommunications service area National interstate highway system
Perceptual	Has areas defined by people's opinions, attitudes, or perceptions Not based on measureable data More likely than other regions to change over time	Midwest the North Middle East Southern California New England

1. Which of the following is a formal region?

    A. Washington, DC
    B. A national railroad system
    C. The South
    D. An electric power grid

2. Which of the following is a perceptual region?

    A. Brazil
    B. A metropolitan transit system
    C. The South
    D. A mountain range

3. Airline system maps are a type of functional region because

    A. air travel provides a particular use.
    B. airports are located in or near cities.
    C. airlines respond to customers' opinions.
    D. airlines fly over national borders.

Answers are on page 807.

Human Migration

A major part of geography is the study of human migration. Migration is the movement of people from one place to another.

The most important question in the study of migration is why people move from one place to another. Most often people move in search of economic opportunities, either in terms of work or higher wages. An example of this is the arrival of European immigrants to the United States during the 19th century, when American businesses needed workers for factories during the Industrial Revolution. Sometimes people move to be close to family, as when members of the same family are separated or forced to relocate. An example of this is the movement of large numbers of Europeans at the end of World War II due to political changes resulting from the war. Sometimes people move to escape war or religious persecution. An example of this is the voyage of the Pilgrims from Great Britain to the American colonies in the 17th century.

Geographers also study how people, goods, and resources are transported from one place to another. This may include the shipment of products by land, sea, or air. In the early days, explorers used sailing routes to establish trading posts. Later, the study of transportation allowed governments and corporations to gain better insight into foreign markets. Today, studying this kind of movement allows researchers to determine how regions and economies develop over time. It also allows governments to find more effective means of transportation.

Cultural Diffusion

In addition to the movement of people and goods, geographers also study the movement of ideas, such as art, music, philosophy, and religion. One example is the influence of Greek culture on the ancient world, most notably on the Roman Empire, which borrowed heavily from the Greeks. Another example is the Western influence on Japan, which borrowed ideas from Europe during its rapid industrialization in the 19th and 20th centuries. One modern example includes the vast influence of American culture across the world through technologies such as Facebook and Twitter. Another modern example is the influence of British television on American pop culture. The simplest example of ideas moving from one place to another is through books. Broadly speaking, all of these are cases of **cultural diffusion**, or the spreading out of culture, cultural traits, or practices from a central point.

Language is an element of culture, and language has been affected by cultural diffusion as well. Chinese has strongly influenced Korean and Japanese, with Chinese words having been adopted by both Korea and Japan. The French language, which for centuries was spoken by the upper classes across Europe, dominates the arts even today. And originating in the high-tech industry of the United States, the word *google* has become a verb virtually everywhere in the world.

Language can also influence the way people think and, therefore, how cultures develop. For example, because the Russian language contains extra distinctions between light and dark colors, Russians are better able to identify shades of colors, such as blue, than those who speak other languages. Some cultures have no words for numbers but instead rely on terms such as *few* or *many* to keep track of quantities. Understanding how language influences cultures and the way people think helps researchers not only learn more about cultures but also to better understand how cultures communicate.

Cultural Diffusion

Directions: Use the chart and what you read in "Cultural Diffusion" to complete the writing assignment that follows.

Examples of Cultural Diffusion

Silk and silk production	Originated in ancient China and became its major export
	Brought from China to ancient Rome on a network of trading routes known as the Silk Road
	Spread from ancient China to ancient India and eventually to Europe in the 1300s
Arabic numerals	Originated in India around the 500s
	Introduced to Europe through Arab mathematicians around the 1100s
	Used everywhere in the world today
Baseball	Introduced to Japan from the United States in the 1870s by American teachers
	Formed first professional Japanese leagues in 1936
	Has become one of Japan's most watched and played sports, with teams from elementary school to the professional level
Fast food restaurants	Spread throughout the world by American fast food companies
	Can be found in major cities of the world

Write one or two paragraphs that explain and give three examples of cultural diffusion. When you write your response, be sure to follow these steps:

- Support your explanation with multiple pieces of evidence using information from the chart and your reading of "Cultural Diffusion."

- Organize and present information in a sensible sequence.

- Show clear connections between main points and supporting details.

- Follow standard English conventions in regard to grammar, spelling, punctuation, and sentence structure.

Write your response in the box. This task may take 25 minutes to complete.

Posttests

How to Use the Posttests

Now that you have finished studying the lessons and exercises in this book, it is time to measure your readiness to begin an intensive GED© test review. There are four Posttests in this section, one in each GED Test subject area: Reasoning Through Language Arts (RLA), Mathematical Reasoning, Science, and Social Studies. When you take these Posttests, your results will help you to determine how well prepared you are to begin your intensive study program for the GED test and which subjects you most need to focus on.

To make the best use of these Posttests, follow these four steps:

1. Take the Posttests one at a time. Do not try to work through all four Posttests in one session.

2. Take each Posttest under test conditions. Find a quiet place where you will not be disturbed. Work though the Posttest from beginning to end in one sitting. Mark your answers directly on the test pages. Observe the time limit given at the start of the test. If you have not finished the Posttest when time runs out, mark the last question you answered and then note how much longer it takes you to complete the test. This information will tell you if you need to speed up your pace, and if so, by how much.

3. Answer every question. On the real GED test, there is no penalty for wrong answers, so it makes sense to answer every question, even if you have to guess. If you don't know an answer, see if you can eliminate one or more of the answer choices. The more choices you can eliminate, the better your chance of guessing correctly!

3. Check your answers in the Posttest Answer Keys section at the back of this book. Pay particular attention to the explanations for questions you missed.

The number of questions and time limit for each Posttest are shown in the following chart.

Posttest	Number of Questions	Time Limit
Reasoning Through Language Arts (RLA)	35	60 minutes
Mathematical Reasoning	30	60 minutes
Science	25	60 minutes
Social Studies	30	45 minutes

Reasoning Through Language Arts (RLA)

This Reasoning Through Language Arts (RLA) Posttest is designed to help you determine how well prepared you are to begin your intensive GED® test study program.

This practice test has 35 items. The questions are designed to measure the same skills as the ones on the real exam. Many are based on nonfiction or literary reading passages.

Most of the questions are in multiple-choice format, but you will also see questions in the "drop-down" format that is used for some questions on the real exam. On the real GED test, you will indicate your answers by clicking on the computer screen. For this paper-and-pencil practice test, mark your answers directly on the page.

To get a good idea of how you will do on the real exam, take this test under actual exam conditions. Complete the test in one session and follow the given time limit. If you do not complete the test in the time allowed, you will know that you need to work on improving your pacing.

Try to answer as many questions as you can. There is no penalty for wrong answers, so guess if you have to. In multiple-choice questions, if you can eliminate one or more answer choices, you can increase your chances of guessing correctly.

After you have finished the test, check your answers in the Posttest Answer Keys section that begins on page 751.

Now turn the page and begin the Reasoning Through Language Arts (RLA) Posttest.

Reasoning Through Language Arts (RLA)

35 Questions (various formats) | **60 Minutes**

Directions: The following memo contains several numbered blanks, each marked "Select. . . ." Beneath each one is a set of choices. Indicate the choice from each set that is correct and belongs in the blank. (**Note:** On the real GED® test, the choices will appear as a "drop-down" menu. When you click on a choice, it will appear in the blank.)

MEMO

To: All Staff

From: Human Resources, Informational Technology Division

Re: New Timekeeping System

Effective Monday, July 14, the timekeeping system at ACD Staffing Solutions will change. Over the weekend, the IT department will outfit each computer with a timekeeping program. Employees will

1. Select.... ▼

1. Select.... ▼
log in, and out, at the beginning, and end, of the workday, and they will log out, and back in, for their lunch hour.
log in and out at the beginning and end of the workday they will log out and back in for their lunch hour.
log in and out at the beginning and end of the workday. They will log out and back in for their lunch hour.
log in and out at the beginning and end of the workday, they will log out and back in for their lunch hour.

Allan Remington of IT will be conducting a training session this Thursday morning at 10:30 to familiarize employees with the new system. | 2. Select.... ▼ |

2. Select.... ▼
An hour-long session, you should make sure you clear your calendar to accommodate it and avoid conflicts.
Make sure you clear your calendar to accommodate an hour-long training session and avoid conflicts.
Cleared, your calendar should accommodate an hour-long training session and avoid conflicts.
Make sure that you clear your calendar accommodating an hour-long training session and avoid conflicts.

If you miss the session due to unavoidable circumstances, such as illness, you must contact the Human Resources department to schedule a make-up session.

At the training session, each employee will receive login information specific to 3. Select.... ▼.

3. Select....	▼
their own computer	
his or her own computer	
his own computer	
one's own computer	

Do not attempt to log on to your computer on July 14 unless you have first gone through a training session. *Do not* attempt to log on to your computer using 4. Select.... ▼

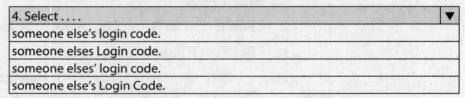

4. Select....	▼
someone else's login code.	
someone elses Login code.	
someone elses' login code.	
someone else's Login Code.	

The timekeeping system will also track employees' personal use of company computers (e.g., personal email, shopping, bill-paying). Effective July 14, an employee may spend his or her lunch hour on the computer for personal use. Employees may log an additional 30 minutes of personal use on the computer during work hours.

Employees 5. Select.... ▼

5. Select....	▼
who are found to have spent longer than the allotted time on personal computer use has one of two options,	
who are found to have spent longer than the allotted time on personal computer use have one of too options.	
who is found to have spent longer than the allotted time on personal computer use will has one of to options.	
who are found to have spent longer than the allotted time on personal computer use will have one of two options.	

Their paycheck will be reduced by that amount of time, or they may make up the time.

If there is a special family situation that you think will require an excessive amount of personal computer time, | 6. Select.... ▼ |

6. Select....
nevertheless, please contact the Human Resources department and discuss it when you get in touch with them so they can understand what your situation is.
however, please contact the Human Resources department about it.
furthermore, please contact and make an appointment with the Human Resources department for purposes of discussing the situation with a member of the department
whereas, please contact the Human Resources department at which time a member of the Human Resources Department will talk with you about the fact that you need more computer time for personal reasons.

While we recognize that some activities cannot be managed after-hours, we believe this timeframe for computer use should be more than adequate to cover most employees' personal needs. ACD Staffing Solutions | 7. Select.... ▼ |

7. Select....
has created this policy to meet employee needs without harming the customer service of which we are proud and on which our reputation is based.
are creating this policy to meet employee needs without harming the customer service of which they are proud and on which their reputation is based.
created this policy to meet employee needs without harming the customer service of which we are so proud and our reputation is based on.
will be creating this policy to meet employee needs without harm to the customer service of which we are so proud and having a great reputation.

Directions: Read the passage and then answer questions 8–15.

Job Interviewing Tips

1 A company you are interested in working for has offered you a job interview. You are excited but probably nervous, too. Here are some important tips for being calm and collected on the big day.

Before the Interview

2 Career counselors say a good job interview starts well before the job seeker and interviewer meet. Preparation can be as important as the interview itself. Researching and practicing are the first steps to making the most of a job interview.

Research

3 Research both the company and the position for which you are being interviewed. Employers say they are impressed by well-informed job seekers. Before arriving for an interview, you should know what the company does, how large it is, what changes it has undergone recently, and what role you could play in its organization.

4 Try to learn about the company's goals and values. With these facts, you can show how your qualifications match the company's needs. The company's own website and the public library are often excellent resources for this kind of information.

Practice

5 Have a friend play the part of the interviewer and ask you questions about your training and any previous employment, why you think you are qualified for the job, and what you hope to contribute to the company. The questions should be realistic, neither too harsh nor too easy to answer. Your answers should be brief but detailed enough so you are giving the information an interviewer would actually need in order to learn about you and your qualifications. Keep track of any questions that you do not know how to answer or that you answer hesitantly. These are weak spots that you will need to improve before the interview.

Before You Go

6 On the day of the interview, give yourself plenty of time to get ready for and travel to the interview. Plan to arrive 10 to 15 minutes early. (Some career counselors suggest making a test run to the interview site in advance to familiarize yourself with the travel route.)

7 Consider carrying a briefcase to the interview. In addition to giving you a professional look, a briefcase serves a function: you can carry things in it you will want at the interview. These include a pen and paper to record important information, such as the proper spelling of the interviewer's name and the time and date of follow-up interviews; copies of your résumé or application and references; and examples of your work, such as writing samples.

Butterflies

8 Most people are nervous when interviewing. But remember: You have been asked to interview for the job because the employer believes you could be right for it. The interview is your chance to confirm that belief and establish rapport. To reduce nervousness, interviewers recommend getting a good night's sleep and maintaining your usual morning routine—for example, if you never eat breakfast, don't eat a hearty morning meal on interview day.

9 They also recommend calling to mind some of your happiest memories or proudest moments before arriving for the interview. And they remind job seekers that each opening you interview for is not the only one that exists. More than one company recruits for jobs. If one interview doesn't go well, another will.

During the Interview

First Impressions

10 The interview begins the moment you arrive. Everyone you meet, from the receptionist to the hiring manager, will form an impression of you. To ensure the impression is positive, remember that your words and mannerisms will affect the image you project. When greeting people, smile warmly and shake hands. Make eye contact and maintain good posture. Don't create a negative impression by using slang, chewing gum, smoking cigarettes, or giving curt, one-word answers.

11 Standard politeness is important in an interview because the interviewer knows very little about you. To be safe, never use the interviewer's first name unless you are invited to do so, and do not sit down until the interviewer does.

Responding to Questions

12 After introductions, the interviewer will probably explain the job in more detail, discuss the company, or initiate friendly conversation. Throughout the interview, maintain eye contact and keep your answers to the point. Do not bring up anything that does not directly relate to the question the interviewer asks.

13 Also, be sure to ask one or two thoughtful questions about the company, its goals, and what kind of work environment is typical for the job for which you are being interviewed. You can base your questions on the research you did about the company prior to the interview. This shows that you have a strong interest in working for this particular company.

14 Before leaving the interview, make sure you understand the next step in the hiring process. Find out whether there will be another round of interviews, whether you should provide additional information, and when a hiring decision will be made. Finally, be sure to thank the interviewer. And if you are interested in the job, say so.

8. According to the passage, what is the first step that potential job seekers should take in the interview process?

   A. They should rehearse for the interview by having a friend play the role of the interviewer.
   B. They should smile and make eye contact as they greet everyone from the receptionist to the hiring manager.
   C. They should ask thoughtful questions about the company, its goals, and its workplace environment.
   D. They should research the company and the position for which they might be hired.

9. What main idea can you infer from the details in the passage?

   A. A successful job interview requires careful preparation and planning.
   B. A job seeker should look professional in order to impress employers.
   C. The job interview is a rite of passage for most young Americans.
   D. The process of finding a suitable job involves much time and expense.

Use paragraph 1 from the previous passage to answer question 10.

A company you are interested in working for has offered you a job interview. You are excited but probably nervous, too. Here are some important tips for being calm and collected on the big day.

10. How do these sentences contribute to the overall structure of the passage?

    A. They grab the reader's attention with a humorous anecdote about job interviews.
    B. They sum up the most important ideas and bring the passage to its conclusion.
    C. They introduce the topic and let readers know what information will follow.
    D. They clarify and extend ideas discussed in the previous section of the passage.

11. Which sentence accurately summarizes the information in the section "Before You Go" (paragraphs 6–7)?

    A. Before the interview, look online to find information about the company and the position.
    B. On the day of the interview, plan to arrive early and bring a briefcase with papers and other supplies.
    C. During the interview, make a good impression by greeting people warmly and making eye contact.
    D. As the interview concludes, ask one or two thoughtful questions about the company and its goals.

12. Which generalization can be supported by the details in paragraph 9?

    A. Employers prefer to hire people who are cheerful and pleasant.

    B. Companies are constantly looking for and interviewing for new recruits.

    C. Job seeking requires a positive attitude and a willingness to fail.

    D. Interviews will go well if you remember that other jobs are available.

13. In the section called "First Impressions," what is the relationship between paragraphs 10 and 11?

    A. Paragraph 10 defines what a first impression is, and paragraph 11 provides several anecdotes about making good first impressions.

    B. Paragraph 10 states an opinion about the importance of first impressions, and paragraph 11 provides examples of a good first impression.

    C. Paragraph 10 introduces the idea of making an impression, and paragraph 11 explains how to form a positive one.

    D. Paragraph 10 describes a job seeker who makes a bad first impression, and paragraph 11 describes one who makes a good impression.

14. Which detail from the text supports the idea that a job interview is a formal situation?

    A. "On the day of the interview, give yourself plenty of time to get ready for and travel to the interview."

    B. "Standard politeness is important in an interview because the interviewer knows very little about you."

    C. "Everyone you meet, from the receptionist to the hiring manager, will form an impression of you."

    D. "Throughout the interview, maintain eye contact and keep your answers to the point."

15. How does the overall structure of the passage support the author's purpose?

    A. The author uses a cause-effect structure to illustrate how planning can make a job interview go well.

    B. The author uses a problem-solution structure to identify potential interview mishaps and offer advice.

    C. The author uses an order of importance structure to stress the most important interview tips first.

    D. The author uses a sequence structure to demonstrate the interview process step-by-step.

Directions: Read the passage and then answer questions 16–21.

Excerpt adapted from "The Decision to Go to the Moon"

by John F. Kennedy

1 We set sail on this new sea because there is new knowledge to be gained, and new rights to be won, and they must be won and used for the progress of all people. For space science, like nuclear science and all technology, has no conscience of its own. Whether it will become a force for good or ill depends on man, and only if the United States occupies a position of pre-eminence can we help decide whether this new ocean will be a sea of peace or a new terrifying theater of war. I do not say that we should or will go unprotected against the hostile misuse of space any more than we go unprotected against the hostile use of land or sea, but I do say that space can be explored and mastered without feeding the fires of war, without repeating the mistakes that man has made in extending his writ around this globe of ours.

2 There is no strife, no prejudice, no national conflict in outer space as yet. Its hazards are hostile to us all. Its conquest deserves the best of all mankind, and its opportunity for peaceful cooperation many never come again. But why, some say, the moon? Why choose this as our goal? And they may well ask why climb the highest mountain? Why, thirty-five years ago, fly the Atlantic? We choose to go to the moon. We choose to go to the moon in this decade and do the other things, not because they are easy, but because they are hard, because that goal will serve to organize and measure the best of our energies and skills, because that challenge is one that we are willing to accept, one we are unwilling to postpone, and one which we intend to win, and the others, too.

3 It is for these reasons that I regard the decision last year to shift our efforts in space from low to high gear as among the most important decisions that will be made during my incumbency in the office of the Presidency. . . .

4 The *Mariner* spacecraft now on its way to Venus is the most intricate instrument in the history of space science. The accuracy of that shot is comparable to firing a missile from Cape Canaveral and dropping it in this stadium between the 40-yard lines.

5 Transit satellites are helping our ships at sea to steer a safer course. Satellites have given us unprecedented warnings of hurricanes and storms, and will do the same for forest fires and icebergs.

6 We have had our failures, but so have others, even if they do not admit them. And they may be less public.

7   To be sure, we are behind, and will be behind for some time in manned flight. But we do not intend to stay behind, and in this decade, we shall make up and move ahead.

8   The growth of our science and education will be enriched by new knowledge of our universe and environment, by new techniques of learning and mapping and observation, by new tools and computers for industry, medicine, the home as well as the school. Technical institutions, such as Rice, will reap the harvest of these gains.

9   And finally, the space effort itself, while still in its infancy, has already created a great number of new companies, and tens of thousands of new jobs. Space and related industries are generating new demands in investment and skilled personnel, and this city and this state, and this region, will share greatly in this growth. . . . During the next five years the National Aeronautics and Space Administration expects to double the number of scientists and engineers in this area, to increase its outlays for salaries and expenses to $60 million a year; to invest some $200 million in plant and laboratory facilities; and to direct or contract for new space efforts over $1 billion from this center in this city.

16. What is President Kennedy's purpose for giving this speech?

   A. To justify the allocation of millions of dollars to fund an unpopular space exploration program
   B. To engage the American public in a dialogue about the benefits of investing in space technology
   C. To present the reasoning behind his support for the development of a US space program
   D. To remind the American people of their country's long history as explorers and innovators

17. Which of these is the underlying premise of Kennedy's speech?

   A. The United States is best qualified to lead the world's efforts to explore outer space.
   B. The United States alone is prepared to defend the world from an alien invasion.
   C. The United States must overcome obstacles if it is to be the first nation to reach outer space.
   D. The United States is more committed to sending humans into space than other nations.

18. Why does President Kennedy mention the *Mariner* spacecraft and the transit satellites in paragraphs 6 and 7?

   A. To support his claim that Americans are interested in space exploration
   B. To identify American failures in the fields of science and technology
   C. To illustrate ways space technology is already enriching American lives
   D. To suggest that the United States is falling behind in the space race

19. Which sentence signals that Kennedy is making a transition in the speech?

   A. "We choose to go to the moon in this decade and do the other things, not because they are easy, but because they are hard. . . ."
   B. "For the eyes of the world now look into space . . . and we have vowed that we shall not see it governed by a hostile flag of conquest."
   C. "Space and related industries are generating new demands in investment and skilled personnel, and this city . . . will share greatly in this growth."
   D. "It is for these reasons that I regard the decision last year to shift our efforts in space from low to high gear. . . ."

20. When Kennedy refers in paragraph 3 to outer space as "this new sea" and "this new ocean," what is he suggesting?

   A. Outer space is a place filled with natural resources.
   B. Outer space is vast new territory to be explored.
   C. Outer space is a big, dark, and danger-filled void.
   D. Outer space is all that separates us from aliens.

21. What can be inferred from the final paragraph (paragraph 9) of President Kennedy's speech?

   A. Space exploration will inspire American children to study science.
   B. Space exploration will bring Americans a renewed sense of national pride.
   C. Space exploration will give a boost to the American economy.
   D. Space exploration will test American technological know-how.

Directions: Read the following two passages and then answer questions 22–27.

Early Voting Damages American Democracy

1 In 2012, almost one-third of the votes were cast early, more than double the number in 2000. Yet early voting has many practical and psychological drawbacks ranging from voter fraud to damaging an important American ritual. It is time to reverse the trend and get rid of early voting in the 33 states and the District of Columbia where it is now in place.

2 In practical terms, early voting does not accomplish its stated goal, greater voter participation. A study at the University of Wisconsin examined voter patterns in 2004 and 2008 (both presidential election years). They concluded that early voting led to *lower* voter turnout.

3 Early voting is more expensive for candidates. It wastes valuable funds by mailing materials or buying airtime to show ads to people who have already voted. Election campaigns are already too expensive, and many good candidates already drop out too soon due to lack of funds. One more drain on the campaign war chest is one more nail in the coffin of democracy.

4 Early voting always invites voter fraud. In Nevada, some who tried to vote early for the Republican Senate nominee got the Democrat candidate's name on their electronic voting machines instead. Some citizens complained about the problem, but did everyone? It's likely that some people voted, unwittingly, against their candidate of choice. In fact, Nevada's voting machines are serviced by a union whose president was a frequent visitor to the White House, and which gave 95.3 percent of its campaign contributions in 2008 to Democrats.

5 Equally important is the emotional effect on voters. Election Day is a day of national awareness, of civic pride in the workings of democracy. As Election Day nears, the excitement level ramps up. Candidates make their final push, and a media marathon ensues to get out the message one last time. Early voting changes the nature of this important national ritual.

6 If a significant number of people have already voted, who cares what the candidate has to say 48 hours before Election Day? (Similarly, if new, unflattering revelations come to light, it's too late to undo one's vote in the early voting system.)

7 One reform to the voting system that did seem to have a good effect on voter turnout was allowing voters to register on Election Day. This encouraged people who thought they could not vote to come out and vote.

8 Without the pressure of Election Day, voters feel no sense of urgency and may even forget to vote. Preserving a narrow window of opportunity to vote preserves the voting process. Early voting is an idea whose time has come—and gone.

Early Voting: Promotes Good Government

9 On Election Day 2004, long lines of voters and hours-long waits at Ohio polling places inconvenienced many, including those who could ill-afford to spend the time—hourly workers, people who had to pick up children from day care, and more.

10 Administrative confusion added to the frustration. Some people were directed to the wrong polling place. Others discovered that they were disqualified from voting because of confusing or recently changed laws.

11 What should have been a simple, efficient exercise in carrying out one's civic duty was, instead, chaos. And many simply could not wait, which means they could not exercise their right to vote.

12 Early voting can lessen these problems and should be adopted throughout the United States. It would increase voter participation, and in that way it would promote good government.

13 The details of early voting vary from state to state but the principle is the same: voters have a given period of time to vote by mail, online, or in some cases on-site, before Election Day. (Early voting differs from absentee balloting, which has been in place for decades. Absentee ballots are for voters who know they will not be able to reach their polling place on Election Day, such as soldiers stationed overseas.)

14 Early voting is gaining popularity with each passing year. Thirty-three states and the District of Columbia allow some form of early voting. In Washington, Colorado, and Oregon, voting by mail is the only option.

15 Mike Brickner, senior policy director of the Ohio ACLU, thinks that a more perfect democracy is one in which citizens can choose to vote, rather than have that choice taken away by circumstance. And indeed, by Election Day 2005, early voting legislation had been passed in Ohio, noticeably reducing the problems of 2004.

16 In the 1970s, Oregon and California became the first states to pass early voting legislation. The trend migrated eastward, and as of 2014 the latest state to pass early voting laws was Massachusetts. Its early voting laws are due to take effect in 2016. Kentucky is one of the few states that does not have early voting.

17 On average, early voting periods last for 19 days but can range from 4 to 45 days, ending a few days before Election Day. The numbers vary from state to state. In several states, polling places must open at least one weekend during the early voting period to accommodate those who can't come during the week.

18 States must bow to the pressures and responsibilities of citizens' lives and adopt early voting as an option in all states. It would greatly benefit citizens.

22. What is the main idea of the first passage?

    A. Early voting is a detriment to the democratic process.
    B. Early voting is a source of conflict among voters.
    C. Early voting is an issue with both supporters and detractors.
    D. Early voting is an idea whose time has come.

23. How does the author of the first passage build his or her argument about early voting?

    A. By focusing on some of the negative outcomes that are associated with early voting
    B. By highlighting statistics that prove the increasing popularity of early voting among local and state jurisdictions
    C. By appealing to readers' sense of national pride and unity of purpose on Election Days
    D. By citing incidents of voter inconvenience and frustration during past Election Days

24. Which claim made by the author of the first passage lacks the support of valid evidence?

    A. Early voting does not increase voter turnout.
    B. Early voting increases expenses for candidates.
    C. Early voting dampens voters' enthusiasm.
    D. Early voting allows voters to register on Election Day.

25. Which detail mentioned in the second passage supports its main idea?

    A. Early voting is different from absentee balloting.
    B. Early voting laws are easing problems on Election Day.
    C. Early voting is available via mail ballots in some states.
    D. Early voting laws are not yet on the books in Kentucky.

26. Which word is closest in meaning to *exercise* as it is used in the third paragraph of the second passage?

    A. Exert
    B. Worry
    C. Apply
    D. Cause

27. Unlike the author of the first passage, the author of the second passage believes that

    A. states should get rid of early voting.
    B. election fraud is more likely to occur during early voting.
    C. all citizens will participate in early voting.
    D. early voting laws should be passed in every state.

Directions: Read the passage and then answer questions 28–31.

Adapted from "Farmer in the Dell"
from *Half Portions*

by Edna Ferber

1   Old Ben Westerveld was taking it easy. Every muscle taut, every nerve tense, his keen eyes vainly straining to pierce the blackness of the stuffy room— there lay Ben Westerveld in bed, taking it easy. And it was hard. Hard. He wanted to get up. He wanted so intensely to get up that the mere effort of lying there made him ache all over. His toes were curled with the effort. His fingers were clenched with it. His breath came short, and his thighs felt cramped. Nerves. But old Ben Westerveld didn't know that. What should a retired and well-to-do farmer of fifty-eight know of nerves, especially when he has moved to the city and is taking it easy?

2   If only he knew what time it was. Here in Chicago you couldn't tell whether it was four o'clock or seven unless you looked at your watch. To do that it was necessary to turn on the light. And to turn on the light meant that he would turn on, too, a flood of querulous protest from his wife, Bella, who lay asleep beside him.

3   When for forty-five years of your life you have risen at four-thirty daily, it is difficult to learn to loll. To do it successfully you must be a natural-born loller to begin with, and revert. Bella Westerveld was and had. So there she lay, asleep. Old Ben wasn't and hadn't. So there he lay, terribly wide-awake, wondering what made his heart thump so fast when he was lying so still. If it had been light, you could have seen the lines of strained resignation in the aging muscles of his patient face.

4   They had lived in the city for almost a year, but it was the same every morning. He would open his eyes, start up with one hand already reaching for the limp, drab, work-worn garments that used to drape the chair by his bed. Then he would remember and sink back while a great wave of depression swept over him. Nothing to get up for. Store clothes on the chair by the bed. He was taking it easy.

5   Back home on the farm in southern Illinois he had known the hour the instant his eyes opened. Here the flat next door was so close that the bedroom was in twilight even at midday. On the farm he could tell by the feeling—an intangible thing, but infallible. He could gauge the very quality of the blackness that comes just before dawn. The crowing of the cocks, the stamping of the cattle, the twittering of the birds in the old elm whose branches were etched eerily against his window in the ghostly light—these things he had never needed. He had known. But here . . . the very darkness

had a strange quality. A hundred unfamiliar noises misled him. There were no cocks, no cattle, no elm. Above all, there was no instinctive feeling. Once, when they first came to the city, he had risen at twelve-thirty, thinking it was morning, and had gone clumping about the flat waking up everyone and loosing from his wife's lips a stream of acid vituperation that seared even his case-hardened sensibilities. The people sleeping in the bedroom of the flat next door must have heard her.

6   "You big rube! Getting up in the middle of the night and stomping around like cattle. You'd better build a shed in the backyard and sleep there if you're so dumb you can't tell night from day."

7   Even after thirty-three years of marriage he had never ceased to be appalled at the coarseness of her mind and speech—she who had seemed so mild and fragile and exquisite when he married her. He had crept back to bed, shamefacedly. He could hear the couple in the bedroom of the flat just across the little court grumbling and then laughing a little, grudgingly, and yet with appreciation. That bedroom, too, had still the power to appall him. Its nearness, its forced intimacy, were daily shocks to him whose most immediate neighbor, back on the farm, had been a quarter mile away. The sound of a shoe dropped on the hardwood floor, the rush of water in the bathroom, the murmur of nocturnal confidences, the fretful cry of a child in the night, all startled and distressed him whose ear found music in the roar of the thresher and had been soothed by the rattle of the tractor. . . .

8   Before he had begun to take it easy six o'clock had seen the entire mechanism of his busy little world humming smoothly and sweetly, the whole set in motion by his own big, work-calloused hands. Those hands puzzled him now. He often looked at them curiously and in a detached sort of way as if they belonged to someone else. So white they were, and smooth and soft, with long, pliant nails that almost never broke off from rough work as they used to. . . .

9   Those big, capable hands, now dangling so limply from inert wrists, had wrested a living from the soil; those strangely unfaded blue eyes had the keenness of vision which comes from scanning great stretches of earth and sky; the stocky, square-shouldered body suggested power unutilized.

28. Which quotation supports the story's theme?

    A. "Its nearness, its forced intimacy, were daily shocks to him whose most immediate neighbor . . . had been a quarter mile away."

    B. "And to turn on the light meant that he would turn on, too, a flood of querulous protest from his wife, Bella. . . ."

    C. "Those big, capable hands, now dangling so limply from inert wrists, had wrested a living from the soil. . . ."

    D. "He could hear the couple in the bedroom of the flat just across the little court grumbling and then laughing a little. . . ."

29. How does the story's setting affect Ben Westerveld?

   A. It excites him.
   B. It depresses him.
   C. It angers him.
   D. It soothes him.

30. What can be inferred about Bella Westerveld?

   A. She regrets having moved from the farm to the big city.
   B. She is a deeply self-aware and thoughtful individual.
   C. She has retained the mild personality of her girlhood.
   D. She lacks empathy and respect for her husband.

Directions: Use this excerpt from paragraph 7 to answer question 31.

Even after thirty-three years of marriage he had never ceased to be appalled at the coarseness of her mind and speech—she who had seemed so mild and fragile and exquisite when he married her. He had crept back to bed, shamefacedly.

31. Which word could replace *shamefacedly* to reflect the character's true feelings about living in the city?

   A. Despondently
   B. Peacefully
   C. Stubbornly
   D. Furiously

Directions: Read the passage and then answer questions 32–35.

Excerpt adapted from *Main Street*

by Sinclair Lewis

1 [Her husband] Kennicott startled her by chuckling, "D'you realize the town after the next is Gopher Prairie? Home!"

2 That one word—home—it terrified her. Had she really bound herself to live, inescapably, in this town called Gopher Prairie? And this thick man beside her, who dared to define her future, he was a stranger! She turned in her seat, stared at him. Who was he? Why was he sitting with her?

He wasn't of her kind! His neck was heavy; his speech was heavy; he was twelve or thirteen years older than she; and about him was none of the magic of shared adventures and eagerness. She could not believe that she had ever slept in his arms. That was one of the dreams which you had but did not officially admit.

3   She told herself how good he was, how dependable and understanding. She touched his ear, smoothed the plane of his solid jaw, and, turning away again, concentrated upon liking his town. It wouldn't be like these barren settlements. It couldn't be! Why, it had three thousand population. That was a great many people. There would be six hundred houses or more. And——The lakes near it would be so lovely. She'd seen them in the photographs. They had looked charming . . . hadn't they?

4   As the train left . . . she began nervously to watch for the lakes—the entrance to all her future life. But when she discovered them, to the left of the track, her only impression of them was that they resembled the photographs.

5   A mile from Gopher Prairie . . . she could see the town as a whole. With a passionate jerk she pushed up the window, looked out. . . .

6   And she saw that Gopher Prairie was merely an enlargement of all the hamlets[1] which they had been passing. Only to the eyes of a Kennicott was it exceptional. . . . The fields swept up to it, past it. It was unprotected and unprotecting; there was no dignity in it, nor any hope of greatness. Only the tall red grain elevator and a few tinny church-steeples rose from the mass. It was a frontier camp. It was not a place to live in, not possibly, not conceivably.

7   The people—they'd be as drab as their houses, as flat as their fields. She couldn't stay here. She would have to wrench loose from this man, and flee.

8   She peeped at him. She was at once helpless before his mature fixity,[2] and touched by his excitement as he . . . stooped for their bags, came up with flushed face, and gloated, "Here we are!"

9   She smiled loyally, and looked away. The train was entering town. . . . Now the train was passing the grim storage-tanks for oil, a creamery, a lumberyard, a stockyard muddy and trampled and stinking. Now they were stopping at a squat red frame station, the platform crowded with unshaven farmers and with loafers—unadventurous people with dead eyes. She was here. She could not go on. It was the end—the end of the world. She sat with closed eyes, longing to push past Kennicott, hide somewhere in the train, flee on toward the Pacific.

[1] hamlets: small villages
[2] fixity: the quality of being fixed or stable

10   Something large arose in her soul and commanded, "Stop it! Stop being a whining baby!" She stood up quickly; she said, "Isn't it wonderful to be here at last!"

11   He trusted her so. She would make herself like the place. And she was going to do tremendous things——

32. What can be inferred about the relationship between the two characters?

    A. They are an old, happily married couple.
    B. They are unhappily married and middle-aged.
    C. They have recently married, perhaps in haste.
    D. They have plans to be married in Gopher Prairie.

33. Which statement reflects a theme of the story?

    A. You should run away from the things that upset you.
    B. One should not judge a place by its appearance.
    C. Life is a great adventure even in moments of doubt.
    D. Reality can be at odds with one's expectations.

34. What effect does the setting have on the story's female character?

    A. It leads her to make a sudden and life-changing decision.
    B. It forces her to see that she has married the wrong person.
    C. It makes her understand that she is a shallow young woman.
    D. It causes her personality to change from cheerful to anxious.

35. What is the meaning of the word *touched* as it is used in paragraph 8?

    A. Surprised
    B. Moved
    C. Sickened
    D. Amused

This is the end of the Reasoning Through Language Arts (RLA) Posttest.

Mathematical Reasoning

Now that you have reviewed some of the basic topics covered by the GED® test in Mathematical Reasoning, take this Posttest to measure your current mathematical reasoning skills.

This practice test has 30 items in various formats. The questions are designed to measure the same skills as the ones on the real exam. Most are in a multiple-choice or free-response format, but you will also see some questions in the "drop-down" format that is used for some questions on the real exam. On the real GED test, you will indicate your answers by clicking on the computer screen. For this paper-and-pencil practice test, mark your answers directly on the page.

Take this test under actual exam conditions. Complete the test in one session and limit your time to 60 minutes. If you do not complete the test in the time allowed, you will know that you need to work on improving your pacing. Try to answer as many questions as you can. There is no penalty for wrong answers, so guess if you have to. In multiple-choice questions, if you can eliminate one or more answer choices, you can increase your chances of guessing correctly.

After you have finished the test, check your answers in the Posttest Answer Keys section that begins on page 753.

Now turn the page and begin the Mathematical Reasoning Posttest.

Mathematical Reasoning

30 Questions (various formats) | **60 Minutes**

Directions: For multiple-choice questions, choose the best answer. For free-response questions, write your answer in the blank. For "drop-down" questions, follow the directions given.

1. There are 63 candy bars in seven boxes. How many candy bars are there in each box?

   A. 3
   B. 6
   C. 7
   D. 9

2. Estimate 513×284 by rounding each factor to the nearest hundred.

   _____

3. Write the number 14,721 in words.

   _____

   _____

4. Which of the following is a proper fraction?

   A. $\dfrac{5}{5}$

   B. $\dfrac{8}{3}$

   C. $\dfrac{4}{11}$

   D. $1\dfrac{1}{5}$

5. Add: $3\dfrac{3}{4} + 1\dfrac{1}{2}$

   _____

6. Austin traveled 120 kilometers (km) in $2\frac{1}{2}$ hr. What is his average speed?

_____

7. What is the decimal equivalent of $5\frac{3}{5}$?
   A. 5.6
   B. 0.56
   C. 5.06
   D. 6.5

8. Sarah buys three t-shirts on sale. Each t-shirts costs $9.98. What was the total cost of the purchase?

_____

9. Multiply: $23.61 \times 1,000$

_____

Question 10 contains two blanks marked "Select.... ▼" Beneath each blank are four choices. Indicate the choice that is correct and belongs in the blank. (**Note:** On the real GED® test, the choices will appear as a "drop-down" menu. When you click on a choice, it will appear in the blank.)

10. $-7-(-3) =$ Select.... ▼ , while $-7 + (-3) =$ Select.... ▼ .

Select.... ▼
−10
−4
4
10

Select.... ▼
−10
−4
4
10

11. $-72 \div -6 =$
    A. 12
    B. −12
    C. 66
    D. −66

12. Evaluate: $7 - 3 + 14 \div 7 \times 12 \div 3$

_____

13. Find the product: $(2x-3)(5-4x)$

  A. $8x^2-2x-15$
  B. $-8x^2+22x-15$
  C. $8x^2+22x-15$
  D. $-8x^2-2x-15$

14. Factor $32x^5-162x$ completely.

_____

15. Find the quotient: $\dfrac{6x^2+x-15}{3x+5}$

_____

16. Solve: $2(x+4)<5(x-20)$

  A. $x<6$
  B. $x>6$
  C. $x<36$
  D. $x>36$

17. Solve: $\dfrac{4}{5}(5+x)=\dfrac{1}{4}(3x-5)$

_____

18. The fine for speeding is $10 for every mile per hour the speed is above 55 miles per hour. Write a function for the fine for speeding as a function of the speed, x.

  A. $f(x)=\$10(55-x)$
  B. $f(x)=\$10(x-55)$
  C. $f(x)=\$10x-55$
  D. $f(x)=55x-10$

19. What is the ratio of 5 in. to 2 ft?

  A. $\dfrac{5}{2}$

  B. $\dfrac{2}{5}$

  C. $\dfrac{5}{24}$

  D. $\dfrac{24}{5}$

20. Out of 25 students in a class, 5 students receive a grade of A on the science test. What percent of the students did NOT receive an A on the science test?

_____

21. 16% of what number is 192?

_____

Questions 22 and 23 contain blanks marked "Select.... ▼" Beneath each blank are four choices. Indicate the choice that is correct and belongs in the blank. (Note: On the GED® test, the choices will appear as a "drop-down" menu. When you click on a choice, it will appear in the blank.)

22. Select the measures of central tendency for this data set: 1, 6, 5, 11, 10, 14, 21, 5, 8.

The mean is Select.... ▼ , the median is Select.... ▼ ,

Select.... ▼
5
8
9
11

Select.... ▼
6
8
10
11

and the mode is Select.... ▼ .

Select.... ▼
5
10
14
21

23. The probability of flipping a fair coin 4 times and getting H-H-H-H is

Select .... ▼ , while the probability of flipping the same coin

Select .... ▼
1/2
1/4
1/8
1/16

and getting H-T-H-T is Select .... ▼ .

Select .... ▼
1/2
1/4
1/8
1/16

24. There are 5 white balls, 6 blue balls, and 11 green balls in a jar. If one ball is picked at random, what is the probability that it will NOT be a green ball?

A. $\dfrac{1}{11}$

B. $\dfrac{5}{6}$

C. $\dfrac{11}{11}$

D. $\dfrac{1}{2}$

25. The diameter of the sun is approximately 140,000,000,000 cm. Which of the following correctly represents the diameter of the sun in scientific notation?

A. 1.4×10^{-12} cm
B. 1.4×10^{12} cm
C. 1.4×10^{-11} cm
D. 1.4×10^{11} cm

26. Simplify: $\dfrac{10^7 \cdot 10^3}{10^2}$

27. Simplify: 5^{-2}

28. Arrange these measurements in order from longest to shortest:

1 kilometer, 100 millimeters, 7 centimeters, 1 meter, 100 meters, 1,000 centimeters.

Write your answer in the blanks.

_____ < _____ < _____

< _____ < _____ < _____

Question 29 contains two blanks marked "Select.... ▼" Beneath each blank are three choices. Indicate the choice that is correct and belongs in the blank. (**Note:** On the GED® test, the choices will appear as a "drop-down" menu. When you click on a choice, it will appear in the blank.)

29. The area of a triangle with height 5 and a base of 10 is Select.... ▼

Select .... ▼
less than
equal to
greater than

that of a triangle of height 10 and base 5, and is Select.... ▼ the area

Select .... ▼
less than
equal to
greater than

of a triangle with height 10 and base $2\frac{1}{2}$.

30. Arrange these geometric solids in order from least to greatest in volume:

- cube 1 cm on a side
- sphere 1 centimeter in radius
- cylinder with height 1 cm and base 1 cm radius
- cone with base radius 1 cm height 1 cm

(*Hint:* The volume of a sphere is given by $V = \frac{4}{3}\pi r^3$. The volume of a cylinder is given by $V = \pi r^2 h$. The volume of a cone is given by $V = \frac{1}{3}\pi r^2 h$.)

Write your answer in the blanks.

volume of _____ < volume of _____

< volume of _____ < volume of _____

This is the end of the Mathematical Reasoning Posttest.

Science

This Science Posttest is designed to help you determine how well prepared you are to begin your intensive GED® test study program.

This practice test has 25 items. The questions are designed to measure the same skills as the ones on the real exam. Most of the questions are in multiple-choice format, but you will also see some free-response questions. On the real GED test, you will indicate your answers by clicking on the computer screen. For this paper-and-pencil practice test, mark your answers directly on the page.

Take this test under actual exam conditions. Complete the test in one session and follow the given time limit. If you do not complete the test in the time allowed, you will know that you need to work on improving your pacing.

Try to answer as many questions as you can. There is no penalty for wrong answers, so guess if you have to. In multiple-choice questions, if you can eliminate one or more answer choices, you can increase your chances of guessing correctly.

After you have finished the test, check your answers in the Posttest Answer Keys section that begins on page 754.

Now turn the page and begin the Science Pretest.

POSTTEST

Science

25 Questions (various formats) | **60 Minutes**

Directions: Read each passage carefully. Look closely at any illustrations. For multiple-choice questions, choose the best answer. For the free-response questions, write your answer in the boxes provided.

Questions 1–3 are based on the following passage and diagram.

Energy is the ability to make things happen or do work. It can be found in many forms. Energy can be divided into types—potential and kinetic energy. Potential energy is the stored energy that can be used to do work. The opposite of stored energy is moving energy, or kinetic energy. An example of potential and kinetic energy is illustrated in this diagram of a swing.

Kinetic energy is the energy created by moving objects. The following equation is used for calculating kinetic energy:

$$KE = 0.5 \times m \times v^2$$

where m = mass (kg) and v = velocity (m/s)

For question 1, write your answer in the box.

1. Based on the passage and the diagram, where are potential energy and kinetic energy at their minimum and maximum?

Cut Copy Paste Undo Redo

2. The swing in the diagram moves at a velocity of 5 m/s. The approximate weight of the swing is 1.5 kg. What is the resulting kinetic energy from this moving swing?

   A. 2.50 J
   B. 3.75 J
   C. 12.50 J
   D. 18.75 J

3 If the swing's speed increased from 5 m/s to 15 m/s, by how many times is its kinetic energy increased?

   A. 3 times
   B. 6 times
   C. 9 times
   D. 15 times

Question 4 is based on the following passage.

How do we know we will have enough resources such as food, water, and land in the future? Earth's resources have been and continue to be affected by the growing human population. The world has more than seven billion people today. Humans first changed the ecosystems by cutting down forests for agriculture and by taming animals. The environment was forever altered with the Industrial Age and the burning of fossil fuels like oil and gas. Development of urban areas and increased resource consumption add harmful substances to the ecosystem. All of these human activities are disrupting nutrient cycles and the recycling of essential substances, such as water, carbon, and nitrogen, in ecosystems.

As cities grow, the natural water cycle becomes unbalanced because much of the water from rainfall does not return to rivers and oceans. The concrete and asphalt on city streets do not allow water to seep into the ground. Water also gets polluted from industrial processes.

When forests are cut down for fuel or for building supplies, fewer trees are available to absorb carbon dioxide and to release oxygen into the atmosphere. Destruction of forests also destroys the natural habitats of many plant and animal species that depend on the trees for food and shelter.

The carbon cycle is another cycle affected by human activities. Industries and automobiles burn oil and other carbon-based fuels. This releases more carbon into the atmosphere than can be taken in by green plants. The overabundance of carbon dioxide (CO_2) in the atmosphere is the cause of the "greenhouse effect." The carbon dioxide and other gases retain heat like a thermal blanket around the planet. Climate change is a topic of debate because there are also natural sources of CO_2 release, such as decomposition, forest fires, earthquakes, ocean release, volcanic eruptions, and lightning. But the rate of carbon release today is unprecedented.

4. Explain how using resources carefully and at a slower rate could help reduce the effects of human impact on ecosystems. Include evidence from the text to support your answer.

Write your response in the box. This task may require approximately 10 minutes to complete.

✂ Cut 📋 Copy 📋 Paste ↶ Undo ↷ Redo

Questions 5–7 are based on the following passage.

A star's brightness or magnitude can be used to determine the star's position in the universe. Scientists use two kinds of magnitude to measure a star's brightness—apparent magnitude and absolute magnitude. Apparent magnitude is how bright a star appears when viewed from our planet Earth. Absolute magnitude compares stars as if they were next to each other, at a standard distance from Earth of 32.6 light-years.

5. Which is TRUE about a star that is very far from Earth?

   A. It has a small absolute magnitude and a large apparent magnitude.
   B. It has a large apparent magnitude.
   C. It has a large absolute magnitude and a large apparent magnitude.
   D. It has a small apparent magnitude.

6. Which statement is TRUE about two stars that have similar absolute magnitudes?

   A. They must have similar apparent magnitudes.
   B. They are equally bright when viewed from Earth.
   C. They may not have similar apparent magnitudes.
   D. The star closer to Earth will have a smaller apparent magnitude.

7. Star G has an apparent magnitude of 7.0 and an absolute magnitude of 6.0. Star H has an apparent magnitude of 6.0 and an absolute magnitude of 7.0. Which is TRUE when viewing the two stars from Earth?

   A. The absolute magnitudes of Star G and Star H are the same.
   B. Star H appears brighter than Star G.
   C. Star G appears brighter than Star H.
   D. Star G and Star H appear equally bright.

Questions 8–10 are based on the following passage.

Autotrophs, such as plants, algae, and some bacteria, can make their own food using the process of photosynthesis. This process is shown in the following chemical equation:

$$6CO_2 + 6H_2O + \text{light energy} \rightarrow C_6H_{12}O_6 + 6O_2$$

All aerobic organisms, including plants, carry out cellular respiration. This process is shown in the following chemical equation:

$$C_6H_{12}O_6 + 6O_2 \rightarrow 6CO_2 + 6H_2O + \text{ATP energy}$$

8. Which statement is TRUE about the process of photosynthesis?

   A. Photosynthesis removes carbon dioxide from the atmosphere.
   B. Chemical energy is an important input of photosynthesis.
   C. Plants release large amounts of carbon dioxide into the atmosphere.
   D. Photosynthesis uses oxygen to build sugars and other organic molecules.

9. Which statement is TRUE about the process of cellular respiration?

   A. Organisms release large amounts of oxygen into the atmosphere.
   B. Chemical energy is an important output of cellular respiration.
   C. Cellular respiration removes carbon dioxide from the atmosphere.
   D. Cellular respiration uses carbon dioxide to build organic molecules.

10. How are the reactants and products of photosynthesis and cellular respiration related to each other?

    A. Cellular respiration releases carbon dioxide, while photosynthesis uses oxygen.
    B. Cellular respiration requires solar energy, while photosynthesis uses sugars.
    C. Cellular respiration produces oxygen, while photosynthesis requires oxygen.
    D. Cellular respiration produces carbon dioxide, while photosynthesis uses carbon dioxide.

Questions 11–13 are based on the energy pyramid.

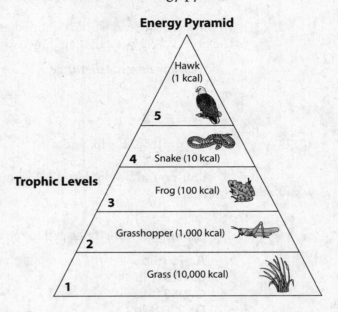

Energy Pyramid

Hawk (1 kcal)

5

4 Snake (10 kcal)

Trophic Levels

3 Frog (100 kcal)

2 Grasshopper (1,000 kcal)

1 Grass (10,000 kcal)

11. Which flowchart best describes the flow of energy through this pyramid?

   A. Producer → predator → herbivore → predator → consumer
   B. Producer → primary consumer → secondary consumer → tertiary consumer → quaternary consumer
   C. Producer → secondary consumer → primary consumer → quaternary consumer
   D. Producer → primary predator → secondary herbivore → tertiary consumer

12. In the energy pyramid, which organism shown is NOT a carnivore?

   A. Snake
   B. Hawk
   C. Grasshopper
   D. Frog

13. How much energy is transferred from one trophic level to another in the energy pyramid?

   A. 1 percent
   B. 5 percent
   C. 10 percent
   D. 15 percent

Questions 14–16 are based on the following passage.

In physical science, work is defined as the force applied to an object to move the object. Work is calculated by using the formula:

Work = Force × distance

or

$W = F \times d$

where W = ft-lb, F = lb, and d = ft

A 50-pound boulder and a 25-pound bag of concrete are to be moved three feet.

14. How much work is needed to move the boulder?

    A. 75 ft-lb
    B. 125 ft-lb
    C. 150 ft-lb
    D. 200 ft-lb

15. How much work is needed to move the concrete?

    A. 75 ft-lb
    B. 100 ft-lb
    C. 150 ft-lb
    D. 200 ft-lb

16. What percent more work would be done if you moved the boulder six feet instead of three feet?

    A. 25 percent more
    B. 30 percent more
    C. 50 percent more
    D. 100 percent more

17. An urban area suddenly experiences a period of high temperatures. During this time, scientists note an increase of sunspots. Which statement may support a correlation between these observations?

    A. Sunspots do not affect Earth's temperature.
    B. An increase in sunspots causes lower temperatures on Earth.
    C. A decrease in sunspots causes higher temperatures on Earth.
    D. An increase in sunspots causes higher temperatures on Earth.

18. Which is the best evidence for Wegener's theory of continental drift?

    A. The seven continents once formed a single giant landmass.
    B. Volcanoes form new islands in the Pacific Ocean.
    C. Large meteors have slammed into Earth, forming giant craters.
    D. Waves from violent storms erode continental shorelines.

Questions 19–22 are based on the following passage.

In physical science, momentum is a measure of how hard it is to stop an object. Momentum (p) is the product of an object's mass and its velocity or

$$p = m \times v$$

The unit measurement of p is kg•m/s.

Conservation of momentum is demonstrated through collisions. The total momentum of a system before a collision is equal to the total momentum of the system after the collision:

$$P_{before} = P_{after}$$

where p is momentum

A 4,000-kg car traveling at 4 m/s collides with a 7,000-kg truck traveling in the same direction at 2 m/s. A 4,000-kg van traveling at 2.5 m/s is also involved in the collision.

19. Before the collision, which vehicle had the greatest momentum?

    A. The car had the greatest momentum.
    B. The truck had the greatest momentum.
    C. The van had the greatest momentum.
    D. The three vehicles had the same momentum.

20. How much momentum does the truck have before the collision?

    A. 1,400 kg•m/s
    B. 1,600 kg•m/s
    C. 14,000 kg•m/s
    D. 16,000 kg•m/s

21. How much momentum does the truck have after the collision?

    A. 11,000 kg•m/s
    B. 14,000 kg•m/s
    C. 16,000 kg•m/s
    D. Not enough information

22. How much combined momentum do the three vehicles have after the collision?

    A. 24,000 kg•m/s
    B. 26,000 kg•m/s
    C. 30,000 kg•m/s
    D. 40,000 kg•m/s

Questions 23–25 are based on the following passage.

Natural selection is a mechanism for evolution to occur. It is also a way for groups of reproducing organisms to become better suited or adapted to their environment. Many of the interesting features of organisms are due to the work of natural selection. Such adaptations are favorable features that allow organisms to better survive and reproduce in their environment.

23. Which statement is part of the process of evolution by natural selection?

    A. Those individuals with beneficial genetic variations survive and reproduce better than those without them.

    B. Some organisms that acquire new physical characteristics during their lifetime can transmit those characteristics to their offspring.

    C. Nature prefers the less-fit organisms and selects against the fittest organisms.

    D. Populations produce a small group of offspring that have all the necessary resources to survive.

24. Which trait is MOST likely to be an adaptation for a plant living under drought or water-scarce conditions?

    A. Large leaves

    B. Poisonous leaves

    C. Thick stems

    D. Sharp thorns

25. Which level of organization can evolve by natural selection?

    A. Cell

    B. Individual

    C. Population

    D. Community

This is the end of the Science Posttest.

Social Studies

This Social Studies Posttest is designed to help you determine how well prepared you are to begin your intensive GED® test study program.

This practice test has 30 items. The questions are designed to measure the same skills as the ones on the real exam. Many are based on historical documents or on short reading passages on social studies topics. Some are based on a table, a diagram, or a map.

Most of the questions are in multiple-choice format, but you will also see questions in the fill-in-the-blank and "drop-down" formats that are used for some questions on the real exam. On the real GED® test, you will indicate your answers by clicking on the computer screen. For this paper-and-pencil practice test, mark your answers directly on the page.

Take this test under actual exam conditions. Complete the test in one session and follow the given time limit. If you do not complete the test in the time allowed, you will know that you need to work on improving your pacing.

Try to answer as many questions as you can. There is no penalty for wrong answers, so guess if you have to. On multiple-choice questions, if you can eliminate one or more answer choices, you can increase your chances of guessing correctly.

After you have finished the test, check your answers in the Posttest Answer Keys section that begins on page 755.

Now turn the page and begin the Social Studies Posttest.

Social Studies

30 Questions (various formats) | **45 Minutes**

Directions: For multiple-choice questions, choose the best answer. For other questions, follow the directions provided.

1. In what type of government do rulers derive their power by divine authority?

   A. Republic
   B. Democracy
   C. Oligarchy
   D. Theocracy

Indicate the choice that is correct and belongs in the blank. (**Note:** On the real GED® test, the choices will appear as a "drop-down" menu. When you click on a choice, it will appear in the blank.)

2. An administrative organization that relies on nonelected officials and regular procedures is called a [Select .... ▼]

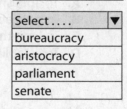

   Select .... ▼
   bureaucracy
   aristocracy
   parliament
   senate

3. Which of the following is NOT a consequence of the rise to power of tyrants in ancient Greece?

   A. Rule by tyrants sometimes led to the rise of an oligarchy.
   B. Rule by tyrants eventually allowed more people to participate in government.
   C. Rule by tyrants led to a renewal of government by monarchs.
   D. Rule by tyrants sometimes led to the development of democracy.

Fill in the blank.

4. In ancient Rome the focal point of politics was the _____,
a ruling body of patricians who served for life.

Use the passage for question 5.

Possibly the most enduring legacy of the Roman Republic was its system
of natural law. The Romans were the first to codify concepts of natural law,
or universal law, establishing that all Roman citizens, and by extension all
people, had some basic rights. Many of these Roman standards of justice
endure today in the world's democratic countries.

5. Which of the following is considered a basic right of all people today in the
United States?

A. Free speech
B. Military service
C. College education
D. Regular employment

6. Why did English aristocrats form a parliament?

A. To abolish constitutional rule
B. To gain absolute power for themselves
C. To limit the power of the king
D. To establish a democracy

POSTTEST

Use the table for questions 7 and 8.

Early Foundations and Influences on American Government

Name of Document	What It Did
Magna Carta (1215)	Guaranteed fundamental rights to individuals, such as trial by jury and due process of law (protection against a government arbitrarily taking a person's life, liberty, or property)
Mayflower Compact (1620)	Established an agreement among English colonists to obey the laws of Plymouth Colony
Petition of Right (1628)	Limited the power of the king; government could no longer imprison or punish individuals unless they had broken the law; government could not impose martial law in peacetime or force soldiers to be housed by citizens without the citizens' consent
English Bill of Rights (1689)	Prevented potential abuses of power by the monarchy; guaranteed an individual's right to a fair trial, to petition the government, to bear arms, and to not be subject to cruel punishment; established free parliamentary elections

7. Which of the above documents was drafted by settlers in North America?

   A. Magna Carta
   B. English Bill of Rights
   C. Petition of Right
   D. Mayflower Compact

8. What important concept is represented in the English Bill of Rights?

   A. The right to inherit property is common to all people.
   B. People have rights granted by the king.
   C. People can participate in government by voting for representatives.
   D. A government has the duty to ensure that citizens are happy.

Use the passage for questions 9 and 10.

The US government was founded on the ideals of shared power, between branches of government, between state government and the federal government, and between citizens and their elected representatives. Citizen rights were protected, but citizens also had certain duties, including the duty to obey the law, perform jury duty, pay taxes, and obtain an education.

9. Which is an example of a duty that American citizens have?

   A. Buying a house
   B. Opening a bank account
   C. Running for elected office
   D. Serving on a jury

10. Why do citizens in a democracy have a duty to obtain an education?

   A. Because they vote and need to be informed on issues
   B. Because they are required by law to attend school
   C. Because the country needs qualified professionals
   D. Because schools are financed by taxpayers

11. Over time, the US Constitution expanded voting rights to include more people. Which of the following groups received the right to vote with the ratification of the Nineteenth Amendment in 1920?

   A. Non-landowning free men
   B. Male citizens of all races
   C. All citizens 18 years or older
   D. Women

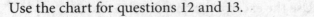

Use the chart for questions 12 and 13.

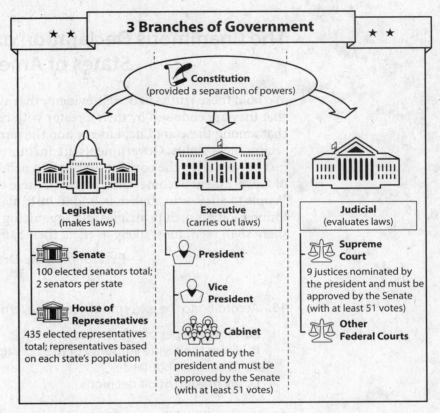

12. Which is a responsibility of the executive branch?

A. Appointing members to the House of Representatives
B. Nominating justices for the Supreme Court
C. Approving justices for the Supreme Court
D. Evaluating laws proposed by the legislative branch

13. Which is an example of the system of checks and balances?

A. States with greater populations have more members in the House of Representatives.
B. The executive branch includes a vice president and a cabinet.
C. The Senate must approve the president's nominations for the Supreme Court.
D. There are only nine Supreme Court justices, but they serve for life.

14. Why did the Pilgrims travel to North America in 1620?

A. To establish new trade routes
B. To claim new territory
C. For travel and adventure
D. To escape religious persecution

Use the excerpt for questions 15 and 16.

The unanimous Declaration of the thirteen united States of America

We hold these truths to be self-evident, that all men are created equal, that they are endowed by their Creator with certain unalienable Rights, that among these are Life, Liberty and the pursuit of Happiness.—That to secure these rights, Governments are instituted among Men, deriving their just powers from the consent of the governed, —That whenever any Form of Government becomes destructive of these ends, it is the Right of the People to alter or to abolish it, and to institute new Government, laying its foundation on such principles and organizing its powers in such form, as to them shall seem most likely to effect their Safety and Happiness.

—*Excerpt from the Declaration of Independence, 1776*

15. According to the excerpt, where do governments get their powers?

    A. From the people by their consent
    B. From the divine authority of their Creator
    C. Through inheritance
    D. By making good decisions

16. Which of the following BEST defines the concept of "unalienable Rights"?

    A. Obligations citizens have to their government
    B. Rights governments grant to citizens
    C. Universal rights people are born with
    D. Rights that only some citizens share

Use the excerpts for questions 17 and 18.

In 1896, the Supreme Court established the doctrine of "separate but equal" in the case of *Plessy v. Ferguson.* The ruling established the legal basis for racial segregation in the South.

We consider the underlying fallacy of the plaintiff's argument to consist in the assumption that the enforced separation of the two races stamps the colored race with a badge of inferiority. If this be so, it is not by reason of anything found in the act, but solely because the colored race chooses to put that construction upon it . . . Legislation is powerless to eradicate racial instincts or to abolish distinctions based upon physical differences, and the attempt to do so can only result in accentuating the difficulties of the present situation.

—*Excerpt from Plessy v. Ferguson, 1896*

In 1954 the Supreme Court overturned the concept of "separate but equal" in the case of *Brown v. Board of Education,* making segregation illegal in public schools.

Segregation of white and colored children in public schools has a detrimental effect upon the colored children. The impact is greater when it has the sanction of law, for the policy of separating the races is usually interpreted as denoting the inferiority of the negro group. . . . We conclude, that, in the field of public education, the doctrine of "separate but equal" has no place. Separate educational facilities are inherently unequal.

—*Excerpt from Brown v. Board of Education, 1954*

17. Which phrase in *Plessy v. Ferguson* suggests that the Supreme Court regarded segregation as natural?

- **A.** "Underlying fallacy"
- **B.** "Racial instincts"
- **C.** "Badge of inferiority"
- **D.** "Enforced separation"

18. What is one similarity between the Supreme Court cases of *Plessy v. Ferguson* and *Brown v. Board of Education*?

- **A.** Both cases deal with segregation based on race.
- **B.** Both cases maintained that segregation is harmful.
- **C.** Both cases endorse the concept of "separate but equal."
- **D.** Both cases uphold enforced separation of whites and blacks.

19. In which of the following cases did the Supreme Court rule that abortion is legal in certain instances?

    A. *Mapp v. Ohio*
    B. *Gideon v. Wainwright*
    C. *Roe v. Wade*
    D. *Miranda v. Arizona*

Indicate the choice that is correct and belongs in the blank. (Note: On the real GED® test, the choices will appear as a "drop-down" menu. When you click on a choice, it will appear in the blank.)

20. The Silk Road was a 4,000-mile-long trade route that connected

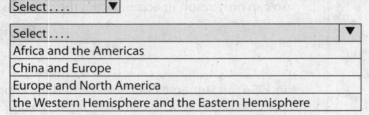

Select.... ▼
Africa and the Americas
China and Europe
Europe and North America
the Western Hemisphere and the Eastern Hemisphere

21. Which of the following BEST explains why coins were invented?

    A. Coins made long-distance trade easier.
    B. Coins were made from precious metals.
    C. Paper currency was too fragile.
    D. Merchants could identify the origin of a coin.

Fill in the blank.

22. According to the theory of _____, the prosperity of a nation depended on a large supply of gold and silver.

POSTTEST

Use the map for questions 23 and 24.

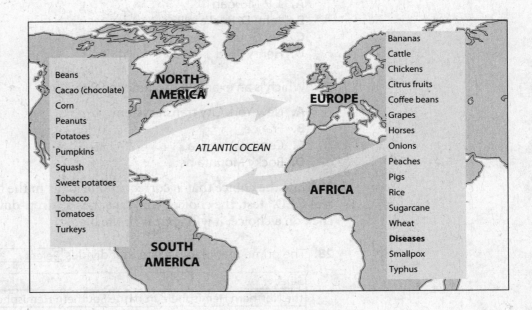

23. Which of the following goods traveled from North America to Europe?

    A. Onions and grapes
    B. Corn and squash
    C. Horses and pigs
    D. Bananas and olives

24. Based on the map, how might the Columbian Exchange have affected Native Americans?

    A. Native Americans began to travel abroad.
    B. New food sources made Native Americans healthier.
    C. Nomadic Native American tribes settled in towns.
    D. Native Americans began using horses for transport.

25. All of the following are consequences of the Industrial Revolution *except*

    A. labor became highly systematized.
    B. cities and towns expanded.
    C. the price of manufactured goods rose.
    D. a new middle class developed.

26. Who initiated the use of the assembly line to mass-produce automobiles?

- **A.** J. P. Morgan
- **B.** John D. Rockefeller
- **C.** Jay Gould
- **D.** Henry Ford

27. Which is an example of a functional region?

- **A.** New York City transit system
- **B.** France
- **C.** Central America
- **D.** Rocky Mountains

Indicate the choice that is correct and belongs in the blank. (**Note:** On the real GED® test, the choices will appear as a "drop-down" menu. When you click on a choice, it will appear in the blank.)

28. The prime meridian is a line that divides $\boxed{\text{Select}\ldots\ \blacktriangledown}$

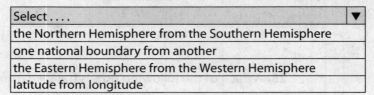

Select.... ▼
the Northern Hemisphere from the Southern Hemisphere
one national boundary from another
the Eastern Hemisphere from the Western Hemisphere
latitude from longitude

29. What is one advantage a map has over a globe?

- **A.** Maps accurately represent the curve of Earth's surface.
- **B.** Maps show Earth's land areas and bodies of water in accurate shapes.
- **C.** Only maps have lines of longitude and latitude.
- **D.** Maps can show small areas more accurately than globes.

Use the following passage for question 30.

Federalism

Federalism describes the relationship between the national, or federal, government and the states. Under federalism, state and national governments work together to enforce laws. Powers that are held by both the states and the federal government are called concurrent powers. When states and the national government both have power over the same issue, the Constitution says that federal law trumps state laws. According to the Tenth Amendment to the Constitution, which was passed as part of the Bill of Rights, any powers that are not given to the national government belong to the states. These clauses form the basis of the relationship between the federal and state governments, but the relationship has shifted over the course of the nation's history.

30. Which is an example of federalism?

    A. Voters cast their votes for state governor.
    B. A city council votes to prohibit the sale of bottled water.
    C. The federal government gives money to the states to support public education.
    D. The governor signs a bill passed by the state legislature.

This is the end of the Social Studies Posttest.

Reasoning Through Language Arts (RLA) Posttest

1. **log in and out at the beginning and end of the workday. They will log out and back in for their lunch hour.** The sentence is not a run-on or a sentence fragment, and it correctly avoids the unnecessary use of commas.

2. **Make sure you clear your calendar to accommodate an hour-long training session and avoid conflicts.** The modifiers in the sentence are logically positioned, and its ideas are balanced, or parallel.

3. **his or her own computer** The phrase "each employee" requires the pronouns *his* or *her*.

4. **someone else's login code.** The correct possessive form is "someone else's." There is no reason to capitalize the words *login* and *code*.

5. **who are found to have spent longer than the allotted time on personal computer use will have one of two options.** This choice is correct because it uses the plural verb *are* to match the plural subject *employees,* and it correctly uses the homonym *two.*

6. **however, please contact the Human Resources department about it.** This choice is correct because it is the only answer choice that correctly uses a conjunctive adverb to avoid wordiness.

7. **has created this policy to meet employee needs without harming the customer service of which we are proud and on which our reputation is based.** This choice is correct because it shows agreement between the subject and its verb, and it uses parallel construction.

8. Choice **D** is correct. The author clearly states that "researching and practicing" are the first steps to making the most of a job interview.

9. Choice **A** is correct. Each section of the passage and its details support the idea that job seekers need to plan and prepare for an interview so that it will be successful.

10. Choice **C** is correct. The sentences, which appear at the beginning of the passage, introduce the topic and suggest the details that will follow.

11. Choice **B** is correct. The section focuses specifically on the day of the interview and how to prepare for it.

12. Choice **C** is correct. The passage touches on mental tricks job seekers can use to prepare for interviews, and it explains that not every job interview will go well or result in a job.

13. Choice **C** is correct. Paragraph 11 extends and clarifies the idea of a first impression, which is introduced in paragraph 10.

14. Choice **B** is correct. The author's emphasis on politeness suggests that an interview is a formal situation.

15. Choice **D** is correct. The author uses sequence to explain the steps a job seeker should take before, during, and after a job interview.

16. Choice **C** is correct. Much of Kennedy's speech is devoted to the economic and nationalistic reasons for developing a US space program.

17. Choice **A** is correct. The excerpt's emphasis on American leadership and peaceful intentions suggests Kennedy's underlying premise that the United States is the nation best equipped to explore space.

18. Choice **C** is correct. The spacecraft and satellites are specific examples Kennedy uses to illustrate both the accuracy of American technology and its usefulness in everyday life.

19. Choice **D** is correct. This sentence signals a transition from Kennedy's discussion of why the United States needs to embark on a space program to the results of his decision to start one.

20. Choice **B** is correct. The metaphor of outer space as a sea or an ocean suggests that Kennedy thinks space is new territory to be explored and mapped as the world's waterways once were.

21. Choice **C** is correct. Kennedy's use of statistics help him present a picture of a prosperous United States whose economy is fueled by the demand for science and technology products.

22. Choice **A** is correct. The writer of the first passage is against early voting. He or she calls it "damaging to an important American ritual."

23. Choice **A** is correct. For support of the main idea, the writer of the first passage focuses on a set of negative outcomes—low voter turnout, needless campaign expenses, the potential for voter fraud, and a decreased sense of urgency on Election Day.

24. Choice **C** is correct. Although the writer of the first passage claims that early voting undermines voters' sense of urgency, he or she offers no substantial evidence in the form of an anecdote, statistic, or expert opinion.

25. Choice **B** is correct. This is the only detail that supports the writer's thesis that early voting can lessen problems voters experience on Election Day.

26. Choice **C** is correct. When one exercises the right to vote, one is applying that right.

27. Choice **D** is correct. The writer of the second passage strongly believes that every state should pass laws to allow early voting because early voting allows more voters enough time to get to the polls.

28. Choice **C** is correct. The details in the story all focus on Ben's unhappiness about "taking it easy" in the city after years of satisfyingly hard physical work on the farm.

29. Choice **B** is correct. The narrator describes Ben's daily ritual of waking to realize that he was no longer living on his farm: "Then he would remember and sink back while a great wave of depression swept over him. Nothing to get up for."

30. Choice **D** is correct. Bella is capable of releasing upon Ben "a stream of acid vituperation that seared even his case-hardened sensibilities." She insults and berates him. She clearly has no respect or fellow feelings for her husband.

31. Choice **A** is correct. The character is depressed and unnerved by city life. The word *disheartened* captures that feeling.

32. Choice **C** is correct. The male character is identified as the female character's husband, but her reaction to him ("And this thick man beside her, who dared to define her future, he was a stranger! She turned in her seat, stared at him. Who was he? Why was he sitting with her?") suggests that she perhaps married him before getting to know him well.

33. Choice **D** is correct. As the narrator explains, the female character spends the duration of the train trip trying to reconcile her expectations of her new hometown, based on photographs, and the rough, barren landscape and towns she sees along the tracks.

34. Choice **A** is correct. While on the train to Gopher Prairie, the female character wants to flee, but when she finally sees the town, she makes a conscious decision: "Something large arose in her soul and commanded, 'Stop it! Stop being a whining baby!' She stood up quickly; she said, 'Isn't it wonderful to be here at last!'"

35. Choice **B** is correct. The woman is touched, or moved by, her husband's excitement as they approach the town.

Mathematical Reasoning Posttest

1. Choice **D** is correct.

2. 150,000

3. fourteen thousand, seven hundred twenty-one

4. Choice **C** is correct.

5. $5\frac{1}{4}$

6. 48 km/hr

7. Choice **A** is correct.

8. $29.94

9. 23,610

10. −4, −10

11. Choice **A** is correct.

12. 12

13. Choice **B** is correct.

14. $2x(4x^2 + 9)(2x + 3)(2x - 3)$

15. $2x - 3$

16. Choice **D** is correct.

17. $x = -105$

18. Choice **B** is correct.

19. Choice **C** is correct.

20. 80%

21. 1,200

22. 9, 8, 5

23. $\frac{1}{16}, \frac{1}{16}$

24. Choice **D** is correct.

25. Choice **D** is correct.

26. 100,000,000

27. $\frac{1}{25}$

28. 1 km, 100 m, 1,000 cm, 1 m, 100 mm, 7 cm

29. equal to, greater than

30. cube, cone, cylinder, sphere

Science Posttest

1. Answers should explain that potential energy is at its maximum at point A and its minimum at point B. Kinetic energy is at its maximum at point B and its minimum at point A.

2. Choice **D** is correct.

3. Choice **C** is correct.

4. Answers should explain that people can reduce harmful impact on the environment by carefully controlling the use of natural resources. For example, by preventing the destruction of forests, they can preserve the trees that contribute oxygen to the atmosphere and provide habitats for other species. By limiting the burning of fossil fuels, they can reduce the amount of carbon dioxide that is released into the atmosphere, thus slowing the buildup of greenhouse gases that can cause climate change.

5. Choice **D** is correct.

6. Choice **C** is correct.

7. Choice **C** is correct.

8. Choice **A** is correct.

9. Choice **B** is correct.

10. Choice **D** is correct.

11. Choice **B** is correct.

12. Choice **C** is correct.

13. Choice **C** is correct.

14. Choice **C** is correct.

15. Choice **A** is correct.

16. Choice **D** is correct.

17. Choice **D** is correct.

18. Choice **A** is correct.

19. Choice **A** is correct.

20. Choice **C** is correct.

21. Choice **D** is correct.

22. Choice **D** is correct.

23. Choice **A** is correct.

24. Choice **C** is correct.

25. Choice **C** is correct.

Social Studies Posttest

1. Choice **D** is correct. Theocracy is a form of monarchy in which rulers derive their power from the gods.

2. The correct answer is "bureaucracy."

3. Choice **C** is correct. The rise to power of tyrants helped bring an end to the rule of monarchs and aristocrats in ancient Greece.

4. The correct answer is "Senate."

5. Choice **A** is correct. The right to free speech is considered to be a basic right that applies to all people.

6. Choice **C** is correct. English aristocrats formed a parliament to create a governing body that would check the powers of the king.

7. Choice **D** is correct. The Mayflower Compact was drafted by the English colonists who settled Plymouth Colony in Massachusetts.

8. Choice **C** is correct. The English Bill of Rights established free parliamentary elections, making it possible for people to participate more fully in government.

9. Choice **D** is correct. Citizens have the right to a fair trial, and to accomplish this, people have the duty to serve on juries.

10. Choice **A** is correct. Because citizens in a democracy elect officials to represent their interests, they have a duty to know about the issues that most affect the country.

11. Choice **D** is correct. The Nineteenth Amendment granted women the right to vote in 1920.

12. Choice **B** is correct. The president nominates justices to serve on the Supreme Court.

13. Choice **C** is correct. By voting to accept or reject a nomination for the Supreme Court, the Senate can check the power of the executive branch.

14. Choice **D** is correct. The Pilgrims were separatists from the Church of England. They left England to escape persecution for their religious beliefs.

15. Choice **A** is correct. The Declaration of Independence states that governments "derive their just powers from the consent of the governed."

16. Choice **C** is correct. The phrase "unalienable Rights" refers to the belief in natural rights, the idea that all people are born with certain rights.

17. Choice **B** is correct. The phrase "racial instincts" suggests that the Supreme Court regarded the doctrine of "separate but equal" as something that developed naturally, as part of a distinction "based on physical differences."

18. Choice **A** is correct. Both cases focused on the issue of segregation between African Americans and whites.

19. Choice **C** is correct. In *Roe v. Wade* the Supreme Court ruled that states could not regulate abortion in the first three months of pregnancy.

20. The correct answer is "China and Europe."

21. Choice **A** is correct. Coins could easily be carried by merchants, which enabled them to expand trade across long distances.

22. The correct answer is "mercantilism."

23. Choice **B** is correct. The map uses arrows and symbols to show that corn and squash were exported from North America to Europe.

24. Choice **D** is correct. In the Columbian Exchange, Europeans brought horses to the Americas. Native Americans soon learned that horses were useful for travel and transport, and even for making war.

25. Choice **C** is correct. During the Industrial Revolution, mass production and improved transportation lowered the price of consumer goods.

26. Choice **D** is correct. Henry Ford initiated the use of the assembly line to mass-produce automobiles.

27. Choice **A** is correct. A functional region is an area defined by a particular use or service, usually related to a business or economic activity, such as a city transit system.

28. The correct answer is "the Eastern Hemisphere from the Western Hemisphere."

29. Choice **D** is correct. The larger the map, the more inaccurate it is, but maps can show small areas of the Earth more accurately than globes.

30. Choice **C** is correct. One example of cooperation between the federal and state governments is the financial support provided by the federal government to the states to support state-run public education.

Reasoning through Language Arts (RLA)

Chapter 1 Parts of Speech and Sentence Basics

Exercise 1: Parts of Speech (page 8)

1. Choice **B** is correct.
2. Choice **A** is correct.
3. Choice **B** is correct.
4. Choice **A** is correct.
5. Choice **D** is correct.
6. Choice **B** is correct.
7. Choice **C** is correct.
8. Choice **B** is correct.
9. Choice **A** is correct.
10. Choice **C** is correct.

Exercise 2: Parts of Speech, continued (page 9) (Part 1)

Nouns	Pronouns	Verbs	Adjectives	Adverbs
Ms. Jay	she	hears	messy	lately
cat	they	eat	sad	here
boat	it	loves	hin	then

Part 2

Answers may vary because examples may vary, but the parts of speech should be as follows.

1. wooden; adjective
2. drove; verb
3. marvelous; adjective
4. slowly; adverb
5. snack; noun

Exercise 3: Four Types of Sentences (page 10)

2. ?; question
3. .; command
4. ?; question
5. .; statement
6. !; exclamation

Exercise 4: Subjects and Verbs (page 12)

2. subject: states; verb: meet
3. subject: you; verb: reach
4. subject: monument; verb: marks
5. subject: you; verb: stand

Exercise 5: Subject-Verb Agreement (page 15)

Answers are listed *subject* and then *verb*.

2. length; is
3. It; is
4. You; do
5. Japan; has
6. It; qualifies
7. Delaware Aqueduct; puts
8. New York City; gets
9. Water; flows
10. Nobody; finds

Exercise 6: Compound Subjects (page 17)

Answers are listed *subject* and then *verb*.

2. Subjects: candidates, debate moderator; verb: has

3. Subjects: Fluids, food; verb: are

4. Subjects: Fall, spring; verb: are

Exercise 7: Interrupters (page 18)

Answers are listed *subject* and then *verb*.

2. Subject: baggers; verb: are

3. Subject: people; verb: strain

4. Subject: roar; verb: makes

Exercise 8: Subject-Verb Agreement (page 19)

Part 1

2. ~~was~~ were

3. ~~Does~~ Do

4. ~~do~~ does

5. ~~are~~ is

6. ~~is~~ are

7. ~~provide~~ provides

8. ~~do take~~, does take

Part 2

1. are

2. provides

3. Are

4. have

5. prevent

6. claim

Exercise 9: Sentence Fragments (page 21)

Answers for items 2 and 4 will vary. Sample answers are shown.

2. SF, The platform is at the top of the tower.

3. CS

4. SF, She pushed off from the platform.

5. CS

Chapter 2 More About Parts of Speech

Exercise 1: Identifying Common and Proper Nouns (page 24)

Suggested answers; answers will vary.

2. Atlantic Ocean

3. Mrs. Briggs

4. New York City

5. Labor Day

Exercise 2: Forming Singular Nouns and Plural Nouns (page 26)

2. ~~Guide;~~ Guides

3. ~~condition;~~ conditions

4. ~~supply;~~ supplies

5. ~~ax;~~ axes

6. ~~foot;,~~ feet

EXERCISE ANSWER KEYS

Exercise 3: Forming Possessive Nouns (page 27)

2. player's
3. chemists'
4. men's
5. students'
6. diver's
7. wolves'
8. Ross's

Exercise 4: Using Subject Pronouns and Object Pronouns (page 29)

2. She
3. They
4. It
5. it
6. her
7. him
8. them

Exercise 5: Forming Possessive Pronouns (page 30)

2. his
3. its
4. them
5. my

Exercise 6: Pronoun Agreement (page 32)

2. them
3. They
4. their
5. Our

6. its
7. his or her

Exercise 7: Choosing the Correct Verb Tense (page 33)

2. started
3. shows
4. continue
5. will pay

Exercise 8: Forming Tenses of Regular Verbs (page 35)

2. loved, will love
3. collected, will collect
4. sailed, will sail
5. placed, will place

Exercise 9: Forming Tenses with Irregular Verbs (page 38)

2. set
3. has driven
4. went
5. had lost
6. stood
7. saw
8. has heard
9. ran
10. read
11. became

Exercise 10: Fixing Errors: Irregular Verbs (page 39)

2. rode
3. came

4. known

5. drew

6. wrote

Exercise 11: Irregular Verbs: *Be, Have,* and *Do* (page 42)

2. Am

3. will be

4. has been

5. has

6. had

7. will have

8. do

9. did

10. had done

Exercise 12: Forming Continuous Tenses (page 44)

2. were failing

3. is providing

4. is hoping

5. are getting

6. was dropping

7. was ignoring

8. was enjoying

Exercise 13: Placing Adjectives (page 45)

Part 1

2. The weather that summer was strange and damaged crops throughout the northeastern United States.

3. The cause of the unusual weather was perplexing and remained a mystery for nearly a century.

4. Some scientists were insightful and concluded that the cause was the eruption of Mount Tambora a year earlier.

Part 2

Answers will vary. Suggested answers are below.

2. roaring; five

3. youngest; beautiful

4. three; last

Exercise 14: Placing Adverbs (page 48)

2. **b.** The twins swim nightly. **c.** The twins swim inside.

3. **a.** The rosebush blooms lushly. **c.** The rosebush blooms outside.

Exercise 15: Adjective or Adverb? (page 50)

2. Underline: wildly. Circle: scattered. Blank: adverb

3. Underline: peaceful. Circle: landscape. Blank: adjective

4. Underline: fearfully. Circle: quake. Blank: adverb

5. Underline: calm. Circle: cameraman. Blank: adjective

6. Underline: quickly. Circle: subside. Blank: adverb

7. Underline: frequently. Circle: filmed. Blank: adverb

Chapter 3 Constructing Sentences

Exercise 1: Creating Compound Sentences, Compound Subjects, and Compound Predicates (page 54)

2. Neighboring states and neighboring towns can be one time zone apart.

3. The United States had 300 different time zones in the early 19th century, and it has four time zones today.

4. In earlier centuries, towns and villages established the correct time based on the position of the sun.

5. Today's system of time zones standardizes timekeeping across the United States and makes it easier to tell time consistently.

Exercise 2: Combining Sentences with Conjunctive Adverbs (page 57)

Answers will vary. Suggested answers are shown.

2. We sent e-mails to Jim for two months; finally, he wrote back.

3. Getting through this day has been tough; similarly, this has been an extremely difficult week.

4. I enjoy playing tennis; likewise, I like to watch it on television.

5. A hurricane can flatten houses; conversely, the air inside the eye of the hurricane remains eerily calm.

6. The weather forecast predicted bitterly cold temperatures all week; nevertheless, we went to the local pond every afternoon to go ice-skating.

Exercise 3: Combining Sentences with Subordinating Conjunctions (page 59)

2. We cannot wrap up this wedding ceremony until you both say, "I do."

3. When we saw the coast emerging from the fog, we knew we would reach shore soon.

4. If you want to excel at anything, you have to work hard.

5. Although I am a defensive driver, I could not avoid the car that ran the stop sign.

6. I forgave him because his apology was so heartfelt.

7. I can't decide if I should vote for one of the two-party candidates or for the independent candidate.

Exercise 4: Editing for Parallel Structure (page 61)

2. When you come to an intersection, a stop sign is a signal to slow down and look both ways.

3. Inventor Thomas Edison claimed that genius is 1 percent inspiration and 99 percent perspiration.

4. (no error)

5. Running, biking, and swimming are three ways to stay in shape.

Exercise 5: Editing Wordy Sentences (page 62)

Answers may vary.

2. The car we bought was a bargain.

3. There is a house in my neighborhood that has been for sale for a long time.

4. The voters waited in line to cast their ballots for the candidates of their choice.

5. My favorite shoes are currently on sale.

Exercise 6: Editing for Illogical Word Order (page 64)

1. **b.** We nearly lost all our money. We almost lost all our money.

2. **a.** Walking quickly tones your muscles. Walking fast tones your muscles.

   b. Walking tones your muscles quickly. A fast way to tone your muscles is by walking.

Exercise 7: Editing Misplaced Modifiers (page 65)

2. Circle: *in the storybook*. The pirate in the storybook found a chest of gold.

3. Circle: *on china plates*. Jacob served cake on china plates to his guests.

Exercise 8: Editing Dangling Modifiers and Split Infinitives (page 67)

2. DM. Circle: *Peering through the darkness*. Peering through the darkness, he saw the door stood only a few feet away.

3. SI. Circle: *to quickly slip*. He was going to have to slip out quickly, or all hope was lost.

4. DM. Circle: *sneaking toward the door*. As he was sneaking toward the door, his sword slipped out of his hand.

Exercise 9: Correcting Comma Usage (page 68)

Part 1

1. According to rumors, the couple's wedding will take place in France.

2. My uncle Carlos, an architect for 20 years, designed a new school.

3. We planted a garden with corn, peas, tomatoes, and my favorite, squash.

4. First, Tyrone will visit his aunt in California, and then he will travel to Seattle.

5. New York, Los Angeles, and Chicago are the three largest American cities, but Houston is not far behind.

Part 2

1. Before we went to dinner, we went out to the mall.

2. NC

3. The giraffe, native to Africa, is one of the zoo's most popular exhibits.

4. Denise came to the dance studio, but the class had already started.

5. Riding in a hot-air balloon is the most exciting thing we've ever done.

Exercise 10: Revising Run-On Sentences (page 70)

Answers may vary.

2. R. The snowstorm started at 10:00 in the morning. Only a few flakes drifted down from the clouds at first.

3. S

4. R. By nightfall, the snowdrifts had buried our car, and the street had turned into an arctic landscape.

5. R. At 9:00, the first snowplows rumbled down our street, and they opened up a path for the cars to get through.

6. R. In the morning, people emerged from their homes, and they spent the next two hours shoveling snow to free their cars from the deep drifts.

EXERCISE ANSWER KEYS

Chapter 4 Building Paragraphs

Exercise 1: Identifying a Topic Sentence (page 72)

1. Sentence B

2. Sentence D

Exercise 2: Adding Supporting Sentences (page 73)

Answers will vary. A sample paragraph follows.

My favorite way to spend my free time is playing soccer. Soccer is a great team sport, like baseball, hockey, and volleyball. I enjoy playing soccer because I love the competition, I love the thrill of kicking the ball, and I also love working with my teammates.

Exercise 3: Providing Sufficient Support (page 75)

Answers may vary but must include detailed examples such as the ones below.

1. Talking on the phone and texting while driving distract you from what is happening to your car and other vehicles—and have caused terrible accidents.

2. Beeping and ringing phones in the theater distract the audience, and sometimes they distract performers during live shows.

3. Smartphones, with their tempting access to Facebook and Instagram, lure you away from your work, interrupt your concentration, and lower your productivity.

Exercise 4: Removing Off-Topic Sentences (page 76)

Underline sentence 1. Cross out sentence 2.

Exercise 5: Editing Inconsistent Verb Tenses (page 78)

Paragraph 2

Next year she ~~visits~~ *will visit* the history museum. The museum will feature a traveling exhibit about dinosaurs. Stephanie ~~planned~~ *plans* to be first in line to see it.

Paragraph 3

Because she ~~will work~~ *works* during the week, weekends are generally the only time she goes on one of her outings. Sometimes she ~~ventured~~ *ventures* out alone, and sometimes a friend accompanies her.

Exercise 6: Making Transitions Between Paragraphs (page 79)

1. Choice **B** is correct.

2. Choice **C** is correct.

3. Choice **D** is correct.

Exercise 7: Splitting a Paragraph (page 81)

Topic sentences: 1. The Hispanic Americans who entered Congress between 1977 and 2012 represent the greatest increase in their ethnic group in congressional history. 2. Demographic changes and political reforms likely caused this change.

Slash after *This means that nearly 60 percent of the Hispanic Americans in congressional history were elected after 1976.*

Exercise 8: Arranging a Paragraph in Logical Order (page 83)

Passage A: 4, 1, 3, 2

Passage B: 1, 4, 3, 2

Exercise 9: Editing Paragraphs (page 84)

Sentences (4) and (10) should be crossed off.

A slash should be added after sentence (6), where the paragraph should be divided into 2 paragraphs.

Sentence (5) is the topic sentence of the first paragraph. Sentence (8) is the topic sentence of the second paragraph.

The correct order of sentences is 5, 1, 3, 2, 6, 8, 7, 9.

(5) Living conditions on Antarctica are extremely harsh. (1) Almost the entire continent is covered by ice and snow, with high winds and extreme cold. (3) Therefore, it is a dangerous climate for humans. (2) There are no towns or cities in Antarctica. (6) In fact, humans have never set up permanent homes there.

(8) Antarctica is, however, the permanent home of a surprising number of animals and plants. (7) Penguins and seals live along the coastline, as do whales and many varieties of fish. (9) In addition, while there are no trees or bushes, many smaller plants have existed there for centuries.

Chapter 5 Building Vocabulary

Exercise 1: Alphabetizing Words (page 86)

Part 1

1. avenue, boulevard, court, lane, street, terrace
2. Austin, Boston, Milwaukee, Omaha, Phoenix, Seattle
3. aluminum, brass, copper, gold, iron, tin

Part 2

1. globe, gloom, glory, glove, glow
2. act, action, active, actress, actual
3. wash, water, weave, weight, welcome

Exercise 2: Using Guide Words (page 87)

2. after
3. before
4. after
5. same page

Exercise 3: Finding Related Words (page 88)

2. discern
3. soft
4. leader
5. banish

Exercise 4: Identifying Parts of Speech (page 90)

2. noun, verb
3. adjective, noun
4. preposition
5. noun, verb
6. preposition, adverb
7. pronoun

Exercise 5: Determining Multiple Meanings (page 91)

2. **a.** swing back and forth **b.** control over

3. **a.** TV show **b.** software put into the computer

4. **a.** stop working in protest **b.** make a musical sound

5. **a.** bend the body forward **b.** front of a boat

Exercise 6: Building Words with Prefixes (page 93)

Part 1

2. *inter–*; interchangeable

3. *fore–*; forewarn

4. *mid–*; midsection

Part 2

1. a

2. c

3. b

Exercise 7: Prefixes Meaning "Not" (page 95)

2. Circle: *in*; not excusable

3. Circle: *im*; not perfect

4. Circle: *ir*; not rational

5. Circle: *dis*; not approve

6. Circle: *anti*; not a hero

Exercise 8: Prefixes Showing Time or Position (page 96)

Part 1

1. d

2. a

3. b

4. c

5. g

6. e

7. f

Part 2

1. e

2. d

3. f

4. a

5. g

6. b

7. c

Exercise 9: Prefixes Showing Number (page 97)

1. c

2. e

3. a

4. f

5. d

6. b

Exercise 10: Building Words with Suffixes (page 99)

1. e

2. g

3. a

4. h

5. d

6. b

7. c

8. f

Exercise 11: Identifying Latin and Greek Roots (page 101)

Part 1

2. ceed
3. cred
4. hydr
5. ceed
6. scope
7. scribe
8. sphere
9. ceive
10. scribe
11. cede
12. sphere

Part 2

1. b
2. d
3. f
4. a
5. g
6. c
7. h
8. e

Exercise 12: Using Latin and Greek Roots to Determine Meaning (page 102)

1. b
2. c
3. a

Exercise 13: Synonyms (page 103)

2. column
3. demonstrate
4. hot
5. seafood
6. instructing

Exercise 14: Antonyms (page 104)

Part 1

1. hushed
2. ignore
3. agreement
4. sharp
5. doubtful

Part 2

2. hunter
3. toppled
4. aggressively

Exercise 15: Using Contractions (page 106)

2. I'd
3. can't
4. they're
5. we'll

Exercise 16: Using Homonyms Correctly (page 108)

	Incorrect	Correct
2.	To, there, you're	Too, their, your
3.	no error	no error
4.	Their, knew	There, new
5.	You're	Your
6.	Its	It's

Chapter 6 Understanding What You Read

Exercise 1: Using Context Clues (page 110)

Part 1

1. Choice **C** is correct.
2. Choice **B** is correct.
3. Choice **A** is correct.
4. Choice **D** is correct.

Part 2

1. Choice **D** is correct.
2. Choice **C** is correct.
3. Choice **D** is correct.

Exercise 2: Understanding Connotation and Denotation (page 112)

	Negative	**Positive**
1.	isolated	quiet
2.	job	career
3.	egotistical	proud
4.	stubborn	persistent
5.	childish	young
6.	indecisive	thoughtful

Exercise 3: Identifying Key Words (page 114)

Answers may vary slightly

1. Amelia Earhart

   disappeared

   Pacific Ocean

   1937

   mysteriously

2. Beethoven

   wrote greatest symphony

   after he went deaf

3. secretary of state

   expressed hope

   journalists

   relations in the Middle East

Exercise 4: Identifying the Main Idea in a Paragraph (page 116)

Part 1

Main idea: Your skin is the organ that comes into contact with the rest of the world.

Supporting detail answers will vary. Examples of three supporting details include:

1. holds bodily fluids in, preventing dehydration
2. keeps harmful germs out
3. nerve endings that help you feel

Part 2

Answers may vary.

1. art and music instruction at Middle School 233
2. Arts education at Middle School 233 has reduced violence and improved attendance.

Exercise 5: Identifying the Main Idea in a Passage (page 118)

Answers may vary in wording.

1. A bee colony is a good example of working together in harmony.
2. Worker bees work as hard and as long as they can.
3. Ants are similar to bees.

4. Ants, however, are more advanced than bees in some ways.

Main Idea of Passage

Ants are like bees in that they work together to build their societies; however, they are more intelligent than bees. Therefore, they are the "rulers of the insect world."

Exercise 6: Summarizing (page 120)

Answers may vary.

1. humans

   collect things

in childhood, especially

anywhere and everywhere

by observing and looking closely

because they follow their interests

2. Answers will vary. *Sample answer:* The urge to collect things is a natural human desire. It often springs from a child's interest in the world and can focus on anything that seems interesting. The desire to collect makes a child observe closely and, through close observation, learn a lot about the surrounding world.

3. Choice **D** is correct.

Chapter 7 The Writing Process

Exercise 1: Brainstorming and Idea Maps (page 124)

Answers will vary. Brainstorm should include both pros and cons.

Exercise 2: Writing a Thesis Statement (page 125)

Part 1

Underline: Our government should take the extra step and make cigarettes illegal for the sake of everyone's safety.

Part 2

1. Choice **D** is correct.

Exercise 3: The Writing Process (page 128)

Answers will vary.

Be sure to include a prewriting exercise, a rough draft, and a final draft. The draft should be focused on the main idea throughout, have an introduction, multiple paragraphs that include at least two types of supporting evidence, and a conclusion that summarizes the essay.

Chapter 8 Informational Texts

Exercise 1: Understanding Audience, Purpose, and Evidence (page 132)

What to Look for	Text Evidence
Title	Rare Butterflies in Danger
Headings	none
Definitions	"An endangered species is any animal or plant in danger of disappearing completely from Earth"
Examples	Schaus swallowtail on endangered species list for 20 years; only 75 recorded in three years; live on only one island
Explanations	"Their survival is hindered by habitat destruction, insecticide use, droughts, hurricanes, and illegal collection"; "breeding may increase their numbers"
Descriptions or Visuals	Dark brown with yellow marks, rusty patch on wing

Audience: people interested in endangered species

Purpose: to give an example of an endangered species and tell why it is endangered

Exercise 2: Chronological Order (page 135)

1. **A**. Underline: single term, second president

   B. Underline: two terms as president

   C. Underline: third president, 1801–1809

   D. Underline: first president

Chronological order: D, B, A, C

Author's purpose: Answers will vary. To trace the conflict about the proper functions of governmental power through the first three presidencies

2. **A**. Underline: Separate

   B. Underline: Then, sort

   C. Underline: Finally

   D. Underline: First

   E. Underline: Later

Chronological order: D, B, A, E, C

Author's purpose: Answers will vary. To explain the recycling procedure to readers

Exercise 3: Comparing and Contrasting (page 137)

1. Money spent on eating at home, money spent on dining out

2. People with the highest 20 percent of household incomes

3. People in the lowest income group

4. Answers will vary. Sample answer: All consumers spend more on eating at home than on dining out, although people in higher income groups spend more on dining out than people in lower income households.

Exercise 4: Cause and Effect (page 139)

Part 1

	Circle:	Underline:
2.	3.9 GPA	graduated in the top 10 percent
3.	streaming	fewer people go to theaters to see movies
4.	changes in the climate	migratory patterns of birds are changing
5.	writes great short stories	won the fiction contest

Part 2

1. How oceans affect weather, hurricanes, climate

2. A. Oceans control weather by heating and cooling the air. B. Oceans control weather by controlling wind speed and direction.

3. Boxes in chart should include three of the following: water supply; food supply; trade shipments; property values; civilization's growth; civilization's death.

Exercise 5: Problem and Solution (page 141)

Problem: How should young people respond to violence around them?

Solutions: Answers may vary but should include at least three of the following: help friends calm down; deal with the situation in a nonviolent way; stop an argument from getting violent; express that they do not agree with bullying or other forms of violence; get help from others, like trusted adults; support others who have been victims of violence.

Exercise 6: Using Different Formats (page 144)

1. 1808 [timeline]

2. 1863 [timeline]

3. Fifteenth Amendment [timeline]

4. **(a)** Lowest: 1790—none produced; highest: 1860; **(b)** Lowest: 1790; highest: 1860

5. Answers will vary. Sample answer: Banning the importing of slaves

Exercise 7: Workplace Documents (page 146)

Answers may vary.

This company will shortly be opening a new branch office in Chicago, Illinois. Four people will be chosen to transfer to this office. If you wish to be a transfer candidate, please make your transfer application to the Human Resources Department by Friday, January 15.

Chapter 9 Texts Intended to Argue or Persuade

Exercise 1: Identifying an Author's Point of View (page 148)

Answers for underlining details may vary. Examples may include "Globally, enormous progress has been made"; "Yet disparities endure"; "obtaining an education remains particularly tough for women and girls."

Author's purpose: The author's purpose is to point out where progress has been made in eliminating the gender gap in education, and where there is a need for more progress.

Author's point of view: While progress in elementary education has been solid, much more needs to be done to help more women become literate.

Exercise 2: Understanding Evidence (page 151)

Answers will vary.

1. The oceans are essential to all life, so we must protect them.

2. "The entire system is interdependent, and we ignore that fact at our peril."

3. He uses facts: The ocean provides us with food, affects the air, provides jobs for humans, and contains many species.

4. He uses an anecdote about growing up learning about the ocean.

Exercise 3: Identifying Logical Fallacies (page 155)

1. False dichotomy
2. Straw man or ad hominem
3. Stereotyping
4. Ad populum
5. Overgeneralization
6. Red herring
7. Circular logic

Exercise 4: Identifying an Underlying Premise (page 156)

1. Choice **B** is correct.

Exercise 5: Refuting an Opposing Argument (page 157)

Answers will vary.

Counterargument 1: While it is true that businesses benefit from advertising, it's less clear that consumers need to be constantly encouraged to buy more, especially when times are tough, and people need to save money.

Counterargument 2: Eliminating advertising seems excessive; however, limiting it can encourage other virtues than consumerism.

Exercise 6: Comparing and Contrasting Texts on the Same Topic (page 159)

1.

Essay 1

Answers will vary. Sample answer: **Author's purpose:** To show that surveillance cameras are bad for society

Main idea: Surveillance cameras erode privacy and infringe on civil rights without improving safety.

Essay 2

Author's purpose: To show that surveillance cameras are good for society

Main idea: Surveillance cameras are a good resource for protecting public safety.

2. Answers may vary. Sample answers are shown below.

Claims (Pro)	Supporting Evidence
1. Decrease of violence in Washington, DC	1. Dept. of Justice study
2. Protect most vulnerable	2. Camera footage helped prevent a kidnapping and murder

Claims (Con)	Supporting Evidence
1. Unclear who owns footage	1. No government laws to regulate
2. Criminals use footage to commit crimes	2. Neil Richards says cameras can be hacked.

3. Choice **A** is correct.
4. Choice **A** is correct.
5. Choice **C** is correct.
6. Answers will vary. Sample response: In Essay 1, approval of surveillance cameras is linked to people's reaction to fear after the Boston Marathon bombing. In Essay 2, however, the cameras are mentioned as leading directly to apprehending the perpetrators.

Exercise 7: Analyzing Persuasive Texts (page 164)

Part 1

1. Choice **E** is correct.
2. Choice **D** is correct.
3. Choice **A** is correct.
4. Choice **B** is correct.
5. Choice **C** is correct.

Part 2

1. Choice **A** is correct.

2. Choice **D** is correct.

Chapter 10 Understanding Fiction

Exercise 1: Plot (page 170)

1. Choice **C** is correct.

2. Choice **A** is correct.

3. Choice **C** is correct.

4. Choice **A** is correct.

Exercise 2: Characterization (page 172)

1. Hungry: **d.** "day and a half without food"

   Alone: **c.** "friendless and unknown"; "vagabond and outcast"

   Poor: **b.** "penniless"; "paid his last coin in passage money"

   Unemployed: **a.** "unsuccessful miner suddenly reduced to the point of soliciting work"

2. Choice **B** is correct.

3. Choice **D** is correct.

Exercise 3: Setting and Tone (page 174)

1. Choice **B** is correct.

2. Answers will vary: "bees humming dreamily," "sun shining steadily," "heaven's happiness."

3. repetition in sentences 3 or 12 (also sentences 7 and 8); parallelism in sentence 10

4. Choice **B** is correct.

3. Choice **C** is correct.

4. Answers will vary: "evil spirit," "cold mist," "unwholesome."

Exercise 4: Author's Point of View (page 176)

1. Third-person limited

2. First person

3. Third-person omniscient

Exercise 5: Theme (page 178)

1. Choice **C** is correct.

2. Choice **B** is correct.

3. Choice **B** is correct.

4. Choice **B** is correct.

5. Choice **D** is correct.

Mathematical Reasoning

Chapter 1 Whole Numbers

Exercise 1: Place Value (page 185)

1. B
2. A
3. D
4. C
5. A
6. 8; 0; 9; 7
7. 1; 7; 9; 2; 6
8. ones
9. ten thousands
10. thousands
11. ten thousands
12. millions
13. ones; hundreds
14. thousands; tens
15. hundreds; ones
16. **a.** 7 tens   **b.** 0 thousands
17. **a.** 2 hundreds   **b.** 1 thousands
18. **a.** 0 tens   **b.** 1 ones
19. 3 millions
20. 9 hundred thousands

Exercise 2: Reading and Writing Whole Numbers (page 187)

1. C
2. D
3. D
4. C
5. C
6. 6,423
7. 25,382
8. 705,209
9. 6,200,692
10. 30,100,301
11. 4,700,000
12. 450,000
13. 326,050,125
14. 21,812
15. 3,491,930
16. 350,383
17. two hundred thousand, three hundred four
18. three hundred fifty thousand, three hundred fifty-nine
19. twenty-three thousand, eight hundred twenty-two
20. eight thousand, nine hundred thirty-four

Exercise 3: Adding Whole Numbers (page 191)

1. 108
2. 99
3. 99
4. 849
5. 388
6. 2,897
7. 100
8. 238
9. 661
10. 1,710

11. 12,610	**14. D**
12. 10,989	**15. D**
13. C	

19. 4,024	**22.** 189,200
20. 80,808	**23.** 741,600
21. 99,000	**24.** 407,682

Exercise 4: Subtracting Whole Numbers (page 194)

1. 61	**16.** 8,950
2. 44	**17.** 841
3. 35	**18.** 2,622
4. 108	**19.** 279
5. 351	**20.** 177
6. 118	**21.** 89
7. 57	**22.** 191
8. 69	**23.** 91
9. 29	**24.** 81
10. 2	**25.** 1,081
11. 22	**26.** 5,001
12. 49	**27. A**
13. 191	**28. B**
14. 284	**29. B**
15. 395	**30. C**

Exercise 5: Multiplying Whole Numbers (page 201)

1. 72	**10.** 729
2. 24	**11.** 738
3. 36	**12.** 36
4. 56	**13.** 280
5. 35	**14.** 648
6. 28	**15.** 801
7. 69	**16.** 1,989
8. 369	**17.** 17,472
9. 81	**18.** 5,887

Exercise 6: Dividing Whole Numbers (page 204)

1. 9	**9.** 623
2. 71	**10.** 8,657r2
3. 0	**11.** 80
4. undefined	**12.** 990
5. 21	**13. A**
6. 58	**14. C**
7. 49r3	**15. A**
8. 309r2	

Exercise 7: Rounding Whole Numbers (page 206)

1. 60	**6.** 9,000,000
2. 2,000	**7.** 100
3. 830,000	**8.** 1,000
4. 3,490	**9.** 700,000
5. 800	**10.** 970,000

Exercise 8: Estimating with Whole Numbers (page 208)

1. 110	**10.** 11,000
2. 170	**11.** 6,000
3. 60	**12.** 4,000
4. 5,100	**13. D**
5. 1,400	**14. B**
6. 3,700	**15. B**
7. 3,600,000	**16. B**
8. 5,000	**17. C**
9. 13,000	

ANSWERS

Exercise 9: Whole Numbers Review (page 210)

1. 3; 8; 0; 9
2. 6; 7; 9; 8
3. 9 tens
4. 2 ten thousands
5. 8 thousands
6. 4 hundred thousands
7. 1 millions
8. 4,908
9. 5,005,575
10. 250,351
11. 21,813
12. 4,220,000
13. twenty-two thousand, four hundred eighty-two
14. two hundred thousand, four hundred three
15. one million, five hundred thirty-two thousand

16. 33
17. 54
18. 365
19. 799
20. 3,003
21. 14,390
22. 7,490
23. 93,009
24. 60
25. 21
26. 818
27. 266
28. 2,105
29. 3,390

30. 4,910
31. 36
32. 88
33. 736
34. 7,550
35. 91,000
36. 8,096
37. 150,000
38. 10,295
39. 15
40. 8
41. 101
42. 6r6
43. 147
44. 72
45. 40r4
46. 120
47. 13
48. 3
49. 17
50. 11
51. 30
52. 60
53. 680

54. 200
55. 300
56. 4,000
57. 9,000
58. 830,000
59. 18,000,000
60. 9,000,000
61. 10
62. 200
63. 0
64. 0
65. 40
66. 80
67. 21,600
68. 240
69. 900
70. 140,000
71. 500
72. 400
73. 7,000
74. 6,000
75. 20,000
76. 1,000

Chapter 2 Fractions

Exercise 1: Understanding Fractions (page 217)

1. B
2. A
3. D
4. C
5. A
6. $\frac{2}{8}$
7. $\frac{3}{8}$
8. $\frac{1}{7}$

ANSWERS

9. $\frac{1}{4}$ **10.** $\frac{3}{4}$

11.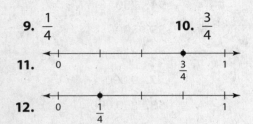

12.

7. 20   **12.** 10

8. 3   **13.** 9

9. 5   **14.** 8

10. 8   **15.** 10

11. 9

Exercise 2: Proper and Improper Fractions and Mixed Numbers (page 223)

1. $\frac{3}{2}$ **11.** $2\frac{4}{5}$

2. $\frac{7}{4}$ **12.** $17\frac{1}{3}$

3. $\frac{13}{5}$ **13.** $4\frac{7}{9}$

4. $\frac{6}{4}$ **14.** $6\frac{9}{13}$

5. $\frac{13}{8}$ **15.** $1\frac{5}{18}$

6. $1\frac{1}{2}$ **16.** $\frac{29}{8}$

7. $1\frac{3}{4}$ **17.** $\frac{29}{11}$

8. $2\frac{3}{5}$ **18.** $\frac{27}{4}$

9. $1\frac{2}{4}$ **19.** $\frac{37}{3}$

10. $1\frac{5}{8}$ **20.** $\frac{63}{5}$

Exercise 3: Equivalent Fractions (page 226)

1. C   **4.** C

2. D   **5.** C

3. D   **6.** 4

Exercise 4: Reducing Fractions to Lowest Terms (page 231)

1. C

2. D   **11.** $\frac{2}{3}$

3. D

4. D   **12.** $\frac{1}{4}$

5. 2   **13.** $\frac{3}{4}$

6. 5

7. 3   **14.** $\frac{1}{3}$

8. 2

9. 2   **15.** $\frac{1}{2}$

10. $\frac{4}{5}$

Exercise 5: Comparing Fractions (page 236)

1. <   **11.** 10, 15. 20, 25, 30

2. >   **12.** 6, 9, 12, 15, 18

3. =   **13.** 16, 24, 32, 40, 48

4. >   **14.** 12, 18, 24, 30, 36

5. =   **15.** 8, 12, 16, 20, 24

6. <   **16.** 10

7. >   **17.** 24

8. <   **18.** 24

9. >   **19.** 30

10. =   **20.** 12

Exercise 6: Adding and Subtracting Like Fractions (page 238)

1. $\dfrac{5}{12}$

2. $\dfrac{5}{8}$

3. $\dfrac{4}{5}$

4. $\dfrac{2}{3}$

5. $\dfrac{5}{8}$

6. $\dfrac{3}{5}$

7. $\dfrac{7}{8}$

8. $\dfrac{11}{12}$

9. $\dfrac{3}{4}$

10. $\dfrac{8}{3}$

11. $1\dfrac{1}{4}$

12. 1

13. $1\dfrac{1}{5}$

14. 2

15. $1\dfrac{1}{2}$

16. $\dfrac{1}{4}$

17. $\dfrac{1}{4}$

18. $\dfrac{2}{5}$

19. $\dfrac{1}{2}$

20. 0

Exercise 7: Adding and Subtracting Unlike Fractions (page 241)

1. $7, 2, \dfrac{9}{14}$

2. $2, \dfrac{5}{8}$

3. $2, \dfrac{3}{4}$

4. $12, 10, \dfrac{2}{15}$

5. $2, \dfrac{3}{8}$

6. $3, 2, \dfrac{5}{6}$

7. $15, 8, \dfrac{7}{20}$

8. $3, \dfrac{4}{9}$

9. $4, \dfrac{15}{16}$

10. $4, 3, \dfrac{7}{12}$

11. $\dfrac{3}{8}$

12. $\dfrac{1}{10}$

13. $\dfrac{5}{12}$

14. $\dfrac{11}{30}$

15. $\dfrac{7}{8}$

16. $\dfrac{5}{6}$

17. $\dfrac{1}{4}$

18. $1\dfrac{1}{2}$

19. $\dfrac{1}{4}$

20. $\dfrac{19}{20}$

Exercise 8: Adding and Subtracting Mixed Numbers (page 244)

1. $8\dfrac{5}{12}$

2. $1\dfrac{2}{3}$

3. $7\dfrac{5}{8}$

4. $3\dfrac{1}{2}$

5. $5\dfrac{1}{4}$

6. $3\dfrac{3}{4}$

7. $7\dfrac{1}{3}$

8. $2\dfrac{11}{12}$

9. 4

10. $2\dfrac{5}{8}$

11. B

12. C

Exercise 9: Multiplying Fractions (page 246)

1. $\dfrac{5}{12}$

2. $\dfrac{8}{15}$

3. $\dfrac{7}{32}$

4. $\dfrac{6}{25}$

5. $\dfrac{6}{35}$

6. $\dfrac{3}{8}$

7. $\dfrac{2}{21}$

8. $\dfrac{1}{15}$

ANSWERS

9. $\dfrac{5}{14}$

10. $\dfrac{2}{15}$

11. $\dfrac{1}{3}$

12. $\dfrac{4}{15}$

13. $\dfrac{1}{2}$

14. $\dfrac{1}{4}$

15. $\dfrac{1}{18}$

16. $\dfrac{2}{7}$

17. $\dfrac{1}{4}$

18. $\dfrac{2}{11}$

19. $\dfrac{2}{5}$

20. $\dfrac{1}{15}$

21. **A**

22. **D**

Exercise 10: Multiplying Fractions, Whole Numbers, and Mixed Numbers (page 248)

1. $1\dfrac{4}{5}$

2. $4\dfrac{1}{2}$

3. $2\dfrac{1}{2}$

4. $3\dfrac{3}{4}$

5. 1

6. $1\dfrac{1}{4}$

7. $3\dfrac{3}{4}$

8. $4\dfrac{3}{8}$

9. $\dfrac{2}{3}$

10. 6

11. $\dfrac{3}{4}$

12. $3\dfrac{1}{3}$

13. $1\dfrac{2}{3}$

14. $1\dfrac{3}{4}$

15. $\dfrac{1}{2}$

16. $\dfrac{7}{8}$

17. $\dfrac{27}{32}$

18. $1\dfrac{1}{8}$

19. **A**

20. **D**

Exercise 11: Dividing Fractions (page 250)

1. $\dfrac{8}{3}$

2. $\dfrac{3}{2}$

3. $\dfrac{8}{7}$

4. $\dfrac{5}{3}$

5. $\dfrac{7}{6}$

6. $\dfrac{2}{1}$

7. $\dfrac{2}{3}$

8. $2\dfrac{1}{2}$

9. $1\dfrac{1}{15}$

10. $\dfrac{1}{4}$

11. $1\dfrac{7}{8}$

12. 6

Exercise 12: Dividing Fractions, Whole Numbers, and Mixed Numbers (page 252)

1. $\dfrac{3}{8}$

2. $\dfrac{2}{3}$

3. $\dfrac{7}{6}$

4. $\dfrac{1}{4}$

5. $\dfrac{1}{9}$

6. $\dfrac{1}{5}$

7. $\dfrac{4}{7}$

8. $\dfrac{3}{8}$

9. $\dfrac{5}{16}$

10. $\dfrac{2}{5}$

11. $\dfrac{5}{9}$

12. $\dfrac{3}{5}$

13. $\dfrac{1}{15}$

14. $\dfrac{3}{4}$

15. $\dfrac{3}{20}$

16. $\dfrac{1}{2}$

17. $\dfrac{1}{16}$

18. $\dfrac{2}{5}$

19. 2

20. $\frac{1}{3}$

21. $1\frac{7}{8}$

22. $1\frac{1}{14}$

12. $\frac{13}{8}$

13. $\frac{11}{5}$

14. <

15. <

16. =

17. $\frac{2}{5}$

18. $1\frac{5}{12}$

19. $4\frac{3}{4}$

20. $\frac{1}{2}$

21. $\frac{1}{2}$

22. $3\frac{5}{6}$

23. $\frac{1}{4}$

24. $2\frac{1}{22}$

25. $1\frac{2}{5}$

26. $\frac{2}{3}$

27. $6\frac{2}{3}$

28. $\frac{1}{2}$

Exercise 13: Fraction Review (page 253)

1. $\frac{4}{6}$

2. $\frac{2}{3}$

3. $\frac{2}{5}$

4. 2

5. 10

6. 9

7. $\frac{3}{5}$

8. $\frac{1}{3}$

9. $\frac{1}{4}$

10. $\frac{1}{3}$

11. $\frac{6}{4}$

Chapter 3 Decimals

Exercise 1: The Place Value System (page 259)

1. hundredths

2. thousandths

3. ten thousandths

4. tens

5. tenths

6. thousandths

7. ten thousandths

8. $2 + 0.4 + 0.03$

9. $7 + 0.8 + 0.009$

10. $10 + 4 + 0.5 + 0.01$

11. $10 + 2 + 0.9 + 0.09 + 0.009$

12. $1 + 0.001$

13. $0.52

14. $0.41

15. $0.76

16. $0.25

Exercise 2: Necessary and Unnecessary 0s (page 262)

1. 0.0<u>9</u>

2. 0.0<u>0</u>3

3. 0.080

4. 6.<u>0</u>08

5. 4.7<u>0</u>8

6. 0.07<u>0</u>

7. 0.3<u>00</u>

8. 0.05<u>00</u>

9. 6.8<u>00</u>

10. 4.78<u>0</u>

Exercise 3: Reading and Writing Decimals (page 263)

1. seven tenths

2. four tenths

3. three hundredths

4. six hundredths

ANSWERS

5. thirty-four hundredths

6. seventy-six hundredths

7. nine thousandths

8. fifty-six thousandths

9. three and two hundred fourteen thousandths

10. seven hundredths of a dollar

11.	0.6	19.	6.25
12.	0.08	20.	14.17
13.	0.45	21.	6.003
14.	0.002	22.	4.034
15.	0.034	23.	13.047
16.	0.426	24.	9.625
17.	2.4	25.	67.234
18.	7.03		

Exercise 4: Decimal/Fraction Conversions (page 267)

1.	$\frac{29}{1000}$	6.	0.31
		7.	0.021
2.	$\frac{13}{25}$	8.	2.19
		9.	7.429
3.	$\frac{651}{1000}$	10.	9.001
		11.	0.75
4.	$17\frac{1}{1000}$	12.	1.2
5.	$23\frac{401}{1000}$		

Exercise 5: Comparing Decimals (page 268)

1.	>	4.	=
2.	>	5.	>
3.	>	6.	>

7.	<	9.	<
8.	>	10.	<

Exercise 6: Rounding Decimals (page 270)

1.	9 cm	10.	21.8 kg
2.	$22	11.	5.67 m
3.	24 mpg	12.	$1.68
4.	$8	13.	8.50
5.	22 kg	14.	$21.64
6.	2.5	15.	1.67 m
7.	$13.3	16.	3; 3.4; 3.44
8.	43.7 km	17.	8; 8.2; 8.22
9.	$7.8	18.	5; 4.5; 4.52

Exercise 7: Estimating with Decimals (page 272)

1.	14	6.	6
2.	2	7.	D
3.	16	8.	C
4.	2	9.	A
5.	36		

Exercise 8: Basic Arithmetic Operations with Decimals (page 278)

1.	0.8	9.	8.665
2.	1.1	10.	11.914
3.	10.87	11.	0.4
4.	$3.13	12.	1.1
5.	$8.23	13.	0.38
6.	5.7	14.	$9.67
7.	7.834	15.	$1.66
8.	8.71	16.	3.484

ANSWERS

17. 2.675

18. 3.23

19. 0.994

20. 0.27

21. 0.14

22. 33

23. 16.2

24. $86.8

25. 8.82

26. 13.11

27. 2.0992

28. 723

29. 2,480

30. 5.7

31. 600

32. 20

33. 20

34. 4

35. 0.23

36. 80

37. 2.1

38. 0.102

39. 0.0842

40. 0.4914

41. 0.18

42. 0.11

43. 0.43

44. 0.83

45. 0.478

46. 0.632

47. 0.533

48. 0.549

Exercise 9: Word Problems with Decimals (page 279)

1. A

2. A

3. B

4. C

5. C

6. D

7. B

8. D

9. B

10. C

Exercise 10: Decimal Review (page 281)

1. thousandths

2. tenths

3. ones

4. $3 + 0.5 + 0.02$

5. $9 + 0.01 + 0.001$

6. $10 + 2 + 0.2 + 0.001$

7. three thousandths

8. seven tenths

9. fourteen hundredths

10. sixteen thousandths

11. 0.3

12. 0.30

13. 0.012

14. $\dfrac{19}{100}$

15. $\dfrac{501}{1000}$

16. $\dfrac{1}{4}$

17. 0.01

18. 0.011

19. 3.03

20. 3.1

21. >

22. <

23. >

24. >

25. >

26. =

27. 14; 14.3; 14.27

28. 7; 7.1; 7.12

29. 22

30. 6

31. 128

32. 15

33. 9.683

34. 9.215

35. 10.705

36. 0.89

37. 50.075

38. 2.55

39. 1.41

40. 249

41. 35.28

42. 20.4

43. 22

44. 36

ANSWERS

Chapter 4 Integers

Exercise 1: Definitions (page 286)

1. 7.25

2. $7\frac{1}{2}, \frac{4}{3}, -3.5$

3. None should be circled.

4–8. Pairs 4 and 6 are opposite integers.

Exercise 2: Integers and the Number Line (page 287)

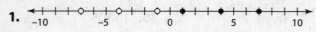

1.

2.

3.

Exercise 3: Absolute Value (page 288)

1. 7   4. −8

2. 9   5. 0

3. −4

Exercise 4: Ordering Integers (page 289)

1. −11, −5, −4, −3, −2, 3, 12

2. −5.2, −4, −1, 0, 1, 5

3. −6, −4, −3, −1, 1, 3, 5, 6, 7

4. $-2\frac{1}{2}$, 0, 1, 2, 3, 4, 5

5. <

6. <

7. >

8. >

9. <

10. >

11. >

12. =

13. $|-8|$

14. $|-7|$

15. 8

16. All three are equal.

17. $|-3|$

Exercise 5: Adding Integers (page 292)

1. 10   7. 19

2. 1   8. −28

3. −1   9. −2

4. −14   10. 3

5. 4   11. 5

6. 16   12. 6

Exercise 6: Subtracting Integers (page 294)

1. 4   9. −4

2. 8   10. 3

3. −4   11. −12

4. 8   12. 16

5. −8   13. −5

6. −4   14. −6

7. −8   15. 17

8. 4   16. −27

Exercise 7: Multiplying and Dividing Integers (page 297)

1. −28   4. 15

2. −12   5. 3

3. 10   6. −5

7. −4

8. −3

9. 540

10. −90

Exercise 8: Integers and Exponents (page 298)

1. negative

2. positive

3. positive

4. negative

5. negative

6. positive

Exercise 9: Distance on the Number Line (page 299)

1. 7 and 4

2. −5 and 5

3. 4 and −9

4. 8 and −9

5. 9 and 0

Exercise 10: Order of Operations (page 301)

1. 162

2. −1

3. 29

4. 1,586

Chapter 5 Expressions and Polynomials

Exercise 1: Evaluating Numerical Expressions (page 304)

1. 0

2. 0.5

3. 19

4. 13

5. 11

6. 0

7. 10

8. 2

9. 3

10. 5

Exercise 2: Evaluating Algebraic Expressions (page 306)

1. 88

2. 8

3. 4

4. 8

5. 5

6. 16

7. 153.86

8. 523.33

9. −32

10. 33,660

Exercise 3: Writing Expressions (page 308)

1. $\dfrac{10}{3+1} = \dfrac{10}{4} = \$2.50$

2. $2 \cdot 30 + 0.28d$

3. $lw = l \cdot \dfrac{l}{2} = \dfrac{l^2}{2}$

4. $\$200 + 0.03s$

5. $2(4+1)-1$

6. $45 + t - \dfrac{t}{2}$

7. A number plus six hundredths times the number

8. The square root of x squared plus y squared

9. A number V divided by h

10. A divided by r squared

Exercise 4: Adding and Subtracting Monomials (page 310)

1. $5x$

2. $9x^2$

3. $12x$

4. Can't combine; not like terms

5. $7xy$

6. $65x^3$

7. Can't combine; not like terms

8. $6sr^3$

9. $(a+b)x$

10. $2x^6$

11. $2x$

12. $2x^2$

13. $5x$

14. Can't combine; not like terms

15. $2xy$

16. $25x^3$

17. Can't combine; not like terms

18. $-2sr^3$

19. $(b-a)x$

20. 0

Exercise 5: Multiplying and Dividing Monomials (page 312)

1. $6x^2y$

2. $36x^5$

3. $30x^4$

4. x^3y^3z

5. $15x^2y^3$

6. 2

7. $4x^2$

8. $2xy$

9. $32x^4$

10. xyz

Exercise 6: Adding and Subtracting Polynomials (page 313)

1. $2x^2+5x+12$

2. $2x^2-1$

3. $5x^2+x$

4. $8x^2+5x+7$

5. x^2+7x-1

6. $9x^2+x+9$

7. $4x^2$

8. $4x^2-2x-5$

9. $13x^2+7x-3$

10. $8x^2+5xy+7y^2$

11. x^2+x+3

12. x^2-x-3

13. $5x+2$

14. $-x^2-5x$

15. $3x+3$

16. $-x^2+5x-17$

17. x^2-x+3

18. $x^2+4x-12$

19. $2x^2+2x+3$

20. $2x^2-xy-y^2$

Exercise 7: Multiplying Polynomials (page 317)

1. $2x^4$

2. $-2x^3$

3. $9x^3$

4. $15x^2y^2$

5. $-2x^3y^3$

6. $10x^2$

7. $4x^2$

8. $6x^5$

9. $42x^2$

10. $3x^3y^2$

11. $9x^2+27x+27$

12. $-4x^2+14x$

13. $4x^3-10x^2$

14. $15x^3+35x$

15. $3x^3-15x^2+18x$

16. x^3+2x^2-8x

17. $3x^4-4x^2$

18. $25x^4-10x^3$

19. $35x^3-60x^2+45x$

20. $12x^2y^3+2x^3y^2$

21. $6x^2+33x+27$

22. $4x^2-2x-42$

23. $9x^3+9x^2-25x-25$

24. $15x^3+20x^2-35x$

25. $25x^2-36$

26. $2x^3+6x^2-6x+8$

27. $2x^3-8x^2+16x-16$

28. $-8x^2+32x-14$

29. $25x^2-60x+36$

30. x^4-y^4

Exercise 8: Dividing Polynomials (page 321)

1. $2x$

2. $4x + 2$

3. $-x^2 - 2x - 3$

4. $5 + x$

5. $x + y$

6. $3x$

7. $8x^3 + 4x^2 + 2x$

8. $x + 3$

9. $3x^2 - 1$

10. x

11. $x + 3$

12. $x - 3$

13. $x - 1$

14. $2x + 1$

15. $2x + 2$

16. $x - 2$

17. $3x - 2$

18. $x + 2$

19. $2x - 2$

20. $4x - 2$

Exercise 9: Factoring Polynomials (page 328)

1. $2x(x - 2)$

2. $4y(x - 2)$

3. $9x^2(3x + y)$

4. $4(3 - 2x)$

5. $7y(2 - x)$

6. $x(yz + 2x)$

7. $2x(x^2 - 2x + 2)$

8. $2(x - 2y + 3z)$

9. $3xy(1 + 2y + 3x)$

10. $3x(2x^2 + x + 2)$

11. $(x + 1)(x + 2)$

12. $(x + 1)(x + 3)$

13. $(x + 4)(x + 3)$

14. $(x + 4)(x - 2)$

15. $(x - 1)(x - 2)$

16. $(x - 3)(x - 2)$

17. $(x - 4)(x - 2)$

18. $(x - 4)(x + 5)$

19. $(x - 3)(x + 6)$

20. $(x - 2)(x + 3)$

21. $(x + 2)(2x + 3)$

22. $(2x + 1)(3x + 1)$

23. $4(x + 1)(x + 2)$

24. $(3x + 2)(2x + 3)$

25. $(x - 2)(4x + 3)$

26. $(2x - 1)(3x + 1)$

27. $(3x + 2)(x + 1)$

28. $2(x - 1)(2x - 1)$

29. $3(x + 1)(4x + 3)$

30. $(2x + 1)(x - 2)$

31. $2x(x + 2)(x + 3)$

32. $3x(x - 2)(x + 2)$

33. $(2x + 3)(2x + 3)$

34. $2(x + 2)(x + 2)$

35. $(x - 3)(x + 5)$

36. $(2x - 3)(x - 4)$

37. $2x(x - 1)(x + 1)$

38. $(3x + 2)(3x - 2)$

39. $(2x + 5)(3x - 4)$

40. $2x(x - 3)(3x - 1)$

Chapter 6 Equations and Functions

Exercise 1: Solving Linear Equations and Inequalities by Adding or Subtracting (page 335)

1. 98

2. $3\frac{1}{9}$

3. 102.1

4. 3.9

5. 0.954

6. 5.55

7. 18

8. $2\frac{1}{2}$

9. $11\frac{13}{16}$

10. $13\frac{3}{4}$

11. $x > -2.5$

12. $x \leq 24\frac{1}{2}$

13. $x \leq 41$

14. $x < 16\frac{1}{8}$

15. $x \geq 107$

16. $x < 212$

17. $x > 8.25$

18. $x \leq \frac{21}{32}$

19. $x < 1\frac{15}{16}$

20. 2,029

Exercise 2: Solving Linear Equations and Inequalities by Multiplying or Dividing (page 338)

1. -4

2. 62.5

3. -18

4. 300

5. 200

6. 5.01

7. $-1,089$

8. 8

ANSWERS

9. 187.5

10. −14

11. $x \geq 13$

12. $x > 10$

13. $x \geq 0.1$

14. $x \leq -60$

15. $x < 37.5$

16. $x \leq 40$

17. $x > -40$

18. $x \geq 75$

19. $x \geq -40$

20. $x > 40$

17. $x > 1$

18. $x \geq 4$

19. $x \leq 22$

20. $x \leq 6$

Exercise 3: Solving Linear Equations and Inequalities with Combined Operations (page 340)

1. 5

2. 30

3. −1,000

4. 125

5. 12

6. 425

7. 13.44

8. $\frac{1}{8}$

9. 58

10. 25

11. $x \geq 6$

12. $x \geq 20$

13. $x \leq 200$

14. $x > 55$

15. $x \leq 1\frac{8}{9}$

16. $x \geq 30$

17. $x > -8$

18. $x > 600$

19. $x > 10$

20. $x \leq 14$

Exercise 4: Solving Linear Equations and Inequalities with Multiple Operations and Parentheses (page 344)

1. 5

2. 3

3. 3.5

4. 3.5

5. 12

6. −6

7. 6

8. −150

9. 10

10. 7.5

11. $x \leq 4$

12. $x < 6$

13. $x \leq 10$

14. $x \leq 5$

15. $x \geq 13$

16. $x \leq 3$

Exercise 5: Using Equations to Solve Problems (page 350)

1. s = short side length, l = long side length, $s = \frac{l}{2} - 1$

2. s = son's age now, j = Jay's age now, $s + 3 > \frac{1}{2}(j + 3)$

3. n = the first integer, $n + n + 1 + n + 2 = 27$ or $3n + 3 = 27$

4. n = the first even integer, $n + n + 2 = 168$

5. p = the cost of the pizza, t = the cost of the tea, $\frac{p+t}{3} < 5$

6. s = short side, l = long side, $s = \frac{l}{3}$

7. $3.50

8. > 15

9. $1,410

10. < 350 miles

11. 25

12. 99

13. 9 liters

14. 2 pounds

15. $3.815

16. 13.477 metric tons

17. Not possible

18. 45%

19. 5.6 hours

20. 180 miles per hour

21. 110.5 miles

22. About 8.7 miles per hour

23. a. 8 miles **b.** 2 hours

Exercise 6: Functions (page 362)

1. $y = 34x - 27$ is a function since it is a linear equation.

2. $y = -150x$ is a function since it is a linear equation.

3. The table represents a function, as there is only one y for each x.

4. It is not a function. There are two different y values, one for $x = 1$ and another for $x = 2$.

5. It is a function. Even though $x = 1$ is listed twice, the same y is listed both times.

6. It is a function; it satisfies the vertical line test.

7. It is not a function; it does not satisfy the vertical line test.

8. It is a function; it satisfies the vertical line test.

9. It is not a function; a vertical line does not satisfy the vertical line test.

10. It is not a function; it fails the vertical line test.

Chapter 7 Ratios, Proportions, and Percent

Exercise 1: Understanding Ratios (page 368)

1. 1:3	7. A
2. 2:1:4	8. D
3. 1:4	9. C
4. 1:6:3	10. A
5. 5:2	11. B
6. B	12. A

Exercise 2: Understanding Unit Rates (page 371)

1. $0.26 per ounce	6. B
2. $0.69 per bottle	7. D
3. $0.12 per pencil	8. B
4. $1.39 per pound	9. D
5. $0.78 per bunch	10. C

Exercise 3: Equivalent Ratios (page 373)

1. C	4. C
2. D	5. C
3. D	6. 4

7. 21	12. 4
8. 3	13. 1
9. 7	14. 3
10. 8	15. 5
11. 9	

Exercise 4: Comparing Ratios (page 375)

1. <	6. <
2. >	7. >
3. =	8. <
4. >	9. >
5. =	10. =

Exercise 5: Understanding Proportions (page 378)

1. C	6. 3
2. D	7. 2
3. D	8. 7
4. 2	9. 3.125
5. 5	10. 4

11. C

12. D

13. C

14. D

15. B

Exercise 6: Understanding Percent (page 385)

1. 23%

2. 49%

3. 25%

4. 36%

5. 20%

6. $\frac{1}{25}$

7. $\frac{19}{100}$

8. $\frac{33}{50}$

9. $1\frac{1}{2}$

10. $1\frac{3}{10}$

11. 0.05

12. 0.16

13. 0.27

14. 4.23

15. 1.1

16. 11.76

17. 130

18. 60

19. 40.05

20. 173.5

21. 144.44

22. 37.18

23. 48.64

24. B

25. C

26. $3,900

27. 25%

28. 0.5%

29. 45 mL

30. $240

31. 15%

32. 25%

Exercise 7: Ratio, Proportion, and Percent Review (page 388)

1. 3:7

2. 2:5:7

3. 3:8

4. B

5. A

6. D

7. $2.08 per bottle

8. $0.86 per pound

9. B

10. C

11. 12

12. 9

13. 21

14. 2

15. >

16. =

17. <

18. 6

19. 12

20. 24

21. C

22. B

23. D

24. 20%

25. 800

26. 14%

27. 990

28. 130%

29. 9.88

30. 144.2

31. 43.6

32. 25

33. 6,900

34. $25

35. 12%

Chapter 8 Data Analysis and Probability

Exercise 1: Data Types (page 395)

1. Continuous

2. Discrete

3. Continuous

4. Continuous

5. Discrete

6. Continuous

7. Discrete

8. Continuous

9. Continuous

10. Continuous

Exercise 2: Data Representation: Tables (page 398)

#	Name	Age at Inauguration	Age at Death	Party
	**Age at Inauguration and At Death for American Presidents since 1900**			

#	Name	Age at Inauguration	Age at Death	Party
25	McKinley, W.	54	58	R
26	Roosevelt, T.	42	60	R
27	Taft, W.	51	72	R
28	Wilson, W.	56	67	D
29	Harding, W.	55	57	R
30	Coolidge, C.	51	60	R
31	Hoover, H.	54	90	R
32	Roosevelt, F.	51	63	D
33	Truman, H.	60	88	D
34	Eisenhower, D.	62	78	R
35	Kennedy, J.	43	46	D
36	Johnson, L.	55	64	D
37	Nixon, R.	56	81	R
38	Ford, J.	61	93	R
39	Carter, J.	52	*	D
40	Reagan, R.	69	93	R
41	Bush, G. H.	64	*	R
42	Clinton, W.	46	*	D
43	Bush, G. W.	54	*	R
44	Obama, B.	47	*	D

Exercise 3: Histograms (page 400)

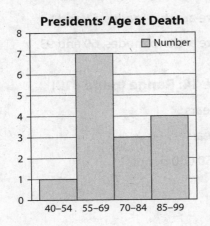

Presidents' Age at Death

Exercise 4: Bar Charts (page 401)

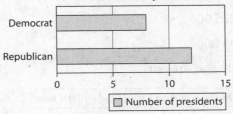

Presidents' Party Affiliation

Exercise 5: Reading Histograms and Bar Charts (page 402)

1. 50–54
2. 65–69
3. 11
4. after turning 55
5. 55

Exercise 6: Data Representation: Line Graphs (page 405)

1.

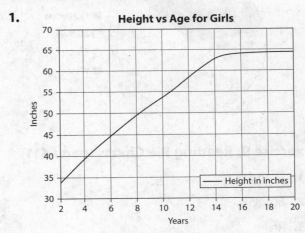

Height vs Age for Girls

2.

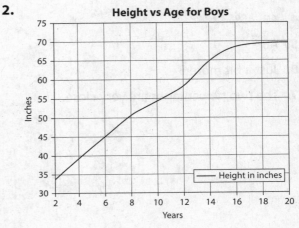

Height vs Age for Boys

Exercise 7: Reading Line Graphs (page 408)

1. $180,000
2. $225,000
3. $45,000
4. July and August
5.

Quarter	Ending Date (end of)	Total Sales
1	March	$50,000
2	June	$120,000
3	September	$200,000

Exercise 8: Creating a Pie Chart (page 410)

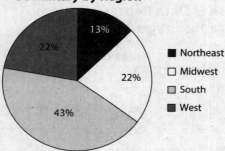

Percentage of Recruits to US Military by Region

- Northeast
- Midwest
- South
- West

Exercise 9: Reading Pie Charts (page 411)

1. O and A
2. 80–85%
3. Rh+
4. 40–45%
5. AB–
6. Just a bit more B+
7. The two percentages are very close.

Exercise 10: Data Representation: Pictograms (page 414)

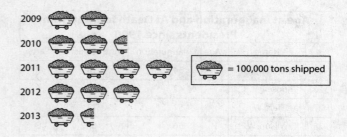

= 100,000 tons shipped

Exercise 11: Mean (page 416)

1. 54.2 years
2. 71.3 years
3. 54.8 years

Exercise 12: Median (page 417)

1. 54 years
2. 67 years
3. Day 183
4. 50%
5. Nothing
6. 15.5

Exercise 13: Mode (page 418)

1. There are two modes, 51 and 54.
2. There are two modes, 60 and 93.

Exercise 14: Range (page 419)

1. 26 years
2. 47 years
3. 37,750,000 people

ANSWERS

Exercise 15: Midrange (page 420)

1. 55.5 years
2. 69.5 years
3. 19,457,000 people

Exercise 16: Counting Outcomes (page 422)

1. $\frac{1}{3} = 33.3\%$

2. $\frac{3}{10} = 30\%$

3. $\frac{1}{2} = 50\%$

4. $\frac{3}{10} = 30\%$

5. $\frac{1}{7,000,000} = 0.000014\%$

6. $\frac{2}{9} = 22.22\%$

7. $\frac{7}{9} = 77.77\%$

8. $\frac{11}{28} = 39.3\%$

9. $\frac{1}{13} = 7.7\%$

10. $\frac{1}{4} = 25\%$

11. $\frac{3}{4} = 75\%$

12. $\frac{5}{9} = 55.6\%$

13. $\frac{1}{9} = 11.1\%$

14. $\frac{1}{9} = 11.1\%$

15. $\frac{7}{12} = 58.3\%$

Exercise 17: Combining Probabilities: Addition Rules (page 424)

1. 0.7

2. $\frac{11}{20} = 55\%$

3. $\frac{25}{52} = 48\%$

4. $\frac{3}{4} = 75\%$

5. $\frac{7}{8} = 87.5\%$

Exercise 18: Combining Probabilities: Multiplication Rules (page 427)

1. Independent
2. Dependent
3. Independent
4. Dependent
5. Dependent
6. Independent
7. Independent
8. Independent

Exercise 19: Probability Review (page 428)

1. $\frac{1}{64} = 1.56\%$

2. $\frac{1}{64} = 1.56\%$

3. $0.128 = 12.8\%$

4. $\dfrac{1}{169} = 0.59\%$

5. $\dfrac{1}{221} = 0.45\%$

6. $\dfrac{2197}{132,600} = 1.66\%$

7. $\dfrac{1}{36} = 2.78\%$

8. $\dfrac{1}{81} = 1.23\%$

9. 0%

10. $\dfrac{1}{20} = 5\%$

Chapter 9 Exponents and Roots

Exercise 1: Positive Integer Exponents (page 430)

1. c^6

2. $(2y)^3$

3. $(3xy)^6$

4. $(a^2y)^4$

5. $(5a^2bc)^5$

Exercise 2: Properties of Exponents: The Product Rule (page 431)

1. x^{12}

2. a^{10}

3. $(2xy)^8$

4. $15p^5q^7$

5. $a^3b^7c^2$

6. $24x^8y^5z^7$

Exercise 3: Properties of Exponents: The Quotient Rule (page 432)

1. p^6

2. $(2d)^5$

3. $4x^2$

4. $\dfrac{3}{2}x^3y^2$

5. $8r^3$

6. a^3b^3

Exercise 4: Properties of Exponents: The Power Rule (page 433)

1. x^8

2. 5^{18}

3. $(4q)^{15}$

4. b^{27}

5. k^2

6. x^8

Exercise 5: Properties of Exponents: The Factor Rule (page 434)

1. x^3y^3

2. $64a^6b^6$

3. $9x^8$

4. $s^{20}t^{14}$

5. x^8y^6

6. $p^{17}q^9$

Exercise 6: Properties of Exponents: The Fraction Rule (page 435)

1. $\dfrac{16}{81}$

2. $\dfrac{x^7}{y^7}$

3. $\dfrac{49x^2}{81y^2}$

4. $\dfrac{x^{12}}{y^{24}}$

5. $\dfrac{27a^{12}}{125b^6}$

6. $\dfrac{32x^5}{y^{10}z^5}$

Exercise 7: Properties of Exponents (page 436)

1. $(-3x)^{10}$

2. $-2a^{14}$

3. $x^7y^5z^6$

4. x^3z^2

5. a^7bc

6. 2^{10}

7. $\dfrac{a^3}{125}$

8. $-x^{10}$

9. $\dfrac{8}{27}$

10. $18x^{12}$

11. $\dfrac{6}{5}x^5y$

12. $3x^2y^2z$

ANSWERS

Exercise 8: Zero and Negative Integer Exponents (page 438)

1. $\dfrac{1}{2^9}$

2. 64

3. 1

4. 1

5. 1

6. 3^{12}

7. $\dfrac{1}{2^{20}}$

8. $\dfrac{1}{5^8}$

9. $\dfrac{6}{m^2 n^5}$

10. $\dfrac{2x^6}{3y^2}$

11. $\dfrac{1}{m^5 n^3}$

12. $\dfrac{1}{a^6 b^6}$

Exercise 9: Scientific Notation (page 439)

1. 3×10^{-4}

2. 1.1×10^5

3. 5.2×10^6

4. 2.3×10^2

5. 2.12×10^6

6. 0.0079

7. 0.00009

8. 210

9. 61,000

10. 0.7

11. A

12. B

13. B

14. C

15. D

Exercise 10: Roots (page 443)

1. 30

2. 14

3. 27

4. 21

5. 11

6. −15

7. 6

8. 3

9. 8.5

10. 10.5

11. 6.5

12. 9

13. 5

14. −2

15. −4

16. B

17. A

18. C

19. D

20. D

Exercise 11: Exponents and Roots Review (page 445)

1. m^5

2. $(3yz)^3$

3. $(-2x)^{12}$

4. $-8m^{14}$

5. $(x^2 yz)^{10}$

6. $m^7 n^2$

7. 3^9

8. $\dfrac{a^3}{27}$

9. $-a^{15}$

10. $\dfrac{27}{125}$

11. $10x^{10}$

12. $3a$

13. $\dfrac{1}{27}$

14. 125

15. 1

16. 1

17. 2^{15}

18. $\dfrac{1}{3^{25}}$

19. $15a^4$

20. $\dfrac{x^{10}}{2y^4}$

21. 7×10^{-5}

22. 1×10^4

23. 2.2×10^7

24. 8,100

25. 0.005

26. 40

27. 16

28. 23

29. −10

30. 7

ANSWERS

Chapter 10 Measurement and Geometry

Exercise 1: The Metric System in Detail (page 450)

1. 18.5 centimeters
2. 13.55 meters
3. 8.245 kilograms
4. 450 milliliters
5. 1,250 grams
6. 25.4 millimeters
7. 0.350 liters
8. 0.00245 meters
9. 0.850 meters
10. 0.72 meters

Exercise 2: Using a Metric Ruler (page 452)

1. 4.8 centimeters; 48 millimeters
2. 8.1 centimeters; 81 millimeters
3. 12.4 centimeters; 124 millimeters
4. 1.1 centimeters; 11 millimeters

Exercise 3: Using a US System Ruler (page 454)

1. $1\frac{1}{4}$ inches

2. $1\frac{1}{2}$ inches

3. $1\frac{5}{8}$ inches

4. $2\frac{3}{4}$ inches

Exercise 4: Unit Conversions Using Dimensional Analysis (page 458)

1. $1\frac{1}{2}$ pounds

2. 24 cups

3. 201.2 meters

4. 130.5 miles
5. 27.78 meters per second
6. 96.6 kilometers per hour
7. 51 by 102
8. 183 centimeters and 244 centimeters
9. 69.3 inches
10. 188 centimeters

Exercise 5: Angles (page 460)

1. B
2. 60°
3. C

4.

Exercise 6: Relationships for Intersecting Lines (page 466)

1. a. 108° b. 72° c. 108° d. 72°
   e. 108° f. 72° g. 108°

2. There are no errors. The student's work is correct

Exercise 7: Triangles (page 468)

1. a, d, e
2. b, g, l
3. d, f, j

ANSWERS

4. c, h

5. $P = 15$ units; $A = 8.75$ square units

6. $P = 21$ units; $A = 14$ square units

7. $P = 15$ units; $A = 3.5$ square units

8. $P = 20$ units; $A = 17.5$ square units

Exercise 8: Quadrilaterals (page 472)

a. 5 **b.** 10 **c.** 90° **d.** 7

e. 7 **f.** 90° **g.** 90° **h.** 9

i. 6 **j.** 120° **k.** 60°

1. $P = 22$ units; $A = 24$ square units

2. $P = 26$ units; $A = 28$ square units

3. $P = 24$ units; $A = 36$ square units

4. $P = 44$ units; $A = 121$ square units

Exercise 9: Circles (page 473)

1. 38.5 square units

2. 38.5 square units

3. 10.5 square units

4. 59.5 square units

5. 11.8 square units

6. $P = 6.282$ inches; $A = 3.141$ square inches

7. 2.36 square inches

Exercise 10: Geometric Bodies in Three Dimensions (page 477)

1. $A = 1005.12$ square units; $V = 2412.29$ cubic units

2. $A = 126$ square units; $V = 81$ cubic units

3. $A = 88$ square units; $V = 48$ cubic units

4. $A = 312$ square units; $V = 264$ cubic units

Exercise 11: Cones and Pyramids (page 479)

1. Cone: $A = 151.6$ square units; $V = 117.3$ cubic units

2. Pyramid: $A = 156$; $V = 96$

Exercise 12: Complex Constructions (page 481)

1. a. $A = 316$ m² (square meters)

   b. $V = 126.4$ m³ (cubic meters)

2. a. $V \approx 3282$ ft³ (cubic feet) of concrete

   b. $A = 3109$ ft² (square feet) will need to be sealed

3. $A = 2,200$ m² (square meters) of cloth

4. $V \approx 609,285$ m³ (cubic meters)

5. a. $A = 551.1$ ft²

   b. 21 buffalo hides

Science

Chapter 1 Life Science

Exercise 1: Restating Ideas (page 488)

There are several ways to simplify these sentences. Here are some sample answers. If you are not sure whether your answer is correct, check with your teacher.

1. You need to use a heating element to make the water turn from a liquid to a gas.

2. Once nuclear power became available, electric companies did not need to use coal or gas to make electricity.

3. People who report the news argue that cell phones can be bad for a person's health.

Exercise 2: Fact vs. Opinion (page 492)

1. F The most recent US census lists New York as the most populous city.

2. O This is an opinion; if these two were being compared for safety, the number of accidents over a period of time could be measured.

3. F You can prove this by reading about the state of Arizona.

4. O A statement that something is "the greatest" is usually an opinion.

5. F This can be proven by measuring the distance with a laser.

6. F You can prove (or disprove) this by measuring your foot and arm.

7. O Statements that use the term "better" to compare items are opinions.

8–10. Answers will vary.

Exercise 3: Forming Everyday Hypotheses (page 493)

Your answers should be similar to these sample answers. If you are not sure whether your answer is correct, check with your teacher.

1. Since the food is not cooking on the gas grill, you could hypothesize that the gas tank attached to the grill is empty.

2. Feeling lightheaded and low on energy during your morning run may make you hypothesize that your body is weak from lack of nutrition.

3. You could hypothesize that since you can see people hiding in the darkness of your parents' house and balloons are floating around, your parents are throwing you a surprise party.

Exercise 4: Forming Scientific Hypotheses (page 494)

Your answers may be worded differently, but your hypotheses should be similar to these answers. If you are not sure whether your answer is correct, check with your teacher.

1. The soap in the creek is coming from the town, and the arsenic and oil are coming from the manufacturing plant. Upstream past the city, no soap is in the creek, and upstream from the manufacturing plant the water is clean.

2. Amelie's magnet only picks up objects made of iron or steel, and not all metals.

Exercise 5: Errors in Experiments (page 497)

Your answers should be similar to these sample answers. If you are not sure whether your answer is correct, check with your teacher.

1. **The subjects are not similar OR conditions of the experiment were not kept the same**

   The gardener used two different kinds of flowers, so the subjects of the experiment were dissimilar. She could not tell if the roses wilted because of the distilled water or because of something else; perhaps the plants were unhealthy or the temperatures were unsuitable for growing roses.

2. **Not enough subjects in the test OR the experiment results were not reproduced**

   The mailroom worker sent only a few envelopes through the machine, which is not a large enough test to see if the machine would work properly. The worker needed to run several more envelopes through the machine to try to reproduce his success rate.

Exercise 6: Making Decisions Using the Scientific Method (page 499)

Your answers should be similar to these examples. If you are not sure whether your answer is correct, check with your teacher.

1. Why didn't the women who milked cows catch smallpox?

2. Milkmaids got cowpox, but they didn't catch smallpox.

3. Getting cowpox kept you from catching smallpox.

4. Jenner tested his hypothesis by injecting healthy people with cowpox to see if they would also catch smallpox.

5. Cowpox protects people from catching smallpox.

Exercise 7: Cells (page 504)

1. (a) pili

   (b) cell membrane

   (c) cell wall

   (d) chromosomes

   (e) nucleus

   (f) chlorophyll

   (g) vacuole

2. Choice **B** is correct. Cell theory does not state that all cells have a nucleus. Only complex eukaryotic cells like plant and animal cells have a nucleus.

Exercise 8: History of Life (page 509)

1. Choice **B** is correct. Scales are a special type of skin that prevents the adult reptile from drying out.

2. Choice **A** is correct. Organisms found in the same class are also in the same phylum and kingdom.

3. (a) mammals

   (b) order

   (c) reptiles

   (d) vertebrates

   (e) amphibians

   (f) Age of Mammals

   (g) fossil record

Exercise 9: Life Functions and Energy Intake (page 512)

1. Choice **C** is correct. Plants that have chlorophyll output oxygen through the process of photosynthesis.

2. Choice **C** is correct. Plants and other autotrophs take in inorganic carbon dioxide, light energy, and inorganic water to make food in the form of sugar molecules.

3. (a) plants (or *animals*)

   (b) animals (or *plants*)

   (c) ATP

   (d) mitochondria

   (e) eukaryotic

Exercise 10: Reproduction (page 517)

1. Choice **C** is correct. Haploid cells, or sex cells, each have half of a chromosome pair. Each one combines with another sex cell to complete the chromosome pair.

Exercise 11: Gene Expression (page 521)

1. Choice **A** is correct. Translation is decoding the mRNA into an amino acid sequence to build a protein.

Exercise 12: Genetics and Heredity (page 523)

1. **e.** meiosis I

2. **a.** telophase

3. **f.** interphase

4. **c.** anaphase

5. **b.** mitosis

6. **d.** metaphase

	B	b
b	1. _____ Bb _____	2. _____ bb _____
b	3. _____ Bb _____	4. _____ bb _____

7. **C.** There is a 50 percent chance the child will have green eyes. Boxes #1 and #3 each have a dominant *B* gene for blue eyes. This results in a blue-eye color. Only two *b* genes lead to green eyes.

8. A T A–C C G–A T A–G A C–C C C–C T G

Exercise 13: Skeletal and Muscular Systems (page 527)

1. **c.** tendon

2. **e.** ligament

3. **f.** smooth muscle

4. **g.** bone marrow

5. **a.** cartilage

6. **d.** tissue

7. **b.** involuntary

Exercise 14: Respiratory and Circulatory Systems (page 530)

1. Choice **C** is correct. One of the main purposes of respiration is to bring oxygen into the body and bloodstream to deliver it to all the body cells.

2. Choice **B** is correct. The atria (plural of *atrium*) are the parts of the heart that first receive blood from either the body (right atrium) or the lungs (left atrium).

3. Choice **D** is correct. The respiratory system takes in oxygen from the air and delivers it by the circulatory system to body cells such as muscle cells.

Exercise 15: Digestive System (page 532)

1. **e.** villi

2. **g.** saliva

3. **d.** peristalsis

4. **f.** enzyme

5. **b.** bile

6. **c.** chyme

7. **a.** colon

8. Choice **A** is correct. Ingestion occurs in the mouth, digestion begins here too, absorption mainly occurs in the small intestine, and undigested material is eliminated by the colon.

9. Choice **B** is correct. Proteins are first digested in the stomach and then further broken down in the small intestine.

Exercise 16: Nervous System (page 535)

1. Choice **C** is correct. Sensory nerves receive information about the environment, including heat to the touch. The somatic system controls voluntary movement through impulses sent through motor nerves from the brain.

2. Choice **B** is correct. A synapse is an extremely small gap between an axon and the receptors of another neuron. Nerve impulses are messages that are sent from one neuron to another.

3. Choice **D** is correct. The axon extends from the cell body to the next neuron.

Exercise 17: Homeostasis (page 537)

1. **(a)** set point

   (b) homeostasis

   (c) negative

   (d) effectors

Exercise 18: Health (page 540)

1. **f.** vitamin

2. **d.** water

3. **a.** mineral

4. **e.** protein

5. **g.** carbohydrate

6. **b.** amino acid

7. **c.** lipid

Exercise 19: Evolution (page 544)

1. Choice **B** is correct. The fossil record is not complete, but it provides evidence that organisms have changed over time. Older organisms in older rock layers are not the same as those living today, nor are they like the fossils found in younger rock layers.

2. Choice **C** is correct. Based on the information provided, the best hypothesis would be that South America and Africa were once a large landmass that separated earlier than 250 million years ago.

3. Choice **B** is correct. Some plants in dense forests such as the rainforest evolved climbing stems to compete for sunlight for photosynthesis. Large leaves and not small leaves are also beneficial to capture sunlight.

4. Choice **A** is correct. Populations can evolve by natural selection if there are genetically variable traits in the population and differential reproductive success of organisms due to the presence or absence of these traits.

Exercise 20: Sequencing Events (page 546)

1. The oven's heating element increases the temperature within the oven.

2. After the particles begin vibrating quickly, the particles collide with one another.

3. Heat transfers from the metal in the oven to the metal in the pan.

4. The collision of particles causes the conduction of heat.

Exercise 21: Cause and Effect (page 549)

Your answers for questions 1 and 2 should be similar to these examples. If you are not sure whether your answer is correct, check with your teacher.

1. **Effect 1:** A severe decrease in rainfall might cause lakes and rivers to have lower water levels.

   Effect 2: This decrease may lead local governments to limit use of water for irrigation.

2. **Cause 1:** The use of motorcycle helmet may have been required due to an increase in motorcycle accident–related deaths.

Cause 2: New laws are now requiring the use of motorcycle helmets.

3. O A statement that something is "the greatest" is usually an opinion.

4. F You can prove this by reading your state's driver's manual.

5. F You can prove this by researching who wrote *Hamlet*.

Exercise 22: Populations (page 552)

1. Choice **B** is correct. Carrying capacity is the maximum population size sustained by a specific environment.

2. Choice **B** is correct. Biotic factors are living organisms like fish. Abiotic factors are nonliving factors that include sunlight, soil, and humidity (water).

3. Choice **A** is correct. When births exceed deaths, the population grows.

4. Choice **D** is correct. Both lines 2 and 3 show population growth slowing down and leveling off and/or fluctuating at a set point called the carrying capacity. Line 1 shows unlimited, exponential growth and no carrying capacity.

Exercise 23: Community Interactions (page 555)

1. Choice **A** is correct. The vine receives a benefit while not helping or hurting the tree.

2. Choice **B** is correct. The elephants and rhinoceros are competing for a limited resource.

3. Choice **B** is correct. The bison provide a food source for the cowbirds while the cowbird protects the bison from insects.

Exercise 24: Ecosystems (page 560)

1. Choice **B** is correct. Only 10% of the energy stored in the insects is passed to the frogs, and only 10% of that 10% (= approximately 1% of the original amount) is passed to the snakes that eat the frogs.

2. Choice **B** is correct. Proteins help algae grow. Nitrogen is used to build proteins. Nitrogen can only be acquired by algae after its modification by decomposers such as bacteria in the water. Oxygen is depleted after the excessive growth of the algae population, but not initially.

3. Choice **C** is correct. Deforestation is the mass removal of forests that would otherwise release oxygen into the atmosphere.

Chapter 2 Physical Science

Exercise 1: Diagrams (page 564)

1. Cornea

2. Lens

3. Aqueous humor

Exercise 2: Tables (page 565)

1. The correct answer is "AB." People with AB blood type can accept blood from everyone.

2. The correct answer is "A and B." People with either of these two blood types can receive a kidney from a type O donor as well as from people with their own blood type, and people with these blood types can donate to a patient with AB blood and to people with their own blood type.

Exercise 3: Line Graphs (page 568)

1. The *x-axis* represents months in a year or unit of time.

2. June—the average price of gas reached $2.04.

3. Answers may vary. One possible reason for the high price of gas in June is that people tend to begin taking car trips for vacations in June, increasing the demand for gas. Another reason may be that crude oil prices reached their highest price during this month.

Exercise 4: Bar Graphs (page 569)

1. Physics has the smallest enrollment.

2. About 100 more students enrolled in Econ than in Poly Sci.

3. Line graphs are best used for linear data that show a direct relationship. That is, as the *x-axis* value increases, the *y-axis* value changes. The enrollment data are best shown in a bar graph because each category or group (course) is unique.

Exercise 5: Energy (page 574)

1. Choice **D** is correct. The nutrients we eat contain stored energy that can be converted into a usable form of energy for our cells.

2. Choice **D** is correct. The equation for GPE is mass × height × 9.8 m/s², the gravitational constant. GPE = 100 kg × 10 m × 9.8 m/s² = 9,800 J.

3. Choice **B** is correct. The equation for kinetic energy is KE = 0.5 × mass (kg) × velocity (m/s)². Because you know the value for KE (187.5 J) and velocity (50 m/s), you solve for mass:

   187.5 J = 0.5 × mass × (50 m/s)²

   mass = 187.5 J / (0.5 × (50 m/s)²)
   $\quad\quad$ = 187.5 J/(0.5 × 2,500 m²/s²)

   mass = 0.150 kg

Exercise 6: Thermodynamics (page 575)

1. Choice **C** is correct. The first law of thermodynamics is more commonly known as the law of conservation of energy.

Exercise 7: Simple Machines (page 578)

1. Choice **D** is correct. The work done is calculated by multiplying the force, 800 lbs, by the distance, 30 ft.

2. Choice **D** is correct. A knife acts like a wedge when it cuts objects into smaller pieces.

3. **f.** light bulb

4. **e.** crane

5. **d.** seesaw

6. **c.** slope

7. **b.** doorstop

8. **a.** doorknob

Exercise 8: Newton's Laws of Motion (page 581)

1. Choice **B** is correct. The equation to determine force (in Newtons) is $F = m \times a$. Inserting the known values gives you an equation of F = 0.150 kg × 10 m/s² = 1.5. kg·m/s² = 1.5 N

2. Choice **B** is correct.

Exercise 9: Momentum (page 583)

1. Choice **A** is correct. The total momentum after the collision equals 50 kg·m/s + 100 kg·m/s, or 150 kg·m/s. The total momentum before the collision must also equal 150 kg·m/s. Object A had a momentum $p_a = m \times v$ prior to the collision of 10 kg × 8 m/s, or 80 kg·m/s. Object B must have had a momentum equal to 150 kg·m/s minus 80 kg·m/s, or 70 kg·m/s. Since object B has a mass of 10 k/g, solving for the velocity in m/s equals 70 divided by 10 = 7 m/s.

EXERCISE ANSWER KEYS

2. Choice **C** is correct. The car has more momentum than the bicycle because the car has more mass than the bicycle.

Exercise 10: Forces and Energy (page 584)

1. The correct responses are "equal" and "opposite."

Exercise 11: Noncontact Forces (page 586)

1. Choice **B** is correct. Newton's law of universal gravitation states that as the distance between two objects increases, the amount of gravitational force decreases.

Exercise 12: Electricity and Magnetism (page 587)

1. **b.** flow of electricity

2. **d.** movement of electrons

3. **c.** magnet built by wrapping a coil around a metal core

4. **a.** object attracted to metal

Exercise 13: Properties of Waves (page 591)

1. The correct answer is "transverse." This is the type of wave caused when the disturbance moves perpendicularly to the direction of the wave.

2. The correct answer is 1 m/s. The wave takes 3 s to move along a 3-m rope.

3. The correct answers are "compressions" and "rarefactions." These properties define the motion of a longitudinal wave.

4. The correct answers are "crest" and "amplitude." The amplitude is the distance from the state of rest of the medium to the topmost part of the wave.

Exercise 14: Digital Information and Waves (page 592)

1. Choice **B** is correct. Digital information is stored electronically, which allows the potential for hackers at a remote location to steal the information. Analog systems use physical tapes to store information, so a thief must physically enter the storage area.

Exercise 15: Electromagnetic Radiation (page 594)

1. The correct answers are "particle" and "diffraction."

2. Choice **C** is correct. Refraction is the bending of waves from one medium to another medium.

Exercise 16: Effects of Electromagnetic Radiation (page 595)

1. Choice **D** is correct. X-rays and gamma waves have short wavelengths that can damage living cells. Longer wavelengths as in microwaves and infrared rays do not cause the same damage.

Exercise 17: Atoms and Their Properties (page 600)

1. **d.** electron

2. **f.** proton

3. **b.** neutron

4. **e.** atomic number

5. **a.** nucleus

6. **c.** isotope

7. Choice **A** is correct. Each of the elements has a different number of protons, but they all have one electron in the outer shell.

Exercise 18: Conservation of Mass (page 601)

1. The correct answer is 58.44 g. One sodium atom + one chlorine atom → one sodium chloride atom. This is the same as 1 mole of sodium + 1 mole of chlorine → 1 mole of sodium chloride. Replace with the atomic masses: 22.99 g sodium + 35.45 g chlorine → 58.44 g sodium chloride.

Exercise 19: Chemical Bonding (page 603)

1. Choice **C** is correct. The potassium atom gives up one electron to the bromine atom, and as a result, the potassium atom becomes positively charged.

2. Choice **C** is correct. When a covalent bond is formed, energy is released.

Exercise 20: Chemical Reactions (page 606)

1. Choice **C** is correct.

2. Choice **B** is correct.

3. Choice **C** is correct. There are 4 sodium (Na) atoms and 2 oxygen (O) atoms on the reactants side of the chemical equation.

Exercise 21: Reaction Rates (page 607)

1. Choice **A** is correct. A catalyst decreases the energy of the reaction, which speeds up the reaction rate.

Exercise 22: Chemical Equilibrium (page 608)

1. Choice **B** is correct. An endothermic reaction absorbs heat, which pushes the reaction to the right. This will increase the output of the product.

Exercise 23: Nuclear Processes (page 611)

1. Choice **D** is correct. Radioactive decay occurs in unstable isotopes in which the nucleus has more protons than neutrons. This describes alpha decay.

2. Choice **C** is correct. Fission can occur naturally with an unstable nucleus.

3. Choice **B** is correct. Nuclear fusion has a greater output of energy than nuclear fission. Radioactive decay is a different nuclear process from nuclear fusion.

Chapter 3 Earth and Space Science

Exercise 1: The Big Bang Theory (page 614)

1. Choice **C** is correct. In the phenomenon called redshift, as objects move away from an observer, their light appears redder in color than that of objects that are not moving or moving in other directions.

Exercise 2: Stars and Elements (page 616)

1. Choice **B** is correct. The apparent magnitude is the measurement of a star's brightness as seen from Earth. Since A1000 and B1000 appear equally bright, but A1000 is farther away, A1000 would have a greater absolute magnitude. Because A1000 is a red giant, it outputs a thousand times more light than B1000, which is about the size of our sun.

Exercise 3: The Sun (page 617)

1. Choice **D** is correct. Although sunspots are a cooler region on the surface of the sun, they have an effect of creating more solar radiation, which is responsible for heating Earth.

Exercise 4: The Sun–Earth System (page 619)

1. Choice **A** is correct. The equation $P^2 = a^3$, where P is a planet's orbital period and a is its radius of orbit, reflects a direct relationship between these two values. The longer it takes a planet to orbit the sun, the greater its average distance from the sun.

2. Choice **D** is correct. Nicolaus Copernicus developed the heliocentric model that states that the sun is the center of the universe.

Exercise 5: The History of Planet Earth (page 623)

1. Choice **C** is correct. The solar nebula formed from the big bang and then hydrogen and helium swirling in the nebula formed the sun, heavier elements formed asteroids that developed into the terrestrial planets, and lighter gases swirling in the outer areas of the nebula formed the Jovian planets.

2. Choice **A** is correct. Continental drift explains why Pangaea broke up into separate continents, and it explains why the North American continent continues to drift slowly away from the European continent.

Exercise 6: The Hydrosphere (page 625)

1. Choice **C** is correct. Carbon dioxide dissolves into the ocean surfaces through the carbon cycle.

Exercise 7: Earth's Atmosphere and the Weather (page 627)

1. Choice **B** is correct. The destructive forces of tornadoes and hurricanes displace and sometimes destroy wildlife populations by destroying ecosystems and habitats.

Exercise 8: The Lithosphere (page 632)

1. Choice **C** is correct. In mass wasting, rock slides and avalanches can cause igneous rocks to slam into other rocks, breaking them down into sediments.

2. Choice **B** is correct. The mantle makes up more than 80 percent of Earth's total mass.

Exercise 9: Interactions of Earth's Systems (page 634)

1. Choice **A** is correct. Earthquakes are violent events, but they do not cause changes in the climate.

Exercise 10: Climate and Weather (page 635)

1. Choice **B** is correct. By definition, weather occurs within a very short time frame such as hours, days, or weeks. It is a snapshot of a point in time. The time frame for climate is considerably longer—months, years, or longer.

Exercise 11: Natural Resources and Human Activity (page 637)

1. Choice **B** is correct. Increased carbon dioxide levels in the atmosphere have the effect of trapping solar radiation, which raises global temperatures. In the arctic regions of the North and South Poles, higher temperatures lead to melting of glaciers and polar ice caps.

Exercise 12: Reducing Human Impact on the Earth (page 639)

1. Choice **C** is correct. The process of fracking creates jobs and produces cleaner-burning fuel with costs rivalling those of imported oil. However, environmentalists claim that the process of fracking can destroy water sources and stress ecosystems.

Social Studies

Chapter 1 US Civics and Government

Exercise 1: Early Forms of Government (page 644)

1. Choice **C** is correct.

2. Choice **A** is correct.

3. Choice **B** is correct.

Exercise 2: Athenian Democracy (page 646)

1. Choice **B** is correct.

2. Choice **A** is correct.

3. Choice **D** is correct.

Exercise 3: The Roman Republic (page 649)

1. Choice **B** is correct.

2. Choice **D** is correct.

3. Choice **C** is correct.

Exercise 4: The Rise of Modern Government (page 652)

1. Choice **D** is correct.

2. Choice **B** is correct.

3. Choice **A** is correct.

Exercise 5: The US Government (page 654)

The paragraph should include the main idea that civil rights in the United States expanded as a result of the Fifteenth, Nineteenth, and Twenty-Sixth Amendments. Each of these amendments extended the right to vote. In 1870, the Fifteenth Amendment guaranteed that the right to vote cannot be denied "on account of race, color, or previous condition of servitude." The Fifteenth Amendment, however, did not grant voting rights to women. This civil right was not guaranteed until the Nineteenth Amendment was ratified in 1920. Civil rights were again extended in 1971 with the ratification of the Twenty-Sixth Amendment, which set the voting age at 18.

Chapter 2 US History

Exercise 1: Ideas from Greece and England (page 658)

1. Choice **B** is correct.

2. Choice **D** is correct.

Exercise 2: The Mayflower Compact (page 659)

1. Choice **C** is correct.

2. Choice **A** is correct.

3. Choice **B** is correct.

Exercise 3: The Declaration of Independence (page 661)

1. Choice **B** is correct.

2. Choice **C** is correct.

3. Choice **D** is correct.

Exercise 4: The Constitution of the United States (page 664)

1. Answers will vary. The Constitution was written to provide the structure for a new government, to establish justice, ensure domestic tranquility, provide for the common defense, promote the general welfare, and secure the blessings of liberty.

2. Answers will vary. The phrase "We the People" is significant because it makes clear that the new government of the United States is a government of all the people, not just that of a few.

Exercise 5: *Plessy v. Ferguson* (page 666)

1. Answers will vary. The justices argued that African Americans placed the badge of inferiority on themselves, and that the law was not to blame.

2. Answers will vary. This Supreme Court would not support a civil rights bill, as the justices argued that neither the Constitution nor any law could force equality, especially if one race was inferior to another.

Exercise 6: *Brown v. Board of Education* (page 667)

1. Choice **A** is correct.

2. Answers may vary, but they might include the idea that diversity improves learning and social development, or that it makes for a more equal society.

3. Answers will vary. Segregation instills a sense of state-endorsed inferiority in African-American students. This sense of inferiority hurts student learning and achievement, placing African Americans at a disadvantage, thus promoting inequality. For this reason segregation is unconstitutional.

Exercise 7: The Warren Court (page 669)

1. Choice **b** is correct.

2. Choice **a** is correct.

3. Choice **d** is correct.

4. Choice **c** is correct.

5. Answers will vary. Possible answer: The Warren Court was activist because it used its constitutional power to effect social change in the United States on issues such as civil and criminal rights.

Exercise 8: *Roe v. Wade* (page 670)

1. Answers will vary. Possible answer: Justice Byron White's objection to *Roe v. Wade* was based on the idea that the Supreme Court overstepped its constitutional powers, and by making abortion legal, it was diminishing the power of the states.

2. Answers will vary.

Chapter 3 Economics

Exercise 1: Foundations of Economics (page 674)

1. Choice **B** is correct.

2. Choice **C** is correct.

3. Choice **A** is correct.

4. Choice **B** is correct.

Exercise 2: The First Global Economic System (page 676)

1. Choice **D** is correct.

2. Choice **A** is correct.

3. Choice **D** is correct.

4. Choice **C** is correct.

Exercise 3: The Rise of Modern Economics (page 679)

1. Choice **B** is correct.

2. Choice **D** is correct.

3. Choice **C** is correct.

Exercise 4: Developments in American Economics (page 681)

1. Choice **A** is correct.

2. Choice **B** is correct.

Exercise 5: The Globalized Economy (page 684)

1. Answers will vary but might include discussion on the decline in global conflict, the rise of shared prosperity, and the growing interconnectedness of the world.

2. Answers will vary but might include discussion on the rise of income inequality and corporations putting profit ahead of workers' rights and environmental concerns.

Chapter 4 Geography and World History

Exercise 1: Environment and Society (page 687)

1. Choice **D** is correct.

2. Choice **C** is correct.

3. The correct answer is "Euphrates."

4. Choice **B** is correct.

Exercise 2: Geographic Concepts and Tools (page 689)

1. Choice **A** is correct.

2. Choice **C** is correct.

3. Choice **A** is correct.

Exercise 3: Cultural Diffusion (page 692)

Answers will vary. The response should explain that cultural diffusion is the spreading out of culture, cultural traits, or practices from a central point and include three examples of cultural diffusion drawn from the chart and the text under the heading "Cultural Diffusion."

Examples of cultural diffusion should be presented in chronological order. The response should follow standard English conventions for grammar, spelling, punctuation, and sentence structure.